דברים

DEUTERONOMY

DEUTERONOMY

Commentary by

W. GUNTHER PLAUT

THE TORAH

A
Modern
Commentary

V

Union of American Hebrew Congregations

NEW YORK

LIBRARY OF CONGRESS CATALOGING IN PUBLICATION DATA

PLAUT, W. GUNTHER, 1912–
(DEVARIM)

דברים—DEUTERONOMY.
(*His* The Torah; 5)

Includes original Hebrew text and the Jewish Publication
Society's English translation of Deuteronomy and the corresponding Haftarot for each Sabbath, both the traditional ones and two
alternatives chosen by the author from a wider range of biblical
sources.

Bibliography: p.

1. Bible. O.T. Deuteronomy—Commentaries.

I. Bible. O.T. Deuteronomy. Hebrew. 1980.

II. Bible. O.T. Deuteronomy. English. Jewish Publication Society. 1980.

III. Jewish Publication Society of America.

IV. Jews. Liturgy and ritual. Haftarot (Reform, Plaut). Pt. 5.
English & Hebrew. 1980.
V. Jews. Liturgy and ritual. Reform rite, Plaut.

VI. Title.

VII. Title: Deuteronomy.

BS1225.3.P55   vol. 5   [BS1275.3]   222'.1077s
ISBN 0-8074-0045-9   [222'.15077]   80-22928

MANUFACTURED IN THE UNITED STATES OF AMERICA

PUBLICATION OF
THIS VOLUME OF

The Torah: A Modern Commentary

has been made possible
by the generosity of

RABBI LEON FRAM

Other volumes in this series
have been made possible by the
generosity of the
Falk Foundation, Kivie Kaplan,
Maurice Saltzman, the
Miriam Stern Fox Fund,
Samuel H. Block, and
members of
Holy Blossom Temple,
Toronto

Preface

As in the preparation of previous volumes, I have had the constant and perceptive help of three distinguished scholars who acted as consultants: Professors Alexander Guttmann and Matitiahu Tsevat (Hebrew Union College - Jewish Institute of Religion) and, above all, Professor William W. Hallo (Yale University) who also contributed a special introductory essay to this book. A larger Board of Advisors, chaired by Rabbi Robert I. Kahn (Houston), read the manuscript critically. Its members were Professors Sheldon H. Blank (HUC - JIR, Cincinnati), Stanley Gevirtz (HUC - JIR, Los Angeles), and Harry M. Orlinsky (HUC - JIR, New York), Rabbis Samuel E. Karff (Houston), Bernard H. Mehlman (Boston), and Frederick C. Schwartz (Chicago). Rabbi Leonard A. Schoolman of the headquarters of the Union of American Hebrew Congregations in New York gave the book his particular attention and helped it along to final publication.

Despite the assistance rendered by the consultants and advisors, the responsibility for all materials in the commentary proper, their formulation and selection, rests solely with the author.

I wish to acknowledge with special gratitude the editorial assistance rendered by Mrs. Louise B. Stern and, from the UAHC Department of Publication, Mesdames Josette Knight, Annette Abramson, and Esther Fried Africk. Two presidents of the Union, Rabbi Maurice N. Eisendrath ז״ל and Rabbi Alexander M. Schindler gave me their unfailing support, as did Messrs. Ralph Davis and Stuart L. Benick, UAHC Publication Department. Mrs. Kitty Cohen (of Toronto) assisted me in meticulously preparing the manuscript. Finally, I wish to thank the staff of the Library of HUC - JIR in Cincinnati for their courteous and ever-ready help. The persistent encouragement I received from my wife cannot be adequately expressed.

With this volume the project which I began sixteen years ago comes to its conclusion: the first Jewish commentary on the Torah published in North America has now reached the first stage of completion. I hope that, as the years go on, there will be other stages: opportunities for revisions and corrections and additions based on new insights. For the knowledge of Torah can never be complete and its ever renewed study remains a duty, a pleasure, and a privilege.

תודה לאל עליון

W. G. P.

Erev Shavuot 5740
May 1980

CONTENTS

PART IV   Final Appeal and Farewell

PART V   Epilogue
The Death of Moses

Introducing Deuteronomy

DUDLEY WEINBERG ז"ל and W. GUNTHER PLAUT[1]

Name

Deuteronomy is the fifth of the five books of the Torah. The name is derived from the Greek and means "second law," which is the way the Septuagint translated the expression *mishneh ha-torah* in 17:18 (our translation renders these words as "a copy of this Teaching"). As in the other books of the Torah, the Hebrew name is taken from the first sentence of chapter 1; it is known as דְּבָרִים (*devarim*, words), for the book begins by saying, "These are the words. . . ."

Content

Deuteronomy is presented as a series of farewell speeches by Moses and ends with a description of his death. With few exceptions the book exhibits an integrated flow of narrative, exhortation, liturgy, law, and poetry. It addresses itself to Israel at a crucial period of its history and aims at national solutions which will guarantee the achievement of the nation's highest goals: peace, prosperity,

and security—both material and spiritual—under the suzerainty of the One God.

The book may be divided in a number of ways. One possibility is taking the text as being organized around four titles: 1:1; 4:44; 28:69; and 33:1. A more frequent division, which has been adopted in this commentary, distinguishes five parts: a prologue which reviews the past and a first sermon which stresses Israel's relationship to God (chapters 1:1–4:43); a second, long discourse which presents laws of ritual and civil character and a long catalogue of consequences (chapters 4:44–11:25); a third discourse (chapters 11:26–28:69); a final appeal and farewell by Moses (chapters 29–33); and a brief epilogue describing the leader's death (chapter 34).

In presenting the text in such a manner, one should remember that the need for systematizing which modern people feel when they approach a subject did not exist in the same way in ancient days. One of the reasons for this difference lies in the fact that today we *read* the material, while the early traditions of Israel were transmitted at first in *oral* form. Such transmission required aids to memory—and these might consist of assonances, word plays, and other mnemotechnical devices.[2] Or again, the text might be governed by its relationship to older, pre-existing traditions. In any case, one should at all times be on guard against judging these matters from a contemporary point of view. For instance, it has been claimed that Moses'

---

[1] When Rabbi Dudley Weinberg died in 1976, he left behind the draft of an introduction to his planned commentary on Deuteronomy. I have incorporated many of his notes, in this introduction, as a memorial to a dear friend and unique spiritual leader.

[2] For example, 22:13–29 deals with the actual or putative loss of virginity and related circumstances of sexual intercourse. In the midst of these laws (in verse 22) the subject of adultery is briefly introduced, and then the text returns to its former concerns.

first sermon elaborates on the first commandment and that the subsequent text deals with the rest of the Decalogue. Such analysis may satisfy the modern inquirer, but it has little to do with the structure of the ancient text.

Characteristics

That text, however, does have some overriding characteristics, and it features certain subjects which are either unique to Deuteronomy or which, by style and emphasis, give it a particular flavor. At the core stands the covenantal concept: At Horeb,[3] God concluded a pact with Israel and the mutuality of their intentions and obligations flows from this covenant.

God is One and is Israel's Master; He is to be the people's object of love and undivided loyalty. Idolatry is decried time and again and so are magic and the dark arts of the sorcerer. "You shall love the Lord your God" (6:5) spells out Israel's basic obligation which is amplified by a set of ordinances that the people must carefully observe. If they love and obey God, He will raise them above the nations, not because Israel is superior to other peoples, but because Israel is in possession of a special teaching. Torah makes Israel unique, and the Giver of Torah will protect this unequalled covenantal partner. But should the latter break the oath of loyalty, the direst consequences will occur, and both heaven and earth are called upon to witness these awesome threats.

The unique God and His unique people—the theme is not altogether new, for it forms the subject of the revelation at Horeb-Sinai (Exod. 19 and 20). In Deuteronomy, however, monotheism is central and God's Chosen Ones are time and again reminded that theirs is an unequalled opportunity. Their task is not easy and it is weighted with warnings of certain retribution for misdeeds. But the people are not adrift on an uncharted sea; they have guides to help them.

First and foremost among these is the Book itself, open and accessible to all who care to learn its teachings. Torah is not an esoteric doctrine beyond the people's reach; rather, it is "very close to you, in your mouth and in your heart, to observe it" (30:14).

Then there is Moses, friend and intimate of God whose representative he is. He is more than a transmitter of the divine word; he is prophet, intermediary, and fiery advocate for his people. Exodus and Numbers hint at his special status which at times approaches the level of semidivinity—such as the glow that emanates from his face (Exod. 34:29–33). In Deuteronomy, these supernatural traits of Moses are less in evidence, but his importance as leader and interpreter is stressed more than in the other books. In fact, Moses is shown to be surprisingly unhesitating in emphasizing his own role.

Finally, there are the priests who will aid the people in their quest of divine favor. They belong to the family of Aaron the Levite and have a variety of functions. Prime amongst these is the singular privilege of officiating at the central sanctuary. No longer may the people bring sacrifices at various shrines; now only one altar is permitted to them. The centralization of the cult is an important characteristic of Deuteronomy, and a contemplation of the reasons for this rule leads us squarely into a consideration of the origins of the book as a whole.

Time and Authorship

Traditional Judaism and Orthodox Christianity believe that Moses authored the Book of Deuteronomy, perhaps with the exception

---

[3] In Deuteronomy, God's mountain is generally called Horeb rather than Sinai. In the other books of the Torah, Horeb is traced to E, and Sinai to J and P. The

of chapter 34, or parts thereof, where Moses' death is recounted. These traditionalists further believe that the great leader wrote only what his divine Mentor instructed him to set down. In this view, Deuteronomy—like the other four books—is literally God's work, brought to earth by Moses His servant.

Our commentary does not accept this position. Rather, it holds that the whole Torah was the result of many centuries of growth, a fusion of sources and traditions, orally transmitted at first and then committed to writing. What God's and Moses' roles were in this process is a separate question. Nowhere can this development be followed more clearly than in the composition of Deuteronomy, for it is the only one of the five books of the Torah which enjoys a fairly unambiguous historical setting.

A radical religious reformation, which was carried out in 621 B.C.E. by King Josiah who reigned in Judah from 640–608, is reported in II Kings 22 and 23. This reformation displayed a remarkable resemblance to certain provisions which occur only in Deuteronomy. Some of these provisions differ with or at least vary from legislation which is contained in the other Torah books. For example, Josiah abolished the ancient practice of worshiping and offering sacrifices at the "high places" and established the Temple in Jerusalem as the sole sanctuary in which sacrifices could be properly offered. Deuteronomy is the only book of the Torah which contains legislation to that effect. Similarly, the prohibition of the worship of the heavenly bodies was stringently forbidden by Josiah. This too is a matter with which Deuteronomy is much concerned (17:3). Further, Deuteronomy 16:1–8 requires that Passover be celebrated in Jerusalem, while

Exodus 12 provides that it be observed at home. Josiah arranged Passover to be celebrated in Jerusalem in accordance with the law in Deuteronomy; and II Kings 23:22 f. records that such a Passover had not been celebrated during the entire period of the judges and of the monarchy, which is to say, for nearly four centuries.

According to the account in II Kings 22 and 23, King Josiah's reform was predicated on the discovery of a document called "Book of Teaching" (Sefer ha-Torah). This "Book of Teaching" is reported to have been found by the High Priest Hilkiah while the Temple was being repaired on orders of the king (II Kings 22:8). Precisely what this book was is not stated; however, the intriguing correspondence between the account of Josiah's reform and the Book of Deuteronomy is heightened by the fact that the expression "Book of Teaching" occurs nowhere else except in Deuteronomy and refers to Deuteronomy itself (29:20).

II Kings 23:1–2 describes that King Josiah assembled the leadership and the people of Judah and how they entered into a covenant with God, pledging themselves to abide loyally by the rules set down in the newly discovered book. The language of this passage is highly reminiscent of several passages in Deuteronomy in which the people are summoned to pledge their devotion and loving loyalty to God (e.g., 10:12–11:32 and 29:9–30:20).

What was the "Book of Teaching" which was discovered during the reign of Josiah and which provided the platform for his religious revolution in 621 B.C.E.? While biblical scholars are agreed that Josiah's "book" was not precisely the same text which is contained in Deuteronomy as we know it today, they are also largely agreed that there is an inescapable connection between the two. Modern scholars speculate about the exact contents of Josiah's "book," but most agree that it

close relation of Deuteronomy to the (northern) E-source is observable elsewhere as well. See further footnotes 5 and 9.

contained the core of what subsequently, through a continuing process of addition and editing, ultimately became our Book of Deuteronomy.

Assuming that the account of the discovery of the Torah book in II Kings 22:8 is historically accurate (or at least reflects a genuinely historical situation), we still are faced with some unanswered questions. How did the book which the High Priest Hilkiah "discovered" during the process of Temple repair come to be "hidden"? When and by whom was it written?

A significant clue is found in the biblical account of an earlier reform, similar to that which Josiah undertook. It occurred under the sponsorship of King Hezekiah who reigned in Judah from 715–687 B.C.E.[4] He too had mounted an assault against idolatry and the places and objects of idolatrous worship (II Kings 18:3–6). He too had attempted to centralize worship in the Jerusalem Temple (II Kings 18:22). Hezekiah's reform may well have been the occasion for the composition— or at least the beginning of the composition —of the Torah book whose discovery later helped to prompt and to provide the program for King Josiah's reform.

It is possible that the fall of Samaria and the Northern Kingdom, which occurred a few years before Hezekiah's accession, contributed to the monarch's reform. Northerners may have brought a basic document with them when they fled to Jerusalem—for Deuteronomy does indeed show affinity to the E-tradition which is believed to hail from the North. The centralization of the cult which was to have distinguished the shrine of Shechem now focused on Jerusalem.[5]

In addition, the reforms of Hezekiah were closely related to his foreign policy and constituted an aspect of his rebellion against his Assyrian overlords—a rebellion that caused the invasion of Judah by Sennacherib, in 701 B.C.E. For instance, the centralization of

the cult which Hezekiah undertook increased his access to large amounts of money deposited in the Temple treasury. This in turn made him assume a greater degree of political independence, but, while the Assyrians quelled his insurrection, his religious reforms remained in place during his lifetime.

A radical change occurred during the reign of his successors, Manasseh and Amon, especially since Assyria—under the kingship of Esarhaddon—obtained a stature of great power and extended its suzerainty as far west and south as Egypt and as far east as Elam.[6] Perhaps it was Manasseh's desire to conform more closely to the religious practices of his masters (though they did not apparently require such adjustments from their vassals); perhaps his and Amon's personal inclinations played a role—at any rate, in their reigns idolatrous practices were reintroduced, and an idol was placed in the Temple itself. Manasseh supported the Assyrians, tentatively at first and then vigorously, and his policy was carried on by his son Amon. Two years after his accession Amon was murdered, possibly by religious traditionalists or possibly by an anti-Assyrian conspiracy, or perhaps a combination of these forces. The result was the installation of Josiah as king who in stages reformed the cult and at the same time managed to dis-

[4] There is some controversy over the year of his ascendancy to the throne; some scholars put it somewhat earlier.
[5] So Jacob Milgrom, HUCA, 47 (1976), pp. 1–17, on the basis of linguistic terminology. According to his reconstruction, the book was reworked by P (after the reversal of Manasseh) and in this new form became state law under Josiah. M. Or, Beth Mikra, 73 (1978), pp. 218–220, adds the observation that the sefer found by Hilkiah probably contained chapters (scrolls?) from Exodus.
[6] This development may be followed in the essay of Carl D. Evans, "Judah's Foreign Policy from Hezekiah to Josiah," Scripture in Context: Essays on the Comparative Method, ed. C. D. Evans, W. W. Hallo, J. B. White (Pittsburgh Theological Monograph Series, vol. 34, 1980; Pittsburgh: Pickwick Press).

tance himself from Assyria, which was now entering into a period of political weakness. The climax of Josiah's reforms was the discovery of Deuteronomy and the spread of his ideas into cities of the former Northern Kingdom of Israel. This was possible because Assyria had already lost effective control of Judah and her neighboring territories.

What then can we say about the time of Deuteronomy's composition?

It is possible to assume that some traditions in the book were quite old and that they were subsequently molded to fit the special needs of changing times. Thus, the centralization of the cult in Jerusalem under Hezekiah may have been one consequence of the destruction of the Northern Kingdom in 721 B.C.E., a few years before the king ascended the throne. The emphasis on the Aaronide priesthood may have been the result of a power struggle among priestly families; while the strong exhorting voice calling the people to the worship of the One God may have belonged to an "underground" movement during the reigns of Manasseh and Amon. In Josiah's time, a full hundred years after the Northern Kingdom was destroyed and its people led away by the Assyrians, a religious revival combined with favorable political circumstances to bring forth a document which may have been the core of what we have come to know as the Book of Deuteronomy.[7]

What of Moses?

The Book of Deuteronomy begins with the assertion that Moses was delivering his final summary address to the people in the land of Moab (present-day Kingdom of Jordan) as they were about to cross the Jor-

dan River to take possession of the land which had for so long been promised them and in which Israel would at last find rest and security. That this assertion, which is frequently repeated in Deuteronomy, is a fiction seems obvious. It is not Moses who is the speaker or the preacher in Deuteronomy, although the ultimate inspiration for much that is said in Deuteronomy may well be traced back to him. Nor are the auditors of the Deuteronomic preacher the survivors of the wilderness experience which was about to achieve its culmination in Israel's homecoming. The fiction, however, speaks its own truth, and in that sense it is no fiction at all. If the conviction of modern scholarship concerning the time of Deuteronomy's composition is correct—and both historical and archeological evidence seems to confirm that conviction—then the "fiction" addresses itself to a real life situation which existed during the later period of the monarchy in Judah. That it does so, in terms of principles which were derived from ancient traditions which transcended the immediately addressed situation, was essential to the role of Deuteronomy in the development of biblical and postbiblical Judaism. The "fiction" of Deuteronomy was a summons to do God's will whenever it was heard; instruction from the past called forth a response in the present. The period of Josiah's reign, like the situation of the Israelites on the Steppes of Moab, was one marked by radical renewal, hope, and change. It too seemed like the fulfillment of a promise and was surely so understood by those who lived through it and attempted to interpret its meaning both at the time itself and in retrospect.

At the same time, the very persistence of Moses in the awareness of the people and of the compilers and preservers of their traditions lend enormous weight to the conviction that the real and historical Moses, difficult as the recovery of his genuine biog-

[7] The document which Hilkiah and Shaphan brought to Josiah must have been much shorter than the present Deuteronomy, for it had two readings in one day and possibly three (II Kings 22:8-10; 23:1-2).

raphy may be, was the true generator of the religion of Israel, the effective founder of the people of Israel, the inspired genius whose insights and career in many ways shaped the ideal, not only of the Jewish people, but of the entire Western world. While Deuteronomy did not flow directly from the pen of Moses, it did in part flow from his spirit. Why else would the actual authors of Deuteronomy have attributed their Torah book to him? Why else would the ultimate compilers of the entire Torah text have presented Moses as its earthly author and as God's chosen messenger whose mission was to proclaim His uniqueness and unity and to bring Israel into covenant with Him alone? Moses is not diminished by critical historical and literary analysis of the biblical text. If anything, his stature is enlarged and his life, although we may know very little of its details, looms large in history and especially in the consciousness of his people for whom he became *Mosheh Rabbenu*, Moses our teacher.

And what of the divine role in the text? This question has been discussed at some length in our commentary on Exodus 19 and in our Introduction to Genesis. We hold that the Torah is a record of Israel's striving to meet God and understand His will. In centuries of search, of finding and forgetting, of inspiration and desperation, God touched the soul of His people and the sparks of these meetings burn in the pages of the Torah. Deuteronomy is such a record of encounters, and it clearly stands—more than the other Torah books—in the tradition of Israel's prophets. When the prophets proclaimed, "Thus says the Lord," it was not a gratuitous attribution by the speaker; it was felt as reality and partook of it. Last but not least, as time went on, the belief that indeed God had spoken through Moses gained a firm hold and this belief developed its own dynamism, shaping the fate of a believing people. They *knew* what God wanted of them and tried to carry out His will as best they could.

Relation to Other Torah Books

Were the other Torah books already formulated when Deuteronomy came into being? The question cannot be answered with certainty; in fact, nowhere do scholars disagree more widely than in the dating of the various strands that went into the making of the Torah.[8] Formerly it was generally accepted among critical scholars that J, E, and D preceded P, the latter representing the most recent major source, which was assumed to belong to exilic or postexilic days (sixth and fifth centuries B.C.E.). Others disagree and believe P to be much earlier.

This commentary proceeds from the theory that major elements of the J, E, and P-traditions were already in existence when the D-texts were first formulated, representing partly an expansion, partly a departure from the former.[9] It is possible and even likely that Deuteronomy's core (chapters 5–26, 28) was set down as a book before the other four books of the Torah were formulated as distinct documents. When eventually they were, there came into existence a "Tetrateuch" (four books) which stood side by side with Deuteronomy. The latter was then enlarged with a prologue (chapters 1–4), an insert (chapter 27), and a

[8] These strands are usually named E (which in Genesis uses the word *Elohim* for God, and which had its origins in northern Israel); J (for the source that stresses the divine name YHWH, probably of southern Judahite origin); P (for the tradition that created most of Leviticus and other passages of archival and sacrificial content). The strands that went into the making of Deuteronomy are usually signed as D.

[9] The formulation of the Sabbath commandment (5:15) represents an expansion; the permission to eat meat at profane occasions, away from a sacrificial context (12:15), represents a departure from former practice.

concluding section (chapters 29–34). In this form the Book of Deuteronomy was joined to the Tetrateuch to form the Pentateuch (five books) or Torah, thereby bringing the major traditions concerning Moses together in one large work.[10] This process was not completed until after the exiles had returned from Babylon, perhaps in the fifth or fourth century B.C.E. The redactors of this work remain unknown; with Franz Rosenzweig we may refer to them as R, for *Rabbenu*, our teacher(s).[11]

Literary Aspects

As indicated, narrative, exhortation, liturgy, law, and poetry form the literary genres of the book. Narration occurs at the beginning and end and in chapter 27, and poetry only in chapter 32. Sometimes an exhortation has a narrative reference point, such as the passage in which Israel is asked to remember forever what Amalek had done, and the text then briefly recounts the relevant events (25:17–19). There is liturgy, such

as the thanksgiving ritual and recitation (chapter 26) and the reenactment of a covenantal ceremony marked by blessings and curses (chapter 27). All these materials, including many of the laws, are couched in a language which is different from that found in the other books of the Torah. The sentences are marked by more clauses, and the phrases have often a poetic quality, featuring a kind of prose meter with assonances which give the text a special rhythm and sense of ceremony.[12]

The style is highly rhetorical, the speaker pleads and urges, threatens and comforts, exhorts and, at the last, invokes the very heavens to be his witnesses.[13] The text has all the earmarks of preaching and uses a series of key expressions such as: "Hear, O Israel"; "do not try the Lord"; "be careful, then"; "give heed"; "remember"; "guard yourselves." The phrases are sometimes long and repetitive, but this only serves to heighten the oratorical effect of the whole. Special grammatical forms—such as the ending *un* in the plural imperfect of the third person—add the flavor of the unusual. The closest parallels are found in the prose style of Jeremiah and in the so-called "Early Prophets," that is, the books from Joshua to Kings. The affinity of this latter group to Deuteronomy has caused many scholars to say that it came from a "Deuteronomic school," whose theological interests were distinct from and were somewhat at variance with those who produced the Tetrateuch.[14] But scholarly agreement ends here. Some hold that the Deuteronomic school was centered in rural areas, among the Levites, while others detect telling parallels with the kind of "wisdom language" known at the court and in the city.[15]

The core of Deuteronomy (chapters 5–26) consists of laws which have their parallels in other ancient Near Eastern codes. They consist of casuistic and apodictic law. The former

[10] In Deuteronomy, however, the word תּוֹרָה (translated as "teaching") refers to Deuteronomy, not to the Pentateuch (which in this form did not yet exist).
[11] The literature on biblical criticism is immense. Concise surveys may be found in Kenneth A. Kitchen, *Ancient Orient and Old Testament* (London: Tyndale Press, 1966), pp. 112–138; Roland de Vaux, *The Bible and the Ancient Near East* (Darton, Longman, and Todd, 1972), pp. 31–48; on Deuteronomy, see Moshe Weinfeld, *Encyclopaedia Judaica*, Vol. 5, cols. 1574 ff.; N. Lohfink, *Interpreter's Dictionary of the Bible*, Supplement, pp. 229 ff.
[12] Lohfink, *Interpreter's Dictionary of the Bible*, p. 229. In classical languages this is called "artistic prose."
[13] The technical term by which this style is often described is "parenesis" (from the Greek *ainos*, speech), a type of exhortation.
[14] See especially M. Weinfeld, *Deuteronomy and the Deuteronomic School* (Oxford: Clarendon Press, 1972). Peake's *Commentary on the Bible* (London: Thomas Nelson and Sons, 1962), p. 269, says: "Just as Genesis to Numbers is the P-Bible, so Deuteronomy to II Kings is the D-Bible."
[15] The former opinion is expounded by Gerhard von Rad, the latter by George E. Mendenhall.

is much more frequent and states the cases and conditions under which the law is to be operative, for instance: "When you take the field against your enemies . . ." (20:1). Apodictic law is stated without conditional clauses, as in the Decalogue and elsewhere: "You shall not have in your pouch alternate weights" (25:13), or "You shall not boil a kid in its mother's milk" (14:21).[16]

How do these laws relate to the Book of the Covenant which is generally considered the oldest of the legal codes in the Torah (Exod. 21–23)? The Deuteronomist, though fully conversant with this code, yet departs from it significantly. Compare, for instance, the way a Hebrew slave is to be treated. Both Exodus 21:2–6 and Deuteronomy 15:12–18 agree on the need to free such a servant at the end of six years but disagree on whether the slave is entitled to compensation. Exodus says no, Deuteronomy (which extends the law also to female slaves) says yes. In this and similar instances, the Deuteronomist clearly amends older laws, especially those which have a moral and religious underpinning.[17] The majority of the casuistic laws in Exodus are not mentioned at all in Deuteronomy, probably because these belonged to a corpus of law common to the neighboring nations which the Deuteronomic circle expected to remain operative.[18] For the whole framework of the covenant bears a close resemblance to Hittite suzerain-vassal treaties of the second millennium and neo-Assyrian treaties of the time when Deuteronomy germinated.[19]

In sum, Deuteronomy is the heir of old traditions which it molded in accordance with new social and political needs and did so in a prophetic spirit which gave it the urgency of religious imperatives. As time went on, these characteristics especially impressed themselves on the soul of Israel, for they made clear that even the smallest rule had the purpose of purifying the Lord's people and that the nation as a whole, collectively, had a responsibility for the future. The ringing cadences were believed to have been the words of Moses, the greatest figure of Israel's past, and were thereby given added stature. God himself was seen to stand behind leader and law. When Deuteronomy was at last joined to the Tetrateuch and became the fifth book of the Torah, it continued the saga which had started with Creation, had proceeded to the fashioning of Israel, and, with the death of Moses, now completed the first stage of a universal history. Israel, as God's co-worker, was to be forever ready to help the Creator perfect the work of His hands. Torah was the way, and a willing people thereby held the key both to its own fate and to the future of the world.

[16] On casuistic and apodictic law see A. Alt, *Essays on Old Testament History and Religion* (Garden City: Doubleday, 1968), and the survey by R. Sonsino, *Journal of Reform Judaism* (Summer 1979), pp. 117–123.
[17] Already Rashi, in his commentary on the Exodus passages, recognized the expanding nature of the Deuteronomic law.
[18] The revolutionary nature of Deuteronomic law is propounded by Weinfeld, *Deuteronomy, passim*, who holds that the book came to replace rather than complement the older law. Two other radical theorists may be mentioned. Ellis Rivkin, *The Shaping of Jewish History* (New York: Charles Scribner's Sons, 1971), considers Deuteronomy as an attempt to end prophetic privilege and install Moses as the one unequalled prophet whose words were immutable. This revolution failed, for Jeremiah and Ezekiel continued independently to interpret the divine will. But another, later revolution succeeded, that of a group of anonymous leaders who installed the Aaronides as God's sole priests and did so by creating the Pentateuch and thus saved a disintegrating YHWH religion (pp. 17–41). Morton Smith, *Palestinian Parties and Politics That Shaped the Old Testament* (New York and London: Columbia University Press, 1971), on the other hand, considers Deuteronomy to have been a religious and political success. It represented the "God Alone" party which taught God's jealous love for Israel. In doing so it altered older traditions, proclaimed Israel to be a separate people, and established monotheism as Israel's religion (pp. 48–56).
[19] This aspect is discussed in greater detail in William W. Hallo's essay, which follows. See there also for a discussion on kingship in Deuteronomy.

On Reading This Commentary

Note first of all that text and commentary do not appear in the usual continuous fashion but are divided into a prologue, three major parts, and an epilogue, altogether 28 separate sections. While this division has no precise warrant in prior practice,[20] it has been introduced for convenience of study and for those synagogues which do not read the entire traditional weekly portion. In attempting thus to divide the book both by reason of length and by subject matter, our arrangement frequently differs from the division into chapters which originated with medieval Christian scholarship.

Readers of the Bible are usually unaware that what they are reading is not "the" original version of the manuscript and that the translation they use is actually a kind of commentary on the Hebrew text which it means to render.

There is no original manuscript available which was written by any of the authors of the Bible. The oldest extant parchment scroll of the Torah dates from the tenth century C.E., which is as much as 1,500 or more years later than the likely time of its final composition. Quite naturally, much happens to a text in the course of oral transmission and copying by hand, and one must not be astonished that a number of variants and versions arose. It is a great tribute to the care and devotion which were lavished on the text that the variants are relatively minor and the scribal corruptions rather few. Our commentary uses the Masoretic version. The Masoretes, so called because they transmitted the *Masorah* (מָסוֹרָה) or textual tradition,

were scholars who over the centuries attempted to ascertain and preserve the best text. One of these versions, produced in Tiberias in the tenth century C.E., found general acceptance and is the standard Hebrew text in synagogue use today.

Because the knowledge of classical Hebrew diminished or disappeared among many Jews after they returned from the Babylonian exile, the need for translations arose. In the course of centuries there appeared translations in Aramaic (Targum) which was the popular language of postexilic Jews, Greek (Septuagint), Latin (Vulgate), Syriac (Peshitta), Arabic, and in modern times in every written language of man. The important ancient translations often give us significant clues about the original from which they were translated, for there are differences between them. What is even more important is to recognize that every translator interprets the original text, for he renders it as he understands (or misunderstands) it.

This becomes particularly apparent when one follows modern translations. For instance, there are great differences between the famous and beloved English King James Version (published in 1611 and often called "Authorized," i.e., for the Church of England) and later renditions such as the American version, or the German Luther Bible and the translation by Rosenzweig and Buber. Many of these differences are stylistic since the language of translation has itself undergone vast changes; others are due to new insights into the philology of ancient days and the political, social, and economic circumstances to which the text refers.

The translation of Deuteronomy used is the New Jewish Version, published by the

---

[20] It resembles to some degree the divisions of the old triennial cycle of Torah readings.

XXI

Jewish Publication Society (revised printing, 1967), with the kind permission of the publishers. This translation, in addition to its scholarly and linguistic merits, has been made particularly valuable by the publication of the translators' *Notes on the New Translation of the Torah* (1969, referred to as JPS *Notes*) which explain in detail why certain translations were chosen and others rejected.

In addition to the introductory essays, the Hebrew text, and translation, this book is composed of the following parts:

1] THE TEXTUAL NOTES. These appear below and immediately following the text and are arranged by verse and number for easy reference to the text itself. The notes may be called "textual," i.e., they attempt to give the "plain meaning" (*peshat*) of words and sentences without going into deeper interpretations (which are reserved for the commentary proper). In the notes you will find explanations of terms, names, references to other biblical books, and notations on linguistic difficulties. It should be remembered that the notes comment, not only on the English translation, and try to make it understandable, but also—and primarily—on the underlying Hebrew text. For instance, the Hebrew text uses word plays and assonances extensively, and these can rarely be translated into another language. The reader should also remember that the Torah tradition was originally transmitted by word of mouth so that many so-called etymological explanations of personal and place names may have served as popular memory devices. For instance, *Kayin* (Cain) is said to come from *kaniti* (I have gained) although linguistically there is no connection.

2] THE COMMENTARY. The brief essays which accompany each unit are largely interpretative: they attempt to explain the intent of the Torah, how Jewish tradition saw these meanings, and how relevant they are today. The author has chosen and concentrated on a few themes in each section; he is aware that in so choosing he has omitted other themes which the reader might wish to have had included.

Just as the notes frequently offer alternative explanations, so does the commentary itself. Sometimes this is done because we really have at present no sure way of establishing one particular interpretation as *the* meaning; at other times the author feels that the Torah leaves us purposely with parallel or even contradictory ideas. If this seems unlikely to a modern reader who is used to a systematic and logical exposition of a subject, it must be remembered that the Torah is not a treatise, essay, or exposition, but poetry, prose, epic, and historic memory created in a prescientific age fundamentally different from ours. Where we are prone to say "either, or," the Bible may say "both" and let the unresolved tension between the two stand without further comment. This sometimes lends the Torah a special quality of opaqueness which those who look for one and only one meaning are bound to miss.

3] THE GLEANINGS. Appended to all sections are gleanings from world literature which have a bearing on the text. Here especially will be found selections from that vast compendium of ancient Jewish lore and homily called Midrash[21] and also some writings from Christian and Moslem sources as well as contemporary observations not included in the commentary proper. (Where the source is not identified, the author himself is to be credited.) The gleanings are generally only brief excerpts; they are intended to sug-

---

[21] The total collection, spread over many sources, will be written Midrash (with a capital M), while an individual homily will be written midrash (plural: *midrashim*).

gest something of the vast range of response elicited by the Torah. It is hoped that the reader will be moved to explore these areas further.

4] FOOTNOTES. Occasionally the text of commentary and gleanings is expanded by brief additions. These are indicated by superior notes in the text—such as[5]—and are printed at the bottom of the page.

5] THE REFERENCES. Notes, commentary, gleanings, and footnotes contain references only to the Bible (where no book is mentioned the reference is to Deuteronomy). We follow the standard way of noting biblical passages; for instance, chapter 12, verse 3, is listed as 12:3.

All other sources may be found in the references which, for easier readability, are grouped together at the end of the volume. These references—indicated by bracketed numbers such as [15]—are not meant primarily for scholars; hence they do not usually give alternative sources, divergent readings, and the like. They refer, wherever possible, to works which have appeared in English or English translation and to others only where no translation is available. (For abbreviations and principal bibliographical references, see back matter.)

References to commentaries on Genesis, Exodus, Leviticus, and Numbers which do not bear an author's name are to the books by B. J. Bamberger (*Leviticus*, 1979) and by the author (*Genesis*, 1974; *Numbers*, 1979; *Exodus*), published by the Union of American Hebrew Congregations. A single volume containing all five commentaries appeared mid-1981.

6] HAFTAROT. The synagogue, and subsequently the church, established a tradition which provides that on each Sabbath and holy day a special portion be read from the Bible. At Jewish services, a section from the Torah, called *sidrah* or *parashah*, and an additional selection from the Earlier and Later Prophets, called *haftarah* (originally signifying dismissal of the congregation), are publicly read. Tradition has divided Deuteronomy into 11 *sidrot*, the cycle of which begins on the Sabbath preceding Tishah b'Av.

The *haftarot* appear without commentary at the end of the book, together with alternate selections. These nontraditional additions are provided to give congregations a wider range of acquaintance with the Bible and draw also on the Book of Psalms which is not represented in the *haftarah* cycles of the traditional synagogue.

Transliterations

When comment is made on a Hebrew word or phrase, the latter is usually rendered in Hebrew characters. Transliterations are utilized only where they are deemed of special help to the reader who is unfamiliar with Hebrew.

This commentary has adopted the simplified transliteration proposed by Prof. Werner Weinberg of Hebrew Union College - Jewish Institute of Religion and brought it into consonance with the usage of the Union of American Hebrew Congregations. Based on the Sephardic pronunciation, it makes no distinction between ס and שׂ, between ח and כ, ט and ת, nor between כ and ק. צ is represented by tz; ב appears as v, and ח and כ as ch. It does not always take note of א or ע except when two vowels inside a word should be separated and could be mispronounced, in which case a hyphen or an apostrophe is introduced (as in רֹאִי, ro-i, or מוֹעֵד, mo'ed). The *dagesh* is omitted except where it is an aid to pronunciation (*shabbat* rather than *shabat*). Also omitted is the resting *sheva*; the moving *sheva* is shown as e when it represents a syllable (as in שְׁמַע, *shema*). Half

vowels are transliterated as full vowels (as in אֱמֶת, *emet*). Other vowels are rendered as follows:

_ and _		as a
_ and _		as e
_ and י_		as i
וֹ and ·		as o
וּ and _		as u

The letter י is represented as y, except in י_ and י_ in which cases it is sometimes omitted.

There are a few Hebrew words which have become part of common usage, and therefore their usual spelling has been maintained. This is especially true for proper names, e.g., Ishmael rather than Yishmael. Also, the definite article *ha* (or *he*) has been separated from its noun by the introduction of a hyphen in order to facilitate the reading (*ha-yashar* rather than *hayashar*) except in some cases where by virtue of common usage the hyphen has been omitted.

Deuteronomy
and Ancient Near Eastern Literature

WILLIAM W. HALLO

Deuteronomy occupies a unique position in the Hebrew Bible and in the history of biblical scholarship. More nearly than any other biblical book, it can lay claim to having been a book in its own right before it was incorporated into the canon; it is the least hypothetical of the documents which the documentary hypothesis claims as the original components of the Pentateuch. Deuteronomy, or at least its central core (here Parts II and III), preserves in its essence the "book of the law" found by Hilkiah the High Priest and turned over to King Josiah of Judah in the eighteenth year of his reign (621 B.C.E.) according to one of the most fundamental tenets of modern biblical criticism.

But beyond this there is little scholarly agreement. The authorship of Deuteronomy has been variously attributed to the priestly circles that found it; to the prophetic movement whose influence is said to be evident in it; to the royal court that needed it to counter precisely the exclusive prophetic claims to speak for God; to the party of scribes and wise men who wanted a new morality based on universal norms, or contrariwise to a zealous group of exiles from the defeated northern kingdom of Israel striving to preserve pre-monarchic traditions and purify them from the corrupting cosmopolitanism of the surrounding world.

In formal and stylistic terms, too, Deuteronomy has been subject to very divergent modern interpretations: as a lengthy sermon on the theme of collective responsibility; as the libretto of a recurrent cultic ceremony celebrating the renewal of the covenant; as a lawbook superseding or supplementing the "Covenant Code" of Exodus; as a declaration of independence from human (Assyrian) overlordship and of vassalage instead to God; as an integral and concluding part of the Pentateuch or contrariwise as the introduction to the "Deuteronomic" history of the Former Prophets (Joshua through Kings).[1]

These and other issues will probably never be resolved by appeal to the biblical text alone. Here as elsewhere, the comparative and archeological evidence must be thrown into the balance. It will be marshaled here in accordance with the structural analysis of the text offered in the commentary and with the literary genres adduced in the various proposed comparisons.

---

[1] Moshe Weinfeld, "Deuteronomy—The Present State of Inquiry," *Journal of Biblical Literature*, 86 (1967), pp. 249–262 [hereafter cited as *JBL*]; idem, *Deuteronomy and the Deuteronomic School* (Oxford, 1972).

Deuteronomy as Homily

Ostensibly the Book of Deuteronomy presents itself to us in the guise of a homily, i.e., a religious discourse addressed to a congregation. Indeed, with the exception of a few narrative introductions, inserts, and transitions, all of the book is phrased in the first person as a direct address by Moses or, rather, as three successive sermons (chs. 1–4, 5–28, 29–31),[2] a song (32), and a blessing of the twelve tribes (33). Only the concluding notice of Moses' death (34) falls outside this framework (see below).

Such a framework is unique in biblical literature. All the other narratives involving Moses and the legislation attributed to him are phrased in the third person, and this is generally true of the other historical figures in the Bible. Only the literary prophets speak in the first person, but their biographies tend to retreat behind the transcendental events and messages that are their primary concern. Even apocalyptic and apocryphal literature, although more receptive to the "autobiographical" style, did not follow the model of Deuteronomy. On the contrary, the Temple Scroll recently edited from the finds at Qumran took pains to eliminate all references to Moses and rephrased the Deuteronomic record in third person terms.[3]

The parenetic or hortatory style of Deuteronomy seems, in fact, less at home in Israel than in Greece, where rhetoric first evolved as a fine art in the orations of an Isocrates or a Demosthenes, and where historians like Thucydides and Xenophon sprinkled their narratives with lengthy speeches and exhortations, not, to be sure, claiming to be verbatim transcripts of the original words, but aspiring in an imaginative way to suggest what the protagonists, given their character and the circumstances, might have said on a given occasion. There are, as a result, scholars who would like to see Greek models as inspiring the literary structure and legislative content of the Book of Deuteronomy.[4] In comparative terms, this represents a "minimalist" view. As usual, it is open to challenge.

For in point of fact the style of Deuteronomy is not so much oratorical or autobiographical as pseudo-autobiographical. That is to say, the figure of Moses is presented in such colorless terms that it is clearly no more than a literary device for supporting the thread of injunction and narrative. Only a truly "maximalist" position would take the Mosaic authorship of the book literally. More specifically, the choice of Moses for this literary purpose is evidently dictated by the intention of imparting the highest possible authority to a legislative program by attributing it to the great lawgiver himself. In this respect, the most suggestive literary models are to be found, not in the contemporary west, but in the older Near East.

In Egypt, where every official tended to decorate his tomb with an autobiographical obituary,[5] there early evolved a sophisticated form of fictitious narrative in the first person, the most famous examples being the tales of Sinuhe and Wen-Amon.[6] And in more blatantly pseudepigraphical autobiography, the great leaders of a hoary antiquity are made to speak in texts that are patently of much later date, and pretend to furnish either an eye-witness account of their "own"

---

[2] In the present commentary, chs. 1–4 are treated as a prologue and 5–28 as two separate discourses (5–11 and 12–28, with ch. 27 as an insert).

[3] Baruch A. Levine, "The Temple Scroll," *Bulletin of the American Schools of Oriental Research*, 232 (1978), pp. 5–23. [Hereafter cited as *BASOR*.]

[4] Morton Smith, "East Mediterranean Law Codes of the Early Iron Age," *H. L. Ginsberg Volume (Eretz-Israel*, 14, Jerusalem, 1978), pp. 38–43.

[5] See the examples in James B. Pritchard, *Ancient Near Eastern Texts* (3rd ed., Princeton, 1969), pp. 227 f., 230, 233 f., 329 f. [Hereafter cited as Pritchard, *ANET*.]

[6] *Ibid.*, pp. 18–22 and 25–29 respectively.

time or an accurate prophecy of the then future (already past), or both in succession. The tradition of seven lean years is preserved in a Ptolemaic text thus attributed to Pharaoh Djoser of the Old Kingdom.[7]

But the genre is most at home in the literature of Babylonia and Assyria, where the tradition of first person royal inscriptions went back to the beginnings of the second millennium, and easily spawned fictitious royal autobiographies by imitation. The great kings of the Akkad dynasty were cast in this role, notably Sargon and Naram-Sin, but also some less celebrated rulers of the later third and second millennia. The authority of these ancient worthies was presumably invoked in order to enhance the credibility of the texts attributed to them, just as in the case of Deuteronomy.[8]

Deuteronomy as Cult Libretto

But if such pseudo-autobiographies provide a model of sorts for the form and the

framework of the book, we must look further for the source of its particular function. The words attributed to Moses in Deuteronomy are addressed by him to the entire people of Israel as it prepared to cross the Jordan into the Promised Land. They therefore assume a definite purpose, a programmatic function. Their intent is to lay down a virtual constitution for the people when they take possession of the land. The Decalogue and some of the laws previously given in the wilderness are repeated or supplemented to the accompaniment of reiterated exhortations of a general requirement to do God's will and a specific new injunction to prepare to centralize the entire cult at a single place of God's choosing.

Such cultic centralization, although "anticipating" the ultimate role of Jerusalem and possible Mesopotamian analogies,[9] also reflects the older realities of Israel's past, the tradition of primary shrines that had united the tribes on the cultic plane ever since the conquest and settlement of the Promised Land, even while they remained largely fragmented on the political plane. Shechem, Shilo, Bethel, and Gilgal appear to have played this role successively in the period of the Judges and Samuel,[10] although recent opinion questions this reconstruction.[11] All of them are located in the central highlands today referred to variously as "Samaria" or the "West Bank" which were then occupied by the "Rachel tribes"— Benjamin, Ephraim, and (half of) Manasseh. They were thus relatively accessible to the more outlying tribes on the coast, in the Galilee, Transjordan, and Judea, but they were clearly in the territory of the later northern kingdom and shared its particular interests.[12]

Such a "northern" bias has been detected also in the theology of Deuteronomy. The conspicuous stress on the love-relationship between God and Israel shows affinities with

[7] Ibid., pp. 31 f.

[8] Ibid., p. 119; cf. A. K. Grayson, *Babylonian Historical-Literary Texts* (Toronto Semitic Texts and Studies, 3, 1975), pp. 7–9.

[9] Weinfeld, "Cult Centralization in Israel in the Light of Neo-Babylonian Analogy," *Journal of Near Eastern Studies*, 23 (1964), pp. 202–212. [Hereafter cited as *JNES*.]

[10] George W. Anderson, "Israelite Amphictyonies," *Translating and Understanding the Old Testament*, ed. H. T. Frank and W. L. Reed (1970), pp. 135–151.

[11] Roland de Vaux, "Was There an Israelite Amphictyony?" *Biblical Archaeology Review*, 3/2 (1977), pp. 40–47. Cf. already Harry M. Orlinsky, "The Tribal System of Israel and Related Groups in the Period of the Judges," *Studies and Essays in Honor of Abraham A. Neuman* (1962), pp. 375–387; reprinted in *Oriens Antiquus*, 1 (1962), pp. 11–20, and in *Essays in Biblical Culture and Biblical Translation* (1974), pp. 66–77. (See there, p. 77, for additional references.)

[12] J. H. Hayes and J. M. Miller, eds., *Israelite and Judaean History* (Philadelphia: The Westminster Press, 1977), pp. 297—308; Jacob Weingreen, "The Theory of the Amphictyony in Pre-Monarchial Israel," *Journal of the Ancient Near Eastern Society*, 5 (1973), pp. 427–434.

the northern prophet Hosea.[13] The outspoken opposition to idolatry reflects, like that of the "Elohistic" or northern source of the Tetrateuch, the greater exposure of the cosmopolitan north to indigenous and foreign polytheistic cults. The use of "place" (*māqōm*) to identify (any) sacred locale is in marked distinction to the southern "height" (*bāmā*) in this sense. (In post-biblical Hebrew, "*the* place" even became a substitute for the divine name.) Above all, the stress on God's name contrasts with the central role of God's glory in the priestly source.[14]

It has therefore been argued that the Book of Deuteronomy reflects an attempt by the prophetic circles in the north to elevate Moses to the status of the first and greatest prophet (cf., e.g., Hosea 12:14; Deut. 18:18), and to picture him as mediator for a cult ceremony at which the covenant was established or renewed. Indeed, Deuteronomy would be the libretto of such a ceremony, while passages such as Joshua 24 would represent shorter synopses together with stage directions.

But even on this uniquely Israelite interpretation of the overall function of the book, essential elements in it owe something to Near Eastern precedent. The amphictyonic principle, named for the classical Greek leagues of Delos, Delphi, etc., has been detected also in King Solomon's provisioning system (I Kings 4:7–19) and at the court of his younger Egyptian contemporary Sheshonq I (the biblical Shishak), though it is debated who copied it from whom;[15] its earliest manifestation may go back to the end of the third millennium in Sumer.[16] The notion of "establishing the name," so central to Deuteronomy, echoes earlier Sumerian, Akkadian, and Phoenician idioms, where it refers to acquiring legitimacy or fame, especially by the king.[17] This analogy suggests that a traditional royal prerogative was here being bestowed on God. And the

"place" of God's choosing with which this name is invariably linked in Deuteronomy is similarly evocative of the cult places literally referred to as the "place where the king stands."[18] Thus the conception of Deuteronomy as the text of a periodic cultic renewal of the covenant by the tribes of Israel finds some support in the comparative data.

Deuteronomy as Lawbook

The core of Deuteronomy is formed by its legislation, repeating and supplementing the Covenant Code in Exodus, the Holiness Code in Leviticus, and scattered priestly laws in Numbers. The Greek (and English) name of the whole book, based on the Hebrew of 17:18 (cf. also Joshua 8:32), reflects the central importance of this "repetition of the law" (New Jewish Version: "a copy of this Teaching"). And the phrase "as God commanded/promised/swore," repeated more than thirty times in the text, sounds like a

[13] For other interpretations of the relationship, see William L. Moran, "The Ancient Near Eastern Background of the Love of God in Deuteronomy," *Catholic Biblical Quarterly*, 25 (1963), pp. 77–87; J. W. McKay, "Man's Love of God in Deuteronomy and the Father/ Teacher-Son/Pupil Relationship," *Vetus Testamentum*, 22 (1972), pp. 426–435. [Hereafter cited as VT.]

[14] E. W. Nicholson, *Deuteronomy and Tradition* (Philadelphia: Fortress Press, 1967); idem, "The Centralisation of the Cult in Deuteronomy," VT, 13 (1963), pp. 380–389.

[15] D. B. Redford, "Studies in Relations between Palestine and Egypt during the First Millennium B.C. I. The Taxation System of Solomon," *Studies on the Ancient Palestinian World* (Toronto Semitic Texts and Studies, 2, 1972), pp. 141–156. Alberto R. Green, "Israelite Influence at Shishak's Court?" BASOR, 233 (1979), pp. 59–62.

[16] William W. Hallo, "A Sumerian Amphictyony," *Journal of Cuneiform Studies*, 14 (1960), pp. 88–114. [Hereafter cited as JCS.]

[17] Shalom M. Paul, "Psalm 72:5—A Traditional Blessing for the Long Life of the King," *JNES*, 31 (1972), p. 354.

[18] Richard S. Ellis, "Mountains and Rivers," *Bibliotheca Mesopotamica*, 7 (Malibu, 1977), pp. 29–34.

recurrent footnote, alluding to the previous formulations in the rest of the Pentateuch.[19]

But the "Deuteronomic code" is not only the most crucial portion of the book, it is also the oldest or, more precisely, the portion most explicitly indebted to older models. This is true in the first place of the overall structure of the material. Like the other biblical codes and, more particularly, like their cuneiform antecedents, the Deuteronomic code is encased within a prologue and epilogue, the former largely hortatory in character, the latter prominently featuring catalogues of blessings for compliance and curses for non-compliance with the code. The internal arrangement of the individual laws proceeds generally from the cultic legislation (chs. 12–14) to criminal, civil, and procedural law (15–25), each grouped in broad legal categories which, according to a new interpretation, follow the order of topics in the Decalogue in ch. 5, whose provisions are conspicuously not repeated here.[20]

A similar order (albeit in reverse) and comparable groupings were already imposed on the Laws of Hammurabi by the scholars of his time or a little later.[21] More telling still is the testimony of individual enactments, adduced here by way of illustration only.

At its outset, the code provides for the centralization of the cult, but mitigates the new law by allowing "profane slaughter" outside the central sanctuary (12:21; cf. 12:15) thus maintaining the distinction from sacred slaughter which set Israel apart from its neighbors.[22] The specific prohibition against the consumption of pork (14:8) was based on the unclean character of the pig, not, as elsewhere in the ancient world, on its sacred nature and cultic uses, attested occasionally also by biblical allusions[23] and by bones and artistic representations uncovered by excavations at Palestinian sites which were under Egyptian or Assyrian rule or influence.[24]

The laws of the sabbatical year (ch. 15) elaborate on those of Leviticus 25 and like them represent an essentially Israelite institutionalization of what had at best been vaguely comparable precedents in the Old Babylonian dynasty of Hammurabi.[25] His son Samsu-iluna and his descendant Ammi-saduqa promulgated edicts which appear to have provided for remission of certain debts and release of certain debt-slaves, but not at regular intervals.[26]

The judiciary envisaged in Deuteronomy has been compared to the reform of King Jehoshaphat of Judah (ca. 870–850 B.C.E.) as described in II Chronicles 19:4–11 (see commentary to 16:18–20 and 17:8–13). But both enactments, involving priests as well as judges in an elaborate hierarchy, have an analogy of sorts in the Edict of Horemheb (late fourteenth century B.C.E.), last pharaoh of the great Eighteenth Dynasty in Egypt's empire period.[27] The law of the king which follows (17:14–20; cf. I Samuel 8:9, 11; 10:25)

[19] J. Milgrom, "Profane Slaughter and the Composition of Deuteronomy," *Hebrew Union College Annual*, 47 (1976), pp. 1–17.

[20] Stephen A. Kaufman, "The Structure of the Deuteronomic Law," *Maarav*, 1 (1979), pp. 105–158.

[21] J. J. Finkelstein, "A Late Old Babylonian Copy of the Law of Hammurapi," *JCS*, 21 (1967), pp. 39–48.

[22] Hallo, "The Concept of Consumption," in essay to Commentary on Leviticus.

[23] J. M. Sasson, "Isaiah LXVI, 3–4a," *VT*, 26 (1976), pp. 199–207.

[24] De Vaux, "The Sacrifice of Pigs in Palestine and in the Ancient Near East," in de Vaux, *The Bible and the Ancient Near East*, translated by D. McHugh (Garden City: Doubleday, 1971), ch. 14, pp. 252–269; Alfred von Rohr Sauer, "The Cultic Role of the Pig in Ancient Times," *In Memoriam Paul Kahle*, ed. Matthew Black and Georg Fohrer (Beiheft zur Zeitschrift für die alttestamentliche Wissenschaft, 103, 1968), pp. 201–207.

[25] Hallo, "The Laws of Sanctification," in essay to Commentary on Leviticus.

[26] Finkelstein, "The Edict of Ammiṣaduqa: A New Text," *Revue d'Assyriologie et d'Archéologie Orientale*, 63 (1969), pp. 45–64. [Hereafter cited as *RA*.]

[27] Kurt Pflüger, "The Edict of King Haremhab," *JNES*, 5 (1946), pp. 260–268.

may similarly have drawn its immediate inspiration from a specific Judean reign, but again its ultimate antecedents have been sought in Canaanite political practice, notably in respect of conscription for military services and public works and of royal control over real and movable property and over the tithing of income.[28]

The issue of "prophetic credentials" is taken up next (18:9–22; cf. already ch. 13) and silhouetted against the multifarious divination techniques encountered among the indigenous populations. Of all these techniques, the most intriguing may be that of interrogating "ghosts and familiar spirits," almost invariably linked together throughout the Hebrew Bible. The translations of these terms sound quite colorless in English, but in the Septuagint they appear as engastrímythos, literally stomach-talker or ventriloquist, and terato-skópos, literally diviner by prodigies or monstrous births, revealing something of their long history still dimly familiar to the Hellenistic world. New evidence, especially in Hittite, suggests that the "ghosts" in question were conjured up out of pits dug in the ground to the accompaniment of elaborate rituals.[29] As for teratoscopy (even if it is a mistranslation in Greek), this practice of divining the future from monstrous deformities encountered (or imagined) at the birth of infants or (more often) of domesticated animals was highly developed in ancient Mesopotamia. Not only were such freak births duly reported to the court, but elaborate cuneiform handbooks systematically interpreted the centuries of observations of such births and the "results" that had attended them.[30]

The cities of refuge (19:1–13) were an essentially unique Israelite innovation. Although the concept of asylum was familiar to the classical world in connection with temples and specifically altars, and the very word asylum comes from the Greek word for "inviolable," yet the notion of whole cities set aside for the purpose (cf. Numbers 35; Joshua 20 ff.; I Chronicles 6) was strange to Greek ears and translated with a term borrowed from the language of banishment and exile. In Deuteronomy, where the cities are chosen on the basis of their location and not of their sacred character (as Levitical cities), the contrast with the classical world is even more conspicuous. But there may be a remote precedent in Mesopotamian lore, where the distant forest is described as a city on the one hand and on the other as a place of detention, protection, refuge, or sanctuary.[31]

The cities of refuge were primarily designed to break the traditional chain of blood-vengeance, a motive sometimes attributed also to the legislation regarding unsolved homicide, which is found only in Deuteronomy (21:1–9). The alleged parallels from Nuzi similarly apply the principle of collective liability, but only in cases of burglary or the killing of livestock.[32] Closer precedents are found, rather, in the Hittite laws. Here the earlier version of paragraph 6 provides for compensation to the heir of the victim from the owner of the land on which

[28] I. Mendelsohn, "Samuel's Denunciation of Kingship in the Light of the Akkadian Documents from Ugarit," BASOR, 143 (1956), pp. 17–27. Cf. also John Gray, "Canaanite Kingship in Theory and Practice," VT, 2 (1952), pp. 193–220.
[29] Harry A. Hoffner, Jr., "Second Millennium Antecedents to the Hebrew 'ōb," JBL, 86 (1967), pp. 384–401; idem; "The Hittites and Hurrians," Peoples of Old Testament Times, ed. D. J. Wiseman (Oxford, 1973), pp. 197–228; esp. p. 216.
[30] Erle Leichty, The Omen Series Summa Izbu (Texts from Cuneiform Sources, 4, New York, 1970).
[31] Hallo, "Notes from the Babylonian Collection I: Nungal in the Egal," JCS, 31 (1979), pp. 161–165.
[32] Cyrus H. Gordon, "An Akkadian Parallel to Deuteronomy 21:1 ff.," RA, 33 (1936), pp. 1–6. "Biblical Customs and the Nuzi Tablets," Biblical Archaeologist, 3 (1940), pp. 1–12; reprinted in The Biblical Archaeologist Reader, 2 (1964), ed. D. N. Freedman and E. F. Campbell, Jr., pp. 21–33.

the body is found. But the later version provides, as in Deuteronomy, for the contingency that it was found in open country between settlements, in which event the nearest settlement (within stated limits) bears the responsibility.[33]

The treatment of female captives (21:10–14) is again unparalleled in the other biblical codes. The Deuteronomic provision directs the woman to shave her hair, clip her nails, and change her garment before entering her new state as wife of her captor. This is in keeping with the symbolic role which hair, nails, and (the fringes of one's) garment play elsewhere in the Bible and in the earlier Near East. They are, in effect, the personality in effigy or in miniature. In Mesopotamia, fingernails or fringes were used to validate a contract (in the absence of a seal),[34] and the hair and fringes to "identify" a witness who reported a dream of ominous significance to the court.[35] Shaving off the peculiar hairdo required of slaves was also an element in the ceremony of manumission.

Deuteronomy condemns as "abhorrent to the Lord" more offenses than any of the other biblical codes, though Proverbs is also familiar with the concept. Abominations, sins, or taboos against this or that deity are common clichés likewise in Sumerian wisdom literature and in Akkadian religious texts.

But, while the taboo concept was thus common to Israelites and Mesopotamians, they had very different notions of what constituted a taboo. In Israel, the very practices most sacred to foreign deities were often regarded as abominations to God. One of the practices condemned in these terms is transvestism, the adoption of clothes of the opposite sex (22:5). This appears to be a direct reaction to an aspect of the cult of the Canaanite goddess Ashtarte and her Mesopotamian equivalents Ishtar and Inanna, or to its more innocent literary and dramatic reflexes ("travesty").[36] Much the same could be said in regard to cultic prostitution (23:18 f.).[37]

Absent such explicit reaction against practices sanctioned or even commanded by Near Eastern usage, much of the specifically Deuteronomic legislation was of a more obviously humanitarian cast, and therefore not "justified" in specific terms. Indeed, it often paralleled traditional Near Eastern usage as documented in literature and records if not specifically in law. This "humanitarianism" extends in the first place to animals, as in the prohibition against yoking of ox and ass together (22:10), not found in the comparable rules about "unnatural mixtures" in Leviticus 19:19, but reminiscent of the proverbial juxtaposition of ox and ass in Sumerian literature (e.g., Lugalbanda Epic, 164 f.). The prohibition against muzzling the threshing oxen was already observed by the early Sumerians according to actual account texts on the one hand (see commentary to 25:4) and the so-called "Farmer's Almanac" on the other; this didactic collection of agricultural lore also seems already to provide for leaving the gleanings of the harvest (cf. 24:19 f.) for the destitute.[38] The prohibition against interest between fellow-Israelites (23:20 f.) seems less a case of xenophobia than of a time-honored practice of waiving interest in cases of "a loan between gentlemen" attested in a four-

[33] Pritchard, *ANET*, p. 189; H. A. Hoffner, Jr., "Some Contributions of Hittitology to Old Testament Study," *Tyndale Bulletin*, 20 (1969), pp. 27–55.
[34] Ferris J. Stephens, "The Ancient Significance of Ṣîṣith," *JBL*, 50 (1931), pp. 59–70.
[35] Pritchard, *ANET*, pp. 623–626; 629–632; esp. letters a, b, m, n, p.
[36] W. H. Ph. Römer, "Randbemerkungen zur Travestie von Deut. 22,5," *Studies . . . Beek* (Studia Semitica Neerlandica, 16, 1974), pp. 217–222.
[37] E. M. Yamauchi, "Cultic Prostitution," in *Orient and Occident: Essays Presented to Cyrus H. Gordon* (Alter Orient und Altes Testament, Vol. 22, 1973), pp. 213–222.
[38] Samuel N. Kramer, *The Sumerians* (Chicago: The University of Chicago Press, 1963), pp. 296 f., 342.

teenth- or thirteenth-century letter found at Ugarit.[39]

Legislation regarding women is prominent in Deuteronomy, providing additional protection as well as further constraints not found in the comparable provisions of earlier biblical or Near Eastern codes, but sometimes attested as customary law by the testimony of actual court cases. Thus the elaborate protection of the bride against unjustified aspersions on her virginity (22:13–19) is paralleled by a dossier of contracts and litigation regarding just such a case from eighteenth-century Babylonia.[40] The penalty exacted from the wife embroiled with her husband's antagonist (25:11 f.) seems less excessive in light of the clear precedent in the notoriously cruel Assyrian laws as codified about the end of the twelfth century B.C.E., or of the even earlier but less certain parallel alleged from a court case at fifteenth-century Nuzi.[41] Such parallels could be multiplied at will by additional examples.

Deuteronomy as Covenant

Libraries and archives thus furnish a wealth of detail about the customary and statutory law of the ancient Near East, and its preservation and reemergence in the legal formulations of Deuteronomy. But these essentially isolated relics from a remote antiquity cannot serve to date and evaluate the book as such. For this purpose, we must look rather to the peroration of Moses' homily (27–31), which at one time may have concluded the original book. The idea of setting up large stones and coating them with plaster before inscribing them (27:2) is now attested by archeological finds from the eighth century B.C.E. in the northern Sinai[42] and in Transjordan.[43] The latter find also features a long list of curses and assigns a prominent role to Shagar-and-Ishtar as a composite goddess of fertility (and the starry

heavens) which is echoed by the cognate nouns for "offspring" and "calving" in the catalogue of blessings and curses in ch. 28 (4, 18, 51; cf. 7:13).

But the closest connections of this catalogue are with the treaties imposed on their vassals by the Assyrian kings of the first millennium, most notably Esarhaddon (680–669 B.C.E.). In numerous exemplars dated three years before his death, he adjured each of his Iranian vassals to fealty to himself and, after his demise, to his designated successor, on pain of suffering a lengthy succession of fearsome curses.[44] Some of these curses occur in virtually identical form and even in the same order in Deuteronomy.[45] And the efficacy of such curses was described in what has been aptly termed "one of the most striking parallels . . . between cuneiform and biblical literature in any period."[46]

When it is remembered that the entire reign of Esarhaddon fell within the long reign of Manasseh; that this ruler was (by necessity if not by choice)[47] a particularly loyal vassal

[39] Pritchard, *ANET*, p. 629.
[40] Hallo, "The Slandered Bride," *Studies Presented to A. Leo Oppenheim* (Chicago, 1964), pp. 95–105.
[41] Pritchard, *ANET*, p. 181, 8; Gordon, "A New Akkadian Parallel to Deuteronomy 25:11–12," *The Journal of the Palestine Oriental Society*, 15 (1935), pp. 29–34.
[42] Ze'ev Meshel and Carol Meyers, "The Name of God in the Wilderness of Zin," *Biblical Archaeologist* 39 (1976), pp. 6–10; Meshel, "Did Yahweh Have a Consort? The New Religious Inscriptions from the Sinai," *Biblical Archaeology Review*, 5/2 (1979), pp. 24–35.
[43] Jacob Hoftijzer, "The Prophet Balaam in a 6th-Century [sic] Aramaic Inscription," *Biblical Archaeologist*, 39 (1976), pp. 11–17; cf. B. A. Levine, "The Deir ʿAlla Plaster Inscriptions" (in press).
[44] Pritchard, *ANET*, pp. 534, 541. See also Gleanings to ch. 28.
[45] Weinfeld, "Traces of Assyrian Treaty Formulae in Deuteronomy," *Biblica*, 46 (1965), pp. 417–427; R. Frankena, "The Vassal-Treaties of Esarhaddon and the Dating of Deuteronomy," *Oudtestamentische Studiën*, 14 (1965), pp. 122–154.
[46] Moran, *op. cit.*, p. 83, referring to the Annals of Assurbanipal (*ANET*, p. 300, lines 11–16) compared with Deut. 29:23–25.
[47] Carl D. Evans, "Judah's Foreign Policy from Heze-

of Assyria; and that the Assyrians concluded vassal treaties with their western neighbors not unlike those preserved for their vassals on the eastern frontier[48]—then it is tempting to conclude that the kingdom of Judah became only too familiar, under Manasseh, with the form of such treaties. What the anti-Assyrian party did, on this assumption, was to employ this form to declare Judah's independence of Assyria and its allegiance to God.

This interpretation of matters holds good whether the form was original to Assyria or to some antecedent Syrian tradition, and whether the declaration was drafted under Hezekiah or Manasseh or Josiah, as variously proposed. But it fits best the situation in Josiah's eighteenth year when the "book of the law" was discovered in the Temple (II Kings 22–23). For by then Assyria was in retreat; Judah had recovered much of the territory of the old northern kingdom; and Josiah was ready to apply a "pattern of usurpation" known as early as Old Babylonian times in Mesopotamia that included, among other steps, shifting allegiance from a foreign king to the deity of one's own nation or city.[49] The same device was still employed in Maccabean times in Israel and in Renaissance times in Europe.[50]

Deuteronomy as History

The original core of Deuteronomy can thus be defined by its literary affinities to external models, but that core was successively embedded in larger biblical contexts by the editorial addition of the miscellaneous appendices that now conclude the book. Of these the earliest may well have been the notice of Joshua's appointment to succeed Moses (31:14 f.) followed, first in prose (vv. 16–30) and then in poetry (ch. 32), by classic formulations of the Deuteronomistic view of history: that adherence to the covenant promises national weal, while apostasy ensures disaster. This doctrine reflects a cyclical view of history which far antedates Deuteronomy, and in which periods of prosperity and disaster follow each other in inevitable succession, often in consequence of the cultic piety displayed or, on the contrary, withheld by a given king with respect to a particular deity or shrine. Where Deuteronomy differed was in extending the obligations from the exclusively cultic sphere to the whole realm of legal and ethical norms, and from the sole figure of the king to the nation as a whole.

Deuteronomy's doctrine of collective responsibility so thoroughly informed the historical books that follow it in the canon (Joshua through Kings) that it is reasonable to reconstruct a stage when they were editorially linked together by the passages in question. If so, however, the link was broken again by the insertion of the blessing of Moses (ch. 33), an ancient poem that may have been designed to parallel the equally ancient poem at the end of Genesis (Gen. 49) and thus to confer on Deuteronomy the same kind of literary and religious status that Genesis already enjoyed. The notice of Moses' death (ch. 34) probably originally belonged at the end of Numbers as the conclusion of a "triteuch" consisting of Exodus-Leviticus-Numbers or of a "tetrateuch" running from Genesis to Numbers. Its removal to the end of Deuteronomy allowed that book to serve as the conclusion of the

kiah to Josiah," in *Scripture in Context: Essays on the Comparative Method*, ed. Evans, Hallo, and John B. White (Pittsburgh Theological Monograph Series 34, 1980), pp. 157–178.
[48] Cf. *ANET*, pp. 532–534.
[49] Hallo and William K. Simpson, *The Ancient Near East: A History* (New York: Harcourt Brace Jovanovich, Inc., 1971), pp. 86 f. and n. 48.
[50] Marco Treves, "The Reign of God in the Old Testament," *VT*, 19 (1969), pp. 230–243.

biography of Moses and, ultimately, of the whole Pentateuch.

The successive stages of literary history which eventually produced the Book of Deuteronomy can thus be reconstructed with some degree of probability. Each of them reveals formal and functional ties to the literature of the surrounding Near East, and each adds new dimensions that together lend the book its distinctive character.

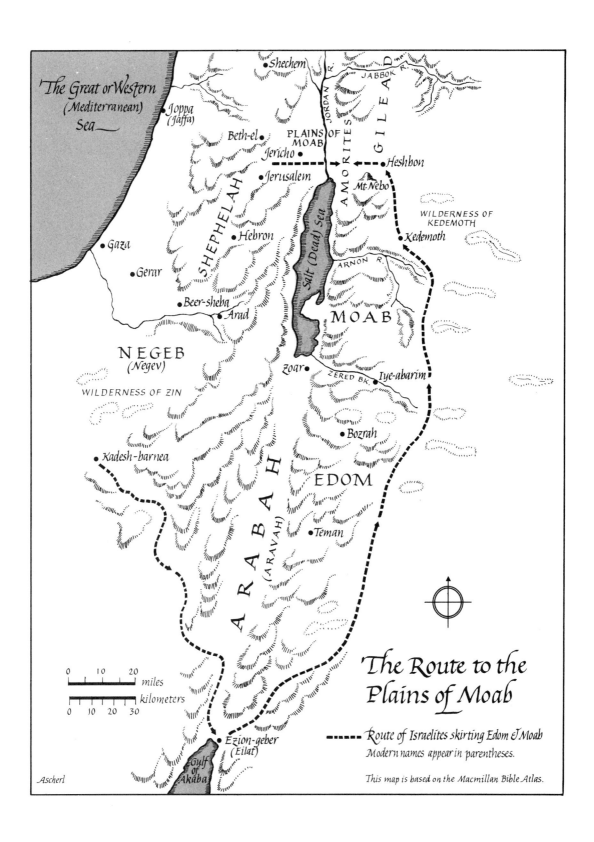

The Great or Western
(Mediterranean)
Sea

Joppa
(Jaffa)

Shechem

JABBOK R.

GILEAD

JORDAN R.

Beth-el

PLAINS OF
MOAB

Jericho

Heshbon

Jerusalem

Mt. Nebo

AMORITES

WILDERNESS OF
KEDEMOTH

Gaza

Hebron

SHEPHELAH

Salt (Dead) Sea

Kedemoth

Gerar

ARNON R.

Beer-sheba

Arad

MOAB

NEGEB
(Negev)

Zoar

ZERED BK.

Iye-abarim

WILDERNESS OF ZIN

Bozrah

Kadesh-barnea

EDOM

A R A B A H
(ARAVAH)

Teman

The Route to the
Plains of Moab

- - - - Route of Israelites skirting Edom & Moab
Modern names appear in parentheses.

This map is based on the Macmillan Bible Atlas.

0   10   20   miles
0 10 20 30 kilometers

Ezion-geber
(Eilat)

Gulf
of
Akaba

Ascherl

PART I

Prologue

FIRST DISCOURSE

The prologue to Deuteronomy (Chapters 1–4:43) prepares the stage for the instructions, laws, warnings, blessings, and curses that Moses delivers to the Children of Israel. It is set in the time immediately preceding his death; the place where he delivers them is the plateau of Moab, east of Jericho, across the Jordan River (see map).

The prologue recalls the historical preambles of certain ancient Near Eastern treaties.* It can be conveniently divided into four parts: (1) recounting time and place (1:1–5); (2) first review of Israel's wanderings in the desert and God's unceasing care (1:6–45); (3) continued review and Moses' own part in the people's unfolding history (1:46–3:29); (4) summation (4:1–43).

Most of the content of the prologue represents a recounting of events well known to the readers of Exodus, Leviticus, and especially Numbers, and both the similarities and the differences in these accounts have a bearing on how one may judge the origin and composition of the Book of Deuteronomy as a whole (see "Introducing Deuteronomy").

The prologue states at once that what follows was spoken by Moses. This commentary takes the view (discussed earlier, see introduction) that, while Mosaic traditions may be at the core of the book, the text itself was composed many centuries later. Both prologue and epilogue were written from a post-Mosaic and cis-Jordanian point of view. But by the time they were set down the name and figure of Moses were firmly identified with the events described and the laws bearing his name were believed to have originated with God. These ascriptions developed their own dynamics and in time became sacred history which had a decisive effect on the minds and hearts of subsequent generations.

---

* These treaties—like those made by Assyrian King Esarhaddon in 672 B.C.E.—specify the parties to the treaty; the past benefits bestowed by the suzerain and his rights to exclusive loyalty and obedience; and finally the blessings which arise from compliance as well as the consequences which will follow any noncompliance. The basis of Deuteronomy is the treaty-covenant between God and Israel, upon whom He lavishes His protective love. Israel's faithfulness to the covenant will assure this protection in perpetuity [1]. (See also W. W. Hallo's essay above.)

The Setting

The introductory section provides the setting; like the rest of the prologue it reveals little of the thrust and fervor of the later chapters of Deuteronomy.* A matter-of-fact recital plays down the high emotions, the triumphs, and tragedies of Israel's past. Only later on will the text move from this low-keyed historical review to an ever-greater intensity of rhetoric.

(The weekly portion, *Devarim*, begins here.)

---

* This suggests that the entire introductory portion of Deuteronomy (chapters 1–4) is from a tradition other than that which produced the book's main portion.

א אֵלֶּה הַדְּבָרִים אֲשֶׁר דִּבֶּר מֹשֶׁה אֶל־כָּל־יִשְׂרָאֵל בְּעֵבֶר הַיַּרְדֵּן בַּמִּדְבָּר בָּעֲרָבָה מוֹל סוּף בֵּין־פָּארָן

ב וּבֵין־תֹּפֶל וְלָבָן וַחֲצֵרֹת וְדִי זָהָב: אַחַד עָשָׂר יוֹם

ג מֵחֹרֵב דֶּרֶךְ הַר־שֵׂעִיר עַד קָדֵשׁ בַּרְנֵעַ: וַיְהִי בְּאַרְבָּעִים שָׁנָה בְּעַשְׁתֵּי־עָשָׂר חֹדֶשׁ בְּאֶחָד לַחֹדֶשׁ דִּבֶּר מֹשֶׁה אֶל־בְּנֵי יִשְׂרָאֵל כְּכֹל אֲשֶׁר צִוָּה יְהוָה

ד אֹתוֹ אֲלֵהֶם: אַחֲרֵי הַכֹּתוֹ אֵת סִיחֹן מֶלֶךְ הָאֱמֹרִי

Devarim

Deuteronomy 1

1–4

1] These are the words that Moses addressed to all Israel on the other side of the Jordan.—Through the wilderness, in the Arabah near Suph, between Paran and Tophel, Laban, Hazeroth, and Di-zahab,   2] it is eleven days from Horeb to Kadesh-barnea by the Mount Seir route.—   3] It was in the fortieth year, on the first day of the eleventh month, that Moses addressed the Israelites in accordance with the instructions that the LORD had given him for them,   4] after he had defeated Sihon

---

1:1] *Words.* דְּבָרִים (*devarim*), here in the broad sense of "discourse" and referring to the whole book.

On the other side of the Jordan. The Hebrew בְּעֵבֶר has a more general meaning: "The region by the Jordan" [1].

Arabah. (Aravah) The depression that runs from Lake Kinneret to the Gulf of Akaba. In the Torah, as in modern Israel, the name is attached only to the valley south of the Dead Sea.

Near Suph. The geographical references that follow are difficult to identify. Thus Suph means "reed," but most likely there were no reeds in Moab where verse 5 places the speaker; similarly, Hazeroth is known to us as a place in the Sinai peninsula only (see Num. 33:17); and the otherwise unknown Di-zahab might mean a place where gold (*zahav*) was found, except that we have no records of gold finds in the area.

The Midrash suggests that the place names were symbolic expressions. For instance, Di-zahab was seen to refer to the place where Israel sinned with the golden calf [2].

2] *Eleven days . . . by the Mount Seir route.* If Mount Horeb (Sinai) is today's Jebel Musa, a journey of eleven days' travel by foot would traverse 160 miles (256 km) to Kadesh-barnea; while a route via Seir (east of the Aravah) would consume more time. The mountain where the covenant was proclaimed is usually called Horeb in Deuteronomy and in the source called E; while in J and P its name is Sinai (see our Commentary on Exodus).

Malbim interprets "eleven days" to mean the time it took Moses to deliver his message at the places mentioned.

Kadesh-barnea. Excavations suggest that in all likelihood it lay some 50 miles (80 km) south of Beer-sheba. It was the Israelites' headquarters for most of their forty years of wandering.

3] *Eleventh month.* Shevat, counting from the spring season, i.e., the month of Nisan.

4] *Sihon king of the Amorites.* See the story told in Num. 21:21–31. Amorites here refers to an ethnic

אֲשֶׁר יוֹשֵׁב בְּחֶשְׁבּוֹן וְאֵת עוֹג מֶלֶךְ הַבָּשָׁן אֲשֶׁר־יוֹשֵׁב

ה בְּעַשְׁתָּרֹת בְּאֶדְרֶעִי: בְּעֵבֶר הַיַּרְדֵּן בְּאֶרֶץ מוֹאָב

הוֹאִיל מֹשֶׁה בֵּאֵר אֶת־הַתּוֹרָה הַזֹּאת לֵאמֹר:

king of the Amorites who dwelt in Heshbon and Og king of Bashan who dwelt at Ashtaroth [and] Edrei.   **5]** On the other side of the Jordan, in the land of Moab, Moses undertook to expound this Teaching. He said:

group that inhabited Transjordan. See also verse 6.

Heshbon. East of Jericho.

Og king of Bashan. See Num. 21:33 ff. Bashan is the area northeast of Lake Kinneret and north of the Yarmuk River.

Ashtaroth (and) Edrei. The Hebrew text does not contain the word "and," but that two different places were meant is clear from Josh. 12:4; 13:12, 31. Ashtaroth can be identified with today's Tel Ashtarah, 15 miles north of Der'a, which is 30 miles east of Lake Kinneret.

5] *Moab.* The land east of the Dead Sea.

Moses undertook. The Hebrew הוֹאִיל has the connotation of doing it gladly, or eagerly.

This Teaching. תּוֹרָה (torah) has a number of meanings. It can (especially in the plural, *torot*) describe a set of laws; here it most likely refers to the whole Book of Deuteronomy.

Today the most frequent meaning is the Pentateuch, i.e., the Five Books of Moses; and finally Torah (without the article) refers to the entire body of Jewish law and lore.

These Are the Words

In its earliest days, Torah represented essentially an oral tradition. Even after it was committed to writing, the majority of the people were not literate and therefore received the tradition primarily through the spoken word. To them, words indicated the beginning of God's creative process— "God said, 'Let there be light,' and there was light"—and the Ten Words proclaimed at Sinai were understood as a direct continuation of this process: even as words were instrumental in the world's creation, so were they in the creation and perfection of the Creator's people. And since the words that Moses had spoken (or was believed to have spoken) were taken to be a resonance of the divine will, those who transmitted them made certain that they would be preserved as accurately as possible. Even when new and revolutionary ideas were introduced in these traditions [3] the old words were carefully guarded. This led frequently to textual contradictions, but in time these were considered as merely apparent, not real, for Deuteronomy and all of the Torah were seen as the single emanation of the divine mind. A proper understanding would therefore explain any perceived inconsistencies.

There were other variations as well, which were entirely due to the problems of physical transmission and which led to textual discrepancies, so that even after the words were fixed in written form different manuscripts testified to different oral traditions. The Torah scrolls which nowadays are entirely uniform in content are based on the prescriptions of the so-called Masoretes ("transmitters"), who flourished in Palestine in the eighth to tenth centuries c.e., and whose rules as to what constituted the best tradition became accepted among Jews.[1] On the whole, it is remarkable how faithfully all sacred texts were preserved, and this was especially true of the most sacred of all, the Torah. Great and loving care was lavished on transmitting it faithfully, and we may assume that a similar degree of faithfulness was brought to bear on its earlier, oral transmission.

In the introduction above, the problem of the origin and the historic context of Deuteronomy were discussed at some length. Whatever was the content of the book found by King Josiah, we may be certain that much of the manuscript was based on oral traditions which reached back into earlier times. The history of Judaism, and especially of its beginnings, was bound up in words spoken and heard, expressed and interpreted, and the capacity to hear and understand was the essential counterpart of speech. Characteristically, the *Shema* ("Hear, O Israel! The Lord is our God, the Lord alone." Deut. 6:4) became a central expression of Israel's faith. Thus, when the Book of Deuteronomy opens with the phrase "These are the words," it places the human ability to formulate moral concepts and to heed their command at the head of the message that Moses delivered to his people.

---

[1] Since by that time Christianity was already launched on its own independent course, Christian manuscripts and translations were based on Hebrew sources which occasionally differed to some degree (though generally not in a significant manner) from the norm established later by the Masoretes.

All

We are told that Moses addressed his words to "all Israel" (verse 1). How could he address so large a multitude and be heard?

A traditional view held that a miracle made this possible (similar to the way Judah's voice was said to have carried through all Egypt when he spoke in behalf of Benjamin) [4]. But another commentator, calling our attention to the fact that "all Israel" frequently occurs in Deuteronomy, notes especially 31:11–12, where the preceding verses describe "all Israel" to consist of Joshua, the elders, and the priests, i.e., the notables who bore responsibility for the people. It was these whom Moses addressed.

SOLOMON EPHRAIM LENCICZ [5]

These

The opening word of Deuteronomy is אֵלֶּה (*eleh*, these). By way of *gematria*,[2] אלה adds up to 36. Tradition has it that the world is sustained by thirty-six righteous persons,[3] even as it is sustained by "these" words of Torah.

ITTURE TORAH [7]

Bees

דְּבָרִים (*devarim*, words) may be vocalized to read דְּבֹרִים (*devorim*, bees). Just as bee's honey is sweet and its sting sharp, so are the words of Torah.

MIDRASH [8]

Before and After

When Moses was younger he thought of himself as a man of few words (Exod. 4:10), but after he had received the Torah he changed and spoke about it often and at length.

MIDRASH [9]

Reproof

(Deuteronomy contains many words of reproof which were repeated frequently in various ways.) Moses spoke as he did because he knew himself to be near death, for otherwise a leader ought not to reprove and reprove again and again.

RASHI

(When a preacher was reminded of Rashi's comment he replied: When I preach I feel as if each day is my dying day.) [10]

Moses, the friend of Israel, rebuked the people, while Balaam, the enemy of Israel, blessed the people (Num., chs. 22–24). Thus the authenticity of both was beyond question.

MIDRASH [11]

Twice and Once

Twice we are told that Moses *reiterated* the substance of the Torah ("These are the words," verse 1; "Moses addressed...," verse 3), and once that he *explained* the teaching (verse 5). In this you may find a hint of the traditional prescription to prepare oneself for the reading of the text of the weekly scriptural portion by studying it twice in the original Hebrew and once in the Aramaic exposition (called Targum).

CHASIDIC [12]

Moses and Elijah

It says that "Moses undertook to expound" (verse 5). One can rearrange the letters הוֹאִיל (undertook) to read אֵלִיָּהוּ (Elijah). In time to come, Elijah, the forerunner of the Messiah, will explain difficult questions left unexpounded by Moses.

CHASIDIC [13]

---

[2] A Hebrew term derived from the Greek and related by some to our "geometry" but more likely from *grammateiae*, "script," or from *ge*, "earth," and *metria*, "measurement" [6]. It describes a method which connects a word with the numerical value of its letters. Thus אלה equals 36 (א=1, ל=30, ה=5).

[3] In the Hebrew system of writing numbers, 36 is ל״ו (*lamed-vav*); hence the thirty-six righteous are called "lamed-vavniks."

First Review

Moses prefaces his exposition of the Torah by recollecting the history of Israel during the forty years in the wilderness. In this review he includes his own role, especially his inability to enter the Promised Land. Along with the generation already dead, he bears the sting of God's displeasure and stern judgment.

In addressing Israel, Moses says "you" both to those in his hearing who will be allowed to cross over into Canaan and also to those who already perished in the desert. For in his view, what happened to the fathers is an integral part of the children's fate; the obligations of Sinai undertaken by the forebears are binding upon their descendants. Moses will express this thought later on more succinctly: "I make this covenant, with its sanctions, not with you alone, but both with those who are standing here with us this day before the Lord our God and with those who are not with us here this day," that is, with those not yet born (29:13–14). This chronological continuum, combined with the idea of collective, national responsibility for the covenant, is the framework upon which Deuteronomy rests (see further below).

It should be noted that, although the sin of idolatry is prominently mentioned in later chapters, here in the prologue it is the sin of losing faith which Moses singles out. In his review of the wanderings this failure is the target of his critique, one which is constantly before his mind, for he too shares its consequences.

יְהוָֹה אֱלֹהֵינוּ דִּבֶּר אֵלֵינוּ בְּחֹרֵב לֵאמֹר רַב־לָכֶם

שֶׁבֶת בָּהָר הַזֶּה: פְּנוּ וּסְעוּ לָכֶם וּבֹאוּ הַר הָאֱמֹרִי

וְאֶל־כָּל־שְׁכֵנָיו בָּעֲרָבָה בָהָר וּבַשְּׁפֵלָה וּבַנֶּגֶב וּבְחוֹף

הַיָּם אֶרֶץ הַכְּנַעֲנִי וְהַלְּבָנוֹן עַד־הַנָּהָר הַגָּדֹל נְהַר

פְּרָת: רְאֵה נָתַתִּי לִפְנֵיכֶם אֶת־הָאָרֶץ בֹּאוּ וּרְשׁוּ

אֶת־הָאָרֶץ אֲשֶׁר נִשְׁבַּע יְהוָֹה לַאֲבֹתֵיכֶם לְאַבְרָהָם

לְיִצְחָק וּלְיַעֲקֹב לָתֵת לָהֶם וּלְזַרְעָם אַחֲרֵיהֶם:

וָאֹמַר אֲלֵכֶם בָּעֵת הַהִוא לֵאמֹר לֹא־אוּכַל לְבַדִּי

שְׂאֵת אֶתְכֶם: יְהוָֹה אֱלֹהֵיכֶם הִרְבָּה אֶתְכֶם וְהִנְּכֶם

Deuteronomy 1
6–10

6] The Lord our God spoke to us at Horeb, saying: You have stayed long enough at this mountain. 7] Start out and make your way to the hill country of the Amorites and to all their neighbors in the Arabah, the hill country, the Shephelah, the Negeb, the seacoast, the land of the Canaanites, and the Lebanon, as far as the Great River, the river Euphrates. 8] See, I place the land at your disposal. Go, take possession of the land that the Lord swore to your fathers, Abraham, Isaac, and Jacob, to give to them and to their offspring after them.

9] Thereupon I said to you, "I cannot bear the burden of you by myself. 10] The Lord your God has multiplied you until you are today as numerous as the stars in

---

1:6] *The Lord our God.* The combination of God's personal name (YHVH) and the generic appellation (Elohim) occurs frequently in Deuteronomy. About the meaning of YHVH, see at Exod. 6; on Elohim, see at Exod. 3 and Gen. 2.

7] *Hill country of the Amorites.* In Assyrian sources, the areas of Syria and Palestine appear as lands of the Amorites; in Deuteronomy the term is more restricted. See verse 4.

Shephelah. "Lowlands," the western foothills of the Judean mountains. The cities in this area are listed in Josh. 15:33–44.

Negeb. נֶגֶב (Negev), the southland; today the

term covers the area from Beer-sheba to Eilat.

Euphrates. The text has in mind the territory occupied in Solomonic days. See further at 11:24.

8] *See.* The word is frequently employed in Deuteronomy as an introduction; it begins the *sidrah* רְאֵה (11:26). Compare the English "Look here...."

Swore to your fathers. Abraham, Isaac, and Jacob (see Gen. 15:18; 26:3 f.; 28:13 f.).

9] *Thereupon.* In another tradition, what is related here took place before the revelation at Sinai, and at the advice of Jethro (Exod. 18).

הַיּוֹם כְּכוֹכְבֵי הַשָּׁמַיִם לָרֹב: יְהוָה אֱלֹהֵי אֲבוֹתֵכֶם יֹסֵף עֲלֵיכֶם כָּכֶם אֶלֶף פְּעָמִים וִיבָרֵךְ אֶתְכֶם

יא

כַּאֲשֶׁר דִּבֶּר לָכֶם: אֵיכָה אֶשָּׂא לְבַדִּי טָרְחֲכֶם

יב

וּמַשַּׂאֲכֶם וְרִיבְכֶם: הָבוּ לָכֶם אֲנָשִׁים חֲכָמִים וּנְבֹנִים

יג

וִידֻעִים לְשִׁבְטֵיכֶם וַאֲשִׂימֵם בְּרָאשֵׁיכֶם: וַתַּעֲנוּ אֹתִי

יד

וַתֹּאמְרוּ טוֹב־הַדָּבָר אֲשֶׁר־דִּבַּרְתָּ לַעֲשׂוֹת: וָאֶקַּח אֶת־רָאשֵׁי שִׁבְטֵיכֶם אֲנָשִׁים חֲכָמִים וִידֻעִים וָאֶתֵּן אֹתָם רָאשִׁים עֲלֵיכֶם שָׂרֵי אֲלָפִים וְשָׂרֵי מֵאוֹת וְשָׂרֵי חֲמִשִּׁים וְשָׂרֵי עֲשָׂרֹת וְשֹׁטְרִים לְשִׁבְטֵיכֶם:

טו

וָאֲצַוֶּה אֶת־שֹׁפְטֵיכֶם בָּעֵת הַהִוא לֵאמֹר שָׁמֹעַ בֵּין אֲחֵיכֶם וּשְׁפַטְתֶּם צֶדֶק בֵּין־אִישׁ וּבֵין־אָחִיו וּבֵין גֵּרוֹ:

טז

Deuteronomy 1

11–16

the sky.— **11]** May the LORD, the God of your fathers, increase your numbers a thousandfold, and bless you as He promised you.— **12]** How can I bear unaided the trouble of you, and the burden, and the bickering! **13]** Pick from each of your tribes men who are wise, discerning, and experienced, and I will appoint them as your heads." **14]** You answered me and said, "What you propose to do is good." **15]** So I took your tribal leaders, wise and experienced men, and appointed them heads over you: chiefs of thousands, chiefs of hundreds, chiefs of fifties, and chiefs of tens, and officials for your tribes. **16]** I further charged your magistrates as follows, "Hear out your fellow men, and decide justly between any man and a

---

11] *May the Lord . . .* An interjection; similar to expressions like "My father, may he rest in peace," or ". . . may he live to 120 years."

13] *Pick.* In this version the people—not, as recorded in Numbers, God or Moses—chose the spies.

Experienced. Or, "known to you (for their ability)" [1].

16] *Magistrates.* Rendered "judges" in the biblical Book of Judges. No special responsibility for them

was recorded in Exodus, where they were treated like other officials. On the other hand, the Exodus account (18:13 ff.) gives the credit for instituting the judicial system to Jethro, Moses' father-in-law, while the Deuteronomic version overlooks Jethro. Verses 16 and 17 establish basic principles of justice based on complete equality.

Hear out. From this the Talmud derived the rule that a judge should not listen to one party before the other one has arrived [2].

יז לֹא־תַכִּירוּ פָנִים בַּמִּשְׁפָּט כַּקָּטֹן כַּגָּדֹל תִּשְׁמָעוּן לֹא
תָגוּרוּ מִפְּנֵי־אִישׁ כִּי הַמִּשְׁפָּט לֵאלֹהִים הוּא וְהַדָּבָר

יח אֲשֶׁר יִקְשֶׁה מִכֶּם תַּקְרִבוּן אֵלַי וּשְׁמַעְתִּיו: וָאֲצַוֶּה
אֶתְכֶם בָּעֵת הַהִוא אֵת כָּל־הַדְּבָרִים אֲשֶׁר תַּעֲשׂוּן:

יט וַנִּסַּע מֵחֹרֵב וַנֵּלֶךְ אֵת כָּל־הַמִּדְבָּר הַגָּדוֹל וְהַנּוֹרָא
הַהוּא אֲשֶׁר רְאִיתֶם דֶּרֶךְ הַר הָאֱמֹרִי כַּאֲשֶׁר צִוָּה

כ יְהוָה אֱלֹהֵינוּ אֹתָנוּ וַנָּבֹא עַד קָדֵשׁ בַּרְנֵעַ: וָאֹמַר
אֲלֵכֶם בָּאתֶם עַד־הַר הָאֱמֹרִי אֲשֶׁר־יְהוָה אֱלֹהֵינוּ

כא נֹתֵן לָנוּ: רְאֵה נָתַן יְהוָה אֱלֹהֶיךָ לְפָנֶיךָ אֶת־הָאָרֶץ
עֲלֵה רֵשׁ כַּאֲשֶׁר דִּבֶּר יְהוָה אֱלֹהֵי אֲבֹתֶיךָ לָךְ

כב אַל־תִּירָא וְאַל־תֵּחָת: וַתִּקְרְבוּן אֵלַי כֻּלְּכֶם וַתֹּאמְרוּ

Deuteronomy 1
17–22

fellow Israelite or a stranger.   17] You shall not be partial in judgment: hear out low and high alike. Fear no man, for judgment is God's. And any matter that is too difficult for you, you shall bring to me and I will hear it."   18] Thus I instructed you, at that time, about the various things that you should do.

19] We set out from Horeb and traveled the great and terrible wilderness that you saw, along the road to the hill country of the Amorites, as the LORD our God had commanded us. When we reached Kadesh-barnea,   20] I said to you, "You have come to the hill country of the Amorites which the LORD our God is giving to us.   21] See, the LORD your God has placed the land at your disposal. Go up, take possession, as the LORD, the God of your fathers, promised you. Fear not and be not dismayed."

22] Then all of you came to me and said, "Let us send men ahead to reconnoiter

17] *Low and high alike.* Lower and upper classes are to be treated without distinction. Another understanding: Give equal attention to all cases, whether involving small or large amounts [3].

Fear no man. When truth is at stake.

19] *Kadesh-barnea.* See at 1:2.

21] *See.* The Hebrew here changes from plural to singular, a stylistic device frequent in the book.

22] *You came to me.* In Num. 13 the initiative was God's, and the fault lay in part with the spies who

14

נִשְׁלְחָה אֲנָשִׁים לְפָנֵינוּ וְיַחְפְּרוּ־לָנוּ אֶת־הָאָרֶץ

וְיָשִׁבוּ אֹתָנוּ דָּבָר אֶת־הַדֶּרֶךְ אֲשֶׁר נַעֲלֶה־בָּהּ וְאֵת

כג הֶעָרִים אֲשֶׁר נָבֹא אֲלֵיהֶן: וַיִּיטַב בְּעֵינַי הַדָּבָר

וָאֶקַּח מִכֶּם שְׁנֵים עָשָׂר אֲנָשִׁים אִישׁ אֶחָד לַשָּׁבֶט:

כד וַיִּפְנוּ וַיַּעֲלוּ הָהָרָה וַיָּבֹאוּ עַד־נַחַל אֶשְׁכֹּל וַיְרַגְּלוּ

כה אֹתָהּ: וַיִּקְחוּ בְיָדָם מִפְּרִי הָאָרֶץ וַיּוֹרִדוּ אֵלֵינוּ

וַיָּשִׁבוּ אֹתָנוּ דָבָר וַיֹּאמְרוּ טוֹבָה הָאָרֶץ אֲשֶׁר־יְהֹוָה

כו אֱלֹהֵינוּ נֹתֵן לָנוּ: וְלֹא אֲבִיתֶם לַעֲלֹת וַתַּמְרוּ אֶת־

כז פִּי יְהֹוָה אֱלֹהֵיכֶם: וַתֵּרָגְנוּ בְאָהֳלֵיכֶם וַתֹּאמְרוּ

בְּשִׂנְאַת יְהֹוָה אֹתָנוּ הוֹצִיאָנוּ מֵאֶרֶץ מִצְרָיִם לָתֵת

כח אֹתָנוּ בְּיַד הָאֱמֹרִי לְהַשְׁמִידֵנוּ: אָנָה אֲנַחְנוּ עֹלִים

* כח מלרע.

Deuteronomy 1
23–28

the land for us and bring back word on the route we shall follow and the cities we shall come to." **23]** I approved of the plan, and so I selected twelve of your men, one from each tribe. **24]** They made for the hill country, came to the wadi Eshcol, and spied it out. **25]** They took some of the fruit of the land with them and brought it down to us. And they gave us this report, "It is a good land that the LORD our God is giving to us."

26] Yet you refused to go up, and flouted the command of the LORD your God. **27]** You sulked in your tents and said, "It is because the LORD hates us that He brought us out of the land of Egypt, to hand us over to the Amorites to wipe us out. **28]** What kind of place are we going to? Our kinsmen have taken the heart

discouraged the people, while here the people alone are to blame.

Hoffmann reconciles the differences by seeing Moses in Numbers as a historian and in Deuteronomy as a moralist.

23] *I approved.* God's role in the scheme is not a

part of Moses' story; hence many scholars find this to be added proof of different traditions.

24] *Wadi Eshcol.* Probably somewhere in the vicinity of Hebron; see also Num. 13:23–24.

27] *You sulked.* Others, "murmured."

15

אַחֵינוּ הֵמַסּוּ אֶת־לְבָבֵנוּ לֵאמֹר עַם גָּדוֹל וָרָם מִמֶּנּוּ
עָרִים גְּדֹלֹת וּבְצוּרֹת בַּשָּׁמָיִם וְגַם־בְּנֵי עֲנָקִים רָאִינוּ
כט שָׁם: וָאֹמַר אֲלֵכֶם לֹא־תַעַרְצוּן וְלֹא־תִירְאוּן מֵהֶם:
ל יְהוָה אֱלֹהֵיכֶם הַהֹלֵךְ לִפְנֵיכֶם הוּא יִלָּחֵם לָכֶם
לא כְּכֹל אֲשֶׁר עָשָׂה אִתְּכֶם בְּמִצְרַיִם לְעֵינֵיכֶם: וּבַמִּדְבָּר
אֲשֶׁר רָאִיתָ אֲשֶׁר נְשָׂאֲךָ יְהוָה אֱלֹהֶיךָ כַּאֲשֶׁר יִשָּׂא־
אִישׁ אֶת־בְּנוֹ בְּכָל־הַדֶּרֶךְ אֲשֶׁר הֲלַכְתֶּם עַד־בֹּאֲכֶם
לב עַד־הַמָּקוֹם הַזֶּה: וּבַדָּבָר הַזֶּה אֵינְכֶם מַאֲמִינִם
לג בַּיהוָה אֱלֹהֵיכֶם: הַהֹלֵךְ לִפְנֵיכֶם בַּדֶּרֶךְ לָתוּר לָכֶם
מָקוֹם לַחֲנֹתְכֶם בָּאֵשׁ לַיְלָה לַרְאֹתְכֶם בַּדֶּרֶךְ אֲשֶׁר
לד תֵּלְכוּ־בָהּ וּבֶעָנָן יוֹמָם: וַיִּשְׁמַע יְהוָה אֶת־קוֹל

Deuteronomy 1
29–34

out of us, saying, 'We saw there a people stronger and taller than we, large cities with walls sky-high, and even Anakites.' "

29] I said to you, "Have no dread or fear of them.   30] None other than the LORD your God, who goes before you, will fight for you, just as He did for you in Egypt before your very eyes,   31] and in the wilderness, where you saw how the LORD your God carried you, as a man carries his son, all the way that you traveled until you came to this place.   32] Yet for all that, you have no faith in the LORD your God,   33] who goes before you on your journeys—to scout the place where you are to encamp—in fire by night and in cloud by day, in order to guide you on the route you are to follow."

34] When the LORD heard your loud complaint, He was angry. He vowed:

28] *Walls sky-high.* So they appeared to the nomads.

Anakites. In popular mythology a people of gigantic stature, but anthropology provides no evidence that such people lived in Palestine in biblical times; see our commentary on Num. 13:22.

31] *As a man carries his son.* The image of God as father and Israel as child recurs in Deut. 8:5 and 32:11, and elsewhere in the Bible. A similar image depicts God carrying Israel as on eagles' wings (Exod. 19:4).

32] *Yet for all that.* Despite God's proven care you did not believe His promise [4].

לה] דְּבָרֵיכֶם וַיִּקְצֹף וַיִּשָּׁבַע לֵאמֹר: אִם־יִרְאֶה אִישׁ
בָּאֲנָשִׁים הָאֵלֶּה הַדּוֹר הָרָע הַזֶּה אֵת הָאָרֶץ הַטּוֹבָה

לו] אֲשֶׁר נִשְׁבַּעְתִּי לָתֵת לַאֲבֹתֵיכֶם: זוּלָתִי כָּלֵב בֶּן־
יְפֻנֶּה הוּא יִרְאֶנָּה וְלוֹ־אֶתֵּן אֶת־הָאָרֶץ אֲשֶׁר דָּרַךְ־בָּהּ

לז] וּלְבָנָיו יַעַן אֲשֶׁר מִלֵּא אַחֲרֵי יְהֹוָה: גַּם־בִּי הִתְאַנַּף

לח] יְהֹוָה בִּגְלַלְכֶם לֵאמֹר גַּם־אַתָּה לֹא־תָבֹא שָׁם: יְהוֹשֻׁעַ
בִּן־נוּן הָעֹמֵד לְפָנֶיךָ הוּא יָבֹא שָׁמָּה אֹתוֹ חַזֵּק כִּי־

לט] הוּא יַנְחִלֶנָּה אֶת־יִשְׂרָאֵל: וְטַפְּכֶם אֲשֶׁר אֲמַרְתֶּם לָבַז
יִהְיֶה וּבְנֵיכֶם אֲשֶׁר לֹא־יָדְעוּ הַיּוֹם טוֹב וָרָע הֵמָּה

* לח מלעיל.

Deuteronomy 1
35—39

35] Not one of these men, this evil generation, shall see the good land that I swore to give to your fathers— 36] none except Caleb son of Jephunneh; he shall see it, and to him and his descendants will I give the land on which he set foot, because he remained loyal to the LORD.

37] Because of you the LORD was incensed with me too, and He said: You shall not enter it either. 38] Joshua son of Nun, who attends you, he shall enter it. Imbue him with strength, for he shall allot it to Israel. 39] Moreover, your little ones who you said would be carried off, your children who do not yet know good from bad, they shall enter it; to them will I give it and they shall possess it.

36] *None except Caleb.* Clearly a tradition different from Num. 14:6–7, 30, where both Caleb and Joshua are named as the dissenters (assigned to the P-source, in contrast to Num. 14:24, which is ascribed to J/E and singles out only Caleb). In Deuteronomy Caleb alone is distinguished for his faith, whereas Joshua's selection as the successor of Moses and his entrance into the Land (verse 38) are not connected with this incident.

On which he set foot. Hebron and vicinity; see Josh. 14:13 ff.

37] *Incensed with me too.* Num. 20 reported the condemnation of Moses to have taken place at Meribah, at the incident of the rock, during the thirty-ninth year of wandering. But here Moses appears to have been punished at Kadesh-barnea, in the second year, for the sins of the people or for some other unreported reason [5].

39] *Your children.* Who were under twenty years of age; see at 2:14.

From this the Rabbis inferred that youths under twenty were not punished for transgressions judged by the divine court [6].

מ יָבֹאוּ שָׁמָּה וְלָהֶם אֶתְּנֶנָּה וְהֵם יִירָשׁוּהָ: וְאַתֶּם פְּנוּ
מא לָכֶם וּסְעוּ הַמִּדְבָּרָה דֶּרֶךְ יַם־סוּף: וַתַּעֲנוּ וַתֹּאמְרוּ
אֵלַי חָטָאנוּ לַיהֹוָה אֲנַחְנוּ נַעֲלֶה וְנִלְחַמְנוּ כְּכֹל
אֲשֶׁר־צִוָּנוּ יְהֹוָה אֱלֹהֵינוּ וַתַּחְגְּרוּ אִישׁ אֶת־כְּלֵי
מב מִלְחַמְתּוֹ וַתָּהִינוּ לַעֲלֹת הָהָרָה: וַיֹּאמֶר יְהֹוָה אֵלַי
אֱמֹר לָהֶם לֹא תַעֲלוּ וְלֹא תִלָּחֲמוּ כִּי אֵינֶנִּי בְּקִרְבְּכֶם
מג וְלֹא תִּנָּגְפוּ לִפְנֵי אֹיְבֵיכֶם: וָאֲדַבֵּר אֲלֵיכֶם וְלֹא
שְׁמַעְתֶּם וַתַּמְרוּ אֶת־פִּי יְהֹוָה וַתָּזִדוּ וַתַּעֲלוּ הָהָרָה:
מד וַיֵּצֵא הָאֱמֹרִי הַיֹּשֵׁב בָּהָר הַהוּא לִקְרַאתְכֶם וַיִּרְדְּפוּ
אֶתְכֶם כַּאֲשֶׁר תַּעֲשֶׂינָה הַדְּבֹרִים וַיַּכְּתוּ אֶתְכֶם
מה בְּשֵׂעִיר עַד־חָרְמָה: וַתָּשֻׁבוּ וַתִּבְכּוּ לִפְנֵי יְהֹוָה וְלֹא־
שָׁמַע יְהֹוָה בְּקֹלְכֶם וְלֹא הֶאֱזִין אֲלֵיכֶם:

Deuteronomy 1
40–45

40] As for you, turn about and march into the wilderness, toward the Sea of Reeds.

41] You replied to me, saying, "We stand guilty before the Lord. We will go up now and fight, just as the Lord our God commanded us." And you all girded yourselves with war gear and recklessly started for the hill country. **42]** But the Lord said to me: Warn them, "Do not go up and do not fight, since I am not in your midst; else you will be routed by your enemies." **43]** I spoke to you, but you would not listen; you flouted the Lord's command and willfully marched into the hill country. **44]** Then the Amorites who lived in those hills came out against you like so many bees and chased you, and they crushed you at Hormah in Seir. **45]** Again you wept before the Lord; but the Lord would not heed your cry or give ear to you.

41] *Recklessly.* The Hebrew word occurs nowhere else in the Bible; the translation is suggested by the context.

44] *At Hormah in Seir.* With several ancient versions one should read "from Seir to Hormah" (מִשֵּׂעִיר instead of בְּשֵׂעִיר). Seir was the name most frequently applied to the Edomite mountains east of the Aravah; here it means probably a mountain near Jerusalem (see Josh. 15:10). Hormah was a place in the general vicinity of Beersheba; both the meaning of the name and the exact location are in doubt (see at Num. 21:3).

The Nature of Jewish Law

At the very beginning of Moses' recollections stands a brief statement on the principles of judicial procedure (verses 16 and 17); the courts must deal justly; give both sides a fair hearing; make no distinction between people of great or little status;[1] and apply one standard to Israelite citizen and resident alien when they have a lawsuit with each other.

These principles are then drawn together by enunciating their common basis: "judgment is God's." Biblical legislation assumes the divine origin of the law and covers its content as well as its administration. The law is of one piece and does not, therefore, know of any distinction between moral, ritual, and mere "legal" norms. What Israel must do is revealed and willed by God.[2] Transgression of His will is sinful and fraught with consequences human and divine; morality, ritual, and law are part of one single structure and are indistinguishable in the Torah and the Prophets. The latter often laid heavy emphasis on ethical behavior, but in doing so they did not negate the unified nature of Israelite law. This unity was developed and carried over into that highly complex system of later Jewish law which, when eventually codified in Mishnah and Talmud, became known as halachah, the way in which a Jew was to order his life in accordance with divine will, as understood by the Rabbis in subsequent centuries.

Traditional Jewish law to this day maintains this view of halachah; in it there are no distinctions (except for the purpose of systematic organization) that separate the laws governing the relations between God and the individual from those between human beings, or ritual from civil and criminal law. Thus, fasting on Yom Kippur and loving one's neighbor are both commanded in the halachah; the latter mitzvah is no more "ethical" than the former, for both are considered emanating from one divine source, and therefore halachah is, by its very nature, "ethical."

Reform Judaism brought a different perspective to Jewish law. While recognizing that the Torah presented the unitary principle of law as "God's judgment," it could not overlook either that human hands shaped the Torah or the human contribution made in later centuries to its development. In doing so it attempted to distinguish between various laws and gave a higher priority to moral norms than to ritual demands. The teachings of the Prophets became especially important to Reform because they stressed above all the need for social ethics and moral attitudes, and in turn the ritual aspects of halachah took a distinctly secondary place. Still, Reform always perceived its practices and perspectives to be guided by the biblical injunction: Whatever we do must be just, for justice is the will of God.

From the days of the formulation of the Torah this obligation has rested on every individual as well as on the whole people. God's judgment falls on all Israel if too many of its leaders and members transgress His law. The Jewish "ought" is at the same time personal and collective, for the nation has been and remains a partner to the covenant, the covenant which was concluded between the Lord and the totality of Israel who proclaimed: "All that the Lord has spoken we will do!" (Exod. 19:8)

---

[1] The text has also been understood as referring to matters of large and small financial consideration; see note on verse 17.

[2] Non-Israelites too must observe certain basic, self-evident laws (called by Tradition the Noahide laws); see our commentary on Gen. 8:15–9:29.

Two Generations

A striking feature of Moses' oration is the way in which he addressed the generation about to enter the Land. Clearly, his warnings were addressed to people whose fathers and mothers had perished in the wilderness, because by their lack of faith they had shown themselves unworthy of God's trust. But while Moses spoke to the people before him and recited to them the sins of the past, he slipped into a remarkable identification of past and present. In recounting the crucial incident of the spies (which eventually led to the condemnation of the old generation) he might have been expected to say: "Then all of them came to me and said . . ." (verse 22), or "They refused to go up . . ." (verse 26), or "I said to them . . ." (verse 29). But in every case, instead of using "them" and "they," Moses used "you," addressing the new generation as if *they* had been the sinners, who must now be cautioned not to repeat the earlier transgression.

This appears to be more than a stylistic peculiarity. Even as the text changes frequently from plural to singular and back again—thus reflecting the close relation between individual and collective responsibility—so it views Israel's past and present as a single continuum. The covenant was originally concluded with those now dead, but its force continued unabated and it will apply to future generations as well: "I make this covenant . . . both with those who are standing here with us this day before the Lord our God and with those who are not with us here this day" (29:13–14). The history of the Jewish people possessed then, and has continued to exhibit, a quality which identifies past and present, in that the obligations of the people are in fact a-historical. They are not bound by time.

Therefore, when Moses begins his exhortations, his prologue deals not with idolatry (a theme to which he will later insistently turn) but rather with lack of faith and trust. Once before the people had stood at the gates of Canaan but had disbelieved God's promise; Moses now cautions them not to repeat the same sin. For this reason he does not single out the incident of the golden calf, which had loomed so large as a virtual abandonment of the covenant; rather, he begins with the challenge to the present generation to trust God's providence. "You" made a fatal error once before, he says, don't do it again. You are now the fathers and mothers of Israel, and in the future our people will identify with you as you do with your own forebears. Your responsibility is therefore not to yourselves alone, it is to the generations yet unborn who will be able to say even as you do now: "*We* stood at Sinai."[3]

---

[3] See also the words of the Haggadah: In every generation, each person should feel as though he himself/she herself had gone forth from Egypt, as it is said (Exod. 13:8), "because of what the Lord did *for me* when *I* went free from Egypt."

GLEANINGS

Blessing and Reproof

Moses begins his exhortation with a blessing (verse 11), in order to make his reproof more palatable.　　　　　　　　　M. HACOHEN [7]

One of the reasons Jerusalem was destroyed was that people did not reprove one another.

TALMUD [8]

How

Three uttered their prophecy by using the word אֵיכָה (*echah*, how):

Moses, who said: "How can I alone bear the trouble of you" (verse 12);

Isaiah, who said: "How has the faithful city become a harlot" (1:21); and

Jeremiah, who said: "How does the city sit solitary" (Lam. 1:1).[4]

The Sages connected all three "hows" by bringing them into a liturgical relationship with one another. They arranged the Book of Lamentations, which deals with the destruction of the Temple, to be read on the 9th of Av; and the passages from Deuteronomy and Isaiah to be the scriptural readings for the Sabbath before Tishah b'Av.

The Stranger

It says "Decide justly between any man . . . or a stranger" (verse 16). The Hebrew reads literally "*his* stranger"—as if the stranger lived in his house and was therefore doubly dependent on him. The following story is based on this reading.

The wife of a rabbi prepared to lodge a complaint against her maid. The rabbi accompanied her wife to the magistrate. Was this not beneath his dignity? she asked. His answer: No, I intend to represent the maid who, being "our" stranger, needs someone to take her part so that justice will be done.　　　　　　　AFTER J. H. HERTZ

Seven Qualities

Judges must exhibit seven qualities: they must be wise, discerning, and experienced[5] (verse 13); they must be capable, fear God, be trustworthy, and spurn ill-gotten gain (Exod. 18:21).

MAIMONIDES [9]

"Experienced" (verse 13) means that they must be in close contact with the people, which is to say, they must love them.　　ITTURE TORAH [10]

Decide Justly (verse 16)

וּשְׁפַטְתֶּם צֶדֶק could be understood to mean "judge righteousness." There are times when the way righteousness is executed needs itself judging and weighing in the balance.　　CHASIDIC [11]

The Judgment of Moses

Why in verse 37 does Moses say that he was punished *because of the people*, while in Num. 20 it is recounted how he was punished for *his own particular sin*? The answer is that God was incensed with him as with everyone else, except Joshua and Caleb, when He judged Israel as unfit to enter the Land. Moses was one of the people and suffered their fate, but God waited for a propitious time to announce His judgment to Moses.[6]

YALKUT ME'AM LO'EZ [12]

---

[4] Tradition ascribed the authorship of Lamentations to Jeremiah.

[5] See verse 15, for an alternate understanding of יְדֻעִים.

[6] This represents one of many rabbinic and post-rabbinic attempts to explain why the apparently minor transgression related in Num. 20 brought on such drastic divine retribution (see our commentary on that chapter).

The Secret of Moses' Blessing

Students of the text delighted to find hidden connections. Thus, they asked, how could Moses bestow a blessing of thousandfold power (verse 11)? They argued in this way:

In gematria the letters in Moses equal the letters in El Shaddai (a name for God: משה and אל שדי both add up to 345).[7] Now the letters in אל שדי when written out fully look thus: אלף, למד, שין, דלת, יוד. Add these letters together and you find they amount to 999! Moses loved Israel with divine love and thus, adding his own benediction, he could bestow this extravagant thousandfold blessing.   CHASIDIC [13]

---

[7] מ=40, ש=300, ה=5;   א=1, ל=30, ש=300, ד=4, י=10.

Second Review

The purpose of the long recital with which Moses begins his exhortation is to lay before the people a clear view of their fate, a fate closely tied to the will of God. He recalls how they wandered in the desert for forty years, thirty-eight of which were punishment for their fathers' lack of trust in God; how the Guardian of Israel had brought the old generation out of Egypt in a display of wonders and terrors never experienced by any other nation; how He had taken them to Sinai and told them what they needed to do so that they might merit divine approval and enter the Promised Land—and how they had proven themselves unworthy of the divine trust. They acted cowardly when given the opportunity to conquer the land, their cowardice springing from their lack of faith that God would sustain them. Their failure was a failure of nerve: to believe in the saving power of the Lord. In consequence, the whole generation of the Exodus was condemned to die in the wilderness, and Moses himself was included in the judgment. Like the captain of a sinking ship, he was to perish with his people whom he had not prepared properly for their task.

The section ends with Moses recounting how his own plea, to be allowed to enter the Promised Land, was rejected by God. With this the prologue comes to an end, and in chapter 4 we will read the beginning of Moses' first major oration.

It is important to view this recital also in the light of ancient Near Eastern treaty patterns. These usually contained a declaration that granted land and rule to the vassal and then, as here, proceeded to a description of the land and its boundaries [1].

(A new weekly portion, *Va'etchanan*, begins with 3:23.)

מו וַתֵּשְׁבוּ בְקָדֵשׁ יָמִים רַבִּים כַּיָּמִים אֲשֶׁר יְשַׁבְתֶּם:

א וַנֵּפֶן וַנִּסַּע הַמִּדְבָּרָה דֶּרֶךְ יַם־סוּף כַּאֲשֶׁר דִּבֶּר

ב יְהֹוָה אֵלָי וַנָּסָב אֶת־הַר־שֵׂעִיר יָמִים רַבִּים: וַיֹּאמֶר

ג יְהֹוָה אֵלַי לֵאמֹר: רַב־לָכֶם סֹב אֶת־הָהָר הַזֶּה פְּנוּ

ד לָכֶם צָפֹנָה: וְאֶת־הָעָם צַו לֵאמֹר אַתֶּם עֹבְרִים

בִּגְבוּל אֲחֵיכֶם בְּנֵי־עֵשָׂו הַיֹּשְׁבִים בְּשֵׂעִיר וְיִירְאוּ

ה מִכֶּם וְנִשְׁמַרְתֶּם מְאֹד: אַל־תִּתְגָּרוּ בָם כִּי לֹא־אֶתֵּן

לָכֶם מֵאַרְצָם עַד מִדְרַךְ כַּף־רָגֶל כִּי־יְרֻשָּׁה לְעֵשָׂו

ו נָתַתִּי אֶת־הַר שֵׂעִיר: אֹכֶל תִּשְׁבְּרוּ מֵאִתָּם בַּכֶּסֶף

וַאֲכַלְתֶּם וְגַם־מַיִם תִּכְרוּ מֵאִתָּם בַּכֶּסֶף וּשְׁתִיתֶם:

46] Thus, after you had remained at Kadesh all that long time,

1] we marched back into the wilderness, toward the Sea of Reeds, as the LORD had spoken to me, and skirted the hill country of Seir a long time.

2] Then the LORD said to me: 3] You have been skirting this hill country long enough; now turn north. 4] And charge the people as follows: You will be passing through the territory of your kinsmen, the descendants of Esau, who live in Seir. Though they will be afraid of you, be very careful 5] not to start a fight with them. For I will not give you of their land so much as a foot can tread on; I have given the hill country of Seir as a possession to Esau. 6] What food you eat you shall obtain from them for money; even the water you drink you shall procure from

2:1] *Toward the Sea of Reeds.* Its location is disputed; see our commentary on Exod. 13:18.

4] *Territory of your kinsmen.* The report in Num. 20:14 ff. differs: there, Edom is depicted as having refused Israel its request to pass through.
Traditional interpreters explain the discrepancy in this way: the account in Numbers tells of what happened thirty-eight years before, in Deuteronomy of what happened recently; according to this view the Edomites had altered their policies. Another interpretation denies that Seir (Esau) is identical with Edom [2].

5] *Seir as a possession to Esau.* While Moab and Ammon were bequeathed to Lot (in that Moab and Ammon were traced back to Lot, Gen. 19:37–38). Israel was not the only people to receive its land as a divine patrimony.

כִּי יְהוָה אֱלֹהֶיךָ בֵּרַכְךָ בְּכֹל מַעֲשֵׂה יָדֶךָ יָדַע
לֶכְתְּךָ אֶת־הַמִּדְבָּר הַגָּדֹל הַזֶּה זֶה אַרְבָּעִים שָׁנָה

ח יְהוָה אֱלֹהֶיךָ עִמָּךְ לֹא חָסַרְתָּ דָּבָר: וַנַּעֲבֹר מֵאֵת
אַחֵינוּ בְנֵי־עֵשָׂו הַיֹּשְׁבִים בְּשֵׂעִיר מִדֶּרֶךְ הָעֲרָבָה
מֵאֵילַת וּמֵעֶצְיֹן גָּבֶר   ס   וַנֵּפֶן וַנַּעֲבֹר דֶּרֶךְ מִדְבַּר

ט מוֹאָב: וַיֹּאמֶר יְהוָה אֵלַי אַל־תָּצַר אֶת־מוֹאָב וְאַל־
תִּתְגָּר בָּם מִלְחָמָה כִּי לֹא־אֶתֵּן לְךָ מֵאַרְצוֹ יְרֻשָּׁה

י כִּי לִבְנֵי־לוֹט נָתַתִּי אֶת־עָר יְרֻשָּׁה: הָאֵמִים לְפָנִים

יא יָשְׁבוּ בָהּ עַם גָּדוֹל וְרַב וָרָם כָּעֲנָקִים: רְפָאִים
יֵחָשְׁבוּ אַף־הֵם כָּעֲנָקִים וְהַמֹּאָבִים יִקְרְאוּ לָהֶם

Deuteronomy 2
7–11

them for money.   7] Indeed, the LORD your God has blessed you in all your under-takings. He has watched over your wanderings through this great wilderness; the LORD your God has been with you these past forty years: you have lacked nothing.

8] We then moved on, away from our kinsmen, the descendants of Esau, who live in Seir, away from the road of the Arabah, away from Elath and Ezion-geber; and we marched on in the direction of the wilderness of Moab.   9] And the LORD said to me: Do not harass the Moabites or engage them in war. For I will not give you any of their land as a possession; I have given Ar as a possession to the descendants of Lot.—

10] It was formerly inhabited by the Emim, a people great and numerous, and as tall as the Anakites.   11] Like the Anakites, they are counted as Rephaim;

8] *We then moved on.* Marching from the northern end of the Gulf of Akaba through the Aravah toward the southern end of the Dead Sea; from there turning eastward, then north again toward Moab.

Ezion-geber. Its original location is in doubt. For a time it was believed to have been near or identical with Elath (modern Eilat); but lately the island of Jazirat-Farun, in the northern end of the Gulf of Akaba, has been accepted as the more likely site [3]. See also at Num. 33:35.

Tradition prescribes that in the writing of the Torah a space be inserted between Ezion-geber and the words following. Why the Masoretes introduced this is not clear. Perhaps at one time a new sentence started here.

9] *Ar.* An important Moabite city.

10] *Formerly.* Verses 10–12 are an editorial aside, as if written in parentheses.

Emim. They are here listed as "Rephaim" (while in Gen. 14:5 they were thought to be distinct from them). The explanation has the flavor

יב אֵמִים: וּבְשֵׂעִיר יָשְׁבוּ הַחֹרִים לְפָנִים וּבְנֵי עֵשָׂו
יִירָשׁוּם וַיַּשְׁמִידוּם מִפְּנֵיהֶם וַיֵּשְׁבוּ תַחְתָּם כַּאֲשֶׁר
עָשָׂה יִשְׂרָאֵל לְאֶרֶץ יְרֻשָּׁתוֹ אֲשֶׁר־נָתַן יְהוָה לָהֶם:
יג עַתָּה קֻמוּ וְעִבְרוּ לָכֶם אֶת־נַחַל זָרֶד וַנַּעֲבֹר אֶת־
יד נַחַל זָרֶד: וְהַיָּמִים אֲשֶׁר־הָלַכְנוּ מִקָּדֵשׁ בַּרְנֵעַ עַד
אֲשֶׁר־עָבַרְנוּ אֶת־נַחַל זֶרֶד שְׁלֹשִׁים וּשְׁמֹנֶה שָׁנָה עַד־
תֹּם כָּל־הַדּוֹר אַנְשֵׁי הַמִּלְחָמָה מִקֶּרֶב הַמַּחֲנֶה
טו כַּאֲשֶׁר נִשְׁבַּע יְהוָה לָהֶם: וְגַם יַד־יְהוָה הָיְתָה בָּם

Deuteronomy 2
12–15

but the Moabites call them Emim.   12] Similarly, Seir was formerly inhabited by the Horites; but the descendants of Esau dispossessed them, wiping them out and settling in their place, just as Israel did in the land they were to possess, which the LORD had given to them.—

13] Up now! Cross the wadi Zered!

So we crossed the wadi Zered.   14] The time that we spent in travel from Kadesh-barnea until we crossed the wadi Zered was thirty-eight years, until that whole generation of warriors had perished from the camp, as the LORD had sworn concerning them.   15] Indeed, the hand of the LORD struck them, to root them out from the camp to the last man.

---

of folk memory and popular commentary. See further in W. W. Hallo's essay, above.

13] *Up now!* Moses resumes his recital of past events.

Wadi Zered. A stream near the Moabite border; its identity is in doubt.

14] *Thirty-eight years.* As in the Book of Numbers, no statement is made about any happenings during this period. The generation of the Exodus died and so did the knowledge of their latter-day lives, for now it was their children who constituted Is-

rael's future and the chronicler's attention shifts to them. Tradition fixed the 15th of Av as the date when Israel was given permission to proceed to Canaan, and for centuries the day was celebrated with great joy [4].

On that day the marriageable women dressed in white and danced with the young men, inviting them to choose their partners for marriage. It was also the day of wood-offering, when priests and people brought firewood to the altar for use at sacrifices.

Whole generation of warriors had perished. "Warriors" is not to be understood technically as if only

26

טז לְהָמָּם מִקֶּרֶב הַמַּחֲנֶה עַד תֻּמָּם: וַיְהִי כַאֲשֶׁר־תַּמּוּ
יז כָּל־אַנְשֵׁי הַמִּלְחָמָה לָמוּת מִקֶּרֶב הָעָם: ס וַיְדַבֵּר
יח יְהֹוָה אֵלַי לֵאמֹר: אַתָּה עֹבֵר הַיּוֹם אֶת־גְּבוּל מוֹאָב
יט אֶת־עָר: וְקָרַבְתָּ מוּל בְּנֵי עַמּוֹן אַל־תְּצֻרֵם וְאַל־
תִּתְגָּר בָּם כִּי לֹא־אֶתֵּן מֵאֶרֶץ בְּנֵי־עַמּוֹן לְךָ יְרֻשָּׁה
כ כִּי לִבְנֵי־לוֹט נְתַתִּיהָ יְרֻשָּׁה: אֶרֶץ־רְפָאִים תֵּחָשֵׁב
אַף־הִוא רְפָאִים יָשְׁבוּ־בָהּ לְפָנִים וְהָעַמֹּנִים יִקְרְאוּ
כא לָהֶם זַמְזֻמִּים: עַם גָּדוֹל וְרַב וָרָם כָּעֲנָקִים וַיַּשְׁמִידֵם
כב יְהֹוָה מִפְּנֵיהֶם וַיִּירָשֻׁם וַיֵּשְׁבוּ תַחְתָּם: כַּאֲשֶׁר עָשָׂה
לִבְנֵי עֵשָׂו הַיֹּשְׁבִים בְּשֵׂעִיר אֲשֶׁר הִשְׁמִיד אֶת־הַחֹרִי

Deuteronomy 2
16–22

16] When all the warriors among the people had died off, 17] the LORD spoke to me, saying: 18] You are now passing through the territory of Moab, through Ar. 19] You will then be close to the Ammonites; do not harass them or start a fight with them. For I will not give any part of the land of the Ammonites to you as a possession; I have given it as a possession to the descendants of Lot.—

20] It, too, is counted as Rephaim country. It was formerly inhabited by Rephaim, whom the Ammonites call Zamzummim, 21] a people great and numerous and as tall as the Anakites. The LORD wiped them out, so that [the Ammonites] dispossessed them and settled in their place, 22] as He did for the descendants of Esau who live in Seir, when He wiped out the Horites before them, so that

males perished. Rather, the word should be understood as "people over twenty," which conforms with Num. 14:21 ff.

19] *Land of the Ammonites.* In the area of today's Amman, east of the Jordan, northeast of the Dead Sea. To the south of it was Moab and further south was Edom.

20] *It, too.* Verses 20–23 are another editorial aside.

Zamzummim. Likely identical with the Zuzim of Gen. 14:5. It has been suggested that the name imitated some speech habit of the people (compare the Greek *barbaros* and Latin *barbarus* as terms for foreign people).

מִפְּנֵיהֶם וַיִּירָשֻׁם וַיֵּשְׁבוּ תַחְתָּם עַד הַיּוֹם הַזֶּה:

כג וְהָעַוִּים הַיֹּשְׁבִים בַּחֲצֵרִים עַד־עַזָּה כַּפְתֹּרִים הַיֹּצְאִים

כד מִכַּפְתֹּר הִשְׁמִידֻם וַיֵּשְׁבוּ תַחְתָּם: קוּמוּ סְּעוּ וְעִבְרוּ

אֶת־נַחַל אַרְנֹן רְאֵה נָתַתִּי בְיָדְךָ אֶת־סִיחֹן מֶלֶךְ־

חֶשְׁבּוֹן הָאֱמֹרִי וְאֶת־אַרְצוֹ הָחֵל רָשׁ וְהִתְגָּר בּוֹ

כה מִלְחָמָה: הַיּוֹם הַזֶּה אָחֵל תֵּת פַּחְדְּךָ וְיִרְאָתְךָ עַל־

פְּנֵי הָעַמִּים תַּחַת כָּל־הַשָּׁמָיִם אֲשֶׁר יִשְׁמְעוּן שִׁמְעֲךָ

כו וְרָגְזוּ וְחָלוּ מִפָּנֶיךָ: וָאֶשְׁלַח מַלְאָכִים מִמִּדְבַּר

קְדֵמוֹת אֶל־סִיחוֹן מֶלֶךְ חֶשְׁבּוֹן דִּבְרֵי שָׁלוֹם לֵאמֹר:

* כד ס' דנושה.

they dispossessed them and settled in their place, as is still the case.   23] So, too, with the Avvim who dwelt in villages in the vicinity of Gaza: the Caphtorim, who came from Crete, wiped them out and settled in their place.—

24] Up! Set out across the wadi Arnon! See, I give into your power Sihon the Amorite, king of Heshbon, and his land. Begin the occupation: engage him in battle.   25] This day I begin to put the dread and fear of you upon the peoples everywhere under heaven, so that they shall tremble and quake because of you whenever they hear you mentioned.

26] Then I sent messengers from the wilderness of Kedemoth to Sihon king of

23] *Avvim.* A people not further identified. Their land was not to be conquered by Israel until the end of Joshua's life (Josh. 13:3).

Gaza. About 50 miles (80 km) south of Tel Aviv-Jaffa. An important town on the road from Mesopotamia to Egypt, mentioned already in the el-Amarna letters of fourteenth century B.C.E.

Caphtorim who came from Crete. Literally, "from Caphtor." The identity of Caphtor and Crete is a longstanding assumption, but without final proof.

Some believe Caphtor to mean Cappadocia, an area in today's eastern Turkey.

24] *Up!* Moses resumes his narrative.

Begin the occupation. The meaning of רָשׁ (*rash*) is deduced from the context.

26] *I sent messengers.* Rehearsing the story told in Num. 21:21 ff.

Kedemoth. Not mentioned previously. It appears in Josh. 13:18 and I Chron. 6:64 as located in the territory of Reuben (east of the Jordan River).

כו אֶעְבְּרָה בְאַרְצֶךָ בַּדֶּרֶךְ בַּדֶּרֶךְ אֵלֵךְ לֹא אָסוּר

כז יָמִין וּשְׂמֹאול: אֹכֶל בַּכֶּסֶף תַּשְׁבִּרֵנִי וְאָכַלְתִּי וּמַיִם

כט בַּכֶּסֶף תִּתֶּן־לִי וְשָׁתִיתִי רַק אֶעְבְּרָה בְרַגְלָי: כַּאֲשֶׁר

עָשׂוּ־לִי בְּנֵי עֵשָׂו הַיֹּשְׁבִים בְּשֵׂעִיר וְהַמּוֹאָבִים הַיֹּשְׁבִים

בְּעָר עַד אֲשֶׁר־אֶעֱבֹר אֶת־הַיַּרְדֵּן אֶל־הָאָרֶץ אֲשֶׁר־

ל יְהוָה אֱלֹהֵינוּ נֹתֵן לָנוּ: וְלֹא אָבָה סִיחֹן מֶלֶךְ חֶשְׁבּוֹן

הַעֲבִרֵנוּ בּוֹ כִּי־הִקְשָׁה יְהוָה אֱלֹהֶיךָ אֶת־רוּחוֹ

וְאִמֵּץ אֶת־לְבָבוֹ לְמַעַן תִּתּוֹ בְיָדְךָ כַּיּוֹם הַזֶּה: ס

לא וַיֹּאמֶר יְהוָה אֵלַי רְאֵה הַחִלֹּתִי תֵּת לְפָנֶיךָ

אֶת־סִיחֹן וְאֶת־אַרְצוֹ הָחֵל רָשׁ לָרֶשֶׁת אֶת־אַרְצוֹ:

Deuteronomy 2
27–31

* כז מלא ו'.

Heshbon with an offer of peace, as follows,   27] "Let me pass through your country. I will keep strictly to the highway, turning off neither to the right nor to the left. 28] What food I eat you will supply for money, and what water I drink you will furnish for money; just let me pass through—   29] as the descendants of Esau who dwell in Seir did for me, and the Moabites who dwell in Ar—that I may cross the Jordan into the land that the LORD our God is giving us."

30] But Sihon king of Heshbon would not let us pass through, because the LORD had stiffened his will and hardened his heart in order to deliver him into your power—as is now the case.   31] And the LORD said to me: See, I begin by placing Sihon and his land at your disposal. Begin the occupation; take possession of his land.

27] *Keep strictly to the highway.* Literally, "I will keep to the highway, to the highway"—and will not stray from it.

28] *Pass through.* The story resembles the account in Num. 20:18 ff. as far as the payments are concerned, but it differs in that it does not seem to know of the delegation which was sent and the refusal it met. Another version of the account appears in Judg. 11:19–22.

30] *Stiffened his will.* Like Pharaoh's. On the theological problem—how God can restrict a person's free will and yet punish him as if he were free—see our commentary on Exod. 4:19–6:1.

לב וַיֵּצֵא סִיחֹן לִקְרָאתֵנוּ הוּא וְכָל־עַמּוֹ לַמִּלְחָמָה יָהְצָה:

לג וַיִּתְּנֵהוּ יְהֹוָה אֱלֹהֵינוּ לְפָנֵינוּ וַנַּךְ אֹתוֹ וְאֶת־בָּנָו* וְאֶת־

לד כָּל־עַמּוֹ: וַנִּלְכֹּד אֶת־כָּל־עָרָיו בָּעֵת הַהִוא וַנַּחֲרֵם אֶת־כָּל־עִיר מְתִם וְהַנָּשִׁים וְהַטָּף לֹא הִשְׁאַרְנוּ שָׂרִיד:

לה רַק הַבְּהֵמָה בָּזַזְנוּ לָנוּ וּשְׁלַל הֶעָרִים אֲשֶׁר לָכָדְנוּ:

לו מֵעֲרֹעֵר אֲשֶׁר עַל־שְׂפַת־נַחַל אַרְנֹן וְהָעִיר אֲשֶׁר בַּנַּחַל וְעַד־הַגִּלְעָד לֹא הָיְתָה קִרְיָה אֲשֶׁר שָׂגְבָה

לז מִמֶּנּוּ אֶת־הַכֹּל נָתַן יְהֹוָה אֱלֹהֵינוּ לְפָנֵינוּ: רַק אֶל־אֶרֶץ בְּנֵי־עַמּוֹן לֹא קָרָבְתָּ כָּל־יַד נַחַל יַבֹּק וְעָרֵי הָהָר וְכֹל אֲשֶׁר־צִוָּה יְהֹוָה אֱלֹהֵינוּ:

* לג בָּנָיו קרי.

32] Sihon with all his men took the field against us at Jahaz,   **33]** and the LORD our God delivered him to us and we defeated him and his sons and all his men. **34]** At that time we captured all his towns, and we doomed every town—men, women, and children—leaving no survivor.   **35]** We retained as booty only the cattle and the spoil of the cities that we captured.   **36]** From Aroer on the edge of the Arnon valley, including the town in the valley itself, to Gilead, not a city was too mighty for us; the LORD our God delivered everything to us.   **37]** But you did not encroach upon the land of the Ammonites, all along the wadi Jabbok and the towns of the hill country, just as the LORD our God had commanded.

32] *At Jahaz.* According to the Mesha stone, it was located not far from Dibon. Mesha, king of Moab, erected the stele to commemorate his victory over Israel (ninth century B.C.E.).

34] *We doomed.* Or, "proscribed" (so translated in Num. 21:2), meaning: We utterly destroyed them, reserving no booty except what was to be deposited in the sanctuary as an offering, and taking no prisoners. What was to be doomed could not be sold or redeemed; Lev. 27:28.

35] *We retained . . . the cattle.* But, when later on

Jericho was conquered under Joshua's leadership, cattle too were doomed (Josh. 6:21). Amalek was to be treated in like manner (I Sam. 15:3).

36] *Aroer.* About 10 miles (16 km) from the Dead Sea.

37] *Wadi Jabbok.* It divided the tribe of Gad, on its south side, from one-half the tribe of Manasseh on the north. The story of Jacob's wrestling with the angel and his meeting with Esau was located here (Gen. 32:23).

א וַנֵּ֣פֶן וַנַּ֔עַל דֶּ֖רֶךְ הַבָּשָׁ֑ן וַיֵּצֵ֣א עוֹג֩ מֶלֶךְ־הַבָּשָׁ֨ן
ב לִקְרָאתֵ֜נוּ ה֧וּא וְכָל־עַמּ֛וֹ לַמִּלְחָמָ֖ה אֶדְרֶ֑עִי׃ וַיֹּ֨אמֶר
יְהֹוָ֜ה אֵלַ֗י אַל־תִּירָ֣א אֹת֔וֹ כִּ֣י בְיָדְךָ֞ נָתַ֧תִּי אֹת֛וֹ
וְאֶת־כָּל־עַמּ֖וֹ וְאֶת־אַרְצ֑וֹ וְעָשִׂ֣יתָ לּ֔וֹ כַּאֲשֶׁ֣ר עָשִׂ֗יתָ
ג לְסִיחֹן֙ מֶ֣לֶךְ הָֽאֱמֹרִ֔י אֲשֶׁ֥ר יוֹשֵׁ֖ב בְּחֶשְׁבּֽוֹן׃ וַיִּתֵּן֩
יְהֹוָ֨ה אֱלֹהֵ֜ינוּ בְּיָדֵ֗נוּ גַּ֛ם אֶת־ע֥וֹג מֶלֶךְ־הַבָּשָׁ֖ן וְאֶת־
ד כָּל־עַמּ֑וֹ וַנַּכֵּ֕הוּ עַד־בִּלְתִּ֥י הִשְׁאִֽיר־ל֖וֹ שָׂרִֽיד׃ וַנִּלְכֹּ֤ד
אֶת־כָּל־עָרָיו֙ בָּעֵ֣ת הַהִ֔וא לֹ֤א הָֽיְתָה֙ קִרְיָ֔ה אֲשֶׁ֥ר
לֹא־לָקַ֖חְנוּ מֵֽאִתָּ֑ם שִׁשִּׁ֥ים עִיר֙ כָּל־חֶ֣בֶל אַרְגֹּ֔ב
ה מַמְלֶ֖כֶת ע֥וֹג בַּבָּשָֽׁן׃ כָּל־אֵ֜לֶּה עָרִ֧ים בְּצֻרֹ֛ת חוֹמָ֥ה
גְבֹהָ֖ה דְּלָתַ֣יִם וּבְרִ֑יחַ לְבַ֛ד מֵעָרֵ֥י הַפְּרָזִ֖י הַרְבֵּ֥ה
ו מְאֹֽד׃ וַנַּחֲרֵ֣ם אוֹתָ֔ם כַּאֲשֶׁ֣ר עָשִׂ֔ינוּ לְסִיחֹ֖ן מֶ֣לֶךְ

Deuteronomy 3
1–6

1] We made our way up the road toward Bashan, and Og king of Bashan with all his men took the field against us at Edrei.   2] But the LORD said to me: Do not fear him, for I am delivering him and all his men and his country into your power, and you will do to him as you did to Sihon king of the Amorites, who lived in Heshbon.

3] So the LORD our God also delivered into our power Og king of Bashan, with all his men, and we dealt them such a blow that no survivor was left.   4] At that time we captured all his towns; there was not a town that we did not take from them: sixty towns, the whole district of Argob, the kingdom of Og in Bashan   5]—all those towns were fortified with high walls, gates, and bars—apart from a great number of unwalled towns.   6] We doomed them as we had done in the case of

---

3:1] *We made our way.* The war against Og was recounted in Num. 21:33 ff.

Bashan. See at Deut. 1:4.

4] *Sixty towns.* Probably a round figure meaning

"many towns" [5].

Argob. Josephus identified it with Jaulan (Golan) [6].

5] *Unwalled towns.* See also Ezek. 38:11.

ז חֶשְׁבּוֹן הַחֲרֵם כָּל־עִיר מְתִם הַנָּשִׁים וְהַטָּף: וְכָל־

ח הַבְּהֵמָה וּשְׁלַל הֶעָרִים בַּזּוֹנוּ לָנוּ: וַנִּקַּח בָּעֵת הַהִוא
אֶת־הָאָרֶץ מִיַּד שְׁנֵי מַלְכֵי הָאֱמֹרִי אֲשֶׁר בְּעֵבֶר

ט הַיַּרְדֵּן מִנַּחַל אַרְנֹן עַד־הַר חֶרְמוֹן: צִידֹנִים יִקְרְאוּ

י לְחֶרְמוֹן שִׂרְיֹן וְהָאֱמֹרִי יִקְרְאוּ־לוֹ שְׂנִיר: כֹּל עָרֵי
הַמִּישֹׁר וְכָל־הַגִּלְעָד וְכָל־הַבָּשָׁן עַד־סַלְכָה וְאֶדְרֶעִי

י״א עָרֵי מַמְלֶכֶת עוֹג בַּבָּשָׁן: כִּי רַק־עוֹג מֶלֶךְ הַבָּשָׁן
נִשְׁאַר מִיֶּתֶר הָרְפָאִים הִנֵּה עַרְשׂוֹ עֶרֶשׂ בַּרְזֶל הֲלֹה
הוּא בְּרַבַּת בְּנֵי עַמּוֹן תֵּשַׁע אַמּוֹת אָרְכָּהּ וְאַרְבַּע

* יא כתיב בה׳.

Sihon king of Heshbon; we doomed every town—men, women, and children—
7] and retained as booty all the cattle and the spoil of the towns.

8] Thus we seized, at that time, from the two Amorite kings, the country beyond the Jordan, from the wadi Arnon to Mount Hermon   (9) Sidonians call Hermon Sirion, and the Amorites call it Senir),   10] all the towns of the Tableland and the whole of Gilead and Bashan as far as Salcah and Edrei, the towns of Og's kingdom in Bashan.—   (11] Only Og king of Bashan was left of the remaining Rephaim. His bedstead, an iron bedstead, is now in Rabbah of the Ammonites; it is nine cubits long and four cubits wide, by the standard cubit!)

8] *Beyond the Jordan.* On this expression see at Deut. 1:1.

From the wadi Arnon. Which flows into the Dead Sea, near its middle.

To Mount Hermon. The highest peak in the northern mountains adjacent to Palestine, 9,232 feet (2,797 meters) high.

9] *Sidonians call.* Clearly an editorial aside and therefore bracketed in the English text. The Sidonians were often called Phoenicians; Sidon was a port city south of today's Beirut.

10] *Tableland.* The plains of Moab.

Salcah. The city is generally identified with modern Salkhad, southeast of Edrei (see at Deut. 1:4).

11] *Only Og.* This folkloric note pictures Og as the survivor of a race of giants (similarly in Josh. 12:4 and 13:12).

Some believe that "bedstead" was a euphemism for Og's sarcophagus.

Rabbah. Also called Rabbat-B'nei-Ammon. In the Hellenistic period it was one of several cities named Philadelphia (after Ptolemy Philadelphos). Today it is the site of Jordan's capital, Amman.

Standard cubit. Literally, "a man's cubit," pos-

יב אֵמּוֹת רָחְבָּהּ בְּאַמַּת־אִישׁ: וְאֶת־הָאָרֶץ הַזֹּאת יָרַשְׁנוּ
בָּעֵת הַהִוא מֵעֲרֹעֵר אֲשֶׁר־עַל־נַחַל אַרְנֹן וַחֲצִי הַר־

יג הַגִּלְעָד וְעָרָיו נָתַתִּי לָראוּבֵנִי וְלַגָּדִי: וְיֶתֶר הַגִּלְעָד
וְכָל־הַבָּשָׁן מַמְלֶכֶת עוֹג נָתַתִּי לַחֲצִי שֵׁבֶט הַמְנַשֶּׁה
כֹּל חֶבֶל הָאַרְגֹּב לְכָל־הַבָּשָׁן הַהוּא יִקָּרֵא אֶרֶץ

יד רְפָאִים: יָאִיר בֶּן־מְנַשֶּׁה לָקַח אֶת־כָּל־חֶבֶל אַרְגֹּב
עַד־גְּבוּל הַגְּשׁוּרִי וְהַמַּעֲכָתִי וַיִּקְרָא אֹתָם עַל־שְׁמוֹ

טו אֶת־הַבָּשָׁן חַוֺּת יָאִיר עַד הַיּוֹם הַזֶּה: וּלְמָכִיר נָתַתִּי

טז אֶת־הַגִּלְעָד: וְלָראוּבֵנִי וְלַגָּדִי נָתַתִּי מִן־הַגִּלְעָד וְעַד־

12] And this is the land which we apportioned at that time: The part from Aroer along the wadi Arnon, with part of the hill country of Gilead and its towns, I assigned to the Reubenites and the Gadites.   13] The rest of Gilead, and all of Bashan under Og's rule—the whole Argob district, all that part of Bashan which is called Rephaim country—I assigned to the half-tribe of Manasseh.   14] Jair son of Manasseh received the whole Argob district (that is, Bashan) as far as the boundary of the Geshurites and the Maacathites, and named it after himself, Havvoth-jair—as is still the case.   15] To Machir I assigned Gilead.   16] And to the Reubenites and the Gadites I assigned the part from Gilead down to the wadi Arnon, the middle of

sibly figured from the tip of the middle finger to the end of the elbow, similar to the way a yard was figured before it became fixed definitively. There were several cubits, none of which can be precisely reconstructed. The legendary bed was some thirteen to sixteen feet long and six to seven feet wide [7].

12] *This is the land.* The description proceeds from south to north in verses 12–13, and in reverse in verses 14–16. Reuben had settled in the southern-most portion, south and east of the Dead Sea;

Gad settled north of it, and Manasseh occupied the rich land north of Gad, now located mostly in Syria.

14] *Geshurites and Maacathites.* Two Canaanite tribes dwelling in the western part of Manasseh's territory, that is, in the Golan.

Havvoth-jair. Literally, "villages of Jair." According to Num. 32:39 ff. and other passages, the area was known as Gilead.

15] *Machir.* The only son of Manasseh (Jacob's grandson) is here used to represent the tribe.

33

נַחַל אַרְנֹן תּוֹךְ הַנַּחַל וּגְבֻל וְעַד יַבֹּק הַנַּחַל גְּבוּל
בְּנֵי עַמּוֹן: וְהָעֲרָבָה וְהַיַּרְדֵּן וּגְבֻל מִכִּנֶּרֶת וְעַד
יָם הָעֲרָבָה יָם הַמֶּלַח תַּחַת אַשְׁדֹּת הַפִּסְגָּה מִזְרָחָה:
וָאֲצַו אֶתְכֶם בָּעֵת הַהִוא לֵאמֹר יְהֹוָה אֱלֹהֵיכֶם
נָתַן לָכֶם אֶת־הָאָרֶץ הַזֹּאת לְרִשְׁתָּהּ חֲלוּצִים תַּעַבְרוּ
לִפְנֵי אֲחֵיכֶם בְּנֵי־יִשְׂרָאֵל כָּל־בְּנֵי־חָיִל: רַק נְשֵׁיכֶם
וְטַפְּכֶם וּמִקְנֵכֶם יָדַעְתִּי כִּי־מִקְנֶה רַב לָכֶם יֵשְׁבוּ
בְּעָרֵיכֶם אֲשֶׁר נָתַתִּי לָכֶם: עַד אֲשֶׁר־יָנִיחַ יְהֹוָה
לַאֲחֵיכֶם כָּכֶם וְיָרְשׁוּ גַם־הֵם אֶת־הָאָרֶץ אֲשֶׁר יְהֹוָה
אֱלֹהֵיכֶם נֹתֵן לָהֶם בְּעֵבֶר הַיַּרְדֵּן וְשַׁבְתֶּם אִישׁ

* כ סבורין לכם.

the wadi being the boundary, and up to the wadi Jabbok, the boundary of the Ammonites.

17] [We also seized] the Arabah, from the foot of the slopes of Pisgah on the east, to the edge of the Jordan, and from Chinnereth down to the sea of the Arabah, the Dead Sea.

18] At that time I charged you, saying, "The LORD your God has given you this country to possess. You must go as shocktroops, warriors all, at the head of your Israelite kinsmen. **19]** Only your wives, children, and livestock—I know that you have much livestock—shall be left in the towns I have assigned to you, **20]** until the LORD has granted your kinsmen a haven such as you have, and they too have taken possession of the land that the LORD your God is giving them, beyond the

17] *Pisgah.* A mountain range northeast of the Dead Sea, where later on Moses will die (34:1–5).

Chinnereth. A city from which Lake Kinneret (also called Sea of Galilee or Lake Tiberias) received its name.

Dead Sea. Literally, "Salt Sea," the lowest spot on earth. Its water is heavily salinated and only microscopic life exists in it.

18] *I charged you.* I charged the two and a half tribes.

Shock-troops. חֲלוּצִים (chalutzim). In modern Hebrew the term has come to mean "pioneers."

19] *I know that you have.* The kind of interjection a speaker is likely to make.

34

כא לִירִשְׁתָּהּ אֲשֶׁר נָתַתִּי לָכֶם: וְאֶת־יְהוֹשׁוּעַ צִוֵּיתִי בָּעֵת
הַהִוא לֵאמֹר עֵינֶיךָ הָרֹאֹת אֵת כָּל־אֲשֶׁר עָשָׂה
יְהוָה אֱלֹהֵיכֶם לִשְׁנֵי הַמְּלָכִים הָאֵלֶּה כֵּן־יַעֲשֶׂה יְהוָה
כב לְכָל־הַמַּמְלָכוֹת אֲשֶׁר אַתָּה עֹבֵר שָׁמָּה: לֹא תִּירָאוּם
כִּי יְהוָה אֱלֹהֵיכֶם הוּא הַנִּלְחָם לָכֶם:

Haftarah Devarim, p. 419

ס ס ס

כג וָאֶתְחַנַּן אֶל־יְהוָה בָּעֵת הַהִוא לֵאמֹר: אֲדֹנָי יְהוִה
כד אַתָּה הַחִלּוֹתָ לְהַרְאוֹת אֶת־עַבְדְּךָ אֶת־גָּדְלְךָ וְאֶת־
יָדְךָ הַחֲזָקָה אֲשֶׁר מִי־אֵל בַּשָּׁמַיִם וּבָאָרֶץ אֲשֶׁר־
כה יַעֲשֶׂה כְמַעֲשֶׂיךָ וְכִגְבוּרֹתֶךָ: אֶעְבְּרָה־נָּא וְאֶרְאֶה אֶת־
הָאָרֶץ הַטּוֹבָה אֲשֶׁר בְּעֵבֶר הַיַּרְדֵּן הָהָר הַטּוֹב הַזֶּה

ואתחנן

Va'etchanan

Deuteronomy 3
21–25

Jordan. Then you may return each to the homestead that I have assigned to him."

21] I also charged Joshua at that time, saying, "You have seen with your own eyes all that the LORD your God has done to these two kings; so shall the LORD do to all the kingdoms into which you shall cross over.   22] Do not fear them, for it is the LORD your God who will battle for you."

23] I pleaded with the LORD at that time, saying,   24] "O Lord GOD, You who let Your servant see the first works of Your greatness and Your mighty hand, You whose powerful deeds no god in heaven or on earth can equal!   25] Let me, I pray, cross over and see the good land on the other side of the Jordan, that good hill

---

24] *O Lord God.* אֲדֹנָי יְהוִה. Usually יהוה is voweled יְהוָה, but when following the word Adonai its voweling is that of אֱלֹהִים (*Elohim*), and the two words are pronounced *Adonai Elohim*.

No god in heaven. There is none whom others call "god" who can equal Israel's Lord (see further at Exod. 20:3).

25] *Hill country.* The Judean hills.

35

כו וְהַלְּבָנֹן: וַיִּתְעַבֵּר יְהֹוָה בִּי לְמַעַנְכֶם וְלֹא שָׁמַע
אֵלָי וַיֹּאמֶר יְהֹוָה אֵלַי רַב־לָךְ אַל־תּוֹסֶף דַּבֵּר

כז אֵלַי עוֹד בַּדָּבָר הַזֶּה: עֲלֵה רֹאשׁ הַפִּסְגָּה וְשָׂא
עֵינֶיךָ יָמָּה וְצָפֹנָה וְתֵימָנָה וּמִזְרָחָה וּרְאֵה בְעֵינֶיךָ

כח כִּי־לֹא תַעֲבֹר אֶת־הַיַּרְדֵּן הַזֶּה: וְצַו אֶת־יְהוֹשֻׁעַ
וְחַזְּקֵהוּ וְאַמְּצֵהוּ כִּי־הוּא יַעֲבֹר לִפְנֵי הָעָם הַזֶּה

כט וְהוּא יַנְחִיל אוֹתָם אֶת־הָאָרֶץ אֲשֶׁר תִּרְאֶה: וַנֵּשֶׁב
בַּגַּיְא מוּל בֵּית פְּעוֹר: פ

country, and the Lebanon." **26]** But the LORD was wrathful with me on your account and would not listen to me. The LORD said to me, "Enough! Never speak to Me of this matter again! **27]** Go up to the summit of Pisgah and gaze about, to the west, the north, the south, and the east. Look at it well, for you shall not go across yonder Jordan. **28]** Give Joshua his instructions, and imbue him with strength and courage, for he shall go across at the head of this people and he shall allot to them the land that you may only see."

29] Meanwhile we stayed on in the valley near Beth-peor.

26] *The Lord was wrathful.* וַיִּתְעַבֵּר is a word play on אֶעְבְּרָה (verse 25): God's anger is a response to Moses' plea.

The Lord said to me. The interplay between God and Moses was greatly expanded by the Midrash; see Gleanings at chapter 34.

29] *Beth-peor.* Where Israel sinned with the women of Moab (Num. 25:1 ff.) and where Moses will be buried (Deut. 34:6). It probably was near Heshbon, but the exact location is unknown.

Variant Traditions

The stories here related are found also in the Book of Numbers, and there is general agreement between these accounts. However, in Moses' recollections a series of colorful and informative asides are included, which deal in part with history and geography and in part with folklore, such as the remarkable bedstead of Og. Another and important difference is the role assigned to Caleb and Joshua. The Deuteronomic account of Israel's faithlessness singles out Caleb alone as the one who by his demonstrated faith had merited the right to enter Canaan. He had opposed the majority and had insisted that Israel could overcome all obstacles if only they trusted God's word. Joshua too was spared, not because (as in Num. 14:6) he had stood with Caleb against the multitude, but because he was Moses' lieutenant and he alone was trained to lead the nation.

Another difference is the way Moses was punished. In Deuteronomy, Moses suffered exclusion from Canaan because, as a leader, he shared his people's fate. In Numbers, Moses was punished for his individual sin—though what precisely the sin was is not clear (see Commentary on Numbers, chapter 20). Further differences occur in the descriptions of Israel's relationship with Edom and Moab (see at 2:4 and 2:28).

In all these cases it is apparent that there were variant traditions about Israel's wanderings which in time were joined. Their confluence—in a process that lasted many hundreds of years—resulted eventually in the text as we have it now. In general, the Deuteronomic account of Israel's wanderings is more detailed, more given to relating folklore, and more hortatory than Numbers, for its primary aim is to give moral instructions. Yet despite these differences the basic stories are the same. After the disastrous incident with the spies when Israel had refused to go forward, the people wandered about the Negev and the Sinai peninsula, and not until the old generation had died did they prepare for a new thrust. During their fortieth year in the wilderness they went northward, taking a route to the east of the Aravah, through the hills and plains of today's Kingdom of Jordan. They skirted Edom (east of the Negev) on its eastern side and then attacked the realms of Sihon and Og, conquering them and settling two and a half tribes on their territories. These wars mark the end of Israel's wanderings for, when Moses will have finished his last instructions and will have died east of the Jordan, his successor Joshua will lead the people into Canaan and begin the long struggle to occupy the whole land—a struggle that was not to be finished until the time of David and Solomon, more than two hundred years later.

God's Realm

In two important passages the second chapter concerns itself with the extension of God's realm beyond Israel. The influence that God has over Israel's fate is of course the foundation of all biblical thinking about Him. It is taken for granted that God's power was unlimited as far as His chosen ones were concerned; He could and did destroy Israel's enemies when it pleased Him. The whole Exodus story was a demonstration of His might and a paean to His glory. God and Israel were the focus; the Egyptians and other nations appeared to merit God's attention only in relation to Israel.[1]

---

[1] This is so, even though there is never any question that God created the nations; see Gen. 10 and 11. Only once in the first four books of the Torah is there another dimension, when it is said that the inhabit-

Now, in 2:5 and 2:19, a new note is struck. Israel is specifically instructed not to touch Edom and Ammon, for these are given as inalienable possessions to their inhabitants: Edom to the descendants of Esau (Isaac's older son and Jacob's brother), and Ammon to the offspring of Lot (Abraham's nephew). To be sure, this makes the Edomites and Ammonites Israel's kinsmen, but it is not the relationship alone that causes God to concern himself with them. After all, Moab too, like Ammon, is pictured as Lot's inheritance (stained though it was, Gen. 19:37–38), but Moab's land is never considered sacrosanct. It is subject to conquest like all of Canaan whose inhabitants are by divine preordination destined to be conquered by the Israelites.

The permanent allotment of the lands of Edom and Ammon to their inhabitants introduces a concept which later prophets (especially the Second Isaiah) stressed with great force: it is God's unique quality that He holds sway over all the nations, cares for them, and judges them. He is the one single God, He is God alone (Deut. 6:4), and there is no power beside Him. Other gods are false, and their adoration futile. Here, then, monotheism is proclaimed in its full force, and the Book of Deuteronomy devotes much space to its proclamation. Deut. 2:5 and 2:19 are notations made on the canvas of Israel's story and they hint at the fuller development which Moses will give to the theme of the all-embracing One God of the world.

ants of Canaan will forfeit the land because of their misdeeds—implying that otherwise they had a divine right of possession. Not until Deuteronomy, however, does this dimension come into full view.

GLEANINGS

Alive or Dead

The word מְתִים (men) is very similar to the word מֵתִים (dead). This shows that the difference between alive and dead is small, it is merely the position of the dots under the מ.

ITTURE TORAH [8]

Va'etchanan

The opening word of the weekly portion (3:23) is a form which suggests a reflexive sense, such as "I got myself to plead."

Said the Rabbi of Tsans, in like manner: "Before I begin to pray, I pray that I may be able to pray." [9]

At That Time (Deut. 3:23)

Moses prayed "at that time." When is "that time" for prayer? Any time, and not when it appears convenient. Moses prayed then and there—learn from him.

ISRAEL SALANTER [10]

Gematria

According to tradition, Moses spoke 515 prayers for וָאֶתְחַנַּן equals 515 by gematria, and so does תְּפִלָּה (prayer). Now, if God is present in prayer (add יהוה = 26) you obtain 541, a number equivalent to the letters in יִשְׂרָאֵל (Israel).[2] If Israel clings to God in prayer, it will gain true life.

CHATAM SOFER [11]

Note that the word for song (שִׁירָה) also adds up to 515,[3] for song and prayer go together.

M. HACOHEN [12]

What Moses Saw

Moses saw "the good land" (3:25), that is, the good *in* the land, unlike the spies who saw the bad in it.

CHASIDIC [13]

Moses encompassed with his gaze more than Joshua or his successor would actually tread upon. His vision was larger than subsequent reality.

M. HACOHEN [14]

That Good Hill Country (Deut. 3:25)

Throughout the Hebrew Scripture we find a deep love of mountains and mountain scenery. The Rabbis even introduced a special blessing to be recited on beholding lofty mountains.[4] Thus the Psalmist sang: "I turn my eyes to the mountains; from where will my help come?" (121:1)

AFTER J. H. HERTZ

Enough! (Deut. 3:26)

According to a midrash, Moses failed to understand God's judgment and even ventured to say: "If that is the way it is to be, then all men are alike and there is no difference between the righteous and the sinner, and all is accidental."[5]

---

[2] ו=6, א=1, ת=400, ח=8, נ=50 (twice);

ת=400, פ=80, ל=30, ה=5;

י=10, ה=5, ו=6, ה=5;

י=10, שׂ=300, ר=200, א=1; ל=30.

[3] שׁ=300, י=10, ר=200, ה=5

[4] "Blessed are You, Lord God, Ruler of the universe, Author of the work of Creation."

[5] This is similar to the midrashic interpretation given to Gen. 4 by Jonathan ben Uzziel, who ascribes the same outburst to Cain; see our Commentary on Genesis, chapter 4, Gleanings.

39

God cut him short and said "Enough! Never speak to Me of this matter again!"   TANCHUMA [15]

"Enough!" is a warning which implies man's need to realize that all he can do is do his part; this is enough. Man cannot ever hope to fulfill all his human wishes. He must accept whatever gratification comes from his particular role in the work of achieving God's will, even if he will not taste the fruit of his labor.   THE BIBLE READER [16]

Summary: To Observe the Law

Moses now proceeds from a consideration of the past to a summary of the fundamental requirements which God asks of Israel. Such a resumé could have stood at the end of the book; its placement here appears as an intrusion in a text that perhaps once continued directly with the second discourse starting with verse 44. This intrusion is emphasized by the further addition of three verses (41–43) dealing with cities of refuge, a subject that has no connection with what precedes or follows.

The summary sets forth the completeness of Torah as well as its uniqueness, qualities that characterize the treaty-covenant between God and Israel, with the Torah serving as the instrument ratifying this relationship. The first part of chapter 4 is itself cast in this covenantal framework and may be said to be, in this respect, a miniature of the whole Book of Deuteronomy:* It has a prologue (verses 1–8); it specifies the parties and how they came to make the covenant (9–14); it sets forth the request for undivided loyalty to the King (15–18); it issues warnings, with a first intimation of future exile (19–29); it sets forth rewards (30–31) [1].

The recital of the treaty is climaxed by an eloquent statement of God's power and an appeal to observe the law "that it may go well with you and your children" (verse 40).

---

* A similar and more complete parallel to the treaty form will be found below, in chapter 29. See also Hallo's essay above.

א וְעַתָּה יִשְׂרָאֵל שְׁמַע אֶל־הַחֻקִּים וְאֶל־הַמִּשְׁפָּטִים אֲשֶׁר
אָנֹכִי מְלַמֵּד אֶתְכֶם לַעֲשׂוֹת לְמַעַן תִּחְיוּ וּבָאתֶם
וִירִשְׁתֶּם אֶת־הָאָרֶץ אֲשֶׁר יְהֹוָה אֱלֹהֵי אֲבֹתֵיכֶם נֹתֵן
ב לָכֶם: לֹא תֹסִפוּ עַל־הַדָּבָר אֲשֶׁר אָנֹכִי מְצַוֶּה אֶתְכֶם
וְלֹא תִגְרְעוּ מִמֶּנּוּ לִשְׁמֹר אֶת־מִצְוֺת יְהֹוָה אֱלֹהֵיכֶם
ג אֲשֶׁר אָנֹכִי מְצַוֶּה אֶתְכֶם: עֵינֵיכֶם הָרֹאֹת אֵת אֲשֶׁר־
עָשָׂה יְהֹוָה בְּבַעַל פְּעוֹר כִּי כָל־הָאִישׁ אֲשֶׁר הָלַךְ
אַחֲרֵי בַעַל־פְּעוֹר הִשְׁמִידוֹ יְהֹוָה אֱלֹהֶיךָ מִקִּרְבֶּךָ:
ד וְאַתֶּם הַדְּבֵקִים בַּיהֹוָה אֱלֹהֵיכֶם חַיִּים כֻּלְּכֶם הַיּוֹם:

Deuteronomy 4

1–4

1] And now, O Israel, give heed to the laws and rules which I am instructing you to observe, so that you may live to enter and occupy the land that the LORD, the God of your fathers, is giving you.   2] You shall not add anything to what I command you or take anything away from it, but keep the commandments of the LORD your God that I enjoin upon you.   3] You saw with your own eyes what the LORD did in the matter of Baal-peor, that the LORD your God wiped out from among you every person who followed Baal-peor;   4] while you, who held fast to the LORD your God, are all alive today.

4:1] *Laws and rules.* The Torah frequently places *chukim* and *mishpatim* next to each other, but the distinction between them is not fully established. A number of theories have been developed: (1) that *chukim* deal with the basic relationship of man to God, the world, and himself, and *mishpatim* with man's relation to his fellow man, as expressed in civil and criminal law; (2) that the reasons for *mishpatim* are clear, whereas those for *chukim* are hidden (for instance, why the consumption of pork is prohibited [2]); (3) that *chukim* are those laws that restrict our sensual life and aim at creating a people of personal purity (for instance, laws of *kashrut* or those defining sexual transgressions [3]); (4) and, most likely, that *mishpatim* represents case law and *chukim*

apodictic law, "engraved" for all time. See further our commentary on Exod. 21:1.

So that you may live. The offer of rewards is an important aspect of the covenant model and therefore a normal accompaniment of the law, though doing God's will for His sake rather than for reward is a higher form of human response.

3] *The matter of Baal-peor.* Baal-peor, a local Moabite deity whom many Israelites worshiped in a moment of weakness (Num. 25:1–5). The sinful practices may have been sexual orgies.

4] *You . . . held fast.* This phrase was taken into the liturgy and is recited in traditional services before the blessings over the Torah.

ה רְאֵה לִמַּדְתִּי אֶתְכֶם חֻקִּים וּמִשְׁפָּטִים כַּאֲשֶׁר צִוַּנִי
יְהֹוָה אֱלֹהָי לַעֲשׂוֹת כֵּן בְּקֶרֶב הָאָרֶץ אֲשֶׁר אַתֶּם
ו בָּאִים שָׁמָּה לְרִשְׁתָּהּ: וּשְׁמַרְתֶּם וַעֲשִׂיתֶם כִּי הִוא
חָכְמַתְכֶם וּבִינַתְכֶם לְעֵינֵי הָעַמִּים אֲשֶׁר יִשְׁמְעוּן
אֵת כָּל־הַחֻקִּים הָאֵלֶּה וְאָמְרוּ רַק עַם־חָכָם וְנָבוֹן
ז הַגּוֹי הַגָּדוֹל הַזֶּה: כִּי מִי־גוֹי גָּדוֹל אֲשֶׁר־לוֹ אֱלֹהִים
קְרֹבִים אֵלָיו כַּיהֹוָה אֱלֹהֵינוּ בְּכָל־קָרְאֵנוּ אֵלָיו:
ח וּמִי גּוֹי גָּדוֹל אֲשֶׁר־לוֹ חֻקִּים וּמִשְׁפָּטִים צַדִּיקִם
כְּכֹל הַתּוֹרָה הַזֹּאת אֲשֶׁר אָנֹכִי נֹתֵן לִפְנֵיכֶם הַיּוֹם:
ט רַק הִשָּׁמֶר לְךָ וּשְׁמֹר נַפְשְׁךָ מְאֹד פֶּן־תִּשְׁכַּח אֶת־
הַדְּבָרִים אֲשֶׁר־רָאוּ עֵינֶיךָ וּפֶן־יָסוּרוּ מִלְּבָבְךָ כֹּל

Deuteronomy 4
5–9

5] See, I have imparted to you laws and rules, as the LORD my God has commanded me, for you to abide by in the land which you are about to invade and occupy. 6] Observe them faithfully, for that will be proof of your wisdom and discernment to other peoples, who on hearing of all these laws will say, "Surely, that great nation is a wise and discerning people." 7] For what great nation is there that has a god so close at hand as is the LORD our God whenever we call upon Him? 8] Or what great nation has laws and rules as perfect as all this Teaching that I set before you this day?

9] But take utmost care and watch yourselves scrupulously, so that you do not forget the things that you saw with your own eyes and so that they do not fade from your mind as long as you live. And make them known to your children and

6] *Observe them faithfully.* Literally, "observe and do them," a juxtaposition which has led tradition to identify "observe" as the duty to study, which complements the duty to "do" [4].

7] *A god so close at hand.* אֱלֹהִים is constructed with the plural קְרֹבִים suggesting that one should

understand "god(s)" and not "God." But this conclusion is not compelling, for in Gen. 20:13 the same construction occurs, but clearly God (and not any god) is meant [5].

9] *Your mind.* The Hebrew says literally "your heart," for the heart was thought to be the seat of intelligence.

43

יְמֵי חַיֶּיךָ וְהוֹדַעְתָּם לְבָנֶיךָ וְלִבְנֵי בָנֶיךָ: יוֹם אֲשֶׁר
עָמַדְתָּ לִפְנֵי יְהֹוָה אֱלֹהֶיךָ בְּחֹרֵב בֶּאֱמֹר יְהֹוָה
אֵלַי הַקְהֶל־לִי אֶת־הָעָם וְאַשְׁמִעֵם אֶת־דְּבָרָי אֲשֶׁר
יִלְמְדוּן לְיִרְאָה אֹתִי כָּל־הַיָּמִים אֲשֶׁר הֵם חַיִּים

יא עַל־הָאֲדָמָה וְאֶת־בְּנֵיהֶם יְלַמֵּדוּן: וַתִּקְרְבוּן וַתַּעַמְדוּן
תַּחַת הָהָר וְהָהָר בֹּעֵר בָּאֵשׁ עַד־לֵב הַשָּׁמַיִם חֹשֶׁךְ

יב עָנָן וַעֲרָפֶל: וַיְדַבֵּר יְהֹוָה אֲלֵיכֶם מִתּוֹךְ הָאֵשׁ קוֹל
דְּבָרִים אַתֶּם שֹׁמְעִים וּתְמוּנָה אֵינְכֶם רֹאִים זוּלָתִי

יג קוֹל: וַיַּגֵּד לָכֶם אֶת־בְּרִיתוֹ אֲשֶׁר צִוָּה אֶתְכֶם לַעֲשׂוֹת
עֲשֶׂרֶת הַדְּבָרִים וַיִּכְתְּבֵם עַל־שְׁנֵי לֻחוֹת אֲבָנִים:

Deuteronomy 4
10–13

to your children's children: 10] The day you stood before the LORD your God at Horeb, when the LORD said to me, "Gather the people to Me that I may let them hear My words, in order that they may learn to revere Me as long as they live on earth, and may so teach their children."   11] You came forward and stood at the foot of the mountain. The mountain was ablaze with flames to the very skies, dark with densest clouds.   12] The LORD spoke to you out of the fire; you heard the sound of words but perceived no shape—nothing but a voice.   13] He declared to you the covenant which He commanded you to observe, the Ten Commandments;

10] *You stood.* Moses identifies his audience with the previous generation (see above, commentary on 1:6–46, "Two Generations").

Gather the people. "Assemble" would be better, as a parallel to 9:10; 10:4; 18:16, where יוֹם הַקְהֵל is rendered as "day of the Assembly."

Revere Me. This does not convey the full meaning of the word. In the biblical view, man's relationship to God goes beyond reverence. יָרֵא means to stand in awe and deference, amazement, trembling, and fear.

11] *The very skies.* Literally, "heart of heaven."

13] *The covenant.* בְּרִית (berit) denotes the fundamental relationship of God with Israel; see below, verse 37, and our commentary on Exod. 19:1–25, "The Covenant."

Ten Commandments. They represent the covenant but are not identical with it. On the term, see at Exod. 20.

יד וְאֹתִי צִוָּה יְהֹוָה בָּעֵת הַהִוא לְלַמֵּד אֶתְכֶם חֻקִּים

וּמִשְׁפָּטִים לַעֲשֹׂתְכֶם אֹתָם בָּאָרֶץ אֲשֶׁר אַתֶּם עֹבְרִים

טו שָׁמָּה לְרִשְׁתָּהּ: וְנִשְׁמַרְתֶּם מְאֹד לְנַפְשֹׁתֵיכֶם כִּי לֹא

רְאִיתֶם כָּל־תְּמוּנָה בְּיוֹם דִּבֶּר יְהֹוָה אֲלֵיכֶם בְּחֹרֵב

טז מִתּוֹךְ הָאֵשׁ: פֶּן־תַּשְׁחִתוּן וַעֲשִׂיתֶם לָכֶם פֶּסֶל תְּמוּנַת

יז כָּל־סָמֶל תַּבְנִית זָכָר אוֹ נְקֵבָה: תַּבְנִית כָּל־בְּהֵמָה

אֲשֶׁר בָּאָרֶץ תַּבְנִית כָּל־צִפּוֹר כָּנָף אֲשֶׁר תָּעוּף

יח בַּשָּׁמָיִם: תַּבְנִית כָּל־רֹמֵשׂ בָּאֲדָמָה תַּבְנִית כָּל־דָּגָה

יט אֲשֶׁר־בַּמַּיִם מִתַּחַת לָאָרֶץ: וּפֶן־תִּשָּׂא עֵינֶיךָ הַשָּׁמַיְמָה

וְרָאִיתָ אֶת־הַשֶּׁמֶשׁ וְאֶת־הַיָּרֵחַ וְאֶת־הַכּוֹכָבִים כֹּל

צְבָא הַשָּׁמַיִם וְנִדַּחְתָּ וְהִשְׁתַּחֲוִיתָ לָהֶם וַעֲבַדְתָּם אֲשֶׁר

Deuteronomy 4
14–19

and He inscribed them on two tablets of stone.   14] At the same time the LORD
commanded me to impart to you laws and rules for you to observe in the land which
you are about to cross into and occupy.

15] For your own sake, therefore, be most careful—since you saw no shape when
the LORD your God spoke to you at Horeb out of the fire—   16] not to act wickedly
and make for yourselves a sculptured image in any likeness whatever: the form of
a man or a woman,   17] the form of any beast on earth, the form of any winged
bird that flies in the sky,   18] the form of anything that creeps on the ground, the
form of any fish that is in the waters below the earth.   19] And when you look
up to the sky and behold the sun and the moon and the stars, the whole heavenly

14] *To impart to you.* Moses conveys all divine
laws to Israel as God's intermediary, with the exception of the Ten Commandments, which are, at
least in part, transmitted directly by God.

16] *Sculptured image.* For the purpose of idolatry.

18] *Waters below the earth.* The ancients believed
the earth to be flat and resting on water.

19] *Sun and the moon.* Which were worshiped in
various countries. Thus the moon god was adored
in Ur, whence Abraham's family came.

חָלַק יְהֹוָה אֱלֹהֶיךָ אֹתָם לְכֹל הָעַמִּים תַּחַת כָּל־
כ הַשָּׁמָיִם: וְאֶתְכֶם לָקַח יְהֹוָה וַיּוֹצִא אֶתְכֶם מִכּוּר
הַבַּרְזֶל מִמִּצְרָיִם לִהְיוֹת לוֹ לְעַם נַחֲלָה כַּיּוֹם הַזֶּה:
כא וַיהֹוָה הִתְאַנַּף־בִּי עַל־דִּבְרֵיכֶם וַיִּשָּׁבַע לְבִלְתִּי עָבְרִי
אֶת־הַיַּרְדֵּן וּלְבִלְתִּי־בֹא אֶל־הָאָרֶץ הַטּוֹבָה אֲשֶׁר
כב יְהֹוָה אֱלֹהֶיךָ נֹתֵן לְךָ נַחֲלָה: כִּי אָנֹכִי מֵת בָּאָרֶץ
הַזֹּאת אֵינֶנִּי עֹבֵר אֶת־הַיַּרְדֵּן וְאַתֶּם עֹבְרִים וִירִשְׁתֶּם
כג אֶת־הָאָרֶץ הַטּוֹבָה הַזֹּאת: הִשָּׁמְרוּ לָכֶם פֶּן־תִּשְׁכְּחוּ
אֶת־בְּרִית יְהֹוָה אֱלֹהֵיכֶם אֲשֶׁר כָּרַת עִמָּכֶם וַעֲשִׂיתֶם

Deuteronomy 4

20–23

host, you must not be lured into bowing down to them or serving them. These the LORD your God allotted to the other peoples everywhere under heaven; **20]** but you the LORD took and brought out of Egypt, that iron blast furnace, to be His very own people, as is now the case.

21] Now the LORD was angry with me on your account and swore that I should not cross the Jordan and enter the good land that the LORD your God is giving you as a heritage. **22]** For I must die in this land; I shall not cross the Jordan. But you will cross and take possession of that good land. **23]** Take care, then, not to forget the covenant that the LORD your God concluded with you, and not to make for

---

Allotted to the other peoples. This appears to suggest that non-Israelites are permitted to worship such deities, and that in this sense everything has its origin with God, even the practice of idolatry, which He has allotted to other nations [6].

The Talmud adds, however, that idolaters—by yielding to the opportunity—are causing their own destruction. Luzzatto considered the text to stress God's way of leading men upward.

20] *His very own people.* עַם נַחֲלָה, literally, "people

of (His) inheritance." In 7:6 and 14:2 Israel is called סְגֻלָּה, (His) treasured people. On the concept of chosenness see at Exod. 19:5.

21] *And swore.* This was not related in Num. 20:12. See above, commentary on 2:1–3:29, "Variant Traditions," on the two traditions about the punishment of Moses.

Tradition harmonizes the discrepancy by saying that the judgment in Numbers was pronounced by God in the form of an oath [7].

לָכֶם פֶּסֶל תְּמוּנַת כֹּל אֲשֶׁר צִוְּךָ יְהֹוָה אֱלֹהֶיךָ:

כד כִּי יְהֹוָה אֱלֹהֶיךָ אֵשׁ אֹכְלָה הוּא אֵל קַנָּא: פ

כה כִּי־תוֹלִיד בָּנִים וּבְנֵי בָנִים וְנוֹשַׁנְתֶּם בָּאָרֶץ וְהִשְׁחַתֶּם וַעֲשִׂיתֶם פֶּסֶל תְּמוּנַת כֹּל וַעֲשִׂיתֶם הָרַע בְּעֵינֵי

כו יְהֹוָה־אֱלֹהֶיךָ לְהַכְעִיסוֹ: הַעִידֹתִי בָכֶם הַיּוֹם אֶת־הַשָּׁמַיִם וְאֶת־הָאָרֶץ כִּי־אָבֹד תֹּאבֵדוּן מַהֵר מֵעַל הָאָרֶץ אֲשֶׁר אַתֶּם עֹבְרִים אֶת־הַיַּרְדֵּן שָׁמָּה לְרִשְׁתָּהּ לֹא־תַאֲרִיכֻן יָמִים עָלֶיהָ כִּי הִשָּׁמֵד

כז תִּשָּׁמֵדוּן: וְהֵפִיץ יְהֹוָה אֶתְכֶם בָּעַמִּים וְנִשְׁאַרְתֶּם מְתֵי מִסְפָּר בַּגּוֹיִם אֲשֶׁר יְנַהֵג יְהֹוָה אֶתְכֶם שָׁמָּה:

Deuteronomy 4
24–27

* כן סבורין כאשר.

yourselves a sculptured image in any likeness, against which the LORD your God has enjoined you.   24] For the LORD your God is a consuming fire, an impassioned God.

25] Should you, when you have begotten children and children's children and are long established in the land, act wickedly and make for yourselves a sculptured image in any likeness, causing the LORD your God displeasure and vexation,   26] I call heaven and earth this day to witness against you that you shall soon perish from the land which you are crossing the Jordan to occupy; you shall not long endure in it, but shall be utterly wiped out.   27] The LORD will scatter you among the peoples, and only a scant few of you shall be left among the nations to which the

24] *Impassioned God.* Older translations had "jealous"; see at Exod. 20:5.

25] *Should you.* Traditional interpreters take this to be a prophecy, critical scholars as a passage arising out of some devastating experience.

Long established. Literally, "grown old"; when you will have lost your spiritual keenness.

26] *I call heaven and earth.* A frequent expression in Deuteronomy, having legal force as in vassal treaties. Heaven and earth function as witnesses [8]. See also at 32:1.

47

כח וַעֲבַדְתֶּם־שָׁם אֱלֹהִים מַעֲשֵׂה יְדֵי אָדָם עֵץ וָאֶבֶן
אֲשֶׁר לֹא־יִרְאוּן וְלֹא יִשְׁמְעוּן וְלֹא יֹאכְלוּן וְלֹא
כט יְרִיחֻן: וּבִקַּשְׁתֶּם מִשָּׁם אֶת־יְהֹוָה אֱלֹהֶיךָ וּמָצָאתָ כִּי
ל תִדְרְשֶׁנּוּ בְּכָל־לְבָבְךָ וּבְכָל־נַפְשֶׁךָ: בַּצַּר לְךָ וּמְצָאוּךָ
כֹּל הַדְּבָרִים הָאֵלֶּה בְּאַחֲרִית הַיָּמִים וְשַׁבְתָּ עַד־יְהֹוָה
לא אֱלֹהֶיךָ וְשָׁמַעְתָּ בְּקֹלוֹ: כִּי אֵל רַחוּם יְהֹוָה אֱלֹהֶיךָ
לֹא יַרְפְּךָ וְלֹא יַשְׁחִיתֶךָ וְלֹא יִשְׁכַּח אֶת־בְּרִית אֲבֹתֶיךָ
לב אֲשֶׁר נִשְׁבַּע לָהֶם: כִּי שְׁאַל־נָא לְיָמִים רִאשֹׁנִים
אֲשֶׁר־הָיוּ לְפָנֶיךָ לְמִן־הַיּוֹם אֲשֶׁר בָּרָא אֱלֹהִים אָדָם
עַל־הָאָרֶץ וּלְמִקְצֵה הַשָּׁמַיִם וְעַד־קְצֵה הַשָּׁמָיִם

Deuteronomy 4
28–32

LORD will drive you.   **28]** There you will serve man-made gods of wood and stone, that cannot see or hear or eat or smell.

29] But if you search there for the LORD your God, you will find Him, if only you seek Him with all your heart and soul—   **30]** when you are in distress because all these things have befallen you and, in the end, return to the LORD your God and obey Him.   **31]** For the LORD your God is a compassionate God: He will not fail you nor will He let you perish; He will not forget the covenant which He made on oath with your fathers.

32] You have but to inquire about bygone ages that came before you, ever since God created man on earth, from one end of heaven to the other: has anything as

28] *There you will serve.* In exile Israel will be forced to practice the very idolatry they had voluntarily chosen in Canaan.

29] *But if you search . . . you will find.* The image of searching and finding is found in Jer. 29:13 and Isa. 55:6.

30] *In the end.* The expression projects Israel's return to God in the course of time; it does not here have the posthistorical sense that later prophets gave it.

31] *A compassionate God.* See at Exod. 34:6.

32] *Ever since God created man.* From this, the halachah derived restrictions about inquiries into what happened *before* creation and into the nature of heaven and hell [9].

הֲנִהְיָה כַּדָּבָר הַגָּדוֹל הַזֶּה אוֹ הֲנִשְׁמַע כָּמֹהוּ:

לג הֲשָׁמַע עָם קוֹל אֱלֹהִים מְדַבֵּר מִתּוֹךְ־הָאֵשׁ כַּאֲשֶׁר־

לד שָׁמַעְתָּ אַתָּה וַיֶּחִי: אוֹ הֲנִסָּה אֱלֹהִים לָבוֹא לָקַחַת

לוֹ גוֹי מִקֶּרֶב גּוֹי בְּמַסֹּת בְּאֹתֹת וּבְמוֹפְתִים וּבְמִלְחָמָה

וּבְיָד חֲזָקָה וּבִזְרוֹעַ נְטוּיָה וּבְמוֹרָאִים גְּדֹלִים כְּכֹל

אֲשֶׁר־עָשָׂה לָכֶם יְהוָה אֱלֹהֵיכֶם בְּמִצְרַיִם לְעֵינֶיךָ:

לה אַתָּה הָרְאֵתָ לָדַעַת כִּי יְהוָה הוּא הָאֱלֹהִים אֵין

לו עוֹד מִלְּבַדּוֹ: מִן־הַשָּׁמַיִם הִשְׁמִיעֲךָ אֶת־קֹלוֹ לְיַסְּרֶךָּ

וְעַל־הָאָרֶץ הֶרְאֲךָ אֶת־אִשּׁוֹ הַגְּדוֹלָה וּדְבָרָיו שָׁמַעְתָּ

לז מִתּוֹךְ הָאֵשׁ: וְתַחַת כִּי אָהַב אֶת־אֲבֹתֶיךָ וַיִּבְחַר

Deuteronomy 4
33–37

* לג כך צריך לבטא.

grand as this ever happened, or has its like ever been known? **33]** Has any people heard the voice of a god speaking out of a fire, as you have, and survived? **34]** Or has any god ventured to go and take for himself one nation from the midst of another by prodigious acts, by signs and portents, by war, by a mighty and an outstretched arm and awesome power, as the LORD your God did for you in Egypt before your very eyes? **35]** It has been clearly demonstrated to you that the LORD alone is God; there is none beside Him. **36]** From the heavens He let you hear His voice to discipline you; on earth He let you see His great fire; and from amidst that fire you heard His words. **37]** And because He loved your fathers, He chose their

33] *And survived.* Ordinarily human beings cannot behold the Divine and live (Exod. 33:20). Only Israel was granted moments of exception (Exod. 20:19).

34] *Outstretched arm.* See Exod. 6:6.

35] *Clearly demonstrated.* Literally, "you have been shown to know." The phrase has entered the liturgy for Shemini Atzeret-Simchat Torah [10].

37] *Because He loved your fathers.* The love was an unconditional grant extended to Abraham, Isaac, and Jacob and remained so for their descendants. But Deuteronomy made the grant of land dependent on Israel's compliance with the law [11].

בְּזַרְעוֹ אַחֲרָיו וַיּוֹצִאֲךָ בְּפָנָיו בְּכֹחוֹ הַגָּדֹל מִמִּצְרָיִם:

לח לְהוֹרִישׁ גּוֹיִם גְּדֹלִים וַעֲצֻמִים מִמְּךָ מִפָּנֶיךָ לַהֲבִיאֲךָ

לט לָתֶת־לְךָ אֶת־אַרְצָם נַחֲלָה כַּיּוֹם הַזֶּה: וְיָדַעְתָּ הַיּוֹם

וַהֲשֵׁבֹתָ אֶל־לְבָבֶךָ כִּי יְהוָה הוּא הָאֱלֹהִים בַּשָּׁמַיִם

מ מִמַּעַל וְעַל־הָאָרֶץ מִתַּחַת אֵין עוֹד: וְשָׁמַרְתָּ אֶת־

חֻקָּיו וְאֶת־מִצְוֹתָיו אֲשֶׁר אָנֹכִי מְצַוְּךָ הַיּוֹם אֲשֶׁר

יִיטַב לְךָ וּלְבָנֶיךָ אַחֲרֶיךָ וּלְמַעַן תַּאֲרִיךְ יָמִים

עַל־הָאֲדָמָה אֲשֶׁר יְהוָה אֱלֹהֶיךָ נֹתֵן לְךָ

כָּל־הַיָּמִים:
פ

מא אָז יַבְדִּיל מֹשֶׁה שָׁלֹשׁ עָרִים בְּעֵבֶר הַיַּרְדֵּן מִזְרָחָה

Deuteronomy 4
38–41

offspring after them; He Himself, in His great might, led you out of Egypt,   38] to drive from your path nations greater and more populous than you, to take you into their land and give it to you as a heritage, as is still the case.   39] Know therefore this day and keep in mind that the LORD alone is God in heaven above and on earth below; there is no other.   40] Observe His laws and commandments, which I enjoin upon you this day, that it may go well with you and your children after you, and that you may long remain in the land that the LORD your God is giving you for all time.

41] Then Moses set aside three cities on the east side of the Jordan,   42] to

Their offspring. Literally, "his offspring," referring either to the Fathers as a collective or to one of them, possibly Jacob, who gave the people his name [12].

38] *As is still the case.* Referring to the abiding love of God.

Von Rad reads the phrase as applying to Israel's occupation of the land and says that the editor "forgot the fiction that it was Moses speaking" [13].

39] *Know therefore.* The sentence has entered the daily liturgy and concludes the first paragraph of the *Aleinu* [14].

41] *Then Moses set aside.* According to Num. 35:10 ff. (see commentary there) six cities of refuge were to be set aside, three of them on the eastern side of the Jordan where three tribes had already settled. The Talmud speculates that the sparsely populated eastern territories needed as many

מב שֶׁמֶשׁ: לָנֻס שָׁמָּה רוֹצֵחַ אֲשֶׁר יִרְצַח אֶת־רֵעֵהוּ
בִּבְלִי־דַעַת וְהוּא לֹא־שֹׂנֵא לוֹ מִתְּמֹל שִׁלְשֹׁם וְנָס
מג אֶל־אַחַת מִן־הֶעָרִים הָאֵל וָחָי: אֶת־בֶּצֶר בַּמִּדְבָּר
בְּאֶרֶץ הַמִּישֹׁר לָרֻאוּבֵנִי וְאֶת־רָאמֹת בַּגִּלְעָד לַגָּדִי
וְאֶת־גּוֹלָן בַּבָּשָׁן לַמְנַשִּׁי:

Deuteronomy 4
42–43

* מב סבורין האלה.
* מג כך צריך לבטא.

which a manslayer could escape, one who unwittingly slew a fellow man without having been hostile to him in the past; he could flee to one of these cities and live: 43] Bezer, in the wilderness in the Tableland, belonging to the Reubenites; Ramoth, in Gilead, belonging to the Gadites; and Golan, in Bashan, belonging to the Manassites.

cities of refuge as the rest of the country together because of the high incidence of crime [15]. Already Hosea called Gilead a land "covered with footprints of blood" (6:8).

43] *Bezer ... Ramoth ... Golan.* Their precise location is not known. Bezer was southeast of the Dead Sea; Ramoth, near today's Amman; Golan, somewhere on the Golan Heights.

Neither Add Nor Detract

One of the laws which in time assumed crucial significance reads: "You shall not add anything to what I command you or take anything away from it . . ." (4:2). It is possible that such an injunction was at first directed to the scribes, warning them to keep the text exactly as they found it, with its apparent contradictions, mistakes in spelling, duplications, and incomprehensible passages. A similar rule was already in effect in ancient Egypt, a thousand years prior to the Exodus, and is also reflected in the Akkadian Epic of Erra. There it is said of the poet who had been taught a poem that "he left nothing out nor did he add a single line" [16]. In Jeremiah's vision the prophet was cautioned not to leave out a single word when he transmitted divine instruction; and a proverb, in exalting God's teaching, said, "Add not to His words." Two other passages clearly established the rule as applying to the essence of God's work and word: Koheleth proclaimed that whatever God did was "for ever," and another passage in Deuteronomy enjoined the Israelites to be careful and observe only what they had been taught, neither more nor less.[1]

In later centuries, both 4:2 and 13:1 became proof texts for limiting changes in and interpretations of the Torah laws. Special note was taken of the fact that 4:2 is phrased in the plural while 13:1 is couched in the singular. Thus the former was understood to be addressed to the leaders of the community who were warned not to pass off their injunctions as equivalent to the Torah itself and to let the people know at all times what was of rabbinic and what of pentateuchal origin (מִדְּרַבָּנָן and מִדְּאוֹרַיְיתָא) [17]. On the other hand, 13:1 was seen to address itself to each individual, exhorting him to complete and meticulous observance [18]. But rabbinic law was not in itself seen as innovative, it only made the intent of the Torah "clearer" (though often it did so innovatively).

Another reading of the two verses became even more important, for it understood 4:2 as prohibiting changes in the number of the commandments—there were according to tradition 613 mitzvot in the Torah—so that there should not be 612 or 614; and 13:1 was seen to mean that each individual mitzvah was to be carried out as specified and was not to be tampered with.[2] Thus, since an authoritative interpretation of the laws of phylacteries had arrived at four paragraphs that were to be inscribed on the parchment, this was to remain an unalterable rule, as were four double threads in the ritual fringes [19]. Moreover, the general rule was declared applicable both in Eretz Yisrael and in the Diaspora.

The Course of Jewish Law

To be sure, no community could survive and grow without an organic development of its laws. Halachah—the body of written and oral law—became the instrument by which the Jewish people ordered their lives. While the Written Torah remained unchanged and unchangeable, the Oral Torah interpreted it, thereby expanding and contracting it in accordance with the needs of new times. The Rabbis created a set of guidelines that spelled out the possibilities of such interpretation; for instance, they determined how analogies were to be used, how legal inferences were to be made, or how the repetition of certain laws affected their content. At first, out of deference to the strict injunc-

---

[1] Jer. 26:2; Prov. 30:6; Eccles. 3:14; Deut. 13:1.

[2] This became particularly important because the Christian church had declared these and similar provisions of the Torah as no longer binding, for in its view the "Old Covenant" (at Sinai) had been set aside by the "New Covenant" (through Jesus).

tions of Deut. 4:2 and 13:1, none of these rabbinic rules and their conclusions was permitted to be written down, but by the year 200 C.E. this restriction was abandoned and the basic code of Jewish life was committed to writing. The result was the Mishnah, which combined into its six sections[3] every aspect of Jewish living, from the regulation of the liturgy to civil and criminal law to family purity. Now the Mishnah became the foundation for legal discussions in the academies and for decisions in the courts, and after three more centuries two bodies of recorded debates and decisions were assembled: one in Palestine (the Palestinian or Jerusalem Talmud—"talmud" meaning study or learning) and the other in Babylon (the Babylonian Talmud). The latter became the commanding, fundamental document for all subsequent ages. It is a vast-ranging commentary on the Mishnah, but it does not usually adhere strictly to the subject at hand and instead covers every conceivable area of human knowledge, Jewish law, popular custom, theological and moral considerations—all arranged rather loosely, reflecting the unstructured discussions of the Sages rather than the rigorous systematizing of an editor.

The Talmud now was the edifice in which Jewish life dwelt, and at once it itself became the object of study, comment, and argument. Scholars wrote legal opinions (responsa) and composed commentaries, and in time abstracts appeared that attempted to summarize all previous contributions to talmudic knowledge and to set down clearly what laws a Jew ought to observe. Of these attempts the code of Maimonides (twelfth century) achieved the greatest authority and deeply influenced Jewish practice during the following centuries, until the appearance of Joseph Karo's *Shulchan Aruch* (sixteenth century). From then on the latter was universally considered the authoritative handbook of Jewish law and life. After its appearance it quickly became the object of scholarly commentary; it was considered extensively in responsa and continues in this capacity until today. Most of the halachah it contains is represented in both its biblical and its rabbinic provisions as binding, for it is taken to be the will of God.

This system was by nature highly conservative, since the Torah, being considered divine, was in principle unamendable, and even the most ingenious interpretation could not alter a rule beyond a certain point. Moreover, the Oral Torah, too, shared in the divine nature of the law and therefore in its resistance to change. Still, the process worked well enough as long as Jews lived in a basically conservative and frequently restricted environment, where faith and custom provided the framework of existence. But with the beginning of Enlightenment, at the end of the eighteenth century, Western Jewry left its traditional habitat, both physically and culturally, and this placed enormous strains on the halachah. Its guardians were highly defensive and refused to find legal justifications for even the most minor changes. In consequence, an increasing number of Jews looked for means of adjusting the law to an emerging modern industrial society. The result was the development of Reform Judaism, which amended the law while assuring the preservation of its spirit. The new movement saw its greatest advance in North America, where at the beginning of the twentieth century its members discarded many of the 613 mitzvot, even when they were explicitly stated in or founded on the Written Torah. For them,

---

[3] *Zeraim* (Seeds), *Mo-ed* (Feasts), *Nashim* (Women), *Nezikin* (Damages), *Kodashim* (Hallowed Things), *Tohorot* (Cleanness).

the provisions of Deut. 4:2 and 13:1 had ceased to be operative, especially—though not exclusively—in the area of ritual practice.[4] Their emphasis was on the moral component of Judaism, which they found championed by the biblical prophets.

Reform Judaism thus largely separated itself from halachic Judaism, which has continued to be vigorously represented by Orthodoxy. Conservatism occupies a middle ground; it stands with Reform in recognizing the human and therefore changeable aspect of the law, while it tries to effect these changes within the framework of the halachah. There has also been a turn toward a greater incorporation of halachic principles within the Reform movement, albeit on a basis that allows for individual decision within the framework of a mitzvah system [20]. The rules laid down by the Deuteronomist have thus experienced a long and varied development, and they continue to be at issue in contemporary Judaism.[5]

---

[4] Such as the careful observance of dietary laws, the wearing of fringes, or rules pertaining to the descendants of priestly families.

[5] In fact, the nature of mitzvah and its theological foundations are a serious problem to Reform Judaism and have been the subject of varying interpretations [21].

GLEANINGS

Never Closed

It says (verse 7) that God is close at hand whenever Israel does call on Him. To "call" on God means to pray, which teaches that the gates of prayer are never closed.　　　MIDRASH [22]

The Uniqueness of Torah (verse 8)

When other nations follow their laws they are merely law-abiding; when Israel observes the Torah it is at the same time engaged in the praise of God.　　　CHASIDIC [23]

But Take Utmost Care (verse 9)

Moses warns Israel, the very people who were vouchsafed great miracles, against idolatry. From this you may learn that however pious a person is he is always in potential danger of idolatry and should never fully trust himself.

Literally, verse 9 reads, "Only watch yourself and watch your soul scrupulously."[6] Why the dual warning to both "watch *yourself*" and "watch your *soul* scrupulously"? The word "yourself" refers to your body to which you need give only ordinary attention, and there is little doubt that you will do so. But, when it comes to your soul, you are likely to neglect it, hence "watch your soul scrupulously."　　　CHASIDIC [24]

The Chain of Generations

Torah is to be taught to children and children's children (verse 9). He who teaches his child Torah is considered as if he taught Torah not only to his child but to his child's children and their children, to the end of time.

A grandchild taught by his grandfather is considered as if he had received the Torah at Sinai.　　　TALMUD [25]

The Image

Verse 23 reads strangely in the Hebrew, for in effect it warns us not to make a sculptured image of His mitzvot! It means that mitzvot should not become like idols of wood and stone, without soul and spirit.　　　CHASIDIC [26]

Gematria

Verses 25 and following contain the prediction that Israel will fall away from God and then be exiled. This will happen when the people are "long established" (וְנוֹשַׁנְתֶּם) in the Land. The Hebrew letters of the word add up to 852[7]—the number of years Israel would dwell in the Land. Actually, however, the people were exiled already after 850 years, that is, two years ahead of the prediction. By not letting the time run out to its full length God avoided also bringing the full force of verse 26 to bear on them, namely, that they would be "utterly wiped out."　　　RASHI [27]

Searching and Finding (verse 29)

Every promise found in the Torah also contains a command. Thus the promise "The Lord your God is bringing you into a good land . . ." (8:7) entails the command to go and settle in the

---

[6] The word נַפְשְׁךָ is a Hebrew idiom for "your self," but it is here interpreted literally as if it meant "your soul."

[7] וּ= 6, נ= 50, וּ= 6, שׁ=300, נּ=50, תּ=400, ם=40.

55

Promised Land. So here: "If you search" implies the mitzvah to search without delay.

M. HACOHEN [28]

Distress

In the Hebrew of verse 30 the words "when you are in distress"—בַּצַּר לְךָ—are phrased in the singular (לְךָ, not לָכֶם). Distress confined to an individual is true distress.[8]

MIDRASH [30]

This Day

We are to know God "this day" (verse 39), meaning the duty to rediscover every day that the Lord is God.

CHASIDIC [31]

---

[8] Note the proverb: "Distress shared by the community is in itself half a consolation"[29].

PART II

Second Discourse

With the second discourse, the Book of Deuteronomy rises to its heights of oratory. Moses appears as the preacher par excellence, his exhortations are issued with increased insistence. Time and again his commands, issued in God's name, are accompanied by promises as well as imprecations: if the Children of Israel obey the Lord all will be well with them, but, if they leave the path of Torah and mitzvot, disaster will overtake them. In the first discourse, God's past protection was cited as the chief warrant for Israel's compliance with His will; now the law itself is repeated in essence and held up as a unique guide to ethical behavior. God is the focus of exclusive adoration and the seat of ethical concern, and thus the foundations of ethical monotheism (as it has come to be known) are linked to Moses.* "Hear, O Israel" is the ringing address thrice repeated, and "You shall love the Lord your God" stands forth as the opening theme of the discourse. Again it is the nation as a whole which is held responsible for the actions of its members: the measure of their individual adherence to the covenant forms the basis for God's judgment on all Israel, for good and for evil.

While there is general agreement that Moses' first discourse ended with 4:43 (the postscript about the cities of refuge), there is no agreement as to where the second discourse begins and where it ends. Thus, verses 44 to the end of chapter 4 are obviously an introduction of some kind, but this introduction is at once followed by another one (5:1) which appears to be unrelated to it. It may therefore be that 4:44–49 belonged somewhere else, possibly at the beginning of the whole Book of Deuteronomy [1]. Further, the address itself is seen by some to extend up to and including chapter 26 and by others to reach even farther, to 30:20. The majority of scholars, however, believe 11:25 to be the termination of this discourse, a division we have adopted.

Its content can be broadly divided as follows: (1) general introduction, describing the locus (4:44–49); the Decalogue, with introductory and concluding exhortations (chapter 5); (2) the *Shema*, with introduction and follow-up (6:1–19); duty to rehearse the Exodus from Egypt (6:20–25);

---

* See "Introducing Deuteronomy" on the controversy whether Moses' ideas preceded those of the Prophets and were incorporated in Deuteronomy or whether the book was to a large extent the consequence of later teaching, with Moses' name linked to it to give it added authority.

(3) warning not to be tempted by mixed marriage and idolatry (chapter 7); (4) duty not to forget God's goodness toward Israel (chapter 8); (5) recollection of the golden calf episode, of the fashioning of the second tablets, of Israel's stubbornness (9:1–10:11); (6) further exhortation to faith (10:12–11:25).

Again and again Moses recounts God's continuing care for His people and Israel's consequent obligation to obey His will. For Israel is not an ordinary nation; it has a special relationship with the Lord, and out of this relationship comes its potential for holiness and love. It is its task to make the potential actual, and thus the love of God becomes a command, centered upon the Holy One who is the protecting as well as demanding partner of the covenant. (The Deuteronomic view of history is discussed in W. W. Hallo's essay, above.)

The Decalogue

A fter a brief introduction the second discourse presents a recollection of the covenant at Horeb and of the Ten Commandments. Inasmuch as the Decalogue has been discussed in detail in Exodus 20, the notes below will summarize the earlier commentary and then discuss the differences between the two versions. These differences are most pronounced in the Sabbath commandment, which gives the need for human (instead of God's) rest as the reason for observance.

Traditional commentaries explain the divergencies as purposeful, in that the two versions together are seen to reveal the full meaning of the divine will. This commentary, on the other hand, understands the Exodus Decalogue to represent one sacred tradition and the one in Deuteronomy, another. This explains also why the former speaks of the revelation having taken place at Sinai while the latter places it at Horeb.[1] The latter also stresses the great role that Moses played in the transmission, for his position as intermediary between God and the people is an important aspect of the Deuteronomic version. (On this aspect, see introduction, above.)

It has been suggested that the Decalogue was at one stage of Israel's history part of a sacral recital. If so, it ceased to have this function when the synagogue service was fixed. The Decalogue did not become part of the obligatory daily liturgy, although it is included as an additional reading in Reform, Conservative, and Orthodox prayer books. Perhaps this ambivalent status arose from the fear that the Ten Commandments

[1] On the significance of this difference, see our commentary on Exod. 3:1.

might be considered the heart of Judaism and that the other mitzvot could be disregarded.[2] Once this caution was fully understood the unique position of the Decalogue was given its due emphasis, and it became customary for the congregation to rise in respect when the Ten Words were read from the Torah.[3]

[2] Such a view was held by the Karaitic sect.   [3] In the weekly portions *Yitro* and *Va'etchanan* and on the festival of Shavuot.

מד וְזֹאת הַתּוֹרָה אֲשֶׁר־שָׂם מֹשֶׁה לִפְנֵי בְּנֵי יִשְׂרָאֵל:

מה אֵלֶּה הָעֵדֹת וְהַחֻקִּים וְהַמִּשְׁפָּטִים אֲשֶׁר דִּבֶּר מֹשֶׁה

מו אֶל־בְּנֵי יִשְׂרָאֵל בְּצֵאתָם מִמִּצְרָיִם: בְּעֵבֶר הַיַּרְדֵּן

בַּגַּיְא מוּל בֵּית פְּעוֹר בְּאֶרֶץ סִיחֹן מֶלֶךְ הָאֱמֹרִי

אֲשֶׁר יוֹשֵׁב בְּחֶשְׁבּוֹן אֲשֶׁר הִכָּה מֹשֶׁה וּבְנֵי יִשְׂרָאֵל

מז בְּצֵאתָם מִמִּצְרָיִם: וַיִּירְשׁוּ אֶת־אַרְצוֹ וְאֶת־אֶרֶץ עוֹג

מֶלֶךְ־הַבָּשָׁן שְׁנֵי מַלְכֵי הָאֱמֹרִי אֲשֶׁר בְּעֵבֶר הַיַּרְדֵּן

מח מִזְרַח שָׁמֶשׁ: מֵעֲרֹעֵר אֲשֶׁר עַל־שְׂפַת־נַחַל אַרְנֹן וְעַד־

מט הַר שִׂיאֹן הוּא חֶרְמוֹן: וְכָל־הָעֲרָבָה עֵבֶר הַיַּרְדֵּן

מִזְרָחָה וְעַד יָם הָעֲרָבָה תַּחַת אַשְׁדֹּת הַפִּסְגָּה: פ

Deuteronomy 4
44–49

44] This is the Teaching that Moses set before the Israelites: 45] these are the exhortations, laws, and rules that Moses addressed to the people of Israel, after they had left Egypt,   46] beyond the Jordan, in the valley at Beth-peor, in the land of Sihon king of the Amorites, who dwelt in Heshbon, whom Moses and the Israelites defeated after they had left Egypt.   47] They had taken possession of his country and that of Og king of Bashan—the two kings of the Amorites who were on the east side of the Jordan,   48] from Aroer on the banks of the wadi Arnon, as far as Mount Sion, that is, Hermon;   49] also the whole Arabah on the east side of the Jordan, as far as the Sea of the Arabah, at the foot of the slopes of Pisgah.

4:44] *This is the Teaching.* וְזֹאת הַתּוֹרָה (*vezot ha-Torah*). This general term is replaced in verse 45 (which forms an introduction from another source) by "exhortations, laws, and norms."

Verse 44 is recited at synagogue services as the Torah scroll is lifted up and shown to the congregation; it is followed by the words:

עַל־פִּי יְהוָה בְּיַד־מֹשֶׁה

"At the command of the Lord through Moses" (Num. 4:37).

46] *Land of Sihon.* Victories over Sihon and Og loomed large in the memory of the people, for they established the nation's military competence and constituted the opening phase in the conquest of the Promised Land (see 1:4; 3:2).

48] *Aroer.* See 2:36; 3:8.

Mount Sion. (שִׂיאֹן) Probably a name for Mount Hermon and not to be confused with Zion (צִיּוֹן). The Sidonians called it Sirion; see 3:9.

49] *Pisgah.* The introduction to the discourse

א וַיִּקְרָא מֹשֶׁה אֶל־כָּל־יִשְׂרָאֵל וַיֹּאמֶר אֲלֵהֶם שְׁמַע
יִשְׂרָאֵל אֶת־הַחֻקִּים וְאֶת־הַמִּשְׁפָּטִים אֲשֶׁר אָנֹכִי דֹּבֵר
בְּאָזְנֵיכֶם הַיּוֹם וּלְמַדְתֶּם אֹתָם וּשְׁמַרְתֶּם לַעֲשֹׂתָם:
ב יְהוָה אֱלֹהֵינוּ כָּרַת עִמָּנוּ בְּרִית בְּחֹרֵב: לֹא אֶת־
אֲבֹתֵינוּ כָּרַת יְהוָה אֶת־הַבְּרִית הַזֹּאת כִּי אִתָּנוּ
אֲנַחְנוּ אֵלֶּה פֹה הַיּוֹם כֻּלָּנוּ חַיִּים: פָּנִים בְּפָנִים
ד דִּבֶּר יְהוָה עִמָּכֶם בָּהָר מִתּוֹךְ הָאֵשׁ: אָנֹכִי עֹמֵד
בֵּין־יְהוָה וּבֵינֵיכֶם בָּעֵת הַהִוא לְהַגִּיד לָכֶם אֶת־
ה דְּבַר יְהוָה כִּי יְרֵאתֶם מִפְּנֵי הָאֵשׁ וְלֹא־עֲלִיתֶם

Deuteronomy 5
1–5

1] Moses summoned all the Israelites and said to them: Hear, O Israel, the laws and rules that I proclaim to you this day! Study them and observe them faithfully!

2] The LORD our God made a covenant with us at Horeb.   3] It was not with our fathers that the LORD made this covenant, but with us, the living, every one of us who is here today.   4] Face to face the LORD spoke to you on the mountain out of the fire—   5] I stood between the LORD and you at that time to convey the LORD's words to you, for you were afraid of the fire and did not go up the mountain—saying:

ends with a reference to the place where Moses will die.

5:1]   *Hear, O Israel.* First of the several times this address is issued. Perhaps it was at one time a formal call to assembly.

3]   *Not with our fathers.* That is to say, not with them alone, who are now dead, but also with us, the living. Such elliptical style occurs in other places as well. (On the idea that the covenant bound also those not present, see below, at 29:13.)

4]   *Face to face.* This tradition stands in contrast to what the next verse and also verses 20 ff. state,

namely, that Moses was God's spokesman.

Nachmanides (Moses ben Nachman Gerondi) reconciles the contradiction by repeating the tradition that Israel heard only the first two commandments directly from God, and the Talmud suggests that God was like the Torah reader at a worship service and Moses the translator and interpreter [1].

5]   *You were afraid.* As recounted in Exod. 20:15–18.

And did not go up. Here, Israel's fear is given as reason. In Exod. 19:12, 13, 23, it was because of God's warning, reflecting two different traditions.

וַ בָּהָר לֵאמֹר: ס אָנֹכִי יְהֹוָה אֱלֹהֶיךָ אֲשֶׁר
ז הוֹצֵאתִיךָ מֵאֶרֶץ מִצְרַיִם מִבֵּית עֲבָדִים: לֹא יִהְיֶה־
ח לְךָ אֱלֹהִים אֲחֵרִים עַל־פָּנָי: לֹא־תַעֲשֶׂה־לְךָ פֶסֶל
כָּל־תְּמוּנָה אֲשֶׁר בַּשָּׁמַיִם מִמַּעַל וַאֲשֶׁר בָּאָרֶץ מִתַּחַת
ט וַאֲשֶׁר בַּמַּיִם מִתַּחַת לָאָרֶץ: לֹא־תִשְׁתַּחֲוֶה לָהֶם וְלֹא
תָעָבְדֵם כִּי אָנֹכִי יְהֹוָה אֱלֹהֶיךָ אֵל קַנָּא פֹּקֵד עֲוֹן
י אָבוֹת עַל־בָּנִים וְעַל־שִׁלֵּשִׁים וְעַל־רִבֵּעִים לְשֹׂנְאָי: וְעֹשֶׂה

Deuteronomy 5
6–10

6] I the Lord am your God who brought you out of the land of Egypt, the house of bondage: **7]** You shall have no other gods beside Me.

8] You shall not make for yourself a sculptured image, any likeness of what is in the heavens above, or on the earth below, or in the waters below the earth.   **9]** You shall not bow down to them or serve them. For I the Lord your God am an impassioned God, visiting the guilt of the fathers upon the children, upon the third and upon the fourth generations of those who reject Me,   **10]** but showing kindness

6] *I the Lord.* Rather, "I am the Lord. . . ." Jewish tradition generally considered this verse, and this verse alone, as the first commandment. It serves also as a preamble in the manner of ancient Near Eastern proclamations. God's claim on His people is as Redeemer, not Creator, and, though it is meant for the whole community, it is (in Hebrew) addressed to the individual Israelite.

7] *You shall have no other gods beside Me.* The opening phrase of the second commandment which extends through verse 10. The singularity of God is a central theme of Deuteronomy, "the commandment of all commandments, in its rigor without parallel in religious history" [2]. It establishes God's exclusive right to Israel's loyalty.

8] *A sculptured image, any likeness.* With the in-

tent to adore it. Though idols were not generally identified as actual gods, they represented them in surrogate fashion: Images were given "life" in special mouth-opening ceremonies, which were renewed periodically by mouth washing. The idols were "fed," and there is evidence that they were buried when damaged. In contrast, יְהֹוָה could not be represented in any form since the world itself was His creation. This commandment does not prohibit plastic works as such, else verse 9 would be unnecessary. Still, the strict construction given to this commandment by the Jews (and by Moslems as well) prevented them for many centuries from developing the sculptured arts freely (see further our commentary on Exod. 20:4).

9] *Impassioned God.* Denoting passion rather than possessiveness (so in the older rendering "jealous God").

חֶסֶד לַאֲלָפִים לְאֹהֲבַי וּלְשֹׁמְרֵי מִצְוֹתָו: ס

יא לֹא תִשָּׂא אֶת־שֵׁם־יְהוָֹה אֱלֹהֶיךָ לַשָּׁוְא כִּי לֹא יְנַקֶּה

יב יְהוָֹה אֵת אֲשֶׁר־יִשָּׂא אֶת־שְׁמוֹ לַשָּׁוְא: ס שָׁמוֹר

אֶת־יוֹם הַשַּׁבָּת לְקַדְּשׁוֹ כַּאֲשֶׁר צִוְּךָ יְהוָֹה אֱלֹהֶיךָ:

יג שֵׁשֶׁת יָמִים תַּעֲבֹד וְעָשִׂיתָ כָּל־מְלַאכְתֶּךָ: וְיוֹם

יד הַשְּׁבִיעִי שַׁבָּת לַיהוָֹה אֱלֹהֶיךָ לֹא־תַעֲשֶׂה כָל־

Deuteronomy 5

11–14

* יי מצותי.

to the thousandth generation of those who love Me and keep My commandments.

11] You shall not swear falsely by the name of the LORD your God; for the LORD will not clear one who swears falsely by His name.

12] Observe the sabbath day and keep it holy, as the LORD your God has commanded you. 13] Six days you shall labor and do all your work, 14] but the seventh day is a sabbath of the LORD your God: you shall not do any work—you,

11] *Not swear falsely.* The commandment may originally have referred to a custom of swearing "by the life of God," and that therefore such an oath demanded extreme caution [3]. However, the meaning of the Hebrew is in doubt; it may not at all relate to swearing falsely but to taking God's name in vain or to abusing it—forbidding magical, profane, or even casual use of the divine name. Proponents of the latter interpretation point out that the ninth commandment, which deals with false witness, implies the prohibition of swearing falsely.

The second commandment dealt with the misuse of image, the third turns to the misuse of God's name—a transition from the visual to the verbal. The divine name is part of the divine essence; hence care must be taken lest one diminish the sanctity of God by misusing His name. Jewish tradition subsequently introduced severe restrictions in any pronouncement of the Name (see our commentary on Exodus 20:7).

12] *Observe.* שָׁמוֹר (shamor); in the Exodus version the opening word of the fourth commandment is זָכוֹר (zachor, remember). Tradition treats this difference as purposeful and suggests that "remember" refers to positive acts, like sanctification through candles and wine and Sabbath joy, and "observe" to abstinence from any form of labor. The commandment is the only one that exhibits significant differences between the two versions, and, although critical scholars believe them to be due to varying traditions, rabbinic opinion insisted that the Deuteronomic version was in some miraculous fashion proclaimed together with the text reported in Exodus 20 [4]. Both שָׁמוֹר and זָכוֹר are infinitives absolute serving as imperatives (compare the German *Aufpassen!*). On the origins of the Sabbath and its observance in history see at Exodus 20.

Keep it holy. By setting it apart. In Jewish tradition the expression לְקַדְּשׁוֹ implies the duty to sanctify the Sabbath with a benediction (*Kiddush*).

As the Lord your God has commanded you. This phrase is not found in the Exodus version.

14] *Not do any work.* Jewish tradition defined this in detail, developing a catalogue of thirty-nine

מְלָאכָה אַתָּה וּבִנְךָ־וּבִתֶּךָ וְעַבְדְּךָ־וַאֲמָתֶךָ וְשׁוֹרְךָ
וַחֲמֹרְךָ וְכָל־בְּהֶמְתֶּךָ וְגֵרְךָ אֲשֶׁר בִּשְׁעָרֶיךָ לְמַעַן
טו יָנוּחַ עַבְדְּךָ וַאֲמָתְךָ כָּמוֹךָ: וְזָכַרְתָּ כִּי־עֶבֶד הָיִיתָ
בְּאֶרֶץ מִצְרַיִם וַיֹּצִאֲךָ יְהֹוָה אֱלֹהֶיךָ מִשָּׁם בְּיָד
חֲזָקָה וּבִזְרֹעַ נְטוּיָה עַל־כֵּן צִוְּךָ יְהֹוָה אֱלֹהֶיךָ
טז לַעֲשׂוֹת אֶת־יוֹם הַשַּׁבָּת: ס כַּבֵּד אֶת־אָבִיךָ
וְאֶת־אִמֶּךָ כַּאֲשֶׁר צִוְּךָ יְהֹוָה אֱלֹהֶיךָ לְמַעַן יַאֲרִיכֻן
יָמֶיךָ וּלְמַעַן יִיטַב לָךְ עַל הָאֲדָמָה אֲשֶׁר־יְהֹוָה
יז אֱלֹהֶיךָ נֹתֵן לָךְ: ס לֹא תִּרְצָח: ס וְלֹא

Deuteronomy 5
15–17

your son or your daughter, your male or female slave, your ox or your ass, or any of your cattle, or the stranger in your settlements, so that your male and female slave may rest as you do.   15] Remember that you were a slave in the land of Egypt and the Lord your God freed you from there with a mighty hand and an outstretched arm; therefore the Lord your God has commanded you to observe the sabbath day.

16] Honor your father and your mother, as the Lord your God has commanded you, that you may long endure, and that you may fare well, in the land that the Lord your God is giving you.

17] You shall not murder.

main types of prohibited labor (see commentary at Exod. 20:10).

15] *Remember.* The reason given for the commandment constitutes the main difference from Exodus. See below.

16] *Honor your father and your mother.* The fifth commandment in Jewish tradition, it completes the first tablet, which deals mainly with the rela-

tionship of humans to God. The commandment makes the honor given to parents a prerequisite for Israel's continued stay in the Holy Land.

And that you may fare well. The phrase is not found in Exodus.

17] *You shall not murder.* See commentary on Exod. 20:13. The older translation was "You shall not kill." But while in English there is a distinction between "kill" (which may be authorized by the

תִּנְאָף: ס וְלֹא תִגְנֹב: ס וְלֹא־תַעֲנֶה בְרֵעֲךָ עֵד

שָׁוְא: ס וְלֹא תַחְמֹד אֵשֶׁת רֵעֶךָ ס וְלֹא תִתְאַוֶּה

בֵּית רֵעֶךָ שָׂדֵהוּ וְעַבְדּוֹ וַאֲמָתוֹ שׁוֹרוֹ וַחֲמֹרוֹ וְכֹל אֲשֶׁר

You shall not commit adultery.

You shall not steal.

You shall not bear false witness against your neighbor.

18] You shall not covet your neighbor's wife. You shall not crave your neighbor's house, or his field, or his male or female slave, or his ox, or his ass, or anything that is your neighbor's.

---

state or be accidental) and "murder" (which is unauthorized and malicious), the Hebrew רָצַח cannot be clearly distinguished from the more frequent הָרַג [5]. However, the commandment deals obviously with homicide, and hence those supporting pacifism or the abolition of capital punishment cannot justifiably base themselves on this word but must look to other reasons.

You shall not commit adultery. This, like the commandment that follows, is connected with the preceding by the conjunctive וְ, linking the injunctions stylistically more closely than in Exodus 20 where the וְ is absent. The seventh commandment and the eighth and ninth are in this version part of verse 17, while in other versions they are separate, thus giving the chapter three additional verses. (This alternate counting is indicated below by bracketed numbers.)

The command raises the purity of family life to the highest level of importance. In time this became a distinguishing aspect of Israel's social structure, complementing the honor rendered to parents and the sense of responsibility felt for all members of the family. The commandment applies to men and women: both are punished when found guilty of adultery (Lev. 20:10), the man having violated someone else's marriage; the woman, her own (for men could enter multiple marriages while women could not).

You shall not steal. The Rabbis interpreted the eighth commandment as referring to the theft of persons and Lev. 19:11 to the theft of property [6].

You shall not bear false witness. The prohibition covers not only the act of witnessing in court, it addresses itself also to the character of a person. Lying injures both liar and society and when practiced in judicial proceedings is doubly injurious. Says a midrash: "Everything in the world was created by God except the art of lying" [7].

The text here uses שָׁוְא instead of שֶׁקֶר as in Exodus. The difference appears to be stylistic only.

18] [21] *You shall not covet your neighbor's wife.* "Wife" is placed here before "house"; in Exodus the order is reversed, "house" being understood as "household" (of which the wife was considered a part). Here, the wife is clearly distinguished from material possessions others might crave. The commandment is the most inward of the Ten Words.

You shall not crave. תִתְאַוֶּה (titaveh), a stylistic variance of תַחְמֹד (tachmod, covet).

Your neighbor's house. A neighbor's possessions are ready-at-hand objects for what people covet.

It has been suggested that this command was a warning issued to a nomadic or seminomadic community not to become entirely sedentary [8].

Or his field. These words are not in the Exodus version.

יט לְרֵעֶךָ: ס אֶת־הַדְּבָרִים הָאֵלֶּה דִּבֶּר יְהוָה אֶל־
כָּל־קְהַלְכֶם בָּהָר מִתּוֹךְ הָאֵשׁ הֶעָנָן וְהָעֲרָפֶל קוֹל
גָּדוֹל וְלֹא יָסָף וַיִּכְתְּבֵם עַל־שְׁנֵי לֻחֹת אֲבָנִים וַיִּתְּנֵם
כ אֵלָי: וַיְהִי כְּשָׁמְעֲכֶם אֶת־הַקּוֹל מִתּוֹךְ הַחֹשֶׁךְ וְהָהָר
בֹּעֵר בָּאֵשׁ וַתִּקְרְבוּן אֵלַי כָּל־רָאשֵׁי שִׁבְטֵיכֶם
כא וְזִקְנֵיכֶם: וַתֹּאמְרוּ הֵן הֶרְאָנוּ יְהוָה אֱלֹהֵינוּ אֶת־
כְּבֹדוֹ וְאֶת־גָּדְלוֹ וְאֶת־קֹלוֹ שָׁמַעְנוּ מִתּוֹךְ הָאֵשׁ הַיּוֹם
כב הַזֶּה רָאִינוּ כִּי־יְדַבֵּר אֱלֹהִים אֶת־הָאָדָם וָחָי: וְעַתָּה
לָמָּה נָמוּת כִּי תֹאכְלֵנוּ הָאֵשׁ הַגְּדֹלָה הַזֹּאת אִם־
יֹסְפִים אֲנַחְנוּ לִשְׁמֹעַ אֶת־קוֹל יְהוָה אֱלֹהֵינוּ עוֹד
כג וָמָתְנוּ: כִּי מִי כָל־בָּשָׂר אֲשֶׁר שָׁמַע קוֹל אֱלֹהִים
כד חַיִּים מְדַבֵּר מִתּוֹךְ־הָאֵשׁ כָּמֹנוּ וַיֶּחִי: קְרַב אַתָּה

Deuteronomy 5
19–24

19] The LORD spoke those words—those and no more—to your whole congregation at the mountain, with a mighty voice out of the fire and the dense clouds. He inscribed them on two tablets of stone, which He gave to me. **20]** When you heard the voice out of the darkness, while the mountain was ablaze with fire, you came up to me, all your tribal heads and elders, **21]** and said, "The LORD our God has just shown us His majestic Presence, and we have heard His voice out of the fire; we have seen this day that man may live though God has spoken to him. **22]** Let us not die, then, for this fearsome fire will consume us; if we hear the voice of the LORD our God any longer, we shall die. **23]** For what mortal ever heard the voice of the living God speak out of the fire, as we did, and lived? **24]** You go

---

19][22] *Those words.* The Decalogue.

Those and no more. Our translation connects these words (וְלֹא יָסָף), which are found at the end of the phrase, to "The Lord spoke those words"; but others understand that after the Ten Commandments had been proclaimed God no longer

spoke "with a mighty voice out of the fire and the dense clouds" [9].

He inscribed them. As told in Exod. 32:16 and in Deut. 9:9–10.

22][25] *Let us not die.* See 4:33.

69

וּשְׁמַ֣ע אֵ֣ת כָּל־אֲשֶׁ֣ר יֹאמַ֗ר יְהֹוָ֣ה אֱלֹהֵ֔ינוּ וְאַ֣תְּ תְּדַבֵּ֣ר
אֵלֵ֗ינוּ אֵ֣ת כָּל־אֲשֶׁ֣ר יְדַבֵּ֗ר יְהֹוָ֣ה אֱלֹהֵ֖ינוּ אֵלֶ֑יךָ
כה וְשָׁמַ֖עְנוּ וְעָשִֽׂינוּ: וַיִּשְׁמַ֤ע יְהֹוָה֙ אֶת־ק֣וֹל דִּבְרֵיכֶ֔ם
בְּדַבֶּרְכֶ֖ם אֵלָ֑י וַיֹּ֨אמֶר יְהֹוָ֜ה אֵלַ֗י שָׁמַ֙עְתִּי֙ אֶת־ק֤וֹל
דִּבְרֵ֣י הָעָ֣ם הַזֶּ֔ה אֲשֶׁ֥ר דִּבְּר֖וּ אֵלֶ֑יךָ הֵיטִ֖יבוּ כָּל־אֲשֶׁ֥ר
כו דִּבֵּֽרוּ: מִֽי־יִתֵּ֡ן וְהָיָה֩ לְבָבָ֨ם זֶ֜ה לָהֶ֗ם לְיִרְאָ֥ה אֹתִ֛י
וְלִשְׁמֹ֥ר אֶת־כָּל־מִצְוֺתַ֖י* כָּל־הַיָּמִ֑ים לְמַ֨עַן יִיטַ֤ב לָהֶם֙
כז וְלִבְנֵיהֶ֖ם לְעֹלָֽם: לֵ֖ךְ אֱמֹ֣ר לָהֶ֑ם שׁ֥וּבוּ לָכֶ֖ם
כח לְאָהֳלֵיכֶֽם: וְאַתָּ֗ה פֹּה֙ עֲמֹ֣ד עִמָּדִ֔י וַאֲדַבְּרָ֣ה אֵלֶ֗יךָ
אֵ֧ת כָּל־הַמִּצְוָ֛ה וְהַֽחֻקִּ֥ים וְהַמִּשְׁפָּטִ֖ים אֲשֶׁ֣ר תְּלַמְּדֵ֑ם
וְעָשׂ֣וּ בָאָ֔רֶץ אֲשֶׁ֥ר אָנֹכִ֛י נֹתֵ֥ן לָהֶ֖ם לְרִשְׁתָּֽהּ:

* כד המ' בקמץ.

closer and hear all that the LORD our God says, and then you tell us everything that the LORD our God tells you, and we will willingly do it."

25] The LORD heard the plea that you made to me, and the LORD said to me, "I have heard the plea that this people made to you; they did well to speak thus. 26] May they always be of such mind, to revere Me and follow all My commandments, that it may go well with them and with their children forever! 27] Go, say to them, 'Return to your tents.' 28] But you remain here with Me, and I will give you the whole Instruction—the laws and the rules—which you shall impart to them, for them to observe in the land that I am giving them to possess."

26] [29] *May they ... be.* The verse is clearly based on the assumption that human beings possess the freedom to follow or not to follow God's commands [10]; see below.

To revere. The Hebrew is stronger, it conveys also a sense of awe and fear. (See above, at 4:10.)
27] [30] *Return to your tents.* From which the people had been absent for three days (Exod. 19:15).
28] [31] *The whole Instruction.* In the Torah, מִצְוָה

(*mitzvah*) describes that which God has commanded; the Rabbis determined that there were 613 such Torah mitzvot [11].

Which you shall impart. Jewish tradition finds here its warrant for the basic belief that God's will was transmitted authentically by Moses and his successors when they interpreted (and interpret) the mitzvot of the Torah.

To observe in the land. A large portion of the

כט וּשְׁמַרְתֶּם לַעֲשׂוֹת כַּאֲשֶׁר צִוָּה יְהֹוָה אֱלֹהֵיכֶם אֶתְכֶם
ל לֹא תָסֻרוּ יָמִין וּשְׂמֹאל: בְּכָל־הַדֶּרֶךְ אֲשֶׁר צִוָּה
יְהֹוָה אֱלֹהֵיכֶם אֶתְכֶם תֵּלֵכוּ לְמַעַן תִּחְיוּן וְטוֹב
לָכֶם וְהַאֲרַכְתֶּם יָמִים בָּאָרֶץ אֲשֶׁר תִּירָשׁוּן:

Deuteronomy 5

29–30

29] Be careful, then, to do as the LORD your God has commanded you. Do not turn aside to the right or to the left: 30] follow only the path that the LORD your God has enjoined upon you, so that you may thrive and that it may go well with you, and that you may long endure in the land you are to occupy.

positive commandments in Deuteronomy could be observed only
in the Land of Israel [12].

The Commandment of Social Conscience

Both versions of the Sabbath commandment state the reason why the day has been specially set aside and they state it differently. In Exodus, Israel is bidden to imitate God the Creator: even as He rested on the seventh day so must His chosen ones. Once a week they are to reenact the creative process and thus renew their own creative power. Here, in Deuteronomy, the duty to observe the Sabbath is linked not to God the Creator but to God the Redeemer. In remembering its own liberation from Egyptian slavery, Israel is to recall that all servants are human and therefore must extend the duty and privilege of Sabbath rest to them as well. Week after week the humanity of the servant is brought into the focus of social conscience. In consequence, Judaism became a religion in which social justice, equity, and decency occupied a central position.

In Genesis (2:1–3) the Sabbath is shown to be the seal of Creation and becomes God's sanctified time as well; in Exodus 20 the fourth commandment makes the day Israel's sanctified time, a supernaturally defined span that depends on no celestial or terrestrial occurrence. Even as God "renews daily the work of creation," so Israel renews weekly its awareness and appreciation of this ongoing process. In Deuteronomy, on the other hand, the Sabbath is founded, not on prehistoric creation, but on the historic creation of His people from the mire of slavery, and thus the day is humanized and its humanization is extended to all members of Israel's society. Exodus proclaims Israel's freedom from the tyranny of time; Deuteronomy, from human tyranny—and both proclamations rest in the sovereignty of God.

The day then, in remembrance and observance, is anchored in God's kingship, His manifestation outside and inside history. In Exodus the day's foundation is universal, in Deuteronomy it is bound up with Israel's experience; in Exodus the day's observance is aimed at rekindling human awe before the miracle of existence, in Deuteronomy the quality of gratitude is the focus, and out of this gratitude arises the obligation to safeguard the humanity of others.[1] Yet, on another level, the two foundations of the Sabbath—creation and redemption—are joined by the mortar of revelation. The Sabbath *Kiddush* praises God as the Giver of mitzvot (i.e., the God of Revelation) who assigned the day to Israel as a reminder of the work of creation and a remembrance of the Exodus from Egypt.

We do not know whether the Sabbath was observed in Israel long before the fourth commandment raised its celebration to the status of divinely ordained duty. It is, however, likely that the original phrasing of the commandment was simply, "Observe (or, remember) the Sabbath day to keep it holy," and that two different yet related traditions arose, each of which gave the day its own special foundation. In the confluence of these traditions the unique character of the Jewish Sabbath was shaped, a day linking heaven and earth, the creation of the world and that of Israel, the creature of eternity and of history, the focus on self and on others. The Sabbath proclaims God's sovereignty over time, and in both Exodus and Deuteronomy Israel is bidden to extend this mastery,

---

[1] The very term *tzedakah*, which describes the act of caring for the less privileged, contains the dual elements of human charity and divinely sanctioned obligation. It should be emphasized, however, that social concern is found in other books of the Torah as well; see, for instance, our commentary on the Covenant Code, Exod. 21:1 ff.

viewed through the prism of creation and redemption, to the realm of human practice. The Sabbath thus helped to mold Israel's consciousness of both time and humanity [13].

The Doctrine of Free Will

The chapter contains a verse (5:26) which in time became the proof text for the doctrine of human free will. Moses reports God as *hoping* that Israel would always revere Him and follow His commandments.[2] This obviously implies that God does not *know* whether or not Israel will do His will, for Israel—like all humanity—is free to obey or not to obey. It is the theme first touched upon in the story of the Garden of Eden and of Cain and Abel, and then drawn into question in the Exodus story of Pharaoh whose heart was "hardened" by God. But here, in Deuteronomy, the biblical text is unequivocal, for all that God can do is hope. He can guide, urge, and even threaten Israel, but He cannot force it to walk the right path. In the realm of nature rigid laws exist that determine the relationship between cause and effect, but no such laws prevail in the ethical realm. The doctrine was expressed pithily in the talmudic saying, "Everything is determined by Heaven, except the fear of Heaven" [14]. God cannot command the

moral will of His children. In this view, then, there appears to be a limit to God's foreknowledge; He may be omniscient in all other ways, but He cannot determine what decisions human beings will make.[3]

But granting that humans are free, is God also? Can He make choices that do not square with human conceptions of justice and yet, simply because they are divine choices, claim ethical rightness on a higher level? An early discussion of this problem was posed by the story of Akiba's martyrdom. Because he insisted on teaching Torah, despite an imperial Roman decree forbidding it, he was sentenced to death and flayed alive. When Moses (being shown Akiba's fate in a vision) questioned God's apparent acquiescence in Akiba's martyrdom, God replied: "Silent! Such is My will" [17]. Ultimately, although we can—and even must—question God (as did Abraham and Job), we cannot penetrate the mystery of His will. We may (as the philosopher Saadia did) suppose that God and humanity are bound by the same laws of justice, but we cannot hope to understand the reason for many divine choices. This limitation is an aspect of our mortality, and our concern must be focused on the *quality* of our human choices, believing that we are indeed free to determine it.

---

[2] In the Hebrew text God says מִי־יִתֵּן, literally, "Who might grant" that Israel be of such a mind. Says Biur: God too can express a wish of this kind, for freedom of will was given to man.

[3] Rabbi Akiba, however, taught that while there is human free will God already knows what the outcome will be: "Everything is foreseen, yet freedom of choice exists" [15]. According to a thoroughly mechanistic view of life, moral freedom is an illusion, however. No one is ever really free to do anything, for everyone is programed by heredity, training, environment, electrical and chemical stimuli, etc., to

act in strictly predictable fashion—*if* we had all the information available to make the prediction. Judaism rejects this approach and holds to the premise that there is a realm, however narrow, where human beings are free to make ethical choices. The medieval philosopher Abraham Ibn Daud considered divine ignorance in this respect to be a defect of creation. On the other hand, Bachya ibn Pakuda, who wrote a popular treatise on the ethical life (*Duties of the Heart*), believed that, even if God himself had determined our human choices in advance, we still had to act *as if* true freedom of will existed [16].

The Refuge

Why does the opening statement of Moses' discourse ("This is the Teaching," 4:44) come immediately after the rules for manslayer and blood avenger (4:41–43)? Even as the latter cannot pursue as long as the former has found refuge in one of the special "cities of refuge," so the Angel of Death cannot slay as long as a person is in his "city of refuge," that is, while studying Torah. It was told that the Angel of Death found Rabbi Chisda sitting on a branch of a tree, immersed in his studies, and because of this had no power over him. But when the branch broke Chisda interrupted his studies and in that moment the Angel of Death overcame him.

BASED ON THE TALMUD [18]

Face to Face

Moses recalls that God spoke to Israel "face to face." One would expect the expression פָּנִים אֶל פָּנִים, but it says פָּנִים בְּפָנִים (literally, "face *in* face"), expressing even greater directness. The Presence is not only turned to the other, but penetrates into the other.   S. R. HIRSCH [19]

Grandeur

The Decalogue belongs to humanity's truly great possessions, and one ought to speak of it only in the simplest words, since no encomium can describe it. It is the core and soul of Moses' lifework, the cornerstone of Israel's religion, and, through it, the fundamental law for the ethical development of humanity.   E. AUERBACH [20]

Critique of Moses

Moses should not have said "I stood between the Lord and you" (5:5), for in so saying he was thinking of his own importance and became not a link but a barrier. Only God can utter "I."

But is there no moment when there is room for the human "I"? There is. When the Evil Impulse whispers "You are unworthy to fulfill the precepts of the Torah," answer: "I *am* worthy."

CHASIDIC [21]

I Am the Lord Your God (5:6)

The suffix ךָ[4] refers to Israel collectively, and at the same time to each Israelite individually. The Midrash says: Even as thousands look at a great portrait and each one feels that it looks at *him*, so every Israelite at Horeb felt that the Divine Voice was addressing him.   J. H. HERTZ [22]

Oaths

The last letters of תִשָּׂא אֶת־שֵׁם are the anagram of אֱמֶת. Not only are false oaths prohibited, true ones too ought to be avoided.

CHASIDIC [23]

(This play on letters was meant to find scriptural warrant for the prevailing practice not to testify under oath—even when this entailed severe financial loss—for fear of using God's name for mundane purposes.)

God's Possession

Sabbath is the day that belongs to God in a special way, a day not desecrated by human usage. Not a word is said about observing it in a cultic fashion. Hence one may speculate that in Israel's older days abstinence from "using" the day was the main observance, whereby the day was demonstratively "returned to God."

G. VON RAD [24]

---

[4] אֱלֹהֶיךָ, "your (singular) God," not אֱלֹהֵיכֶם, "your (plural) God."

The Feast of Creation

The Sabbath is the feast of creation, but of a creation wrought for the sake of redemption. The feast instituted at the close of creation is creation's meaning and goal.   F. ROSENZWEIG [25]

Observe the Sabbath Day

The word שָׁמוֹר means "Keep in mind" (as in Gen. 37:11). All week one should keep the Sabbath in mind.   CHASIDIC [26]

But another interpretation holds the opposite view: "Remember" (Exodus version) the Sabbath during the week and "observe" it (Deuteronomy version) when it occurs.

Together

"Remember" and "Observe" (that is, both versions of the Sabbath commandment) were miraculously pronounced together by God, though the human mouth and ear cannot duplicate it.   RASHI [27]

So also in the Sabbath hymn, *Lecha Dodi*, "Observe" and "Remember": the One God caused us to hear them as one single word.

Even after Death

Parents should be honored even after their death. A meritorious child can redeem an unworthy parent, so that child and parent may dwell together in *Gan Eden*.   ZOHAR [28]

Return to Your Tents (5:27)

"Here at Sinai," says God, "you showed Me reverence; now let Me see what you do when you return home."   CHASIDIC [29]

How to Teach

God asks Moses to remain with Him (5:28). The Hebrew literally says to "stand" with Him. A teacher while teaching should stand or sit with dignity. God, so to speak, was himself "standing" with Moses while teaching him.   TALMUD [30]

The Shema

Moses had opened his second discourse with a restatement of the Decalogue; now he turns to the major theme of the address, the elaboration of the second commandment, "You shall have no other gods before Me." He begins his ringing appeal with *Shema Yisrael*, words that have become deeply imbedded in the consciousness of Jews, however far away they may be from the traditions of their faith. "Hear, O Israel" and "You shall love the Lord your God" are the cornerstones of Judaism's edifice, which have been given added exposure through Christianity and Islam. In the Gospels the love of God is quoted as one of two pillars of human obligation [1], and in Islam the declaration "There is no god but Allah" is a rewording of the *Shema* and, as in Jewish tradition, it has become the watchword of its faith.

The *Shema* (the expression sometimes encompasses only verse 4, sometimes verses 4–9, and, in the liturgy, these plus additional Torah selections) has been called "Judaism's greatest contribution to the religious thought of mankind" [2], the source from which Judaism time and again drew its strength for inspiration and rejuvenation [3], "the great text of monotheism" [4]. It derived its importance both from its intrinsic meaning and from the place it assumed in Jewish liturgy and history. Repeated morning and night, as well as in moments of gravest crisis and at death's door, it has sustained every generation of Jews and deepened their commitment to the One saving and caring God. Yet, despite the centrality which the *Shema* has been accorded in Jewish tradition, its exact meaning (therefore, its translation) is not entirely certain, nor is the reason for the particular writing of its Hebrew text (the third letters of the first and last words are enlarged). We have here, as perhaps nowhere else in the Torah in like degree, an example of original text and later tradition coalescing and impinging upon each other to a remarkable degree, raising four verses, inconspicuously imbedded in Moses' discourse, to a position of eminence rivaled only by the Ten Commandments.

The *Shema* is followed by three brief "sermons," verses 10–15, 16–19, and 20–25. There are some scholars who believe that the original Book of Deuteronomy began here and extended through chapter 11.

וְזֹאת הַמִּצְוָה הַחֻקִּים וְהַמִּשְׁפָּטִים אֲשֶׁר צִוָּה יְהוָֹה ×
אֱלֹהֵיכֶם לְלַמֵּד אֶתְכֶם לַעֲשׂוֹת בָּאָרֶץ אֲשֶׁר אַתֶּם
עֹבְרִים שָׁמָּה לְרִשְׁתָּהּ: לְמַעַן תִּירָא אֶת־יְהוָֹה ב
אֱלֹהֶיךָ לִשְׁמֹר אֶת־כָּל־חֻקֹּתָיו וּמִצְוֹתָיו אֲשֶׁר אָנֹכִי
מְצַוְּךָ אַתָּה וּבִנְךָ וּבֶן־בִּנְךָ כֹּל יְמֵי חַיֶּיךָ וּלְמַעַן
יַאֲרִכֻן יָמֶיךָ: וְשָׁמַעְתָּ יִשְׂרָאֵל וְשָׁמַרְתָּ לַעֲשׂוֹת ג
אֲשֶׁר יִיטַב לְךָ וַאֲשֶׁר תִּרְבּוּן מְאֹד כַּאֲשֶׁר דִּבֶּר
יְהוָֹה אֱלֹהֵי אֲבֹתֶיךָ לָךְ אֶרֶץ זָבַת חָלָב וּדְבָשׁ: פ
שְׁמַע יִשְׂרָאֵל יְהוָֹה אֱלֹהֵינוּ יְהוָֹה אֶחָד: ד

Deuteronomy 6
1–4

* ד ע' ד' רבתי.

1] And this is the Instruction—the laws and the rules—that the LORD your God has commanded [me] to impart to you, to be observed in the land which you are about to cross into and occupy, 2] so that you, your son, and your son's son may revere the LORD your God and follow, as long as you live, all His laws and commandments which I enjoin upon you, to the end that you may long endure. 3] Obey, O Israel, willingly and faithfully, that it may go well with you and that you may increase greatly [in] a land flowing with milk and honey, as the LORD, the God of your fathers, spoke to you.

4] Hear, O Israel! The LORD is our God, the LORD alone.

6:1] *Instruction.* מִצְוָה (*mitzvah*) here covers laws (חֻקִּים, *chukim*) and rules (מִשְׁפָּטִים, *mishpatim*), but other translations are possible, making *mitzvah* a coordinate of the other terms and covering a specific type of legislation [5].

2] *Revere.* See comment on 5:26.

3] *Willingly and faithfully.* A free translation, literally, "If you listen and are careful to do."

A land flowing with milk and honey. Ibn Ezra suggests that this phrase should be connected with the end of verse 1. On the meaning of "milk and honey," see at Exod. 3:8 and Num. 13:27.

4] *The Lord is our God, the Lord alone.* In this translation of the *Shema* two affirmations are made: one, that the Divinity is Israel's God, and two, that it is He alone and no one else. Other translations render "The Lord our God, the Lord is One" (stressing the unity of God) or "The Lord our God is one Lord" (that is, neither divisible nor to be coupled with other deities, like Zeus with Jupiter) [6].

ה וְאָהַבְתָּ אֵת יְהוָה אֱלֹהֶיךָ בְּכָל־לְבָבְךָ וּבְכָל־נַפְשְׁךָ

ו וּבְכָל־מְאֹדֶךָ: וְהָיוּ הַדְּבָרִים הָאֵלֶּה אֲשֶׁר אָנֹכִי

ז מְצַוְּךָ הַיּוֹם עַל־לְבָבֶךָ: וְשִׁנַּנְתָּם לְבָנֶיךָ וְדִבַּרְתָּ

בָּם בְּשִׁבְתְּךָ בְּבֵיתֶךָ וּבְלֶכְתְּךָ בַדֶּרֶךְ וּבְשָׁכְבְּךָ

ח וּבְקוּמֶךָ: וּקְשַׁרְתָּם לְאוֹת עַל־יָדֶךָ וְהָיוּ לְטֹטָפֹת בֵּין

ט עֵינֶיךָ: וּכְתַבְתָּם עַל־מְזֻזֹת בֵּיתֶךָ וּבִשְׁעָרֶיךָ: ס

5] You shall love the LORD your God with all your heart and with all your soul and with all your might.   **6]** Take to heart these instructions with which I charge you this day.   **7]** Impress them upon your children. Recite them when you stay at home and when you are away, when you lie down and when you get up.   **8]** Bind them as a sign on your hand and let them serve as a symbol on your forehead; **9]** inscribe them on the doorposts of your house and on your gates.

5] *Your heart.* Your intellect.

Your soul. Your affective capacity; see above, at 4:29.

The Talmud understands "your soul" to mean "your life": we are obligated to love God even if He takes our life [7]. The story of Rabbi Akiba's death is a dramatic example of such love; see Gleanings below.

Your might. Your physical strength.

However, according to tradition this means one's material possessions [8]. The Rabbis ruled that while there is a limit to the obligation to lay down one's life (it needs to be done only to avoid committing murder, adultery, and idolatry), there is no such limitation on the amount of money that must be sacrificed in order to avoid violations of the Torah law. (Under ordinary circumstances people were to contribute no more than 20 per cent of their substance [9].)

7] *Impress.* Others, "teach diligently." Our translation derives וְשִׁנַּנְתָּם from שנן, to sharpen, to make an incision, a meaning reflected precisely by the German *einschärfen*. But perhaps a better derivation is from שָׁנָה, repeat, and the rendition therefore should be "Recite (or repeat) them to your children" [10].

8] *Sign on your hand.* Originally this was a figure of speech, but Jewish tradition interpreted it to command the wearing of hand-phylacteries (*tefillin shel yad*; see commentary on Exod. 13:9).

Symbol on your forehead. טֹטָפֹת (*totafot*) may have derived originally from women's ornaments, as shown on Nimrud ivories [11]. This injunction too was understood literally as the command to wear head-phylacteries (*tefillin shel rosh*; see commentary on Exod. 13:16).

The two sets of tefillin consist of small boxes to which leather straps are attached for affixing the boxes to hand and head during morning worship. The boxes contain parchments with the *Shema* and other scriptural selections inscribed on them. (For details, see Commentary on Exodus, chapter 13.)

9] *Inscribe them on the doorposts.* Jewish tradition takes this to be a command to put a *mezuzah* on

י וְהָיָה כִּי יְבִיאֲךָ יְהֹוָה אֱלֹהֶיךָ אֶל־הָאָרֶץ אֲשֶׁר נִשְׁבַּע
לַאֲבֹתֶיךָ לְאַבְרָהָם לְיִצְחָק וּלְיַעֲקֹב לָתֶת לָךְ

יא עָרִים גְּדֹלֹת וְטֹבֹת אֲשֶׁר לֹא־בָנִיתָ: וּבָתִּים מְלֵאִים
כָּל־טוּב אֲשֶׁר לֹא־מִלֵּאתָ וּבֹרֹת חֲצוּבִים אֲשֶׁר לֹא־
חָצַבְתָּ כְּרָמִים וְזֵיתִים אֲשֶׁר לֹא־נָטַעְתָּ וְאָכַלְתָּ

יב וְשָׂבָעְתָּ: הִשָּׁמֶר לְךָ פֶּן־תִּשְׁכַּח אֶת־יְהֹוָה אֲשֶׁר

יג הוֹצִיאֲךָ מֵאֶרֶץ מִצְרַיִם מִבֵּית עֲבָדִים: אֶת־יְהֹוָה

יד אֱלֹהֶיךָ תִּירָא וְאֹתוֹ תַעֲבֹד וּבִשְׁמוֹ תִּשָּׁבֵעַ: לֹא
תֵלְכוּן אַחֲרֵי אֱלֹהִים אֲחֵרִים מֵאֱלֹהֵי הָעַמִּים אֲשֶׁר

Deuteronomy 6
10–14

10] When the LORD your God brings you into the land which He swore to your fathers, Abraham, Isaac, and Jacob, to give you—great and flourishing cities which you did not build,   **11]** houses full of all good things which you did not fill, hewn cisterns which you did not hew, vineyards and olive groves which you did not plant—and you eat your fill,   **12]** take heed that you do not forget the LORD who freed you from the land of Egypt, the house of bondage.   **13]** Revere only the LORD your God and worship Him alone, and swear only by His name.   **14]** Do not follow other gods, any gods of the peoples about you

the doors of one's dwelling [12]. *Mezuzah* is the Hebrew word for the doorpost itself but has given its name to the small container and its parchment, on which are written the words of Deut. 6:4–9 and 11:13–21.

10]   *Great and flourishing cities.* This was a view of Canaan as seen from the outside.

11]   *You eat your fill.* Medieval commentators were greatly puzzled with this verse since it appeared

to give the Israelites permission to eat the Canaanites' (non-kosher) food [13]. The words are cited in the *Birkat ha-Mazon* (Grace after Meals).

13]   *Worship Him.* In Hebrew, עבד denoted originally physical service and later spiritual (worship) service as well. (The same dual meaning of the word service is found in English, in the Aramaic *pelach*, and the Latin-based cultivate-cult.)

Swear only by His Name. And by none other. The word "only" is not in the Hebrew text but is implied [14].

טו סְבִיבוֹתֵיכֶם: כִּי אֵל קַנָּא יְהֹוָה אֱלֹהֶיךָ בְּקִרְבֶּךָ

פֶּן־יֶחֱרֶה אַף־יְהֹוָה אֱלֹהֶיךָ בָּךְ וְהִשְׁמִידְךָ מֵעַל

טז פְּנֵי הָאֲדָמָה: ס לֹא תְנַסּוּ אֶת־יְהֹוָה אֱלֹהֵיכֶם

יז כַּאֲשֶׁר נִסִּיתֶם בַּמַּסָּה: שָׁמוֹר תִּשְׁמְרוּן אֶת־מִצְוֺת

יח יְהֹוָה אֱלֹהֵיכֶם וְעֵדֹתָיו וְחֻקָּיו אֲשֶׁר צִוָּךְ: וְעָשִׂיתָ

הַיָּשָׁר וְהַטּוֹב בְּעֵינֵי יְהֹוָה לְמַעַן יִיטַב לָךְ וּבָאתָ

וְיָרַשְׁתָּ אֶת־הָאָרֶץ הַטֹּבָה אֲשֶׁר־נִשְׁבַּע יְהֹוָה לַאֲבֹתֶיךָ:

יט לַהֲדֹף אֶת־כָּל־אֹיְבֶיךָ מִפָּנֶיךָ כַּאֲשֶׁר דִּבֶּר

כ יְהֹוָה: ס כִּי־יִשְׁאָלְךָ בִנְךָ מָחָר לֵאמֹר מָה

הָעֵדֹת וְהַחֻקִּים וְהַמִּשְׁפָּטִים אֲשֶׁר צִוָּה יְהֹוָה אֱלֹהֵינוּ

Deuteronomy 6
15–20

15]—for the LORD your God in your midst is an impassioned God—lest the anger of the LORD your God blaze forth against you and He wipe you off the face of the earth.

16] Do not try the LORD your God, as you did at Massah.   **17]** Be sure to keep the commandments, exhortations, and laws which the LORD your God has enjoined upon you.   **18]** Do what is right and good in the sight of the LORD, that it may go well with you and that you may be able to occupy the good land which the LORD your God promised on oath to your fathers,   **19]** and that your enemy may be driven out before you, as the LORD has spoken.

20] When, in time to come, your son asks you, "What mean the exhortations, laws, and rules which the LORD our God has enjoined upon you?"

15] *Impassioned God.* On this, see at Exod. 20:5.

Lest . . . He wipe you off. Spoken as a hyperbole to emphasize the seriousness of the consequence.

16] *Massah.* "Trial," see Exod. 17:1 ff. Israel had grumbled about the dearth of water and had dared Moses to provide a miracle—thereby "trying" God himself.

18] *Do what is right and good.* The Rabbis developed an important ethical principle from this verse, holding that it was not sufficient to do the "right" or legal thing, but that one needed to go beyond and do also what was "good" or moral. See below, Gleanings [15].

20] *Your son asks you.* The question has been taken into the Passover Haggadah and is ascribed

82

כא אֶתְכֶם: וְאָמַרְתָּ לְבִנְךָ עֲבָדִים הָיִינוּ לְפַרְעֹה
כב בְּמִצְרָיִם וַיֹּצִיאֵנוּ יְהוָה מִמִּצְרַיִם בְּיָד חֲזָקָה: וַיִּתֵּן
יְהוָה אוֹתֹת וּמֹפְתִים גְּדֹלִים וְרָעִים בְּמִצְרַיִם
כג בְּפַרְעֹה וּבְכָל־בֵּיתוֹ לְעֵינֵינוּ: וְאוֹתָנוּ הוֹצִיא מִשָּׁם
לְמַעַן הָבִיא אֹתָנוּ לָתֶת לָנוּ אֶת־הָאָרֶץ אֲשֶׁר נִשְׁבַּע
כד לַאֲבֹתֵינוּ: וַיְצַוֵּנוּ יְהוָה לַעֲשׂוֹת אֶת־כָּל־הַחֻקִּים
הָאֵלֶּה לְיִרְאָה אֶת־יְהוָה אֱלֹהֵינוּ לְטוֹב לָנוּ כָּל־
כה הַיָּמִים לְחַיֹּתֵנוּ כְּהַיּוֹם הַזֶּה: וּצְדָקָה תִּהְיֶה־לָּנוּ כִּי־
נִשְׁמֹר לַעֲשׂוֹת אֶת־כָּל־הַמִּצְוָה הַזֹּאת לִפְנֵי יְהוָה
אֱלֹהֵינוּ כַּאֲשֶׁר צִוָּנוּ:

Deuteronomy 6
21–25

21] you shall say to your son, "We were slaves to Pharaoh in Egypt and the LORD freed us from Egypt with a mighty hand.   **22]** The LORD wrought before our eyes marvelous and destructive signs and portents in Egypt, against Pharaoh and all his household;   **23]** and us He freed from there, that He might take us and give us the land that He had promised on oath to our fathers.   **24]** Then the LORD commanded us to observe all these laws, to revere the LORD our God, for our lasting good and for our survival, as is now the case.   **25]** It will be therefore to our merit before the LORD our God to observe faithfully this whole Instruction, as He has commanded us."

to the Wise Son. The answer he receives in verse 21 is similar to the one given the Simple Son (Exod. 13:14). See also Gleanings below.

25] *Merit.* צְדָקָה (*tzedakah*), a word usually denoting "right" or "just" action, but occasionally meaning "merit" as here and in Gen. 15:6, Deut. 24:13. Those who acknowledge God are counted as being "right" in their relation to Him [16].

The words "in the sight of the Lord" appear later in the Hebrew text but are moved up in the translation for better understanding.

The Shema—Its Meaning

The six words of the *Shema* (6:4) have become the best-known words in Judaism's liturgy, the "watchword" of Israel's faith, and this despite the fact that their precise meaning is not clear at all. In the Hebrew text, after the opening call "Hear, O Israel," the affirmation itself states tersely: "Lord our God Lord *echad*." The uncertainty of the meaning arises from the absence of punctuation and the nature of juxtaposing these Hebrew words without an explicative verb, as well as from the various emphases that can be ascribed to the word *echad*: one, alone, unique. Thus, the text can be understood to say:

יהוה is our God, and יהוה alone;

יהוה is our God, one indivisible יהוה;

יהוה our God is a unique יהוה;

יהוה is our God, יהוה is unique (in His extraordinariness).

Despite these variant meanings—or perhaps because of them!—the words assumed a position of centrality in Jewish thinking and liturgical practice, and this position became assured and hallowed through Rabbi Akiba's martyrdom (see Gleanings). Since that time Jews have repeated the *Shema* on countless other occasions as they sanctified God's name through their death; and they continue to speak the six words (usually with the words that follow and other selections; see further below) at prayer services throughout the year, affix them to their doorposts, and inscribe them on their phylacteries.

While in earliest days the existence of other gods was accepted by Israel, the uniqueness of the Lord became an article of faith as time went on: יְהֹוָה not only was Israel's personal guardian, He was also superior to all other deities—if in fact these could be said to exist at all (an idea that had been discarded by the time Deuteronomy was codified). God was now acknowledged as singular or unique or extraordinary, who in His wisdom had bound himself to the people Israel. In repeating the *Shema* the Jew directed himself to this special relationship, he gloried in it, and pledged his very life to witness to the Holy One. Jewish devotional manuals often advised the worshiper to keep the possibility of martyrdom in mind and, in reciting the watchword as well as the words following it, to concentrate on God's incomparable greatness as Creator and Giver of the Torah. Thus, Alexander Suskind of Grodno suggested that one remember these thoughts:

"I believe with perfect faith, pure and true, that You are one and unique and that You have created all worlds, upper and lower, without end, and You are in past, present, and future. I make You King over each of my limbs that it might keep and perform the precepts of Your holy Torah and I make You King over my children and children's children to the end of time. I will, therefore, command my children and grandchildren to accept the yoke of Your Kingdom, Divinity, and Lordship upon themselves, and I will command them to command their children, in turn, up to the last generation to accept, all of them, the yoke of Your Kingdom, Divinity, and Lordship" [17].

The *Shema* thus came to be like a precious gem, in that the light of faith made its words sparkle with rich brilliance of varied colors. Negatively, it underscored the Jew's opposition to polytheism and pagan ethics, to the dualism of the Zoroastrians, the pantheism of the Greeks, and the trinitarianism of the Christians. Positively, the One God was seen to imply one humanity and therefore demanded the brotherhood of all; it spoke of the world as the stage for the ethical life and linked monotheism and morality. It meant that God undergirded all laws for nature and for mankind; hence heaven and earth as well as human history were His domain. And, if humanity found itself still unredeemed, God's presence would reach beyond history into the time of messianic redemption: "The Lord shall reign over all the earth; on that day the Lord shall be One and His name shall be One" (Zech. 14:9; cf. Zeph. 3:9).[1] These principles were seen by generations of Jews as rays shining forth from the *Shema*, as from a diamond set into a crown of faith and proven true and enduring in human history.

The Love of God [18]

It is one of the characteristics of Deuteronomy that it stresses the duty to love God as well as to acknowledge Him as Israel's savior, the singular Deity in the world who rules it in solitary splendor. "You must love the Lord your God with all your heart and with all your soul and with all your might"—this is the great theme to which the book returns time and again. The duty presupposes, by its nature, a reciprocal relationship, for God loves Israel and has loved it since patriarchal days—a love freely extended to a people whom He chose mysteriously, inexplicably (4:37; 7:7–8). But no love—neither divine nor human—can exist in a vacuum; without mutual loyalty its roots dry up and its flowers wither. And since God is by nature a faithful God (אֵל נֶאֱמָן), it is *Israel's* loyalty which needs to be nurtured and strengthened. As in marriage, love rests on loyalty and trust, and although love itself cannot be forced [19] the uniquely desirable relationship it engenders is constantly held up to Israel. In that sense, it becomes a "must"

for disenchanted love often turns to anger, and even the Divine Lover is caught in this tension of opposites.[2] Hosea, Jeremiah, and the Second Isaiah, as well as the rabbinic view of the Song of Songs, saw God and Israel in a quasi-conjugal relationship: bliss is in store for the bride (identified with Israel) who deserves the love of her bridegroom (God), but woe to her if she betrays her trust. She will be cast out, thrust into darkness, and only a merciful lover, remembering their past affection, can restore her to her former position (see Hosea 2; Jeremiah 2, 3, 31:2–6; Isaiah 49:14–54:8).

The duty to love God is on occasion coupled with the caution to fear Him (so in 10:12 and in 11:13–21, which constitutes the second paragraph in the morning and evening *Shema*). Both love and fear can motivate us to do God's will, but of the two, according to the Rabbis, love is superior; still, fear needs to be instilled in those whose moral development is imperfect[3] [22].

How then can one love God? From ancient to modern times writers have given much attention to this question. The Midrash holds that we best express this love when we conduct ourselves in such a manner as to make God beloved by others [23]. It is our attention to the mitzvot that will make us as well as others aware of the One in Whose name they are performed, and, the greater our devotion and concentration upon the mitzvah and its Giver, the more likely we will be to enter into the context of pure love. For, while love as such cannot be the subject of command, actions leading to love—

---

[1] This phrase culminates the Aleinu (or "Adoration") and occurs in all three daily prayer services.

[2] Such tension is expressed also in ancient Near Eastern vassal-suzerain treaties, where political loyalty was generally expressed by the term "love" [20].

[3] It should be kept in mind, however, as B. J. Bamberger has shown [21], that neither "love" nor "fear," as we use the terms today, is a proper rendering of the biblical terms אַהֲבָה and יִרְאָה. They indicate action more than an inward state, overt demonstrations of loyalty to God, and hence are two sides of the same coin. Both together denote what we would call "active religion."

both ours and others'—can be. Each mitzvah done in the right spirit is an act of loving God. It can be done everywhere and anywhere, wherever the opportunity for mitzvot exists, and it is, therefore, not exclusively the consequence of spiritual contemplation.[4] "You must love the Lord your God" is the command to do godly deeds, which will vouchsafe the capacity and will to love the Lover of Israel.

The Shema in Jewish Liturgy

As indicated above, the single line of the *Shema* (6:4) holds a position of importance in Jewish practice unparalleled by any other verse. It is recited at evening and morning services on various occasions, on retiring at night and at the end of Yom Kippur, where it is almost at once followed by the sevenfold exclamation "The Lord is God!" (I Kings 18:39). It is a custom among Orthodox Jews to cover the eyes while saying the words, in order to increase one's concentration and to linger on the last letter (ד) which is written large in the Hebrew text. (But the *Shema* need not be said in Hebrew; one's obligation is fulfilled by saying it in any language.) The Talmud prescribes that the sentence be spoken clearly and precisely; the fires of hell, it says with metaphoric emphasis, are cooled for those who observe this rule [25].

Already at an early time it became a custom to read verse 4 twice daily together with verses 5–9 as well as nine other verses from chapter 11 (13–21), and five from Numbers (15:37–41).[5] These readings together became known as the *Shema* in a liturgical sense and were surrounded by benedictions extolling God as Creator, faithful Lover, and Protector of Israel. Tradition prescribed the hours during which the *Shema* had to be recited: the evening prayers were to be said between nightfall and dawn, and the morning *Shema* from dawn on until one-quarter of the day had passed [27].

It was natural that so important a text became the subject of controversy and special practices. The schools of Hillel and Shammai (at the beginning of the Common Era) argued over the bodily position one ought to assume while reciting the *Shema*. Shammai held that verse 7 was to be taken literally: at night speak the words lying down, and in the morning standing up; while Hillel (whose teaching prevailed) ruled that one should not change one's position during the recital [28]. Reform practice provides for the congregation to stand in order to emphasize the importance of the *Shema*, while in Orthodox and most Conservative synagogues it is recited sitting down.[6] Another difference has developed around the response customarily made to the public proclamation of the *Shema*: "Praised be the Lord's name for ever and ever." In Reform synagogues this response is spoken or sung aloud, in others it is said *sotto voce*, except on Yom Kippur.

And, finally, traditional prayer books provide that an individual person preface the

---

[4] The medieval moralist Bachya ibn Pakuda was one of the minority who believed that the love of God could be achieved only if one divorced himself from worldly pursuits. "What does the love of God consist of? The soul's complete surrender of its own accord to the Creator in order to cleave to His supernal light ... then it will become completely preoccupied with His service and have no place for any other thought, sending forth not even one of the limbs of its body on any other service but that drawn to by His will;

loosening the tongue but to make mention of Him and praise Him out of love of Him and longing for Him" [24].

[5] In Reform services, the latter two paragraphs are omitted and only two verses (Num. 15:40–41) are recited to conclude Deut. 6:4–9 [26].

[6] However, congregations stand for the *Shema* during special parts of a service which in themselves require standing: the *Musaf Kedushah*, the Torah service, and the concluding proclamations of Yom Kippur.

Shema with the three words *El Melech ne-eman* (O God, faithful King!). This practice seems to have been instituted in order to raise the number of words found in the three paragraphs of the *Shema* (which amounts to two hundred forty-five) to two hundred forty-eight, thus equaling the number of positive mitzvot in the Torah—another indication that these words were seen to be at the heart of the Jewish faith.

GLEANINGS

The Death of Rabbi Akiba (about 138 C.E.)

The wicked government (the Romans) issued a decree forbidding the Jews to study and practice the Torah. Pappus ben Judah came and found Rabbi Akiba publicly bringing gatherings together and occupying himself with the Torah. He said to him: "Akiba, are you not afraid of the government?" He replied: "I will answer you with a parable. A fox was once walking alongside a river, and he saw fishes going in swarms from one place to another. He said to them: 'From what are you fleeing?' They replied: 'From the nets cast for us by men.' He said to them: 'Would you like to come up on to the dry land so that you and I can live together in the way that my ancestors lived with your ancestors?' They replied: 'Are you the one that they call the cleverest of animals? You are not clever but foolish. If we are afraid in the element in which we live, how much more in the element in which we would die!' So it is with us. If such is our condition when we sit and study the Torah, of which it is written, 'For that is your life and the length of your days' (Deut. 30:20), if we go and neglect it how much worse off we shall be!"

It is related that soon afterward Rabbi Akiba was arrested and thrown into prison, and Pappus ben Judah was also arrested and imprisoned next to him. He said to him: "Pappus, who brought you here?" He replied: "Happy are you, Rabbi Akiba, that you have been seized for busying yourself with the Torah! Alas for Pappus who has been seized for busying himself with idle things!" When Rabbi Akiba was taken out for execution, it was the hour for the recital of the *Shema* and,

while they combed his flesh with iron combs, he was accepting upon himself the kingship of heaven.[7]

His disciples said to him: "Our teacher, even to this point?" He said to them: "All my days I have been troubled by this verse, 'with all your soul,' which I interpret 'even if He takes your soul.' I said: When shall I have the opportunity of fulfilling this? Now that I have the opportunity shall I not fulfill it?" He prolonged the word *echad*[8] until he expired while saying it. A heavenly voice went forth and proclaimed: "Happy are you, Akiba, that your soul has departed with the word *echad*!"
TALMUD [29]

Hearing and Seeing

Israel's original knowledge rested on seeing ("You have been *shown* that you might know," 4:35), by being made eyewitnesses to the revelation at Sinai. Since that time, however, tradition rests on hearing and not on a continuation of natural phenomena—hence, "*Hear*, O Israel!"
AFTER S. R. HIRSCH [30]

Majuscules

Why are the last letters of שְׁמַע and אֶחָד written large in all Torah scrolls? We no longer know the reason, but the following have been suggested:

To remind us to concentrate on the thought that lies between the ע and the ד;

The large ע: so that one should read שְׁמַע and not שֶׁמָּא ("Perhaps, O Israel . . .");

The large ד: so that one should read אֶחָד and not אַחֵר ("another").[9]

---

[7] Meaning, he recited the *Shema*.

[8] The last word of verse 4.

[9] Conversely, in Exod. 34:14 the ר is written large,

so that one should not read אָחָד, which instead of "Do not bow down to any other god" would be perverted into: "Do not bow down to the one God."

Together, ע and ד read עֵד (ed, witness), to emphasize that the Jew who pronounces the Shema witnesses to the Holy One.   SFORNO AND OTHERS

God's Glory

God said to Israel, "My children, everything I have created I have created in pairs: heaven and earth, sun and moon, Adam and Eve, this world and the world-to-come. But My glory is one and unique in the world—hence ". . . the Lord alone."   MIDRASH [31]

One

He is One. Nobody will dispute that this doctrine is absolutely necessary for complete devotion, admiration, and love toward God. For devotion, admiration, and love spring from the superiority of one over all else.   SPINOZA [32]

Thou art One, the beginning of all computation, the base of all construction.

Thou art One, and in the mystery of Thy Oneness the wise of heart are astonished, for they know not what it is.

Thou art One, and Thy Oneness neither diminishes nor increases, neither lacks nor exceeds.

Thou art One, but not as the one that is counted or owned, for number and chance cannot reach Thee, nor attribute, nor form.

Thou art One, but my mind is too feeble to set Thee a law or a limit, and therefore I say: "I will take heed to my ways, that I sin not with my tongue."

Thou art One, and Thou art exalted above abasement and falling—not like a man, who falls when he is alone.

SOLOMON IBN GABIROL [33]

Modern Jewish monotheistic belief has been so thoroughly explored in the previous centuries that a consensus has emerged among believers as to what it implies and what it rejects. Judaism stands or falls on the rejection of polytheism as it is compatible with dualism or trinitarianism. . . . Moderns will be sceptical, to say the least, regarding the kabbalistic systems and will regard chasidic pantheism as logically obscure. The believing Jew still recites the Shema as plying the pure monotheistic doctrine on which Judaism as a religion is based.   L. JACOBS [34]

He is the One, and therefore man must decide for Him, in contrast to and over and against all else, and must serve Him only and no power of nature or fate. . . . It is the grasp of this singular Reality, the awareness of this singular Truth, this will and courage to decide for the One and Only, rather than the multiple and the many, which is the soul of monotheism.   LEO BAECK [35]

A Doctrine of Faith

I believe with perfect faith that the Creator, blessed be His name, is One only and that there is no unity in any manner like His, and that He alone is our God, who was, is, and will be.

MAIMONIDES [36]

In poetic form, the principle appears as the second stanza of the hymn Yigdal, by Meir Leoni (based on Maimonides):

One He is, no unity like His,
Mysterious and unending in His unity.

To Love God

The meaning of the love of God is that a man should be longing and yearning after the nearness of God, blessed be He, and striving to reach His holiness, in the same manner as he would pursue any object for which he feels a strong passion. He should feel that bliss and delight in mentioning His name, in uttering His praises, and in occupying himself with the words of the Torah, which a lover feels toward the wife of his youth, or the father toward his only son.   LUZZATTO [37]

This is the way the Psalmist describes his yearning:

Like a hind crying for water,
My soul cries for You, O God;
My soul thirsts for God, the living God. . . .

PSALM 42:2–3

Man cannot love God as he loves another human being. Love of God involves a holy fear or reverence (6:13), and it expresses itself in that devoted and single-minded loyalty which issues in wholehearted and obedient service. The love of

God without obedience is not love.

G. E. WRIGHT [38]

"You must love the Lord" means to do His commandments out of love, and "with all your heart" challenges us to do it with both our good and evil inclinations.[10]

MIDRASH [39]

What, then, is the way to love Him and revere Him? When man contemplates His works and His wonderful, great creatures and fathoms through them His inestimable and boundless wisdom, he will immediately love, and praise, and exalt, and will be seized by a keen longing passion to know Him—as David said: "My soul thirsts for God, the living God" (Ps. 42:3).

What is suitable love? To love God with an exceedingly great and very intense love until one's soul is knit with the love of God and one is constantly obsessed by it. As in a state of love-sickness, in which the mind cannot be diverted from the beloved, the lover is constantly obsessed by his love, lying down or rising up, eating or drinking. Even more so will the lovers of God experience this constant obsession in their heart, as we are bidden to love "with all your heart and with all your soul," and as Solomon expressed allegorically "I am love-sick" (Song of Songs 5:8); the entire Song of Songs is, in fact, an allegorical expression of this love.

MAIMONIDES [40]

Defiant Love

The story was told of a man who had lost his wife and children in a pogrom. He addressed God as follows: "Master of the universe, You have done much to make me forsake my faith. Know then that in spite of it all I am a Jew, and a Jew I will remain, and nothing You will yet do to me will avail You anything and turn me away from loving You."

SHELOMO IBN VERGA [41]

Unity and Love

The juxtaposition of verse 4 (God's unity) and verse 5 (the love of God) suggests that, when we recognize Him as One, we are challenged to love Him as the source of all that happens to us—both good and evil.

MALBIM [42]

Sequence

It says (6:6) "Take to heart" and then (6:7) "Impress them upon your children." Only when you yourself take them to heart will you be able to impress them upon your children, as the saying is, "Words that come from the heart can enter the heart."

ALSHECH [43]

A Difficulty

How is it possible to command the love of God when it is dependent on an inner urge? Suppose such an urge is absent? However, every person has the potential somewhere buried within him, hence the commandment means to bolster the spirit so that the slumbering love of God may be uncovered.

SEFAT EMET [44]

The Commandment

Of course, love cannot be commanded. No third party can command it or extort it. No third party can, but the One can. The commandment to love can only proceed from the mouth of the Lover. Only the Lover can and does say: love me! —and He really does so. In His mouth the commandment to love is not a strange commandment; it is none other than the voice of love itself. The love of the Lover has, in fact, no word to express itself other than the commandment.

F. ROSENZWEIG [45]

Love People First

Three times the Torah asks us to love: twice, in Leviticus (19:18, 34), we are commanded to love human beings; then, in Deuteronomy, our love is directed toward God. Only after we have learned to love people can we come to love God.

CHASIDIC [46]

Before beginning one's prayers one should concentrate on the thought of loving one's fellow creatures.   ISAAC BEN SOLOMON LURIA (HA-ARI) [47]

Our God (Deut. 6:4)

The "our" appears to limit God's universality. Hence we must take special care to proclaim His unity.

YALKUT SHIMONI [48]

---

[10] This is derived from the word לְבָבְךָ (rather than לְבְּךָ, which has only one ב).

90

He is "our God" now, and not yet the God of all nations, but in the future He will be "the Lord alone."   RASHI [49]

Sharpen

The duty to "impress" means to teach incisively, to sharpen the intellect of one's child on the words of Torah.   ZOHAR [50]

Do Not Try the Lord (Deut. 6:16)

This means: Do not test one of God's prophets by challenging him to perform miracles.

                                   MAIMONIDES [51]

Do What Is Right and Good (Deut. 6:18)

(The Rabbis did not consider "right" and "good" as synonyms. Rather, they took "good" to be an extension and widening of "right.")

This is a new command, not implied in any previous mitzvah. It means the (moral) obligation to go, when necessary, beyond what is (legally) required of us.   RASHI [52]

According to one opinion, Jerusalem was destroyed because its inhabitants acted merely according to the letter of the law and did not go beyond it.   TALMUD [53]

The Wise and the Wicked Sons

(The Haggadah assigns the question of 6:20 to the Wise Son,[11] but—according to the Masorah —he too says "you" like the Wicked Son. What then is the distinction?)

The Wise Son says "you" because the law was enjoined before his own time; at the same time he acknowledges that God stands behind the law. The Wicked Son (Exod. 12:26) does not acknowledge the latter.   TOSEFET BERACHAH [55]

[11] The Haggadah distinguishes the Wise Son from the Wicked in that the former identifies with his people while the latter does not. (He says, "What does this mean to *you*," excluding himself [54].)

ואתחנן–עקב

Dealing with Idolatry

The seventh chapter addresses the chief religious problem of the anticipated occupation of Canaan: how is Israel to deal with the idolaters
and idolatries they will find in the land? For the first time since Egypt,
the people will be exposed to and come in close contact with a foreign
culture that will be a potential snare to the invaders, whose own religious
practices are not as yet firmly established. The rules for occupation are
therefore extreme in their simplicity: those who endanger Israel's spiritual
survival are to be destroyed; mixed marriage with the inhabitants is to
be avoided; the pagan images and their sanctuaries are to be demolished.
If Israel will follow these prescriptions, all will be well and blessings will
attend it, but, if not, the very destruction due the enemy will be visited
on Israel itself. God will prove himself both faithful and vengeful, as circumstances demand, for His Chosen People stand in an ambience not du-
plicated elsewhere and unrelated to their power or their numbers.

These provisions have to be seen and understood in their own context
and must not be judged by the need and experience of a later age. Only
when we consider them as applicable to our own time does contemporary
judgment become opportune. The clash of cultures is a problem in contemporary Israel, and so is the frequent occurrence of mixed marriages
in the Diaspora, while idolatry, with which the ancients were greatly
concerned, is no longer an issue. Still, this subject raises questions about
the God whom the Torah depicts as desiring the death of idolaters and
who commands "Show them no pity!"

(A new weekly portion, *Ekev,* begins with 7:12.)

א כִּי יְבִיאֲךָ יְהֹוָה אֱלֹהֶיךָ אֶל־הָאָרֶץ אֲשֶׁר־אַתָּה בָא־
שָׁמָּה לְרִשְׁתָּהּ וְנָשַׁל גּוֹיִם־רַבִּים מִפָּנֶיךָ הַחִתִּי
וְהַגִּרְגָּשִׁי וְהָאֱמֹרִי וְהַכְּנַעֲנִי וְהַפְּרִזִּי וְהַחִוִּי וְהַיְבוּסִי
ב שִׁבְעָה גוֹיִם רַבִּים וַעֲצוּמִים מִמֶּךָּ: וּנְתָנָם יְהֹוָה
אֱלֹהֶיךָ לְפָנֶיךָ וְהִכִּיתָם הַחֲרֵם תַּחֲרִים אֹתָם לֹא־
ג תִכְרֹת לָהֶם בְּרִית וְלֹא תְחָנֵּם: וְלֹא תִתְחַתֵּן בָּם
בִּתְּךָ לֹא־תִתֵּן לִבְנוֹ וּבִתּוֹ לֹא־תִקַּח לִבְנֶךָ:

1] When the LORD your God brings you to the land that you are about to invade and occupy, and He dislodges many nations before you—the Hittites, Girgashites, Amorites, Canaanites, Perizzites, Hivites, and Jebusites, seven nations much larger than you— **2]** and the LORD your God delivers them to you and you defeat them, you must doom them to destruction: grant them no terms and give them no quarter. **3]** You shall not intermarry with them: do not give your daughters to their sons or

---

7:1] *Hittites*. The great Hittite empire of Anatolia (central Turkey) collapsed about the time of the Israelite conquest of Canaan (about 1200 B.C.E.) and its survivors fled into northern Syria. There they formed city-states jointly with Arameans invading from the south. (These are the Hittites referred to in neo-Assyrian inscriptions.) In the Bible, "Hittites" is more often than not used as an ideological pejorative with little specific ethnic content (compare the use of Ishmaelite, Midianite, Medanite; see our Commentary on Genesis, chapter 37) [1].

Girgashites. They are not known in sources outside the Bible. According to the Midrash the Israelites did not, however, encounter them during their conquest, for the Girgashites were said to have emigrated to Africa [2].

Amorites. See at 1:4, 7.

Canaanites. Here apparently a term for those natives who had no other tribal loyalty. In other contexts "Canaanites" is a general word for the inhabitants of the land.

Perizzites. Living in central Canaan, around Bethel and Shechem (see Josh. 17:15; Judg. 1:4 f.). The name may indicate "people who dwell in the open countryside" (see 3:5).

Hivites. They also lived near Shechem, and around Gibeon (Gen. 34:2; Josh. 9:7; 11:19).

Jebusites. Who lived in and around Jebus, which was the old name for Jerusalem. The Jebusites were not dislodged until King David's time, a little before 1000 B.C.E. (II Sam. 5:6).

Seven nations. This is the only time in the Torah that all the seven are listed together.

2] *Doom them to destruction*. On the problem raised by this verse and verse 16, see commentary below, "The Treatment of Conquered Nations."

ד כִּי־יָסִיר אֶת־בִּנְךָ מֵאַחֲרַי וְעָבְדוּ אֱלֹהִים אֲחֵרִים

ה וְחָרָה אַף־יְהֹוָה בָּכֶם וְהִשְׁמִידְךָ מַהֵר: כִּי־אִם־כֹּה

תַעֲשׂוּ לָהֶם מִזְבְּחֹתֵיהֶם תִּתֹּצוּ וּמַצֵּבֹתָם תְּשַׁבֵּרוּ

ו וַאֲשֵׁירֵהֶם תְּגַדֵּעוּן וּפְסִילֵיהֶם תִּשְׂרְפוּן בָּאֵשׁ: כִּי

עַם קָדוֹשׁ אַתָּה לַיהֹוָה אֱלֹהֶיךָ בְּךָ בָּחַר יְהֹוָה

אֱלֹהֶיךָ לִהְיוֹת לוֹ לְעַם סְגֻלָּה מִכֹּל הָעַמִּים אֲשֶׁר

ז עַל־פְּנֵי הָאֲדָמָה: לֹא מֵרֻבְּכֶם מִכָּל־הָעַמִּים חָשַׁק

יְהֹוָה בָּכֶם וַיִּבְחַר בָּכֶם כִּי־אַתֶּם הַמְעַט מִכָּל־

Deuteronomy 7

4–7

take their daughters for your sons.   4] For they will turn your children away from Me to worship other gods, and the LORD's anger will blaze forth against you and He will promptly wipe you out.   5] Instead, this is what you shall do to them: you shall tear down their altars, smash their pillars, cut down their sacred posts, and consign their images to the fire.

6] For you are a people consecrated to the LORD your God: of all the peoples on earth the LORD your God chose you to be His treasured people.   7] It is not because you are the most numerous of peoples that the LORD set His heart on you

4] *Away from Me.* Moses speaks here like a prophet, as if with God's voice.

5] *Their altars.* Such altars have been unearthed by archeologists [3].

Pillars. A row of some ten free-standing slabs was found at Gezer [4]. Most likely they represented seats of the deity. It has been suggested that the "memorial chapel" at Hazor was destroyed by the Israelites to fulfill this commandment [5].

Sacred posts. Usually made of wood, these *asherim* (dedicated to the goddess Asherah) were found near altar sites and represented sacred trees.

6] *His treasured people.* עַם סְגֻלָּה (*am segullah*), a term related to the Akkadian *sugullu* which means "property" (or "cattle," which was usually a person's main possession; see further at Exod. 19:5). According to Buber, the term meant "a possession which is withdrawn from general family property because one invididual has a special relation to it and a special claim on it" [6].

7] *Not because you are the most numerous.* God operates sometimes in contradiction to what the "natural" order appears to suggest or demand; "an act of paradoxical divine love" [7].

ח הָעַמִּים: כִּי מֵאַהֲבַת יְהֹוָה אֶתְכֶם וּמִשָּׁמְרוֹ אֶת־
הַשְּׁבֻעָה אֲשֶׁר נִשְׁבַּע לַאֲבֹתֵיכֶם הוֹצִיא יְהֹוָה אֶתְכֶם
בְּיָד חֲזָקָה וַיִּפְדְּךָ מִבֵּית עֲבָדִים מִיַּד פַּרְעֹה מֶלֶךְ־

ט מִצְרָיִם: וְיָדַעְתָּ כִּי־יְהֹוָה אֱלֹהֶיךָ הוּא הָאֱלֹהִים הָאֵל
הַנֶּאֱמָן שֹׁמֵר הַבְּרִית וְהַחֶסֶד לְאֹהֲבָיו וּלְשֹׁמְרֵי

י מִצְוֹתוֹ* לְאֶלֶף דּוֹר: וּמְשַׁלֵּם לְשֹׂנְאָיו אֶל־פָּנָיו
לְהַאֲבִידוֹ לֹא יְאַחֵר לְשֹׂנְאוֹ אֶל־פָּנָיו יְשַׁלֶּם־לוֹ:

יא וְשָׁמַרְתָּ אֶת־הַמִּצְוָה וְאֶת־הַחֻקִּים וְאֶת־הַמִּשְׁפָּטִים
אֲשֶׁר אָנֹכִי מְצַוְּךָ הַיּוֹם לַעֲשׂוֹתָם:

Deuteronomy 7
8–11

* ט מצותיו ק'.

Haftarah Va'etchanan, p. 428

and chose you—indeed, you are the smallest of peoples; **8]** but it was because the LORD loved you and kept the oath He made to your fathers that the LORD freed you with a mighty hand and rescued you from the house of bondage, from the power of Pharaoh king of Egypt.

9] Know, therefore, that only the LORD your God is God, the steadfast God who keeps His gracious covenant to the thousandth generation of those who love Him and keep His commandments, **10]** but who instantly requites with destruction those who reject Him—never slow with those who reject Him, but requiting them instantly. **11]** Therefore, observe faithfully the Instruction—the laws and the rules—with which I charge you today.

Chose you. On the concept of the Chosen People, see at Exod. 19.

8] *The Lord loved you.* His love is the foundation of the command to love Him.

9] *Steadfast God.* הָאֵל הַנֶּאֱמָן (ha-el ha-ne-eman), see at verse 12.
Thousandth generation. The Hebrew לְאֶלֶף דּוֹר

is a stylistic variance of לַאֲלָפִים in the Ten Commandments (Exod. 20:6 and Deut. 5:10).

10] *Instantly.* Literally, "to their faces," that is, while they can see and experience it.

11] *Therefore.* The sentence repeats the introduction of chapter 6, bringing this section to a close (and also the *sidrah Va'etchanan* which ends here).

96

פ פ פ

עקב

יג וְהָיָה עֵקֶב תִּשְׁמְעוּן אֵת הַמִּשְׁפָּטִים הָאֵלֶּה וּשְׁמַרְתֶּם

דברים ז

וַעֲשִׂיתֶם אֹתָם וְשָׁמַר יְהֹוָה אֱלֹהֶיךָ לְךָ אֶת־הַבְּרִית

יב—טו

יג וְאֶת־הַחֶסֶד אֲשֶׁר נִשְׁבַּע לַאֲבֹתֶיךָ: וַאֲהֵבְךָ וּבֵרַכְךָ

וְהִרְבֶּךָ וּבֵרַךְ פְּרִי־בִטְנְךָ וּפְרִי־אַדְמָתֶךָ דְּגָנְךָ

וְתִירֹשְׁךָ וְיִצְהָרֶךָ שְׁגַר אֲלָפֶיךָ וְעַשְׁתְּרֹת צֹאנֶךָ עַל

יד הָאֲדָמָה אֲשֶׁר־נִשְׁבַּע לַאֲבֹתֶיךָ לָתֶת לָךְ: בָּרוּךְ

Ekev
Deuteronomy 7
12—15

תִּהְיֶה מִכָּל־הָעַמִּים לֹא־יִהְיֶה בְךָ עָקָר וַעֲקָרָה

טו וּבִבְהֶמְתֶּךָ: וְהֵסִיר יְהֹוָה מִמְּךָ כָּל־חֹלִי וְכָל־מַדְוֵי

12] And if you do obey these rules and observe them faithfully, the LORD your God will maintain for you the gracious covenant that He made on oath with your fathers: 13] He will love you and bless you and multiply you; He will bless the issue of your womb and the produce of your soil, your new grain and wine and oil, the calving of your herd and the lambing of your flock, in the land that He swore to your fathers to give you. 14] You shall be blessed above all other peoples: there shall be no sterile male or female among you or among your livestock. 15] The LORD will ward off from you all sickness; He will not bring upon you any of the

12] *And if you do.* The new *sidrah Ekev* is named after the second Hebrew word, עֵקֶב, literally, "on the heel of," i.e., in consequence of your obeisance. The catalogue of blessings that begins here and reaches to verse 24 more than counterbalances the brief warnings in verses 4 and 10 (a full catalogue of blessings and curses is presented in chapter 28). It becomes clear—and this remains a prominent theme of Deuteronomy—that God's execution of the covenantal terms depends on Israel. He is the unchanging, faithful God, and

therefore Israel's fate for good or evil depends essentially on the people itself.

The blessings present the familiar recital of protection, fertility of body and soil, health and victory [8].

13] *Calving.* עַשְׁתְּרֹת (*ashterot*), a word related to Ashtoreth, a Canaanite goddess concerned with fertility.

14] *No sterile male or female.* A hyperbolic expression, not to be understood literally.

97

מִצְרַיִם הָרָעִים אֲשֶׁר יָדַעְתָּ לֹא יְשִׂימָם בָּךְ וּנְתָנָם

טז בְּכָל־שֹׂנְאֶיךָ: וְאָכַלְתָּ אֶת־כָּל־הָעַמִּים אֲשֶׁר יְהֹוָה

אֱלֹהֶיךָ נֹתֵן לָךְ לֹא־תָחוֹס עֵינְךָ עֲלֵיהֶם וְלֹא תַעֲבֹד

יז אֶת־אֱלֹהֵיהֶם כִּי־מוֹקֵשׁ הוּא לָךְ: ס כִּי תֹאמַר

בִּלְבָבְךָ רַבִּים הַגּוֹיִם הָאֵלֶּה מִמֶּנִּי אֵיכָה אוּכַל

יח לְהוֹרִישָׁם: לֹא תִירָא מֵהֶם זָכֹר תִּזְכֹּר אֵת אֲשֶׁר־

יט עָשָׂה יְהֹוָה אֱלֹהֶיךָ לְפַרְעֹה וּלְכָל־מִצְרָיִם: הַמַּסֹּת

הַגְּדֹלֹת אֲשֶׁר־רָאוּ עֵינֶיךָ וְהָאֹתֹת וְהַמֹּפְתִים וְהַיָּד

הַחֲזָקָה וְהַזְּרֹעַ הַנְּטוּיָה אֲשֶׁר הוֹצִאֲךָ יְהֹוָה אֱלֹהֶיךָ

כֵּן־יַעֲשֶׂה יְהֹוָה אֱלֹהֶיךָ לְכָל־הָעַמִּים אֲשֶׁר־אַתָּה יָרֵא

Deuteronomy 7
16–19

dreadful diseases of Egypt, about which you know, but will inflict them upon all your enemies.

16] You shall destroy all the peoples that the LORD your God delivers to you, showing them no pity. And you shall not worship their gods, for that would be a snare to you.   **17]** Should you say to yourselves, "These nations are more numerous than we; how can we dispossess them?"   **18]** You need have no fear of them. You have but to bear in mind what the LORD your God did to Pharaoh and all the Egyptians: **19]** the wondrous acts that you saw with your own eyes, the signs and the portents, the mighty hand, and the outstretched arm by which the LORD your God liberated you. Thus will the LORD your God do to all the peoples you now fear.

15] *Dreadful diseases of Egypt.* Probably a reference to dysentery, ophthalmia, and especially elephantiasis; the last was called by the Roman historian Pliny "the particular Egyptian disease" [9].

16] *Destroy.* Literally, "eat," "consume." The idiom occurs also in Num. 13:32 (where the spies report that Canaan "consumes" its inhabitants).

In Num. 14:9, the potential enemy is called "our bread," that is, our prey.

Showing them no pity. See commentary below.

98

כ מִפְּנֵיהֶם: וְגַם אֶת־הַצִּרְעָה יְשַׁלַּח יְהֹוָה אֱלֹהֶיךָ בָּם

כא עַד־אֲבֹד הַנִּשְׁאָרִים וְהַנִּסְתָּרִים מִפָּנֶיךָ: לֹא תַעֲרֹץ

מִפְּנֵיהֶם כִּי־יְהֹוָה אֱלֹהֶיךָ בְּקִרְבֶּךָ אֵל גָּדוֹל וְנוֹרָא:

כב וְנָשַׁל יְהֹוָה אֱלֹהֶיךָ אֶת־הַגּוֹיִם הָאֵל מִפָּנֶיךָ מְעַט

מְעָט לֹא תוּכַל כַּלֹּתָם מַהֵר פֶּן־תִּרְבֶּה עָלֶיךָ חַיַּת

כג הַשָּׂדֶה: וּנְתָנָם יְהֹוָה אֱלֹהֶיךָ לְפָנֶיךָ וְהָמָם מְהוּמָה

כד גְדֹלָה עַד הִשָּׁמְדָם: וְנָתַן מַלְכֵיהֶם בְּיָדֶךָ וְהַאֲבַדְתָּ

אֶת־שְׁמָם מִתַּחַת הַשָּׁמָיִם לֹא־יִתְיַצֵּב אִישׁ בְּפָנֶיךָ

כה עַד הִשְׁמִדְךָ אֹתָם: פְּסִילֵי אֱלֹהֵיהֶם תִּשְׂרְפוּן בָּאֵשׁ

Deuteronomy 7
20—25

* כב סבורין האלה.

20] The Lord your God will also send a plague against them, until those who are left in hiding perish before you. **21]** Do not stand in dread of them, for the Lord your God is in your midst, a great and awesome God.

22] The Lord your God will dislodge those peoples before you little by little; you will not be able to put an end to them at once, else the wild beasts would multiply to your hurt. **23]** The Lord your God will deliver them up to you, throwing them into utter panic until they are wiped out. **24]** He will deliver their kings into your hand, and you shall obliterate their name from under the heavens; no man shall stand up to you, until you have wiped them out.

25] You shall consign the images of their gods to the fire; you shall not covet

20] *Plague.* Others, "hornet," "panic." See at Exod. 23:28.

22] *Little by little.* This is the same prediction found in Exod. 23:29–30 and explains ex-post-facto why God decided not to make the conquest easy. The actual and full acquisition took several hundred years, and the native population was assimilated and not driven off or killed.

In the Book of Judges, various reasons are given for the gradual rather than quick occupation: God wanted to punish Israel (2:3); to test Israel (3:1, 4); to make a new generation taste war (3:2).

99

לֹא־תַחְמֹד כֶּסֶף וְזָהָב עֲלֵיהֶם וְלָקַחְתָּ לָךְ פֶּן תִּוָּקֵשׁ
כו בּוֹ כִּי תוֹעֲבַת יְהֹוָה אֱלֹהֶיךָ הוּא: וְלֹא־תָבִיא תוֹעֵבָה
אֶל־בֵּיתֶךָ וְהָיִיתָ חֵרֶם כָּמֹהוּ שַׁקֵּץ תְּשַׁקְּצֶנּוּ וְתַעֵב
תְּתַעֲבֶנּוּ כִּי־חֵרֶם הוּא: פ

the silver and gold on them and keep it for yourselves, lest you be ensnared thereby; for that is abhorrent to the LORD your God.   26] You must not bring an abhorrent thing into your house, or you will be proscribed like it; you must reject it as abominable and abhorrent, for it is proscribed.

25] *Silver and gold on them.* Nothing was to be used that was at any time connected with the idols.

The Treatment of Conquered Nations

The Torah instructs the Israelites to "doom" the idolatrous nations in Canaan and to show them no pity. This provision is in stark contrast to the pervasive humaneness of the book, and therefore attempts of various kinds have been made to explain or defend this harshness and to make clear how a loving and caring God could be seen to issue such edicts.

An early attempt was made in talmudic days. The Hebrew for "show them no pity" (לֹא תְחָנֵּם) was read as "do not grant them [land]," as if the text read לֹא תַחֲנֵם, that is, do not sell real estate to them—a rendering which leaned on the warning in Exod. 23:33 not to let them dwell "in your land" [10]. But even if one would deem this interpretation feasible (which it is not, in view of the clear Masoretic text), one could not argue away the provision of Deut. 20:16 which, using another word, unequivocally says, "You shall not let a soul remain alive."

The text has further been defended on the grounds of necessity: unless the native people were done away with, they would ensnare Israel with their idolatrous practices, and the maintenance of the Sinaitic covenant was a task overshadowing all else. God's plans for humanity could not and cannot be measured by human considerations. To emphasize this point, S. R. Hirsch interpreted the twice-issued injunction of verses 2 and 16 to show that repetition was needed because it went so much against the sensibilities of the Israelites [11]. However, no student of history can easily accept such a reading, for all too many humans have fallen victim to inquisitors and crusading warriors who pretended to act out of the highest religious motives.

And already in talmudic times the notion was rejected that an Almighty God would agree to wipe idolatry off the face of the earth, though He had the power to do so.

One comes closer to an understanding of the Torah if one abandons efforts to shield it from criticism and sees it in the light of its own time, its values, and standards.[1] "The custom to 'dedicate' an enemy to the deity, or to ban him, or after a victory to annihilate him, is told us of various Near Eastern nations[2] as well as of the Greeks, Romans, Celts, and Germans. Since the sensitivities of the ancients were not offended by the rigor of this procedure, Moses could use this harsh war practice as a means to shield Israel from pagan infection" [13].

But even this interpretation does not do the text full justice, for it ascribes to Moses a point of view which may not have been his at all. Moreover, and most important: the unyielding tenor of these provisions stands in sharp contrast to the fact that such a policy of annihilation was never carried out—the Canaanites were *not* annihilated. In fact, in Judg. 3:1, God himself is said to have abrogated His original command (see above, at verse 22). Later, in retrospect—taking Deuteronomy to be a post-settlement and not a Mosaic document—the reader was told that the rampant idolatry which characterized Israel's history for centuries could have been avoided had the native peoples been destroyed. Note that the sermon warns the Israelites not to intermarry with the idolaters —the very idolaters who were supposed to be doomed!

A proper understanding, then, would view these passages as retrojections of what could and might have been, and the senti-

---

[1] This approach is easier for the liberal who sees the Torah as a human document than for a fundamentalist who considers it the word of God.

[2] The Mesha stone (ninth century B.C.E.) tells of Nebo's 7,000 Israelites—"men, boys, women, girls, and maidservants"—being "devoted" to Ashtar-Chemosh [12].

ments were acceptable in view of the common practices of the times.

Mixed Marriage

The practice of encouraging endogamy (marriage within the group) was not unique to Israel, but, because the Jewish people down to the present age have generally supported it and have discouraged exogamy (marriage out of the group), the purpose and desirability of such practices continue to be debated. It is important, however, to avoid the projection of latter-day religious, psychological, and sociological opinions onto the discussion of the biblical text.

An example of such projection is the talmudic discussion of the warning in verse 3, not to intermarry with the sons and daughters of the seven Canaanite nations. The Talmud, proceeding from the practice of avoiding marriage with *any* other nation and assuming that such was already the case in biblical days, reasoned as follows: Since marriage with unconverted Gentiles of any kind was prohibited, verse 3 could only mean to issue an additional restriction, namely, not to marry Canaanites, *even if converted* [14]. This is similar to the discussion about Abraham's observance of the prohibition of mixing milk and meat, which is postbiblical, and rests on biblical law which is post-Abrahamitic [15].

There is no question that endogamy was encouraged amongst the Israelites from earliest days on. This may be gathered from the stories of Abraham (instructing his servant to find a wife for his son from his own family) or Rebekah (whose unhappiness over Esau's marriages to foreign women was especially recorded; Gen. 26:34–35). But, at the same time, exogamous alliances did take place throughout the early centuries of Israel's existence; thus, Moses, Solomon, and Ahab took foreign wives, as did the tribal forefathers Simeon and Joseph. Not until the time of Ezra, that is, about 400 B.C.E., after the exiles' return from Babylon, were such marriages deemed socially and politically so undesirable that they had to be dissolved (see Ezra 9). In this phase of history, the consolidation of religious commitment through strictly enforced endogamy appeared as a necessary policy, one which persisted thereafter into modern times.[3]

We may assume, therefore, that Deuteronomy attempted to codify a principle but that as in other matters the actual carrying out of the law fell far short of the ideal. At stake was the religious purity of both people and land, buttressed by the conviction that only a nation totally consecrated to God could be His partner in the covenant. For it was not enough for Israel to merely exist and survive with a national identity; it was to be a special people, a "holy nation"—and therefore only families in whose midst God and Torah-conscious generations would be reared could be entrusted with this task. The prohibition against out-marriages[4] *was religious* in nature, it had nothing to do with racial ideas, and with superiority only in the sense that Israel had a unique relation with the Holy One which needed to be protected at all costs [16].

Endogamous marriage represented no problems for Diaspora Jews in host societies that disapproved of or forbade mixed marriages. But, when such restraints were removed and Jews themselves became less

---

[3] The Book of Ruth may have been written to counteract this development and may have been written as a defense of exogamy.

[4] See further, for instance, Num. 25:1 ff.; 31:15 f.; Josh. 23:7; Judg. 3:6; I Kings 2:1.

attentive to traditional ways, the rate of exogamous marriages increased sharply. Once exogamous patterns become established they develop their own dynamic thrust. While the great majority of Jews continue to endorse the old biblical prohibitions, at least in theory, there is no agreement on how to treat the actual spread of mixed marriages and how to keep their offspring in the Jewish fold. In the Reform movement especially, the discussion of means and ends has been vigorous, with no resolution in sight [17]. The problem is ultimately an expression of the tension of contrasting tendencies in Jewish history: its expanding and contracting heartbeats, the broadening and the narrowing of peoplehood. Together they give the biblical concern an abiding relevancy.

GLEANINGS

Mixed Marriage

Though the halachah prohibits mixed marriage for both men and women and does not recognize such marriages as religiously valid, it considers the children of Jewish mothers and gentile (unconverted) fathers as Jewish, and the offspring of Jewish fathers and gentile (unconverted) mothers as gentile.[5]

Reform Judaism, though it too continues to discourage mixed marriages, recognizes their validity once they have been contracted and accepts the offspring of these unions as Jewish if the parents—and, later, the children themselves—affirm their Jewish identity [19].

Today

In the Hebrew text the words "observe" and "today" stand together, לַעֲשׂוֹתָם הַיּוֹם, as a reminder to observe God's commandments today and not to delay them until tomorrow (that is, after death).　　　　　TALMUD [20]

Observe Them Faithfully (Deut. 7:12)

Israel's obedience is required for the totality of Torah, and not for one command in preference to another. No mitzvah is "superior" or "inferior": "Be heedful of a light precept as of a grave one, for you do not know the measure of reward for each command."　　　MISHNAH AND MIDRASH [21]

The Last Mitzvah

The Baal Shem Tov explained the opening words of the *sidrah* וְהָיָה עֵקֶב (verse 12), as if they meant "and the end shall be . . . ."[6] Therefore, he concluded, consider every mitzvah as the last you will be able to perform in your life.

M. HACOHEN [22]

Plural and Singular (verse 12)

The warning "If, then, *you* obey . . ." is in Hebrew couched in the plural, but the reward, "God will keep with *you* the gracious covenant," in the singular. One can warn all, but only individuals can perform the mitzvah and merit the reward.　　　　　　CHASIDIC [23]

Halachah

(Verse 25 commands the destruction of heathen images. Does this include pagan antiques?)

If the pagans themselves have abandoned or mutilated their idols they have destroyed their status as forbidden images and the statues may be acquired or kept. An idolater can abrogate the status of an idol, an Israelite cannot.

TALMUD [24]

The Sanctity of One's Home (verse 26)

The prohibition to bring idols into one's house implies the prohibition to sell the house to an idolater. (However, this obtains only in Eretz Yisrael.)　　　　　　TALMUD [25]

---

[5] The proof text (a combination of verses 3 and 4) is interpreted this way: the Hebrew of verse 4 begins with a masculine construction, saying literally "when *he* (the gentile husband) turns your son away from Me." Thus, though the child has a gentile father (and a Jewish mother), he is still called "your son" (i.e., an acknowledged Jew). For lack of the reverse expression, the child of a gentile mother is regarded as gentile [18].

[6] Understanding עֵקֶב to mean "end" (literally, "heel").

The Good Life

The discourse now turns to the inner dimensions of Israel's existence. If it is lived in accordance with God's will, its material rewards will be readily apparent, but these will not tell the whole story. Moses hopes that Israel will come to understand the munificence of God and the generous protection He has afforded His children and will appreciate that their good fortune is due primarily to Him and not to their own power. The forty long years they spent in the desert were a necessary education for them, so that they might learn that human dependence on God must be total, that "man does not live on bread alone, but that man may live on anything that the Lord decrees" (8:3). Thus it is not only Israel's actions that are important, but also its state of mind, its humility, its feeling of essential powerlessness in the face of the Lord's might.

The land Israel will inherit (or, in Josianic days,[1] land already inherited) is called "a good land"(8:7), whose wealth is described in detail. That very wealth, however, has its dangers, and Israel is warned that affluence is likely to engender false pride. Once again, the by now familiar threat is repeated: If despite God's favors in past and present the people turn to other gods, the divine wrath will be unleashed and Israel "shall certainly perish" (8:19).

A brief postscript (9:1–5) emphasizes once more that it was God whose will bestowed the land on Israel and that a contributing factor in Israel's

---

[1] In the seventh century B.C.E., when Deuteronomy was most likely composed (see introduction).

successful occupation of the land was the wickedness of the native peoples, their immorality and idolatry, which caused them to lose their title to the Holy Land.[2] This statement implies, of course, that Israel too will possess Canaan only as long as it justifies God's trust and does not defile the sacredness of the soil.

[2] The idea that possession of Canaan depends on the morality of the inhabitants is found also in Gen. 15:16 and Lev. 18:24 ff.

א כָּל־הַמִּצְוָה אֲשֶׁר אָנֹכִי מְצַוְּךָ הַיּוֹם תִּשְׁמְרוּן לַעֲשׂוֹת
לְמַעַן תִּחְיוּן וּרְבִיתֶם וּבָאתֶם וִירִשְׁתֶּם אֶת־הָאָרֶץ
ב אֲשֶׁר־נִשְׁבַּע יְהֹוָה לַאֲבֹתֵיכֶם: וְזָכַרְתָּ אֶת־כָּל־הַדֶּרֶךְ
אֲשֶׁר הוֹלִיכֲךָ יְהֹוָה אֱלֹהֶיךָ זֶה אַרְבָּעִים שָׁנָה
בַּמִּדְבָּר לְמַעַן עַנֹּתְךָ לְנַסֹּתְךָ לָדַעַת אֶת־אֲשֶׁר
ג בִּלְבָבְךָ הֲתִשְׁמֹר מִצְוֹתָו* אִם־לֹא: וַיְעַנְּךָ וַיַּרְעִבֶךָ
וַיַּאֲכִלְךָ אֶת־הַמָּן אֲשֶׁר לֹא־יָדַעְתָּ וְלֹא יָדְעוּן אֲבֹתֶיךָ
לְמַעַן הוֹדִיעֲךָ כִּי לֹא עַל־הַלֶּחֶם לְבַדּוֹ יִחְיֶה הָאָדָם
ד כִּי עַל־כָּל־מוֹצָא פִי־יְהֹוָה יִחְיֶה הָאָדָם: שִׂמְלָתְךָ
לֹא בָלְתָה מֵעָלֶיךָ וְרַגְלְךָ לֹא בָצֵקָה זֶה אַרְבָּעִים

Deuteronomy 8
1–4

* ב מצותיו ק׳.

1] You shall faithfully observe all the Instruction that I enjoin upon you today, that you may thrive and increase and be able to occupy the land which the LORD promised on oath to your fathers.

2] Remember the long way that the LORD your God has made you travel in the wilderness these past forty years, that He might test you by hardships to learn what was in your hearts: whether you would keep His commandments or not. 3] He subjected you to the hardship of hunger and then gave you manna to eat, which neither you nor your fathers had ever known, in order to teach you that man does not live on bread alone, but that man may live on anything that the LORD decrees.   4] The clothes upon you did not wear out, nor did your feet swell these

8:2] *That He might test you by hardships.* Literally, "in order to afflict you for the purpose of testing you." The same word עַנּוֹת (*anot,* afflict) is used for the hardships imposed on Israel by the Egyptians (Exod. 1:11). In Egypt the afflictions were the work of an oppressor; in the desert they were instituted by God for Israel's sake.

3] *Manna.* See Exodus, chapter 16. Whatever explanations of the natural background of this food may be offered (such as believing it to have been an exudation and secretion by symbiotic insects living on tamarisks), the Torah perceived of manna as a supernatural gift. The test referred to in the preceding verse consisted of seeing whether Israel could accommodate itself to continued dependence on God [1].

4] *Clothes . . . did not wear out.* A hyperbole describing God's miraculous care.

ה שָׁנָה: וְיָדַעְתָּ עִם־לְבָבֶךָ כִּי כַּאֲשֶׁר יְיַסֵּר אִישׁ אֶת־

ו בְּנוֹ יְהֹוָה אֱלֹהֶיךָ מְיַסְּרֶךָּ: וְשָׁמַרְתָּ אֶת־מִצְוֺת

ז יְהֹוָה אֱלֹהֶיךָ לָלֶכֶת בִּדְרָכָיו וּלְיִרְאָה אֹתוֹ: כִּי

יְהֹוָה אֱלֹהֶיךָ מְבִיאֲךָ אֶל־אֶרֶץ טוֹבָה אֶרֶץ נַחֲלֵי

ח מַיִם עֲיָנֹת וּתְהֹמֹת יֹצְאִים בַּבִּקְעָה וּבָהָר: אֶרֶץ

חִטָּה וּשְׂעֹרָה וְגֶפֶן וּתְאֵנָה וְרִמּוֹן אֶרֶץ־זֵית שֶׁמֶן

ט וּדְבָשׁ: אֶרֶץ אֲשֶׁר לֹא בְמִסְכֵּנֻת תֹּאכַל־בָּהּ לֶחֶם

לֹא־תֶחְסַר כֹּל בָּהּ אֶרֶץ אֲשֶׁר אֲבָנֶיהָ בַרְזֶל

י וּמֵהֲרָרֶיהָ תַּחְצֹב נְחֹשֶׁת: וְאָכַלְתָּ וְשָׂבָעְתָּ וּבֵרַכְתָּ

אֶת־יְהֹוָה אֱלֹהֶיךָ עַל־הָאָרֶץ הַטֹּבָה אֲשֶׁר נָתַן־לָךְ:

Deuteronomy 8
5–10

forty years.   **5]** Bear in mind that the LORD your God disciplines you just as a man disciplines his son.   **6]** Therefore keep the commandments of the LORD your God: walk in His ways and revere Him.

7] For the LORD your God is bringing you into a good land, a land with streams and springs and fountains issuing from plain and hill;   **8]** a land of wheat and barley, of vines, figs, and pomegranates, a land of olive trees and honey;   **9]** a land where you may eat food without stint, where you will lack nothing; a land whose rocks are iron and from whose hills you can mine copper.   **10]** When you have eaten your fill, give thanks to the LORD your God for the good land which He has given you.

The Rabbis, however, understood this verse literally: If God could provide manna He could (and did) make the clothes of children grow along with them [2].

8] *A land of wheat and barley.* They continue to be the two chief field crops grown in the land today.

9] *Whose rocks are iron.* The reference is unclear, for iron was not mined in Canaan but was imported.

10] *Give thanks.* The obligation to thank God after the conclusion of a meal (בִּרְכַּת הַמָּזוֹן) is based on this verse (see Gleanings).

108

יא הִשָּׁ֣מֶר לְךָ֗ פֶּן־תִּשְׁכַּ֖ח אֶת־יְהוָ֣ה אֱלֹהֶ֑יךָ לְבִלְתִּ֣י שְׁמֹ֤ר
מִצְוֺתָיו֙ וּמִשְׁפָּטָ֣יו וְחֻקֹּתָ֔יו אֲשֶׁ֛ר אָנֹכִ֥י מְצַוְּךָ֖ הַיּֽוֹם׃

יב פֶּן־תֹּאכַ֖ל וְשָׂבָ֑עְתָּ וּבָתִּ֥ים טוֹבִ֛ים תִּבְנֶ֖ה וְיָשָֽׁבְתָּ׃

יג וּבְקָרְךָ֤ וְצֹֽאנְךָ֙ יִרְבְּיֻ֔ן וְכֶ֥סֶף וְזָהָ֖ב יִרְבֶּה־לָּ֑ךְ וְכֹ֥ל
יד אֲשֶׁר־לְךָ֖ יִרְבֶּֽה׃ וְרָ֖ם לְבָבֶ֑ךָ וְשָֽׁכַחְתָּ֙ אֶת־יְהוָ֣ה
אֱלֹהֶ֔יךָ הַמּוֹצִיאֲךָ֛ מֵאֶ֥רֶץ מִצְרַ֖יִם מִבֵּ֥ית עֲבָדִֽים׃

טו הַמּוֹלִֽיכֲךָ֞ בַּמִּדְבָּ֣ר ׀ הַגָּדֹ֣ל וְהַנּוֹרָ֗א נָחָ֤שׁ ׀ שָׂרָף֙ וְעַקְרָ֔ב
וְצִמָּא֖וֹן אֲשֶׁ֣ר אֵֽין־מָ֑יִם הַמּוֹצִ֤יא לְךָ֙ מַ֔יִם מִצּ֖וּר
טז הַֽחַלָּמִֽישׁ׃ הַמַּֽאֲכִ֨לְךָ֥ מָן֙ בַּמִּדְבָּ֔ר אֲשֶׁ֥ר לֹא־יָדְע֖וּן
אֲבֹתֶ֑יךָ לְמַ֣עַן עַנֹּֽתְךָ֗ וּלְמַ֙עַן֙ נַסֹּתֶ֔ךָ לְהֵיטִֽבְךָ֖
יז בְּאַחֲרִיתֶֽךָ׃ וְאָמַרְתָּ֖ בִּלְבָבֶ֑ךָ כֹּחִי֙ וְעֹ֣צֶם יָדִ֔י עָ֤שָׂה

Deuteronomy 8

11–17

11] Take care lest you forget the LORD your God and fail to keep His commandments, His rules, and His laws, which I enjoin upon you today. 12] When you have eaten your fill, and have built fine houses to live in, 13] and your herds and flocks have multiplied, and your silver and gold have increased, and everything you own has prospered, 14] beware lest your heart grow haughty and you forget the LORD your God—who freed you from the land of Egypt, the house of bondage; 15] who led you through the great and terrible wilderness with its *seraph* serpents and scorpions, a parched land with no water in it, who brought forth water for you from the flinty rock; 16] who fed you in the wilderness with manna, which your fathers had never known, in order to test you by hardships only to benefit you in the end— 17] and you say to yourselves, "My own power and the might of my

---

15] *Seraph serpents.* The meaning of "seraph" is uncertain; some render it "fiery," a presumed reference to snake bites that caused an inflammation of the skin. See at Num. 21:6.

יח לִי אֶת־הַחַיִל הַזֶּה: וְזָכַרְתָּ אֶת־יְהוָה אֱלֹהֶיךָ כִּי הוּא
הַנֹּתֵן לְךָ כֹּחַ לַעֲשׂוֹת חָיִל לְמַעַן הָקִים אֶת־בְּרִיתוֹ
אֲשֶׁר נִשְׁבַּע לַאֲבֹתֶיךָ כַּיּוֹם הַזֶּה: פ

יט וְהָיָה אִם־שָׁכֹחַ תִּשְׁכַּח אֶת־יְהוָה אֱלֹהֶיךָ וְהָלַכְתָּ
אַחֲרֵי אֱלֹהִים אֲחֵרִים וַעֲבַדְתָּם וְהִשְׁתַּחֲוִיתָ לָהֶם
כ הַעִדֹתִי בָכֶם הַיּוֹם כִּי אָבֹד תֹּאבֵדוּן: כַּגּוֹיִם אֲשֶׁר
יְהוָה מַאֲבִיד מִפְּנֵיכֶם כֵּן תֹּאבֵדוּן עֵקֶב לֹא תִשְׁמְעוּן
בְּקוֹל יְהוָה אֱלֹהֵיכֶם:

א שְׁמַע יִשְׂרָאֵל אַתָּה עֹבֵר הַיּוֹם אֶת־הַיַּרְדֵּן לָבֹא
לָרֶשֶׁת גּוֹיִם גְּדֹלִים וַעֲצֻמִים מִמֶּךָּ עָרִים גְּדֹלֹת
ב וּבְצֻרֹת בַּשָּׁמָיִם: עַם־גָּדוֹל וָרָם בְּנֵי עֲנָקִים אֲשֶׁר

own hand have won this wealth for me." **18]** Remember that it is the Lord your God who gives you the power to get wealth, in fulfillment of the covenant that He made on oath with your fathers, as is still the case.

19] If you do forget the Lord your God and follow other gods to serve them or bow down to them, I warn you this day that you shall certainly perish; **20]** like the nations that the Lord will cause to perish before you, so shall you perish—because you did not heed the Lord your God.

1] Hear, O Israel! You are about to cross the Jordan to invade and dispossess nations greater and more populous than you: great cities with walls sky-high; **2]** a people great and tall, the Anakites, of whom you have knowledge; for you

---

18] *As is still the case.* Moses emphasizes that the covenant continues to exist.

9:1] *Walls sky-high.* See at 1:28.

2] *Anakites of whom you have knowledge.* Because the messengers who spied out the land told you about them; see Num. 13:28; Deut. 1:28.

אַתָּה יָדַעְתָּ וְאַתָּה שָׁמַעְתָּ מִי יִתְיַצֵּב לִפְנֵי בְּנֵי

ג עֲנָק: וְיָדַעְתָּ הַיּוֹם כִּי יְהוָֹה אֱלֹהֶיךָ הוּא־הָעֹבֵר

לְפָנֶיךָ אֵשׁ אֹכְלָה הוּא יַשְׁמִידֵם וְהוּא יַכְנִיעֵם לְפָנֶיךָ

וְהוֹרַשְׁתָּם וְהַאֲבַדְתָּם מַהֵר כַּאֲשֶׁר דִּבֶּר יְהוָֹה לָךְ:

ד אַל־תֹּאמַר בִּלְבָבְךָ בַּהֲדֹף יְהוָֹה אֱלֹהֶיךָ אֹתָם

מִלְּפָנֶיךָ לֵאמֹר בְּצִדְקָתִי הֱבִיאַנִי יְהוָֹה לָרֶשֶׁת אֶת־

הָאָרֶץ הַזֹּאת וּבְרִשְׁעַת הַגּוֹיִם הָאֵלֶּה יְהוָֹה מוֹרִישָׁם

ה מִפָּנֶיךָ: לֹא בְצִדְקָתְךָ וּבְיֹשֶׁר לְבָבְךָ אַתָּה בָא

לָרֶשֶׁת אֶת־אַרְצָם כִּי בְּרִשְׁעַת הַגּוֹיִם הָאֵלֶּה יְהוָֹה

Deuteronomy 9
3–5

have heard it said, "Who can stand up to the children of Anak?"   3] Know then this day that none other than the LORD your God is crossing at your head, a devouring fire; it is He who will wipe them out. He will subdue them before you, that you may quickly dispossess and destroy them, as the LORD promised you. 4] And when the LORD your God has thrust them from your path, say not to yourselves, "The LORD has enabled me to occupy this land because of my virtues"; it is rather because of the wickedness of those nations that the LORD is dispossessing them before you.   5] It is not because of your virtues and your rectitude that you will be able to occupy their country, but because of the wickedness of those nations

3] *A devouring fire*. A figure of speech recalling the image of the pillar of fire that led the people by night (Exod. 40:38).

Quickly. In 7:22, Israel was told that the land could be conquered only "little by little." The two promises may be examples of different foci: in the earlier passage the emphasis was on the explanation of failure; here the stress is on anticipated success.

Most modern scholars see the two verses as arising from different sources; similarly, the Book of Joshua stresses the quickness of the conquest, and the Book of Judges its slowness.

4] *Rather because of the wickedness of those nations*. The phrase duplicates verse 5 and may be the erroneous addition of a scribe; it is missing in the Septuagint. See also above, footnote 2.

אֱלֹהֶיךָ מוֹרִישָׁם מִפָּנֶיךָ וּלְמַעַן הָקִים אֶת־הַדָּבָר אֲשֶׁר נִשְׁבַּע יְהֹוָה לַאֲבֹתֶיךָ לְאַבְרָהָם לְיִצְחָק וּלְיַעֲקֹב:

the Lord your God is dispossessing them before you, and in order to fulfill the oath that the Lord made to your fathers, Abraham, Isaac, and Jacob.

Not on Bread Alone

The saying "Man does not live on bread alone" (8:3) is firmly ensconced in the English language, but the meaning which those who quote it wish to convey thereby is not at all what the Torah itself expresses. Popularly spoken, the quotation only encompasses the first part of the sentence and has come to mean: human beings are not fulfilled by material things alone; there is another, spiritual dimension of life which makes it truly worthwhile. The full text hardly allows for this interpretation,[1] though what it means precisely may be in some doubt.

There is no question about the broader meaning of the text: God taught you in the wilderness that He could meet your needs by whatever means He chose. He gave you manna to show you that you would be sustained through His providence, whether you had bread or not. This time He sent manna, another time He could choose to care for you in a different way. Such is the general import of the statement; it fits the context which relates God's desire to educate His people in a true understanding of their own limitations on the one hand and His limitless power on the other [3].

There is another dimension to the Hebrew text. Literally, the second half of the verse says that man lives עַל כָּל־מוֹצָא פִי־יְהֹוָה, "by any product of God's mouth." Our translation renders the idiom properly as "anything that the Lord decrees," that is, God's word and will are the cause of every material thing, just as the world itself came into being by His word. The process of creation was dependent on God's word (Gen. 1), and so is Israel, whom He has fashioned.[2]

Chastisements of Love

In stating that God tried Israel by hardships in the wilderness (8:2–3) the Torah enunciates an important principle of faith. When Israel suffered, it says, it suffered because God in His very love of Israel so willed it. The Psalmist put it this way:

> Happy is the man whom You discipline,
> O Lord . . .
> To give him tranquillity in times of
> misfortune.
>
> (94:12–13)

or:

> It was good for me that I was humbled,
> so that I might learn Your laws.
>
> (119:71)

By chastisements of love (יִסּוּרִין שֶׁל אַהֲבָה, *yisurin shel ahavah*), as tradition came to call them, a loving Father educates and purifies His children. In doing so, He too may be said to experience suffering, to weep over the bitter effects of the afflictions He himself has brought about; nonetheless He must do what divine necessity demands [4].

In postbiblical and early medieval times this doctrine came to explain the realities of human suffering in general and Israel's calamities in particular. It allowed for the protests of a Job who questioned the justice of God, but who in the end surrendered to the superior wisdom of the One before whom he stood in awe though he could not fathom His design. This, so the doctrine held, was Israel's fate. Chosen by divine decision it had become God's stake in the perfection of the human race, and, if the Children of Israel had to endure sufferings to merit this choice, it was worth the price. This teaching, while it

---

[1] It should be noted, however, that Ibn Ezra comes close to it when he says that human beings are sustained by what emanates from the heavenly spheres (עֶלְיוֹנִים) and these emanations are of a spiritual nature.

[2] An Egyptian source speaks of the god Ptah, "who maintains all humans with his food, in whose power are length of days, fate, and riches; one lives from that which issues from his mouth."

offered a total defense of God, also demanded total faith and to a significant extent had to surrender the human understanding of what constituted justice on this earth.

Maimonides's opposition to this teaching did much to weaken its hold on rabbinic and popular belief [5]. He distinguished between three types of suffering: (1) those caused by natural causes, like earthquakes—they are part of our physical existence which itself is ultimately destructible; (2) those caused by social corruption, like wars—these are society's burden and responsibility; and, finally, (3) that suffering we bring upon ourselves. In this analysis *yisurin shel ahavah* have no place at all and were therefore to be rejected as a general explanation of injustice, evil, and suffering—even though in some few instances, such as the case stated in Deut. 8:2–3, they were accepted as an authentic interpretation of divine and human reality.

Nowadays, after Auschwitz, the broader doctrine has disappeared; manifestly it could not be held that a benevolent God caused the destruction of six million of His people for their own good. In the light of such changes in the nature of belief, the abiding validity of the biblical statement itself must also be drawn into the question. In the Torah's telling, Moses believed God to have been a disciplining Father to Israel, an interpretation which we today need not find compelling. This theology, cogent for many centuries, will hardly convince the modern reader whose concept of God differs from the Bible's premise of an all-powerful Lord who deals with His people as they deserve and He determines.

The Source of Wealth

In no small measure the discourse presents a severe indictment of Israel's society. While it is phrased as a warning of something that will happen in the future, the history of Deuteronomy suggests a different setting: brought to light (and probably written) during the reign of King Josiah, the book meant to address first and foremost its own time. If therefore Moses is portrayed as speaking of the corrosive effects of affluence (8:11 ff.) we may see in this a comment on conditions prevailing in Judah in the seventh century B.C.E. Then, as many times later, physical well-being led people to regard their own power as the chief source of their wealth. In doing so they lost sight of its ultimate wellspring, the gracious providence of God. In ringing terms the sermon calls the people to greater humility and lessened pride: "Remember that it is the Lord your God who gives you the power to get wealth" (8:18).

It was also a time when the Promised Land was seen to have richly provided for its inhabitants. Its agriculture was flourishing, and even the Negev had its share of productive communities. Its hills were amply forested, the water supply was sufficient, and a modicum of mineral resources had been tapped. It was, as the Torah states emphatically, "a good land" (verse 7), and it would continue to be a source of blessing if its inhabitants would see themselves as stewards of God's gift and remain worthy of it by dint of their faithful observance of the covenant.

GLEANINGS

Grace before and after Meals

8:10 is the proof text for the בִּרְכַּת הַמָּזוֹן (*Birkat ha-Mazon*, the blessings spoken at the conclusion of a meal). The Rabbis extended the obligation and ruled that one should bless Him beforehand as well [6]. The purpose of these mitzvot is to make one realize that nature and human effort alone do not fully sustain us. Hence it was considered a sacrilege to "enjoy the gifts of this world without a benediction" [7].

Before the Meal

The halachah greatly elaborated on the variety of prayers which were to be said on different occasions, especially before a meal. The benedictions over bread and wine are the most frequently used, in fact, saying "*Ha-Motzi*"[3] became a term for pronouncing any prior blessing over food. Having spoken the *berachah* over bread one need not say blessings for other foods in the ensuing meal, except if one drinks wine over which the customary *berachah* should always be said—even if one drinks it in the middle of the meal [8].

After the Meal

According to the halachah, these blessings are obligatory if one has eaten as little as a *shiur zayit*, the measure of an olive; but the full grace is said only if some bread has been consumed. The blessings speak of God's grace, of gratitude for the Land of Israel as well as other signs of divine goodness, of Jerusalem to be rebuilt, and of hope for messianic redemption. Deut. 8:10 is recited in an early part of this litany of thanks, which may be spoken in any language. A shortened form of the *Birkat ha-Mazon* is provided for

those occasions when no bread was eaten or when it is not feasible to recite the entire version. Conservative and Reform synagogues have published such briefer forms of grace for public occasions, as do the (Reform) *Shabbat Manual* and *Gates of the House* for home use. The Reform Haggadah features both the shorter and longer versions [9].

Doubled

By blessing God we double our enjoyment of the food. JUDAH HALEVI [10]

On Bread (Deut. 8:3)

Note that it says *on* and not *by* bread alone. Man is bidden not to stake his life merely on gaining a livelihood: eating in order to work, working in order to eat. His true purpose should be learning in order to teach, observe, do, and uphold Torah in truth and faith. CHATAM SOFER [11]

Satisfaction

Your readiness to thank God after a meal is part of having "eaten your fill" (8:10).

The command addresses itself not merely to those who have satisfied their hunger but also, and especially, to those who are habitually well sated. CHASIDIC [12]

Lest Your Heart Grow Haughty (Deut. 8:14)

The greatest haughtiness is that of excessive piety. CHASIDIC [13]

Even Now

The translation says that God "*freed* you from the land of Egypt" (8:14), but the Hebrew reads literally "*frees* you"[4] even now. It is a reminder

---

[3] So called after the key verb in the *berachah* over bread: הַמּוֹצִיא לֶחֶם מִן הָאָרֶץ, "Who brings forth bread from the earth" (based on Ps. 104:14).

[4] הַמּוֹצִיאֲךָ (present participle) instead of הוֹצִיאֲךָ (past tense).

115

that God's liberation of His people has never ceased. CHASIDIC [14]

Insensitivity

In addressing Israel, Moses tells them, "You are about to cross the Jordan" (9:1). Thereby he hinted that they, but not he himself, would be so privileged, and he hoped that they might intercede for him with God. However, the people failed him; they were insensitive to his plea.

MIDRASH [15]

The Stiff-Necked People

Moses continues his appeal to the people by reminding them of their repeated trespasses. Of these, the incident of the golden calf stands out as a particularly odious offense against God, and Moses recalls it in some detail in order to buttress his main point: the Israelites are a stiff-necked people and God's favor has been bestowed upon them not because of their merits but rather despite their moral failures.

As befits an oration, it is weighted with judgmental epithets like "provoked," "sinful," "wicked," "defiant." The account is personal and emotional, quite in contrast to the tale in Exodus 32 which speaks in detached, objective tones.

Perhaps more than at any other time, Moses stresses his own role as intermediary between God and the people. Had it not been for him, he says, there would have been nothing to stop the avenging anger of the Lord against both Israel and Aaron. This emphasis on the leader's unique role is a distinguishing aspect of Deuteronomy. It is in fact presented with such insistence that later commentators wondered about the presumed modesty of the man Moses.

The disquisition is interrupted by four verses, 10:6–9. While Moses' address speaks of "I" and "we," the interlude switches to the impersonal "they." The passage brings us an important notation on the function of the Levites which rounds out what we have learned about them in other parts of the Torah.

י וְיָדַעְתָּ כִּי לֹא בְצִדְקָתְךָ יְהוָה אֱלֹהֶיךָ נֹתֵן
לְךָ אֶת־הָאָרֶץ הַטּוֹבָה הַזֹּאת לְרִשְׁתָּהּ כִּי עַם־
קְשֵׁה־עֹרֶף אָתָּה: זְכֹר אַל־תִּשְׁכַּח אֵת אֲשֶׁר־
הִקְצַפְתָּ אֶת־יְהוָה אֱלֹהֶיךָ בַּמִּדְבָּר לְמִן־הַיּוֹם אֲשֶׁר־
יָצָאתָ מֵאֶרֶץ מִצְרַיִם עַד־בֹּאֲכֶם עַד־הַמָּקוֹם הַזֶּה
ח מַמְרִים הֱיִיתֶם עִם־יְהוָה: וּבְחֹרֵב הִקְצַפְתֶּם אֶת־
ט יְהוָה וַיִּתְאַנַּף יְהוָה בָּכֶם לְהַשְׁמִיד אֶתְכֶם: בַּעֲלֹתִי
הָהָרָה לָקַחַת לוּחֹת הָאֲבָנִים לוּחֹת הַבְּרִית אֲשֶׁר־
כָּרַת יְהוָה עִמָּכֶם וָאֵשֵׁב בָּהָר אַרְבָּעִים יוֹם
וְאַרְבָּעִים לַיְלָה לֶחֶם לֹא אָכַלְתִּי וּמַיִם לֹא שָׁתִיתִי:

Deuteronomy 9
6–9

6] Know, then, that it is not for any virtue of yours that the LORD your God is giving you this good land to occupy; for you are a stiffnecked people. **7]** Remember, never forget, how you provoked the LORD your God to anger in the wilderness: from the day that you left the land of Egypt until you reached this place, you have continued defiant toward the LORD.

8] At Horeb you so provoked the LORD that the LORD was angry enough with you to have destroyed you. **9]** I had ascended the mountain to receive the tablets of stone, the Tablets of the Covenant that the LORD had made with you, and I stayed on the mountain forty days and forty nights, eating no bread and drinking

9:6] *Stiffnecked people.* Moses quotes the judgment issued by God at the incident of the golden calf (Exod. 32:9).

The Yom Kippur liturgy includes a congregational confession that we are still a stiff-necked people.

8] *At Horeb.* Where the most notable of the rebellions took place, the incident of the golden calf (Exod. 32–34). The murmurings at Marah and Massah had happened earlier.

You ... provoked. Moses addresses either the survivors of these events or the whole people whom he identifies with the past; see above, on Deut. 1:22.

י וַיִּתֵּן יְהֹוָה אֵלַי אֶת־שְׁנֵי לוּחֹת הָאֲבָנִים כְּתֻבִים

בְּאֶצְבַּע אֱלֹהִים וַעֲלֵיהֶם כְּכָל־הַדְּבָרִים אֲשֶׁר דִּבֶּר

יא יְהֹוָה עִמָּכֶם בָּהָר מִתּוֹךְ הָאֵשׁ בְּיוֹם הַקָּהָל: וַיְהִי

מִקֵּץ אַרְבָּעִים יוֹם וְאַרְבָּעִים לַיְלָה נָתַן יְהֹוָה אֵלַי

יב אֶת־שְׁנֵי לֻחֹת הָאֲבָנִים לֻחוֹת הַבְּרִית: וַיֹּאמֶר יְהֹוָה

אֵלַי קוּם רֵד מַהֵר מִזֶּה כִּי שִׁחֵת עַמְּךָ אֲשֶׁר הוֹצֵאתָ

מִמִּצְרָיִם סָרוּ מַהֵר מִן־הַדֶּרֶךְ אֲשֶׁר צִוִּיתִם עָשׂוּ

יג לָהֶם מַסֵּכָה: וַיֹּאמֶר יְהֹוָה אֵלַי לֵאמֹר רָאִיתִי אֶת־

יד הָעָם הַזֶּה וְהִנֵּה עַם־קְשֵׁה־עֹרֶף הוּא: הֶרֶף מִמֶּנִּי

no water.   **10]** And the LORD gave me the two tablets of stone inscribed by the finger of God, with the exact words that the LORD had addressed to you out of the fire on the day of the Assembly.

11] At the end of those forty days and forty nights, the LORD gave me the two tablets of stone, the Tablets of the Covenant.   **12]** And the LORD said to me, "Hurry, go down from here at once, for the people whom you brought out of Egypt have acted wickedly; they have been quick to stray from the path that I enjoined upon them; they have made themselves a molten image."   **13]** The LORD further said to me, "I see that this is a stiffnecked people.   **14]** Let Me alone and

10] *Day of the Assembly.* When the people stood at Horeb (or Sinai). The expression is rare; it occurs again in 10:4 and 18:16.

11] *The Lord gave me.* A repetition of verse 10, a stylistic device not uncommon in the Torah and in ancient Near Eastern literature. It may be best to translate verse 11 in the pluperfect: "Now when the Lord had given me. . . ."

   Tablets of the Covenant. On which the Ten Com-

mandments were inscribed.

12] *A molten image.* A calf (verse 16).

14] *Let Me alone.* The exclamation must be understood as a challenge to Moses to appease the divine anger, though Moses has not yet pleaded Israel's case [1]. The parallel passage in Exod. 32:10 uses a different idiom (הַנִּיחָה לִי instead of הֶרֶף מִמֶּנִּי) to express the same meaning.

וָאַשְׁמִידֵם וָאֶמְחֶה אֶת־שְׁמָם מִתַּחַת הַשָּׁמָיִם וָאֶעֱשֶׂה

טו אוֹתְךָ לְגוֹי־עָצוּם וָרָב מִמֶּנּוּ: וָאֵפֶן וָאֵרֵד מִן־הָהָר

וְהָהָר בֹּעֵר בָּאֵשׁ וּשְׁנֵי לוּחֹת הַבְּרִית עַל שְׁתֵּי יָדָי:

טז וָאֵרֶא וְהִנֵּה חֲטָאתֶם לַיהוָה אֱלֹהֵיכֶם עֲשִׂיתֶם לָכֶם

עֵגֶל מַסֵּכָה סַרְתֶּם מַהֵר מִן־הַדֶּרֶךְ אֲשֶׁר־צִוָּה יְהוָה

יז אֶתְכֶם: וָאֶתְפֹּשׂ בִּשְׁנֵי הַלֻּחֹת וָאַשְׁלִכֵם מֵעַל שְׁתֵּי

יח יָדָי וָאֲשַׁבְּרֵם לְעֵינֵיכֶם: וָאֶתְנַפַּל לִפְנֵי יְהוָה

כָּרִאשֹׁנָה אַרְבָּעִים יוֹם וְאַרְבָּעִים לַיְלָה לֶחֶם לֹא

* יד קמץ בטרחא.

I will destroy them and blot out their name from under heaven, and I will make you a nation far more numerous than they."

15] I started down the mountain, a mountain ablaze with fire, the two Tablets of the Covenant in my two hands. 16] I saw how you had sinned against the LORD your God: you had made yourselves a molten calf; you had been quick to stray from the path that the LORD had enjoined upon you. 17] Thereupon I gripped the two tablets and flung them away with both my hands, smashing them before your eyes. 18] I threw myself down before the LORD—eating no bread and

15] *I started down.* God had told Moses what was happening in the camp, and now Moses sees for himself. The repetition may be compared to the prayer which Abraham's servant delivers and which is then essentially repeated as it is realized in fact (Gen. 24).

17] *Smashing them.* Since the covenant had been broken by the people, the "Tablets of the Covenant" were no longer applicable. The smashing was a vivid reflection of the people's defection, comparable to the later custom of tearing up a contract when its terms have been violated.

The Rabbis disagreed on whether Moses was justified in destroying God's handiwork; see at

Exodus 32, Gleanings.

18] *As before.* Moses had fasted for forty days and nights in the mountain; now—on reaching the tribes below—he commenced a second period of abstinence, in order to plead the people's cause and to expiate their sins. Later on he will ascend again and begin a third period of fasting after which he will descend once more, this time with the second tablets. The three times forty days and nights of self-abnegation amount to a total of one hundred twenty, paralleling the one hundred twenty years of Moses' life (on this figure see Gen. 6:3 and commentary there) [2].

אָכַלְתִּי וּמַיִם לֹא שָׁתִיתִי עַל כָּל־חַטַּאתְכֶם אֲשֶׁר

חֲטָאתֶם לַעֲשׂוֹת הָרַע בְּעֵינֵי יְהֹוָה לְהַכְעִיסוֹ: כִּי

יָגֹרְתִּי מִפְּנֵי הָאַף וְהַחֵמָה אֲשֶׁר קָצַף יְהֹוָה עֲלֵיכֶם

לְהַשְׁמִיד אֶתְכֶם וַיִּשְׁמַע יְהֹוָה אֵלַי גַּם בַּפַּעַם הַהִוא:

וּבְאַהֲרֹן הִתְאַנַּף יְהֹוָה מְאֹד לְהַשְׁמִידוֹ וָאֶתְפַּלֵּל

גַּם־בְּעַד אַהֲרֹן בָּעֵת הַהִוא: וְאֶת־חַטַּאתְכֶם אֲשֶׁר־

עֲשִׂיתֶם אֶת־הָעֵגֶל לָקַחְתִּי וָאֶשְׂרֹף אֹתוֹ בָּאֵשׁ וָאֶכֹּת

אֹתוֹ טָחוֹן הֵיטֵב עַד אֲשֶׁר־דַּק לְעָפָר וָאַשְׁלִךְ אֶת־

עֲפָרוֹ אֶל־הַנַּחַל הַיֹּרֵד מִן־הָהָר: וּבְתַבְעֵרָה וּבְמַסָּה

וּבְקִבְרֹת הַתַּאֲוָה מַקְצִפִים הֱיִיתֶם אֶת־יְהֹוָה:

Deuteronomy 9
19–22

drinking no water forty days and forty nights, as before—because of the great wrong you had committed, doing what displeased the Lord and vexing Him. **19]** For I was in dread of the Lord's fierce anger against you, which moved Him to wipe you out. And that time, too, the Lord gave heed to me— **20]** Moreover, the Lord was angry enough with Aaron to have destroyed him; so I also interceded for Aaron at that time.— **21]** As for that sinful thing you had made, the calf, I took it and put it to the fire; I broke it to bits and ground it thoroughly until it was fine as dust, and I threw its dust into the brook that comes down from the mountain.

22] Again you provoked the Lord at Taberah, and at Massah, and at Kibroth-hattaavah.

19] *And that time, too.* As at Marah (Exod. 15:25) and Massah (Exod. 17:1 ff.).

20] *I also interceded for Aaron.* Neither God's judgment of Aaron nor Moses' intercession is found in the Exodus account.

21] *Brook that comes down.* This too is not in Exo-

dus; there, Moses made Israel swallow the ground-up calf mixed with water, which is not mentioned here.

22] *At Taberah.* See Num. 11:1 ff.
At Massah. See Exod. 17:2 ff. The first rebellion, at Marah, is not mentioned.
At Kibroth-hattaavah. See Num. 11:4–34.

כג וּבִשְׁלֹחַ יְהֹוָה אֶתְכֶם מִקָּדֵשׁ בַּרְנֵעַ לֵאמֹר עֲלוּ
וּרְשׁוּ אֶת־הָאָרֶץ אֲשֶׁר נָתַתִּי לָכֶם וַתַּמְרוּ אֶת־פִּי
יְהֹוָה אֱלֹהֵיכֶם וְלֹא הֶאֱמַנְתֶּם לוֹ וְלֹא שְׁמַעְתֶּם
כד בְּקֹלוֹ: מַמְרִים הֱיִיתֶם עִם־יְהֹוָה מִיּוֹם דַּעְתִּי אֶתְכֶם:
כה וָאֶתְנַפַּל לִפְנֵי יְהֹוָה אֵת אַרְבָּעִים הַיּוֹם וְאֶת־
אַרְבָּעִים הַלַּיְלָה אֲשֶׁר הִתְנַפָּלְתִּי כִּי־אָמַר יְהֹוָה
כו לְהַשְׁמִיד אֶתְכֶם: וָאֶתְפַּלֵּל אֶל־יְהֹוָה וָאֹמַר אֲדֹנָי
יֱהֹוִה אַל־תַּשְׁחֵת עַמְּךָ וְנַחֲלָתְךָ אֲשֶׁר פָּדִיתָ בְּגָדְלֶךָ
כז אֲשֶׁר־הוֹצֵאתָ מִמִּצְרַיִם בְּיָד חֲזָקָה: זְכֹר לַעֲבָדֶיךָ
לְאַבְרָהָם לְיִצְחָק וּלְיַעֲקֹב אַל־תֵּפֶן אֶל־קְשִׁי הָעָם
כח הַזֶּה וְאֶל־רִשְׁעוֹ וְאֶל־חַטָּאתוֹ: פֶּן־יֹאמְרוּ הָאָרֶץ אֲשֶׁר

* כד מ׳ קטנה.

23] And when the LORD sent you on from Kadesh-barnea, saying, "Go up and occupy the land that I am giving you," you flouted the command of the LORD your God; you did not put your trust in Him and did not obey Him.

24] As long as I have known you, you have been defiant toward the LORD.

25] When I lay prostrate before the LORD those forty days and forty nights, because the LORD was determined to destroy you, **26]** I prayed to the LORD and said, "O Lord GOD, do not annihilate Your very own people, whom You redeemed in Your majesty and whom You freed from Egypt with a mighty hand. **27]** Give thought to Your servants, Abraham, Isaac, and Jacob, and pay no heed to the stubbornness of this people, its wickedness, and its sinfulness. **28]** Else the country

23] *From Kadesh-barnea.* From where the spies were sent out; their negative report caused the people to rebel (see Deut. 1:22 ff. and Num. 13–14).

25] *Those forty days and forty nights.* Literally, "the forty days and forty nights that I lay prostrate."

28] *Country . . . will say.* The country's *people* will say: similar ellipses are common in English (e.g., "the whole town will talk").

It may be noted that the Hebrew noun (הָאָרֶץ) is in the feminine singular and the verb (יֹאמְרוּ) in the masculine plural.

הוֹצֵאתָנוּ מִשָּׁם מִבְּלִי יְכֹלֶת יְהוָֹה לַהֲבִיאָם אֶל־
הָאָרֶץ אֲשֶׁר־דִּבֶּר לָהֶם וּמִשִּׂנְאָתוֹ אוֹתָם הוֹצִיאָם

כט לַהֲמִתָם בַּמִּדְבָּר: וְהֵם עַמְּךָ וְנַחֲלָתֶךָ אֲשֶׁר הוֹצֵאתָ
פ בְּכֹחֲךָ הַגָּדֹל וּבִזְרֹעֲךָ הַנְּטוּיָה:

א בָּעֵת הַהִוא אָמַר יְהוָֹה אֵלַי פְּסָל־לְךָ שְׁנֵי־לוּחֹת
אֲבָנִים כָּרִאשֹׁנִים וַעֲלֵה אֵלַי הָהָרָה וְעָשִׂיתָ לְּךָ
ב אֲרוֹן עֵץ: וְאֶכְתֹּב עַל־הַלֻּחֹת אֶת־הַדְּבָרִים אֲשֶׁר
הָיוּ עַל־הַלֻּחֹת הָרִאשֹׁנִים אֲשֶׁר שִׁבַּרְתָּ וְשַׂמְתָּם
ג בָּאָרוֹן: וָאַעַשׂ אֲרוֹן עֲצֵי שִׁטִּים וָאֶפְסֹל שְׁנֵי־לֻחֹת
אֲבָנִים כָּרִאשֹׁנִים וָאַעַל הָהָרָה וּשְׁנֵי הַלֻּחֹת בְּיָדִי:
ד וָאֶכְתֹּב עַל־הַלֻּחֹת כַּמִּכְתָּב הָרִאשׁוֹן אֵת עֲשֶׂרֶת

Deuteronomy 9; 10

29; 1–4

* ב פתח באתנח.

from which You freed us will say, 'It was because the LORD was powerless to bring
them into the land that He had promised them, and because He hated them, that
He brought them out to have them die in the wilderness.' **29]** Yet they are
Your very own people, whom You freed with Your great might and Your outstretched arm."

1] Thereupon the LORD said to me, "Carve out two tablets of stone like the
first, and come up to Me on the mountain; and make an ark of wood.   **2]** I will
inscribe on the tablets the commandments that were on the first tablets which you
smashed, and you shall deposit them in the ark."

3] I made an ark of acacia wood and carved out two tablets of stone like the
first; I took the two tablets with me and went up the mountain.   **4]** The LORD
inscribed on the tablets the same text as on the first, the Ten Commandments

10:1] *Ark of wood.* In Exod. 34:1 we are told that
the ark was made *after* Moses returned from his
second ascent, and not before. Rashi therefore assumed that the Deuteronomy passage indicates
that a temporary ark was made and served as a
receptacle until the permanent one was ready [3].
Others read the account as a telescoped version of
the Exodus story [4].

הַדְּבָרִים אֲשֶׁר דִּבֶּר יְהֹוָה אֲלֵיכֶם בָּהָר מִתּוֹךְ
הָאֵשׁ בְּיוֹם הַקָּהָל וַיִּתְּנֵם יְהֹוָה אֵלָי: וָאֵפֶן וָאֵרֵד
מִן־הָהָר וָאָשִׂם אֶת־הַלֻּחֹת בָּאָרוֹן אֲשֶׁר עָשִׂיתִי וַיִּהְיוּ
שָׁם כַּאֲשֶׁר צִוַּנִי יְהֹוָה: וּבְנֵי יִשְׂרָאֵל נָסְעוּ מִבְּאֵרֹת
בְּנֵי־יַעֲקָן מוֹסֵרָה שָׁם מֵת אַהֲרֹן וַיִּקָּבֵר שָׁם וַיְכַהֵן
אֶלְעָזָר בְּנוֹ תַּחְתָּיו: מִשָּׁם נָסְעוּ הַגֻּדְגֹּדָה וּמִן־הַגֻּדְגֹּדָה
יָטְבָתָה אֶרֶץ נַחֲלֵי־מָיִם: בָּעֵת הַהִוא הִבְדִּיל יְהֹוָה
אֶת־שֵׁבֶט הַלֵּוִי לָשֵׂאת אֶת־אֲרוֹן בְּרִית־יְהֹוָה לַעֲמֹד

Deuteronomy 10
5–8

that He addressed to you on the mountain out of the fire on the day of the Assembly; and the LORD gave them to me.   5] Then I left and went down from
the mountain, and I deposited the tablets in the ark that I had made, where they
still are, as the LORD had commanded me.

6] From Beeroth-bene-jaakan the Israelites marched to Moserah. Aaron died
there and was buried there; and his son Eleazar became priest in his stead.   7] From
there they marched to Gudgod, and from Gudgod to Jotbath, a region of running brooks.

8] At that time the LORD set apart the tribe of Levi to carry the Ark of the

5] *Where they still are.* This translation does not
render the sense of the Hebrew, which says: "And
they remained there"—clearly an anachronism
that betrays the late date of the composition.
In Deuteronomic times the tablets were kept in
the ark which stood in the Holy of Holies in the
Temple where Solomon had brought it (I Kings
8:9).

6] *From Beeroth-bene-jaakan.* This passage poses a
number of further problems: it suddenly interrupts the flow of the discourse; in Num. 33:31–33
the way stations are recounted in different order;
and in Num. 20:22 ff. and 33:38 Aaron was said to
have died at Mt. Hor and not at Moserah.

a. Placement in the text. This is best explained
by considering the passage a mnemotechnical insertion: the preceding subject had been the restoration of God's favor to Israel after the incident
with the golden calf, which involved Aaron and
(in the Exodus account) stressed the loyalty of the
Levites. Hence the notation in verses 6–9 rounds
out the recital [5].

b. Order of way stations. Most likely a variant
tradition is represented here, characterized also by
the mention of Gudgod, which in Num. 33:31–32
is called Hor-haggidgad.

c. Aaron's death. Conventional harmonizers
say that Moserah lay in the vicinity of or at the
foot of a mountain range called Hor, hence no

לִפְנֵי יְהֹוָה לְשָׁרְתוֹ וּלְבָרֵךְ בִּשְׁמוֹ עַד הַיּוֹם הַזֶּה:

ט עַל־כֵּן לֹא־הָיָה לְלֵוִי חֵלֶק וְנַחֲלָה עִם־אֶחָיו יְהֹוָה

י הוּא נַחֲלָתוֹ כַּאֲשֶׁר דִּבֶּר יְהֹוָה אֱלֹהֶיךָ לוֹ: וְאָנֹכִי

עָמַדְתִּי בָהָר כַּיָּמִים הָרִאשֹׁנִים אַרְבָּעִים יוֹם

וְאַרְבָּעִים לָיְלָה וַיִּשְׁמַע יְהֹוָה אֵלַי גַּם בַּפַּעַם הַהִוא

יא לֹא־אָבָה יְהֹוָה הַשְׁחִיתֶךָ: וַיֹּאמֶר יְהֹוָה אֵלַי קוּם

לֵךְ לְמַסַּע לִפְנֵי הָעָם וְיָבֹאוּ וְיִרְשׁוּ אֶת־הָאָרֶץ

אֲשֶׁר־נִשְׁבַּעְתִּי לַאֲבֹתָם לָתֵת לָהֶם: פ

Deuteronomy 10
9–11

Lord's Covenant, to stand in attendance upon the Lord, and to bless in His name, as is still the case.   9] That is why the Levites have received no hereditary portion along with their kinsmen: the Lord is their portion, as the Lord your God spoke concerning them.

10] I had stayed on the mountain, as I did the first time, forty days and forty nights; and the Lord heeded me once again: the Lord agreed not to destroy you. 11] And the Lord said to me, "Up, resume the march at the head of the people, that they may invade and occupy the land that I swore to their fathers to give them."

conflict exists with what is recorded in Numbers. Other scholars consider this divergence as another evidence that variant traditions are involved.

9] No hereditary portion. Meaning, no land. The

Levites were maintained by offerings which people brought to the Temple.

10] I had stayed on the mountain. After ascending with the new tablets. The second stay, like the first, lasted forty days and nights.

Defiance

"As long as I have known you, you have been defiant toward the Lord." These words of Moses are the prophet's ringing indictment of his people (9:24). They are, in his eyes, a stiff-necked lot, prone to sin, provoking God to anger, ungrateful for His many mercies—altogether undeserving of His continuing concern. Only because of their forefathers' merit and the pledge God had made to them, has He not abandoned Israel. If in his own lifetime Moses had cause to be disillusioned with the people he led, how much more so the Deuteronomist who, centuries later, could look back on a nation's record steeped in idolatry, social injustice, and continued disregard of the covenant. It was a dismal picture, calling forth the prophetic ire with which the text bristles.

It cannot be denied that the words here attributed to and projected onto Moses have a deeply pessimistic strain within them. He exhorts his people, but he already knows that they will not heed him. Their obduracy appears to be part of their nature. That nonetheless he (like God himself) persists in loving them is in the end not explicable in rational terms: they belong to each other for good and for evil, and he will fight for them whether they deserve it or not.

In viewing this tension-filled relationship, one must keep in mind that while Israel is the immediate focus there is also a larger perspective. For, throughout the Torah, Israel has a paradigmatic quality, which is to say that as God's people they represent humanity as a whole. At times their fate is even linked to the cosmos itself. Thus, the Israelites' wilderness sojourn, during which they were sustained by God, reenacts humanity's experience in Eden; the building of the Tabernacle parallels (in the key words used) the creation of the world; and Israel's observance of Shabbat rehearses the climactic moments of creation. Similarly, Israel's defiance of God is but an acting out of what the Torah judges to be the general character of man, "how every plan devised by his mind was nothing but evil all the time" (Gen. 6:5). Torah and Prophets may in fact be seen as responding to this condition by providing Israel and humanity with an opportunity to overcome it through covenant and mitzvot.

The stiff-neckedness of Israel is therefore a particular distillation of the spirit of defiance built into the human species. If there is to be any hope for the latter it will only be because Israel begins to fulfill its obligations and responds to the terms of the covenant [6].

The Intermediary

It has become a fundamental aspect of Jewish teaching—in contrast to Christianity's—that people neither need nor can use an intermediary in their relationship with God (see I Sam. 2:25). However, this principle most decidedly did not apply when it came to the position that Moses occupied as a mediator between God and Israel. According to Moses' own account, it was *his* intervention that procured God's forgiveness, it was *his* advocacy then and at other times which saved the people from the effects of divine anger. This puts Moses, the man who could speak with God face to face and who returned from these encounters with their afterglow imprinted on his brow, into a category that can only be described as superhuman, even semidivine.

This special status is underscored by the symbolic use of numbers. Even as Moses will live to the age of a hundred twenty—the ideal life span of biblical tradition—so his entreaties before God lasted one hundred twenty days. During this time of "perfection" he received the commandments and pleaded Israel's cause, all the while observing a total fast which, as tradition pointed out, meant that he was sustained by divine food.

But these superhuman capacities and attributes were counterbalanced by the man's thorough humanity. He had human foibles. The Rabbis wondered why Moses felt impelled to reveal his special role, that is, why he had spoken about his intercession when the people never needed to know about it. Quite clearly, he *wanted* them to know what he had done and was not satisfied to keep them in ignorance of his accomplishments. This was hardly an admirable trait, for which the Sages valiantly tried to find an acceptable explanation (see Gleanings, below).

Despite this, the man Moses has remained somewhat remote. In the consciousness of his people, he is *Mosheh Rabbenu*, Moses our teacher (the only prophet so called), the prophet or rabbi par excellence. But the term conveys awe rather than affection. He was human, to be sure, but his humanity was of a kind that touched the edge of the Divine. After him, in the mainstream of Jewish history, all prophets abided fully in the human realm. God might use them to reach the people, but the people no longer needed them to reach their God. (See further below, commentary on chapter 34.)

A Note on the Levites (Deut. 10:8–9)

The text specifies four duties and privileges which were assigned to "the Levites."[1] The term itself has both a larger and a narrower meaning: it refers sometimes to the whole tribe which includes and features the priests, and at other times only to the non-priestly Levites who assisted the priests in various ways. In Deuteronomy "Levites" generally means levitical *priests* (thus, 31:9 speaks of "the priests, sons of Levi, who carried the Ark of the Lord's Covenant"), and we may therefore assume that in our passage too the *priests* are meant. Their first duty was to carry the Ark;[2] secondly, they were to "stand in attendance upon the Lord," that is, to officiate at cultic functions, like sacrifices; thirdly, they were to bless the people in God's name, a duty specifically assigned to priests in Num. 6:23. A fourth duty, listed not here but farther on (Deut. 33:10), consisted of burning the incense. The Levites were landless and were considered "God's portion" (Num. 18:20). Their sustenance came, so to speak, from the Lord's table: they received their share of the contributions that the people brought to the Temple in both money and kind (see Deut. 18:1–8).

In time, "Levites" came to mean only the non-priests who sang at the Temple service and otherwise attended the priests and performed menial tasks in the sanctuary. The priests themselves were of the levitical family of Zadok and traced their ancestry to Aaron. This development was the result of a long struggle of various factions and families. In 70 C.E. when the Temple was destroyed, most levitical functions, both priestly and non-priestly, ceased, though Jews remained careful to preserve their descent from these families, for in traditional practice some halachic and liturgical rules still apply to them. Reform Judaism no longer observes distinctions of this kind.

[1] For a fuller treatment of the Levites, their service and history, see our commentaries on Lev. 21–22 and Exod. 29 (Gleanings).

[2] But in Num. 3:31 and 4:15 this task is given to the non-priestly family of the Kohathites—clearly a different tradition, which reflects changes that over the centuries occurred in the Temple service.

GLEANINGS

Confession

Our God, God of our ancestors, grant that our prayers may reach You. Do not be deaf to our pleas, for we are not so arrogant and stiffnecked as to say before You, Lord our God and God of all ages, we are perfect and have not sinned; rather do we confess: we have gone astray, we have sinned, we have transgressed.

We are arrogant, brutal, careless, destructive, egocentric, false, greedy, heartless, insolent, and joyless. Our sins are an alphabet of woe.

LITURGY FOR THE DAY OF ATONEMENT [7]

To Know

Better a sinner who knows he is a sinner than a righteous man who knows he is righteous.

CHASIDIC [8]

In Praise of Stubbornness

Why are the Patriarchs mentioned in connection with Israel's stubbornness (Deut. 9:27)? Because they too possessed a measure of it. For without it neither they nor their descendants could have stood up to the whole world.

ISAAC ELIJAH LANDAU [9]

Yom ha-Kahal (Deut. 9:10)

The day of the giving of the Torah was called "Day of Assembly," because never before or after had the people assembled in such unity of spirit.

BASED ON THE ZOHAR [10]

The Order Is All-important

In 10:1 God commanded (in literal translation): "Carve out for yourself . . ."—פְּסָל־לְךָ. In the second commandment (5:8) it says: "(You shall not make) for yourself a sculptured image"— (לֹא תַעֲשֶׂה לְךָ פֶּסֶל). Note that, in one, לְךָ follows פסל and, in the other, it precedes it. From this you may learn that when לְךָ (yourself) comes first it leads to idolatry; when second, to the Tablets of the Law.

CHASIDIC [11]

Both Sets

According to tradition, both the broken and whole sets of the tablets were kept in the ark [12]. From this we learn that one should respect a scholar who has forgotten his learning through adverse circumstances (age, troubles, illness).

TALMUD [13]

Replace Them

God said to Moses: You were the intermediary between Me and My people. You broke the tablets (which were entrusted to you) and you must replace them, "carve out two tablets of stone like the first."[3]

MIDRASH [14]

A Time to Cast Away

It says: "There is . . . a time to every purpose under the heaven . . . a time to cast away stones and a time to gather stones together" (Eccles. 3:1, 5). This is applicable to Moses: there was a time for him to cast away tablets and a time to hew new ones.

MIDRASH [15]

Small מ

In some manuscripts the first מ of מַמְרִים (defiant, Deut. 9:24) is written small[4] to hint that, though Moses accused the people of defiance, he

---

[3] The Midrash connects this with the halachah which rules that, when a cask is broken before delivery to the buyer, the middleman must replace it.

[4] Though not in the Masoretic text; see Minchat Shai.

himself took part of the blame.[5]

CHASIDIC [16]

A Question

Why did Moses tell the people about his prayer and God's answer? Did this not serve to aggrandize himself, inasmuch as without his telling no one would ever have known about it! He needed to teach us a lesson, namely, that when one prays for others such prayer is more likely to be answered than prayer for one's own sake. Note that, when Moses prayed for himself and asked that God reverse the judgment and let him enter the Promised Land, the Lord cut him off by saying "Enough!" (Deut. 3:26) But, when he prayed for Israel for forty days and nights, God let him be and in the end He relented.

This is what the Talmud means when it says: He who prolongs his prayer will not have it return empty.

YALKUT YEHUDAH [17]

---

[5] This is based on Rashi's comment on 1:13, where the Masoretic text reads ואשימם and Rashi's text ואשמם (without י; which could be understood as "their guilt"). This suggested to Rashi that when a people sins the guilt rests first and foremost with its leaders.

The Good Land

The discourse continues with an exhortation along familiar lines: Israel must revere and love God and God only, for He is their proven guardian and savior. Special emphasis is now placed on the land which will be Israel's, for it is not like other lands. It is particularly blessed by being fertile, gifted with ample water, and not subject to the climatic vagaries of Egypt. The text looks at the land from the east side of the Jordan and sees it—with its expanse from north to south—touching the Mediterranean. This is one of several geographic descriptions of the Promised Land given by the Torah and suggests that there were different conceptions of what actual area the Promise was to encompass. In general, "Canaan" was a stereotypical expression used to describe the old borders of the Egyptian province (for a detailed discussion, see our commentary on Num. 34).

The discourse emphasizes once more the Israelite's duty to love the stranger and again gives as the reason for this mitzvah the people's servitude in Egypt.

וְעַתָּה יִשְׂרָאֵל מָה יְהֹוָה אֱלֹהֶיךָ שֹׁאֵל מֵעִמָּךְ כִּי

אִם־לְיִרְאָה אֶת־יְהֹוָה אֱלֹהֶיךָ לָלֶכֶת בְּכָל־דְּרָכָיו

וּלְאַהֲבָה אֹתוֹ וְלַעֲבֹד אֶת־יְהֹוָה אֱלֹהֶיךָ בְּכָל־לְבָבְךָ

וּבְכָל־נַפְשֶׁךָ: לִשְׁמֹר אֶת־מִצְוֺת יְהֹוָה וְאֶת־חֻקֹּתָיו

אֲשֶׁר אָנֹכִי מְצַוְּךָ הַיּוֹם לְטוֹב לָךְ: הֵן לַיהֹוָה

אֱלֹהֶיךָ הַשָּׁמַיִם וּשְׁמֵי הַשָּׁמָיִם הָאָרֶץ וְכָל־אֲשֶׁר־בָּהּ:

רַק בַּאֲבֹתֶיךָ חָשַׁק יְהֹוָה לְאַהֲבָה אוֹתָם וַיִּבְחַר

בְּזַרְעָם אַחֲרֵיהֶם בָּכֶם מִכָּל־הָעַמִּים כַּיּוֹם הַזֶּה:

וּמַלְתֶּם אֵת עָרְלַת לְבַבְכֶם וְעָרְפְּכֶם לֹא תַקְשׁוּ

עוֹד: כִּי יְהֹוָה אֱלֹהֵיכֶם הוּא אֱלֹהֵי הָאֱלֹהִים וַאֲדֹנֵי

12] And now, O Israel, what does the Lord your God demand of you? Only this: to revere the Lord your God, to walk only in His paths, to love Him, and to serve the Lord your God with all your heart and soul,   **13]** keeping the Lord's commandments and laws, which I enjoin upon you today, for your good.   **14]** Mark, the heavens to their uttermost reaches belong to the Lord your God, the earth and all that is on it!   **15]** Yet it was to your fathers that the Lord was drawn in His love for them, so that He chose you, their lineal descendants, from among all peoples—as is now the case.   **16]** Cut away, therefore, the thickening about your hearts and stiffen your necks no more.   **17]** For the Lord your God is God

---

10:12] *Revere.* See above, at 4:10, on יִרְאָה in its basic meaning of fear and trembling. In this verse, both fear and love are combined to form the most desirable relationship with God (see commentary on 6:1–25, "The Love of God").

13] *Your good.* The Torah unhesitatingly holds out rewards for obeisance to God. Maimonides considered this approach a necessary educational device [1].

14] *To their uttermost reaches.* Literally, "and the heaven of heavens."

16] *Cut away . . . the thickening.* Older translations had "circumcise the foreskin of your hearts." "Circumcise" was an idiom used also in regard to lips and ears.

17] *God supreme and Lord supreme.* Literally, "the God of gods and the Lord of lords."

הָאֲדֹנִים הָאֵל הַגָּדֹל הַגִּבֹּר וְהַנּוֹרָא אֲשֶׁר לֹא־יִשָּׂא

יח פָּנִים וְלֹא יִקַּח שֹׁחַד: עֹשֶׂה מִשְׁפַּט יָתוֹם וְאַלְמָנָה

יט וְאֹהֵב גֵּר לָתֶת לוֹ לֶחֶם וְשִׂמְלָה: וַאֲהַבְתֶּם אֶת־הַגֵּר

כ כִּי־גֵרִים הֱיִיתֶם בְּאֶרֶץ מִצְרָיִם: אֶת־יְהֹוָה אֱלֹהֶיךָ

כא תִּירָא אֹתוֹ תַעֲבֹד וּבוֹ תִדְבָּק וּבִשְׁמוֹ תִּשָּׁבֵעַ: הוּא

תְהִלָּתְךָ וְהוּא אֱלֹהֶיךָ אֲשֶׁר־עָשָׂה אִתְּךָ אֶת־הַגְּדֹלֹת

כב וְאֶת־הַנּוֹרָאֹת הָאֵלֶּה אֲשֶׁר רָאוּ עֵינֶיךָ: בְּשִׁבְעִים

נֶפֶשׁ יָרְדוּ אֲבֹתֶיךָ מִצְרָיְמָה וְעַתָּה שָׂמְךָ יְהֹוָה

אֱלֹהֶיךָ כְּכוֹכְבֵי הַשָּׁמַיִם לָרֹב:

דברים י
יח—כב

Deuteronomy 10
18—22

* כ קמץ בז״ק.

supreme and Lord supreme, the great, the mighty, and the awesome God, who shows no favor and takes no bribe,   18] but upholds the cause of the fatherless and the widow, and befriends the stranger, providing him with food and clothing.— 19] You too must befriend the stranger, for you were strangers in the land of Egypt.

20] You must revere the LORD your God: only Him shall you worship, to Him shall you hold fast, and by His name shall you swear.   21] He is your glory and He is your God, who wrought for you those marvelous, awesome deeds that you saw with your own eyes.   22] Your ancestors went down to Egypt seventy persons in all; and now the LORD your God has made you as numerous as the stars of heaven.

Great . . . mighty . . . awesome. These attributes of God are quoted in the daily liturgy, in the first paragraph of the *Tefillah* or main prayer.

Takes no bribe. Do not consider your sacrifice as a means of influencing God's will.

18] *The stranger.* גֵּר (ger), a resident alien who was a free person but without political rights, who would generally be someone from another land

or district. The Rabbis differentiated between such a person (later called *ger toshav*, resident alien) and a *ger tzedek* (righteous alien) who had converted to Judaism [2].

19] *For you were strangers.* See commentary below.

22] *Seventy persons.* So Exod. 1:5.

א וְאָהַבְתָּ אֵת יְהֹוָה אֱלֹהֶיךָ וְשָׁמַרְתָּ מִשְׁמַרְתּוֹ וְחֻקֹּתָיו

ב וּמִשְׁפָּטָיו וּמִצְוֹתָיו כָּל־הַיָּמִים: וִידַעְתֶּם הַיּוֹם כִּי

לֹא אֶת־בְּנֵיכֶם אֲשֶׁר לֹא־יָדְעוּ וַאֲשֶׁר לֹא־רָאוּ אֶת־

מוּסַר יְהֹוָה אֱלֹהֵיכֶם אֶת־גָּדְלוֹ אֶת־יָדוֹ הַחֲזָקָה

ג וּזְרֹעוֹ הַנְּטוּיָה: וְאֶת־אֹתֹתָיו וְאֶת־מַעֲשָׂיו אֲשֶׁר עָשָׂה

בְּתוֹךְ מִצְרָיִם לְפַרְעֹה מֶלֶךְ־מִצְרַיִם וּלְכָל־אַרְצוֹ:

ד וַאֲשֶׁר עָשָׂה לְחֵיל מִצְרַיִם לְסוּסָיו וּלְרִכְבּוֹ אֲשֶׁר

הֵצִיף אֶת־מֵי יַם־סוּף עַל־פְּנֵיהֶם בְּרָדְפָם אַחֲרֵיכֶם

ה וַיְאַבְּדֵם יְהֹוָה עַד הַיּוֹם הַזֶּה: וַאֲשֶׁר עָשָׂה לָכֶם

ו בַּמִּדְבָּר עַד־בֹּאֲכֶם עַד־הַמָּקוֹם הַזֶּה: וַאֲשֶׁר עָשָׂה

Deuteronomy 11
1–6

1] Love, therefore, the LORD your God, and always keep His charge, His laws, His rules, and His commandments.

2] Take thought this day that it was not your children, who neither experienced nor witnessed the lesson of the LORD your God—

His majesty, His mighty hand, His outstretched arm;   **3]** the signs and the deeds that He performed in Egypt against Pharaoh king of Egypt and all his land;   **4]** what He did to Egypt's army, its horses and chariots; how the LORD rolled back upon them the waters of the Sea of Reeds when they were pursuing you, thus destroying them once and for all;   **5]** what He did for you in the wilderness before you arrived in this place;   **6]** and what He did to Dathan

---

11:1] *Keep His charge.* The Hebrew style is distinct in that it uses the same root for both verb and noun: וְשָׁמַרְתָּ מִשְׁמַרְתּוֹ. The word מִשְׁמֶרֶת has also the meaning of "being on watch," conveying here that God's command is like a treasure to be watched.

The same idiom occurs also in Gen. 26:5.

2] *Take thought.* The Hebrew syntax is not clear. Our English translation takes the passage from the second half of verse 2 to verse 6 as an apposition to explain what "the lesson" is. Verse 7 then concludes the first half of verse 2 [3].

Lesson. The word מוּסָר (*musar*) later came primarily to mean ethical teaching in general.

4] *Once and for all.* An idiomatic rendering of the literal "unto this day" [4].

6] *Dathan and Abiram.* Who were leaders in the revolt against Moses. There were two traditions,

134

לְדָתָן וְלַאֲבִירָם בְּנֵי אֱלִיאָב בֶּן־רְאוּבֵן אֲשֶׁר פָּצְתָה
הָאָרֶץ אֶת־פִּיהָ וַתִּבְלָעֵם וְאֶת־בָּתֵּיהֶם וְאֶת־אָהֳלֵיהֶם
וְאֵת כָּל־הַיְקוּם אֲשֶׁר בְּרַגְלֵיהֶם בְּקֶרֶב כָּל־יִשְׂרָאֵל:

ז כִּי עֵינֵיכֶם הָרֹאֹת אֶת־כָּל־מַעֲשֵׂה יְהֹוָה הַגָּדֹל אֲשֶׁר

ח עָשָׂה: וּשְׁמַרְתֶּם אֶת־כָּל־הַמִּצְוָה אֲשֶׁר אָנֹכִי מְצַוְּךָ
הַיּוֹם לְמַעַן תֶּחֶזְקוּ וּבָאתֶם וִירִשְׁתֶּם אֶת־הָאָרֶץ אֲשֶׁר

ט אַתֶּם עֹבְרִים שָׁמָּה לְרִשְׁתָּהּ: וּלְמַעַן תַּאֲרִיכוּ יָמִים
עַל־הָאֲדָמָה אֲשֶׁר נִשְׁבַּע יְהֹוָה לַאֲבֹתֵיכֶם לָתֵת לָהֶם

י וּלְזַרְעָם אֶרֶץ זָבַת חָלָב וּדְבָשׁ: ס כִּי הָאָרֶץ
אֲשֶׁר אַתָּה בָא־שָׁמָּה לְרִשְׁתָּהּ לֹא כְאֶרֶץ מִצְרַיִם

Deuteronomy 11
7–10

and Abiram, sons of Eliab son of Reuben, when the earth opened her mouth and swallowed them, along with their households, their tents, and every living thing in their train, from amidst all Israel—

7] but that it was you who saw with your own eyes all the marvelous deeds that the LORD performed.

8] Keep, therefore, all the Instruction that I enjoin upon you today, so that you may have the strength to invade and occupy the land which you are about to cross into and occupy,   9] and that you may long endure upon the soil which the LORD swore to your fathers to give to them and to their descendants, a land flowing with milk and honey.

10] For the land which you are about to invade and occupy is not like the land

one ascribing the initiative to Dathan and Abiram, the other naming Korah as the ring leader (see our commentary on Num. 16; the Deuteronomist follows the former tradition and omits the mention of Korah).

This omission is explained by the Sages in two ways: one, that only Dathan and Abiram were swallowed by the earth, but not Korah; or that, since Korah's sons were still alive (Num. 26:11), Moses did not wish to offend them by mentioning their father's sin [5].

הוּא אֲשֶׁר יְצָאתֶם מִשָּׁם אֲשֶׁר תִּזְרַע אֶת־זַרְעֲךָ

וְהִשְׁקִיתָ בְרַגְלְךָ כְּגַן הַיָּרָק: וְהָאָרֶץ אֲשֶׁר אַתֶּם

עֹבְרִים שָׁמָּה לְרִשְׁתָּהּ אֶרֶץ הָרִים וּבְקָעֹת לִמְטַר

הַשָּׁמַיִם תִּשְׁתֶּה־מָּיִם: אֶרֶץ אֲשֶׁר־יְהוָה אֱלֹהֶיךָ דֹּרֵשׁ

אֹתָהּ תָּמִיד עֵינֵי יְהוָה אֱלֹהֶיךָ בָּהּ מֵרֵשִׁית הַשָּׁנָה

וְעַד אַחֲרִית שָׁנָה: ס וְהָיָה אִם־שָׁמֹעַ תִּשְׁמְעוּ

אֶל־מִצְוֹתַי אֲשֶׁר אָנֹכִי מְצַוֶּה אֶתְכֶם הַיּוֹם לְאַהֲבָה

אֶת־יְהוָה אֱלֹהֵיכֶם וּלְעָבְדוֹ בְּכָל־לְבַבְכֶם וּבְכָל־

נַפְשְׁכֶם: וְנָתַתִּי מְטַר־אַרְצְכֶם בְּעִתּוֹ יוֹרֶה וּמַלְקוֹשׁ

* יב חסר א'.

of Egypt from which you have come. There the grain you sowed had to be watered by your own labors, like a vegetable garden;   11] but the land you are about to cross into and occupy, a land of hills and valleys, soaks up its water from the rains of heaven.   12] It is a land which the LORD your God looks after, on which the LORD your God always keeps His eye, from year's beginning to year's end.

13] If, then, you obey the commandments that I enjoin upon you this day, loving the LORD your God and serving Him with all your heart and soul,   14] I will grant the rain for your land in season, the early rain and the late. You shall gather

10] *By your own labors.* The translation understands the literal "by your foot" figuratively, thereby sidestepping speculation about the irrigation methods used by the Egyptians (such as: they carried the water from the river on their shoulders and transported it on foot).

11] *Soaks up.* Retains it without wasteful runoffs or flooding. The comparison is made for hortatory purposes and therefore employs exaggeration.

13–21] These verses are the fourth selection inscribed on phylacteries because mention is made of binding these admonitions to hand and fore-head (verse 18). The passage is also recited in the traditional daily liturgy as the second section of the *Shema*, after Deut. 6:4–9.

The Mishnah explains that this order is instituted "so that a person might first accept the yoke of the Kingdom of heaven (Deut. 6) and then the yoke of the mitzvot (Deut. 11) [6].

14] *I will grant.* Moses speaks in God's stead. However, the Samaritan text has *"He will grant."*

Early rain and the late. The former falls in late October and early November, the latter in late March and early April. The height of the rainy season occurs in December and January.

136

טו וְאָסַפְתָּ דְגָנֶךָ וְתִירֹשְׁךָ וְיִצְהָרֶךָ: וְנָתַתִּי עֵשֶׂב בְּשָׂדְךָ

טז לִבְהֶמְתֶּךָ וְאָכַלְתָּ וְשָׂבָעְתָּ: הִשָּׁמְרוּ לָכֶם פֶּן יִפְתֶּה

לְבַבְכֶם וְסַרְתֶּם וַעֲבַדְתֶּם אֱלֹהִים אֲחֵרִים

יז וְהִשְׁתַּחֲוִיתֶם לָהֶם: וְחָרָה אַף־יְהוָֹה בָּכֶם וְעָצַר אֶת־

הַשָּׁמַיִם וְלֹא־יִהְיֶה מָטָר וְהָאֲדָמָה לֹא תִתֵּן אֶת־

יְבוּלָהּ וַאֲבַדְתֶּם מְהֵרָה מֵעַל הָאָרֶץ הַטֹּבָה אֲשֶׁר

יח יְהוָֹה נֹתֵן לָכֶם: וְשַׂמְתֶּם אֶת־דְּבָרַי אֵלֶּה עַל־לְבַבְכֶם

וְעַל־נַפְשְׁכֶם וּקְשַׁרְתֶּם אֹתָם לְאוֹת עַל־יֶדְכֶם וְהָיוּ

יט לְטוֹטָפֹת בֵּין עֵינֵיכֶם: וְלִמַּדְתֶּם אֹתָם אֶת־בְּנֵיכֶם

לְדַבֵּר בָּם בְּשִׁבְתְּךָ בְּבֵיתֶךָ וּבְלֶכְתְּךָ בַדֶּרֶךְ

כ וּבְשָׁכְבְּךָ וּבְקוּמֶךָ: וּכְתַבְתָּם עַל־מְזוּזוֹת בֵּיתֶךָ

Deuteronomy 11

15–20

in your new grain and wine and oil— **15]** I will also provide grass in the fields for your cattle—and thus you shall eat your fill. **16]** Take care not to be lured away to serve other gods and bow to them. **17]** For the LORD's anger will flare up against you, and He will shut up the skies so that there will be no rain and the ground will not yield its produce; and you will soon perish from the good land that the LORD is giving you.

18] Therefore impress these My words upon your very heart: bind them as a sign on your hand and let them serve as a symbol on your forehead, **19]** and teach them to your children—reciting them when you stay at home and when you are away, when you lie down and when you get up; **20]** and inscribe them on

16] *Take care.* It has been suggested that verses 13–15 ought to be read as depending on the clause "If then" and that only in verse 16 the resolution occurs. This would, however, not alter the Torah's apparent idea that rainfall is granted or withheld at God's will. See also chapter 28 [7].

17] *The Lord's anger will flare up.* The description of punishment is as hyperbolic as the promise of plenty.

18] *Your very heart.* Literally, "your heart and soul."

Symbol on your forehead. See at Deut. 6:8.

כא וּבִשְׁעָרֶֽיךָ: לְמַ֫עַן יִרְבּ֣וּ יְמֵיכֶם֙ וִימֵ֣י בְנֵיכֶ֔ם עַ֚ל
הָ֣אֲדָמָ֔ה אֲשֶׁ֨ר נִשְׁבַּ֤ע יְהֹוָה֙ לַאֲבֹתֵיכֶ֔ם לָתֵ֥ת לָהֶ֖ם

כב כִּימֵ֥י הַשָּׁמַ֖יִם עַל־הָאָֽרֶץ: ס כִּ֣י אִם־שָׁמֹ֣ר
תִּשְׁמְר֗וּן אֶת־כׇּל־הַמִּצְוָ֤ה הַזֹּאת֙ אֲשֶׁ֧ר אָנֹכִ֛י מְצַוֶּ֥ה
אֶתְכֶ֖ם לַעֲשֹׂתָ֑הּ לְאַהֲבָ֞ה אֶת־יְהֹוָ֧ה אֱלֹהֵיכֶ֛ם לָלֶ֥כֶת

כג בְּכׇל־דְּרָכָ֖יו וּלְדׇבְקָה־בֽוֹ: וְהוֹרִ֧ישׁ יְהֹוָ֛ה אֶת־כׇּל־
הַגּוֹיִ֥ם הָאֵ֖לֶּה מִלִּפְנֵיכֶ֑ם וִירִשְׁתֶּ֣ם גּוֹיִ֔ם גְּדֹלִ֥ים

כד וַעֲצֻמִ֖ים מִכֶּֽם: כׇּל־הַמָּק֗וֹם אֲשֶׁ֨ר תִּדְרֹ֧ךְ כַּף־רַגְלְכֶ֛ם
בּ֖וֹ לָכֶ֣ם יִהְיֶ֑ה מִן־הַמִּדְבָּ֨ר וְהַלְּבָנ֜וֹן מִן־הַנָּהָ֣ר נְהַר־

כה פְּרָ֗ת וְעַד֙ הַיָּ֣ם הָאַֽחֲר֔וֹן יִהְיֶ֖ה גְּבֻלְכֶֽם: לֹא־יִתְיַצֵּ֥ב
אִ֖ישׁ בִּפְנֵיכֶ֑ם פַּחְדְּכֶ֤ם וּמֽוֹרַאֲכֶם֙ יִתֵּ֣ן ׀ יְהֹוָ֣ה אֱלֹהֵיכֶ֔ם
עַל־פְּנֵ֤י כׇל־הָאָ֨רֶץ֙ אֲשֶׁ֣ר תִּדְרְכוּ־בָ֔הּ כַּאֲשֶׁ֖ר דִּבֶּ֥ר
לָכֶֽם:

Deuteronomy 11
21–25

Haftarah Ekev, p. 436

the doorposts of your house and on your gates—   **21]** to the end that you and your children may endure, in the land that the Lord swore to your fathers to give to them, as long as there is a heaven over the earth.

22] If, then, you faithfully keep all this Instruction that I command you, loving the Lord your God, walking in all His ways, and holding fast to Him,   **23]** the Lord will dislodge before you all these nations: you will dispossess nations greater and more numerous than you.   **24]** Every spot on which your foot treads shall be yours; your territory shall extend from the wilderness to the Lebanon and from the River—the Euphrates—to the Western Sea.   **25]** No man shall stand up to you: the Lord your God will put the dread and the fear of you over the whole land in which you set foot, as He promised you.

24] *Western Sea.* The Mediterranean.

Why Love the Stranger?

In an oft-quoted talmudic passage, R. Eliezer comments on the surprising fact that Scripture asks us no fewer than thirty-six times to love[1] the stranger [8]. This is the more noteworthy when one compares this with other ancient Near Eastern records. There, the protection of *widows* and *orphans* was well entrenched (care of these was a cliché for the humane conduct of kings), but not the concern for *strangers*, which is unique to the Torah. The frequency of this repetition suggests that aliens had a difficult time and that instead of finding acceptance and friendship (let alone love) they experienced rejection. Similarly, the duty to love God was repeated so often because the Israelites continued to be steeped in idolatry. The command "You must love (or befriend) the stranger" must be appreciated in this light.

The Torah gives two explicitly stated reasons for this mitzvah. One, which occurs only once, calls on the Israelite's compassion: "You shall not oppress a stranger, *for you know the feelings of the stranger*, having yourselves been strangers in the land of Egypt" (Exod. 23:9). But, while this reminder of past bitter experience could be expected to create empathy amongst those who had actually been slaves, it was certainly less potent for their descendants.[2]

The second, and related, reason is purely historical and is stated time and again: You were strangers once, and were mistreated, therefore do not do to others what was done to your forefathers. But could this rehearsal of ancient history be expected to produce moral rectitude? Aside from the obvious weakness of this type of motivation, should we not expect the Torah to tell us the real reason for treating the stranger decently is that it is the right and moral thing to do?

That, in fact, is what the Torah does tell us, albeit in its own way which, as so often, is implicit rather than explicit. To be sure, the reference to slavery in Egypt is cast in historical terms, as many commentators pointed out [9], but it is also "religious" in the deepest sense. Nachmanides therefore says: The reminder that we were slaves in Egypt draws our attention to the fact that God hears the cry of the oppressed and saves them as He saved Israel in Egypt [10]. The reference to the Exodus is the Torah's standard method of eliciting Israel's awareness of God's overarching presence, and in two places the text emphasizes it clearly. One, in Lev. 19:34, says: "You shall love him (the stranger) as yourself, for you were strangers in the land of Egypt: *I the Lord am your God.*" The other is found in the text above (Deut. 10:17–19): "For the Lord your God is God supreme and Lord supreme, the great, the mighty, and the awesome God who . . . befriends the stranger, providing him with food and clothing. You too must befriend the stranger, for you were strangers in the land of Egypt."

In the Torah's view, ethics belongs in the

---

[1] Our translation of verses 18 and 19 renders the Hebrew word אָהַב as "befriend," but in Lev. 19:34 it retains the more usual "love," probably because it would be awkward to say that one should "befriend a stranger as oneself." The commandment intends that we should disregard the strangeness of the גֵּר as much as possible and make him feel welcome, that is, *befriend* him. Asking us to *love* him, in the ordinary sense of the English word, would hardly be realistic. (See also Rosenzweig in Gleanings.)

[2] Another Deuteronomic law (26:5–9) and subsequent tradition (as expressed in the Haggadah) required the Israelite to identify himself with the Egyptian experience, and the command to love the stranger was thereby given added emphasis. But the question remains how this identification could be achieved to the point where it decisively influenced social attitudes and actions.

realm of religion because God sets the standards of human behavior. Thus, the esteem for and love of the stranger is a reflection of our love of God [11]. In the alien we **are** first and foremost bidden to discover the presence of the redeeming God and thereby to reinforce our bonds with all humanity.

On the Geography of the Land

This commentary assumes that the text of Deuteronomy reflects a time when the Israelites had long been settled in the land and therefore were well familiar with its advantages and shortcomings (see introduction). When therefore, toward the end of his discourse, Moses is pictured as extolling the physical features of Canaan, we may take this to be a judgment based on experience, made at the time of King Josiah and not, as a fundamentalist view of the Torah would have it, an assessment made from a trans-Jordanian perspective, before the conquest under Joshua. It is noteworthy, then, that the land is said to possess a natural superiority to Egypt, in that it needs a minimum of care because of its rainfall and the retentive condition of the soil; and also in that, instead of the Egyptian flatlands, it possesses an amplitude of hills, valleys, and rivers. This judgment—especially if allowance is made for the poetic license expected in the context of Moses' address—remains an accurate description of Israel's geographic features.

Contrary to popular impression, the average annual rainfall in the land does not differ from that found in temperate zones. The difference lies in the intensity of the rain per hour and its distribution: it falls during forty to sixty days in a season stretching from October to April, while in temperate climes precipitation occurs over some one hundred eighty days spread over twelve months [12]. A further difference lies in the uneven distribution of the rain over the face of the land: in the southern desert there is less than 30 mm. (1.2 in.) rain per annum, while in northern Galilee there may be up to 1,100 mm. (44 in.). The forested areas of Judea and Samaria have a consistently high amount of precipitation. Since in antiquity the forests were far more widespread and the top soil had not yet eroded to the extent it did in later centuries, runoffs must have been fewer and much of the land was deserving of the description that it soaked up the rainwater (Deut. 11:11).

The major geographical feature of the land is its location at the edge of the earth's longest rift valley, which runs from the Zambesi in Central Africa to the Ural Mountains in Soviet Russia, 6,000 km. (3,700 miles) long, forming one vast basin containing primarily streams that do not discharge into the sea. Thus, 70 percent of the rivers and wadis in the mountains girding Israel run into the rift valley. Its lowest point, the Dead Sea, is the lowest surface area on earth.

Moses calls Canaan "a land of hills and valleys." In its topography it is not unlike Greece or Switzerland, where people live in relative proximity to one another, yet—because of the mountains—are also separate and prone to keep individual traditions and dialects alive. The long endurance of tribal differences in Israel was in part a function of its geography.

The land was further distinguished in that it was the land bridge connecting the two major cultural and political centers of the ancient Near East, Egypt and Mesopotamia. The Via Maris (as it was known later on) ran along the Mediterranean, and the King's Highway on the east side of the Jordan. Armies traversed these roads and often fought for them and the cities that guarded their access. In the process, religious and other cultural influences from north and south fructified its people. But ultimately it was neither the natural nor the geopolitical advantages which gave the land its distinction; rather, it was the conviction of its people that they were possessing it as God's gift. To them, it was a supranatural possession whose title could be revoked if the covenant on which it was based was breached—an eternal yet conditional gift, a land "on which the Lord your God always keeps His eye, from year's beginning to year's end" (Deut. 11:12). It reaches, in the words of this exhortation, all the way to the Euphrates, an idealized conception of its extent, or a hope that the days of Solomon's reign would return.[3]

On this note of promise and vision the second discourse of Moses reaches its conclusion.

---

[3] See further at Deut. 2:7 and Commentary on Numbers, chapter 34. P. Diepold distinguishes three Deuteronomic concepts of the extent of the land: a cis-Jordanian, a trans-Jordanian, and a Euphrates tradition [13].

And Now (Deut. 10:12)

Whenever the Torah begins an admonition with "And now..." (וְעַתָּה) it implies the need for repentance.   MIDRASH [14]

What ... (10:12)

"What is it that the Lord your God demands of you?" The "what" (מָה) denotes humility, as when Moses and Aaron say "What are we?" (Exod. 16:7).[4] Hence, in our text too: Humility is *what* the Lord requires.   THE BAAL SHEM TOV [15]

Only This ... (10:12)

God asks "only" reverence, from which we learn that everything is in the power of heaven except man's reverence for God (i.e., the "only" must be supplied by man).   TALMUD [16]

Commented the chasidic leader, Levi Yitzchak of Berditchev, always a staunch defender of Israel: In those days, reverence for God was a small matter for the people (hence the text says "only this"), because they had seen the great deeds of the Lord. And he confronted God: "Give our generation the likes of the Exodus and see how for us too reverence for You will be a small matter!" [17]

Love and Fear[5]

Both are commanded, and only if one serves Him out of both motivations does one serve Him fully.   ISAAC ALFASI [18]

A popular saying went: "Fear without love is incomplete; love without fear is nothing."

A Contradiction

Since we are commanded to make Shabbat a delight (Isa. 58:13), why are congregations exposed to Shabbat sermons which reprove the people and sadden the heart? Because such admonition is called a circumcision of the heart (Deut. 10:16), and we are taught that circumcision is a command to be observed even on Shabbat.   CHASIDIC [19]

God Supreme (10:17)

The Hebrew literally calls Him "God of gods and Lord of lords," because He is beyond any description and conception we might have of His divinity.   CHASIDIC [20]

Neighbor and Stranger

He is "like you" ("as yourself," Lev. 19:18), and thus not "you." You remain you and are to remain just that. But he is not to remain a He for you, and thus a mere It for you. Rather he is like You, like your You, a You like You, an I—a soul.
                                F. ROSENZWEIG [21]

Animals First

In Deut. 11:15 the Torah speaks first of God providing grass for cattle and then says "thus you shall eat your fill." From this, Rabbi Judah taught, in the name of Rav: A person is forbidden to eat until he has fed his cattle.   TALMUD [22]

Responsibility

In the *Shema* the command to teach the children is addressed to the individual (וְשִׁנַּנְתָּם, Deut.

---

[4] One Torah translation renders the verse "*Who are we*...."

[5] Understanding "fear" as "reverence" (יִרְאָה); see above, at 10:12.

6:7), while here it is phrased in the plural (וּלְמַדְתֶּם אֹתָם, Deut. 11:19). From this you learn that the primary responsibility for education rests with the parents, the secondary with the community.

BASED ON THE TALMUD [23]

The Mountains

It is a little land, Canaan, small and slender as scarcely any other historical land. It stretches down from the mountains to the sea and from the mountains to the river. Not the river, which is more boundary than internal influence, but the mountains give the land its determining line. It is a land with a spine, similar to Italy. From the south to the north stretch mountains. In the south, the outposts lie between the Sea of Salt (into which runs the downward-flowing Jordan) and the Great Sea, the Mediterranean; while, in the north, the white mountains of Lebanon form a terminus. Occasionally, in the course of the centuries, the boundaries advanced; but the land always remained small. Everything that occurred in it had an intimacy; only that which was outside seemed distant.[6]

LEO BAECK [24]

---

[6] Baeck here refers to the spiritual state of Israel.

PART III

Third Discourse

While the second discourse was essentially an elaboration of the first and second commandments—stressing the love, respect, and unique adoration due the God of Israel—the text now—comprising the third discourse—turns to other considerations which may be divided into two broad categories: ritual (moral) and civil (social) laws, plus an epilogue. Some of these appear elsewhere in the Torah, others are found only here. For instance, the passages dealing with false prophets occur only in Deuteronomy, whereas rules of permitted and forbidden foods can be found also in Leviticus.

Ritual and Moral Laws

Worship in a central place, 12:1–28
Further injunctions against idolatry, 12:29–13:19; 16:21–17:7
Self-mutilation, 14:1–2
Permitted and forbidden foods, 14:3–21
Tithes, 14:22–29
Release, 15:1–18
Firstlings, 15:19–23
Holy days, 16:1–17
Kindness to animals, 22:1–4, 6–8; 25:4
Unnatural mixtures, 22:5, 9–11
Fringes, 22:12
Unchastity, 22:13–29
Ostracism, 23:1–9
Holiness of the camp, 23:10–15
Temple prostitution, 23:18–19
Skin affection, 24:8–9
Amalek, 25:17–19

Civil, Criminal, and Social Laws

Debts, prevention of poverty, 15:1–11
Laws of slavery, 15:12–18
Judges and courts, 16:18–20
Election of a king, 17:14–20
Priests and Levites, 18:1–8
Prophets, 18:9–22 (also in ch. 13)
Cities of refuge, 19:1–13

Encroachment, 19:14
False testimony, 19:15–21
Rules of war, 20:1–20
Unsolved murder, 21:1–9
Punishment by hanging, 21:22–23
Marriage to captive woman, 21:10–24
Primogeniture, 21:15–17
Rebellious son, 21:18–21
Runaway slaves, 23:16–17
Interest charges, 23:20–21
Vows, 23:22–24
Neighbor's rights, 23:25–26
Remarriage, 24:1–4
Exemption from war service, 24:5
Pledges, 24:6, 10–13, 17–18
Kidnaping, 24:7
Wages, 24:14–15
Personal responsibility, 24:16
Strangers, orphans, and widows, 24:17–22
Excessive punishment, 25:1–3
Levirate marriage, 25:5–10
Assault, 25:11–12
Weights and measures, 25:13–16

Epilogue
　Exhortation, chapter 26
　Pronouncement of blessings and curses, chapters 27–28.

In depicting the bulk of Deuteronomic legislation in this fashion we need to remember that the Torah itself did not deal with such categories of law. Often certain passages obtained their present position as an aid to memory rather than for systematic reasons in the modern sense. But it is noteworthy that, unlike in Mesopotamian codes, laws regarding *persons* generally precede laws of *property*, with procedural regulations following or interspersed.

The Divine Command

Many commentators consider the last seven verses of chapter 11 as the conclusion of the second discourse and not, as we do here, as the beginning of the third. Our reason is primarily literary: the discourse thus opens with the command to pronounce blessings and curses on Mount Gerizim and Mount Ebal, respectively; and, in chapter 27, at the end of the discourse, this command is repeated and treated in detail. The formal, dramatic invocation of the Divine Presence constitutes the framework for the code of special laws which forms the bulk of Deuteronomy. Our division is supported by the rabbinic provision that a new weekly portion (*Re'eh*) begins with 11:26.

כו רְאֵה אָנֹכִי נֹתֵן לִפְנֵיכֶם הַיּוֹם בְּרָכָה וּקְלָלָה: אֶת־
הַבְּרָכָה אֲשֶׁר תִּשְׁמְעוּ אֶל־מִצְוֺת יְהֹוָה אֱלֹהֵיכֶם אֲשֶׁר
כז אָנֹכִי מְצַוֶּה אֶתְכֶם הַיּוֹם: וְהַקְּלָלָה אִם־לֹא תִשְׁמְעוּ
אֶל־מִצְוֺת יְהֹוָה אֱלֹהֵיכֶם וְסַרְתֶּם מִן־הַדֶּרֶךְ אֲשֶׁר
אָנֹכִי מְצַוֶּה אֶתְכֶם הַיּוֹם לָלֶכֶת אַחֲרֵי אֱלֹהִים
כט אֲחֵרִים אֲשֶׁר לֹא־יְדַעְתֶּם: ס וְהָיָה כִּי יְבִיאֲךָ
יְהֹוָה אֱלֹהֶיךָ אֶל־הָאָרֶץ אֲשֶׁר־אַתָּה בָא־שָׁמָּה
לְרִשְׁתָּהּ וְנָתַתָּה אֶת־הַבְּרָכָה עַל־הַר גְּרִזִים וְאֶת־
ל הַקְּלָלָה עַל־הַר עֵיבָל: הֲלֹא־הֵמָּה בְּעֵבֶר הַיַּרְדֵּן

26] See, this day I set before you blessing and curse: **27]** blessing, if you obey the commandments of the LORD your God which I enjoin upon you this day; **28]** and curse, if you do not obey the commandments of the LORD your God, but turn away from the path which I enjoin upon you this day and follow other gods, whom you have not experienced. **29]** When the LORD your God brings you into the land which you are about to invade and occupy, you shall pronounce the blessing at Mount Gerizim and the curse at Mount Ebal.— **30]** Both are on the other side

11:26] *I set before you.* Affirming free choice.

27–28] *Blessing . . . curse.* Details of the procedure are given at the end of the discourse, 27:12 ff. Mount Gerizim (called by the Arabs Jebel al-Tur, 2,849 ft. or 855 m. high) lies to the south of Shechem (modern Nablus), while Mount Ebal (Jebel Islamiya, 3,077 ft. or 923 m. high) is to the north. Gerizim has numerous springs arising at its foot and is the more fertile of the two. Its choice as the mountain of blessing may go back to an old tra- dition that regarded Shechem rather than Sinai and Jerusalem as the chief locale of God's presence. This explains the Samaritan claim that Gerizim is superior in sanctity to Jerusalem [1].

28] *Experienced.* The word יָדַע describes some- times intellectual apprehension and at other times an intimate, living relationship; see Hosea 13:4 and, in sexual respects, Gen. 4:1 (and our com- mentary to Gen. 2:25–3:24, "Sexual Interpreta- tion").

אַחֲרֵי דֶּרֶךְ מְבוֹא הַשֶּׁמֶשׁ בְּאֶרֶץ הַכְּנַעֲנִי הַיֹּשֵׁב
לא בָּעֲרָבָה מוּל הַגִּלְגָּל אֵצֶל אֵלוֹנֵי מֹרֶה: כִּי אַתֶּם
עֹבְרִים אֶת־הַיַּרְדֵּן לָבֹא לָרֶשֶׁת אֶת־הָאָרֶץ אֲשֶׁר־
יְהוָֹה אֱלֹהֵיכֶם נֹתֵן לָכֶם וִירִשְׁתֶּם אֹתָהּ וִישַׁבְתֶּם־בָּהּ:
לב וּשְׁמַרְתֶּם לַעֲשׂוֹת אֵת כָּל־הַחֻקִּים וְאֶת־הַמִּשְׁפָּטִים
אֲשֶׁר אָנֹכִי נֹתֵן לִפְנֵיכֶם הַיּוֹם:

Deuteronomy 11
31–32

of the Jordan, beyond the west road which is in the land of the Canaanites who dwell in the Arabah—near Gilgal, by the terebinths of Moreh.

31] For you are about to cross the Jordan to invade and occupy the land which the LORD your God is giving to you. When you have occupied it and are settled in it, **32]** take care to observe all the laws and rules that I have set before you this day.

30] *Canaanites who dwell in the Arabah—near Gilgal.* The name Gilgal (suggesting rolled stones that formed a marker or monument) was probably applied to several sacred places in Canaan. Similarly, Arabah (or Aravah) may have been used in various senses; Driver suggests that here it meant an area near Jericho where a Gilgal was located, a place that could be seen from the heights of Moab [2].

Terebinths of Moreh. Noted in Gen. 12:6 as standing near Shechem.

GLEANINGS

Singular

The *sidrah* begins with the word "See," which in the Hebrew (רְאֵה) is in the singular. Thereafter, however, the text switches to the plural. The reason is that, while the commandments are set before the whole people (hence the plural address), each individual must "see" and decide whether to obey or disobey.   AFTER BACHYA [3]

This Day (Deut. 11:26)

This signified that the mitzvah of Gerizim and Ebal was to be performed at once, and not after total possession of the land had been achieved. It emphasized that Israel was to live in the land only for the sake of doing mitzvot.

RALBAG (GERSONIDES) [4]

I Set before You Blessing and Curse

Hence the saying: "Sword and book came down from Heaven together." God said: If you observe what is written in the Book you will be saved from the sword, but if not it will slay you.

MIDRASH [5]

In laying two choices before us, God urges us to choose the good and helps us if we strive to achieve it. For He does not deal with us in accordance with strict justice.   MIDRASH [6]

The choice between blessing and curse does not permit of a compromise. They are two opposites between which one must choose.

SFORNO [7]

It says "blessing, if you obey" (verse 27)—it is enough to obey, for this will inevitably lead to the performance of mitzvot. But regarding the curse the text speaks differently. It adds to "curse, if you do not obey" (verse 28) the words, "but turn away." For failure to obey or hear does not always and necessarily lead to actual sin.   CHASIDIC [8]

The words are so couched as to make clear that every acknowledgment of idolatry is tantamount to a denial of the Torah, and every denial of idolatry is an acknowledgment of the Torah.

MIDRASH [9]

Two Mountains

Gerizim and Ebal are two peaks of the Ephraim range of mountains which still show a striking contrast in their appearance. Gerizim to the south of the valley of Shechem presents a smiling green slope rising in fruit-covered terraces to its summit; Ebal on the north side, steep, barren, and bleak, slightly higher than Gerizim. The two mounts lying next to each other form accordingly a most telling instructive picture of blessing and curse. They both rise on one and the same soil, both are watered by one and the same fall of rain and dew, the same air breathes over both of them, the same pollen wafts over both of them, and yet Ebal remains in barren bleakness while Gerizim is clad to its summit in embellishment of vegetation. In the same way, blessing and curse are not conditional on external circumstances but on our own inner receptivity for the one or the other, on our behavior towards that which is to bring blessing.   S. R. HIRSCH [10]

The Central Sanctuary

Moses' third discourse begins with a fundamental tenet which characterizes the Book of Deuteronomy: the overriding need for a central sanctuary. In order to achieve a centralization of sacrificial worship, all other sites and altars were to be dismantled and destroyed. This provision constituted an important development in the religious life of the people: it was part of the constant fight against idolatry, for it struck at the persistence of local pagan cults; and it was also a stage in the unification of the nation in which the central sanctuary played a significant role.

This raised some ancillary problems, chief among them the custom of eating meat only on sacrificial occasions. Since such consumption had taken place in the context of sacrificial worship in various localities, which were at all times in reach of every person, a central sanctuary would prevent an Israelite from eating meat most of the time. Hence the law specifies at once that, while sacrifice would be centralized, the consumption of meat would not. But other offerings, such as firstlings, must be brought to the central site.

The section ends with a warning not to give way to curiosity about foreign religious practices, and with a repetition of the injunction not to add to or detract from the law as presented. In most English versions, 13:1 is reckoned as belonging to chapter 12 (making it 12:32; actually, the verse is a bridge between the two chapters).

א אֵלֶּה הַחֻקִּים וְהַמִּשְׁפָּטִים אֲשֶׁר תִּשְׁמְרוּן לַעֲשׂוֹת
בָּאָרֶץ אֲשֶׁר נָתַן יְהֹוָה אֱלֹהֵי אֲבֹתֶיךָ לְךָ לְרִשְׁתָּהּ

ב כָּל־הַיָּמִים אֲשֶׁר־אַתֶּם חַיִּים עַל־הָאֲדָמָה: אַבֵּד
תְּאַבְּדוּן אֶת־כָּל־הַמְּקֹמוֹת אֲשֶׁר עָבְדוּ־שָׁם הַגּוֹיִם
אֲשֶׁר אַתֶּם יֹרְשִׁים אֹתָם אֶת־אֱלֹהֵיהֶם עַל־הֶהָרִים

ג הָרָמִים וְעַל־הַגְּבָעוֹת וְתַחַת כָּל־עֵץ רַעֲנָן: וְנִתַּצְתֶּם
אֶת־מִזְבְּחֹתָם וְשִׁבַּרְתֶּם אֶת־מַצֵּבֹתָם וַאֲשֵׁרֵיהֶם
תִּשְׂרְפוּן בָּאֵשׁ וּפְסִילֵי אֱלֹהֵיהֶם תְּגַדֵּעוּן וְאִבַּדְתֶּם

ד אֶת־שְׁמָם מִן־הַמָּקוֹם הַהוּא: לֹא־תַעֲשׂוּן כֵּן לַיהֹוָה

ה אֱלֹהֵיכֶם: כִּי אִם־אֶל־הַמָּקוֹם אֲשֶׁר־יִבְחַר יְהֹוָה

Deuteronomy 12
1–5

1] These are the laws and rules which you must carefully observe in the land that the LORD, God of your fathers, is giving you to possess, as long as you live on earth.

2] You must destroy all the sites at which the nations you are to dispossess worshiped their gods, whether on lofty mountains and on hills or under any luxuriant tree.   3] Tear down their altars, smash their pillars, put their sacred posts to the fire, and cut down the images of their gods, obliterating their name from that site.

4] Do not worship the LORD your God in like manner,   5] but look only to

---

12:1] *Laws and rules.* See at 4:1.

Live on earth. Others apply the expression *al ha-adamah* to the land of Israel only [1] (see further in Gleanings).

2] *Lofty mountains . . . hills.* These were traditional places of pagan worship, but in biblical religion, too, elevated places play an important role: Mt. Sinai, Mt. Nebo, Mt. Zion. Driver suggested that in such places one was believed closer to the Divinity [2].

Tree. Sacred trees also were frequent worship sites, and it is likely that the *menorah* was a stylized tree (see commentary on Exod. 25:31 ff.).

3] *Altars . . . pillars.* Rashi suggests that the former consisted of many stones, the latter of single slabs.

Sacred posts. They were called *asherim* because they were dedicated to Asherah (see at 7:5). The command to destroy pagan sites and objects was considered obligatory only in Eretz Yisrael and not, for obvious reasons, outside the Land [3].

4] *In like manner.* That is, on mountains or under trees.

אֱלֹהֵיכֶם מִכָּל־שִׁבְטֵיכֶם לָשׂוּם אֶת־שְׁמוֹ שָׁם לְשִׁכְנוֹ

ו תִדְרְשׁוּ וּבָאתָ שָּׁמָּה: וַהֲבֵאתֶם שָׁמָּה עֹלֹתֵיכֶם

וְזִבְחֵיכֶם וְאֵת מַעְשְׂרֹתֵיכֶם וְאֵת תְּרוּמַת יֶדְכֶם

וְנִדְרֵיכֶם וְנִדְבֹתֵיכֶם וּבְכֹרֹת בְּקַרְכֶם וְצֹאנְכֶם:

ז וַאֲכַלְתֶּם־שָׁם לִפְנֵי יְהֹוָה אֱלֹהֵיכֶם וּשְׂמַחְתֶּם בְּכֹל

מִשְׁלַח יֶדְכֶם אַתֶּם וּבָתֵּיכֶם אֲשֶׁר בֵּרַכְךָ יְהֹוָה

ח אֱלֹהֶיךָ: לֹא תַעֲשׂוּן כְּכֹל אֲשֶׁר אֲנַחְנוּ עֹשִׂים פֹּה

ט הַיּוֹם אִישׁ כָּל־הַיָּשָׁר בְּעֵינָיו: כִּי לֹא־בָאתֶם עַד־

Deuteronomy 12
6–9

the site that the LORD your God will choose amidst all your tribes as His habitation, to establish His name there. There you are to go, **6]** and there you are to bring your burnt offerings and other sacrifices, your tithes and contributions, your votive and freewill offerings, and the firstlings of your herds and flocks. **7]** Together with your households, you shall feast there before the LORD your God, happy in all the undertakings in which the LORD your God has blessed you.

8] You shall not act at all as we now act here, everyman as he pleases, **9]** be-

---

6] *There you are to bring.* Seven kinds of offerings are mentioned:

a. Burnt offerings. The *olah* was consumed entirely by fire (see verse 27); older translations used the term holocaust, "wholly burnt."

b. Other sacrifices. *Zevach*, an offering of which only the blood and some other parts were sacrificed, the rest was eaten; such sacrifices were usually thanks or peace offerings. (A detailed discussion of sacrifices may be found in our Commentary on Leviticus, in the introduction to Part I, "Laws of Sacrifice.")

c. Tithes. The *ma-aser* (from עֶשֶׂר, *eser*, ten) was the tenth of cattle or produce set aside for the Levites and the socially disadvantaged (see at 14:22 ff.) [4].

d. Contributions. *Terumah* ("heave offering") was a general levy brought on the three pilgrim festivals and for special occasions, such as contributions for the building of a sanctuary.

However, in talmudic literature, *terumah* referred mostly to portions given to the priests.

e. Votive offerings. Made to fulfill a vow (*neder*). On the importance and treatment of vows see our commentary on Num. 30:1–16.

f. Freewill offerings. A *nedavah* was a sacrifice made voluntarily, because the worshiper wanted to offer it.

The term has persisted in modern Hebrew and in Yiddish to describe charitable gifts.

g. Firstlings. *Bikkurim*, the first yield of herd and field belonged to God. See below at 15:19.

8] *As we now act here.* These words may be a critique of conditions prevailing in later days (see Judg. 17:6; 21:25).

עַתָּה אֶל־הַמְּנוּחָה וְאֶל־הַנַּחֲלָה אֲשֶׁר־יְהוָה אֱלֹהֶיךָ
נֹתֵן לָךְ: וַעֲבַרְתֶּם אֶת־הַיַּרְדֵּן וִישַׁבְתֶּם בָּאָרֶץ אֲשֶׁר־
יְהוָה אֱלֹהֵיכֶם מַנְחִיל אֶתְכֶם וְהֵנִיחַ לָכֶם מִכָּל־
יא אֹיְבֵיכֶם מִסָּבִיב וִישַׁבְתֶּם־בֶּטַח: וְהָיָה הַמָּקוֹם
אֲשֶׁר־יִבְחַר יְהוָה אֱלֹהֵיכֶם בּוֹ לְשַׁכֵּן שְׁמוֹ שָׁם שָׁמָּה
תָבִיאוּ אֵת כָּל־אֲשֶׁר אָנֹכִי מְצַוֶּה אֶתְכֶם עוֹלֹתֵיכֶם
וְזִבְחֵיכֶם מַעְשְׂרֹתֵיכֶם וּתְרֻמַת יֶדְכֶם וְכֹל מִבְחַר
יב נִדְרֵיכֶם אֲשֶׁר תִּדְּרוּ לַיהוָה: וּשְׂמַחְתֶּם לִפְנֵי יְהוָה
אֱלֹהֵיכֶם אַתֶּם וּבְנֵיכֶם וּבְנֹתֵיכֶם וְעַבְדֵיכֶם
וְאַמְהֹתֵיכֶם וְהַלֵּוִי אֲשֶׁר בְּשַׁעֲרֵיכֶם כִּי אֵין לוֹ חֵלֶק
יג וְנַחֲלָה אִתְּכֶם: הִשָּׁמֶר לְךָ פֶּן־תַּעֲלֶה עֹלֹתֶיךָ בְּכָל־
יד מָקוֹם אֲשֶׁר תִּרְאֶה: כִּי אִם־בַּמָּקוֹם אֲשֶׁר־יִבְחַר יְהוָה

Deuteronomy 12

10—14

cause you have not yet come to the allotted haven that the LORD your God is giving you.   **10]** When you cross the Jordan and settle in the land that the LORD your God is allotting to you, and He grants you safety from all your enemies around you and you live in security,   **11]** then you must bring everything that I command you to the site where the LORD your God will choose to establish His name: your burnt offerings and other sacrifices, your tithes and contributions, and all the choice votive offerings that you vow to the LORD.   **12]** And you shall rejoice before the LORD your God with your sons and daughters and with your male and female slaves, along with the Levite of your settlement, for he has no territorial allotment among you.

13] Take care not to sacrifice your burnt offerings in any place you like,   **14]** but only in the place which the LORD will choose in one of your tribal territories. There

---

12] *Levite of your settlement.* The original idea of settling the Levites in forty-eight special cities ap- parently never materialized. Instead, levitical families lived in all communities and served in the central sanctuary on a rotating basis.

בְּאַחַד שְׁבָטֶיךָ שָׁם תַּעֲלֶה עֹלֹתֶיךָ וְשָׁם תַּעֲשֶׂה כֹּל

טו אֲשֶׁר אָנֹכִי מְצַוֶּךָּ: רַק בְּכָל־אַוַּת נַפְשְׁךָ תִּזְבַּח

וְאָכַלְתָּ בָשָׂר כְּבִרְכַּת יְהֹוָה אֱלֹהֶיךָ אֲשֶׁר נָתַן־לְךָ

בְּכָל־שְׁעָרֶיךָ הַטָּמֵא וְהַטָּהוֹר יֹאכְלֶנּוּ כַּצְּבִי וְכָאַיָּל:

טז רַק הַדָּם לֹא תֹאכֵלוּ עַל־הָאָרֶץ תִּשְׁפְּכֶנּוּ כַּמָּיִם:

יז לֹא־תוּכַל לֶאֱכֹל בִּשְׁעָרֶיךָ מַעְשַׂר דְּגָנְךָ וְתִירֹשְׁךָ

וְיִצְהָרֶךָ וּבְכֹרֹת בְּקָרְךָ וְצֹאנֶךָ וְכָל־נְדָרֶיךָ אֲשֶׁר

יח תִּדֹּר וְנִדְבֹתֶיךָ וּתְרוּמַת יָדֶךָ: כִּי אִם־לִפְנֵי יְהֹוָה

אֱלֹהֶיךָ תֹּאכְלֶנּוּ בַּמָּקוֹם אֲשֶׁר יִבְחַר יְהֹוָה אֱלֹהֶיךָ

בּוֹ אַתָּה וּבִנְךָ וּבִתֶּךָ וְעַבְדְּךָ וַאֲמָתֶךָ וְהַלֵּוִי אֲשֶׁר

בִּשְׁעָרֶיךָ וְשָׂמַחְתָּ לִפְנֵי יְהֹוָה אֱלֹהֶיךָ בְּכֹל מִשְׁלַח

Deuteronomy 12
15–18

you shall sacrifice your burnt offerings and there you shall observe all that I enjoin upon you.   **15]** But whenever you desire, you may slaughter and eat meat in any of your settlements, according to the blessing which the LORD your God has granted you. The unclean and the clean alike may partake of it, as of the gazelle and the deer.   **16]** But you must not partake of the blood; you shall pour it out on the ground like water.

17] You may not partake in your settlements of the tithes of your new grain or wine or oil, or of the firstlings of your herds and flocks, or of any of the votive offerings that you vow, or of your freewill offerings, or of your contributions. **18]** These you must consume before the LORD your God in the place that the LORD your God will choose—you and your son and your daughter, your male and female slaves, and the Levite in your settlements—happy before the LORD your God in all

15]   *The unclean and the clean.* In the ritual sense. Thus, a woman in her menstrual period was considered unclean, and afterwards, her ablutions performed, she was clean.

    The gazelle and the deer. Which are permitted

for food but not for sacrifice. Similarly, an animal with a blemish which disqualified it for sacrifice but not for food would be included in this rule [5].

16]   *Partake of the blood.* See commentary below.

יט יָדֶ֑ךָ: הִשָּׁ֣מֶר לְךָ֔ פֶּֽן־תַּעֲזֹ֖ב אֶת־הַלֵּוִ֑י כָּל־יָמֶ֖יךָ עַל־

כ אַדְמָתֶֽךָ: ס כִּֽי־יַרְחִיב֩ יְהֹוָ֨ה אֱלֹהֶ֥יךָ אֶֽת־גְּבֻלְךָ֮

כַּאֲשֶׁ֣ר דִּבֶּר־לָךְ֒ וְאָמַרְתָּ֙ אֹכְלָ֣ה בָשָׂ֔ר כִּֽי־תְאַוֶּ֥ה

נַפְשְׁךָ֖ לֶאֱכֹ֣ל בָּשָׂ֑ר בְּכָל־אַוַּ֥ת נַפְשְׁךָ֖ תֹּאכַ֥ל בָּשָֽׂר:

כא כִּֽי־יִרְחַ֨ק מִמְּךָ֜ הַמָּק֗וֹם אֲשֶׁ֨ר יִבְחַ֜ר יְהֹוָ֣ה אֱלֹהֶ֘יךָ֘

לָשׂ֣וּם שְׁמ֣וֹ שָׁם֒ וְזָבַחְתָּ֞ מִבְּקָרְךָ֣ וּמִצֹּֽאנְךָ֗ אֲשֶׁ֨ר נָתַ֤ן

יְהֹוָה֙ לְךָ֔ כַּאֲשֶׁ֖ר צִוִּיתִ֑ךָ וְאָֽכַלְתָּ֙ בִּשְׁעָרֶ֔יךָ בְּכֹ֖ל

כב אַוַּ֥ת נַפְשֶֽׁךָ: אַ֗ךְ כַּאֲשֶׁ֨ר יֵֽאָכֵ֤ל אֶֽת־הַצְּבִי֙ וְאֶת־הָ֣אַיָּ֔ל

כג כֵּ֣ן תֹּאכְלֶ֑נּוּ הַטָּמֵא֙ וְהַטָּה֔וֹר יַחְדָּ֖ו יֹאכְלֶֽנּוּ: רַ֡ק

חֲזַ֡ק לְבִלְתִּי֩ אֲכֹ֨ל הַדָּ֜ם כִּ֤י הַדָּם֙ ה֣וּא הַנָּ֔פֶשׁ וְלֹֽא־

כד תֹּאכַ֥ל הַנֶּ֖פֶשׁ עִם־הַבָּשָֽׂר: לֹ֖א תֹּאכְלֶ֑נּוּ עַל־הָאָ֥רֶץ

כה תִּשְׁפְּכֶ֖נּוּ כַּמָּֽיִם: לֹ֣א תֹּאכְלֶ֑נּוּ לְמַ֨עַן֙ יִיטַ֣ב לְךָ֔

* כא חסר י'.

Deuteronomy 12

19–25

your undertakings. **19]** Be sure not to neglect the Levite as long as you live in your land.

20] When the LORD enlarges your territory, as He has promised you, and you say, "I shall eat some meat," for you have the urge to eat meat, you may eat meat whenever you wish. **21]** If the place where the LORD has chosen to establish His name is too far from you, you may slaughter any of the cattle or sheep that the LORD gives you, as I have instructed you; and you may eat to your heart's content in your settlements. **22]** Eat it, however, as the gazelle and the deer are eaten: the unclean may eat it together with the clean. **23]** But make sure that you do not partake of the blood; for the blood is the life, and you must not consume the life with the flesh. **24]** You must not partake of it; you must pour it out on the ground like water: **25]** you must not partake of it, in order that it may go well

20] *I shall eat some meat.* What follows gives a strong hortatory
cast to the injunctions previously issued.

158

כו וּלְבָנֶיךָ אַחֲרֶיךָ כִּי־תַעֲשֶׂה הַיָּשָׁר בְּעֵינֵי יְהוָה: רַק
קָדָשֶׁיךָ אֲשֶׁר־יִהְיוּ לְךָ וּנְדָרֶיךָ תִּשָּׂא וּבָאתָ אֶל־
כז הַמָּקוֹם אֲשֶׁר־יִבְחַר יְהוָה: וְעָשִׂיתָ עֹלֹתֶיךָ הַבָּשָׂר
וְהַדָּם עַל־מִזְבַּח יְהוָה אֱלֹהֶיךָ וְדַם־זְבָחֶיךָ יִשָּׁפֵךְ
כח עַל־מִזְבַּח יְהוָה אֱלֹהֶיךָ וְהַבָּשָׂר תֹּאכֵל: שְׁמֹר
וְשָׁמַעְתָּ אֵת כָּל־הַדְּבָרִים הָאֵלֶּה אֲשֶׁר אָנֹכִי מְצַוֶּךָּ
לְמַעַן יִיטַב לְךָ וּלְבָנֶיךָ אַחֲרֶיךָ עַד־עוֹלָם כִּי תַעֲשֶׂה
כט הַטּוֹב וְהַיָּשָׁר בְּעֵינֵי יְהוָה אֱלֹהֶיךָ: ס כִּי־יַכְרִית
יְהוָה אֱלֹהֶיךָ אֶת־הַגּוֹיִם אֲשֶׁר אַתָּה בָא־שָׁמָּה לָרֶשֶׁת
ל אוֹתָם מִפָּנֶיךָ וְיָרַשְׁתָּ אֹתָם וְיָשַׁבְתָּ בְּאַרְצָם: הִשָּׁמֶר
לְךָ פֶּן־תִּנָּקֵשׁ אַחֲרֵיהֶם אַחֲרֵי הִשָּׁמְדָם מִפָּנֶיךָ וּפֶן־
תִּדְרֹשׁ לֵאלֹהֵיהֶם לֵאמֹר אֵיכָה יַעַבְדוּ הַגּוֹיִם הָאֵלֶּה

Deuteronomy 12
26–30

with you and with your descendants to come, for you will be doing what is right in the sight of the LORD.

26] But such sacred and votive donations as you may have shall be taken by you to the site that the LORD will choose. 27] You shall offer your burnt offerings, both the flesh and the blood, on the altar of the LORD your God; and of your other sacrifices, the blood shall be poured out on the altar of the LORD your God, and you shall eat the flesh.

28] Be careful to heed all these commandments which I enjoin upon you; thus it will go well with you and with your descendants after you forever, for you will be doing what is good and right in the sight of the LORD your God.

29] When the LORD your God has cut down before you the nations which you are about to invade and dispossess, and you have dispossessed them and settled in their land, 30] beware of being lured into their ways after they have been wiped out before you! Do not inquire about their gods, saying, "How did those nations

לא אֶת־אֱלֹהֵיהֶם וְאֶעֱשֶׂה־כֵּן גַּם־אָנִי: לֹא־תַעֲשֶׂה כֵן
לַיהֹוָה אֱלֹהֶיךָ כִּי כָל־תּוֹעֲבַת יְהֹוָה אֲשֶׁר שָׂנֵא
עָשׂוּ לֵאלֹהֵיהֶם כִּי גַם אֶת־בְּנֵיהֶם וְאֶת־בְּנֹתֵיהֶם
יִשְׂרְפוּ בָאֵשׁ לֵאלֹהֵיהֶם:

א אֵת כָּל־הַדָּבָר אֲשֶׁר אָנֹכִי מְצַוֶּה אֶתְכֶם אֹתוֹ
תִשְׁמְרוּ לַעֲשׂוֹת לֹא־תֹסֵף עָלָיו וְלֹא תִגְרַע מִמֶּנּוּ: פ

Deuteronomy 12; 13
31; I

worship their gods? I too will follow those practices." **31]** You shall not act thus toward the Lord your God, for they perform for their gods every abhorrent act that the Lord detests; they even offer up their sons and daughters in fire to their gods. **1]** Be careful to observe only that which I enjoin upon you: neither add to it nor take away from it.

31] *Even ... their sons and daughters.* Tradition took the word גַּם (*gam,* "even," but normally meaning "also") to imply that sacrificing one's parents also fell under the prohibition. In various pagan cultures infirm parents were abandoned to wild animals or otherwise disposed of.

The Centralization of Worship

Traditional interpreters of the Torah aver that the rules, which demand that all sacrifices must be brought to a central sanctuary, anticipate the settlement of Israel in the land. This commentary, however, holds that these regulations are the record of religious developments which took place after the settlement and the results of which the Book of Deuteronomy attempted to codify [6].

In the early days after the conquest, cultic as well as political life was completely decentralized and tribal organizations were the seats of power. With the establishment of the monarchy (just before the year 1000 B.C.E.) a centralized authority began to emerge, but tribal autonomy continued to exist for a long time. In religious matters, too, centralization was slow to come. People worshiped at local shrines, and often they would adopt cultic practices devoted to the local deity and combine them with the worship of Israel's God. This was natural, for there was a belief common to the peoples of the ancient Near East that the gods of a country could not be ignored with impunity. A syncretistic approach to religion—which was prominent especially among the Greeks and, later, the Romans—was a feature of Israel's worship in the early centuries of settlement in Canaan.

In this proliferation of centers, some like Shechem, Shiloh, and Beth-el achieved special status, but they remained local or, at most, regional sanctuaries. With the unification of the tribes under David and the establishment of Jerusalem as the political center of the nation, the drive toward religious centralization also gained strength.[1] In the centuries that followed, unified politics and centralized religious worship became mutually supportive.

However, the process of religious centralization received a setback when the nation split into two kingdoms, Israel and Judah, so that even within Judah (where the Temple of Jerusalem was located) local worship practices persisted and sacrifices continued to be offered at sacred shrines and *bamot* ("heights"). People would come to these various places with their meat and grain offerings and share them with the priestly attendants. In addition, other pagan practices were popular with significant numbers of Israelites, as is shown by the story of the prophet Elijah's contest with four hundred priests of Baal. Toward the latter part of the eighth century King Hezekiah abolished the *bamot*, but they were reintroduced by Manasseh (II Kings 21:3), until Josiah did away with them once and for all (II Kings 23). It was under his rule that the text of a book was found which scholars generally identify with Deuteronomy or its prototype. The text became normative for the cult and called for centralized worship as the will of God. As a concession, the eating of meat was permitted outside the sanctuary, but Jerusalem and its Temple, built by King Solomon three hundred thirty-five years before, became thereafter the focal point of the people's political and religious existence.[2]

[1] From what political foundations this unification developed is a matter of scholarly dispute. One theory posits a league (amphictyony) based at first on six "Leah" tribes, which were later—after the arrival of the "Joseph" group from Egypt—expanded into a twelve-member league. David placed his central shrine in Jerusalem because it was neutral territory and therefore less likely to have tribal opposition.

Opponents of this theory point to the absence of any mention of the league in the books of Judges and Samuel, and to the purely hypothetical nature of the "Leah" group [7].

[2] Jerusalem is not mentioned in Deuteronomy or the rest of the Torah. Only after the Deuteronomic reform (see introduction) was this central worship place firmly ensconced in the Jerusalemic Temple.

Blood and Meat

Three times the Torah deals with the non-sacrificial, everyday consumption of meat (Gen. 9:4; Lev., chapter 17; Deut. 12:20 ff.). Clearly, these passages reveal a development of attitudes, but precisely what this development was is a matter of scholarly controversy.[3]

The eating of animal flesh is probably a late stage in human evolution. Originally humanity was vegetarian; the Creation account reflects this in that it permits the consumption of plants but is silent on animals, which are specifically allowed only after the Flood (Gen. 1:29; 9:4). The idea persisted that blood was the seat of life and had a mysterious quality, and that therefore it was not to be eaten under any circumstances. It was to be poured on the ground where primal earth received it back, or dashed against the altar where, so to speak, God himself accepted it. Only in the latter case could the meat be consumed, for the altar was God's table, where the food could be shared with Him through His representatives. Thus, all slaughter for food had to be sacral in nature.[4]

This rule was feasible as long as sacrifices could be brought to local shrines accessible to the people. But, when the cult was centralized in the Deuteronomic reformation, provision had to be made for those who could not reach the sanctuary to consume meat in a non-sacral way. Such profane slaughter—limited to animals unfit for sacrifice—was therefore now permitted (12:15).

This in turn led to the practice of draining blood from the profanely slaughtered animal to the greatest degree possible, which in post-biblical days resulted in elaborate rules for ritual slaughtering (shechitah), and the washing, salting, and soaking of meat prior to eating it [11].

When the Temple was destroyed in 586 B.C.E. these rules lapsed, and when the exiles returned to Palestine they may have reinstituted local shrines where sacrifices could be offered. After the rebuilding of the Temple this proliferation of worship places conflicted once again with the needs of the central authority, and in time the old Deuteronomic rules were reasserted and remained in force during the existence of the Second Temple, until it was burned by the Romans in the year 70 C.E. Thereafter, rabbinic law created a body of rules that prescribe precisely what constitutes kasher (that is, ritually clean or permissible) meat.[5]

Do Not Inquire

The Torah states in Deut. 12:30 that Israelites are not to inquire about pagan religions and ask, "How did those nations worship their gods?" Such inquiry, it was feared, might lead to imitative idolatrous practices. If Israel was to be purged from paganism, it was best to prohibit the very knowledge of such dangerous ways. This intellectual isolation led in time to a concept of non-Israelite and, later, non-Jewish religions that was not always in consonance with the facts. In this way, it has been suggested, the Torah itself

---

[3] For a detailed analysis, see our Commentary on Leviticus, chapter 17 and H. C. Brichto's study of slaughter, sacrifice, blood, and atonement [8].

[4] According to Brichto, "slaughter on other than a duly designated altar, thus failing acknowledgment of God's lordship over all life, constituted a taboo" [9]. Jacob Milgrom finds the use of the term זבח to offer a clue to the question when and how Deuteronomy

was composed. Elsewhere in the Torah and in cognate languages זבח bears a sacral connotation; but now, in Deut. 12:15 and 21, it is used for profane occasions as well because such slaughter had been previously the custom in northern Israel [10].

[5] For the Reform view on kashrut, see commentaries on Deut. 14:1–15:23, "Dietary Law," and on Lev. 11:1–23.

came to view Canaanite worship in a one-dimensional way and decried it as a complete abomination in the eyes of God. The purpose of this view was clear: In order to establish God as the Supreme Ruler of Israel, all other religious practices and ideologies were ruled out of bounds and their very knowledge considered inadmissible [12].

In the history of nations such protectionism has often been the policy of religious as well as political orthodoxies. Thus, the Inquisition proscribed certain books as dangerous to the Catholic faith and created an Index which, in theory at least, exists to this day. The traditional view of the Torah law under discussion has been that it was instituted as a temporary educational measure needed until the worship of God was firmly established. But, in effect, this protective approach remained operative in postbiblical times as well. A number of "unorthodox" books were excluded from the official biblical canon and of most of them no Hebrew originals survive. They were probably destroyed; some are known to us in other languages (mostly Greek), and of others, perhaps many, no trace remains. Even today, certain Orthodox Jewish communities attempt to isolate their members from access to non-Orthodox writings—both Jewish and non-Jewish; and a strictly Orthodox Jew will not enter a church for any reason whatsoever, lest such a visit violate the injunction "Do not inquire about their gods."

Liberal Jews—like liberals in general—take a different view: they consider the biblical law as no longer applicable in the modern context. They affirm the independence of the human spirit and the freedom of intellectual inquiry. To be sure, unlimited inquiry carries certain risks, but these are worth the price, for the freedom of knowledge is, for liberals, a requisite for a fully free human existence.

GLEANINGS

Inside and Outside

The Torah instructs us about laws which we are to "observe in the land . . ." (12:1). From this you might gather that all commandments are valid only in Eretz Yisrael—therefore the verse says "as long as you live on earth."[6] From this you might conclude that all commandments are valid both inside and outside Eretz Yisrael—hence it says "observe in the land." Since the rule both includes and excludes, one must look at the context. Matters that are personal (such as the prohibition of idolatry) must be observed everywhere, while others (such as the erasure of idolatry) relate only to the Land.   MIDRASH [13]

Utterly

The Hebrew prescription of verse 2 ("You must destroy all the sites") carries an emphasis which might be rendered "You must destroy utterly all the sites." From this we learn that when idolatry is to be uprooted it is to be done root and branch.   TALMUD [14]

Halachah

Verse 3 prescribes that the names of the pagan gods are to be obliterated, and verse 4 that God (and, by implication, His name) is to be treated differently. These verses became the proof texts for a number of halachic rules, known as the rules of מוֹחֵק (mochek, erasing).

Thus, books containing God's name were not to be destroyed but either to be buried or to be stored away (hence the preservation of many ancient manuscripts in storage places called genizot).

Further, the Divine Name, once written, must not be erased. A prefix may be erased (as in לַיהוָֹה), but not a suffix (as in אֱלֹהֶיךָ). Seven divine names fall under this rule: יְהוָֹה (YHVH), אֲדֹנָי (Adonai), אֵל (El), אֱלֹהַּ (Eloha), אֱלֹהִים (Elohim), שַׁדַּי (Shaddai), and צְבָאוֹת (Tzeva-ot, though, strictly speaking, this is not a divine name).   SHULCHAN ARUCH [15]

Eating Flesh

Although humans have unlimited rule over animals, they must restrain themselves from enjoying "the life" of the animal (that is, its blood). We need special strength for this restraint, hence verse 23 says רַק חֲזַק, which literally means "only be strong."   D. HOFFMANN [16]

The Levite

(Verse 19 admonishes Israel not to neglect the Levites.) They are the living nerves and arteries coming out from the centerpoint of the sanctuary by means of which the members are kept in spiritual connection with the brain and heart of the nation. They are the representatives of the sanctuary of the Torah in the midst of the people. Amongst a nation actively engaged in agriculture, cattle breeding, and the industries associated with them, such unproductive members of the community as the Levites could easily fall into disrepute, be looked on as a burden to the community, and remain unrespected and undervalued in their vital importance for the spiritual, moral, and national well-being of the nation. Hence the repeated admonition not to neglect the Levite; the duration of your remaining on your own soil is essentially dependent on the esteem and respect you give the Levite, and the influence you allow him to have on your spiritual and moral development.   S. R. HIRSCH [17]

---

[6] The Midrash thus translates the end of verse 1, as does our version. Another rendering is "as long as you live in that land." The Hebrew text permits either interpretation.

164

False Prophets

The section before us deals with *the* basic problem in prophecy: how to distinguish between the authentic and inauthentic address. The Torah both accepts and rejects what would appear to be the obvious test: Are the prophecies realized as predicted or not?[1] It was clear that even a pretender could chance on a proper anticipation of the future, and in that case how would one know whether the prophets derived their inspiration from God, their own imagination, or from a demonic source? The question itself precluded an unambiguous answer. Even so, there had to be some criterion that would enable the people to distinguish between true and false prophecy. The Torah suggests that the dividing line between the two was loyalty to God. Negatively, if the pretending prophet counseled disobedience of the divine command or even idolatry, then he was *ipso facto* a pretender, regardless of the accuracy of his predictions. Positively, only someone remaining within the ambience of the mitzvot could be considered a true *navi*—but this was where the question rested. After all, an ultimate test of authenticity could be secured only by a divine proclamation, heard by all the people, which would designate a certain person to be God's true servant to whom one needed to listen. Postbiblical Jewish tradition was greatly intrigued by the intractability of the problem and attempted to elucidate what the Torah itself had left vague.[2]

---

[1] Deut. 18:21–22 versus 13:3. While these passages likely came from two different traditions, their juxtaposition in the Torah underlines the ambiguities of prophecy.

[2] In postbiblical times, chapter 13 served, for Jews, as a warning against heresies and, for Christians, as veiled predictions of the appearance of Jesus.

The section falls into three parts. The first deals with the signs a prophet might give; the second, with the possibility that close relatives might lead one astray; and the third, with the fate to be visited on a whole community that has defected. In the last instance, the punishment was to be extreme: total extermination, including even the cattle.

In the notations that follow, the numbers in double brackets refer to the versions where our verse 1 is their 12:32 (as explained previously); thus, 13:2] [1] means that in our text the sentence is in verse 2, in other versions it is in verse 1.

ב כִּי־יָקוּם בְּקִרְבְּךָ נָבִיא אוֹ חֹלֵם חֲלוֹם וְנָתַן אֵלֶיךָ

ג אוֹת אוֹ מוֹפֵת: וּבָא הָאוֹת וְהַמּוֹפֵת אֲשֶׁר־דִּבֶּר אֵלֶיךָ לֵאמֹר נֵלְכָה אַחֲרֵי אֱלֹהִים אֲחֵרִים אֲשֶׁר

ד לֹא־יְדַעְתָּם וְנָעָבְדֵם: לֹא תִשְׁמַע אֶל־דִּבְרֵי הַנָּבִיא הַהוּא אוֹ אֶל־חוֹלֵם הַחֲלוֹם הַהוּא כִּי מְנַסֶּה יְהוָה אֱלֹהֵיכֶם אֶתְכֶם לָדַעַת הֲיִשְׁכֶם אֹהֲבִים אֶת־יְהוָה

ה אֱלֹהֵיכֶם בְּכָל־לְבַבְכֶם וּבְכָל־נַפְשְׁכֶם: אַחֲרֵי יְהוָה אֱלֹהֵיכֶם תֵּלֵכוּ וְאֹתוֹ תִירָאוּ וְאֶת־מִצְוֹתָיו

2] If there appears among you a prophet or a dream-diviner and he gives you a sign or a portent, **3]** saying, "Let us follow and worship another god"—whom you have not experienced—even if the sign or portent that he named to you comes true, **4]** do not heed the words of that prophet or that dream-diviner. For the LORD your God is testing you to see whether you really love the LORD your God with all your heart and soul. **5]** Follow none but the LORD your God, and revere none but Him; observe His commandments alone, and heed only His orders; wor-

13:2] [1] *Prophet.* The Hebrew נָבִיא (*navi*) probably is related to the Akkadian *nabû*, to call, to summon. Akkadian kings were frequently described as "summoned" by a god, and in this sense the Hebrew may be meant (i.e., *navi* would be a passive participle). But some believe *navi* to be an active participle, and hence to have the meaning "speaker" or "announcer" (of God's message, not his own, though he phrases his master's thoughts) [1].

The English "prophet" derives from the Greek *prophetes*, meaning one who speaks out for a god. The popular understanding that a prophet is one who foretells the future does therefore not properly describe the full meaning of the term.

The *navi* received his message in many ways, such as in dreams or visions or by direct address, but only Moses, Israel's foremost prophet, regularly communicated face to face with the Divine (Num. 12:6–8).

Dream-diviner. An accepted profession in Egypt (see our commentary on Gen. 39:1–40:23, "Dreams"). Though its practitioners existed in Israel it did not gain the approbation of the Torah. (While Joseph and Daniel did interpret dreams, they did so only *ad hoc*, at the behest of foreign potentates.)

3] [2] *Experienced.* The word יָדַע is here used in its widest sense; more than intellectual knowledge is involved. See Deut. 11:28.

תִּשְׁמֹרוּ וּבְקֹלוֹ תִשְׁמָ֑עוּ וְאֹתוֹ תַעֲבֹדוּ וּבוֹ תִדְבָּקֽוּן׃

ו וְהַנָּבִיא הַהוּא אוֹ חֹלֵם הַחֲלוֹם הַהוּא יוּמָ֗ת כִּי
דִבֶּר־סָרָה עַל־יְהֹוָה אֱלֹהֵיכֶם הַמּוֹצִיא אֶתְכֶם מֵאֶרֶץ
מִצְרַיִם וְהַפֹּדְךָ מִבֵּית עֲבָדִים לְהַדִּיחֲךָ מִן־הַדֶּרֶךְ
אֲשֶׁר צִוְּךָ יְהֹוָה אֱלֹהֶיךָ לָלֶכֶת בָּהּ וּבִעַרְתָּ הָרָע

ז מִקִּרְבֶּֽךָ׃ ס כִּי יְסִיתְךָ אָחִיךָ בֶן־אִמֶּךָ אֽוֹ־בִנְךָ
אֽוֹ־בִתְּךָ אוֹ אֵשֶׁת חֵיקֶךָ אוֹ רֵעֲךָ אֲשֶׁר כְּנַפְשְׁךָ
בַּסֵּתֶר לֵאמֹר נֵלְכָה וְנַעַבְדָה אֱלֹהִים אֲחֵרִים אֲשֶׁר

ח לֹא יָדַעְתָּ אַתָּה וַאֲבֹתֶיךָ׃ מֵאֱלֹהֵי הָעַמִּים אֲשֶׁר
סְבִיבֹתֵיכֶם הַקְּרֹבִים אֵלֶיךָ אוֹ הָרְחֹקִים מִמְּךָ מִקְצֵה

* ו קמץ ברביעי. 　 * ה קמץ בז"ק.

ship none but Him, and hold fast to Him.　**6]** As for that prophet or dream-diviner, he shall be put to death; for he urged disloyalty to the LORD your God—who freed you from the land of Egypt and who redeemed you from the house of bondage—to make you stray from the path that the LORD your God commanded you to follow. Thus you will sweep out evil from your midst.

7] If your brother, your own mother's son, or your son or daughter, or the wife of your bosom, or your closest friend entices you in secret, saying, "Come let us worship other gods"—whom neither you nor your fathers have experienced— **8]** from among the gods of the peoples around you, either near to you or distant,

6] [5] *Put to death.* The manner of execution is not specified. The Rabbis ruled that it was to be by stoning [2].

Disloyalty. The Hebrew סָרָה derives either from סָרַר (to be defiant; as in Deut. 21:18) or סוּר (to stray).

Sweep out evil. An expression characteristic of Deuteronomy.

7] [6] *Your own mother's son.* Who, in biblical times, was the true "blood brother." Sister and brother who had a mother in common could not marry, but, if they had only a father in common, they could (as Tamar suggested to her half brother Amnon in David's time, II Sam. 13:13).

The Samaritan version reads, "the son of your father or the son of your mother."

ט הָאָרֶץ וְעַד־קְצֵה הָאָרֶץ: לֹא־תֹאבֶה לוֹ וְלֹא תִשְׁמַע
אֵלָיו וְלֹא־תָחוֹס עֵינְךָ עָלָיו וְלֹא־תַחְמֹל וְלֹא־תְכַסֶּה
עָלָיו: י כִּי הָרֹג תַּהַרְגֶנּוּ יָדְךָ תִּהְיֶה־בּוֹ בָרִאשׁוֹנָה
יא לַהֲמִיתוֹ וְיַד כָּל־הָעָם בָּאַחֲרֹנָה: וּסְקַלְתּוֹ בָאֲבָנִים
וָמֵת כִּי בִקֵּשׁ לְהַדִּיחֲךָ מֵעַל יְהֹוָה אֱלֹהֶיךָ הַמּוֹצִיאֲךָ
יב מֵאֶרֶץ מִצְרַיִם מִבֵּית עֲבָדִים: וְכָל־יִשְׂרָאֵל יִשְׁמְעוּ
וְיִרָאוּן וְלֹא־יוֹסִפוּ לַעֲשׂוֹת כַּדָּבָר הָרָע הַזֶּה
יג בְּקִרְבֶּךָ: ס כִּי־תִשְׁמַע בְּאַחַת עָרֶיךָ אֲשֶׁר יְהֹוָה
יד אֱלֹהֶיךָ נֹתֵן לְךָ לָשֶׁבֶת שָׁם לֵאמֹר: יָצְאוּ אֲנָשִׁים
בְּנֵי־בְלִיַּעַל מִקִּרְבֶּךָ וַיַּדִּיחוּ אֶת־יֹשְׁבֵי עִירָם לֵאמֹר
נֵלְכָה וְנַעַבְדָה אֱלֹהִים אֲחֵרִים אֲשֶׁר לֹא־יְדַעְתֶּם:

anywhere from one end of the earth to the other: **9]** do not assent or give heed to him. Show him no pity or compassion, and do not shield him; **10]** but take his life. Let your hand be the first against him to put him to death, and the hand of the rest of the people thereafter. **11]** Stone him to death, for he sought to make you stray from the LORD your God, who brought you out of the land of Egypt, out of the house of bondage. **12]** Thus all Israel will hear and be afraid, and such evil things will not be done again in your midst.

13] If you hear it said, of one of the towns that the LORD your God is giving you to dwell in, **14]** that some scoundrels from among you have gone and subverted the inhabitants of their town, saying "Come let us worship other gods"—whom you

9] [8] *Do not shield him.* As you ordinarily would shield a relative.

10] [9] *Take his life.* After due trial [3].

A number of scholars, following the Septuagint, emend הָרֹג תַּהַרְגֶנּוּ to הַגֵּד תַּגִּידוּ: "but report him" [4].

Let your hand be the first. As in the case of wit-

nesses, Deut. 17:7.

11] [10] *Stone him.* Considered the most severe form of punishment, commensurate with the offense of idolatry.

14] [13] *Scoundrels.* בְּנֵי־בְלִיַּעַל (*bene veliya-al*). The term is not a proper name, as the King James Version and Christian Scriptures suggest [5].

טו וְדָרַשְׁתָּ וְחָקַרְתָּ וְשָׁאַלְתָּ הֵיטֵב וְהִנֵּה אֱמֶת נָכוֹן

טז הַדָּבָר נֶעֶשְׂתָה הַתּוֹעֵבָה הַזֹּאת בְּקִרְבֶּךָ: הַכֵּה תַכֶּה

אֶת־יֹשְׁבֵי הָעִיר הַהִוא לְפִי־חָרֶב הַחֲרֵם אֹתָהּ וְאֶת־

יז כָּל־אֲשֶׁר־בָּהּ וְאֶת־בְּהֶמְתָּהּ לְפִי־חָרֶב: וְאֶת־כָּל־

שְׁלָלָהּ תִּקְבֹּץ אֶל־תּוֹךְ רְחֹבָהּ וְשָׂרַפְתָּ בָאֵשׁ אֶת־הָעִיר

וְאֶת־כָּל־שְׁלָלָהּ כָּלִיל לַיהֹוָה אֱלֹהֶיךָ וְהָיְתָה תֵּל

יח עוֹלָם לֹא תִבָּנֶה עוֹד: וְלֹא־יִדְבַּק בְּיָדְךָ מְאוּמָה

have not experienced— 15] you shall investigate and inquire and interrogate thoroughly. If it is true, the fact is established—that abhorrent thing was perpetrated in your midst— 16] put the inhabitants of that town to the sword and put its cattle to the sword. Doom it and all that is in it to destruction: 17] gather all its spoil into the open square, and burn the town and all its spoil as a holocaust to the LORD your God. And it shall remain an everlasting ruin, never to be rebuilt. 18] Let nothing that has been doomed stick to your hand, in order that the LORD

15] [14] *Investigate . . . inquire . . . interrogate.* From this verse, and from 17:4 and 19:18, the Rabbis established that seven questions were to be asked of witnesses in criminal cases [6].

16] [15] *Put . . . to the sword.* A proper idiomatic translation of לְפִי־חָרֶב; the King James Version rendered literally, "to the edge of the sword," whence the English idiom.

Doom it. See at 7:2. The town that had offended against God was forfeited to Him. However, there is no record that such a case ever occurred in Israel's history. (See also Gleanings.)

17] [16] *An everlasting ruin.* תֵּל עוֹלָם (tel olam). Tel, like its cognates in Akkadian (tillu) and Arabic (tel or tal), means heap or mound but was applied particularly to the characteristic man-made hills which to this day dot the surface of the entire Near East and constitute the superimposed strata of successive levels of human occupation at any given site, each leveled after destruction by natural or human agency. The term generally identifies archeological sites in Arabic-speaking countries (e.g. Tel el Amarna in Egypt), but Tel Aviv (literally, "Mound of Spring") in Israel is named after the Babylonian city mentioned by Ezekiel (3:15; cf. Ezra 2:59 and Nehemiah 7:61).

18] [17] *Stick to your hand.* As with Achan ben Carmi and associates, an incident that nearly engulfed all the people in disaster (Josh. 7:1 ff.).

מִן־הַחֵרֶם לְמַעַן יָשׁוּב יְהוָֹה מֵחֲרוֹן אַפּוֹ וְנָתַן־לְךָ
רַחֲמִים וְרִחַמְךָ וְהִרְבֶּךָ כַּאֲשֶׁר נִשְׁבַּע לַאֲבֹתֶיךָ:
יט כִּי תִשְׁמַע בְּקוֹל יְהוָֹה אֱלֹהֶיךָ לִשְׁמֹר אֶת־כָּל־
מִצְוֹתָיו אֲשֶׁר אָנֹכִי מְצַוְּךָ הַיּוֹם לַעֲשׂוֹת הַיָּשָׁר בְּעֵינֵי
יְהוָֹה אֱלֹהֶיךָ:

may turn from His blazing anger and show you compassion, and in His compassion increase you as He promised your fathers on oath— **19]** for you will be heeding the LORD your God, obeying all His commandments which I enjoin upon you this day, doing what is right in the sight of the LORD your God.

Turn from His blazing anger. Kindled by the city's transgression.

And show you compassion. The whole nation has become infected by the idolatry of one of its cities and therefore stands in need of God's mercy.

Prophets

One must be careful to distinguish between the original meaning of *navi* and the overtones which the accepted and common translation "prophet" has given it (see above, at verse 2). Moses, as Israel's first and most important *navi*, was primarily the announcer and interpreter of the divine will, and only in the later chapters of the book does he speak to the people of their future.

The Bible has no special word to describe a false prophet; both the true servant of God and the pretender are called *navi*.[1] The absence of a clearly distinct terminology reflects the basic difficulty of distinguishing between the two, and in fact farther on (18:21) the Torah formulates the anticipated question: "And should you ask yourselves, 'How can we know that the oracle was not spoken by the Lord?'" The text then proceeds to give the answer: If the future bears out the *navi*'s words, he is authentic (provided he remains within the ambience of the mitzvot), and, if it does not, he is a pretender. This appears to be the basic guideline, and, as chapter 13 makes clear, there are exceptions and cautions which are not easy to apply. Also, even if in the course of time a prediction does come true, how can the hearer know this at the time the prophecy is made? (The case of Hananiah illustrates this problem.[2]) And, to complicate matters even further, authentic prophets too occasionally prove to be wide of the mark. (See, for instance, Zechariah's prediction of Zerubbabel's success, which was not borne out in subsequent history; Zech. 4:6–7.) Not surprisingly, then, the Torah supplies an ambiguous answer to the problem, and, in the end, the good sense of the people must be relied on to clarify the matter.

In order to understand the Torah texts properly it is important to keep in mind that the true business of prophecy was not to predict the future but to confront Israel with the consequences of various alternatives [7]. Further, one must distinguish between the *theory* of the Deuteronomic laws and their practical *application*. In theory, there were the tests of which the text speaks, but, in practice, biblical prophecy usually disregarded them, for it was the larger message which needed to be borne out by experience rather than the details.[3]

Still, there are subsidiary questions raised by the text. For instance, how could a false prophet perform "signs and portents" in the first instance? A number of answers were suggested by tradition:

1. Such a prophet was once a true *navi* but subsequently defected, like Hananiah ben Azzur (Jer. 28) [9].

2. The pretender imitates the true *navi* and "steals his words" [10].

3. There are many who can make accurate

---

[1] The Septuagint introduces the term *pseudoprophetes*, and rabbinic literature speaks of נְבִיאֵי שֶׁקֶר (*nevi-e sheker*), "falsehood purveyors."

[2] Jer. 28. Jeremiah himself, in opposing Hananiah, had therefore no way of disproving the latter's predictions on the spot. The dramatic tests in which Moses (Num. 16) and Elijah (I Kings 18) engaged remain rare exceptions. Equally rare was the application of the criterion set up by Deut. 13. The inauthentic prophet generally spoke as if God himself had sent him; he did not speak in a strange god's name (exceptions are found in I Kings 18; Jer. 2:8; 23:13).

[3] Both in principle and practice, Deuteronomic credentials of prophecy differed from Babylonian mantic. The latter's predictions could not be disproved by experience—at worst, the observations on which such predictions were based might require refinement. It is also noteworthy that, while biblical credentials could (at least in theory) claim total accuracy, moderns would be highly uncomfortable with and suspicious of such "uncanny" prediction [8].

predictions on the basis of natural observation [11].

4. Some people have certain clairvoyant powers [12].

Why were these problems altogether raised by and included in the text? Did they reflect a contemporary set of circumstances which made the guidelines in chapters 13 and 18 necessary? Among the suggestions identifying the historical life situation for these passages (the "Sitz im Leben") are these:

1. There was a religious offensive by Canaanite prophets in the ninth century B.C.E., the time of Elijah (I Kings 18:19).

2. The Baal priests of Samaria undertook a drive for expanded influence at a later time (II Kings 10:23).

3. The Torah seeks to counter the consequences of the Assyrian conquest of the northern kingdom, which introduced heathen practices on a wide scale (after 722 B.C.E.).

The ambiguities which the passages on the false prophets present may be said to be inherent in every case when humans experience—or believe they experience—a contact with the Divine. How could Jacob tell at first whether it was a demon or an angel who was confronting him in the middle of the night? And on what did he base his judgment when he says afterward that it had been a divine being (Gen. 32:31)? God's presence is elusive, and those who say they speak in His name must be tested by their whole message, their proven loyalties, and their character—and even then we may reach the wrong conclusions. Ultimately it must be the people, in their ongoing history, who will distinguish true from false.

GLEANINGS

A Case of Medieval Censorship

A comment on verse 2 by the Baal ha-Turim[4] led to an interesting intervention by the Christian censor. Israel is warned against a false prophet "among you" (בְּקִרְבְּךָ). Said the Baal ha-Turim: "This, by way of gematria [13], hints at 'that woman' (זוּ הָאִשָּׁה; in both cases the sum of letters amounts to 324)." This was the commentator's way of referring to Mary, mother of Jesus.

He then applied the same method to the words "among you a prophet" (בְּקִרְבְּךָ נָבִיא) and continued: "This hints at 'the woman and her son' (זוּ הָאִשָּׁה וּבְנָהּ; in both cases the sum is 387)."

The censor caught the comment, which implied that Jesus was one of the false prophets, and excised everything after the words, "This by way of gematria . . ." and in this way—bereft of all meaning—subsequent editions of the Baal ha-Turim's comment were printed thereafter.[5]

Signs and Portents

According to my religious teaching, miracles are not the distinguishing marks of Truth and do not provide moral certainty about the divine mission of the prophet. For seducers and false prophets too can perform signs, whether through magic, secret arts, or perhaps a misuse of a gift given to them for a good purpose.

MOSES MENDELSSOHN [14]

The Lord . . . Is Testing You (verse 4)

The victorious spread and world dominion of Christianity were at all times a testing for Israel's loyalty to and affection for God and His Torah. Israel has persisted and, in the future, will not waver in its faith.

D. HOFFMANN [15]

Falsifiers

Even as one who falsifies *human* words (i.e., as a witness in a court case) is guilty of death, how much more so is one who falsifies *divine* words.

MIDRASH [16]

Punishment

The Rabbis explained the references to false prophets in chapters 13 and 18 as follows:

A false prophet is one who prophesies what he has not heard and what was not spoken to him; he is executed by man.[6] But one who suppresses his prophecy (like Jonah) or one who ignores the words of a prophet,[7] or a prophet who violates his own words,[8]—his death is caused by Heaven, as it is said, "I Myself will call him to account" (Deut. 18:19).

MISHNAH [18]

One and Many

The injunction in verse 5 (not to follow other gods) is couched in the plural, and in Deut. 10:20 in the singular. There are times when defection from God remains a personal matter, but in times of upheaval the whole community is affected and one must act as part of it to save the religion.

CHASIDIC [19]

---

[4] Jacob ben Asher; he is called "Baal ha-Turim" because of his great halachic work, the *Arba-ah Turim*.

[5] So to this day the most popular of all rabbinic Bibles, the *Mikra'ot Gedolot*. A similar reference to Jesus was also seen to be implied in verse 7, which speaks of "your own mother's son" but does not mention the father.

[6] The former case is illustrated by Zedekiah ben Chenaanah (I Kings 22:11) and the latter by Hananiah (Jer. 28:1 ff.) [17].

[7] See I Kings 20:35-36.   [8] See I Kings 13.

Far and Near

The Hebrew for "Follow . . . the Lord" (verse 5) reads literally "Go *after* the Lord," using the term אַחֲרֵי for "after." This is used when the object is far, and אַחַר when it is near. Why then is אַחַר not used here when one is asked to be close to God?

Because only when one walks אַחֲרֵי God, deeming oneself far from Him, does one merit to be close.

CHASIDIC [20]

How?

Is it really possible to "follow" God, who is described (Deut. 9:3) as a "devouring fire"? Rather, you should follow His attributes: as He clothes the naked, so must you; as He visits the sick, comforts the mourners, and buries the dead, so must you.

TALMUD [21]

Jerusalem

The holy city was not included in the expression "one of the towns" (verse 13), for Jerusalem was established first and foremost as God's habitation, not man's.

RASHI [22]

(According to the Talmud, this is one of ten distinctions of Jerusalem [23].)

Never

The destruction of a whole community because of idolatry (verses 13 ff.) never occurred nor will it ever occur. The sole purpose of the warning is that it might be studied and that one might receive reward for such study.

TOSEFTA [24]

Not to Heed

Anyone who summons us to violate the Torah, adducing signs and wonders in his favor, even if he causes the sun, moon, and stars to stand still as in the days of Joshua, we must pay no heed to him. Whatever success attends him, whatever wealth, honor, and praise he enjoys, we are not to believe his message or subscribe to his teachings, since truth cannot be established by miracles or any visual spectacle.

N. LEIBOWITZ [25]

Of Food, Tithes, and Social Equity

Israel is to become "a kingdom of priests and a holy nation" (Exod. 19:6). The Torah stresses time and again that this end can be reached only if the people acquire a state of purity and create a society of justice, equity, and love. The section before us deals with pathways that lead to this goal and makes it clear that ritual (the method of Israel's striving for purity) and ethics are two equally necessary approaches, for one sustains the other. Ritual acts serve as the framework of ethical behavior, and ethical impulses are in constant need of symbolic reinforcements. Thus, there is a natural relationship between laws of ritual cleanliness in eating and the rules of tithing that govern the nation's care for the Levites and the poor.

Most of the laws in this segment have been stated elsewhere in the Torah. The dietary rules especially and those dealing with the year of remission have been dealt with extensively in Leviticus.* Particular note will, however, be made of the biblical and postbiblical aversion to the swine.

In general, the Deuteronomic emphasis, as revealed in this section, is both on personal holiness (for we must always remember that we are children of God, verse 1) and on humanitarian concerns (for as His children we are responsible for others). This double perspective governs the Jewish understanding of *tzedakah*, its reasons and its benefits (see commentary on 16:18–18:8, "The Pursuit of Justice").

---

* See commentary on Lev. 11:1–23; 25:1–55; and Appendix I.

א בָּנִים אַתֶּם לַיהוָה אֱלֹהֵיכֶם לֹא תִתְגֹּדְדוּ וְלֹא־
ב תָשִׂימוּ קָרְחָה בֵּין עֵינֵיכֶם לָמֵת: כִּי עַם קָדוֹשׁ אַתָּה
לַיהוָה אֱלֹהֶיךָ וּבְךָ בָּחַר יְהוָה לִהְיוֹת לוֹ לְעַם
סְגֻלָּה מִכֹּל הָעַמִּים אֲשֶׁר עַל־פְּנֵי הָאֲדָמָה: ס
ג לֹא תֹאכַל כָּל־תּוֹעֵבָה: זֹאת הַבְּהֵמָה אֲשֶׁר תֹּאכֵלוּ
ה שׁוֹר שֵׂה כְשָׂבִים וְשֵׂה עִזִּים: אַיָּל וּצְבִי וְיַחְמוּר
ו וְאַקּוֹ וְדִישֹׁן וּתְאוֹ וָזָמֶר: וְכָל־בְּהֵמָה מַפְרֶסֶת

1] You are children of the LORD your God. You shall not gash yourselves or shave the front of your heads because of the dead.   **2]** For you are a people consecrated to the LORD your God: the LORD your God chose you from among all other peoples on earth to be His treasured people.

3] You shall not eat anything abhorrent.   **4]** These are the animals that you may eat: the ox, the sheep, and the goat;   **5]** the deer, the gazelle, the roebuck, the wild goat, the ibex, the antelope, the mountain sheep,   **6]** and any other

---

14:1] *Gash yourselves.* Similarly in Lev. 19:28, though with a different Hebrew terminology. Jeremiah makes repeated references to the practice (Jer. 16:6; 41:5; 47:5) [1].

Or shave. Addressed in Lev. 21:5 to the priests only, but here to everybody. In Lev. 19:28 the general rule goes on to forbid the practice of tattooing.

Because of the dead. Apparently these customs were primarily mourning rites.

3] *You shall not eat.* Essentially the same rules as in Lev. 11:2–20.

Abhorrent. The Torah calls certain foods "abhorrent" not because they are naturally abhorrent to humans but because they are prohibited to Israel. Tradition considered the dietary laws to have two main functions: to separate and distinguish Israel from the nations and to sanctify it

through special discipline [2]. (See further in Gleanings.) The word תּוֹעֵבָה (*to-evah*) is generally used to proscribe Canaanite practices [3].

4] *These . . . you may eat.* The permission covers the then most commonly domesticated animals, except pigs and camels, and clearly aims to exclude predators. The text proceeds from individual examples to the general definition, while in Lev. 11:3 only the latter is stated. Scholars differ in their assessment of this difference; some hold it to be due to different sources, others to the proven need for elaboration. Not all the animals enumerated in the text can be identified with certainty, but it may be assumed that the terms described creatures very familiar to the Israelites in Canaan.

5] *Ibex.* A type of wild goat with curved horns.

פַּרְסָה וְשֹׁסַעַת שֶׁסַע שְׁתֵּי פְּרָסוֹת מַעֲלַת גֵּרָה

בַּבְּהֵמָה אֹתָהּ תֹּאכֵלוּ: אַךְ אֶת־זֶה לֹא תֹאכְלוּ ז

מִמַּעֲלֵי הַגֵּרָה וּמִמַּפְרִיסֵי הַפַּרְסָה הַשְּׁסוּעָה אֶת־

הַגָּמָל וְאֶת־הָאַרְנֶבֶת וְאֶת־הַשָּׁפָן כִּי־מַעֲלֵה גֵרָה

הֵמָּה וּפַרְסָה לֹא הִפְרִיסוּ טְמֵאִים הֵם לָכֶם: וְאֶת־ ח

הַחֲזִיר כִּי־מַפְרִיס פַּרְסָה הוּא וְלֹא גֵרָה טָמֵא הוּא

לָכֶם מִבְּשָׂרָם לֹא תֹאכֵלוּ וּבְנִבְלָתָם לֹא תִגָּעוּ: ס

אֶת־זֶה תֹּאכְלוּ מִכֹּל אֲשֶׁר בַּמָּיִם כֹּל אֲשֶׁר־לוֹ סְנַפִּיר ט

וְקַשְׂקֶשֶׂת תֹּאכֵלוּ: וְכֹל אֲשֶׁר אֵין־לוֹ סְנַפִּיר וְקַשְׂקֶשֶׂת י

Deuteronomy 14

7–10

animal that has true hoofs which are cleft in two and brings up the cud—such you
may eat.   7] But the following, which do bring up the cud or have true hoofs
which are cleft through, you may not eat: the camel, the hare, and the daman—
for although they bring up the cud, they have no true hoofs—they are unclean
for you;   8] also the swine—for although it has true hoofs, it does not bring up
the cud—is unclean for you. You shall not eat of their flesh or touch their carcasses.

9] These you may eat of all that live in water: you may eat anything that has
fins and scales.   10] But you may not eat anything that has no fins and scales:
it is unclean for you.

7] *Hare.* It does not in fact chew the cud, but
because of its constant munching appears to do
so.

Daman. A shy small animal of the hyrax family. It too gives the appearance of bringing up the
cud. The biblical statements are based on the
zoological knowledge of the time.

8] *Swine.* The prohibition covers both the wild
boar and the domesticated pig. See further commentary below.

9] *Live in water.* A condensation of Lev. 11:9–12.
The reason for the rule is not clear; its application
prohibits shell fish, eels, lampreys, and water
mammals.

דברים יד
יא–יח

Deuteronomy 14
11–18

יא לֹא תֹאכְלוּ טָמֵא הוּא לָכֶם: ס כָּל־צִפּוֹר טְהֹרָה

יב תֹּאכֵלוּ: וְזֶה אֲשֶׁר לֹא־תֹאכְלוּ מֵהֶם הַנֶּשֶׁר וְהַפֶּרֶס

יג וְהָעָזְנִיָּה: וְהָרָאָה וְאֶת־הָאַיָּה וְהַדַּיָּה לְמִינָהּ: וְאֵת

יד כָּל־עֹרֵב לְמִינוֹ: וְאֵת בַּת הַיַּעֲנָה וְאֶת־הַתַּחְמָס וְאֶת־

טו הַשָּׁחַף וְאֶת־הַנֵּץ לְמִינֵהוּ: אֶת־הַכּוֹס וְאֶת־הַיַּנְשׁוּף

טז וְהַתִּנְשָׁמֶת: וְהַקָּאָת וְאֶת־הָרָחָמָה וְאֶת־הַשָּׁלָךְ:

יז וְהַחֲסִידָה וְהָאֲנָפָה לְמִינָהּ וְהַדּוּכִיפַת וְהָעֲטַלֵּף:

11] You may eat any clean bird.   **12]** The following you may not eat: the eagle, the vulture, and the black vulture;   **13]** the kite, the falcon, and the buzzard of any variety;   **14]** every variety of raven;   **15]** the ostrich, the nighthawk, the sea gull, and the hawk of any variety;   **16]** the little owl, the great owl, and the white owl;   **17]** the pelican, the bustard, and the cormorant;   **18]** the stork, any variety of heron, the hoopoe, and the bat.

11] *Clean bird.* As in Lev. 11:13–19. What constitutes "clean" is not stated, only the unclean birds are enumerated.

The Rabbis attempted to find general rules that could be said to govern the Torah's distinctions. They considered those birds clean which had an extra talon, a craw, and a detachable stomach lining. As for the prohibitions, the rules seem to aim at excluding all predators, as in the case of mammals. The list of permitted birds nowadays includes chicken, goose, duck, turkey, and varieties of the pigeon family. Other birds, though not prohibited by the Bible, have generally been disallowed by common practice and rabbinic rulings. These rules are not, however, universally observed; thus the house sparrow is permitted in some localities but proscribed in others [4].

12] *The eagle.* The identification of a number of the birds that follow is speculative.

13] *The kite.* This word illustrates the difficulties of the Hebrew text. The translation assumes רָאָה (ra-ah, a word otherwise unknown) to be a scribal error for דָּאָה (da-ah, Lev. 11:14), for ר and ד are easily mistaken for one another. In that case, what meaning has דַּיָּה (dayah) in the same verse? It is translated as "buzzard" but may be another scribal variant.

15] *The ostrich.* Which survives now only in Africa, but in biblical times apparently inhabited Canaan.

18] *The bat.* Then believed to be a bird [5].

180

יט וְכֹל שֶׁרֶץ הָעוֹף טָמֵא הוּא לָכֶם לֹא יֵאָכֵלוּ: כָּל־

כא עוֹף טָהוֹר תֹּאכֵלוּ: לֹא תֹאכְלוּ כָל־נְבֵלָה לַגֵּר

אֲשֶׁר־בִּשְׁעָרֶיךָ תִּתְּנֶנָּה וַאֲכָלָהּ אוֹ מָכֹר לְנָכְרִי כִּי

עַם קָדוֹשׁ אַתָּה לַיהוָה אֱלֹהֶיךָ לֹא־תְבַשֵּׁל גְּדִי

בַּחֲלֵב אִמּוֹ:   פ

כב עַשֵּׂר תְּעַשֵּׂר אֵת כָּל־תְּבוּאַת זַרְעֶךָ הַיֹּצֵא הַשָּׂדֶה

Deuteronomy 14
19–22

19] All winged swarming things are unclean for you: they may not be eaten.

20] You may eat only clean winged creatures.

21] You shall not eat anything that has died a natural death; give it to the stranger in your community to eat, or you may sell it to a foreigner. For you are a people consecrated to the LORD your God.

You shall not boil a kid in its mother's milk.

22] You shall set aside every year a tenth part of all the yield of your sowing

---

19] *All winged swarming things.* The reference is probably to forbidden varieties of locusts; compare Lev. 11:20–23 and commentary there [6].

21] *Died a natural death.* An animal that was not slaughtered. As with the Torah's dietary rules in general, this too was less a hygienic than a ritual provision, though it did have salubrious side effects.

Give it to the stranger. Who is not part of the ritual community. The נָכְרִי (*nochri*) is the occasional visitor, while the גֵּר (*ger*) is a resident alien who does share in a number of ritual occasions; hence the provisions for the *ger* are different (Lev. 17:15). This distinction between the two kinds of non-Israelites is important, for it makes it clear beyond question that the permission to give the *nochri* meat from a dead but not slaughtered animal was purely ritual in nature. The *nochri*, as a religious outsider, could receive food that was ritually unfit for the Israelite, even as the former was allowed to eat pork but the latter was not.

You shall not boil. This prohibition occurs twice more in the Torah, and in exactly the same formulation (Exod. 23:19, 34:26; see there for commentary). The purpose of the law is not clear; it probably was to counteract certain idolatrous practices. Rabbinic Judaism developed the command into a cornerstone of dietary law and saw it as a prohibition of eating milk and meat products together—a meaning entirely extraneous to the text.

22] *Tenth part.* The tithe; the English word derives from Old English *teogothian*, "tenth." See commentary below.

Of all the yield. Commentators differed on the extent of the command. Some took verse 22 to state an all-inclusive principle; others saw it limited by verse 23 and therefore applicable only to new grain, wine, and oil [7].

שָׁנָה שָׁנָה: וְאָכַלְתָּ לִפְנֵי יְהֹוָה אֱלֹהֶיךָ בַּמָּקוֹם אֲשֶׁר־
יִבְחַר לְשַׁכֵּן שְׁמוֹ שָׁם מַעְשַׂר דְּגָנְךָ תִּירֹשְׁךָ וְיִצְהָרֶךָ
וּבְכֹרֹת בְּקָרְךָ וְצֹאנֶךָ לְמַעַן תִּלְמַד לְיִרְאָה אֶת־
יְהֹוָה אֱלֹהֶיךָ כָּל־הַיָּמִים: וְכִי־יִרְבֶּה מִמְּךָ הַדֶּרֶךְ
כִּי לֹא תוּכַל שְׂאֵתוֹ כִּי־יִרְחַק מִמְּךָ הַמָּקוֹם אֲשֶׁר
יִבְחַר יְהֹוָה אֱלֹהֶיךָ לָשׂוּם שְׁמוֹ שָׁם כִּי יְבָרֶכְךָ
יְהֹוָה אֱלֹהֶיךָ: וְנָתַתָּה בַּכָּסֶף וְצַרְתָּ הַכֶּסֶף בְּיָדְךָ
וְהָלַכְתָּ אֶל־הַמָּקוֹם אֲשֶׁר יִבְחַר יְהֹוָה אֱלֹהֶיךָ בּוֹ:
וְנָתַתָּה הַכֶּסֶף בְּכֹל אֲשֶׁר־תְּאַוֶּה נַפְשְׁךָ בַּבָּקָר
וּבַצֹּאן וּבַיַּיִן וּבַשֵּׁכָר וּבְכֹל אֲשֶׁר תִּשְׁאָלְךָ נַפְשֶׁךָ
וְאָכַלְתָּ שָּׁם לִפְנֵי יְהֹוָה אֱלֹהֶיךָ וְשָׂמַחְתָּ אַתָּה

כג

כד

כה

כו

Deuteronomy 14
23–26

that is brought from the field.   23] You shall consume the tithes of your new grain and wine and oil, and the firstlings of your herds and flocks, in the presence of the LORD your God, in the place where He will choose to establish His name, so that you may learn to revere the LORD your God forever.   24] Should the distance be too great for you, should you be unable to transport them, because the place where the LORD your God has chosen to establish His name is far from you and because the LORD your God has blessed you,   25] you may convert them into money. Wrap up the money and take it with you to the place that the LORD your God has chosen,   26] and spend the money on anything you want—cattle, sheep, wine, or other intoxicant, or anything you may desire. And you shall feast there, in the presence of the LORD your God, and rejoice with your household.

23] *And the firstlings.* They are not subject to tithing, but are to be eaten at the sanctuary (Deut. 12:17–18).

24] *Because the Lord . . . has blessed you.* With abundant crops.

26] *Other intoxicant.* שֵׁכָר (shechar; whence the word *shikor*, drunk). Drinking alcohol in moderation was approved, but incontinence was strongly condemned. Thus, Isaiah castigates those "who chase liquor from early in the morning" (Isa. 5:11).

כז וּבֵיתֶ֑ךָ וְהַלֵּוִ֤י אֲשֶׁר־בִּשְׁעָרֶ֙יךָ֙ לֹ֣א תַֽעַזְבֶ֔נּוּ כִּ֣י אֵ֥ין

כח ל֛וֹ חֵ֥לֶק וְנַחֲלָ֖ה עִמָּֽךְ׃ ס מִקְצֵ֣ה ׀ שָׁלֹ֣שׁ שָׁנִ֗ים

תּוֹצִיא֙ אֶת־כָּל־מַעְשַׂר֙ תְּבוּאָ֣תְךָ֔ בַּשָּׁנָ֖ה הַהִ֑וא וְהִנַּחְתָּ֖

כט בִּשְׁעָרֶֽיךָ׃ וּבָ֣א הַלֵּוִ֡י כִּ֣י אֵֽין־לוֹ֩ חֵ֨לֶק וְנַחֲלָ֜ה עִמָּ֗ךְ

וְהַגֵּ֤ר וְהַיָּתוֹם֙ וְהָֽאַלְמָנָה֙ אֲשֶׁ֣ר בִּשְׁעָרֶ֔יךָ וְאָֽכְל֖וּ וְשָׂבֵ֑עוּ

לְמַ֤עַן יְבָרֶכְךָ֙ יְהֹוָ֣ה אֱלֹהֶ֔יךָ בְּכָל־מַעֲשֵׂ֥ה יָֽדְךָ֖ אֲשֶׁ֥ר

תַּעֲשֶֽׂה׃ ס

א מִקֵּ֥ץ שֶֽׁבַע־שָׁנִ֖ים תַּעֲשֶׂ֣ה שְׁמִטָּֽה׃ וְזֶה֮ דְּבַ֣ר הַשְּׁמִטָּה֒

ב שָׁמ֗וֹט כָּל־בַּ֙עַל֙ מַשֵּׁ֣ה יָד֔וֹ אֲשֶׁ֥ר יַשֶּׁ֖ה בְּרֵעֵ֑הוּ לֹֽא־

27] But do not neglect the Levite in your community, for he has no hereditary portion as you have. 28] Every third year you shall bring out the full tithe of your yield of that year, but leave it within your settlements. 29] Then the Levite, who has no hereditary portion as you have, and the stranger, the fatherless, and the widow in your settlements shall come and eat their fill, so that the LORD your God may bless you in all the enterprises you undertake.

1] Every seventh year you shall practice remission of debts. 2] This shall be the nature of the remission: every creditor shall remit the due that he claims from

28] *Every third year.* Tradition understood this to mean *"at the end of* every third year"; the sabbatical year—when nothing came in—was omitted from the counting, so that there were two tithing cycles in every seven-year period.

29] *The Levite.* He is listed with the poor, since he has no field allotment of his own.

15:1] *Every seventh year.* Understood as *"at the end of* every seventh year"; parallel to 14:28 [8].
   Remission of debts. The term שְׁמִטָּה (shemitah)

has the root meaning "to let drop." The rendering here as "remission of debts" is derived from the context, for *shemitah* has a wider meaning; see Exod. 23:10 and commentary there. On the release effected by the jubilee year, see Lev. 25 and commentary there.

Just how much of the law was ever enforced, even in early days, is not certain; its abuses were eventually circumvented in the first century C.E. by Hillel, through the device of *prosbul* [9]. Even before that time the remission did not cover such debts as wages owed, loans secured by pledges, or merchandise bought on credit.

יִגֹּשׂ אֶת־רֵעֵהוּ וְאֶת־אָחִיו כִּי־קָרָא שְׁמִטָּה לַיהוָה:

ג אֶת־הַנָּכְרִי תִּגֹּשׂ וַאֲשֶׁר יִהְיֶה לְךָ אֶת־אָחִיךָ תַּשְׁמֵט

ד יָדֶךָ: אֶפֶס כִּי לֹא יִהְיֶה־בְּךָ אֶבְיוֹן כִּי־בָרֵךְ יְבָרֶכְךָ

יְהוָה בָּאָרֶץ אֲשֶׁר יְהוָה אֱלֹהֶיךָ נֹתֵן־לְךָ נַחֲלָה

ה לְרִשְׁתָּהּ: רַק אִם־שָׁמוֹעַ תִּשְׁמַע בְּקוֹל יְהוָה אֱלֹהֶיךָ

לִשְׁמֹר לַעֲשׂוֹת אֶת־כָּל־הַמִּצְוָה הַזֹּאת אֲשֶׁר אָנֹכִי

ו מְצַוְּךָ הַיּוֹם: כִּי־יְהוָה אֱלֹהֶיךָ בֵּרַכְךָ כַּאֲשֶׁר דִּבֶּר־

לָךְ וְהַעֲבַטְתָּ גּוֹיִם רַבִּים וְאַתָּה לֹא תַעֲבֹט וּמָשַׁלְתָּ

ז בְּגוֹיִם רַבִּים וּבְךָ לֹא יִמְשֹׁלוּ: ס כִּי־יִהְיֶה בְךָ

אֶבְיוֹן מֵאַחַד אַחֶיךָ בְּאַחַד שְׁעָרֶיךָ בְּאַרְצְךָ אֲשֶׁר־

Deuteronomy 15
3–7

his neighbor; he shall not dun his neighbor or kinsman, for the remission proclaimed is of the LORD.   3] You may dun the foreigner; but you must remit whatever is due you from your kinsmen.

4] There shall be no needy among you—since the LORD your God will bless you in the land which the LORD your God is giving you as a hereditary portion—   5] if only you heed the LORD your God and take care to keep all this Instruction that I enjoin upon you this day.   6] For the LORD your God will bless you as He has promised you: you will extend loans to many nations, but require none yourself; you will dominate many nations, but they will not dominate you.

7] If, however, there is a needy person among you, one of your kinsmen in any

3] *Dun the foreigner.* The *nochri*, as occasional visitor or tradesman, was not part of the community subject to *shemitah*. The verse makes clear that the law of remission had a ritual as well as a commercial dimension. See above, on 14:21.

4] *There shall be no needy.* To be understood as an exhortation: "There shouldn't really be any needy among you" (in which case *shemitah* for

debts would be unnecessary). The Torah was in no doubt, however, that poverty would in fact continue to exist (see verses 7 ff., and expressly verse 11).

6] *You will extend loans.* A figure of speech describing the extent of Israel's material well-being.

7] *If, however.* If you will not heed God's com-

184

יְהֹוָה אֱלֹהֶיךָ נֹתֵן לָךְ לֹא תְאַמֵּץ אֶת־לְבָבְךָ וְלֹא

ח] תִקְפֹּץ אֶת־יָדְךָ מֵאָחִיךָ הָאֶבְיוֹן: כִּי־פָתֹחַ תִּפְתַּח אֶת־

יָדְךָ לוֹ וְהַעֲבֵט תַּעֲבִיטֶנּוּ דֵּי מַחְסֹרוֹ אֲשֶׁר יֶחְסַר לוֹ:

ט] הִשָּׁמֶר לְךָ פֶּן־יִהְיֶה דָבָר עִם־לְבָבְךָ בְלִיַּעַל לֵאמֹר

קָרְבָה שְׁנַת־הַשֶּׁבַע שְׁנַת הַשְּׁמִטָּה וְרָעָה עֵינְךָ בְּאָחִיךָ

הָאֶבְיוֹן וְלֹא תִתֵּן לוֹ וְקָרָא עָלֶיךָ אֶל־יְהֹוָה וְהָיָה בְךָ

י] חֵטְא: נָתוֹן תִּתֵּן לוֹ וְלֹא־יֵרַע לְבָבְךָ בְּתִתְּךָ לוֹ כִּי

בִּגְלַל הַדָּבָר הַזֶּה יְבָרֶכְךָ יְהֹוָה אֱלֹהֶיךָ בְּכָל־מַעֲשֶׂךָ

יא] וּבְכֹל מִשְׁלַח יָדֶךָ: כִּי לֹא־יֶחְדַּל אֶבְיוֹן מִקֶּרֶב

הָאָרֶץ עַל־כֵּן אָנֹכִי מְצַוְּךָ לֵאמֹר פָּתֹחַ תִּפְתַּח

אֶת־יָדְךָ לְאָחִיךָ לַעֲנִיֶּךָ וּלְאֶבְיֹנְךָ בְּאַרְצֶךָ: ס

Deuteronomy 15
8–11

of your settlements in the land that the LORD your God is giving you, do not harden your heart and shut your hand against your needy kinsman.   8] Rather, you must open your hand and lend him sufficient for whatever he needs.   9] Beware lest you harbor the base thought, "The seventh year, the year of remission, is approaching," so that you are mean to your needy kinsman and give him nothing. He will cry out to the LORD against you, and you will incur guilt.   10] Give to him readily and have no regrets when you do so, for in return the LORD your God will bless you in all your efforts and in all your undertakings.   11] For there will never cease to be needy ones in your land, which is why I command you: open your hand to the poor and needy kinsman in your land.

mands, then there *will* be needy among you. In that case, let debt remission—which is still the subject in view—assist your social conscience.

9] *The seventh year.* "The septenary" would be a more accurate rendering of the Hebrew, which describes the seventh year in terms of the time span it completes.

11] *Never cease to be needy.* A realistic appraisal of Israel's limited capacity to live in all respects as a holy people.

שֶׁשׁ וַעֲבָדְךָ הָעִבְרִיָּה אוֹ הָעִבְרִי אָחִיךָ לְךָ כִּי־יִמָּכֵר יב

וְכִי־ מֵעִמָּךְ חָפְשִׁי תְּשַׁלְּחֶנּוּ הַשְּׁבִיעִת וּבַשָּׁנָה שָׁנִים יג

הַעֲנֵיק רֵיקָם תְּשַׁלְּחֶנּוּ לֹא מֵעִמָּךְ חָפְשִׁי תְשַׁלְּחֶנּוּ יד

בֵּרַכְךָ אֲשֶׁר וּמִיִּקְבֶךָ וּמִגָּרְנְךָ מִצֹּאנְךָ לוֹ תַּעֲנִיק

בְּאֶרֶץ הָיִיתָ עֶבֶד כִּי וְזָכַרְתָּ תִּתֶּן־לוֹ אֱלֹהֶיךָ יְהוָה טו

מְצַוְּךָ אָנֹכִי עַל־כֵּן אֱלֹהֶיךָ יְהוָה וַיִּפְדְּךָ מִצְרַיִם

לֹא אֵלֶיךָ כִּי־יֹאמַר וְהָיָה הַיּוֹם׃ הַזֶּה אֶת־הַדָּבָר טז

לוֹ כִּי־טוֹב וְאֶת־בֵּיתֶךָ אֲהֵבְךָ כִּי מֵעִמָּךְ אֵצֵא

וּבַדֶּלֶת בְּאָזְנוֹ וְנָתַתָּה אֶת־הַמַּרְצֵעַ וְלָקַחְתָּ עִמָּךְ׃ יז

12] If a fellow Hebrew, man or woman, is sold to you, he shall serve you six years, and in the seventh year you shall set him free.   13] When you set him free, do not let him go empty-handed: 14] Furnish him out of the flock, threshing floor, and vat, with which the LORD your God has blessed you.   15] Bear in mind that you were slaves in the land of Egypt and the LORD your God redeemed you; therefore I enjoin this commandment upon you today.

16] But should he say to you, "I do not want to leave you"—for he loves you and your household and is happy with you—   17] you shall take an awl and put it through his ear into the door, and he shall become your slave in

12] *Serve you six years.* This parallels Exod. 21:2 ff. in most respects. Note the equal treatment of the bondwoman and the emphasis on gifts to be given at the time of release. Lev. 25:39–46 adds rules on the release of slaves in the jubilee year [10].

16] *But should he say.* Disdaining his freedom.

17] *Take an awl.* Targum Yerushalmi adds, "pub-licly, in the court house," which brings the law in line with the parallel passage in Exod. 21:6.

In Middle Assyrian laws the piercing of the ear is listed as a punishment for failing to report a harlot's improper attire [11].

In perpetuity. In order to reconcile this provision with the laws of the jubilee year (Lev. 25), tradition interpreted "in perpetuity" to mean "until the jubilee" [12].

וְהָיָה לְךָ עֶבֶד עוֹלָם וְאַף לַאֲמָתְךָ תַּעֲשֶׂה־כֵּן:

יח לֹא־יִקְשֶׁה בְעֵינֶךָ בְּשַׁלֵּחֲךָ אֹתוֹ חָפְשִׁי מֵעִמָּךְ כִּי מִשְׁנֶה שְׂכַר שָׂכִיר עֲבָדְךָ שֵׁשׁ שָׁנִים וּבֵרַכְךָ יְהוָה אֱלֹהֶיךָ בְּכֹל אֲשֶׁר תַּעֲשֶׂה:

יט כָּל־הַבְּכוֹר אֲשֶׁר יִוָּלֵד בִּבְקָרְךָ וּבְצֹאנְךָ הַזָּכָר תַּקְדִּישׁ לַיהוָה אֱלֹהֶיךָ לֹא תַעֲבֹד בִּבְכֹר שׁוֹרֶךָ

כ וְלֹא תָגֹז בְּכוֹר צֹאנֶךָ: לִפְנֵי יְהוָה אֱלֹהֶיךָ תֹאכֲלֶנּוּ שָׁנָה בְשָׁנָה בַּמָּקוֹם אֲשֶׁר־יִבְחַר יְהוָה אַתָּה וּבֵיתֶךָ:

כא וְכִי־יִהְיֶה בוֹ מוּם פִּסֵּחַ אוֹ עִוֵּר כֹּל מוּם רָע לֹא

Deuteronomy 15

18–21

perpetuity. Do the same with your female slave.   18] When you do set him free, do not feel aggrieved; for in the six years he has given you double the service of a hired man. Moreover, the LORD your God will bless you in all you do.

19] You shall consecrate to the LORD your God all male firstlings that are born in your herd and in your flock: you must not work your firstling ox or shear your firstling sheep.   20] You and your household shall eat it annually before the LORD your God in the place that the LORD will choose.   21] But if it has a defect, lameness or blindness, any serious defect, you shall not sacrifice it to the LORD your God.

18] *Do not feel aggrieved.* As will likely be the case. Jeremiah in fact scolds the people for their unwillingness to heed the command (34:14).

19] *All male firstlings.* A postscript as well as a bridge to the laws of Passover which follow. The firstlings of animals have their parallel in the firstlings of produce, and the Passover sacrifice recalls that Israel's first-born children are God's possession.

The provisions agree generally with other Torah passages (Exod. 13:11 ff.; Lev. 27:26 ff.; Num. 18:15 ff.). However, there are differences; e.g., in Numbers the firstlings belong to the priests.

20] *Shall eat.* In a sacrificial ceremony, as verse 21 makes clear.

כב תִּזְבָּחֶנּוּ לַיהוָֹה אֱלֹהֶיךָ: בִּשְׁעָרֶיךָ תֹּאכְלֶנּוּ הַטָּמֵא

כג וְהַטָּהוֹר יַחְדָּו כַּצְּבִי וְכָאַיָּל: רַק אֶת־דָּמוֹ לֹא תֹאכֵל

עַל־הָאָרֶץ תִּשְׁפְּכֶנּוּ כַּמָּיִם: פ

22] Eat it in your settlements, the unclean among you no less than the clean, just like the gazelle and the deer.   **23]** Only you must not partake of its blood; you shall pour it out on the ground like water.

22]   *Like the gazelle and the deer.* This refers to the statement in Deut. 12:15 (see there).

188

Tithes

The command to yield a tenth of one's sustenance to God is rooted in the recognition that He is its source and, that even as He has a special concern for the Levites and the poor, so we too must show it to them. According to Deut. 14:22 ff. tithing was an annual process, and its portions were to be consumed at the sanctuary, but, if the distance from one's home was too great, the produce could be converted into money, and with the proceeds the food for the feast could be purchased at the locale of the sanctuary. Every third year, however, the tithe was kept in the home community and distributed to the Levites and the poor, who depended on such contributions. This procedure differs significantly from that set forth in Num. 18:21. There, tithes are to be given to the Levites who in turn will tithe to the priests.[1]

Scholars have attempted to elucidate the historical development of tithing from the different provisions in Numbers and Deuteronomy, and from the mention made of it in Genesis. It seems certain that the concept of contributing some portion of one's increase as an expression of gratitude to God was very old, reaching into pastoral days (Jacob vows to tithe if God will protect him, Gen. 28:22; see also Gen. 14:20) and finding its parallels in Ugaritic and Mesopotamian practice, where tithes were known as *ma'šaru* and *ešrētu* (later: *ešrû*) respectively [13].

An understanding of sequential developments, however, depends on whether Deuteronomic law preceded the law in Numbers,

or vice versa. If Deuteronomy is considered older, then it would appear that tithing was at first a social institution, and that in time it became sacralized; the secular aspect being reflected in Deuteronomy, and the sacral, with its emphasis on ritual and priests, in Numbers, chapter 18. If, on the other hand, Numbers has the older tradition, then tithing began as a tax for the maintenance of the sanctuary and later became secularized as a social levy.[2]

During the period of the Second Temple, tithes were no longer given to the Levites and instead were transmitted directly to the priests, since there were relatively small numbers of Levites in attendance at the sanctuary. One talmudic opinion saw this altered procedure as a divine punishment for the Levites because so few of them had returned with Ezra from the Babylonian exile [15]. Still later, it became a custom among the pious to tithe voluntarily even from their grain purchases (though only the farmer who grew the produce was obligated to tithe), inasmuch as there was grave suspicion that farmers were lax in their observance of the law. The halachah concerning tithing is contained in a number of mishnaic and Palestinian talmudic treatises, notably *Terumot*, *Demai*, *Ma'aserot*, and *Ma'aser Sheni*.

In medieval times the church levied special tithes on Jewish communities and also applied the biblical prescription to its own faithful. The great European cathedrals were paid for to a large extent by these levies, which were obligatory in many states until the French Revolution. The Eastern Ortho-

---

[1] The Rabbis harmonized the difference by stipulating three tithes: the first tithe was to go to the Levites; a second (*ma-aser sheni*) was to be eaten at the sanctuary by the owner of the land; and a third (*ma-sar ani*, "tithe of the poor") was raised every third year and sixth year, in which case it took the

place of the *ma-aser sheni*. The tithe of produce and animals mentioned in Lev. 27:30–33 was considered as referring to the Deuteronomic law (see commentary in Leviticus).

[2] Our commentary takes the latter position (see introduction) [14].

dox churches never adopted tithing, while Mormons and Seventh Day Adventists practice it to this day.

Dietary Laws

1. *General Rules.*[3] The biblical regulations provide that although all plants are permitted as food not all animals are.

Allowed are:

Four-legged land animals with parted hooves and a regurgitative digestion; fish that have fins and scales (other water animals are forbidden); birds, except those expressly forbidden (mostly predators); some insects.

Forbidden are:

Animals that have died other than by slaughter; a kid boiled in its mother's milk; *sheretz* (swarming or creeping things) like insects and worms with some exceptions; by application, reptiles and amphibians.

Rabbinic tradition developed a complex system of *kashrut* from these basic laws (to which must of course be added the rules of Passover and of fast days).

2. *Purpose.* Five reasons have been identified as underlying the Torah's dietary laws:[4]

a. They were to distinguish the Israelites from their Canaanite neighbors and, later, from the nations. Indeed, such separation became a major consequence of *kashrut* observance.

b. The laws constituted a rigorous discipline by which Israel was to consecrate itself to God.

c. *Kashrut* promotes human hygiene. This position was held by Maimonides and Nachmanides but vigorously opposed by others, notably by Abarbanel (see Gleanings).

d. The main skein that runs through these laws is to arouse in us a sense of hesitation, even guilt, concerning the consumption of meat—a point of view expressed by Rabbi Abraham Kook (see Gleanings).

e. *Kashrut* expresses an aspect of holiness in that it aims at completeness (see further in Gleanings).

It is likely that a number of such purposes, separately or together, added to already existing taboos and helped to form the biblical system, which must be taken in its entirety as an approach to holiness. It was part and parcel of sacred practice without which Israel could not function in its relation to God. The individual laws now found in the Torah had developed over a long time, and in similar fashion later centuries shaped them further into the observances and rules that now form the body of traditional *kashrut*. Reform Jews, in their eclectic approach to halachah, have generally abandoned most biblical and postbiblical restrictions on the consumption of meat, but many still observe the prohibition of eating pork and (less so) shell fish; others take upon themselves the laws of *kashrut* as a personal discipline; and still others observe such practices as a sign of solidarity with fellow Jews. Where food is served in Reform synagogues, the *biblical* rules set forth above are usually observed, while *postbiblical* rules are applied but rarely.

3. *The Prohibition of Pork.* Among all the laws one prohibition stands out and, indeed, in Jewish history assumed special significance: the biblical and postbiblical aversion to the eating of swine's flesh.

It appears from Isaiah 65:4 and 66:3, 17 that during exilic times in Babylonia some Israelites brought swine's blood as an oblation in sacrifices and consumed its meat on such occasions. However, such illicit sacrifices were exceptional [16]. The Egyptians ate or

---

[3] For a detailed discussion, see commentary on Lev. 11; see there also for a consideration of the contemporary liberal view of these laws.

[4] But see the comment of von Rad (below, in Gleanings), which cautions us not to search too deeply for such reasons.

sacrificed swine at full-moon festivals as, according to their mythology, the god Seth was identified with the swine. In Ugarit, the animal was apparently a symbol of strength; among the Greeks the pig was the most frequently sacrificed animal, and Adonis was called the swine-god. In pre-Israelite times in Canaan, the animal was freely raised and consumed, but on the whole there is no evidence that the pig was widely adored among Israel's neighbors.

What brought about the particularly strong aversion in Israel cannot be determined with certainty. In Maccabean times (second century B.C.E.) it had become a strong symbol of anti-Judaism (I Macc. 1:44–50; II Macc. 6:18 ff.); in Christian Scriptures swine were connected with demons [17];

and in talmudic times the ill effects of pork consumption were well known. A proverb said that when ten diseases descended on the world the pig took nine. Swine were despised for their reputed filthy habits, were compared to dogs (which enjoyed low esteem in early days), and a folk saying went: "A gold ring in a swine's snout is like a pretty woman without sense" (Prov. 11:22) [18].

While other nations and religions also forbade the eating of pigs (notably Islam; see Gleanings), nowhere did the prohibition become so invested with emotional weight as in Jewish tradition. Jews were bidden to abstain both from eating pork and from rearing the animal for profit [19], but in modern times the observance of these injunctions has weakened, both in and outside Israel.

GLEANINGS

Children

It says (Deut. 14:1): "You are children of the Lord your God." Rabbi Judah said: You are called His children only if your behavior makes you worthy of the ascription; Rabbi Meir said: You are called His children even if you are unworthy.

TALMUD [20]

The Kite

It is called רָאָה (ra-ah) because the root signals that it sees extraordinarily well. Said a chasidic rabbi about an enemy of Israel: "The Rabbis said that a kite can fly in Babylon and see carcasses in Israel." That kind of bird was already declared unclean by the Torah. ITTURE TORAH [21]

The Way

The Torah says that tithing will lead to a reverence of God. Some come to revere God through observance of Torah, and others come to Torah through reverence. CHASIDIC [22]

Too Far

When is "the place . . . far from you" (verse 24)? When the commandments of the Torah are a burden to you, then God—who is called "the Place of the World"—becomes too far for you.

ALSHECH [23]

Wrap It Up

Why does the Torah have to say "Wrap up the money" (verse 25; the prescription is unnecessary, for people would do it anyway)? To suggest that we should always "wrap up" our money so that we may rule over it, and not it over us.

CHASIDIC [24]

On Tzedakah (Deut. 15:7–11)

Though the giving of tzedakah is a positive commandment, no blessing is spoken when one gives. For the gift may be rejected and the blessing would have been spoken in vain. RASHBA [25]

Even those who do not give from the heart and give only because of shame or social pressure are accounted as having given tzedakah. Many give less than they ought and more than they want.

MEIR BAR-ILAN [26]

The reward for giving will come in the next world; in this world the reward is the joy of performing the mitzvah. KETAV SOFER [27]

In the Hebrew, the command to open our hands to the needy (Deut. 15:8) is constructed in the "doubling" or emphatic form. Why twice? To teach that one should give twice: once before and once after being asked. M. HACOHEN [28]

From the indefinite tense (the infinitive) you may learn that there is no limit on the times that tzedakah needs to be repeated. S. R. HIRSCH [29]

On Dietary Laws

The contemporary reader must not understand this material to represent mere "externalities," which obstruct true piety. On the contrary, it is their very function to serve it. Such rites are rooted in a holistic view that understands what happens in form also to happen in content, and the spiritual to express itself in material, external matters. And, further, he must restrain himself from asking too much about the "reason" and symbolism of the rites—something we are wont to do. Rites remain remarkably stable, while their spiritual context will frequently change.

G. VON RAD [30]

Be it far from me to believe the way they speculate because, if I would accept that, then the divine Torah would be nothing but a kind of abridged hygienic or medico-dietary manual. That is not the way of the divine Torah and the profundity of its purpose. Moreover, do we not see peoples "eating pork, and the detestable thing, and the mouse" (Isa. 66:17), all sorts of fowl and unclean fish, yet sane and sound, a model of health? Then, again, there are quite a number of harmful creatures, like snake, viper, asp, and scorpion, which are not listed in the text. Even among the plants there are some harmful ones, deathly poisonous; yet we find no injunctions in the Torah against eating them. It all sums up to one conclusion: the divine Torah does not intend to legislate healthful prescription but rather cares for promoting the welfare of our soul. The Torah does not employ any terms like harmful, or bad for your health or digestion, but abominable, detestable, impure, unclean, tainted, in order to teach: the dietary laws are not given merely for the protection of the body, but to guard man's spirit, his soul.

ABARBANEL [31]

(Rabbi Kook proceeds from the general idea that humanity was originally vegetarian and that the permission to kill animals for food was a divine and only temporary concession. We are not to forget that when we eat meat we have destroyed life, and in this way he interprets the command in Lev. 17:13 to pour out the blood of the animal and cover it with earth.)

Cover the blood! Hide your shame! These actions will bear fruit and ultimately educate mankind. The mute protest will, when the time is ripe, be transformed into a mighty shout and succeed in its aim. The very nature of the principles of ritual slaughter, with their specific rules and regulations designed to reduce pain, create the atmosphere that you are not dealing with a helpless unprotected object, with an inanimate automat, but with a living soul. A. KOOK [32]

The Holy Days

In six other places does the Torah prescribe the celebration of holy days: three times in Exodus (chapters 12 and 13 in connection with the institution of Passover; 23:14-18; 34:18-25); twice in Leviticus (chapter 16, which deals with the Day of Atonement; and chapter 23); and once in Numbers (28:1–30:1, where the sacrificial order of the holy days is set forth in detail). Here, in Deuteronomy, neither the New Year nor the Day of Atonement is mentioned; the emphasis is on the three pilgrim celebrations—שָׁלֹשׁ רְגָלִים, *shalosh regalim*: Passover (Pesach), Pentecost (Shavuot), and Tabernacles (Sukot)*—all of which require a visit to the central sanctuary.

The pilgrimage itself is a characteristic feature of Deuteronomy, an aspect of its basic aim to make the Temple in Jerusalem the central point of the national cult. Thus, the Passover sacrifice is no longer to be consumed at home or at local shrines, and the festival now combines the originally separate traditions of *pesach* and *matzot*. Regarding Sukot, the absence of any mention of *lulav* and *etrog* or of the wilderness experience—contained in the Leviticus passages—is due either to the Deuteronomic focus on the central sanctuary as the locus of God's presence or to varying traditions about the celebration of the festival.

The term חַג (*chag*), which is in this section affixed to the festivals, is related to the Arabic *haj*, or *hag*, which denotes the required Moslem pilgrimage to Mecca and a title given to someone who has made such a pilgrimage.

---

* On the history of the Pesach festival, see our Commentary on Exodus, chapter 12; and on Shavuot and Sukot, our Commentary on Leviticus, chapter 23.

שָׁמוֹר אֶת־חֹדֶשׁ הָאָבִיב וְעָשִׂיתָ פֶּסַח לַיהוָֹה אֱלֹהֶיךָ א
כִּי בְּחֹדֶשׁ הָאָבִיב הוֹצִיאֲךָ יְהוָֹה אֱלֹהֶיךָ מִמִּצְרַיִם
לָיְלָה: וְזָבַחְתָּ פֶּסַח לַיהוָֹה אֱלֹהֶיךָ צֹאן וּבָקָר ב
בַּמָּקוֹם אֲשֶׁר־יִבְחַר יְהוָֹה לְשַׁכֵּן שְׁמוֹ שָׁם: לֹא־ ג
תֹאכַל עָלָיו חָמֵץ שִׁבְעַת יָמִים תֹּאכַל־עָלָיו מַצּוֹת
לֶחֶם עֹנִי כִּי בְחִפָּזוֹן יָצָאתָ מֵאֶרֶץ מִצְרַיִם לְמַעַן
תִּזְכֹּר אֶת־יוֹם צֵאתְךָ מֵאֶרֶץ מִצְרַיִם כֹּל יְמֵי חַיֶּיךָ:

Deuteronomy 16
1–3

1] Observe the month of Abib and offer a passover sacrifice to the Lord your God, for it was in the month of Abib, at night, that the Lord your God freed you from Egypt.   2] You shall slaughter the passover sacrifice for the Lord your God, from the flock and the herd, in the place where the Lord will choose to establish His name.   3] You shall not eat anything leavened with it; for seven days thereafter you shall eat unleavened bread, bread of distress—for you departed from the land of Egypt hurriedly—so that you may remember the day of your departure

16:1] *Observe the month of Abib.* חֹדֶשׁ (*chodesh*, month) means, strictly speaking, "new moon"—making it likely that Passover was once observed on the first day of the month; see at Exod. 12:2 [1].

אָבִיב (*aviv*) is the old name for the spring month and reflects the Canaanite calendar. Later on, the month became known as Nisan, from *Nisanu* in the Babylonian calendar.

2] *From the flock and the herd.* That is, from sheep and goats (the "flock") and cattle (the "herd"). Exod. 12:3 specifically commands to take a lamb but says nothing about cattle. This difference is evidence of a development from an earlier practice (reflected in Exodus), after wider agricultural options had become available to a well-settled community (reflected in Deuteronomy).

The contrast of the two passages caused the Rabbis a good deal of difficulty, and their various attempts at reconciliation provide an example of their methods: (1) a lamb was to be sacrificed in Egypt; cattle were permitted later [2]; (2) the sacrifice commanded in Exodus was obligatory, the one in Deuteronomy provided an additional voluntary opportunity [3]; (3) the lamb was obligatory for Passover; cattle were used for peace offerings or were consumed at the *minchah* sacrifice when the obligatory *pesach* was insufficient for the company [4].

3] *Anything leavened.* חָמֵץ (*chametz*). What precisely fell under this prohibition became the subject of elaborate halachic rulings (see further at Exod. 12:15).

Unleavened bread. מַצּוֹת (*matzot*, plural form of *matzah*) were used also on occasions other than Passover; see Lev. 2:4 f. [5].

Bread of distress. Or, "bread of affliction," לֶחֶם עֹנִי (*lechem oni*). Early in the Passover Seder the leader lifts up the matzah and says, in Aramaic, "This is the bread of affliction" (הָא לַחְמָא עַנְיָא).

ד וְלֹא־יֵרָאֶה לְךָ שְׂאֹר בְּכָל־גְּבֻלְךָ שִׁבְעַת יָמִים וְלֹא־

יָלִין מִן־הַבָּשָׂר אֲשֶׁר תִּזְבַּח בָּעֶרֶב בַּיּוֹם הָרִאשׁוֹן

ה לַבֹּקֶר: לֹא תוּכַל לִזְבֹּחַ אֶת־הַפָּסַח בְּאַחַד שְׁעָרֶיךָ

ו אֲשֶׁר־יְהֹוָה אֱלֹהֶיךָ נֹתֵן לָךְ: כִּי אִם־אֶל־הַמָּקוֹם

אֲשֶׁר־יִבְחַר יְהֹוָה אֱלֹהֶיךָ לְשַׁכֵּן שְׁמוֹ שָׁם תִּזְבַּח אֶת־

הַפֶּסַח בָּעָרֶב כְּבוֹא הַשֶּׁמֶשׁ מוֹעֵד צֵאתְךָ מִמִּצְרָיִם:

ז וּבִשַּׁלְתָּ וְאָכַלְתָּ בַּמָּקוֹם אֲשֶׁר יִבְחַר יְהֹוָה אֱלֹהֶיךָ

ח בּוֹ וּפָנִיתָ בַבֹּקֶר וְהָלַכְתָּ לְאֹהָלֶיךָ: שֵׁשֶׁת יָמִים

Deuteronomy 16
4–8

from the land of Egypt as long as you live. **4]** For seven days no leaven shall be found with you in all your territory, and none of the flesh of what you slaughter on the evening of the first day shall be left until morning.

5] You are not permitted to slaughter the passover sacrifice in any of the settlements that the LORD your God is giving you; **6]** but at the place where the LORD your God will choose to establish His name, there alone shall you slaughter the passover sacrifice, in the evening, at sundown, the time of day when you departed from Egypt. **7]** You shall cook and eat it at the place which the LORD your God will choose; and in the morning you may start back on your journey home. **8]** After

4] *No leaven.* Here called שְׂאֹר (*se-or*), and not *chametz* as in verse 3, a variation in language but not in meaning.

But, according to the Talmud, this betokens a purposeful difference [6].

Shall be found with you. The Rabbis interpreted "with you" (לְךָ, *lecha*) to cover only "your own leaven in all your territory" and not leaven belonging to others [7].

From this was developed the halachic device of selling one's leavened materials before Passover to a non-Jew, which permitted the seller to keep them in his house during the festival.

On the evening of the first day. The eve before Passover.

6] *In the evening, at sundown.* Similar to Exod. 12:6, "at twilight." According to Rashi this meant "from 6 P.M. on" [8], while Josephus reported 9 to 11 P.M. as the time when his contemporaries celebrated.

The latter's estimate that the number of Passover pilgrims in Jerusalem was 2,700,000 [9] represents a wild exaggeration.

The time of day. מוֹעֵד (*mo-ed*) might also mean "the season (of the year)"; so the old JPS translation.

7] *Start back.* The plain text suggests that the journey toward home started on the first day of the festival. It follows that, at the time of the formulation of the text, travel on a holy day was

תֹּאכַל מַצּוֹת וּבַיּוֹם הַשְּׁבִיעִי עֲצֶרֶת לַיהוָֹה אֱלֹהֶיךָ
לֹא תַעֲשֶׂה מְלָאכָה: ס שִׁבְעָה שָׁבֻעֹת תִּסְפָּר־לָךְ
מֵהָחֵל חֶרְמֵשׁ בַּקָּמָה תָּחֵל לִסְפֹּר שִׁבְעָה שָׁבֻעוֹת:
וְעָשִׂיתָ חַג שָׁבֻעוֹת לַיהוָֹה אֱלֹהֶיךָ מִסַּת נִדְבַת יָדְךָ
אֲשֶׁר תִּתֵּן כַּאֲשֶׁר יְבָרֶכְךָ יְהוָֹה אֱלֹהֶיךָ: וְשָׂמַחְתָּ
לִפְנֵי יְהוָֹה אֱלֹהֶיךָ אַתָּה וּבִנְךָ וּבִתֶּךָ וְעַבְדְּךָ וַאֲמָתֶךָ
וְהַלֵּוִי אֲשֶׁר בִּשְׁעָרֶיךָ וְהַגֵּר וְהַיָּתוֹם וְהָאַלְמָנָה אֲשֶׁר
בְּקִרְבֶּךָ בַּמָּקוֹם אֲשֶׁר יִבְחַר יְהוָֹה אֱלֹהֶיךָ לְשַׁכֵּן

Deuteronomy 16

9–11

eating unleavened bread six days, you shall hold a solemn gathering for the LORD your God on the seventh day: you shall do no work.

9] You shall count off seven weeks; start to count the seven weeks when the sickle is first put to the standing grain. 10] Then you shall observe the Feast of Weeks for the LORD your God, offering your freewill contribution according as the LORD your God has blessed you. 11] You shall rejoice before the LORD your God with your son and daughter, your male and female slave, the Levite in your communities, and the stranger, the fatherless, and the widow in your midst, at the place where the LORD your God will choose to establish His name.

permitted [10]. However, this conclusion did not agree with rabbinic teaching, and, since it considered the halachah to be in total conformity with the Torah, it had to reconcile the text with the rabbinic prohibition. Among the harmonizing interpretations were these: (1) the Torah meant the *second* day of Passover, which in Israel is not observed as a holy day [11]; (2) in the morning the people started back to their inns, either inside or on the outskirts of Jerusalem, where they stayed the night and then went home on the second day [12]; (3) the journey home started on the last, not the first, day [13].

8] *Solemn gathering.* עֲצֶרֶת (*atzeret*). It is also

called מִקְרָא קֹדֶשׁ in Num. 29:12 and חַג in Exod. 13:7. The various terms appear to be interchangeable, though some scholars think they represent various stages of development (see further at Lev. 23:36).

9] *Count off seven weeks.* Rabbinic tradition starts the count on the second day of Passover, which constituted a controversy with the Karaites; see commentary at Lev. 23.

10] *Feast of Weeks.* חַג שָׁבֻעוֹת (*Chag Shavuot*), also called חַג הַקָּצִיר (*Chag ha-Katzir*, Summer Festival) in Exod. 23:16 and in Num. 28:26 יוֹם הַבִּכּוּרִים (*Yom ha-Bikkurim*, Day of the First Fruits).

יב שְׁמוֹ שָׁם: וְזָכַרְתָּ כִּי־עֶבֶד הָיִיתָ בְּמִצְרָיִם וְשָׁמַרְתָּ
וְעָשִׂיתָ אֶת־הַחֻקִּים הָאֵלֶּה: פ

יג חַג הַסֻּכֹּת תַּעֲשֶׂה לְךָ שִׁבְעַת יָמִים בְּאָסְפְּךָ מִגָּרְנְךָ

יד וּמִיִּקְבֶךָ: וְשָׂמַחְתָּ בְּחַגֶּךָ אַתָּה וּבִנְךָ וּבִתֶּךָ וְעַבְדְּךָ
וַאֲמָתֶךָ וְהַלֵּוִי וְהַגֵּר וְהַיָּתוֹם וְהָאַלְמָנָה אֲשֶׁר

טו בִּשְׁעָרֶיךָ: שִׁבְעַת יָמִים תָּחֹג לַיהוָה אֱלֹהֶיךָ בַּמָּקוֹם
אֲשֶׁר־יִבְחַר יְהוָה כִּי יְבָרֶכְךָ יְהוָה אֱלֹהֶיךָ בְּכָל־

טז תְּבוּאָתְךָ וּבְכֹל מַעֲשֵׂה יָדֶיךָ וְהָיִיתָ אַךְ שָׂמֵחַ: שָׁלוֹשׁ
פְּעָמִים בַּשָּׁנָה יֵרָאֶה כָל־זְכוּרְךָ אֶת־פְּנֵי יְהוָה אֱלֹהֶיךָ

Deuteronomy 16
12–16

12] Bear in mind that you were slaves in Egypt, and take care to obey these laws.

13] After the ingathering from your threshing floor and your vat, you shall hold the Feast of Booths for seven days. 14] You shall rejoice in your festival, with your son and daughter, your male and female slave, the Levite, the stranger, the fatherless, and the widow in your communities. 15] You shall hold festival for the LORD your God seven days, in the place that the LORD will choose; for the LORD your God will bless all your crops and all your undertakings, and you shall have nothing but joy.

16] Three times a year—on the Feast of Unleavened Bread, on the Feast of Weeks, and on the Feast of Booths—all your males shall appear before the LORD

13] *Feast of Booths.* חַג הַסֻּכֹּת (*Chag ha-Sukot*). No reason for the booths is given, as in Lev. 23:43, namely, that the Israelites dwelt in booths when they were in the wilderness. In Exod. 23:16 the festival is called חַג הָאָסִיף (*Chag ha-Asif*), Ingathering or Harvest Feast, and in I Kings 8:2 and 65 it is simply called הֶחָג (*He-Chag*, The Festival).

Seven days. From the 15th to the 21st of Tishri. According to Lev. 23:36 and Num. 29:35, the festival concludes with an eighth day observance (*Shemini Atzeret*).

15] *Nothing but joy.* On Passover the people went home after the opening observance; on Sukot they stayed all week.

The opening of verse 14 and the conclusion of verse 15 have become a Hebrew folk song: וְשָׂמַחְתָּ בְּחַגֶּךָ וְהָיִיתָ אַךְ שָׂמֵחַ (*Vesamachta bechagecha vehayita ach sa-me-ach*).

16] *Three times a year.* A résumé; see Exod. 23:17. The Israelites were promised that during these pilgrimages no enemy would attack their homes (Exod. 34:23).

בַּמָּקוֹם אֲשֶׁר יִבְחָר בְּחַג הַמַּצּוֹת וּבְחַג הַשָּׁבֻעוֹת

וּבְחַג הַסֻּכּוֹת וְלֹא יֵרָאֶה אֶת־פְּנֵי יְהֹוָה רֵיקָם: אִישׁ

Deuteronomy 16

כְּמַתְּנַת יָדוֹ כְּבִרְכַּת יְהֹוָה אֱלֹהֶיךָ אֲשֶׁר נָתַן־לָךְ:

17

* טז קמץ בז'ק.

Haftarah Re'eh, p. 445

your God in the place that He will choose. They shall not appear before the LORD empty-handed,   17] but each with his own gift, according to the blessing that the LORD your God has bestowed upon you.

Here the term שָׁלֹשׁ פְּעָמִים (*shalosh pe-amim*) is used, while at other times it is שָׁלֹשׁ רְגָלִים (*shalosh regalim*). The words are plural forms of foot (*regel*) and sole (*pa-am*), and from the rhythmic beat of foot and sole the plurals came to mean "times." Popular etymology later understood the term שָׁלֹשׁ רְגָלִים to have arisen because one went to Jerusalem on foot.

The Pilgrim Festivals in Contemporary Observance

1. *In General.* In Deuteronomy the festivals of Pesach, Shavuot, and Sukot were to be celebrated at the central sanctuary. After its final destruction, in 70 C.E., the celebrations returned to their places of origin, the Jewish homes, and to the new local sanctuaries, the synagogues. The following will set forth in brief outline how contemporary Jews in the Diaspora—and especially Reform Jews—observe these holy days. No attempt will be made to explain the complex halachah that surrounds them today or the details of liturgy characterizing the observances in home and synagogue. It will be clear that the holy days have traversed a long road from biblical to postbiblical days, from medieval to modern times. The Pilgrim Festivals are no longer what they were; they have changed greatly, and there is every reason to believe that they will continue to do so, inside and outside Israel, as long as the Jewish people exhibit a goodly measure of religious dynamism.

Some features are common to all three festivals. They all ask the Jew to alter the patterns of daily existence and set these days aside for worship with family and community and for rejoicing at special celebrations. However, many Jews in the Diaspora continue to work on these holy days and thereby are denied the full enjoyment of their blessings.

While the Torah specifies the precise number of days that each festival is to be observed—Pesach, seven days; Shavuot, one day; Sukot, eight days—the uncertainty of determining the calendar led in ancient days to an extension of these durations. In order not to violate the festival, Diaspora Jews (who did not have the benefit of the monthly announcement of the new moon, made by the Sanhedrin) added an additional day to each. Thus, Pesach was celebrated for eight days, Shavuot for two, and Sukot for nine—the ninth day in effect a second-day Shemini Atzeret, now called Simchat Torah. (In Israel, the three festivals continue to be observed according to the biblical reckoning, and Reform Jews everywhere do likewise, holding that, with the calendar permanently fixed, the cautionary additional days of the Diaspora are no longer required.)

The liturgy for these holy days is enriched by certain additions, chief amongst them the solemn recital and (in traditional synagogues) the enactment of the Priestly Benediction,[1] the Hallel Psalms (113–118), and Yizkor, a special memorial prayer. Also, particular Torah and Haftarah readings are assigned to each festival.

2. *Pesach.* The Jewish home celebration par excellence, Pesach rehearses the birth of the covenant people and celebrates the glories of freedom. The festival begins in the evening of the fourteenth day of Nisan with the Seder, a unique occasion for religious sharing with family, friends, and guests; for enhancing the meaning of Judaism and rejoicing in its beauty; and for a personal experience of the mysterious unfolding of God's role in history and of the wonder of our redemption, past, present, and future.

The Seder is essentially a home celebration, but many synagogues have instituted communal observances in order to accommodate those who cannot celebrate in their homes. Liberal Jews generally do not follow the minutiae with which rabbinic tradition has surrounded the holy day week; as in every other respect, their observance will vary widely, as will the degree of their abstinence from all leaven. They understand the customs and rituals of Pesach to be symbolic reminders of the holy day's underlying

---

[1] In Israel and among Sephardic Jews, however, the benediction is enacted every Shabbat as well.

201

purpose, which remains in the words of the Haggadah,[2] that each generation should consider itself as having been redeemed. Pesach provides the opportunity for reliving the story of liberation, which has its roots in history and makes its urgent demands on the present.

3. *Shavuot.* The festival is observed seven weeks after the second day of Pesach, on the sixth day of Sivan, and has come to signify the day when God revealed His law at Sinai. At first, Shavuot was an agricultural celebration, the Festival of the First Fruits; its identification with the communication of the Ten Commandments (which are read as a Torah selection in the synagogue) came at a later time. The Festival of the First Fruits plays some renewed role in Israel, but the major connection of this aspect with today's observance lies in the reading of the Book of Ruth (which is set at the season of reaping the early harvest).

The festival suffered diminished attention in modern times, until Reform leaders began to fix Confirmation for that day. Thus, in an annual reenactment of the drama at Sinai, young people take upon themselves the obligations of partnership in the covenant and say, "All that the Lord has spoken we will do." As Confirmation day, Shavuot has once again been given a place of honor in the liberal observance.

4. *Sukot.* It is likely that in early days Sukot marked the beginning of the religious year; later it became the major agricultural festival, celebrating the bringing in of the harvest. Its theme is gratitude for God's bounty, and its name betokens its major ritual: the building of *sukot*, frail booths, which are to remind the Jew of the deprivations of the wilderness years as well as of God's providential care. The number of liberal Jews who build their own *sukot* at home is growing, though the primary place of observing the mitzvah still is in the synagogue. Sukot begins on the fifteenth day of Tishri. On the last day, Simchat Torah, the annual Torah reading cycle is completed and begun again at once. The joy exhibited when all the scrolls are removed from the ark and taken around the sanctuary is testimony to the abiding strength of Torah as well as to the deep commitment to study it and make it relevant in one's everyday life.[3]

In modern times Sukot served as the inspiration for the Canadian and American Thanksgivings (the former observed in October, the latter in November).

---

[2] The order of service provided for the Seder.

[3] The observance of Sukot is enhanced by the use of *lulav* (palm, myrtle, and willow) and *etrog* (a citrus fruit).

GLEANINGS

Exodus

Passover! A nation has been commemorating for thousands of years the day of its Exodus from the house of bondage. Throughout all the atrocities of enslavement and despotism, of inquisition, forced conversion, and massacre, the Jewish nation carries in its heart the yearning for freedom and gives this craving a folk expression which shall not pass over a single soul in Israel, a single downtrodden, pauperized soul!

From fathers to sons, throughout all the generations, the Exodus from Egypt is related as a personal reminiscence, thereby retaining its original luster. "In every generation every man must regard himself as if he personally were redeemed from Egypt."

This is the peak of historic consciousness, and history has no greater example of a fusion of individual with group than this ancient pedagogic command. . . . I do not know of any other ancient memory so entirely a symbol of our present and future as the "memory of the Exodus from Egypt."   BERL KATZENELSON [14]

The Season of Joy

However burdensome the Passover minutiae, especially in regard to the prohibition of leaven, became to the Jewish household, the predominant feature was always an exuberance of joy. In the darkest days of medievalism the synagogue and home resounded with song and thanksgiving, and the young imbibed the joy and comfort of their elders through the beautiful symbols of the feast and the richly adorned tale of the deliverance (the Haggadah). The Passover feast with its "night of divine watching" endowed the Jew ever anew with endurance during the dark night of medieval tyranny and with faith in "the Keeper of Israel who slumbereth not nor sleepeth." Moreover, as the springtide of nature fills each creature with joy and hope, so Israel's feast of redemption promises the great day of liberty to those who still chafe under the yoke of oppression.

K. KOHLER [15]

The Center

The center of the Jewish Passover is not the Jewish people as such. Its annual return does not resemble a patriotic festival like the fourteenth of July (in France), the glory of which deserves enthusiasm and even sacrifice. So little is the Seder a national festival that the Haggadah does not even mention the name of Moses the Liberator. No human exploit is indicated. But what is shown as necessary is that the Jew should become conscious of his Jewishness. Not that the members of a nation should unite to celebrate a national liberation, but that the very ideas of liberation and redemption should be removed from the sphere of abstract thought and be considered from the point of view of an experience, which differs from all others, the experience of the Jewish people in Egypt. In all ages, it is the duty of each man to think of himself as one who had himself come out of Egypt.

A. NEHER [16]

Where Is That Mountain?

Where is that mountain of which we read in the
    Bible—
Sinai—on which the Torah was given to Israel?
Perhaps it is in Egypt
where the wild Israelites left the little idols
of the sons of Jacob, the little idols
which stood in the corners of the tents
and rode with the rider
under the saddlecloth; perhaps it is in Egypt—

a land of such affliction
three thousand years or so afterwards
we speak of it to this day.
Blessed are You, Lord, God of the universe,
Who has kept us alive.

Where is that mountain of which we read in the
    Bible—
Sinai—on which the Torah was given to Israel?
Perhaps it is in Palestine;
for Sinai was built out of skeletons
of much suffering,
in which the lives of the Israelites
were like the sands—
that become in the centuries rock, ledges of rock,
a mountain, and at last
the Law,
cut into tables of stone.
Blessed are You, God, King of the universe,
Who has kept Israel alive.

CHARLES REZNIKOFF [17]

Rejoice on Shavuot (Deut. 16:11)
    Do not rejoice merely in what the earth yields
to you, but rather let earth and heaven be joined:
the beautiful blessing is of the earth, the holiness

is of heaven. God brings blessings to you, and you
should raise yourself toward Him in sanctity.

YISRAEL ELDAD [18]

Compassion
    Why is joy commanded for Shavuot and
Sukot, but not for Pesach? Why is the full *Hallel*
said on Sukot, but only the half *Hallel* on Pesach?
Because of the Egyptians who died, as it says: "Do
not rejoice when your enemy falls" (Prov. 24:17).[4]

YALKUT SHIMONI [20]

You Shall Have Nothing but Joy (Deut. 16:15)
    This is not a command but rather a statement
meant to create confidence that even though you
may start rejoicing in poor circumstances you will
end it in well-being.   AFTER RASHI

The verse means: "Let no worries intrude."

SFORNO

The expression "nothing but" (אך, *ach*) is a "di-
minishing" term [21] and here it means: On the
first day we are commanded to take a *lulav*, build
a *sukah*, and to rejoice; for six days to have a
sukah and joy; and on the eighth day "nothing
but joy."   THE GAON OF VILNA [22]

[4] This is a parallel to the talmudic story of God si-
lencing the angels who wanted to rejoice over the
death of the Egyptians, saying: "The work of My
hands is drowning in the sea, and you want to
sing . . .!" [19]

Administration of Law and State, I

The weekly portion *Shofetim*—"magistrates"—begins (at 16:18) an extensive segment dealing with the ethical and administrative norms for providing the community with a suitable structure. The rules imply that, if these provisions are carried out in the spirit of the Torah, Israel will have come closer to the ideal of being God's kingdom of priests. That is the ultimate objective, which is to say that the mere pragmatic suitability of administrative arrangements is not the only reason they are included in the Torah.

The text deals with officials, judicial procedures, and appeals, with monarchy and priesthood. There are also two unconnected inserts on deviant worship practices (16:21 and 17:1) which may at one time have had their place with chapter 13.*

The section shows that the original tribal system had now developed into a centralized one; it roots the monarchy in divine approval; it confirms the judicial status of the Levites; and altogether shows how an older desert-bred people, geared for war, had become a settled society with a civil organization.

---

* Tradition explains the placement by comparing an unjust judge to an idol [1].

שְׁפֹטִים וְשֹׁטְרִים תִּתֶּן־לְךָ בְּכָל־שְׁעָרֶיךָ אֲשֶׁר יְהוָה יח

אֱלֹהֶיךָ נֹתֵן לְךָ לִשְׁבָטֶיךָ וְשָׁפְטוּ אֶת־הָעָם מִשְׁפַּט־

צֶדֶק: לֹא־תַטֶּה מִשְׁפָּט לֹא תַכִּיר פָּנִים וְלֹא־תִקַּח יט

שֹׁחַד כִּי הַשֹּׁחַד יְעַוֵּר עֵינֵי חֲכָמִים וִיסַלֵּף דִּבְרֵי

צַדִּיקִם: צֶדֶק צֶדֶק תִּרְדֹּף לְמַעַן תִּחְיֶה וְיָרַשְׁתָּ כ

אֶת־הָאָרֶץ אֲשֶׁר־יְהוָה אֱלֹהֶיךָ נֹתֵן לָךְ: ס לֹא־ כא

תִטַּע לְךָ אֲשֵׁרָה כָּל־עֵץ אֵצֶל מִזְבַּח יְהוָה אֱלֹהֶיךָ

אֲשֶׁר תַּעֲשֶׂה־לָּךְ: וְלֹא־תָקִים לְךָ מַצֵּבָה אֲשֶׁר שָׂנֵא כב

יְהוָה אֱלֹהֶיךָ: ס

לֹא־תִזְבַּח לַיהוָה אֱלֹהֶיךָ שׁוֹר וָשֶׂה אֲשֶׁר יִהְיֶה בוֹ א

מוּם כֹּל דָּבָר רָע כִּי תוֹעֲבַת יְהוָה אֱלֹהֶיךָ הוּא: ס

שפטים
דברים טז; יז
יח–כב; א

Shofetim
Deuteronomy 16; 17
18–22; 1

18] You shall appoint magistrates and officials for your tribes, in all the settlements that the LORD your God is giving you, and they shall govern the people with due justice. **19]** You shall not judge unfairly: you shall show no partiality; you shall not take bribes, for bribes blind the eyes of the discerning and upset the plea of the just. **20]** Justice, justice shall you pursue, that you may thrive and occupy the land that the LORD your God is giving you.

21] You shall not set up a sacred post—any kind of pole beside the altar of the LORD your God that you may make— **22]** or erect a stone pillar; for such the LORD your God detests.

1] You shall not sacrifice to the LORD your God an ox or a sheep that has any defect of a serious kind, for that is abhorrent to the LORD your God.

16:18] *In all the settlements.* See commentary below.
19] *Plea of the just.* Of those who are in the right.
21] *Sacred post.* An *asherah*; see at Deut. 7:5.

17:1] *Defect of a serious kind.* The underlying idea is that God is to be served with what is perfect. Specific blemishes are enumerated in Lev. 22:17 ff. See also Hallo's essay in Leviticus.

ב כִּי־יִמָּצֵא בְקִרְבְּךָ בְּאַחַד שְׁעָרֶיךָ אֲשֶׁר־יְהוָה אֱלֹהֶיךָ
נֹתֵן לָךְ אִישׁ אוֹ־אִשָּׁה אֲשֶׁר יַעֲשֶׂה אֶת־הָרַע בְּעֵינֵי
ג יְהוָה־אֱלֹהֶיךָ לַעֲבֹר בְּרִיתוֹ: וַיֵּלֶךְ וַיַּעֲבֹד אֱלֹהִים
אֲחֵרִים וַיִּשְׁתַּחוּ לָהֶם וְלַשֶּׁמֶשׁ אוֹ לַיָּרֵחַ אוֹ לְכָל־
ד צְבָא הַשָּׁמַיִם אֲשֶׁר לֹא־צִוִּיתִי: וְהֻגַּד־לְךָ וְשָׁמָעְתָּ
וְדָרַשְׁתָּ הֵיטֵב וְהִנֵּה אֱמֶת נָכוֹן הַדָּבָר נֶעֶשְׂתָה
ה הַתּוֹעֵבָה הַזֹּאת בְּיִשְׂרָאֵל: וְהוֹצֵאתָ אֶת־הָאִישׁ הַהוּא
אוֹ אֶת־הָאִשָּׁה הַהִוא אֲשֶׁר עָשׂוּ אֶת־הַדָּבָר הָרָע
הַזֶּה אֶל־שְׁעָרֶיךָ אֶת־הָאִישׁ אוֹ אֶת־הָאִשָּׁה וּסְקַלְתָּם
ו בָּאֲבָנִים וָמֵתוּ: עַל־פִּי שְׁנַיִם עֵדִים אוֹ שְׁלֹשָׁה
עֵדִים יוּמַת הַמֵּת לֹא יוּמַת עַל־פִּי עֵד אֶחָד:

Deuteronomy 17
2–6

2] If there is found among you, in one of the settlements which the LORD your God is giving you, a man or woman who has affronted the LORD your God and transgressed His covenant—   3] turning to the worship of other gods and bowing down to them, to the sun or the moon or any of the heavenly host, something I never commanded—   4] and you have been informed or have learned of it, then you shall make a thorough inquiry. If it is true, the fact is established, that abhorrent thing was perpetrated in Israel,   5] you shall take the man or the woman who did that wicked thing out to the public place, and you shall stone them, man or woman, to death.—   6] A person shall be put to death only on the testimony of two or more witnesses; he must not be put to death on the testimony of a single witness.—

3] *Sun . . . moon . . . heavenly host.* Solar and astral religion was widespread in the ancient Near East and publicly practiced by Manasseh (II Kings 21:3; II Chron. 33:3 ff.).

4] *The fact is established.* Through proper trial.

5] *Stone them.* As in Deut. 13:11.

6] *Two or more witnesses.* The Hebrew reads literally "two or three." From the unusual "absolute" use of the word שְׁנַיִם (rather than the construct שְׁנֵי עֵדִים as in Deut. 19:15, where civil matters are at issue), the Rabbis concluded that in criminal cases the two witnesses had to testify that they both as a pair had seen the crime committed [2].

ז יַד הָעֵדִים תִּהְיֶה־בּוֹ בָרִאשֹׁנָה לַהֲמִיתוֹ וְיַד כָּל־הָעָם
בָּאַחֲרֹנָה וּבִעַרְתָּ הָרָע מִקִּרְבֶּךָ: פ

ח כִּי יִפָּלֵא מִמְּךָ דָבָר לַמִּשְׁפָּט בֵּין־דָּם לְדָם בֵּין־דִּין
לְדִין וּבֵין נֶגַע לָנֶגַע דִּבְרֵי רִיבֹת בִּשְׁעָרֶיךָ וְקַמְתָּ
וְעָלִיתָ אֶל־הַמָּקוֹם אֲשֶׁר יִבְחַר יְהוָֹה אֱלֹהֶיךָ בּוֹ:

ט וּבָאתָ אֶל־הַכֹּהֲנִים הַלְוִיִּם וְאֶל־הַשֹּׁפֵט אֲשֶׁר יִהְיֶה
בַּיָּמִים הָהֵם וְדָרַשְׁתָּ וְהִגִּידוּ לְךָ אֵת דְּבַר הַמִּשְׁפָּט:

י וְעָשִׂיתָ עַל־פִּי הַדָּבָר אֲשֶׁר יַגִּידוּ לְךָ מִן־הַמָּקוֹם
הַהוּא אֲשֶׁר יִבְחַר יְהוָֹה וְשָׁמַרְתָּ לַעֲשׂוֹת כְּכֹל אֲשֶׁר

Deuteronomy 17

7–10

7] Let the hands of the witnesses be the first against him to put him to death, and the hands of the rest of the people thereafter. Thus you will sweep out evil from your midst.

8] If a case is too baffling for you to decide, be it a controversy over homicide, civil law, or assault—matters of dispute in your courts—you shall promptly repair to the place which the LORD your God will have chosen, **9]** and appear before the levitical priests, or the magistrate in charge at the time, and present your problem. When they have announced to you the verdict in the case, **10]** you shall carry out the verdict that is announced to you from that place which the LORD

7] *Witnesses be the first.* Perhaps this involved a symbolic act on their part, or they were to be the first to do the actual killing.

8] *Promptly repair.* The text uses the word עָלָה, to "go up," probably because Jerusalem lies on elevated ground.

In a figurative sense, *aliyah,* "going up," means today immigration to Israel.

9] *Levitical priests.* Literally, "the priests (who are) the Levites"; they are to serve as a higher court. The expression suggests that at the time of Deuteronomy not all priests were Levites and that this section reflects the power struggle which in time led to the unquestioned assumption of priestly duties and privileges by the Zadokites, a levitical family. Later on, the Zadokites invoked Aaron as their ancestor to legitimate their status. (See further at Num. 25.)

Or the magistrate. He presided in non-ritual matters.

But a traditional source maintained that priests participated in every case, and that a magistrate ruled alone only if no priest was available or if he was unfit and therefore not qualified to judge [3].

יא יוֹרוּךָ: עַל־פִּי הַתּוֹרָה אֲשֶׁר יוֹרוּךָ וְעַל־הַמִּשְׁפָּט
אֲשֶׁר־יֹאמְרוּ לְךָ תַּעֲשֶׂה לֹא תָסוּר מִן־הַדָּבָר אֲשֶׁר־
יב יַגִּידוּ לְךָ יָמִין וּשְׂמֹאל: וְהָאִישׁ אֲשֶׁר־יַעֲשֶׂה בְזָדוֹן
לְבִלְתִּי שְׁמֹעַ אֶל־הַכֹּהֵן הָעֹמֵד לְשָׁרֶת שָׁם אֶת־יְהֹוָה
אֱלֹהֶיךָ אוֹ אֶל־הַשֹּׁפֵט וּמֵת הָאִישׁ הַהוּא וּבִעַרְתָּ
יג הָרָע מִיִּשְׂרָאֵל: וְכָל־הָעָם יִשְׁמְעוּ וְיִרָאוּ וְלֹא יְזִידוּן
יד עוֹד: ס כִּי־תָבֹא אֶל־הָאָרֶץ אֲשֶׁר יְהֹוָה אֱלֹהֶיךָ
נֹתֵן לָךְ וִירִשְׁתָּהּ וְיָשַׁבְתָּה בָּהּ וְאָמַרְתָּ אָשִׂימָה עָלַי
טו מֶלֶךְ כְּכָל־הַגּוֹיִם אֲשֶׁר סְבִיבֹתָי: שׂוֹם תָּשִׂים עָלֶיךָ
מֶלֶךְ אֲשֶׁר יִבְחַר יְהֹוָה אֱלֹהֶיךָ בּוֹ מִקֶּרֶב אַחֶיךָ
תָּשִׂים עָלֶיךָ מֶלֶךְ לֹא תוּכַל לָתֵת עָלֶיךָ אִישׁ נָכְרִי

chose, observing scrupulously all their instructions to you. **11]** You shall act in accordance with the instructions given you and the ruling handed down to you; you must not deviate from the verdict that they announce to you either to the right or to the left. **12]** Should a man act presumptuously and disregard the priest charged with serving there the Lord your God, or the magistrate, that man shall die. Thus you will sweep out evil from Israel: **13]** all the people will hear and be afraid and will not act presumptuously again.

14] If, after you have entered the land that the Lord your God has given you, and occupied it and settled in it, you decide, "I will set a king over me, as do all the nations about me," **15]** you shall be free to set a king over yourself, one chosen by the Lord your God. Be sure to set as king over yourself one of your own people;

11] *Instructions. Ha-torah*, understood in the broad sense.

12] *A man.* It is not clear who this man is, whether a litigant or someone else, and what the punishable offense might be [4].

Act. From this word, tradition ruled that *teaching* alone was not punishable, only if criminal action resulted from it was the penalty invoked [5]. This also meant that unconventional thought was not subject to prosecution.

15] *Of your own people.* This is paralleled in the Constitution of the United States, which provides that only a native-born American may be president.

טז אֲשֶׁר לֹא־אָחִיךָ הוּא: רַק לֹא־יַרְבֶּה־לּוֹ סוּסִים וְלֹא־
יָשִׁיב אֶת־הָעָם מִצְרַיְמָה לְמַעַן הַרְבּוֹת סוּס וַיהֹוָה
אָמַר לָכֶם לֹא תֹסִפוּן לָשׁוּב בַּדֶּרֶךְ הַזֶּה עוֹד:
יז וְלֹא יַרְבֶּה־לּוֹ נָשִׁים וְלֹא יָסוּר לְבָבוֹ וְכֶסֶף וְזָהָב
יח לֹא יַרְבֶּה־לּוֹ מְאֹד: וְהָיָה כְשִׁבְתּוֹ עַל כִּסֵּא מַמְלַכְתּוֹ
וְכָתַב לוֹ אֶת־מִשְׁנֵה הַתּוֹרָה הַזֹּאת עַל־סֵפֶר מִלִּפְנֵי
יט הַכֹּהֲנִים הַלְוִיִּם: וְהָיְתָה עִמּוֹ וְקָרָא בוֹ כָּל־יְמֵי

Deuteronomy 17
16–19

* יט סבירין בה.

you must not set a foreigner over you, one who is not your kinsman.   16] Moreover, he shall not keep many horses or send people back to Egypt to add to his horses, since the LORD has warned you, "You must not go back that way again."   17] And he shall not have many wives, lest his heart go astray; nor shall he amass silver and gold to excess.

18] When he is seated on his royal throne, he shall have a copy of this Teaching written for him on a scroll by the levitical priests.   19] Let it remain with him

16] *Many horses.* A criticism of Solomon who kept fourteen hundred horses (I Kings 10:26 ff.). Horses were imported into Canaan and Egypt by the invading Hyksos in the middle of the second millennium B.C.E. and were primarily used for war chariots, not for ordinary drayage. The Mishnah limits the king to using them for chariots; the Targum considers three horses one too many [6].

Send people back. It has been suggested that this was to discourage the dispatch of mercenary soldiers to Egypt in exchange for horses, and that such Hebrew soldiers became the nucleus of the Elephantine colony [7].

You must not go back. For permanent settlement; commercial trade was permitted [8].

17] *Many wives.* Another criticism of Solomon who "loved many foreign women" and built altars for their deities (I Kings 11). These worship sites were destroyed in the Josianic-Deuteronomic reformation (II Kings 23:13).

However, polygamy itself was not prohibited and was practiced in biblical times and later [9]; it was proscribed in Christian-ruled countries by a decree of Rabbenu Gershom (Germany, 1000 C.E.) and by law in modern Israel.

18] *Copy of this Teaching.* The Book of Deuteronomy. The Septuagint derived the title of the book from this verse, and Maimonides that of his major halachic work (*Mishneh Torah*).

A scroll. סֵפֶר (*sefer*); written on papyrus or leather and rolled up, but the term covered other inscriptions as well.

Written . . . by the levitical priests. The conjunction מִלִּפְנֵי could also mean that the copy was to be made from a copy *before*, that is, in possession of the priests; see I Sam. 10:25, where the prophet is recorded to have written down the law of the kingdom and "laid it up before the Lord." (See also Josh. 8:32. However, the author of the Samuel passage, reporting events of the eleventh century B.C.E., apparently did not know of any Torah prescription to that effect.)

חַיָּיו לְמַעַן יִלְמַד לְיִרְאָה אֶת־יְהֹוָה אֱלֹהָיו לִשְׁמֹר
אֶת־כָּל־דִּבְרֵי הַתּוֹרָה הַזֹּאת וְאֶת־הַחֻקִּים הָאֵלֶּה
לַעֲשֹׂתָם: לְבִלְתִּי רוּם־לְבָבוֹ מֵאֶחָיו וּלְבִלְתִּי סוּר
מִן־הַמִּצְוָה יָמִין וּשְׂמֹאול לְמַעַן יַאֲרִיךְ יָמִים עַל־
מַמְלַכְתּוֹ הוּא וּבָנָיו בְּקֶרֶב יִשְׂרָאֵל: ס

לֹא־יִהְיֶה לַכֹּהֲנִים הַלְוִיִּם כָּל־שֵׁבֶט לֵוִי חֵלֶק וְנַחֲלָה
עִם־יִשְׂרָאֵל אִשֵּׁי יְהֹוָה וְנַחֲלָתוֹ יֹאכֵלוּן: וְנַחֲלָה לֹא־
יִהְיֶה־לּוֹ בְּקֶרֶב אֶחָיו יְהֹוָה הוּא נַחֲלָתוֹ כַּאֲשֶׁר
דִּבֶּר־לוֹ: ס וְזֶה יִהְיֶה מִשְׁפַּט הַכֹּהֲנִים מֵאֵת הָעָם
מֵאֵת זֹבְחֵי הַזֶּבַח אִם־שׁוֹר אִם־שֶׂה וְנָתַן לַכֹּהֵן הַזְּרֹעַ

Deuteronomy 17; 18
20; 1—3

* כ סלא ו'.

and let him read in it all his life, so that he may learn to revere the LORD his God, to observe faithfully every word of this Teaching as well as these laws. **20]** Thus he will not act haughtily toward his fellows or deviate from the Instruction to the right or to the left, to the end that he and his descendants may reign long in the midst of Israel.

1] The levitical priests, the whole tribe of Levi, shall have no territorial portion with Israel. They shall live only off the LORD's offerings by fire as their portion, **2]** and shall have no portion among their brother tribes: the LORD is their portion, as He promised them.

3] This then shall be the priests' due from the people: Everyone who offers a sacrifice, whether an ox or a sheep, must give the shoulder, the cheeks, and the

20] *Not act haughtily.* As if the law bound the people but not him.

18:1] *No territorial portion.* Based on the literal "no portion nor inheritance." Tradition understood: no portion in booty, no inheritance in land [10].

Their portion. Understanding the Hebrew "its portion" as the tribe's. The subject is treated in Lev. 7:31 ff.; see also Num. 18:18 ff.

3] *Shoulder . . . cheeks . . . stomach.* The reason for

211

ד וְהַלְּחָיַיִם וְהַקֵּבָה: רֵאשִׁית דְּגָנְךָ תִּירֹשְׁךָ וְיִצְהָרֶךָ

ה וְרֵאשִׁית גֵּז צֹאנְךָ תִּתֶּן־לּוֹ: כִּי בוֹ בָּחַר יְהֹוָה אֱלֹהֶיךָ
מִכָּל־שְׁבָטֶיךָ לַעֲמֹד לְשָׁרֵת בְּשֵׁם־יְהֹוָה הוּא וּבָנָיו

י כָּל־הַיָּמִים: ס וְכִי־יָבֹא הַלֵּוִי מֵאַחַד שְׁעָרֶיךָ
מִכָּל־יִשְׂרָאֵל אֲשֶׁר־הוּא גָּר שָׁם וּבָא בְּכָל־אַוַּת נַפְשׁוֹ

ז אֶל־הַמָּקוֹם אֲשֶׁר־יִבְחַר יְהֹוָה: וְשָׁרֵת בְּשֵׁם יְהֹוָה
אֱלֹהָיו כְּכָל־אֶחָיו הַלְוִיִּם הָעֹמְדִים שָׁם לִפְנֵי יְהֹוָה:

ח חֵלֶק כְּחֵלֶק יֹאכֵלוּ לְבַד מִמְכָּרָיו עַל־הָאָבוֹת: ס

stomach to the priest.   4] You shall also give him the first fruits of your new grain and wine and oil, and the first shearing of your sheep.   5] For the LORD your God has chosen him and his descendants, out of all your tribes, to be in attendance for service in the name of the LORD for all time.

6] If a Levite would go, from any of the settlements throughout Israel where he has been residing, to the place that the LORD has chosen, he may do so whenever he pleases.   7] He may serve in the name of the LORD his God like all his fellow Levites who are there in attendance before the LORD.   8] They shall receive equal shares of the dues, without regard to personal gifts or patrimonies.

selecting these parts is not clear; see Gleanings for a homiletical interpretation.

The passages in Leviticus and Numbers proscribe breast and right thigh, a difference which the Mishnah tried to reconcile [11].

4] *First fruits.* רֵאשִׁית (reshit), which tradition distinguished from *reshit bikkurim* (Exod. 23:19; 34:26).

First shearing. From which clothes would be made; this was not previously mentioned.

5] *Him and his descendants.* Levi and those presumed to be his descendants, that is, all Levites.

7] *He may serve.* He is free to move anywhere and retain his privileges.

8] *Without regard.* The Hebrew as it stands is obscure and the translation speculative.

The Administration of Justice

1. *Background.* The judicial structure envisaged by Deuteronomy reflects a well-settled, centrally governed society, but at the same time stages of earlier tribal and more fluid conditions may be detected. The very opening phrase (16:18), "You shall appoint ...," still roots ultimate administrative power in the people rather than the king, and the admonitions administered to the ruler (17:18–19) are to remind him that his decisions are limited by old religious norms. Deuteronomy here continues the process of secularizing the state while retaining, as every evolutionary society must, important vestiges of former stages.[1]

In former days, justice had been administered by elders who in difficult matters inquired of God's representatives, the priests. According to the report in II Chron. 19:5–11, King Jehoshaphat, in the ninth century B.C.E., reorganized the system of placing judges in all fortified cities of Judah and created a mixed priestly-secular tribunal in Jerusalem. It appears that our section codifies his reforms. Later, in Roman times, each city had seven judicial officers, with two levitical attendants [12].

2. *The Supreme Court.* Our text (17:8 ff.) speaks of a high court which was to be the final authority in both religious and civil matters. The court, later called Sanhedrin,[2] was divided into the Small Sanhedrin of twenty-three judges and the Grand Sanhedrin of seventy-one. The latter was the Supreme Court of the state.[3] Its powers were considerable; its decisions had the force of law; it ratified the appointments of high priest and king; and its permission was required if the king wanted to engage in a non-obligatory war. Because the court's rulings were frequently innovative, it was in effect also a limited legislative body.[4]

Its main functions were to rule on cultic affairs, such as levitical and priestly duties; it determined the monthly calendar on the basis of testimony at the time of each new moon; it had final authority with respect to the Temple area; and it made sure that the royal Torah scrolls contained the authentic text. In addition, the Sanhedrin was the supreme court in capital cases and in all religious matters that affected the stability of society, such as the impeachment of the High Priest. Inevitably, there were power struggles between court, king, and High Priest, all of whom were used—and often pitted against one another—by the Roman rulers. It was the genius of the Jewish people that despite all political struggles and internal as well as external upheavals the principles of justice which the Torah enunciates were never lost sight of. In the end, when Temple and state were destroyed, the law survived and its principles remained the undergirding framework of Jewish life.

The Monarchy

Not until the prophet Samuel crowned Saul king of Israel, in the eleventh century B.C.E., did the monarchical system of government make its appearance in Jewish history. Samuel himself had opposed the introduction of the monarchy and had presented his argu-

---

[1] This view assumes that Deuteronomy came from a later time than Numbers; see introduction and also commentary on 14:1–15:23, where this conclusion determines how one views the history of tithing.

[2] From the Greek *synedrion*, meaning a council or meeting.

[3] However, rabbinic and Greek sources do not agree on the nature of the Sanhedrin, and its history is a subject of scholarly debate.

[4] Similarly, the American Senate, which is primarily a legislative body, has on occasion important judicial functions (as in the case of impeachments) and must agree to certain appointments and the conduct of war.

ments to the people (I Sam. 8), but he eventually yielded to their desire.[5] The theocracy that was envisaged from early days on did not require a king,[6] but once he was enthroned his powers were wide, much like those among neighboring peoples. The aim of Deuteronomy was therefore to emphasize that for both king and people there existed a superior divine law and that the rulership of Israel was an aspect of carrying out God's covenantal plan. Hence, the king, though he was chosen by the people, was believed to occupy his place only "by grace of God" (the expression is part of a British monarch's title to this day) [15]. In Israel this was more than a formal ascription; it had deep roots in the way God's supreme rulership was understood. And because of this the prophet Nathan could stand up to King David, or Elijah to King Ahab; and indeed because of this the whole institution of prophecy as a critique of state and society became possible.

For underlying the organization of the community was the conviction that Israel was a kingdom of priests, all of whom had access to God. To speak in modern terms, the monarchy in ancient Israel was "constitutional": the Torah was the constitution and God was the King of Kings, including Israel's.

The Pursuit of Justice

"Justice, justice shall you pursue" (18:20) is the distillation of the Torah's prescription for the social ordering of society. No people gave as much loving attention to the overriding importance of law equitably administered and enforced as did Israel. This special concern earned the Jews a reputation for "legalism"—a negative judgment that missed the essence of the biblical and postbiblical understanding of justice.

Human justice has as its goal the establishment of divine equity: it is *tikun olam*, a contribution to the world's perfection. In biblical thought, law did not exist for its own sake; it had its roots in God's will for Israel. To pursue justice meant therefore that one strove to love God, and neither was achievable without the other. Even the Almighty himself needed both justice and love to sustain the world, a principle which tradition saw expressed in the two major names for God: *Elohim*, representing the quality of justice, and *Adonai*, that of love and mercy.[7] But while love, whether of God or of His creatures, resists circumscription, justice admits of and requires firmer delineation. Justice can be ordered, at least to some extent, while love cannot. The achievement of a just society represents a practical goal, and its pursuit may succeed in engendering love as well; a loving society, however, will remain an ideal if it is not founded on law.

Jewish law came to be known as halachah, "the way to go" to fulfill the divine intent. Giving meticulous attention to its minutiae was to be doing His will, and, while in time this preoccupation often became extreme, its ultimate purpose was never in question: it was and remained to carry out Israel's obligation under the covenant to perfect the kingdom of the Almighty. Conversely, to act with lovingkindness was to act justly, for such was one's obligation. *Tzedek*, the word for justice, and *tzedakah*, the word for giving to others, express the same objective. In the Jewish conception, one does not give "charity" merely out of the love of one's heart; one gives *tzedakah*, that which is required be-

---

[5] Tradition explains this by claiming that what Samuel opposed was not the monarchy per se, but only Israel's desire to be like other nations [13].

[6] However, rabbinic literature contains extensive controversies on this subject [14].

[7] See commentary on Gen. 2.

214

cause of being a Jew and because of being human. To give in a loving spirit is of course the highest rung, but giving in any frame of mind satisfies at least the requirements of justice, or of restoring a God-willed balance to the human realm.

(Midrashic and halachic interpretations of the key phrase abound; see Gleanings below.)

GLEANINGS

Magistrates and Officials

Rabbi Eliezer ben Shamua said: Only if there are officials (who can enforce the judgment) can judges function. MIDRASH [16]

It Matters

Do not think: What difference does it make if we pervert justice to acquit our friend or wrest the judgment of the poor or respect the person of the rich? Therefore it says: "You judge for God, not for man" (II Chron. 19:6). Consider what you do, and conduct yourselves in every judgment as if the Holy One blessed be He were standing before you. This is the meaning of the phrase: "He is with you in giving judgment" (*ibid.*). RASHI [17]

Justice, Justice, Shall You Pursue

The principle applies both to a judgment and to a compromise: the latter too must be guided by justice. TALMUD [18]

The double emphasis means: Justice under any circumstance, whether to your profit or loss, whether in word or in action, whether to Jew or non-Jew. It also means: Do not use unjust means to secure justice. BACHYA BEN ASHER [19]

"Justice" is repeated because in matters of justice one may never stand still.
The pursuit of justice is the beginning of justice. Do justly so that justice be engendered. CHASIDIC [20]

The double promise of verse 20 ("that you may thrive and occupy the land") means: To pursue the goal of justice unceasingly with all devotion is Israel's great task in order that its physical and political existence be secured. The significant truth is thereby laid down, that the possession of the land comes into question every minute, and has to be constantly merited afresh (i.e., through justice) by a Jewish state. S. R. HIRSCH [21]

No Sacred Post

The prohibition of 16:21 led to the rule that no tree be planted nor house be built on the Temple mount. MAIMONIDES [22]

Formerly and Now

In the days of the ancestors God was pleased to have them erect stone pillars, but no longer, since the Canaanites used them for their pagan rituals. RASHI [23]

Already Dead

In Deut. 17:6 the Hebrew reads literally: "The dead shall be put to death." The wicked are called dead even when still alive. TALMUD [24]

You Shall Act in Accordance with the Instructions Given You (Deut. 17:11)

The Sages used this as a proof text to justify the blessings which state that God "has commanded us"—to read the Scroll of Esther, to kindle the Shabbat and Chanukah lights[8]—even though there is no record of His command. But "the instructions given you" tell us to follow the Sages. MAIMONIDES [25]

You Must Not Deviate . . . either to the Right or to the Left (Deut. 17:11)

(This phrase became the subject of numerous discussions in rabbinic literature. Some said that

---

[8] We say: . . . וְצִוָּנוּ לְהַדְלִיק נֵר . . .

one must heed the Sages even if they tell us that right is left and left is right, but others held that we need not follow them if we are certain that they are wrong.)

Rabban Gamliel had calculated the new moon for Tishri to fall on one day, while Rabbi Joshua had reckoned it for another day. R. Gamliel, exercising the prerogatives of his office, ordered R. Joshua to come to him with money and walking stick on a day which the latter had calculated to be Yom Kippur, the 10th of Tishri (on which carrying money and stick would be forbidden). After much agonizing, R. Joshua obeyed. R. Gamliel kissed him and said: "Come in peace, my master and my disciple; my master in wisdom, and my disciple because you accepted my words."

MISHNAH [26]

On Monarchy

(Is monarchy a concession made by the Torah or is it a necessary institution? In the controversy alluded to above, none took a stronger anti-monarchical position than the medieval statesman and commentator Abarbanel.)

Even if we should admit that a king is beneficial and necessary for other peoples for the improvement and maintenance of political order—which actually is contrary to the truth—such reasoning does not apply to making kingship necessary for Israel. The general proposition advances three arguments in favor of kingship: (1) as supreme commander of their armed forces, to give them help and comfort against the enemy and to fight for their country; (2) as supreme legislative authority, to provide them with constitution and laws as the occasion warrants it; (3) as supreme judicial tribunal, to sentence and punish, as called for by the circumstances. For these three functions, Israel has no need to appoint a king.[9]

ABARBANEL [27]

Shoulder, Cheek, and Stomach

These were awarded to the priests in honor of Phinehas: the shoulder because he took his spear in his hand (Num. 25:7); the cheek because his prayer averted a plague (Ps. 106:30); and the stomach because of his deed (Num. 25:8).

TALMUD [28]

Another explanation: The cheeks are the first part of the animal; the shoulder the first part of its extremities; and the stomach the first of its inner parts. The object of the command is to strengthen the moral quality of generosity and to weaken the appetite for eating and acquisition.

MAIMONIDES [29]

---

[9] Abarbanel's reasons: God is Israel's supreme commander; Israel has Torah and halachah; and Israel needs no king to establish justice in its midst.

Administration of Law and State, II

In the continued list of laws dealing with the welfare of the community, cultic and judicial matters stand side by side. The Torah makes no distinction between them; both are seen to pertain equally to the fulfillment of Israel's covenantal obligations. Thus, the removal of a sorcerer and the isolation (and protection) of a manslayer in a city of refuge maintain the standards of purity incumbent on the nation. Doing the "right" thing is essential for Israel, and in this perception law is religion and religion is law. This biblical view carried over into rabbinic language, which used the word דָּת (*dat*, law) also to denote religion, and into the halachah, which did not generally distinguish between various kinds of mitzvot.

The segment before us treats of authentic and inauthentic prophets and of the various proscribed kinds of magic. It goes on to state the rules pertaining to the cities of refuge, which parallel but do not duplicate the regulations at the end of the Book of Numbers. A comparison between these two sets of laws makes it possible to retrace the history of this institution. Finally, there is additional criminal and civil law, ending with a repetition of the so-called *lex talionis*.

ט כִּי אַתָּה בָּא אֶל־הָאָרֶץ אֲשֶׁר־יְהֹוָה אֱלֹהֶיךָ נֹתֵן לָךְ
י לֹא־תִלְמַד לַעֲשׂוֹת כְּתוֹעֲבֹת הַגּוֹיִם הָהֵם: לֹא־יִמָּצֵא
בְךָ מַעֲבִיר בְּנוֹ־וּבִתּוֹ בָּאֵשׁ קֹסֵם קְסָמִים מְעוֹנֵן
יא וּמְנַחֵשׁ וּמְכַשֵּׁף: וְחֹבֵר חָבֶר וְשֹׁאֵל אוֹב וְיִדְּעֹנִי
יב וְדֹרֵשׁ אֶל־הַמֵּתִים: כִּי־תוֹעֲבַת יְהֹוָה כָּל־עֹשֵׂה אֵלֶּה
וּבִגְלַל הַתּוֹעֵבֹת הָאֵלֶּה יְהֹוָה אֱלֹהֶיךָ מוֹרִישׁ אוֹתָם

Deuteronomy 18
9–12

9] When you enter the land that the LORD your God is giving you, you shall not learn to imitate the abhorrent practices of those nations.   **10]** Let no one be found among you who consigns his son or daughter to the fire, or who is an augur, a soothsayer, a diviner, a sorcerer,   **11]** one who casts spells, or one who consults ghosts or familiar spirits, or one who inquires of the dead.   **12]** For anyone who does such things is abhorrent to the LORD, and it is because of these abhorrent things that the LORD your God is dispossessing them before you.

18:9] *Abhorrent practices.* Particular examples are enumerated in the following. All of them constitute breaches in the trust relationship between Israel and God.

10] *Consigns . . . to the fire.* "Consigns" is a non-committal translation of מַעֲבִיר; for it is not clear whether this means that the child was actually burnt [1] or was passed between two fires [2]. The prohibition was understood to be directed against the worship of Molech, which was expressly forbidden in Lev. 20:2–5 and 18:21 (see commentary there). In any case, the injunction encompasses certain abhorrent Canaanite cultic practices [3].

Augur. Who predicts from the entrails of animals or from the flight of birds.

Soothsayer. The meaning of the Hebrew is uncertain [4].

Diviner. Forbidden also in Lev. 19:26.

The Midrash thought a מְנַחֵשׁ to be someone who observed omens at certain times, like new moon, Shabbat eve, or end of Shabbat [5]. The old Jewish custom of not starting new ventures on such occasions is probably related to this.

Sorcerer. מְכַשֵּׁף (mechashef) was and has remained the general term for one who uses dark powers.

11] *Casts spells.* According to rabbinic tradition, a snake charmer [6]. Driver understands the root חבר in the usual meaning "connect," "tie together," and renders "one who ties magic knots" [7].

Consults ghosts. Like the witch of En-dor (I Sam. 28). The Septuagint had a realistic view of how ghosts were "consulted" and translated the Hebrew as *engastrimythos* (ventriloquist).

Familiar spirits. Better, following the Septuagint, one who divines by means of freak or monstrous births, a practice well known in Mesopotamia.

Inquires of the dead. A general prohibition of necromancy. One practice was to consult from skulls of the deceased.

12] *Is dispossessing them.* One of the instances

מִפָּנֶיךָ: תָּמִים תִּהְיֶה עִם יְהֹוָה אֱלֹהֶיךָ: כִּי הַגּוֹיִם יג

הָאֵלֶּה אֲשֶׁר אַתָּה יוֹרֵשׁ אוֹתָם אֶל־מְעֹנְנִים וְאֶל־

קֹסְמִים יִשְׁמָעוּ וְאַתָּה לֹא כֵן נָתַן לְךָ יְהֹוָה אֱלֹהֶיךָ:

נָבִיא מִקִּרְבְּךָ מֵאַחֶיךָ כָּמֹנִי יָקִים לְךָ יְהֹוָה אֱלֹהֶיךָ טו

אֵלָיו תִּשְׁמָעוּן: כְּכֹל אֲשֶׁר־שָׁאַלְתָּ מֵעִם יְהֹוָה טז

אֱלֹהֶיךָ בְּחֹרֵב בְּיוֹם הַקָּהָל לֵאמֹר לֹא אֹסֵף לִשְׁמֹעַ

אֶת־קוֹל יְהֹוָה אֱלֹהָי וְאֶת־הָאֵשׁ הַגְּדֹלָה הַזֹּאת לֹא־

אֶרְאֶה עוֹד וְלֹא אָמוּת: וַיֹּאמֶר יְהֹוָה אֵלָי הֵיטִיבוּ יז

* יג בקצת ספרים הת' רבתי.   * טז קמץ בז'ק.

13] You must be wholehearted with the LORD your God.   **14]** Those nations that you are about to dispossess do indeed resort to soothsayers and augurs; to you, however, the LORD your God has not assigned the like.

15] The LORD your God will raise up for you a prophet from among your own people, like myself; him you shall heed.   **16]** This is just what you asked of the LORD your God at Horeb, on the day of the Assembly, saying, "Let me not hear the voice of the LORD my God any longer or see this wondrous fire any more, lest I die."   **17]** Whereupon the LORD said to me, "They have done well in speaking

which specify that moral conduct was a condition for possession of the land and its absence a reason for expulsion. This applied primarily to Israel, but occasionally, as here, to the other dwellers in the land as well.

13] *Wholehearted.* Noah (Gen. 6:9) and Abraham (Gen. 17:1) are called "blameless." The Hebrew תָּמִים (tamim, wholehearted, blameless) is related to תָּם (tam, simple). Israel is to have simple, undivided loyalty to God, unsullied by magic practices.

14] *To you, however.* To Israel are given other means of ascertaining how to face the future: the

Urim and Thummim, the priests, and prophets to whom the text now turns.

15] *A prophet . . . like myself.* This and verse 18 are the only instances where Moses refers to himself as נָבִיא (navi); in the last verse but two in the Torah he is so called also by the author.

Von Rad suggests that the contrast between mantic and prophet "is the result of persistent thought by Israel about the uniqueness of prophetic revelation" [8].

17] *They have done well.* See at Deut. 5:25; the statement differs from the account in Exod. 20:15–18.

אֲשֶׁר דִּבֵּרוּ: נָבִיא אָקִים לָהֶם מִקֶּרֶב אֲחֵיהֶם כָּמוֹךָ יח

וְנָתַתִּי דְבָרַי בְּפִיו וְדִבֶּר אֲלֵיהֶם אֵת כָּל־אֲשֶׁר

אֲצַוֶּנּוּ: וְהָיָה הָאִישׁ אֲשֶׁר לֹא־יִשְׁמַע אֶל־דְּבָרַי אֲשֶׁר יט

יְדַבֵּר בִּשְׁמִי אָנֹכִי אֶדְרֹשׁ מֵעִמּוֹ: אַךְ הַנָּבִיא אֲשֶׁר כ

יָזִיד לְדַבֵּר דָּבָר בִּשְׁמִי אֵת אֲשֶׁר לֹא־צִוִּיתִיו לְדַבֵּר

וַאֲשֶׁר יְדַבֵּר בְּשֵׁם אֱלֹהִים אֲחֵרִים וּמֵת הַנָּבִיא

הַהוּא: וְכִי תֹאמַר בִּלְבָבֶךָ אֵיכָה נֵדַע אֶת־הַדָּבָר כא

אֲשֶׁר לֹא־דִבְּרוֹ יְהוָה: אֲשֶׁר יְדַבֵּר הַנָּבִיא בְּשֵׁם כב

יְהוָה וְלֹא־יִהְיֶה הַדָּבָר וְלֹא יָבֹא הוּא הַדָּבָר אֲשֶׁר

לֹא־דִבְּרוֹ יְהוָה בְּזָדוֹן דִּבְּרוֹ הַנָּבִיא לֹא תָגוּר מִמֶּנּוּ:

thus.   **18]** I will raise up a prophet for them from among their own people, like yourself: I will put My words in his mouth and he will speak to them all that I command him;   **19]** and if anybody fails to heed the words he speaks in My name, I Myself will call him to account.   **20]** But any prophet who presumes to speak in My name an oracle which I did not command him to utter, or who speaks in the name of other gods—that prophet shall die."   **21]** And should you ask yourselves, "How can we know that the oracle was not spoken by the LORD?"—**22]** if the prophet speaks in the name of the LORD and the oracle does not come true, that oracle was not spoken by the LORD; the prophet has uttered it presumptuously: do not stand in dread of him.

19]   *I Myself will call him to account.* According to tradition, this means that the punishment will be by divine judgment, and not by human agency. Perhaps he will die prematurely [9].

21]   *How can we know . . .?* See the discussion in chapter 13. Jeremiah, in his confrontation with the self-styled prophet Hananiah, predicted the death of the latter, and indeed Hananiah died that year (Jer. 28). But such ready proof of inauthenticity was rarely at hand.

The Torah distinguished between two types of false prophets: one, who *thought* he spoke in God's name; and the other, who *deliberately* prophesied in the name of false gods. Chapter 13 deals with the latter, the text above with the former.

א כִּי־יַכְרִית יְהֹוָה אֱלֹהֶיךָ אֶת־הַגּוֹיִם אֲשֶׁר יְהֹוָה
אֱלֹהֶיךָ נֹתֵן לְךָ אֶת־אַרְצָם וִירִשְׁתָּם וְיָשַׁבְתָּ בְעָרֵיהֶם
ב וּבְבָתֵּיהֶם: שָׁלוֹשׁ עָרִים תַּבְדִּיל לָךְ בְּתוֹךְ אַרְצֶךָ
ג אֲשֶׁר יְהֹוָה אֱלֹהֶיךָ נֹתֵן לְךָ לְרִשְׁתָּהּ: תָּכִין לְךָ
הַדֶּרֶךְ וְשִׁלַּשְׁתָּ אֶת־גְּבוּל אַרְצֶךָ אֲשֶׁר יַנְחִילְךָ יְהֹוָה
ד אֱלֹהֶיךָ וְהָיָה לָנוּס שָׁמָּה כָּל־רֹצֵחַ: וְזֶה דְּבַר הָרֹצֵחַ
אֲשֶׁר־יָנוּס שָׁמָּה וָחָי אֲשֶׁר יַכֶּה אֶת־רֵעֵהוּ בִּבְלִי־
ה דַעַת וְהוּא לֹא־שֹׂנֵא לוֹ מִתְּמֹל שִׁלְשֹׁם: וַאֲשֶׁר יָבֹא
אֶת־רֵעֵהוּ בַיַּעַר לַחְטֹב עֵצִים וְנִדְּחָה יָדוֹ בַגַּרְזֶן
לִכְרֹת הָעֵץ וְנָשַׁל הַבַּרְזֶל מִן־הָעֵץ וּמָצָא אֶת־רֵעֵהוּ

Deuteronomy 19
1–5

1] When the LORD your God has cut down the nations whose land the LORD your God is giving you, and you have dispossessed them and settled in their towns and homes,   **2]** you shall set aside three cities in the land that the LORD your God is giving you to possess.   **3]** You shall survey the distances, and divide into three parts the territory of the country that the LORD your God has allotted to you, so that any manslayer may have a place to flee to.   **4]** —Now this is the case of the manslayer who may flee there and live: one who has killed another unwittingly, without having been his enemy in the past.   **5]** For instance, a man goes with his neighbor into a grove to cut wood; as his hand swings the ax to cut down a tree, the ax-head flies off the handle and strikes the other so that he dies. That man

---

19:1] *Settled in their towns and homes.* In Deut. 12:29 it says "settled in their land."

From the addition "and homes" tradition adduced that Israel was permitted to dwell in Canaanite homes despite their having harbored **idolatrous practices** [10].

3] *Divide into three parts.* So that all Israelites would have relatively easy access to the cities of refuge, and the situation noted in verse 6 would not occur.

Any manslayer. Who has killed unintentionally.

וָמֵת הוּא יָנוּס אֶל־אַחַת הֶעָרִים־הָאֵלֶּה וָחָי: פֶּן־
יִרְדֹּף גֹּאֵל הַדָּם אַחֲרֵי הָרֹצֵחַ כִּי־יֵחַם לְבָבוֹ וְהִשִּׂיגוֹ
כִּי־יִרְבֶּה הַדֶּרֶךְ וְהִכָּהוּ נָפֶשׁ וְלוֹ אֵין מִשְׁפַּט־מָוֶת
כִּי לֹא שֹׂנֵא הוּא לוֹ מִתְּמוֹל שִׁלְשׁוֹם: עַל־כֵּן אָנֹכִי
מְצַוְּךָ לֵאמֹר שָׁלֹשׁ עָרִים תַּבְדִּיל לָךְ: וְאִם־יַרְחִיב
יְהוָה אֱלֹהֶיךָ אֶת־גְּבֻלְךָ כַּאֲשֶׁר נִשְׁבַּע לַאֲבֹתֶיךָ וְנָתַן
לְךָ אֶת־כָּל־הָאָרֶץ אֲשֶׁר דִּבֶּר לָתֵת לַאֲבֹתֶיךָ: כִּי־
תִשְׁמֹר אֶת־כָּל־הַמִּצְוָה הַזֹּאת לַעֲשֹׂתָהּ אֲשֶׁר אָנֹכִי
מְצַוְּךָ הַיּוֹם לְאַהֲבָה אֶת־יְהוָה אֱלֹהֶיךָ וְלָלֶכֶת
בִּדְרָכָיו כָּל־הַיָּמִים וְיָסַפְתָּ לְךָ עוֹד שָׁלֹשׁ עָרִים עַל
הַשָּׁלֹשׁ הָאֵלֶּה: וְלֹא יִשָּׁפֵךְ דָּם נָקִי בְּקֶרֶב אַרְצְךָ

shall flee to one of these cities and live.— **6]** Otherwise, when the distance is great, the blood-avenger, pursuing the manslayer in hot anger, may overtake him and kill him; yet he did not incur the death penalty, since he had never been the other's enemy. **7]** That is why I command you: set aside three cities.

8] And when the LORD your God enlarges your territory, as He swore to your fathers, and gives you all the land that He promised to give your fathers— **9]** if you faithfully observe all this Instruction which I enjoin upon you this day, to love the LORD your God and to walk in His ways at all times—then you shall add three more towns to those three. **10]** Thus blood of the innocent will not be shed,

5] *And live.* After he has explained his case to the elders of the city; see Josh. 20:4.

6] *The blood-avenger.* He represents a leftover of an earlier state of judicial practice. He was usually the slain person's nearest kinsman, who, by killing the manslayer, would redress the balance of life. Should he in fact succeed in doing so, he would be guiltless, even if the alleged manslayer would later be found to have been innocent; in that case the whole community was considered at fault for not providing a place to which the accused could have fled in time.

9] *You shall add.* Either a repetition of the command in verse 2, or added for emphasis, or referring to the East Jordanian cities which Moses had set aside (Deut. 4:41–43). In that case there was a total of nine cities of refuge [11].

אֲשֶׁר יְהֹוָה אֱלֹהֶיךָ נֹתֵן לְךָ נַחֲלָה וְהָיָה עָלֶיךָ
דָּמִים: פ

יא וְכִי־יִהְיֶה אִישׁ שֹׂנֵא לְרֵעֵהוּ וְאָרַב לוֹ וְקָם עָלָיו

יב וְהִכָּהוּ נֶפֶשׁ וָמֵת וְנָס אֶל־אַחַת הֶעָרִים הָאֵל: וְשָׁלְחוּ
זִקְנֵי עִירוֹ וְלָקְחוּ אֹתוֹ מִשָּׁם וְנָתְנוּ אֹתוֹ בְּיַד גֹּאֵל

יג הַדָּם וָמֵת: לֹא־תָחוֹס עֵינְךָ עָלָיו וּבִעַרְתָּ דַם־הַנָּקִי

יד מִיִּשְׂרָאֵל וְטוֹב לָךְ: ס לֹא תַסִּיג גְּבוּל רֵעֲךָ
אֲשֶׁר גָּבְלוּ רִאשֹׁנִים בְּנַחֲלָתְךָ אֲשֶׁר תִּנְחַל בָּאָרֶץ

* יא סבירין האלה.

Deuteronomy 19
11–14

bringing bloodguilt upon you in the land that the LORD your God is allotting to you.

11] If, however, a man who is his neighbor's enemy lies in wait for him and sets upon him and strikes him a fatal blow and then flees to one of these towns, 12] the elders of his town shall have him brought back from there and shall hand him over to the blood-avenger to be put to death; 13] you must show him no pity. Thus you will purge Israel of the blood of the innocent, and it will go well with you.

14] You shall not move your neighbor's landmarks, set up by previous genera-

12] *Hand him over*. After a trial. Apparently the avenger functioned as a prosecutor.

13] *Blood of the innocent*. Which "pollutes the land" and cannot be cleansed "except by the blood of him who shed it" (Num. 35:33). Manslaughter did not permit of ransom (Exod. 21:12; Lev. 24:21; only when an animal had killed was it permitted, Exod. 21:30).

14] *Your neighbor's landmarks*. Their removal constituted an act of theft that was included in the imprecations pronounced on Mount Ebal

(Deut. 27:17). Archeologists have found many boundary stones in Canaan as well as in Greece and Mesopotamia.

Set up by previous generations. By the רִאשֹׁנִים (rishonim), the early settlers. The translation projects the application of the law into the future, hence it speaks of property "that *will be* allotted to you." But it is more likely that the verse addressed itself to conditions which had developed during the settlement and aimed at protecting impoverished or otherwise weakened farmers.

The Rabbis extended the law into the ethical realm, to prohibit an infringement of someone's honor and livelihood (see Gleanings).

אֲשֶׁר יְהוָה אֱלֹהֶיךָ נֹתֵן לְךָ לְרִשְׁתָּהּ: ס לֹא־ טו

יָקוּם עֵד אֶחָד בְּאִישׁ לְכָל־עָוֹן וּלְכָל־חַטָּאת בְּכָל־

חֵטְא אֲשֶׁר יֶחֱטָא עַל־פִּי שְׁנֵי עֵדִים אוֹ עַל־פִּי

שְׁלֹשָׁה־עֵדִים יָקוּם דָּבָר: כִּי־יָקוּם עֵד־חָמָס בְּאִישׁ טז

לַעֲנוֹת בּוֹ סָרָה: וְעָמְדוּ שְׁנֵי־הָאֲנָשִׁים אֲשֶׁר־לָהֶם יז

הָרִיב לִפְנֵי יְהוָה לִפְנֵי הַכֹּהֲנִים וְהַשֹּׁפְטִים אֲשֶׁר

יִהְיוּ בַּיָּמִים הָהֵם: וְדָרְשׁוּ הַשֹּׁפְטִים הֵיטֵב וְהִנֵּה עֵד־ יח

שֶׁקֶר הָעֵד שֶׁקֶר עָנָה בְאָחִיו: וַעֲשִׂיתֶם לוֹ כַּאֲשֶׁר יט

זָמַם לַעֲשׂוֹת לְאָחִיו וּבִעַרְתָּ הָרָע מִקִּרְבֶּךָ:

* יט הטעם נסוג אחור.

tions, in the property that will be allotted to you in the land that the LORD your God is giving you to possess.

15] A single witness may not validate against a person any guilt or blame for any offense that may be committed; a case can be valid only on the testimony of two wtnesses or more. **16]** If a man appears against another to testify maliciously and gives false testimony against him, **17]** the two parties to the dispute shall appear before the LORD, before the priests or magistrates in authority at the time, **18]** and the magistrates shall make a thorough investigation. If the man who testified is a false witness, if he has testified falsely against his fellow man, **19]** you shall do to him as he schemed to do to his fellow. Thus you will sweep out evil from

15] *A single witness.* He was insufficient in criminal (as well as in most civil) cases; see Deut. 17:6; Num. 35:30.

Guilt . . . blame . . . offense. Stylistic variations which tradition, however, took to convey different meanings.

16] *Testify maliciously.* Literally, "a witness of violence," that is, who is doing violence to someone by perverting the truth.

17] *The two parties.* According to the Talmud, the two witnesses [12].

19] *As he schemed.* Pharisees and Sadducees debated when this was to be applied. The latter held that the false witness was to be killed only if the person against whom he testified had already been executed; the Pharisees, only if the accused was still alive. The reason for this Pharisaic opin-

כ וְהַנִּשְׁאָרִים יִשְׁמְעוּ וְיִרָאוּ וְלֹא־יֹסִפוּ לַעֲשׂוֹת עוֹד
כא כַּדָּבָר הָרָע הַזֶּה בְּקִרְבֶּךָ: וְלֹא תָחוֹס עֵינֶךָ נֶפֶשׁ
בְּנֶפֶשׁ עַיִן בְּעַיִן שֵׁן בְּשֵׁן יָד בְּיָד רֶגֶל בְּרָגֶל: ס

your midst;   20] others will hear and be afraid, and such evil things will not again be done in your midst.   21] Nor must you show pity: life for life, eye for eye, tooth for tooth, hand for hand, foot for foot.

ion was in turn debated by the Talmud and later commentators [13].

21] *Life for life.* Commonly referred to as *lex talionis*; for commentary see at Exod. 21:23 ff. The best current understanding of this law is that actual talion was not at all intended; rather, the provision represented an instance of public law developing from the private pursuit of justice and that compensation was intended.

More on the Cities of Refuge

Places of refuge,[1] where offenders against the law could find sanctuary, were not entirely unknown in the Mediterranean area, but the elaborate development of the institution was unique to Israel [14].

The original place was a shrine or altar, and the Book of Kings reports two such cases. In one, Adonijah, after his failed usurpation of the throne, fled to the altar where he held on to the horns; whereupon, after King Solomon promised him immunity, he left free and unmolested. In the other, Joab too fled to the Tabernacle, but in his instance Solomon did not respect the sanctuary and had the general killed (I Kings 1:50–53; 2:28–34). Apparently, Joab was considered an intentional manslayer to whom the law of refuge did not apply (Exod. 21:14).

The legislation that we find in the Torah is of a later time. In earlier days, any law breaker could repair to the altar and there find refuge, whether he be an escaped slave, a debtor, or a political offender. The Torah laws came to restrict this privilege to the unintentional manslayer, and in time the town in which the shrine was located was considered an extended place of sanctuary. For the manslayer, confinement to such a city was tantamount to punishment by exile, which ended when the High Priest died. The reason for this termination may have been that his death was deemed an expiation for all the unrequited deaths that had occurred during his regime.

The desire to centralize the cult in Jerusalem led to a reduction and thereafter abolition of outlying shrines, and the six cities—no longer identified as part of the forty-eight levitical cities as in Num. 35—became secular, judicial places of refuge, and no longer did the death of the High Priest play a role. In this way an old institution was transformed to meet changing conditions. We do not know for how long thereafter it enjoyed a viable existence.[2]

Magic and Mantic

Deut. 18:10–11 deal with two distinct types of practices, with magic and mantic.

Magic may be defined as a practice that attempts to utilize mysterious forces which are not controlled (in biblical terms) by God or (in scientific terms) by natural laws. Mantic is the art of divination. By knowing the secrets of certain signs, the practitioner "divines"—that is, he acts with godlike knowledge, but, unlike the purveyor of magic, he does not manipulate the suprahuman or human realms, he only interprets them. Of magic practitioners our chapter mentions those who manipulate gods, nature, and men: sorcerers and spell casters. It further mentions two types of mantic purveyors:

1. Those who consult the past (by getting in touch with the dead, or ghosts, or familiar spirits).
2. Those who predict the future (augurs, soothsayers, diviners, astrologers, dream interpreters, and false prophets who claim to represent God but base their pronouncements on illegitimate sources).

The biblical text decried these activities because they were unauthorized and not because they were believed to have no substance. When God played a role the practice

---

[1] The term עָרֵי מִקְלָט is not found in Deuteronomy but restricted to Numbers. For the basic discussion, see at Num. 35:9–34; also Exod. 21:12–14; see also at Deut. 4:41–43.

[2] One obtains a different view if Deuteronomy is believed to be older than Numbers, as many scholars aver (see "Introducing Deuteronomy").

228

was approved; thus Joseph and Daniel were considered inspired interpreters of dreams; Moses and Aaron were given special "signs" by God himself. The witch of En-dor whom King Saul consulted engaged in an illegal but not an impossible enterprise. Josiah, who had much to do with the codification of Deuteronomy, was a strong opponent of magic and mantic practices, which had been commonplace in the days of Jezebel and Manasseh (II Kings 9:22; 21:6; II Chron. 34:3–7).

Biblical opposition restrained but could not eradicate these activities, and belief in their efficacy persisted into medieval and even modern days. Especially in the Middle Ages, superstitious beliefs and practices of many kinds had as firm a hold on Jews as on their environment, although on the whole they were not experienced as a threat to Judaism, and witch hunts remained confined to the Christian community. Because mystical texts often utilized magic (and sometimes, mantic) concepts and presuppositions, mysticism itself has been viewed with suspicion, but often unfairly so, for in the history of religion the borderline between the authentic and inauthentic has on occasion become blurred. Belief in magic and mantic has waxed and waned, and, since the full mastery of reality must remain beyond human grasp, there will always be those who will attempt to enhance their power and knowledge by resorting to putative forces not subject to the revealed will of God or ordinary laws of nature [15].

GLEANINGS

Astrology

A dichotomy of powers between the gods and a realm beside or beyond them is implicit in all astrology. On the one hand, the heavenly bodies are living gods; therefore, astral phenomena are understood to reflect mythological events. But, besides the gods, immutable laws are operative as well. The influence of the stars follows natural and eternal laws. Within this framework the gods live out their lives. Hence the astral signs can be taken as both divine decisions and fixed laws of the metadivine realm. Because of the growing tendency toward stressing the latter scientific aspect, astrology was able eventually to separate itself entirely from the belief in gods. In Hellenistic times, it was grounded on a doctrine of cosmic sympathy, the mysterious interconnection of all phenomena whose signs are written in the heavens. For many centuries, it was deeply rooted even in the Christian and Jewish worlds. In paganism, however, it served as one of the expressions of the primary, fundamental subjection of the gods to the laws of a higher realm.   Y. KAUFMANN [16]

Magic in Egypt

Egypt was permeated with magical beliefs. It developed an enormous literature on the subject and a ramified manufacture of magical objects. Magic was called upon at every turn in life: to ward off spirits of the dead, demons, scorpions, serpents, wild beasts, fire, rain, injury, sickness, and enemies; to protect women in childbirth and newborn infants; and to ensure the dying man happiness beyond the grave. The gods have an important role as teachers of magical arts to men. Their names, uttered in spells or written on charms, are a chief means of conjuring. They themselves are regarded as charged with the same powers as are found in magical objects and devices. The dead king who "devours the gods" fills his belly with their power and knowledge. Moreover, the gods practice magic in their own right; man merely imitates them.

Y. KAUFMANN [17]

Magic in Biblical and Hellenic Religion

In truth, there is a clear distinction regarding the concept of power between the prophetic-biblical-Jewish ideology and the magical-mystic belief of the Hellenistic world. The might of God is revealed, in the Bible, in the act of creation, and in the historical Providence with which He watched over His people, which serves as a source of hope to those who love and revere Him. The power remains even when He manifests himself—the power of an invisible God, who is immaterial. On the other hand, in the Hellenistic world the power was conceived as something impersonal, which was found in people and substance. It was a visible and material power. Magical acts were a concomitant of the nature of idolatry. Idolatry, in all its forms, believed in the existence of a source of power apart from the godhead, for it did not recognize a god who transcended the existential system that controlled everything and whose will was absolute. Magic flows from the desire to utilize these forces, and idolatry associates man with the deity in the need for magic. Nor does the fact that there was also opposition to sorcery and sorcerers affect the position. Idolatry forbade injurious magic, especially in the case of a rejected and defeated religion.   E. URBACH [18]

You Must Be Wholehearted with the Lord Your God (Deut. 18:13)

Even if no one sees you in your inner chamber and you are only "with your God," you must be wholehearted with Him.   ALSHECH [19]

230

The ת in תָּמִים (wholehearted) is written large. For if you walk wholehearted with God it is as if you sustained the Torah from א to ת.

BAAL HA-TURIM [20]

Five biblical verses convey the essence of Judaism:

"You must be wholehearted with the Lord your God" (Deut. 18:13).

"I have set the Lord always before me" (Ps. 16:8).

"You shall love your neighbor as yourself" (Lev. 19:18).

"In all your ways acknowledge Him" (Prov. 3:6).

"To walk humbly with your God" (Micah 6:8).

In Hebrew, the opening letters of these verses form the word תְּשׁוּבָה, repentance.   CHASIDIC [21]

Only in Israel

The prophet whom God will raise up must be "from among your own people" (Deut. 18:15).

This means also that he must arise in the Land of Israel.   MIDRASH [22]

Cities of Refuge

Everything must be done so that the cities can be reached easily; this includes building roads and making them level.   MAIMONIDES [23]

Moving the Landmark (Deut. 19:14)

The law follows the warning (verse 13) to purge the land of innocent blood. Moving a landmark defiles the land like spilled blood.

D. HOFFMANN [24]

Why is the law necessary when we are already commanded "You shall not steal"? In order to make clear that any infringement of a neighbor's rights is included. The law also prohibits selling one's family graves, even those as yet unoccupied; and it forbids changing the words of a teacher which are pronounced in his name.

MIDRASH [25]

Administration of Law and State, III

Inevitably, the laws regulating the administration of the community return to the subject of war which was then, as it still is, a major means of arranging and rearranging human affairs. These Deuteronomic laws—Hoffmann calls them rules for preserving life, which therefore well fit the context of this section [1]—are designed to check the barbarity of war and "to bring it under the influence of the higher moral spirit of Israel's religion, and to secure recognition for the claims of morality and moderation" [2].

In this connection, the text deals with exemptions from the duty to serve, with the disposition of booty, the treatment of captive nations, and ecologic restrictions. The latter rules—unequaled in intent until modern conventions of war—became the starting point for extensive discussions on human responsibility toward the environment. Together with previous and subsequent passages on the subject of war (Deut. 7:16 ff.; 9:1 ff.; 31:3 ff.), the regulations form a body of "war sermons," as von Rad has described them [3]. They are followed by a prescription belonging to the leftovers of earlier times: the procedures to be observed when a community has a case of unsolved manslaughter on its hands. The cleansing ritual requires a heifer to be sacrificed in a particular way, and the juxtaposition of these rules to those of war emphasizes that all killing defiles the covenantal people whose purity needs constant watching and, when necessary, restoration.

דברים כ
א–ד

Deuteronomy 20
1–4

א כִּי־תֵצֵא לַמִּלְחָמָה עַל־אֹיְבֶךָ וְרָאִיתָ סוּס וָרֶכֶב עַם
רָב מִמְּךָ לֹא תִירָא מֵהֶם כִּי־יְהוָֹה אֱלֹהֶיךָ עִמָּךְ
ב הַמַּעַלְךָ מֵאֶרֶץ מִצְרָיִם: וְהָיָה כְּקָרָבְכֶם אֶל־
ג הַמִּלְחָמָה וְנִגַּשׁ הַכֹּהֵן וְדִבֶּר אֶל־הָעָם: וְאָמַר אֲלֵהֶם
שְׁמַע יִשְׂרָאֵל אַתֶּם קְרֵבִים הַיּוֹם לַמִּלְחָמָה עַל־
אֹיְבֵיכֶם אַל־יֵרַךְ לְבַבְכֶם אַל־תִּירְאוּ וְאַל־תַּחְפְּזוּ
ד וְאַל־תַּעַרְצוּ מִפְּנֵיהֶם: כִּי יְהוָֹה אֱלֹהֵיכֶם הַהֹלֵךְ
עִמָּכֶם לְהִלָּחֵם לָכֶם עִם־אֹיְבֵיכֶם לְהוֹשִׁיעַ אֶתְכֶם:

1] When you take the field against your enemies, and see horses and chariots—forces larger than yours—have no fear of them, for the LORD your God, who brought you from the land of Egypt, is with you.   2] Before you join battle, the priest shall come forward and address the troops.   3] He shall say to them, "Hear, O Israel! You are about to join battle with your enemy. Let not your courage falter. Do not be in fear, or in panic, or in dread of them.   4] For it is the LORD your God who marches with you to do battle for you against your enemy, to bring you victory."

20:1] *When you take the field.* Most likely, these rules applied only to certain types of war, not to life-and-death defensive struggles (see commentary below).

Horses and chariots. Used by the Egyptians and Assyrians; because of the success they vouchsafed, the Israelites too desired to possess them, although their first reliance should have been on God. Isaiah (31:1) inveighs against "those who go down to Egypt for help and rely on horses," and the Psalmist (20:8) says: "They call on chariots, they call on horses, but we call on the name of the Lord our God." See also Deut. 17:16.

2] *The priest.* Tradition called him "the priest anointed for war," a specialist whose status was comparable to that of the High Priest [4].

3] *Hear, O Israel!* The formulaic opening of his address stresses its ritual nature.

4] *God who marches with you.* Either a figure of speech or a reference to the ark which was carried into battle.

A rabbinic scholar held that there were always two arks: one with the tablets of the Ten Commandments which stayed behind and one with the broken tablets which went with the army [5].

ה וְדִבְּרוּ הַשֹּׁטְרִים אֶל־הָעָם לֵאמֹר מִי־הָאִישׁ אֲשֶׁר
בָּנָה בַיִת־חָדָשׁ וְלֹא חֲנָכוֹ יֵלֵךְ וְיָשֹׁב לְבֵיתוֹ פֶּן־יָמוּת
בַּמִּלְחָמָה וְאִישׁ אַחֵר יַחְנְכֶנּוּ: ו וּמִי־הָאִישׁ אֲשֶׁר־נָטַע
כֶּרֶם וְלֹא חִלְּלוֹ יֵלֵךְ וְיָשֹׁב לְבֵיתוֹ פֶּן־יָמוּת בַּמִּלְחָמָה
וְאִישׁ אַחֵר יְחַלְּלֶנּוּ: ז וּמִי־הָאִישׁ אֲשֶׁר אֵרַשׂ אִשָּׁה וְלֹא
לְקָחָהּ יֵלֵךְ וְיָשֹׁב לְבֵיתוֹ פֶּן־יָמוּת בַּמִּלְחָמָה וְאִישׁ

Deuteronomy 20

5–7

5] Then the officials shall address the troops, as follows, "Is there anyone who has built a new house but has not dedicated it? Let him go back to his home, lest he die in battle and another dedicate it. **6]** Is there anyone who has planted a vineyard but has never harvested it? Let him go back to his home, lest he die in battle and another initiate it. **7]** Is there anyone who has paid the brideprice for a wife, but who has not yet married her? Let him go back to his home, lest he die

---

5] *Then the officials.* Representing the king. The people are addressed first by the most important personage, the priest; then by the officials; and finally the lowest in this order, the army commanders, take over (verse 9).

Is there anyone . . .? The exemptions follow an order of ever greater anxiety: the home builder, the farmer (who works four years before he harvests), the newly married, and lastly the coward. In the Maccabean wars these prescriptions were recorded to have been carried out (in the second century B.C.E., I Macc. 3:56).

According to the Talmud, those who claimed an exemption had to submit proof, much like a conscientious objector under American law [6].

Let him go back. Tradition saw this as a command: he *had* to go back, for his anxiety would prove infectious (verse 8). Also, most men in such positions would be too embarrassed to exercise their option [7].

According to von Rad, the reason lay elsewhere: it was believed that someone who had to dedicate

a thing was threatened by demons who were dangerous for others as well [8].

6] *Who . . . has never harvested.* Literally, "profaned," that is, he has not yet removed it from sacred restrictions to his own private use, which could take place only after four years had elapsed since planting (Lev. 19:23–25).

7] *Paid the bride-price.* He was considered legally married, though he had not as yet lived with his wife. The fully married also had a one-year exemption (Deut. 24:5). The ceremony of betrothal was once entirely separate from the marriage; in the traditional wedding of today the two are joined and the ritual begins with a "betrothal blessing," בִּרְכַּת אֵירוּסִין.

Let him go back. According to the Mishnah, the man had to perform noncombatant service, like helping to provide food and water for the army and repairing the roads [9].

In the modern American army, the draft was first directed to the unmarried, but being newly married provided no special exemption.

ח אַחַר יִקָּחֵנָה: וְיָסְפוּ הַשֹּׁטְרִים לְדַבֵּר אֶל־הָעָם
וְאָמְרוּ מִי־הָאִישׁ הַיָּרֵא וְרַךְ הַלֵּבָב יֵלֵךְ וְיָשֹׁב לְבֵיתוֹ
ט וְלֹא יִמַּס אֶת־לְבַב אֶחָיו כִּלְבָבוֹ: וְהָיָה כְּכַלֹּת
הַשֹּׁטְרִים לְדַבֵּר אֶל־הָעָם וּפָקְדוּ שָׂרֵי צְבָאוֹת
י בְּרֹאשׁ הָעָם: ס כִּי־תִקְרַב אֶל־עִיר לְהִלָּחֵם
יא עָלֶיהָ וְקָרָאתָ אֵלֶיהָ לְשָׁלוֹם: וְהָיָה אִם־שָׁלוֹם תַּעַנְךָ
וּפָתְחָה לָךְ וְהָיָה כָּל־הָעָם הַנִּמְצָא־בָהּ יִהְיוּ לְךָ
יב לָמַס וַעֲבָדוּךָ: וְאִם־לֹא תַשְׁלִים עִמָּךְ וְעָשְׂתָה עִמְּךָ
יג מִלְחָמָה וְצַרְתָּ עָלֶיהָ: וּנְתָנָהּ יְהֹוָה אֱלֹהֶיךָ בְּיָדֶךָ
יד וְהִכִּיתָ אֶת־כָּל־זְכוּרָהּ לְפִי־חָרֶב: רַק הַנָּשִׁים וְהַטַּף

Deuteronomy 20
8–14

in battle and another marry her." **8]** The officials shall go on addressing the troops and say, "Is there anyone afraid and disheartened? Let him go back to his home, lest the courage of his comrades flag like his." **9]** When the officials have finished addressing the troops, army commanders shall assume command of the troops.

10] When you approach a town to attack it, you shall offer it terms of peace. **11]** If it responds peaceably and lets you in, all the people present there shall serve you at forced labor. **12]** If it does not surrender to you, but would join battle with you, you shall lay siege to it; **13]** and when the LORD your God delivers it into your hand, you shall put all its males to the sword. **14]** You may, however,

9] *When the officials have finished.* After the ritual, the physical preparations for war begin.

10] *Approach a town.* Which lies outside of Canaan, according to verses 15–16.

Terms of peace. A euphemism for "call to surrender."

11] *Forced labor.* The likely meaning is that the city, through its people, was to perform certain tasks, not that individual citizens were to be impressed.

12] *Lay siege.* This consisted of constructing siege works (see verse 20), such as building mounds for the scaling of the city's walls, attempts to burn the gates (usually made of wood), and to starve the population.

וְהַבְּהֵמָה וְכֹל אֲשֶׁר יִהְיֶה בָעִיר כָּל־שְׁלָלָהּ תָּבֹז לָךְ וְאָכַלְתָּ אֶת־שְׁלַל אֹיְבֶיךָ אֲשֶׁר נָתַן יְהֹוָה אֱלֹהֶיךָ לָךְ:

טו כֵּן תַּעֲשֶׂה לְכָל־הֶעָרִים הָרְחֹקֹת מִמְּךָ מְאֹד אֲשֶׁר

טז לֹא־מֵעָרֵי הַגּוֹיִם־הָאֵלֶּה הֵנָּה: רַק מֵעָרֵי הָעַמִּים הָאֵלֶּה אֲשֶׁר יְהֹוָה אֱלֹהֶיךָ נֹתֵן לְךָ נַחֲלָה לֹא תְחַיֶּה

יז כָּל־נְשָׁמָה: כִּי־הַחֲרֵם תַּחֲרִימֵם הַחִתִּי וְהָאֱמֹרִי הַכְּנַעֲנִי וְהַפְּרִזִּי הַחִוִּי וְהַיְבוּסִי כַּאֲשֶׁר צִוְּךָ יְהֹוָה

יח אֱלֹהֶיךָ: לְמַעַן אֲשֶׁר לֹא־יְלַמְּדוּ אֶתְכֶם לַעֲשׂוֹת כְּכֹל תּוֹעֲבֹתָם אֲשֶׁר עָשׂוּ לֵאלֹהֵיהֶם וַחֲטָאתֶם לַיהֹוָה

יט אֱלֹהֵיכֶם: ס כִּי־תָצוּר אֶל־עִיר יָמִים רַבִּים

Deuteronomy 20
15–19

take as your booty the women, the children, the livestock, and everything in the town—all its spoil—and enjoy the use of the spoil of your enemy which the LORD your God gives you.

15] Thus you shall deal with all towns that lie very far from you, towns that do not belong to nations hereabout. 16] In the towns of the latter peoples, however, which the LORD your God is giving you as a heritage, you shall not let a soul remain alive. 17] No, you must proscribe them—the Hittites and the Amorites, the Canaanites and the Perizzites, the Hivites and the Jebusites—as the LORD your God has commanded you, 18] lest they lead you into doing all the abhorrent things that they have done for their gods and you stand guilty before the LORD your God.

19] When in your war against a city you have to besiege it a long time in order

15] *Very far from you.* Lying outside of Canaan.

16] *Not let a soul remain alive.* See at Deut. 7:2. This is a retrospective command: had you done this you would not have lapsed into idolatry. In the actual invasion no wholesale extermination of the local population took place, although such a

procedure would not have offended against the usual practice of the times.

17] *Proscribe them.* Put them under the ban, for they belong to God and are therefore unfit for human use; see at Lev. 27:29. The Girgashites, mentioned in Deut. 7:1, are not listed here. Tra-

237

לְהִלָּחֵם עָלֶיהָ לְתָפְשָׂהּ לֹא־תַשְׁחִית אֶת־עֵצָהּ לִנְדֹּחַ

עָלָיו גַּרְזֶן כִּי מִמֶּנּוּ תֹאכֵל וְאֹתוֹ לֹא תִכְרֹת כִּי

כ הָאָדָם עֵץ הַשָּׂדֶה לָבֹא מִפָּנֶיךָ בַּמָּצוֹר: רַק עֵץ

אֲשֶׁר־תֵּדַע כִּי־לֹא־עֵץ מַאֲכָל הוּא אֹתוֹ תַשְׁחִית

וְכָרָתָּ וּבָנִיתָ מָצוֹר עַל־הָעִיר אֲשֶׁר־הִוא עֹשָׂה עִמְּךָ

מִלְחָמָה עַד רִדְתָּהּ: פ

א כִּי־יִמָּצֵא חָלָל בָּאֲדָמָה אֲשֶׁר יְהוָה אֱלֹהֶיךָ נֹתֵן לְךָ

ב לְרִשְׁתָּהּ נֹפֵל בַּשָּׂדֶה לֹא נוֹדַע מִי הִכָּהוּ: וְיָצְאוּ

זְקֵנֶיךָ וְשֹׁפְטֶיךָ וּמָדְדוּ אֶל־הֶעָרִים אֲשֶׁר סְבִיבֹת

to capture it, you must not destroy its trees, wielding the ax against them. You may eat of them, but you must not cut them down. Are trees of the field human to withdraw before you into the besieged city?   20] Only trees which you know do not yield food may be destroyed; you may cut them down for constructing siegeworks against the city that is waging war on you, until it has been reduced.

1] If, in the land that the LORD your God is giving you to possess, someone slain is found lying in the open, the identity of the slayer not being known,   2] your elders and magistrates shall go out and measure the distances from the corpse to

dition explained the omission by speculating that this people had meanwhile, in anticipation of Israel's invasion, migrated to Africa [10].

19] *You must not cut them down.* Forbidding deforestation, which was a common practice in ancient warfare (similar to defoliation in modern days) [11]. However, a scorched-earth policy was carried out by the Israelites in a campaign against the Moabites, and the exception was said to have been ordered by God himself; II Kings 3:19.

Are trees . . . human . . . ? Meaning, you are warring against people, not trees.

The Hebrew was understood by some as a positive statement: "a human being is (like) a tree,"

which stresses his close dependence on vegetation [12].

20] *Until it has been reduced.* Tradition took this as a proof text that a siege could be continued even on the Sabbath [13].

21:1] *Someone slain.* חָלָל (chalal) is of the same root as חִלֵּל (chilel, profane). Killing soils the land and must be expiated either by the death of the culprit or, if he is not identified, by a special procedure.

2] *Your elders and magistrates.* Originally, these came from the nearest cities; later they were

238

ג הֶחָלָל: וְהָיָה הָעִיר הַקְּרֹבָה אֶל־הֶחָלָל וְלָקְחוּ זִקְנֵי
הָעִיר הַהִוא עֶגְלַת בָּקָר אֲשֶׁר לֹא־עֻבַּד בָּהּ אֲשֶׁר
ד לֹא־מָשְׁכָה בְּעֹל: וְהוֹרִדוּ זִקְנֵי הָעִיר הַהִוא אֶת־
הָעֶגְלָה אֶל־נַחַל אֵיתָן אֲשֶׁר לֹא־יֵעָבֵד בּוֹ וְלֹא
ה יִזָּרֵעַ וְעָרְפוּ־שָׁם אֶת־הָעֶגְלָה בַּנָּחַל: וְנִגְּשׁוּ הַכֹּהֲנִים
בְּנֵי לֵוִי כִּי בָם בָּחַר יְהוָה אֱלֹהֶיךָ לְשָׁרְתוֹ וּלְבָרֵךְ
ו בְּשֵׁם יְהוָה וְעַל־פִּיהֶם יִהְיֶה כָּל־רִיב וְכָל־נָגַע: וְכֹל
זִקְנֵי הָעִיר הַהִוא הַקְּרֹבִים אֶל־הֶחָלָל יִרְחֲצוּ אֶת־
ז יְדֵיהֶם עַל־הָעֶגְלָה הָעֲרוּפָה בַנָּחַל: וְעָנוּ וְאָמְרוּ

Deuteronomy 21

3–7

the nearby towns.   **3]** The elders of the town nearest to the corpse shall then take a heifer which has never been worked, which has never pulled in a yoke; **4]** and the elders of that town shall bring the heifer down to a rugged wadi, which is not tilled or sown. There, in the wadi, they shall break the heifer's neck.   **5]** The priests, sons of Levi, shall come forward; for the LORD your God has chosen them to minister to Him and to pronounce blessing in the name of the LORD, and every lawsuit and case of assault is subject to their ruling.   **6]** Then all the elders of the town nearest to the corpse shall wash their hands over the heifer whose neck was broken in the wadi.   **7]** And they shall make this declaration:

drawn from cities with courts and from Jerusalem [14].

3] *A heifer.* Similar to one that was offered as a firstling; Deut. 15:19.

4] *Rugged wadi.* Others, "wadi running with water" or "rough valley" [15].
Not tilled or sown. Similar to the restrictions for the heifer.
They. The magistrates. For the meaning of the ritual, see commentary below.

5] *The priests.* Up to this point they have not been mentioned. The text has better continuity without this verse; most likely, it is a later addition.
Case of assault. Or, "of skin affection," see Deut. 17:8 and 24:8.

6] *Wash their hands.* The ritual of purification symbolized their innocence. Thus Psalm 26:6: "I wash my hands in innocence" (see also Ps. 73:13). Hence also the English expression "to wash one's hands of a matter."

יָדֵינוּ לֹא שָׁפְכָה אֶת־הַדָּם הַזֶּה וְעֵינֵינוּ לֹא רָאוּ:

ח כַּפֵּר לְעַמְּךָ יִשְׂרָאֵל אֲשֶׁר־פָּדִיתָ יְהוָה וְאַל־תִּתֵּן דָּם

ט נָקִי בְּקֶרֶב עַמְּךָ יִשְׂרָאֵל וְנִכַּפֵּר לָהֶם הַדָּם: וְאַתָּה

תְבַעֵר הַדָּם הַנָּקִי מִקִּרְבֶּךָ כִּי־תַעֲשֶׂה הַיָּשָׁר בְּעֵינֵי

יְהוָה:

Haftarah Shofetim, p. 450   ‎* ז שפכו קרי.

"Our hands did not shed this blood, nor did our eyes see it done.   8] Absolve, O Lord, Your people Israel whom You redeemed, and do not let guilt for the blood of the innocent remain among Your people Israel." And they will be absolved of bloodguilt.   9] Thus you will remove from your midst guilt for the blood of the innocent, for you will be doing what is right in the sight of the Lord.

7] *Our hands did not shed.* The elders speak in the name of the community.

8] *Absolve.* כַּפֵּר (kapper); the same root appears in the word (Yom) Kippur. The purpose of the process is to restore the city to its condition of guiltlessness.

The Conduct of War

In the biblical view, warfare was unavoidable and sometimes necessary [16]; universal peace was envisioned for posthistorical days (Micah 4:3). Until then, God's people too had to fight, and in such struggles, if they were righteous in purpose and conduct, God's assistance was anticipated. For, since Israel's existence in this world was bound up with God's will, the nation's wars were ultimately His wars: they were holy struggles. Hence, the preparations for war were ritualized, as were the distribution of booty and the treatment of the enemy, and the fight itself was directed by the One who was called "Lord of Hosts." The priest (verse 2) was a kind of antique army chaplain, but his service was not designed to assist the individual soldier; rather, he aimed at binding the fighting men to the purposes of God, and thus he literally "consecrated" or "sanctified" the war. Hence his status approached that of the High Priest [17].

The concept that wars could serve the deity was an old one and not unique to Israel. The "Israel dimension" grew out of specific historic experiences which were seen as manifestations of God's will, as judgments on His own people and on other nations, the divine element operating in the unfolding of history. It is likely that the ritual which developed, and which is codified in our chapter, also had a pragmatic effect in that it helped to unify the nation, for it reminded Israel of its spiritual destiny and spurred it on to greater national devotion.

Later tradition distinguished between various kinds of war and coined a special terminology to describe them. The conquest of the land as well as a defensive war that was fought to assure Israel's survival was called "obligatory" (*milchemet mitzvah*) [18], whereas any other war—such as a preemptive struggle—was merely optional (*milchemet reshut*). The Deuteronomic law of military

exemptions was considered applicable only to the optional war; in a battle for survival no one was excused from serving, not even a bridegroom; he had to go forth from the bridal chamber to do his share in the war [19].

How closely these rules were observed in practice is hard to say; they were doubtlessly at one time part of the cult and faded away when Israel's independence was destroyed.

The Uses of Nature

The text says: "When in your war against a city you have to besiege it a long time in order to capture it, *you must not destroy its trees*, wielding the ax against them. . . . Are trees of the field human to withdraw before you into the besieged city?" The prohibition applied to food-yielding trees only; others were permitted for the construction of siege works (Deut. 20:19–20) [20].

These verses are clearly a limitation on the principle enunciated in Gen. 1:28 that humanity may utilize ("master") the earth's resources to the fullest. For "the earth is the Lord's with all that it holds" (Ps. 24:1), and God reminds His creatures that they must operate within certain laws—for their own benefit as well as that of nature. The Torah had no literal equivalent of our "ecology," but the interdependence of creation and humanity and the dependence of both on God were part of its world view. The institution of the sabbatical year, when the farmer was to let the fields lie fallow so that they might recuperate, not only represented the insights of agricultural experience but had above all a socio-religious dimension. The poor and the stranger were to benefit from this seventh-year cessation, and thereby God reasserted His ownership of the land.

The Rabbis expanded the biblical law considerably and created a whole category of actions that fell under the prohibition of wastefulness, which they called בַּל־תַּשְׁחִית

(bal tashchit).[1] They ruled that the law against cutting down a fruit tree, by extension, also forbade drawing off its sap for the sake of destruction, and thus defoliation of such trees would also be considered contrary to the spirit of the law. When a tree is cut down, as the saying goes, its voice of pain resounds throughout the world.

The halachah went still further. It ruled that spoliation of fruit was forbidden, as was diverting the flow of a river to cause distress to a besieged city; and Maimonides formulated the rules of tradition as follows: All needless destruction is included in this prohibition; for instance, whoever burns a garment, or breaks a vessel needlessly, contravenes the command "You must not destroy" [21]. A talmudic opinion even stated that someone who could get along on corn but insisted on eating wheat (a rarer commodity), or someone who could drink mead but drank wine instead, infringed on the ordinance of bal tashchit [22]. For creation was seen as an ongoing process, and humans at all times were God's co-partners in safeguarding its potential. The Torah uses the example of behavior during warfare to demonstrate the importance of this principle.

Unsolved Manslaughter

The expiatory ritual for unsolved manslaughter, contained in 21:1–9, undoubtedly went back to very ancient times, and there are Hittite laws resembling the Torah in this respect. Underlying these provisions

was the concept that murder stained the land and that without the punishment of the guilty the cultic purity of the community was impaired. The community nearest the place of the evil deed was considered responsible,[2] and a heifer was chosen to ward off the wrath of the Divine. Once the ritual was completed, God's assurance of forgiveness was obtained and the community's purity restored [23].

The expiation ceremony is complemented by Lev. 4:13–15 (provision for cleansing the community from some unspecified sin) and Num., chapter 19 (dealing with the sacrifice of the red heifer). The three passages apparently arose in different ages but served the same general purpose. Traditional commentators considered the law in Leviticus as the overarching rule and the provisions in Numbers and Deuteronomy as specific examples.

They also found the ritual of the eglah arufah (the broken-necked heifer) to have had a practical value. Hoffmann reasoned that it would attract so much public attention and interest that the level of communal responsibility would be raised by this procedure as much as by the execution of the apprehended murderer. Abarbanel said that its shock value would prevent the people from forgetting the act and would keep alive the search for the offender [24]. The Mishnah reports that the procedure ceased when crimes of murder multiplied to such a degree that the ritual was no longer feasible [25].

---

[1] A variant of the phrase in verse 19: lo tashchit, "you must not destroy."

[2] See Gleanings for the talmudic controversy on why the nearest city was thus singled out.

GLEANINGS

Only with Justice

Why do the prescriptions concerning warfare follow the rules of justice in the preceding chapter? To teach that Israel will succeed in war only if it practices justice.   RASHI [26]

Have No Fear (Deut. 20:1)

This is one of the 365 negative commands of the Torah. One who exhibits fear is answerable for the loss of life he occasions by his attitude.

MAIMONIDES [27]

He who fears humans is likely to have forgotten God.   TRADITIONAL [28]

Enemies

God delivers not only from human enemies (20:4) but also helps us to victory in the battle against the evil impulse.   CHASIDIC [29]

Peace

The greatness of peace may be seen from Scripture. Even when it deals with war it commands: When you make war, first proclaim peace (20:10).

Great is peace, for God has placed it in heaven itself, as it is said: "He makes peace in His high places" (Job 25:2).   MIDRASH [30]

Two Views on War

After World War I, in 1924, the Central Conference of American Rabbis resolved:

We believe that war is morally indefensible.

But after World War II, in 1955, the emphasis changed:

We reject the spreading cancer of despair that wracks the soul of mankind with the anguish of inevitable war [31].

Priorities

From the order in which the exemptions from service are listed (20:5–7), one may conclude that a man first ought to build a house, then plant a vineyard, and then proceed to marry.

TALMUD [32]

Homilies

The three exemptions may be likened to a person's return to his religious roots:

To his faith, that is, when a person has acquired its foundations but has not yet lived by it.

To the commandments, that is, if he observes them but not yet for God's sake.

To the Torah, that is, if he engages in its study but not yet for its own sake.

YALKUT ME'AM LO'EZ [33]

The officials ask: "Is there anyone afraid . . .?" (20:8) This means: . . . of the sins he has committed.   MISHNAH [34]

It also refers to someone constantly preoccupied with his guilt.   CHASIDIC [35]

Eglah Arufah (the heifer whose neck is broken, 21:1 ff.)

The ritual of expiating an unsolved murder occasioned an interesting controversy between the Palestinian and Babylonian Rabbis. It concerned the declaration by the elders of the town nearest the scene of the crime who state (verse 7): "Our hands did not shed this blood, nor did our eyes see it done." But was there ever any suspicion that it was the elders who were the slayers?

The Palestinian Rabbis took this to refer to the unknown slayer, meaning: No one came within our jurisdiction whom we neglected to bring to justice. The Babylonian Rabbis referred the text to the victim, meaning: No one came within our jurisdiction for whom we failed to provide protection or whom we left without a livelihood.

MISHNAH [36]

Thus responsibility for wrongdoing does not only lie with the perpetrator himself and even with the accessory. Lack of proper care and attention is also criminal. Whoever keeps to his own quiet corner and refuses to have anything to do with the "evil world," who observes oppression and violence but does not stir a finger in protest, cannot proclaim with a clear conscience that "our hands have not shed this blood."

N. LEIBOWITZ [37]

Low-Key

If Scripture's call to mankind to safeguard the earth is too restrained for the liking of today's ecological activists, we might bear in mind that the Bible originated in an era when nature worship and the adoration of natural forces and phenomena were prevalent. The Bible fought against this Zeitgeist and strove to implant in its audience an awareness of the worth of the human being, a recognition of the preciousness in the eyes of the Lord of human suffering and human happiness. "Man was created in the image of God" and he was not to be broken by fear of the forces of nature or by the tyranny of nature cults. Viewed in this context, the concern of the biblical tradition for nature had to be formulated, of necessity, in a low-keyed message. But the concern was clearly and unmistakably there. Woven into the narrative, written into specific laws, it is remarkable evidence that the Bible is truly our life and the length of our days, that we may dwell on the land which destiny has provided for us (Deut. 30:20).

E. G. FREUDENSTEIN [38]

The Social Weal, I

The section before us contains a series of diverse laws. Most of them (to speak in modern terms) aim at impressing moral values on the social structure so that Israel may in every respect be worthy of being God's people. Others, such as the law of fringes, deal with the special status of Israel as God's people or, as in the laws against unnatural mixtures, with the need to preserve the intent of creation.

The following subjects are treated: rights of women who are captives of war or who no longer enjoy their husbands' love; treatment of a defiant, rebellious son; burial of an executed criminal; consideration for the property of others; unnatural mixtures—among people, crops, animals, and clothing materials; consideration for animals; fringes.

According to Maimonides, the new weekly portion, *Ki Tetze*, which begins here with 21:10, contains seventy-two mitzvot. One of these—dealing with a mother bird and her young—became the center of a famous dispute over the justice of God (see commentary).

ס ס ס

כי תצא

דברים כא
י–יד

Ki Tetze

Deuteronomy 21

10–14

י כִּי־תֵצֵא לַמִּלְחָמָה עַל־אֹיְבֶיךָ וּנְתָנוֹ יְהֹוָה אֱלֹהֶיךָ
יא בְּיָדֶךָ וְשָׁבִיתָ שִׁבְיוֹ: וְרָאִיתָ בַּשִּׁבְיָה אֵשֶׁת יְפַת־תֹּאַר
יב וְחָשַׁקְתָּ בָהּ וְלָקַחְתָּ לְךָ לְאִשָּׁה: וַהֲבֵאתָהּ אֶל־תּוֹךְ
בֵּיתֶךָ וְגִלְּחָה אֶת־רֹאשָׁהּ וְעָשְׂתָה אֶת־צִפָּרְנֶיהָ:
יג וְהֵסִירָה אֶת־שִׂמְלַת שִׁבְיָהּ מֵעָלֶיהָ וְיָשְׁבָה בְּבֵיתֶךָ
וּבָכְתָה אֶת־אָבִיהָ וְאֶת־אִמָּהּ יֶרַח יָמִים וְאַחַר כֵּן
יד תָּבוֹא אֵלֶיהָ וּבְעַלְתָּהּ וְהָיְתָה לְךָ לְאִשָּׁה: וְהָיָה אִם־

10] When you take the field against your enemies, and the LORD your God delivers them into your power and you take some of them captive,   11] and you see among the captives a beautiful woman and you desire her and would take her to wife,   12] you shall bring her into your house, and she shall trim her hair, pare her nails,   13] and discard her captive's garb. She shall spend a month's time in your house lamenting her father and mother; after that you may come to her and possess her, and she shall be your wife.   14] Then, should you no longer want

21:10–14] It should be noted that these verses present ideal and theoretical, rather than practical, legislation. Actual warfare, then and always, gave vent to humanity's basest impulses; killing, rape, and looting were, and remain, its ambience. The Torah must be seen to have here a meliorating purpose, a statement of how God's people, if war became their lot, *should* behave.

Although the text does not say so, later tradition took it to apply to non-obligatory wars, as in Deut. 20:1. Verses 10–14 appear to belong directly after 20:20, where they may have stood at one time. The permission to marry a captive did not extend to Canaanite women, who were not permitted to Israelites (Deut. 7:3).

12] *Trim her hair.* Others, "shave her head." The

procedure signified a change in the woman's status.

The custom persists among some Orthodox women who cut off their hair prior to marriage.

Pare her nails. Many understand this in the opposite sense: "let her nails grow." Commentators have suggested various reasons for the law, such as control of certain idolatrous practices [1]. Note that traditional Jewish law provides generally that a person must bury or burn the parings of nails [2].

13] *Month's time.* To adjust, like a mourner, to her changed status; cf. Num. 20:29; Deut. 34:8.

246

לֹא חָפַצְתָּ בָּהּ וְשִׁלַּחְתָּהּ לְנַפְשָׁהּ וּמָכֹר לֹא־תִמְכְּרֶנָּה בַּכֶּסֶף לֹא־תִתְעַמֵּר בָּהּ תַּחַת אֲשֶׁר עִנִּיתָהּ: ס

טו כִּי־תִהְיֶיןָ לְאִישׁ שְׁתֵּי נָשִׁים הָאַחַת אֲהוּבָה וְהָאַחַת שְׂנוּאָה וְיָלְדוּ־לוֹ בָנִים הָאֲהוּבָה וְהַשְּׂנוּאָה וְהָיָה הַבֵּן הַבְּכֹר לַשְּׂנִיאָה: טז וְהָיָה בְּיוֹם הַנְחִילוֹ אֶת־בָּנָיו אֵת אֲשֶׁר־יִהְיֶה לוֹ לֹא יוּכַל לְבַכֵּר אֶת־בֶּן־הָאֲהוּבָה עַל־פְּנֵי בֶן־הַשְּׂנוּאָה הַבְּכֹר: יז כִּי אֶת־הַבְּכֹר בֶּן־הַשְּׂנוּאָה יַכִּיר לָתֶת לוֹ פִּי שְׁנַיִם בְּכֹל אֲשֶׁר־יִמָּצֵא לוֹ כִּי־הוּא רֵאשִׁית אֹנוֹ לוֹ מִשְׁפַּט הַבְּכֹרָה: ס יח כִּי־יִהְיֶה לְאִישׁ בֵּן סוֹרֵר וּמוֹרֶה אֵינֶנּוּ שֹׁמֵעַ בְּקוֹל אָבִיו וּבְקוֹל אִמּוֹ

Deuteronomy 21
15–18

her, you must release her outright. You must not sell her for money: since you had your will of her, you must not enslave her.

15] If a man has two wives, one loved and the other unloved, and both the loved and the unloved have borne him sons, but the first-born is the son of the unloved one— 16] when he wills his property to his sons, he may not treat as first-born the son of the loved one in disregard of the son of the unloved one who is older. 17] Instead, he must accept the first-born, the son of the unloved one, and allot to him a double portion of all he possesses; since he is the first fruit of his vigor, the birthright is his due.

18] If a man has a wayward and defiant son, who does not heed his father or

15] *Two wives.* The Bible permitted polygamy, though the law indicates that multiple marriage would likely lead to serious problems. Rachel and Leah, Hannah and Peninnah were examples of the "loved" and "unloved" wives (Gen. 29:30–31; I Sam. 1).

The first-born. Under the prevailing rule of primogeniture, the first-born son had certain rights: he inherited a double portion and succeeded the father as head of the family. He could

sell his birthright (as Esau did, Gen. 25:29 ff.) or he could be deprived of it by his father (as Reuben was, Gen. 49:3–4), but only for cause, and not because he was the son of an unloved mother. In that sense, his mother had a stake in seeing her son's prerogatives maintained.

17] *Double portion.* Literally, "two-thirds."

18] *A wayward and defiant son.* This harsh procedure takes to an extreme the provisions found elsewhere in the Torah, where death is provided

יט] וְיִסְּרוּ אֹתוֹ וְלֹא יִשְׁמַע אֲלֵיהֶם: וְתָפְשׂוּ בוֹ אָבִיו וְאִמּוֹ וְהוֹצִיאוּ אֹתוֹ אֶל־זִקְנֵי עִירוֹ וְאֶל־שַׁעַר מְקֹמוֹ:

כ] וְאָמְרוּ אֶל־זִקְנֵי עִירוֹ בְּנֵנוּ זֶה סוֹרֵר וּמֹרֶה אֵינֶנּוּ שֹׁמֵעַ בְּקֹלֵנוּ זוֹלֵל וְסֹבֵא:

כא] וּרְגָמֻהוּ כָּל־אַנְשֵׁי עִירוֹ בָאֲבָנִים וָמֵת וּבִעַרְתָּ הָרָע מִקִּרְבֶּךָ וְכָל־יִשְׂרָאֵל יִשְׁמְעוּ וְיִרָאוּ: ס

כב] וְכִי־יִהְיֶה בְאִישׁ חֵטְא מִשְׁפַּט־מָוֶת וְהוּמָת וְתָלִיתָ אֹתוֹ עַל־עֵץ:

כג] לֹא־תָלִין נִבְלָתוֹ עַל־הָעֵץ כִּי־קָבוֹר תִּקְבְּרֶנּוּ בַּיּוֹם הַהוּא כִּי־קִלְלַת

Deuteronomy 21
19–23

mother and does not obey them even after they discipline him, **19]** his father and mother shall take hold of him and bring him out to the elders of his town at the public place of his community. **20]** They shall say to the elders of his town, "This son of ours is disloyal and defiant; he does not heed us. He is a glutton and a drunkard." **21]** Thereupon the men of his town shall stone him to death. Thus you will sweep out evil from your midst: all Israel will hear and be afraid.

22] If a man is guilty of a capital offense and is put to death, and you impale him on a stake, **23]** you must not let his corpse remain on the stake overnight, but must bury him the same day. For an impaled body is an

for those who strike or curse their parents (Exod. 21:15, 17; Lev. 20:9; Deut. 27:16); although, if "cursing" parents is to be understood as "insulting" them, the treatment of the wayward son would appear less extreme. But there is a possibility that the law is to be seen primarily as a warning, and a Sage of the Talmud flatly declared that the conditions which would cause a court to decree the death penalty "never occurred and never will occur" [3]. A biblical proverb suggests that a defiant son will have a bad end, but it does not refer to a trial:

The eye that mocks at his father,/ And despises to obey his mother,/ The ravens of the valley shall pick it out,/ And the young vultures shall eat it (Prov. 30:17).

20] *A glutton and a drunkard.* Prov. 23:20–21 warn:

Be not among winebibbers,/ Among gluttonous eaters of flesh;/ For the drunkard and the glutton shall come to poverty,/ And drowsiness shall clothe a man with rags.

22] *Impale him on a stake.* Or, "hang him on a gibbet" (New English Bible) or "on a tree" (old JPS translation). The impaling was not itself a form of execution and probably took place only after the offender's execution by other means. The passage may have been placed here because the previous law specified death by stoning, and it is now stated that impaling must follow the stoning.

23] *Bury him the same day.* Tradition expanded this to all burials [4]. See commentary.

אֱלֹהִים תָּלוּי וְלֹא תְטַמֵּא אֶת־אַדְמָתְךָ אֲשֶׁר יְהוָֹה
אֱלֹהֶיךָ נֹתֵן לְךָ נַחֲלָה: ס

א לֹא־תִרְאֶה אֶת־שׁוֹר אָחִיךָ אוֹ אֶת־שֵׂיוֹ נִדָּחִים

ב וְהִתְעַלַּמְתָּ מֵהֶם הָשֵׁב תְּשִׁיבֵם לְאָחִיךָ: וְאִם־לֹא
קָרוֹב אָחִיךָ אֵלֶיךָ וְלֹא יְדַעְתּוֹ וַאֲסַפְתּוֹ אֶל־תּוֹךְ
בֵּיתֶךָ וְהָיָה עִמְּךָ עַד דְּרֹשׁ אָחִיךָ אֹתוֹ וַהֲשֵׁבֹתוֹ לוֹ:

ג וְכֵן תַּעֲשֶׂה לַחֲמֹרוֹ וְכֵן תַּעֲשֶׂה לְשִׂמְלָתוֹ וְכֵן תַּעֲשֶׂה
לְכָל־אֲבֵדַת אָחִיךָ אֲשֶׁר־תֹּאבַד מִמֶּנּוּ וּמְצָאתָהּ לֹא

ד תוּכַל לְהִתְעַלֵּם: ס לֹא־תִרְאֶה אֶת־חֲמוֹר אָחִיךָ
אוֹ שׁוֹרוֹ נֹפְלִים בַּדֶּרֶךְ וְהִתְעַלַּמְתָּ מֵהֶם הָקֵם תָּקִים

Deuteronomy 22
1–4

affront to God: you shall not defile the land that the LORD your God is giving you to possess.

1] If you see your fellow's ox or sheep gone astray, do not ignore it; you must take it back to your fellow.   2] If your fellow does not live near you or you do not know who he is, you shall bring it home and it shall remain with you until your fellow claims it; then you shall give it back to him.   3] You shall do the same with his ass; you shall do the same with his garment; and so too shall you do with anything that your fellow loses and you find: you must not remain indifferent.

4] If you see your fellow's ass or ox fallen on the road, do not ignore it; you must help him raise it.

Affront to God. Because even the lowliest criminal bears the divine image.

Others translate as "is accursed of God" [5].

22:1] *Your fellow's ox.* In Exod. 23:4, "your enemy's," that is, someone of your own people who is your enemy. While either verse could be a broadening of the other, it is likely that we have here two versions of a common law of concern.

2] *Does not live near you.* He lives so far that restoration of the animal would become an undue burden.

4] *Fallen on the road.* The animal must be helped not only for the sake of the owner but for its own sake. This concern is in Jewish tradition called "(concern for the) distress of living creatures" (*tza-ar ba-alei chayim*). See commentary and compare Exod. 23:5.

ה עַמּוֹ: ס לֹא־יִהְיֶה כְלִי־גֶבֶר עַל־אִשָּׁה וְלֹא־יִלְבַּשׁ
גֶּבֶר שִׂמְלַת אִשָּׁה כִּי תוֹעֲבַת יְהוָה אֱלֹהֶיךָ כָּל־
פ עֹשֵׂה אֵלֶּה:

ו כִּי יִקָּרֵא קַן־צִפּוֹר לְפָנֶיךָ בַּדֶּרֶךְ בְּכָל־עֵץ אוֹ
עַל־הָאָרֶץ אֶפְרֹחִים אוֹ בֵיצִים וְהָאֵם רֹבֶצֶת עַל־
הָאֶפְרֹחִים אוֹ עַל־הַבֵּיצִים לֹא־תִקַּח הָאֵם עַל־

ז הַבָּנִים: שַׁלֵּחַ תְּשַׁלַּח אֶת־הָאֵם וְאֶת־הַבָּנִים תִּקַּח־לָךְ

ח לְמַעַן יִיטַב לָךְ וְהַאֲרַכְתָּ יָמִים: ס כִּי תִבְנֶה
בַּיִת חָדָשׁ וְעָשִׂיתָ מַעֲקֶה לְגַגֶּךָ וְלֹא־תָשִׂים דָּמִים

ט בְּבֵיתֶךָ כִּי־יִפֹּל הַנֹּפֵל מִמֶּנּוּ: לֹא־תִזְרַע כַּרְמְךָ
כִּלְאָיִם פֶּן־תִּקְדַּשׁ הַמְלֵאָה הַזֶּרַע אֲשֶׁר תִּזְרָע

*ט קמץ בז"ק.

5] A woman must not put on man's apparel, nor shall a man wear woman's clothing; for whoever does these things is abhorrent to the LORD your God.

6] If, along the road, you chance upon a bird's nest, in any tree or on the ground, with fledglings or eggs and the mother sitting over the fledglings or on the eggs, do not take the mother together with her young.   **7]** Let the mother go, and take only the young, in order that you may fare well and have a long life.

8] When you build a new house, you shall make a parapet for your roof, so that you do not bring bloodguilt on your house if anyone should fall from it.

9] You shall not sow your vineyard with a second kind of seed, else the

---

5] *Man's apparel.* The Hebrew is more general and says "man's gear." (See further in Gleanings.)

Abhorrent. The Hebrew term suggests that transvestism was considered not so much a sexual deviation as an idolatrous practice.

6] *Do not take the mother.* Commentators have suggested various reasons for this law; see commentary.

7] *Have a long life.* The premature death of a lad who observed the commandment caused a second-century C.E. rabbi to lose his faith; see commentary.

8] *Make a parapet.* Modern building codes have similar regulations.

9] *Second kind of seed.* Verses 9–11 reflect the

וּתְבוּאַת הַכָּרֶם: ס לֹא־תַחֲרֹשׁ בְּשׁוֹר־וּבַחֲמֹר ׳
יַחְדָּו: לֹא תִלְבַּשׁ שַׁעַטְנֵז צֶמֶר וּפִשְׁתִּים יַחְדָּו: ס ׳א
גְּדִלִים תַּעֲשֶׂה־לָּךְ עַל־אַרְבַּע כַּנְפוֹת כְּסוּתְךָ אֲשֶׁר ׳ב
תְּכַסֶּה־בָּהּ: ס

crop—from the seed you have sown—and the yield of the vineyard may not be used.   **10]** You shall not plow with an ox and an ass together.   **11]** You shall not wear cloth combining wool and linen.

12] You shall make tassels on the four corners of the garment with which you cover yourself.

biblical aversion to interfering with the established order of nature—in stark contrast with the objectives of modern technology. See further commentary on Lev. 19:19. The Hebrew term כִּלְאַיִם (kil'ayim) is the name of a tractate in Mishnah and Palestinian Talmud, where more than sixty different plants are mentioned, providing thereby an important source for the knowledge of ancient agriculture.

May not be used. Literally, "lest it become sacred," i.e., set aside for God's use. Tradition provided that the yield be burned.

10] *An ox and an ass together.* A law unique to the Torah, which here wants to protect the weaker animal and to prevent the mixing of species, even at work.

Tradition expanded the provision to all animals of different kinds [6].

11] *Wool and linen.* The mixture is called שַׁעַטְנֵז (sha-atnez), a word of unknown origin. The verse may be taken as an explanation of Lev. 19:19 (see commentary there). Since priests, on the other hand, *had* to wear garments made of wool and

linen, this law may be seen to aim at separating the holy from the profane. See further at Exod. 28:15 [7].

12] *Tassels.* Here called *gedilim*, while in Num. 15:37 ff. they are called *tzitzit*; see commentary there. The tassels serve as reminders of God's ever-presence.

Because the command followed directly on the prohibition of *sha-atnez*, the Talmud reasoned that the Torah permitted woolen tassels to be attached to linen garments [8].

Four corners. The normal garment was square or oblong and had four corners. When in time different (tailored) clothes were adopted, the law was believed not to apply to them and, in order to fulfill the commandment, a special four-cornered cloth with tassels (called *talit*) was donned during prayer. There are also observant Jews who at all times wear a "four-corners" garment (called *arba kanfot*), a square cloth with tassels and with a hole in the middle which is slipped over the head and is regularly worn as part of one's clothing (usually as an undergarment). Certain groups of Orthodox Jews make sure that the fringes are seen at all times.

Burying the Dead

Quick burial of the deceased was a matter of great concern in the ancient Near East except in Egypt, where embalming was practiced. The natural process of decomposition was accelerated by the warm climate, and an abundance of birds and other animals that would feed on the cadavers demanded an early burial. One of the curses with which a wayward Israel is threatened is precisely this: "Your carcasses shall become food for all the birds of the sky and all the beasts of the earth, with none to frighten them off" (Deut. 28:26; see also Jer. 22:19).

The sight of unburied bodies was considered an offense not only against human dignity but against God himself. Even a criminal who had been impaled (or hanged) was to be interred before sunset "for an impaled body is an affront to God: you shall not defile the land that the Lord your God is giving you to possess" (Deut. 21:23).

In the biblical conception of afterlife[1] there was room to believe that in death one could be united with the past, especially if one would be buried in the ancestral plot. The acquisition of such a site, usually or frequently a cave, was therefore of prime concern for Abraham after his wife's death, and the Hittites from whom he purchased Machpelah were well aware of his need and exacted an exorbitant price from him (see Gen. 23:15 and our commentary there). Jacob, though he lived in Egypt for seventeen years and died there, was conveyed back to the cave of Machpelah, and Joseph implored his family not to leave his bones behind when the people would depart from Egypt (Gen. 50:25). Such burial assured the dead that they would "sleep with their fathers" and "be gathered to their kin" (I Kings 11:43; Gen. 25:8).

The Bible neither reports nor requires a distinct ritual for interment; the only prescription is contained in Deut 21:23; expressed negatively, it commands not to leave the hanged person overnight, positively, to bury him the same day.[2] Coffins were not used, though in later centuries important personages were placed in stone sarcophagi.[3] The custom of burning the dead (cremation) was not acceptable as a proper way of disposing of the dead.

The story of Saul's death provides an important exception, for the burning of his mutilated body by his followers was done to forestall further indignities, and the remains were buried thereafter (I Sam. 31:12; the account in I Chron. 10:12 omits the burning). To be sure, one of the means of execution prescribed by the Torah was burning the condemned,[4] but it is likely that, once death had occurred, the body was buried and, at most, only the entrails were consumed by fire [11]. In sum, the Bible reflects a deep-rooted respect for the human body, which even in death must be treated with care and consideration. To do so was to honor God in whose image humanity had been created.

Regard for Animals

The passage which commands that a mother bird should be let go, while her young may be taken from the nest (Deut. 22:6–7), is characteristic of the Torah's concern for the feelings and needs of animals.[5]

---

[1] The existence of this belief has been conclusively demonstrated by C. H. Brichto [9].

[2] Jewish tradition expanded the command by way of an *a fortiori* argument to every dead person: If this consideration was to be shown a criminal, how much more so to others [10].

[3] Current practice in Israel prescribes burial in shrouds, without the use of coffins.

[4] On the procedure of burning the condemned, see Gleanings to Lev. 20, "Put to the Fire."

[5] This was the opinion of Maimonides who wrote: "If the mother is let go or escapes of her own ac-

Though it takes for granted that certain animals may be sacrificed and used for food—a recognition of the universal law of survival[6]—it also makes clear that God's mercy extends to all of His creation.

Thus, ox and ass are not to plow under the same yoke (Deut. 22:10; see above); ox, ass, and all cattle are made beneficiaries of Sabbath rest (Deut. 5:14); an animal and its young may not be slaughtered on the same day (Lev. 22:28); an ox is not to be muzzled while threshing the corn (Deut. 25:4), so that it may not be tortured by its inability to satisfy its hunger; the sabbatical year has as one of its purposes to give both persons and beasts a chance to harvest the fallow fields (Lev. 25:6–7); and Balaam's unjust harshness toward his ass is criticized by God's messenger (Num. 22:32). The final line in the Book of Jonah sums up this divine concern: in a rhetorical question God proclaims that His mercy extends to beasts as well as to innocent human beings.

Later Jewish tradition greatly expanded on the need to prevent cruelty to animals and to avoid as much as possible causing "pain to living things" (tza-ar ba-alei chayim). The elaborate laws governing ritual slaughter were in part designed to kill as quickly as possible (see Commentary on Leviticus, chapter 11); and Deut. 11:15, which mentions cattle before people, was interpreted to mean that an owner had to feed his animals before he could sit down to eat [13]. Human beings are to imitate their Creator:

for even as He is merciful so must they practice lovingkindness to all living creatures.

Reward and Punishment

In biblical thought—and especially in the Book of Deuteronomy—God is believed to reward those who do His will and punish those who defy it.[7] Deut. 28 presents a long list of blessings and an even longer one of curses that will be the divine responses to and consequences of Israel's behavior.[8] The fifth commandment promises those who honor father and mother that they will "long endure" in the land that God gives to them (Deut. 5:16). The same reward is held out to those who observe the command concerning the bird's nest, which appears to emphasize the importance the Torah ascribed to this particular rule (Deut. 22:6–7). Although later interpreters tried to soften the unequivocal nature of this promise,[9] its original intent cannot be in doubt: long years on this earth are proof of God's favor.

To be sure, the righteous did not always appear to prosper, nor did the wicked always seem to be the targets of divine wrath. Questions about God's justice were already asked in biblical days—the entire Book of Job is devoted to this problem of "theodicy"—and they have been asked ever since. Because God's ways are not fully disclosed to man, those who did and do take the biblical promises literally are themselves often subjected to severe trials of their faith. Rabbi Elisha ben Abuyah (second century C.E.)

---

cord she will not be pained by seeing that the young are taken away. In most cases this will lead to people leaving everything alone, for what may be taken is in most cases not fit to be eaten" [12]. But others, like Nachmanides, argued that the purpose of the Torah law was not regard for animals as such, but rather to educate human beings in kindness.

[6] Note, however, that the opening chapters of Genesis portray humans as vegetarians; only later, after

the Flood, are they given permission to eat meat. See our commentary on Gen. 1:30.

[7] For a fuller treatment of this subject, see commentary on Lev. 26 and on Deut. 28.

[8] For other examples, see, e.g., Deut. 11:13–21 and Lev. 23.

[9] By saying, for instance, that the "life" referred to was not of this world but beyond the grave and that, in fact, the reward for the fulfillment of precepts

observed a young lad who, at his father's behest, had approached a bird's nest. The boy followed the Torah to the letter, driving away the mother bird and taking her offspring. But, instead of being rewarded with long life for honoring his father and respecting the law of the bird's nest, the lad fell to his death. Elisha thereupon denied that God ruled with justice and defected from traditional Judaism. His colleagues referred to him henceforth as *Acher*, "the other one," thereby avoiding to pronounce his name [16].

Through the story of Acher, the command concerning the bird's nest became a focal point of discussions on biblical theology. It may be doubted that the reward here held out was ever meant to be taken literally; rather, from the beginning, it was primarily hortatory: Do as God says, and He will reward you in His way. But there was no doubt that a reward was to be expected for an observant individual or for Israel as a people. The specifics might be unclear or temporarily unobservable, but biblical faith was unyielding in its assertion that human deeds were subject to divine judgment and its consequences.

does not occur in this world [14]. "The reward of a good deed is (another) good deed, and the consequence of sin is (further) sin" [15].

GLEANINGS

The Real War

The rules of war also apply to a person's war on his evil impulse, which can be overcome and taken prisoner. Hence the Rabbis praise the greatness of those who by repentance turn their sins into the opposite. ISAIAH HURWITZ [17]

The Torah's language (Deut. 21:10) is in the singular, for it directs itself to the fact that a man has no greater enemy than the evil impulse. THE BAAL SHEM TOV [18]

The Wayward and Defiant Son (Deut. 21:18)

(A tradition says that this law was never operative.[10]) If so, why was it written in the Torah? To study (more) and to obtain reward therefrom. TALMUD [19]

This reminds us that it is the way of the wicked to teach their habits to others. CHASIDIC [20]

Hebrew law insisted on respect being paid to parents, and Hebrew moralists did not hesitate to commend the rod as a salutary instrument of education; but the father's authority—though, at least in an earlier age, he could sell his daughter into slavery—was not despotic: he had not, as at Rome, power of life and death over his son; where (as in the case here contemplated) vice and insubordination became intolerable, he could not take the law into his own hands, he must appeal to the decision of an impartial tribunal. S. D. DRIVER [21]

Even more than the rights of children, the rights of parents are guarded by the Torah, which values highly respect for authority. D. HOFFMANN [22]

Bury the Criminal

It says: "An impaled body is an affront to God" (Deut. 21:23). This is similar to two brothers, one of whom was a king and the other a criminal. When the latter was convicted and hanged, people who saw him thought that he was the king. (The meaning of the parable: man is created in God's image.) TALMUD [23]

Your Fellow's Ox

In Exod. 23:4, the command is to restore the animal to an *enemy*, here (Deut. 22:1), to one's *fellow*. Why the different verbiage? When you return the animal to an enemy and extinguish your hatred you will be returning it to your fellow. BACHYA

The final summation is that "you must not remain indifferent" (Deut. 22:3). The Talmud permits certain exceptions to the command as, for instance, when the finder is aged or a sage; but when a human being is lost exceptions do not apply. AKIBA EGER [24]

Transvestism (Deut. 22:5)

The Torah forbids the wearing of apparel customary for the opposite sex. From this rule, tradition concluded that "man's apparel" included implements of war, and a midrash explained that this was the reason for Jael killing Sisera with tent

---

[10] Note, for instance, that in Prov. 30:17 defiance of parents is not characterized as punishable by law, but it is merely said to lead to a bad end.

pin and mallet (Judg. 4:17–21), because as a woman she was not supposed to wield a man's weapon [25].

This also meant that women were precluded from joining the army [26]; note the present-day controversy in Israel over women's exemption from the military. According to Targum Jonathan the rule implied further that women were forbidden the wearing of talit and tefillin (prayer shawl and phylacteries); but the Talmud disagreed and said that women, while exempt from the duty, were not prohibited from using them [27].

On the island of Cos, says Plutarch, priests of Hercules dressed as women; while, in Rome, men who participated in the vernal mysteries of that god did likewise. So too in the cult of Dionysus, males often adopted feminine costume, just as at the annual festival of Oschophoria boys were attired as girls and, at the Skirophoria, men were garbed like women. The same practice is attested also in connection with the cult of Leukippos in Crete....

The origin of the custom is disputed. According to some scholars, it is a method of assimilating the worshiper to the person of the deity (though it is difficult then to explain why the devotees of the male Hercules affected feminine attire). According to others, it is a form of disguise, designed to foil demons and similar noxious spirits. Probably, as Frazer has observed, there is no single origin for all the examples of this practice; in some, the former idea comes into play; in others, the latter. It has also been suggested that, in cases where men wear women's clothes in the performance of magical rites, this reflects the widespread belief that magic (especially when it aims at promoting fertility) is primarily the province of the female sex, and that—at least in some instances—the usage may go back to a time when priesthood was in the hands of women. Also, ... transvestism is a well-known symptom of sexual abnormality ... frequently associated with religious psychosis.

T. GASTER [28]

Operations to correct the problem of transvest-

ism and bisexuality are the subject of various halachic opinions. Generally speaking, elective surgery is frowned upon because of the danger attendant upon it, but there may be cases where exceptions could apply [29].

The Bird's Nest

Why does the Hebrew for "let the mother go" use the verb twice?[11] If you chance on a nest the second time, do not say, "I have already performed the mitzvah." You must fulfill it every time it comes your way.   MIDRASH [30]

The Torah promises long life to those who observe this mitzvah, which is easy to fulfill in that it demands no effort or sacrifice. How much more so, by implication, does the promise extend to those who do difficult mitzvot.   RASHI [31]

As It Might Have Been

(In this fictional treatment the author pictures Elisha ben Abuyah [see above], accompanied by other Sages, witnessing the death of a boy who died while fulfilling the command of bird's nest—even though the Torah promised long life to those who observe it.)

Elisha trembled from head to foot. A cold perspiration covered him. Nausea writhed through his entrails.

The scene he had just witnessed brought with sudden vividness to his mind the tragedy that had befallen Meir's children.[12] The two pictures merged into a unity, insane and incredible. A wild protest stormed up in him against the horror of it, its senseless waste of life, its wanton cruelty.

The Sages turned and slowly mounted the slope together, talking meanwhile, trying to restore their confidence, to solidify a crumbling universe. At first, Elisha did not listen, so stunned was he, so dazed his senses. But, as his mind recovered from its initial disorganization, he heard one of them say, "He will have his length of days. God is just. It is hard to understand, but let us remember that there is a better world, in which it is all day, a day that stretches for eternity."

---

[11] 22:7 reads שַׁלֵּחַ תְּשַׁלַּח.

[12] His friend, Rabbi Meir, had lost two young children.

At once Elisha knew the answer to the question he had never ventured to face before.

A great negation crystallized in him. The veil of deception dissolved before his eyes. The only belief he still cherished disintegrated as had all the others. The last tenuous chord that bound him to his people was severed.

And when the Sages droned on, their words buzzing like flies, revulsion swept Elisha. He could no longer tolerate their deliberate blindness. In cold desperation he silenced them.

"It is all a lie," he said with a terrible quiet in his voice. "There is no reward. There is no Judge. There is no judgment. For there is no God."

The wind blew in from the sea across horror-stricken faces. The sun, weltering so long in its own blood, died slowly.

MILTON STEINBERG [32]

Yoking Ox and Ass Together (Deut. 22:10)

Why was this prohibition instituted? Because, say some, the ass does not have the strength of an ox (and thus would be worked beyond its capacity); others hold that, because the ox chews its cud and the ass does not, the latter would suffer, seeing (as it thinks) that the ox eats all day. But God, being merciful to all His creatures, wants to save them from suffering unduly [33].

The Social Weal, II

Now follow various civil and criminal laws which, as always, aim at raising the level of the people's communal and individual purity. Just as the Torah's ritual prescriptions were related to this objective, so were those laws which are nowadays called moral and/or secular: together they are the basis for making Israel a fit partner in God's covenant.

The subjects covered in this section are: sexual relationships, their civil and criminal aspects and consequences (divorce, *mamzerut*, prostitution); relations with Ammonites, Moabites, and Edomites; physical hygiene as an aspect of ritual purity; escaped slaves; protection of the weak; taking interest; pledges and loans; treatment of laborers; fulfilling one's vow; kidnaping; affirmation of the principle of personal responsibility.

The laws are not arranged in accordance with any perceivable system; occasionally it is clear that two subjects are placed in sequence as an aid to memory, but at other times the reason is not clear. The family law here presented reflects an extended kinship structure and is most likely quite ancient.

כִּי־יִקַּח אִישׁ אִשָּׁה וּבָא אֵלֶיהָ וּשְׂנֵאָהּ: וְשָׂם לָהּ
עֲלִילֹת דְּבָרִים וְהוֹצִא עָלֶיהָ שֵׁם רָע וְאָמַר אֶת־
הָאִשָּׁה הַזֹּאת לָקַחְתִּי וָאֶקְרַב אֵלֶיהָ וְלֹא־מָצָאתִי
לָהּ בְּתוּלִים: וְלָקַח אֲבִי הַנַּעֲרָ וְאִמָּהּ וְהוֹצִיאוּ
אֶת־בְּתוּלֵי הַנַּעֲרָ אֶל־זִקְנֵי הָעִיר הַשָּׁעְרָה: וְאָמַר
אֲבִי הַנַּעֲרָ אֶל־הַזְּקֵנִים אֶת־בִּתִּי נָתַתִּי לָאִישׁ הַזֶּה
לְאִשָּׁה וַיִּשְׂנָאֶהָ: וְהִנֵּה־הוּא שָׂם עֲלִילֹת דְּבָרִים
לֵאמֹר לֹא־מָצָאתִי לְבִתְּךָ בְּתוּלִים וְאֵלֶּה בְּתוּלֵי
בִתִּי וּפָרְשׂוּ הַשִּׂמְלָה לִפְנֵי זִקְנֵי הָעִיר: וְלָקְחוּ זִקְנֵי

* טו, טז הנערה קרי.

13] A man marries a woman and cohabits with her. Then he takes an aversion to her **14]** and makes up charges against her and defames her, saying, "I married this woman; but when I approached her, I found that she was not a virgin." **15]** In such a case, the girl's father and mother shall produce the evidence of the girl's virginity before the elders of the town at the gate. **16]** And the girl's father shall say to the elders, "I gave this man my daughter to wife, but he has taken an aversion to her; **17]** so he has made up charges, saying, 'I did not find your daughter a virgin.' But here is the evidence of my daughter's virginity!" And they shall spread out the cloth before the elders of the town. **18]** The elders of that town shall

22:13] *Takes an aversion.* See commentary below.

14] *She was not a virgin.* The woman was expected to be a virgin, but no stigma for premarital sexual activity was attached to the man. The evidence of bleeding from a ruptured hymen was taken as proof of virginity; see next verse. (On virginity, see at Exod. 22:15.)

15] *The girl's.* The unvocalized text reads נער, which could mean young man, but the word is read נַעֲרָה, girl. This defective spelling occurs throughout the Torah (except in verse 19, which has the expected נערה).

Evidence. Usually blood-stained sheets; their examination by the family was an important post-nuptial ceremony, prevalent in Eastern Europe and North Africa (and probably elsewhere) well into the twentieth century.

יט הָעִיר־הַהִוא אֶת־הָאִישׁ וְיִסְּרוּ אֹתוֹ: וְעָנְשׁוּ אֹתוֹ מֵאָה
כֶסֶף וְנָתְנוּ לַאֲבִי הַנַּעֲרָה כִּי הוֹצִיא שֵׁם רָע עַל
בְּתוּלַת יִשְׂרָאֵל וְלוֹ־תִהְיֶה לְאִשָּׁה לֹא־יוּכַל לְשַׁלְּחָהּ
כ כָּל־יָמָיו: ס וְאִם־אֱמֶת הָיָה הַדָּבָר הַזֶּה לֹא־
כא נִמְצְאוּ בְתוּלִים לַנַּעֲרָ֫: וְהוֹצִיאוּ אֶת־הַנַּעֲרָ אֶל־פֶּתַח
בֵּית־אָבִיהָ וּסְקָלוּהָ אַנְשֵׁי עִירָהּ בָּאֲבָנִים וָמֵתָה כִּי־
עָשְׂתָה נְבָלָה בְּיִשְׂרָאֵל לִזְנוֹת בֵּית אָבִיהָ וּבִעַרְתָּ
כב הָרָע מִקִּרְבֶּךָ: ס כִּי־יִמָּצֵא אִישׁ שֹׁכֵב עִם־אִשָּׁה
בְעֻלַת־בַּעַל וּמֵתוּ גַּם־שְׁנֵיהֶם הָאִישׁ הַשֹּׁכֵב עִם־הָאִשָּׁה

* כ, כא רה קרי.

then take the man and flog him,   **19]** and they shall fine him a hundred [shekels of] silver and give it to the girl's father; for the man has defamed a virgin in Israel. Moreover, she shall remain his wife; he shall never have the right to divorce her.

20] But if the charge proves true, the girl was found not to have been a virgin, **21]** then the girl shall be brought out to the entrance of her father's house, and the men of her town shall stone her to death; for she did a shameful thing in Israel, committing fornication while under her father's authority. Thus you will sweep away evil from your midst.

22] If a man is found lying with another man's wife, both of them—the man and the woman with whom he lay—shall die. Thus you will sweep away evil from Israel.

18] *Flog him.* Tradition stipulated that, while forty stripes were the norm, only thirty-nine should be administered, lest an error occur and the punishment be excessive [1].

19] *A hundred (shekels of) silver.* That is, twice the amount of the dowry stipulated in the case of one who had seduced a virgin (verse 29). Slander was considered a most serious offense.

Give it to the girl's father. He was the head of the family that had been offended by the husband's action [2].

21] *To the entrance of her father's house.* Her family shared in her disgrace for she had not been properly supervised.

22] *Shall die.* The Ten Commandments forbid adultery, without stipulating the penalty. Here, capital punishment is specified but not its exact

כג וְהָאִשָּׁה וּבִעַרְתָּ הָרָע מִיִּשְׂרָאֵל: ס כִּי יִהְיֶה נַעֲרָ
בְתוּלָה מְאֹרָשָׂה לְאִישׁ וּמְצָאָהּ אִישׁ בָּעִיר וְשָׁכַב
כד עִמָּהּ: וְהוֹצֵאתֶם אֶת־שְׁנֵיהֶם אֶל־שַׁעַר הָעִיר הַהִוא
וּסְקַלְתֶּם אֹתָם בָּאֲבָנִים וָמֵתוּ אֶת־הַנַּעֲרָ עַל־דְּבַר
אֲשֶׁר לֹא־צָעֲקָה בָעִיר וְאֶת־הָאִישׁ עַל־דְּבַר אֲשֶׁר־
עִנָּה אֶת־אֵשֶׁת רֵעֵהוּ וּבִעַרְתָּ הָרָע מִקִּרְבֶּךָ: ס
כה וְאִם־בַּשָּׂדֶה יִמְצָא הָאִישׁ אֶת־הַנַּעֲרָ הַמְאֹרָשָׂה וְהֶחֱזִיק
בָּהּ הָאִישׁ וְשָׁכַב עִמָּהּ וּמֵת הָאִישׁ אֲשֶׁר־שָׁכַב עִמָּהּ
כו לְבַדּוֹ: וְלַנַּעֲרָ לֹא־תַעֲשֶׂה דָבָר אֵין לַנַּעֲרָ חֵטְא
מָוֶת כִּי כַּאֲשֶׁר יָקוּם אִישׁ עַל־רֵעֵהוּ וּרְצָחוֹ נֶפֶשׁ

* כג–כו רה קרי.

23] In the case of a virgin who is engaged to a man—if a man comes upon her in town and lies with her,   **24]** you shall take the two of them out to the gate of that town and stone them to death: the girl because she did not cry for help in the town, and the man because he violated his neighbor's wife. Thus you will sweep away evil from your midst.   **25]** But if the man comes upon the engaged girl in the open country, and the man lies with her by force, only the man who lay with her shall die,   **26]** but you shall do nothing to the girl. The girl did not incur the death penalty, for this case is like that of a man attacking another and murdering

nature (nor is it in Lev. 20:10). In Ezekiel's time the culprits were stoned to death (Ezek. 16:40), which is most likely what the Torah intended.

Ibn Ezra deduces this from the proximity of verse 21, where stoning is commanded; but the Talmud, basing itself on linguistic analogy, opined that, whenever מִיתָה without specification was used, strangulation was intended [3].

23] *Engaged to a man.* That is, one for whom a bride-price had been paid; see 20:7. Such a woman was considered as if already married, and there-

fore, if another man had intercourse with her, the two had committed adultery. Sexual relations with a virgin who was not engaged had civil but not criminal consequences; see verse 28 and Exod. 22:15.

In town. Where, so it was presumed, her cry for help would be heard.

However, later Jewish authorities were inclined to believe a woman who claimed that she had resisted her attacker or that resistance would have resulted in certain death (which likelihood constituted a valid excuse) [4].

כז כֵּן הַדָּבָר הַזֶּה: כִּי בַשָּׂדֶה מְצָאָהּ צָעֲקָה הַנַּעֲרָ֫

כח הַמְאֹרָשָׂה וְאֵין מוֹשִׁיעַ לָהּ: ס כִּי־יִמְצָא אִישׁ

נַעֲרָ֫ בְתוּלָה אֲשֶׁר לֹא־אֹרָשָׂה וּתְפָשָׂהּ וְשָׁכַב עִמָּהּ

כט וְנִמְצָאוּ: וְנָתַן הָאִישׁ הַשֹּׁכֵב עִמָּהּ לַאֲבִי הַנַּעֲרָ֫ חֲמִשִּׁים

כֶּסֶף וְלוֹ־תִהְיֶה לְאִשָּׁה תַּחַת אֲשֶׁר עִנָּהּ לֹא־יוּכַל

שַׁלְּחָהּ כָּל־יָמָיו: ס

א לֹא־יִקַּח אִישׁ אֶת־אֵשֶׁת אָבִיו וְלֹא יְגַלֶּה כְּנַף

Deuteronomy 22; 23
27–29; 1

* כז–כט רה קרי.

him.   27] He came upon her in the open; though the engaged girl cried for help, there was no one to save her.

28] If a man comes upon a virgin who is not engaged and he seizes her and lies with her, and they are discovered,   29] the man who lay with her shall pay the girl's father fifty [shekels of] silver, and she shall be his wife. Because he has violated her, he can never have the right to divorce her.

1] No man shall marry his father's former wife, so as to remove his father's garment.

28] *A virgin who is not engaged.* The same principle is stated in Exod. 22:15–16, except that there no fixed bride-price is stipulated. Deuteronomy may reflect a later social structure where money had already become an important measure of values.

29] *She shall be his wife.* If her father agrees (Exod. 22:16).
Divorce her. Literally, "send her away," i.e., to her father's house.

23:1] Some versions have this verse as 22:30 (for instance, King James, New Standard Version, New English Bible), and their numberings of chapter 23 are noted in brackets.
Father's former wife. The prohibition is stated as part of a catalogue of incestual relationships in Lev. 18:8 and 20:11. It is not clear why here, in Deuteronomy, only this and no other close sexual relationship is proscribed, and why no punishment is here indicated as in Leviticus. If Leviticus is the older book, then there must have been a special reason to single out this offense; if Deuteronomy is older, it may be that this particular union was deemed acceptable by some, and the law made sure that it was ranked with the other and long acknowledged sexual taboos.
Remove his father's garment. The opposite of "spreading his garment," which meant taking a woman as a wife; see Ruth 3:9; Ezek. 16:8. By marrying his father's former wife, the son substituted himself for his father. The imagery also has sexual overtones, as in the story of Noah and his sons (Gen. 9:20 ff.).

263

ב אָבִיו: ס לֹא־יָבֹא פְצוּעַ־דַּכָּא וּכְרוּת שָׁפְכָה בִּקְהַל

ג יְהֹוָה: ס לֹא־יָבֹא מַמְזֵר בִּקְהַל יְהֹוָה גַּם דּוֹר

ד עֲשִׂירִי לֹא־יָבֹא לוֹ בִּקְהַל יְהֹוָה: ס לֹא־יָבֹא עַמּוֹנִי
וּמוֹאָבִי בִּקְהַל יְהֹוָה גַּם דּוֹר עֲשִׂירִי לֹא־יָבֹא לָהֶם

ה בִּקְהַל יְהֹוָה עַד־עוֹלָם: עַל־דְּבַר אֲשֶׁר לֹא־קִדְּמוּ
אֶתְכֶם בַּלֶּחֶם וּבַמַּיִם בַּדֶּרֶךְ בְּצֵאתְכֶם מִמִּצְרָיִם
וַאֲשֶׁר שָׂכַר עָלֶיךָ אֶת־בִּלְעָם בֶּן־בְּעוֹר מִפְּתוֹר

ו אֲרַם נַהֲרַיִם לְקַלְלֶךָּ: וְלֹא־אָבָה יְהֹוָה אֱלֹהֶיךָ לִשְׁמֹעַ

Deuteronomy 23
2–6

2] No one whose testes are crushed or whose member is cut off shall be admitted into the congregation of the LORD.

3] No one misbegotten shall be admitted into the congregation of the LORD; none of his descendants, even in the tenth generation, shall be admitted into the congregation of the LORD.

4] No Ammonite or Moabite shall be admitted into the congregation of the LORD; none of their descendants, even in the tenth generation, shall ever be admitted into the congregation of the LORD, **5]** because they did not meet you with food and water on your journey after you left Egypt, and because they hired Balaam son of Beor, from Pethor of Aram-naharaim, to curse you.— **6]** But the

---

2] [1] *Whose testes are crushed.* By an operation, in order to make him a eunuch. This prohibition aimed at preserving Israel's purity and was meant as an attack on an existing institution [5]. Eunuchs had frequently positions of honor and influence; see I Sam. 8:15; Jer. 38:7; Isa. 56:4 f.

3] [2] *Misbegotten.* The meaning of the biblical מַמְזֵר (*mamzer*) is unclear. Later, tradition explained it to mean the offspring of a prohibited union. Leviticus, 18:6–20 and 20:10–21 [6], lists the various forbidden relationships. See commentary there.

4] [3] *Ammonite or Moabite.* Israel's traditional

enemies: hostility toward them continued into Deuteronomic times (however, in Deut. 2:29, Moab is spoken of favorably). In prophetic literature the Moabites are called haughty (see, for instance, Isa. 16:6) and the Ammonites, cruel (Amos 1:13).

Shall ever be admitted. The proscription was not strictly observed—Ruth was a Moabitess!—and the Rabbis ruled that the law applied to Moab's men only, not to its women [7].

5] [4] *Balaam.* The reference is to Num. 22–24.
Pethor of Aram-naharaim. In Num. 22:5, "Pethor . . . by the Euphrates"; here, the location is given more generally: "Aram of Mesopotamia"

264

אֶל־בִּלְעָם וַיַּהֲפֹךְ יְהֹוָה אֱלֹהֶיךָ לְּךָ אֶת־הַקְּלָלָה

לִבְרָכָה כִּי אֲהֵבְךָ יְהֹוָה אֱלֹהֶיךָ: לֹא־תִדְרֹשׁ שְׁלֹמָם ז

וְטֹבָתָם כָּל־יָמֶיךָ לְעוֹלָם: ס לֹא־תְתַעֵב אֲדֹמִי ח

כִּי אָחִיךָ הוּא לֹא־תְתַעֵב מִצְרִי כִּי־גֵר הָיִיתָ בְאַרְצוֹ:

בָּנִים אֲשֶׁר־יִוָּלְדוּ לָהֶם דּוֹר שְׁלִישִׁי יָבֹא לָהֶם בִּקְהַל ט

יְהֹוָה: ס כִּי־תֵצֵא מַחֲנֶה עַל־אֹיְבֶיךָ וְנִשְׁמַרְתָּ י

מִכֹּל דָּבָר רָע: כִּי־יִהְיֶה בְךָ אִישׁ אֲשֶׁר לֹא־יִהְיֶה יא

טָהוֹר מִקְּרֵה־לָיְלָה וְיָצָא אֶל־מִחוּץ לַמַּחֲנֶה לֹא

Deuteronomy 23
7–11

LORD your God refused to heed Balaam; instead, the LORD your God turned the curse into a blessing for you, for the LORD your God loves you.— **7]** You shall never concern yourself with their welfare or benefit as long as you live.

8] You shall not abhor an Edomite, for he is your kinsman. You shall not abhor an Egyptian, for you were a stranger in his land. **9]** Children born to them may be admitted into the congregation of the LORD in the third generation.

10] When you go out as a troop against your enemies, be on your guard against anything untoward. **11]** If anyone among you has been rendered unclean by a nocturnal emission, he must leave the camp, and he must not re-enter the camp.

(*naharaim* meaning "two rivers," that is, Tigris and Euphrates).

7] [6] *You shall never concern yourself.* And, of course, make no alliances with them—possibly a remembrance of the bad experience David had with them (II Sam. 10).

Driver suggests that the emotional quarantine ordered in verse 7 had the effect of preventing active national hatred. We do not hate people in whom we have no interest.

8] [7] *Edomite . . . your kinsman.* He was perceived as a descendant of Esau, Jacob's brother; Gen. 36:1.

You shall not abhor an Egyptian. If Israelites had reason to abhor any nation, it would expectably be Egypt, the nation that had enslaved them. Yet, Egypt was not to be remembered with aversion.

Possibly, there was a psycho-historical echo of guilt in Israel's relationship with Egypt, going back to the days when Joseph and his family had been servants of an exploitative Pharaoh [8].

9] [8] *In the third generation.* Of residence in Israel.

11] [10] *Nocturnal emission.* Such emission was considered ritually polluting; see Lev. 15:16.

יב יָבֹא אֶל־תּוֹךְ הַמַּחֲנֶה: וְהָיָה לִפְנוֹת־עֶרֶב יִרְחַץ בַּמָּיִם

יג וּכְבֹא הַשֶּׁמֶשׁ יָבֹא אֶל־תּוֹךְ הַמַּחֲנֶה: וְיָד תִּהְיֶה לְךָ

יד מִחוּץ לַמַּחֲנֶה וְיָצָאתָ שָּׁמָּה חוּץ: וְיָתֵד תִּהְיֶה לְךָ
עַל־אֲזֵנֶךָ וְהָיָה בְּשִׁבְתְּךָ חוּץ וְחָפַרְתָּה בָהּ וְשַׁבְתָּ

טו וְכִסִּיתָ אֶת־צֵאָתֶךָ: כִּי יְהוָה אֱלֹהֶיךָ מִתְהַלֵּךְ בְּקֶרֶב
מַחֲנֶךָ לְהַצִּילְךָ וְלָתֵת אֹיְבֶיךָ לְפָנֶיךָ וְהָיָה מַחֲנֶיךָ
קָדוֹשׁ וְלֹא־יִרְאֶה בְךָ עֶרְוַת דָּבָר וְשָׁב מֵאַחֲרֶיךָ: ס

טז לֹא־תַסְגִּיר עֶבֶד אֶל־אֲדֹנָיו אֲשֶׁר־יִנָּצֵל אֵלֶיךָ מֵעִם

יז אֲדֹנָיו: עִמְּךָ יֵשֵׁב בְּקִרְבְּךָ בַּמָּקוֹם אֲשֶׁר־יִבְחַר בְּאַחַד

יח שְׁעָרֶיךָ בַּטּוֹב לוֹ לֹא תּוֹנֶנּוּ: ס לֹא־תִהְיֶה קְדֵשָׁה
מִבְּנוֹת יִשְׂרָאֵל וְלֹא־יִהְיֶה קָדֵשׁ מִבְּנֵי יִשְׂרָאֵל:

Deuteronomy 23
12–18

12] Toward evening he shall bathe in water, and at sundown he may re-enter the camp.   **13]** Further, there shall be an area for you outside the camp, where you may relieve yourself.   **14]** With your gear you shall have a spike, and when you have squatted you shall dig a hole with it and cover up your excrement.   **15]** Since the LORD your God moves about in your camp to protect you and to deliver your enemies to you, let your camp be holy; let Him not find anything unseemly among you and turn away from you.

16] You shall not turn over to his master a slave who seeks refuge with you from his master.   **17]** He shall live with you in any place he may choose among the settlements in your midst, wherever he pleases; you must not ill-treat him.

18] No Israelite woman shall be a cult prostitute, nor shall any Israelite man

---

13] [12] *An area.* Hebrew יָד (*yad*), a word which usually means "hand" and sometimes "memorial" (as in *yad vashem*, Isa. 56:5).

16] [15] *A slave.* Who came to you from abroad [9]. The Talmud asserted that this rule obtained also when the owner abroad was an Israelite [10].

18] [17] *Cult prostitute.* Sexual orgies were a well-known part of many peoples' fertility rites and took place even in Jerusalem, until King Josiah put an end to them (II Kings 23:7) [11].

ט לֹא־תָבִיא אֶתְנַן זוֹנָה וּמְחִיר כֶּלֶב בֵּית יְהוָֹה אֱלֹהֶיךָ

לְכָל־נֶדֶר כִּי תוֹעֲבַת יְהוָֹה אֱלֹהֶיךָ גַּם־שְׁנֵיהֶם: ס

כ לֹא־תַשִּׁיךְ לְאָחִיךָ נֶשֶׁךְ כֶּסֶף נֶשֶׁךְ אֹכֶל נֶשֶׁךְ כָּל־

כא דָּבָר אֲשֶׁר יִשָּׁךְ: לַנָּכְרִי תַשִּׁיךְ וּלְאָחִיךָ לֹא תַשִּׁיךְ

לְמַעַן יְבָרֶכְךָ יְהוָֹה אֱלֹהֶיךָ בְּכֹל מִשְׁלַח יָדֶךָ עַל־

כב הָאָרֶץ אֲשֶׁר־אַתָּה בָא־שָׁמָּה לְרִשְׁתָּהּ: ס כִּי־תִדֹּר

נֶדֶר לַיהוָֹה אֱלֹהֶיךָ לֹא תְאַחֵר לְשַׁלְּמוֹ כִּי־דָּרֹשׁ

כג יִדְרְשֶׁנּוּ יְהוָֹה אֱלֹהֶיךָ מֵעִמָּךְ וְהָיָה בְךָ חֵטְא: וְכִי

כד תֶחְדַּל לִנְדֹּר לֹא־יִהְיֶה בְךָ חֵטְא: מוֹצָא שְׂפָתֶיךָ

Deuteronomy 23

19–24

be a cult prostitute.   **19]** You shall not bring the fee of a whore or the pay of a

dog into the house of the LORD your God in fulfillment of any vow, for both are

abhorrent to the LORD your God.

20] You shall not deduct interest from loans to your countryman, whether in

money or food or anything else that can be deducted as interest.   **21]** You may

deduct interest from loans to foreigners; but do not deduct any from loans to your

countryman—so that the LORD your God may bless you in all your undertakings

in the land which you are about to invade and occupy.

22] When you make a vow to the LORD your God, do not put off fulfilling it,

for the LORD your God will require it of you, and you will have incurred guilt;

23] Λwhereas you incur no guilt if you refrain from vowing.   **24]** You must fulfill

19] [18] *Dog.* Here used as a pejorative, to describe a male prostitute. The simile is found in a Phoenician inscription also [12]. Dogs were not domesticated in biblical times and were considered wild beasts.

20] [19] *Deduct interest.* See commentary below. נֶשֶׁךְ (*neshech*) is related to the word for "bite," the interest being seen as taking a bite out of the capital. (Note also the English expression "tax bite.")

Lev. 25:36–37 introduced the additional terms *tarbit* ("increase") and *marbit*, translated as "accrued interest," to be paid at the time of the loan's repayment; *neshech* is rendered as "advance interest."

22] [21] *A vow to the Lord.* Either by promising Him something, or by calling on Him as a witness. "Better not to vow than to vow and not fulfill it" (Eccles. 5:3–4). See Num. 30.

תִּשְׁמֹר וְעָשִׂיתָ כַּאֲשֶׁר נָדַרְתָּ לַיהֹוָה אֱלֹהֶיךָ נְדָבָה

כה אֲשֶׁר דִּבַּרְתָּ בְּפִיךָ: ס כִּי תָבֹא בְּכֶרֶם רֵעֶךָ
וְאָכַלְתָּ עֲנָבִים כְּנַפְשְׁךָ שָׂבְעֶךָ וְאֶל־כֶּלְיְךָ לֹא
כו תִתֵּן: ס כִּי תָבֹא בְּקָמַת רֵעֶךָ וְקָטַפְתָּ מְלִילֹת
בְּיָדֶךָ וְחֶרְמֵשׁ לֹא תָנִיף עַל קָמַת רֵעֶךָ: ס

א כִּי־יִקַּח אִישׁ אִשָּׁה וּבְעָלָהּ וְהָיָה אִם־לֹא תִמְצָא־חֵן
בְּעֵינָיו כִּי־מָצָא בָהּ עֶרְוַת דָּבָר וְכָתַב לָהּ סֵפֶר
ב כְּרִיתֻת וְנָתַן בְּיָדָהּ וְשִׁלְּחָהּ מִבֵּיתוֹ: וְיָצְאָה מִבֵּיתוֹ
ג וְהָלְכָה וְהָיְתָה לְאִישׁ־אַחֵר: וּשְׂנֵאָהּ הָאִישׁ הָאַחֲרוֹן
וְכָתַב לָהּ סֵפֶר כְּרִיתֻת וְנָתַן בְּיָדָהּ וְשִׁלְּחָהּ מִבֵּיתוֹ
אוֹ כִי יָמוּת הָאִישׁ הָאַחֲרוֹן אֲשֶׁר־לְקָחָהּ לוֹ לְאִשָּׁה:

Deuteronomy 23; 24
25–26; 1–3

what has crossed your lips and perform what you have voluntarily vowed to the LORD your God, having made the promise with your own mouth.

25] When you enter your neighbor's vineyard, you may eat your fill of the grapes, as many as you want; but you must not put any in your vessel. **26]** When you find yourself amid your neighbor's standing grain, you may pluck ears with your hand; but you must not put a sickle to your neighbor's grain.

1] A man takes a wife and possesses her. She fails to please him because he finds something obnoxious about her, and he writes her a bill of divorcement, hands it to her, and sends her away from his house; **2]** she leaves his household and becomes the wife of another man; **3]** then this latter man rejects her, writes her a bill of divorcement, hands it to her, and sends her away from his house; or the

25] [24] *When you enter.* Verses 25 and 26 may refer to the law of Lev. 19:9 and 10, which are meant to keep the poor from starving. Or the verses may be seen as continuing the theme of verses 20 and 21: your possessions are never fully your own and must be shared.

The Rabbis debated whether the law applied without restriction, even to a passer-by [13].

24:1] *Bill of divorcement.* Literally, "a document of cutting off." Both the conclusion of an agreement (see Deut. 29:13; and Commentary on Genesis, chapter 16) and its dissolution were described by the word כָּרֵת.

דּ לֹא־יוּכַל בַּעְלָהּ הָרִאשׁוֹן אֲשֶׁר־שִׁלְּחָהּ לָשׁוּב לְקַחְתָּהּ
לִהְיוֹת לוֹ לְאִשָּׁה אַחֲרֵי אֲשֶׁר הֻטַּמָּאָה כִּי־תוֹעֵבָה
הִוא לִפְנֵי יְהֹוָה וְלֹא תַחֲטִיא אֶת־הָאָרֶץ אֲשֶׁר יְהֹוָה
אֱלֹהֶיךָ נֹתֵן לְךָ נַחֲלָה: ס הּ כִּי־יִקַּח אִישׁ אִשָּׁה
חֲדָשָׁה לֹא יֵצֵא בַּצָּבָא וְלֹא־יַעֲבֹר עָלָיו לְכָל־
דָּבָר נָקִי יִהְיֶה לְבֵיתוֹ שָׁנָה אֶחָת וְשִׂמַּח אֶת־אִשְׁתּוֹ
אֲשֶׁר־לָקָח: ו לֹא־יַחֲבֹל רֵחַיִם וָרָכֶב כִּי־נֶפֶשׁ הוּא
חֹבֵל: ס ז כִּי־יִמָּצֵא אִישׁ גֹּנֵב נֶפֶשׁ מֵאֶחָיו מִבְּנֵי
יִשְׂרָאֵל וְהִתְעַמֶּר־בּוֹ וּמְכָרוֹ וּמֵת הַגַּנָּב הַהוּא וּבִעַרְתָּ

man who married her last dies.   4] Then the first husband who divorced her shall
not take her to wife again, since she has been defiled—for that would be abhorrent
to the LORD. You must not bring sin upon the land which the LORD your God is
giving you as a heritage.

5] When a man has taken a bride, he shall not go out with the army or be
assigned to it for any purpose; he shall be exempt one year for the sake of his
household, to give happiness to the woman he has married.

6] A handmill or an upper millstone shall not be taken in pawn, for that would
be taking someone's life in pawn.

7] If a man is found to have kidnaped a fellow Israelite, enslaving him or selling
him, that kidnaper shall die; thus you will sweep out evil from your midst.

4] *She has been defiled.* For her first husband. She
is disqualified because her second marriage appears now as a promiscuous interlude. According
to Nachmanides, the prohibition was intended to
prevent wife swapping.

5] *He shall be exempt.* This appears to be an extension of Deut. 20:5 ff. There the exemption
applies to a betrothed man, here also to one who
is newly married.

6] *Handmill.* Which consists of an upper and
lower millstone. The injunction means: every

family needs its handmill for making bread; therefore do not take it or any part of it away.

The Hebrew is alliterative and therefore easily
memorable: רֵחַיִם—רָכֶב (*rechayim—rechev*).

7] *Kidnaped.* Compare Exod. 21:16. In biblical
days the profit from kidnaping lay in selling the
captive, today it comes from having him ransomed.

The Rabbis applied the commandment "You
shall not steal" to the theft of persons: see at
Deut. 5:17.

דברים כד
ח–יד

ח הָרָע מִקִּרְבֶּֽךָ׃ ס הִשָּׁ֧מֶר בְּנֶֽגַע־הַצָּרַ֛עַת לִשְׁמֹ֥ר מְאֹ֖ד וְלַעֲשׂ֑וֹת כְּכֹל֩ אֲשֶׁר־יוֹר֨וּ אֶתְכֶ֜ם הַכֹּהֲנִ֤ים הַלְוִיִּם֙

ט כַּאֲשֶׁ֥ר צִוִּיתִ֖ם תִּשְׁמְר֥וּ לַעֲשֽׂוֹת׃ זָכ֕וֹר אֵ֧ת אֲשֶׁר־עָשָׂ֛ה יְהֹוָ֥ה אֱלֹהֶ֖יךָ לְמִרְיָ֑ם בַּדֶּ֖רֶךְ בְּצֵאתְכֶ֥ם מִמִּצְרָֽיִם׃ ס

י כִּֽי־תַשֶּׁ֥ה בְרֵֽעֲךָ֖ מַשַּׁ֣את מְא֑וּמָה לֹֽא־תָבֹ֥א אֶל־בֵּית֖וֹ

יא לַעֲבֹ֥ט עֲבֹטֽוֹ׃ בַּח֖וּץ תַּעֲמֹ֑ד וְהָאִ֗ישׁ אֲשֶׁ֤ר אַתָּה֙

יב נֹשֶׁ֣ה ב֔וֹ יוֹצִ֥יא אֵלֶ֛יךָ אֶֽת־הַעֲב֖וֹט הַחֽוּצָה׃ וְאִם־אִ֥ישׁ

יג עָנִ֖י ה֑וּא לֹ֥א תִשְׁכַּ֖ב בַּעֲבֹטֽוֹ׃ הָשֵׁב֩ תָּשִׁ֨יב ל֤וֹ אֶֽת־הַעֲבוֹט֙ כְּב֣וֹא הַשֶּׁ֔מֶשׁ וְשָׁכַ֥ב בְּשַׂלְמָת֖וֹ וּבֵֽרֲכֶ֑ךָּ וּלְךָ֨

יד תִּהְיֶ֣ה צְדָקָ֔ה לִפְנֵ֖י יְהֹוָ֥ה אֱלֹהֶֽיךָ׃ ס לֹא־תַעֲשֹׁ֥ק שָׂכִ֖יר עָנִ֣י וְאֶבְי֑וֹן מֵאַחֶ֕יךָ א֥וֹ מִגֵּרְךָ֖ אֲשֶׁ֥ר בְּאַרְצְךָ֖

Deuteronomy 24
8–14

8] In cases of a skin affection be most careful to do exactly as the levitical priests instruct you. Take care to do as I have commanded them.   9] Remember what the Lord your God did to Miriam on the journey after you left Egypt.

10] When you make a loan of any sort to your neighbor, you must not enter his house to seize his pledge.   11] You must remain outside, while the man to whom you made the loan brings the pledge out to you.   12] If he is a needy man, you shall not go to sleep in his pledge;   13] you must return the pledge to him at sundown, that he may sleep in his cloth and bless you; and it will be to your merit before the Lord your God.

14] You shall not abuse a needy and destitute laborer, whether a fellow country-

---

8] *Skin affection.* Older translations have "leprosy"; see Lev., chapters 13 and 14. The priests dealt with the physiological aspects of the illness as part of ritual impurity.

9] *Miriam.* A reference to the incident recounted in Num. 12.
The verse has been taken as one proof that Leviticus and Numbers are older than Deuteronomy.

This is however not conclusive, for the references may be to well-known traditions rather than to fixed texts [14].

10] *You must not enter.* That is, the lender [15]. Compare Exod. 22:25–26, which is less specific.

12] *Sleep in his pledge.* Do not use or keep his garment, which he gave you as a pledge [16].

בִּשְׁעָרֶיךָ: בְּיוֹמוֹ תִתֵּן שְׂכָרוֹ וְלֹא־תָבוֹא עָלָיו הַשֶּׁמֶשׁ
כִּי עָנִי הוּא וְאֵלָיו הוּא נֹשֵׂא אֶת־נַפְשׁוֹ וְלֹא־יִקְרָא
עָלֶיךָ אֶל־יְהוָה וְהָיָה בְךָ חֵטְא: ס   לֹא־יוּמְתוּ
אָבוֹת עַל־בָּנִים וּבָנִים לֹא־יוּמְתוּ עַל־אָבוֹת אִישׁ
בְּחֶטְאוֹ יוּמָתוּ: ס   לֹא תַטֶּה מִשְׁפַּט גֵּר יָתוֹם וְלֹא
תַחֲבֹל בֶּגֶד אַלְמָנָה: וְזָכַרְתָּ כִּי עֶבֶד הָיִיתָ בְּמִצְרַיִם
וַיִּפְדְּךָ יְהוָה אֱלֹהֶיךָ מִשָּׁם עַל־כֵּן אָנֹכִי מְצַוְּךָ לַעֲשׂוֹת
אֶת־הַדָּבָר הַזֶּה: ס   כִּי תִקְצֹר קְצִירְךָ בְשָׂדֶךָ
וְשָׁכַחְתָּ עֹמֶר בַּשָּׂדֶה לֹא תָשׁוּב לְקַחְתּוֹ לַגֵּר לַיָּתוֹם

Deuteronomy 24
15–19

man or a stranger in one of the communities of your land.   **15]** You must pay him his wages on the same day, before the sun sets, for he is needy and urgently depends on it; else he will cry to the LORD against you and you will incur guilt.

16] Parents shall not be put to death for children, nor children be put to death for parents: a person shall be put to death only for his own crime.

17] You shall not subvert the rights of the stranger or the fatherless; you shall not take a widow's garment in pawn.   **18]** Remember that you were a slave in Egypt and that the LORD your God redeemed you from there; therefore do I enjoin you to observe this commandment.

19] When you reap the harvest in your field and overlook a sheaf in the field, do not turn back to get it; it shall go to the stranger, the fatherless, and the

15]   *You must pay him.* An elaboration of the principle laid down in Lev. 19:13; but this too does not give us warrant to say that Leviticus is the older book; see above at verse 8.

16]   *Only for his own crime.* See commentary below.

17]   *A widow's garment.* Generally, anyone's garment may be taken in pledge, but not a widow's.

19]   *When you reap.* It is an undergirding principle

of the Torah that every citizen shares in the responsibility for easing the life of the poor, and the abolition of poverty is considered the mark of an ideal society (Deut. 15:4). God himself demands justice for the disadvantaged, who thus ground their claim in more than human charity. Compare Lev. 19:9 f. and 23:22.

Verses 19–21 present certain problems that traditional commentators discussed in great detail. If the reason for the law had a social purpose, they said, the poor were hardly protected, for they had

וְלָאַלְמָנָה יִהְיֶה לְמַעַן יְבָרֶכְךָ יְהֹוָה אֱלֹהֶיךָ בְּכֹל מַעֲשֵׂה יָדֶיךָ: ס כִּי תַחְבֹּט זֵיתְךָ לֹא תְפָאֵר אַחֲרֶיךָ לַגֵּר לַיָּתוֹם וְלָאַלְמָנָה יִהְיֶה: כִּי תִבְצֹר כַּרְמְךָ לֹא תְעוֹלֵל אַחֲרֶיךָ לַגֵּר לַיָּתוֹם וְלָאַלְמָנָה יִהְיֶה: וְזָכַרְתָּ כִּי־עֶבֶד הָיִיתָ בְּאֶרֶץ מִצְרָיִם עַל־כֵּן אָנֹכִי מְצַוְּךָ לַעֲשׂוֹת אֶת־הַדָּבָר הַזֶּה: ס

widow—in order that the LORD your God may bless you in all your undertakings.

20] When you beat down the fruit of your olive trees, do not go over them again; that shall go to the stranger, the fatherless, and the widow.   **21]** When you gather the grapes of your vineyard, do not pick it over again; that shall go to the stranger, the fatherless, and the widow.   **22]** Always remember that you were a slave in the land of Egypt; therefore do I enjoin you to observe this commandment.

to depend on the owner's inadvertence. Furthermore, the mitzvah can be carried out only if one is forgetful; hence it does not emanate entirely from free will. Therefore, the true intent of these laws was seen to be the molding of character: people should learn not to want every last piece of produce and profit.

272

The Prohibition of Taking Interest
(Deut. 23:20–21)

In the ancient Near East, interest charges were well known in societies where the social structure had become sufficiently complex. Thus, in the second millennium B.C.E., Babylonian law permitted 20 percent interest on money and 33 1/3 percent on grain [17]. In Greece and Rome, on the other hand, the taking of interest was considered improper; Aristotle considered money a naturally barren commodity and incapable of reproducing itself—hence interest, as its quasi-offspring, was seen by him to be contrary to nature [18].

Torah law, here as well as in Exod. 22:24 and Lev. 25:35–37, added a moral dimension. Loans were originally extended not for commercial but for charitable purposes, and to connect charity with profit appeared as highly improper. Ezekiel (18:13) condemns it bitterly, and the Psalmist (15:5) praises the person who has never lent on interest. But these statements refer to social, not commercial relationships. To foreigners who were in the land presumably for the purpose of trading, the ancient Near Eastern rules applied, permitting (and expecting) interest.

The sentiment against taking interest from one's people persisted into postbiblical days and was in fact expanded by the Rabbis. A person refraining from charging it was praised as one who had accepted the yoke of the Kingdom of Heaven. In time, however, legal subterfuges were approved that permitted interest taking, in order to accommodate changed economic conditions [19]. The medieval Christian church prohibited its believers from taking interest for any purpose, thus leaving the development of commercial capital to the Jews in its midst, and creating thereby the image of the Jew as a greedy moneylender. He was held up to obloquy for such activity, while at the same time the lending process in which he engaged was both encouraged and needed by the ruling power.[1]

Current economic policy does not distinguish effectively between loans for personal reasons, including need, and for commercial enterprises. Today it is often the poor who have no access to free-loan societies or credit unions and, therefore, pay exorbitant interest rates for desperately needed funds—a total reversal of the original intent of the Torah.

Divorce

In biblical as well as talmudic law, it was the man who acquired a wife[2] and who, when it pleased him, sent her away. In only two instances was this male prerogative restricted: when a husband had falsely accused his wife of having had prenuptial intercourse and when a man had slept with a virgin who had not been engaged to someone else (Deut. 22:19; 22:29). Otherwise, except for incest and adultery, the man was free to do as he wanted, for the law reflected a social tradition that was male-oriented and which permitted polygamy.

The bill of divorcement was an instrument created to testify that the woman was entitled to marry again. We no longer know its precise content, but there is every reason to believe that the *get* of the Talmud, which is in use until this day, was itself based on a long tradition (see below, for the text of a *get*). Its core is the husband's declaration that the woman is no longer his wife and therefore free to marry another man. In Hosea's simile the formula was "She is not my wife, neither am I her husband" (Hos.

---

[1] The term "usury" was formerly a synonym for interest and later came to mean excessive interest.

[2] She is *mekudeshet*, sanctified, consecrated, literally "set aside" for him.

2:4), and in Sumerian practice a similar statement was made, probably first as an oral declaration which was then attested to in the written instrument. The Bible does not speak of a financial settlement for the divorcée, but the prevalence of such an arrangement in Mesopotamian law makes it likely that it was taken for granted by the Bible as part of the proceedings [20].

Despite the ease with which a man could send away his wife,[3] permanent union was the biblical ideal and divorce was considered a necessary evil. It occurred probably most frequently when the marriage failed to produce an offspring, it being believed that in such an instance the woman was the infertile partner. On the other hand, one may conclude from Exod. 21:10–11 that a wife had the right to leave her husband if he refused her proper sustenance and the fulfillment of sexual obligations.

A divorced woman returned to her father's house and did not keep her children, who remained with her husband. Also, she was forbidden to a priest (Lev. 21:7), and it may be assumed that divorce was considered a severe reflection on the woman and produced a significant reduction of her social status. In the fifth century B.C.E., divorces became frequent; whether or not this was related to Ezra's injunction to have Israelite men divorce their foreign wives is hard to say (cf. Malachi 2:13–16; Ezra 10:3 ff.).[4] In later centuries, divorce became relatively rare, and when it occurred it carried with it a serious social stigma. Only in more recent days has divorce once again been accepted by Jews as an aspect of the complexities of marriage. But the ideal enunciated by Koheleth has remained normative: "Enjoy life with the wife whom you love, during all the days of your transient existence which have been apportioned to you under the sun: for that is your reward of life and labor that are yours under the sun" (Eccles. 9:9).

Individual and Collective Responsibility (Deut. 24:16)

The very insistence of the Deuteronomic law, that "a person shall be put to death only for his own crime," indicates the need for counteracting certain then prevailing conditions. Indeed, the Bible records a number of incidents that bear this out. In one, Joshua exacts punishment from a whole family (7:24–25); in another, David vows that Joab's murder of Abner will be avenged on the former's clan (II Sam. 3:29); in a third, David surrenders to the Gibeonites members of Saul's family to be killed for acts which Saul committed many years before (II Sam. 21:1 ff.). In contrast, King Amaziah is specifically commended for observing the Torah of Moses, and the writer takes pains to quote the Torah verse verbatim (II Kings 14:6; II Chron. 25:4). Amaziah reigned in Judea in the eighth century B.C.E., and his commendation indicates that the old principle of individual responsibility, enunciated in our passage, was at last taking root in practice.[5] During the days of the Babylonian exile, the prophet Ezekiel (chapter 18)

---

[3] Deut. 24:1 gives the man this right if he finds anything obnoxious in his wife—whether the reason was sexual, behavioral, or whatever. The schools of Hillel and Shammai had a controversy on this matter [21].
[4] Prevailing scholarly opinion places Malachi before Ezra, and hence the former's statement that God detests divorce is independent of Ezra's later procedures. Sirach (second century B.C.E.) encouraged men to terminate their marriages if their wives were ill-spoken and not responsive to correction (Sirach 25:25 f.). In the time of Josephus (first century C.E.), divorces still must have been frequent; "people have many reasons," he wrote [22], a fact attested to by the Mishnah a hundred years later [23].
[5] By the time the books of Kings and Chronicles were composed, Deuteronomy had encoded the old principle, which could now be quoted.

further elaborated on this idea, which became a cornerstone of Israel's conception of justice.

How does the doctrine of individual responsibility relate to the second commandment which states that God will visit the sins of the fathers on the third and fourth generations (Deut. 5:9)? In the latter case, says Driver, "the reference is to the providence of God, operating naturally through the normal constitution of society: children are linked to their parents by ties, physical and social, from which they cannot free themselves; and they suffer, not because they are *guilty* of their fathers' sins, but because by the self-acting operation of natural laws their fathers' sins entail disgrace and misfortune upon them" [24]. The Deuteronomic law, on the other hand, deals with action by a *human* judicial agency and forbids the punishment of children for crimes they have not committed.[6]

[6] It may be noted that the law of Deuteronomy became in the halachah a proof text for criminal court procedure. The text implies, so it was held, that parents and children were not to testify against each other in capital matters, a principle then extended to other relatives [25].

GLEANINGS

She Did Not Cry for Help (Deut. 22:24)

This teaches that a person needs to cry for help, for the cry makes God a partner to one's fate.　　　　　　　　AFTER SEFAT EMET [26]

Gear and Ear

It says (Deut. 23:14): "With your gear . . . cover up." Do not read "your gear" (אֲזֵנֶךָ) but "your ear" (אָזְנֶךָ). For when a person hears dirty talk he should cover his ears.　　　TALMUD [27]

Divorce Law

From the Code of Hammurabi: If a seignor wishes to divorce his wife who did not bear him children, he shall give her money to the full amount of the marriage price and he shall also make good to her the dowry which she brought from her father's house, and then he may divorce her. If he is a peasant, he shall give her one-third mina of silver [28].

From the Halachah: After fixing the time, place, and identities of husband and wife, the bill of divorcement (*get*) says (in excerpt):

"I (the husband) do willingly consent, being under no constraint, to release, set free, and put aside you, my wife . . . in order that you may have permission and authority for yourself to go and marry any man you may desire. No person may hinder you from this day onward, and you are permitted to any man. This shall be for you a bill of dismissal, a letter of release,

and a document of freedom, in accordance with the laws of Moses and Israel."

SHULCHAN ARUCH [29]

Slander

The plague comes to us because we indulge in slander. See what happened to Miriam: she slandered Moses and the plague attacked her (Num. 12). Therefore, the instruction about treating a skin affection (Deut. 24:8) is followed by "Remember what the Lord your God did to Miriam" (verse 9).

R. Yochanan said: If you slander strangers you will end up slandering your own. Let the pious Miriam be a warning to all slanderers.

MIDRASH [30]

You Shall Not Take a Widow's Garment in Pawn (Deut. 24:17)

The Rabbis argued whether it was the intent of the Torah to protect a *poor* widow, or whether the language of the text precluded a consideration of the Torah's intent, and hence the taking of *any* widow's garment was prohibited. The latter interpretation was adopted, and the principle established that one should investigate the Torah's (that is, God's) intent only in matters which were not halachic [31].

When You . . . Overlook a Sheaf (Deut. 24:19)

Even though a person has no deliberate intention of performing a mitzvah, yet he is considered as having performed it (he has overlooked a sheaf and lets it be). How much more meritorious is one who deliberately does a mitzvah.

TOSEFTA [32]

The Social Weal, III

The two chapters that follow complete the book's social, legal, ethical, and ritual prescriptions. They touch on many different areas but are, as always, united by religious concerns.

Socio-legal subjects covered are: obligation to marry the widow of one's deceased brother; honest weights; treatment of Amalek; excessive punishment; unseemly fight.

Ethico-ritual rules: muzzling an ox (kindness to animals); thanksgiving; tithing.

The section ends with an exhortation to observe the covenant which obligates both God and Israel.

(A new weekly portion, *Ki Tavo*, begins with 26:1.)

א כִּי־יִהְיֶה רִיב בֵּין אֲנָשִׁים וְנִגְּשׁוּ אֶל־הַמִּשְׁפָּט וּשְׁפָטוּם

ב וְהִצְדִּיקוּ אֶת־הַצַּדִּיק וְהִרְשִׁיעוּ אֶת־הָרָשָׁע: וְהָיָה אִם־

בִּן הַכּוֹת הָרָשָׁע וְהִפִּילוֹ הַשֹּׁפֵט וְהִכָּהוּ לְפָנָיו כְּדֵי

ג רִשְׁעָתוֹ בְּמִסְפָּר: אַרְבָּעִים יַכֶּנּוּ לֹא יֹסִיף פֶּן־יֹסִיף

לְהַכֹּתוֹ עַל־אֵלֶּה מַכָּה רַבָּה וְנִקְלָה אָחִיךָ לְעֵינֶיךָ:

ד לֹא־תַחְסֹם שׁוֹר בְּדִישׁוֹ: ס

ה כִּי־יֵשְׁבוּ אַחִים יַחְדָּו

וּמֵת אַחַד מֵהֶם וּבֵן אֵין־לוֹ לֹא־תִהְיֶה אֵשֶׁת־הַמֵּת

הַחוּצָה לְאִישׁ זָר יְבָמָהּ יָבֹא עָלֶיהָ וּלְקָחָהּ לוֹ

Deuteronomy 25
1–5

1] When there is a dispute between men and they go to law, and a decision is rendered declaring the one in the right and the other in the wrong— 2] if the guilty one is to be flogged, the magistrate shall have him lie down and be given lashes in his presence, by count, as his guilt warrants. 3] He may be given up to forty lashes, but not more, lest being flogged further, to excess, your brother be degraded before your eyes.

4] You shall not muzzle an ox while it is threshing.

5] When brothers dwell together and one of them dies and leaves no son, the wife of the deceased shall not be married to a stranger, outside the family. Her husband's brother shall unite with her: take her as his wife and perform the levir's

---

25:2] *To be flogged.* בִּן הַכּוֹת (*bin hakot*). *Bin* is a variant of *ben* and usually means "son" (as with Joshua bin Nun); but when it precedes a noun which is not a name, as here, it has the meaning "subject to (flogging)."
The Aramaic equivalent is *bar*: thus, *bar mitzvah* means "subject to mitzvah."

3] *Up to forty lashes.* The words "up to" are not in the Hebrew text and were inserted to comply with the halachic understanding of the verse that thirty-nine blows should be the limit. See at Deut. 22:18. (See further in Gleanings.)

4] *Not muzzle.* Rather, you must allow the animal to eat at will [1].
While it is threshing. The animal was tied to a pivot and walked in circles treading the corn. This method of threshing is still used in countries with nonmechanized agriculture.
Driver calls the law "another example of the humanity which is characteristic of Deuteronomy."

5] *When brothers dwell together.* On common family property.
Her husband's brother shall . . . perform the levir's duty. The word "levir" is the Latin for "hus-

וֹ לְאִשָּׁה וְיִבְּמָהּ: וְהָיָה הַבְּכוֹר אֲשֶׁר תֵּלֵד יָקוּם עַל־
זֹ שֵׁם אָחִיו הַמֵּת וְלֹא־יִמָּחֶה שְׁמוֹ מִיִּשְׂרָאֵל: וְאִם־לֹא
יַחְפֹּץ הָאִישׁ לָקַחַת אֶת־יְבִמְתּוֹ וְעָלְתָה יְבִמְתּוֹ
הַשַּׁעְרָה אֶל־הַזְּקֵנִים וְאָמְרָה מֵאֵן יְבָמִי לְהָקִים
לְאָחִיו שֵׁם בְּיִשְׂרָאֵל לֹא אָבָה יַבְּמִי: וְקָרְאוּ־לוֹ
חֹ זִקְנֵי־עִירוֹ וְדִבְּרוּ אֵלָיו וְעָמַד וְאָמַר לֹא חָפַצְתִּי
טֹ לְקַחְתָּהּ: וְנִגְּשָׁה יְבִמְתּוֹ אֵלָיו לְעֵינֵי הַזְּקֵנִים וְחָלְצָה
נַעֲלוֹ מֵעַל רַגְלוֹ וְיָרְקָה בְּפָנָיו וְעָנְתָה וְאָמְרָה
כָּכָה יֵעָשֶׂה לָאִישׁ אֲשֶׁר לֹא־יִבְנֶה אֶת־בֵּית
יֹ אָחִיו: וְנִקְרָא שְׁמוֹ בְּיִשְׂרָאֵל בֵּית חֲלוּץ הַנָּעַל: ס

Deuteronomy 25
6–10

duty.   6] The first son that she bears shall be accounted to the dead brother, that his name may not be blotted out in Israel.   7] But if the man does not want to marry his brother's widow, his brother's widow shall appear before the elders in the gate and declare, "My husband's brother refuses to establish a name in Israel for his brother; he will not perform the duty of a levir."   8] The elders of his town shall then summon him and talk to him. If he insists, saying, "I do not want to marry her,"   9] his brother's widow shall go up to him in the presence of the elders, pull the sandal off his foot, spit in his face, and make this declaration: Thus shall be done to the man who will not build up his brother's house!   10] And he shall go in Israel by the name of "the family of the unsandaled one."

band's brother," hence the particular relationship and its consequences are called "levirate." The text takes a knowledge of "the levir's duty" for granted and only describes what happens if a brother is unwilling to fulfill it.

A talmudic treatise *Yevamot* deals with the halachah arising from these prescriptions. (See further

in commentary below.)

6] *Shall be accounted.* In apportioning the inheritance [2].

9] *Pull the sandal off.* Hebrew חָלְצָה (*chaltzah*); hence the ceremony is known as *chalitzah*.

יא כִּי־יִנָּצוּ אֲנָשִׁים יַחְדָּו אִישׁ וְאָחִיו וְקָרְבָה אֵשֶׁת
הָאֶחָד לְהַצִּיל אֶת־אִישָׁהּ מִיַּד מַכֵּהוּ וְשָׁלְחָה יָדָהּ
יב וְהֶחֱזִיקָה בִּמְבֻשָׁיו: וְקַצֹּתָה אֶת־כַּפָּהּ לֹא תָחוֹס
יג עֵינֶךָ: ס לֹא־יִהְיֶה לְךָ בְּכִיסְךָ אֶבֶן וָאָבֶן גְּדוֹלָה
יד וּקְטַנָּה: לֹא־יִהְיֶה לְךָ בְּבֵיתְךָ אֵיפָה וְאֵיפָה גְּדוֹלָה
טו וּקְטַנָּה: אֶבֶן שְׁלֵמָה וָצֶדֶק יִהְיֶה־לָּךְ אֵיפָה שְׁלֵמָה
וָצֶדֶק יִהְיֶה־לָּךְ לְמַעַן יַאֲרִיכוּ יָמֶיךָ עַל הָאֲדָמָה
טז אֲשֶׁר־יְהוָה אֱלֹהֶיךָ נֹתֵן לָךְ: כִּי תוֹעֲבַת יְהוָה
אֱלֹהֶיךָ כָּל־עֹשֵׂה אֵלֶּה כֹּל עֹשֵׂה עָוֶל: פ

Deuteronomy 25
11–16

11] If two men get into a fight with each other, and the wife of one comes up to save her husband from his antagonist and puts out her hand and seizes him by his genitals,   **12]** you shall cut off her hand; show no pity.

13] You shall not have in your pouch alternate weights, larger and smaller. **14]** You shall not have in your house alternate measures, a larger and a smaller. **15]** You must have completely honest weights and completely honest measures, if you are to endure long on the soil that the Lord your God is giving you.   **16]** For everyone who does those things, everyone who deals dishonestly, is abhorrent to the Lord your God.

11] *His genitals.* Literally, "his shame parts" (compare the Latin *pudenda*).

Cut off her hand. A punishment not otherwise decreed in the Torah. In the laudable effort to save her husband the woman used what were considered impermissible means. In this conflict of personal need (to defend her husband) with public morality the Torah opted to support the latter. Compare the endorsement given to Phinehas, who responded violently against sexual license; Num. 25:1 ff. (On the question of talion, and the expression "hand for hand," see at Deut. 19:21.)

A talmudic discussion suggests that the law did not apply when the woman's action was the only recourse to save her husband, and that in any case a fine was exacted in lieu of mutilation [3].

13] *Weights.* אֶבֶן (*even*) means generally "stone," for stones often served as weights.

Larger and smaller. One for buying and one for selling. Compare Lev. 19:35.

14] *Measures.* אֵיפָה (*efah*) was a measure for both dry and liquid substances; it was equal to about 36 litres (8 gallons) [4].

יז זָכוֹר אֵת אֲשֶׁר־עָשָׂה לְךָ עֲמָלֵק בַּדֶּרֶךְ בְּצֵאתְכֶם
יח מִמִּצְרָיִם: אֲשֶׁר קָרְךָ בַּדֶּרֶךְ וַיְזַנֵּב בְּךָ כָּל־הַנֶּחֱשָׁלִים
יט אַחֲרֶיךָ וְאַתָּה עָיֵף וְיָגֵעַ וְלֹא יָרֵא אֱלֹהִים: וְהָיָה
בְּהָנִיחַ יְהוָה אֱלֹהֶיךָ לְךָ מִכָּל־אֹיְבֶיךָ מִסָּבִיב בָּאָרֶץ
אֲשֶׁר יְהוָה־אֱלֹהֶיךָ נֹתֵן לְךָ נַחֲלָה לְרִשְׁתָּהּ תִּמְחֶה
אֶת־זֵכֶר עֲמָלֵק מִתַּחַת הַשָּׁמָיִם לֹא תִּשְׁכָּח:

Haftarah Ki Tetze, p. 459

פ   פ   פ

א וְהָיָה כִּי־תָבוֹא אֶל־הָאָרֶץ אֲשֶׁר יְהוָה אֱלֹהֶיךָ נֹתֵן
ב לְךָ נַחֲלָה וִירִשְׁתָּהּ וְיָשַׁבְתָּ בָּהּ: וְלָקַחְתָּ מֵרֵאשִׁית
כָּל־פְּרִי הָאֲדָמָה אֲשֶׁר תָּבִיא מֵאַרְצְךָ אֲשֶׁר יְהוָה

17] Remember what Amalek did to you on your journey, after you left Egypt—
18] how, undeterred by fear of God, he surprised you on the march, when you were famished and weary, and cut down all the stragglers in your rear.   **19]** Therefore, when the LORD your God grants you safety from all your enemies around you, in the land that the LORD your God is giving you as a hereditary portion, you shall blot out the memory of Amalek from under heaven. Do not forget!

1] When you enter the land that the LORD your God is giving you as a heritage, and you occupy it and settle in it,   **2]** you shall take some of every first fruit of the soil, which you harvest from the land that the LORD your God is giving you,

17] *Remember what Amalek did.* The reference is to the events reported in Exod. 17:8-13; see our commentary there. In Deuteronomic days, Amalek—a group of Nomadic tribes in the Negev and Sinai—no longer threatened the Israelites, but the memory of their first battle stamped Amalek forever as the archenemy whose weakened condition was doubtlessly seen as just retribution.

Verses 17-19 form an additional Torah reading on the Sabbath before Purim, which is called *Shab-* *bat Zachor* after the first word in verse 17, *zachor,* remember.

18] *Undeterred by fear of God.* Which has no national limitation and obligates other peoples as well [5].

Stragglers in your rear. This aspect is not mentioned in Exodus.

The word נֶחֱשָׁלִים (*necheshalim,* translated as "stragglers") was probably נֶחֱלָשִׁים (*nechelashim,*

אֱלֹהֶיךָ נֹתֵן לָךְ וְשַׂמְתָּ בַטֶּנֶא וְהָלַכְתָּ אֶל־הַמָּקוֹם

ג אֲשֶׁר יִבְחַר יְהוָה אֱלֹהֶיךָ לְשַׁכֵּן שְׁמוֹ שָׁם: וּבָאתָ
אֶל־הַכֹּהֵן אֲשֶׁר יִהְיֶה בַּיָּמִים הָהֵם וְאָמַרְתָּ אֵלָיו
הִגַּדְתִּי הַיּוֹם לַיהוָה אֱלֹהֶיךָ כִּי־בָאתִי אֶל־הָאָרֶץ

ד אֲשֶׁר נִשְׁבַּע יְהוָה לַאֲבֹתֵינוּ לָתֶת לָנוּ: וְלָקַח הַכֹּהֵן
הַטֶּנֶא מִיָּדֶךָ וְהִנִּיחוֹ לִפְנֵי מִזְבַּח יְהוָה אֱלֹהֶיךָ:

ה וְעָנִיתָ וְאָמַרְתָּ לִפְנֵי יְהוָה אֱלֹהֶיךָ אֲרַמִּי אֹבֵד אָבִי
וַיֵּרֶד מִצְרַיְמָה וַיָּגָר שָׁם בִּמְתֵי מְעָט וַיְהִי־שָׁם לְגוֹי

ו גָּדוֹל עָצוּם וָרָב: וַיָּרֵעוּ אֹתָנוּ הַמִּצְרִים וַיְעַנּוּנוּ

ז וַיִּתְּנוּ עָלֵינוּ עֲבֹדָה קָשָׁה: וַנִּצְעַק אֶל־יְהוָה אֱלֹהֵי
אֲבֹתֵינוּ וַיִּשְׁמַע יְהוָה אֶת־קֹלֵנוּ וַיַּרְא אֶת־עָנְיֵנוּ וְאֶת־

Deuteronomy 26
3–7

put it in a basket and go to the place where the Lord your God will choose to establish His name. **3]** You shall go to the priest in charge at that time and say to him, "I acknowledge this day before the Lord your God that I have entered the land which the Lord swore to our fathers to give us."

4] The priest shall take the basket from your hand and set it down in front of the altar of the Lord your God.

5] You shall then recite as follows before the Lord your God: "My father was a fugitive Aramean. He went down to Egypt with meager numbers and sojourned there; but there he became a great and very populous nation. **6]** The Egyptians dealt harshly with us and oppressed us; they imposed heavy labor upon us. **7]** We cried to the Lord, the God of our fathers, and the Lord heard our plea and saw our

---

enfeebled). Hence: those left behind. Such transpositions occurred frequently and sometimes the transposed word remained as a variant of the original. Thus, the usual word for "lamb" is כֶּבֶשׂ (keves), but כֶּשֶׂב (kesev) also occurs. Or note עָיֵף (ayef, tired) and its variant יָעֵף (ya-ef).

26:3] *The Lord your God*. The speaker says "your God" in deference to the priest.
But the Septuagint has "my God."

5] *Fugitive Aramean*. See commentary below.

עֲמָלֵנוּ וְאֶת־לַחֲצֵנוּ: וַיּוֹצִאֵנוּ יְהוָֹה מִמִּצְרַיִם בְּיָד ח

חֲזָקָה וּבִזְרֹעַ נְטוּיָה וּבְמֹרָא גָּדֹל וּבְאֹתוֹת וּבְמֹפְתִים:

וַיְבִאֵנוּ אֶל־הַמָּקוֹם הַזֶּה וַיִּתֶּן־לָנוּ אֶת־הָאָרֶץ הַזֹּאת ט

אֶרֶץ זָבַת חָלָב וּדְבָשׁ: וְעַתָּה הִנֵּה הֵבֵאתִי אֶת־ י

רֵאשִׁית פְּרִי הָאֲדָמָה אֲשֶׁר־נָתַתָּה לִּי יְהוָֹה וְהִנַּחְתּוֹ

לִפְנֵי יְהוָֹה אֱלֹהֶיךָ וְהִשְׁתַּחֲוִיתָ לִפְנֵי יְהוָֹה אֱלֹהֶיךָ:

וְשָׂמַחְתָּ בְכָל־הַטּוֹב אֲשֶׁר נָתַן־לְךָ יְהוָֹה אֱלֹהֶיךָ יא

וּלְבֵיתֶךָ אַתָּה וְהַלֵּוִי וְהַגֵּר אֲשֶׁר בְּקִרְבֶּךָ: ס כִּי יב

תְכַלֶּה לַעְשֵׂר אֶת־כָּל־מַעְשַׂר תְּבוּאָתְךָ בַּשָּׁנָה

הַשְּׁלִישִׁת שְׁנַת הַמַּעֲשֵׂר וְנָתַתָּה לַלֵּוִי לַגֵּר לַיָּתוֹם

Deuteronomy 26
8–12

plight, our misery, and our oppression.   8] The LORD freed us from Egypt by a mighty hand, by an outstretched arm and awesome power, and by signs and portents.   9] He brought us to this place and gave us this land, a land flowing with milk and honey.   10] Wherefore I now bring the first fruits of the soil which You, O LORD, have given me."

You shall leave it before the LORD your God and bow low before the LORD your God.   11] And you shall enjoy, together with the Levite and the stranger in your midst, all the bounty that the LORD your God has bestowed upon you and your household.

12] When you have set aside in full the tenth part of your yield—in the third year, the year of the tithe—and have given it to the Levite, the stranger, the fatherless,

9] *Milk and honey*. See at Deut. 6:3.

10] *You shall leave it*. The basket which you have brought (verse 4).

11] *You shall enjoy*. At a festive meal, to which the Levites as well as strangers were to be invited.

The offering itself belonged to the priests; Deut. 18:4.

12] *When you have set aside*. The duty of tithing was set forth in Deut. 14:28–29; see there. The gift was followed by a formal declaration of religious compliance.

283

יג וְלָאַלְמָנָה וְאָכְלוּ בִשְׁעָרֶיךָ וְשָׂבֵעוּ: וְאָמַרְתָּ לִפְנֵי
יְהֹוָה אֱלֹהֶיךָ בִּעַרְתִּי הַקֹּדֶשׁ מִן־הַבַּיִת וְגַם נְתַתִּיו
לַלֵּוִי וְלַגֵּר לַיָּתוֹם וְלָאַלְמָנָה כְּכָל־מִצְוָתְךָ אֲשֶׁר
יד צִוִּיתָנִי לֹא־עָבַרְתִּי מִמִּצְוֺתֶיךָ וְלֹא שָׁכָחְתִּי: לֹא־
אָכַלְתִּי בְאֹנִי מִמֶּנּוּ וְלֹא־בִעַרְתִּי מִמֶּנּוּ בְּטָמֵא וְלֹא־
נָתַתִּי מִמֶּנּוּ לְמֵת שָׁמַעְתִּי בְּקוֹל יְהֹוָה אֱלֹהָי עָשִׂיתִי
טו כְּכֹל אֲשֶׁר צִוִּיתָנִי: הַשְׁקִיפָה מִמְּעוֹן קָדְשְׁךָ מִן־
הַשָּׁמַיִם וּבָרֵךְ אֶת־עַמְּךָ אֶת־יִשְׂרָאֵל וְאֵת הָאֲדָמָה
אֲשֶׁר נָתַתָּה לָנוּ כַּאֲשֶׁר נִשְׁבַּעְתָּ לַאֲבֹתֵינוּ אֶרֶץ

and the widow, that they may eat their fill in your settlements, **13]** you shall declare before the LORD your God: "I have cleared out the consecrated portion from the house; and I have given it to the Levite, the stranger, the fatherless, and the widow, just as You commanded me; I have neither transgressed nor neglected any of Your commandments: **14]** I have not eaten of it while in mourning; I have not cleared out any of it while I was unclean, and I have not deposited any of it with the dead. I have obeyed the LORD my God; I have done just as You commanded me. **15]** Look down from Your holy abode, from heaven, and bless Your people Israel and the soil You have given us, a land flowing with milk and honey, as You swore to our fathers."

This confessional litany, called *Viddui Ma-aser* (confession of tithing), was in later centuries assigned to the eve of the last day of Passover in the fourth and seventh years of the sabbatical cycle and pronounced in the Temple in Jerusalem [6].

14] *While in mourning.* That is, while unclean through contact with the dead, and before the necessary ablutions had been made (cf. Hos. 9:4). The translation is one of several that have been suggested, in part because what follows deals with the dead. But Rashbam understands: I did not (eat of it myself) for my own benefit (cf. the Hebrew text of Job 20:10).

Deposited any of it with the dead. As was done in Egypt, where food was buried with the dead for their journey in the afterlife. Such practices appear to have continued in Israel for many centuries [7].

284

טז זָבַת חָלָב וּדְבָשׁ: ס הַיּוֹם הַזֶּה יְהֹוָה אֱלֹהֶיךָ
מְצַוְּךָ לַעֲשׂוֹת אֶת־הַחֻקִּים הָאֵלֶּה וְאֶת־הַמִּשְׁפָּטִים
וְשָׁמַרְתָּ וְעָשִׂיתָ אוֹתָם בְּכָל־לְבָבְךָ וּבְכָל־נַפְשֶׁךָ:
יז אֶת־יְהֹוָה הֶאֱמַרְתָּ הַיּוֹם לִהְיוֹת לְךָ לֵאלֹהִים וְלָלֶכֶת
בִּדְרָכָיו וְלִשְׁמֹר חֻקָּיו וּמִצְוֹתָיו וּמִשְׁפָּטָיו וְלִשְׁמֹעַ
בְּקֹלוֹ: וַיהֹוָה הֶאֱמִירְךָ הַיּוֹם לִהְיוֹת לוֹ לְעַם סְגֻלָּה
יח
יט כַּאֲשֶׁר דִּבֶּר־לָךְ וְלִשְׁמֹר כָּל־מִצְוֹתָיו: וּלְתִתְּךָ עֶלְיוֹן
עַל כָּל־הַגּוֹיִם אֲשֶׁר עָשָׂה לִתְהִלָּה וּלְשֵׁם וּלְתִפְאָרֶת
וְלִהְיֹתְךָ עַם־קָדֹשׁ לַיהֹוָה אֱלֹהֶיךָ כַּאֲשֶׁר דִּבֵּר:

Deuteronomy 26

16–19

16] The LORD your God commands you this day to observe these laws and rules; observe them faithfully with all your heart and soul. **17]** You have affirmed this day that the LORD is your God, that you will walk in His ways, that you will observe His laws and commandments and rules, and that you will obey Him. **18]** And the LORD has affirmed this day that you are, as He promised you, His treasured people which shall observe all His commandments, **19]** and that He will set you, in fame and renown and glory, high above all the nations that He has made; and that you shall be, as He promised, a holy people to the LORD your God.

16] *Observe these laws.* Of chapters 12–26; a final exhortation.

17] *You have affirmed.* As, in return, has God; verse 18. This mutuality is expressed by the causal

form (otherwise unknown) of the word אָמַר. God causes Israel's affirmation and Israel's acceptance causes God's.

18] *His treasured people.* See on Deut. 7:6.

Chalitzah

The duty to preserve both the name and inheritance of a deceased and childless brother by marrying his widow ("the levir's duty") was apparently deeply rooted in Israel's tradition. The Torah text takes both its knowledge and its practice for granted and addresses itself only to the case of a recalcitrant brother and to the public ceremony (chalitzah) which was highlighted by pulling off his sandal and by spitting in his face. The symbolism of the procedure appears to have legal, psychological, and sexual overtones which doubtlessly were at one time clearly understood.

Thus, documents found in Nuzi (Mesopotamia) show that a shoe was used for effecting certain legal transactions, and "lifting the foot" symbolized the release of property[1] [8].

The Book of Ruth (4:7) remembers: "Now this was the custom in former time in Israel concerning redeeming and concerning exchanging, to confirm all things: a man drew off his shoe, and gave it to his neighbor; and this was the attestation in Israel."[2] But, in addition to representing possession, feet and shoes seem to have represented also certain sexual meanings. In Arabic, a woman is sometimes referred to as "a sandal," and by covering or uncovering his feet a man would convey an erotic message. Similarly, the act of spitting may originally not have been designed to humiliate the brother, but rather to have evoked an image of the semen he had withheld, even as did the act of unshoeing [9].

Levirate marriages were performed for many centuries, well into Mishnaic times (second century C.E.) [10]. But there was increasing doubt whether they were socially desirable, especially in view of the express statement in Lev. 18:16 which forbids a man to marry his brother's wife, classifying such a union with other incestuous relationships. The levirate law permits such marriage and, in fact, demands it when the widow has no children, but the exception does not fully relieve the sense of aversion which Lev. 18 expresses. Therefore, in the course of time, chalitzah appeared as a more desirable alternative and its practice, a priority over levirate marriage. Ultimately, the Rabbis made chalitzah a requirement and forbade levirate unions, save in exceptional cases. A ruling in the State of Israel states that the Torah law had to be set aside because "most levirs do not undergo levirate marriage for the sake of fulfilling a mitzvah, and also to preserve peace and harmony in the State of Israel by keeping the laws of Torah uniform for all" [11]. Still, the halachah continues to consider a widow whose brother-in-law has not yet released her through chalitzah as unmarriageable, and this has produced a number of hardship cases.[3] Orthodox rabbis —despite their concern for the widow—have found themselves unable to resolve the obvious contradiction: the widow depends on a brother-in-law to release her from the effects of a law that has been officially declared inoperative.[4]

Reform Judaism has drawn the logical

---

[1] Nowadays, surrendering a key would be a comparable symbolic act.

[2] Some centuries later, the glove of the right hand had taken the place of the shoe, as the Targum to Ruth 4:7 attests. The procedure recorded in the Book of Ruth diverges from the Torah, but the issue was of a somewhat different nature, which apparently demanded different practices.

[3] For instance, the brother-in-law may be a minor who cannot perform chalitzah until he is legally capable to do so.

[4] They have meliorated the Torah demand that the widow spit in the levir's face (she now spits on the ground), but they have not been able to overcome a levir's unavailability or unwillingness to perform chalitzah.

conclusion: It views levirate marriage as an undesirable norm for modern society and therefore considers *chalitzah* no longer necessary.

Thanksgiving

While the festival of Sukot represented the national religious thanksgiving festival (on which the American and Canadian holidays are based), the Torah orders a personal expression of gratitude as well and prescribes the exact words that are to be spoken on such an occasion (26:5–11). Although this is one of the few instances in the Torah where liturgical pronouncements are fixed—another example is the priestly benediction, Num. 6:22–27—its meaning is not clear.

The Israelite is to come to the sanctuary and, so to speak, identify himself historically. He is to begin by saying אֲרַמִּי אֹבֵד אָבִי—three words, none of which is unambiguous in this context. אֲרַמִּי (*Arami*) usually means "Aramean"; אֹבֵד (*oved*) could mean "lost" or "losing," but also "cause to be lost"; אָבִי (*avi*) means "my father" or "my ancestor."

Our translation has "My father was a fugitive Aramean"—which could be a reference to Abraham (who, when he left Haran, could be said to have been an Aramean) or, more likely, to Jacob (who fled from Laban); but the problem is that Abraham was not a fugitive and Jacob no Aramean.

Other translations have "The Aramean (tried to) cause my father to be lost (i.e., to be destroyed)." The Aramean was seen to be Laban, and the "father" was Jacob, whom Laban attempted to undo.

These are complex grammatical questions that render an undisputed interpretation impossible—but then perhaps such is not necessary to obtain. The Torah is repeatedly ambiguous. Here, thanksgiving is to be rooted in the past, with its glories and its difficulties. The facts of near destruction in ages gone by (or in recent memory, as the case may be) were set down as necessary recollections for an Israelite's thanksgiving. Whether the danger to survival came to an Abraham or to a Jacob, whether the ancestor was threatened or merely lost (physically? spiritually?) is less important than that the past needed to be seen as impinging on the present, and that God's beneficent guidance needed to be rehearsed from generation to generation. The very opaqueness of the language may in fact have prevented the obligation from being identified with the remote past only and instead served to render it of continuing significance [12].

GLEANINGS

Flogging (Deut. 25:1–3)

The number of lashes to be administered is "up to forty lashes but no more." (Therefore, only thirty-nine strokes are given so that a mistake in counting may not lead to excessive punishment.)

If the scourged person dies, the one administering the lashes is not culpable, but if he gave even one stroke too many he is culpable and subject to exile.

Excessive beating would cause "your brother" to be degraded in your eyes. After having been flogged he is like your brother.[5]   MISHNAH [14]

A magistrate must watch the flogging to make sure that the culprit can still bear the lashes.

MIDRASH [15]

Those appointed to administer the lashes should be weak in body but strong in understanding.

TALMUD [16]

If we look into the place in the Torah in which the law of flogging occurs and its close connection with the law of not muzzling an ox (which follows it), then the tendency of the teaching here is not so much on flogging as a punishment as it is directed to its limitation. In the laws preceding (24:20 ff.), kindness and consideration are demanded for the socially deprived, and, in the law following (25:4), considerate behavior is demanded even for animals. So here, when a person is to be disciplined, the court is commanded to exercise watchful consideration.   S. R. HIRSCH [17]

Two Times

The word "everyone" occurs twice in 25:16 (which deals with dishonesty). Dishonesty would be a sin even if there were no Torah command (Cain's murder of Abel was a sin even though there was not yet any law), for it is self-evident. Hence it says "everyone," to make clear that the law includes even those who do not know of its existence.   KETAV SOFER [18]

When

(The opening word of 26:1, וְהָיָה, was construed by the Rabbis to indicate a sense of joy, and was applied by them to every occurrence of the word.)

Settling in Eretz Yisrael is one of the gifts vouchsafed to Israel, in recompense for its suffering.

Y. L. EGER [19]

Past and Present

In 26:5 the expression "fugitive" (אֹבֵד) is a present participle. Persecution of Israel existed long ago and has not ceased in our day.

CHASIDIC [20]

Reciprocity

God's "bringing" Israel into the land and "bringing" the first fruits are set into a mutual relationship that is stressed in the prayer itself (26:9–10): "*He brought* us to this place. . . . Wherefore *I now bring* the first fruits of the soil." Thus is expressed the reciprocity between God and the individual members of the people.

M. BUBER [21]

---

[5] The Mishnah states further that if the flogged person befouls himself no further strokes are administered. It was also noted that the numerical value of "your brother" (אָחִיךָ) is 39: א =1, ח =8, י =10, כ =20 [13].

288

Blessings and Curses, I

It is at once apparent that the following section differs from the preceding one, for directives in the second person now give way to a third person framework. Furthermore, the chapter interrupts the flow of chapters 26–28, and it is likely that it once stood after chapter 28.* Such a position would give it the literary function of ending Part III of the Book of Deuteronomy: at its beginning (11:26 ff.) the blessings and curses on Mount Gerizim and Mount Ebal were assigned their role, and now, at the end, this role would be described in detail. Blessings and curses thus form the framework for the special laws contained in Part III, even as a short catalogue of blessings concludes the Book of the Covenant (Exod. 23:20 ff.), and a list of blessings and curses follows the Holiness Code (Lev. 26).

The preparations for the ritual fall into four parts: (1) inscribing the law on stone tablets and placing them on Mount Ebal; (2) erecting the altar; (3) sacrifice and meal of rejoicing by the people; (4) pronouncement of the curses by the Levites and acknowledgment by the people.

For a discussion of blessings and curses, see commentary below and Gleanings to Introduction to Part III.

---

* But von Rad believes that ch. 28 once followed after 27:10. He calls the twelve laws of 27:15–26 "the Shechem Dodecalogue, the oldest list of prohibitions in the Bible" [1].

אַ וַיְצַו מֹשֶׁה וְזִקְנֵי יִשְׂרָאֵל אֶת־הָעָם לֵאמֹר שָׁמֹר

ב אֶת־כָּל־הַמִּצְוָה אֲשֶׁר אָנֹכִי מְצַוֶּה אֶתְכֶם הַיּוֹם: וְהָיָה
בַּיּוֹם אֲשֶׁר תַּעַבְרוּ אֶת־הַיַּרְדֵּן אֶל־הָאָרֶץ אֲשֶׁר־
יְהוָה אֱלֹהֶיךָ נֹתֵן לָךְ וַהֲקֵמֹתָ לְךָ אֲבָנִים גְּדֹלוֹת
ג וְשַׂדְתָּ אֹתָם בַּשִּׂיד: וְכָתַבְתָּ עֲלֵיהֶן אֶת־כָּל־דִּבְרֵי
הַתּוֹרָה הַזֹּאת בְּעָבְרֶךָ לְמַעַן אֲשֶׁר תָּבֹא אֶל־הָאָרֶץ
אֲשֶׁר־יְהוָה אֱלֹהֶיךָ נֹתֵן לְךָ אֶרֶץ זָבַת חָלָב וּדְבַשׁ
ד כַּאֲשֶׁר דִּבֶּר יְהוָה אֱלֹהֵי־אֲבֹתֶיךָ לָךְ: וְהָיָה בְּעָבְרְכֶם
אֶת־הַיַּרְדֵּן תָּקִימוּ אֶת־הָאֲבָנִים הָאֵלֶּה אֲשֶׁר אָנֹכִי
מְצַוֶּה אֶתְכֶם הַיּוֹם בְּהַר עֵיבָל וְשַׂדְתָּ אוֹתָם בַּשִּׂיד:

Deuteronomy 27
1–4

1] Moses and the elders of Israel charged the people, saying: Observe all the Instruction that I enjoin upon you this day. **2]** As soon as you have crossed the Jordan into the land that the Lord your God is giving you, you shall set up large stones. Coat them with plaster **3]** and inscribe upon them all the words of this Teaching. When you cross over to invade the land that the Lord your God is giving you, a land flowing with milk and honey, as the Lord, the God of your fathers, promised you— **4]** upon crossing the Jordan, you shall set up these stones, about

27:2] *As soon as you have crossed.* The prescriptions that follow were not precisely observed by Joshua; thus Mount Gerizim is not mentioned as having a role in his ceremonies—despite the specific statement that Joshua carried out the law of Moses (Josh. 8:30 ff.). One cannot explain this discrepancy with certainty; one possibility is that the author of Deuteronomy (who lived centuries after Joshua and probably later also than the compilation of the Book of Joshua) wanted to point out that the conquest of the land had not always followed divine prescriptions and had, in fact, significantly digressed from them (as also in the matter of extirpating the pagans).

The construction of verses 2–4 is difficult and the translation uncertain.

Coat them with plaster. And afterwards inscribe them, according to Egyptian practice. This method preserved the inscription better than an incision in the stone, which often weathered badly [2].

3] *This Teaching.* According to Josh. 8:32, this appears to mean the Book of Deuteronomy; see also at Deut. 1:5.
Josephus: only the blessings and curses were inscribed [3]; Mishnah: the whole Torah [4]; Saadia: the essential teachings of Torah [5].

ה וּבָנִיתָ שָּׁם מִזְבֵּחַ לַיהוָה אֱלֹהֶיךָ מִזְבַּח אֲבָנִים לֹא־

ו תָנִיף עֲלֵיהֶם בַּרְזֶל: אֲבָנִים שְׁלֵמוֹת תִּבְנֶה אֶת־

מִזְבַּח יְהוָה אֱלֹהֶיךָ וְהַעֲלִיתָ עָלָיו עוֹלֹת לַיהוָה

ז אֱלֹהֶיךָ: וְזָבַחְתָּ שְׁלָמִים וְאָכַלְתָּ שָּׁם וְשָׂמַחְתָּ לִפְנֵי

ח יְהוָה אֱלֹהֶיךָ: וְכָתַבְתָּ עַל־הָאֲבָנִים אֶת־כָּל־דִּבְרֵי

הַתּוֹרָה הַזֹּאת בַּאֵר הֵיטֵב: ס

ט וַיְדַבֵּר מֹשֶׁה וְהַכֹּהֲנִים הַלְוִיִּם אֶל כָּל־יִשְׂרָאֵל לֵאמֹר

הַסְכֵּת וּשְׁמַע יִשְׂרָאֵל הַיּוֹם הַזֶּה נִהְיֵיתָ לְעָם לַיהוָה

י אֱלֹהֶיךָ: וְשָׁמַעְתָּ בְּקוֹל יְהוָה אֱלֹהֶיךָ וְעָשִׂיתָ אֶת־

יא מִצְוֹתָו* וְאֶת־חֻקָּיו אֲשֶׁר אָנֹכִי מְצַוְּךָ הַיּוֹם: ס וַיְצַו

יב מֹשֶׁה אֶת־הָעָם בַּיּוֹם הַהוּא לֵאמֹר: אֵלֶּה יַעַמְדוּ

Deuteronomy 27
5–12

* י מצותיו קרי.

which I charge you this day, on Mount Ebal, and coat them with plaster. **5]** There, too, you shall build an altar to the LORD your God, an altar of stones. Do not wield an iron tool over them; **6]** you must build the altar of the LORD your God of unhewn stones. You shall offer on it burnt offerings to the LORD your God, **7]** and you shall sacrifice there offerings of well-being and eat them, rejoicing before the LORD your God. **8]** And on those stones you shall inscribe every word of this Teaching most distinctly.

9] Moses and the levitical priests spoke to all Israel, saying: Silence! Hear, O Israel! Today you have become the people of the LORD your God: **10]** Heed the LORD your God and observe His commandments and His laws, which I enjoin upon you this day.

11] Thereupon Moses charged the people, saying: **12]** After you have crossed

9] *Levitical priests.* See at 18:1.

לְבָרֵךְ אֶת־הָעָם עַל־הַר גְּרִזִּים בְּעָבְרְכֶם אֶת־הַיַּרְדֵּן
יג שִׁמְעוֹן וְלֵוִי וִיהוּדָה וְיִשָּׂשכָר וְיוֹסֵף וּבִנְיָמִן: וְאֵלֶּה
יַעַמְדוּ עַל־הַקְּלָלָה בְּהַר עֵיבָל רְאוּבֵן גָּד וְאָשֵׁר
יד וּזְבוּלֻן דָּן וְנַפְתָּלִי: וְעָנוּ הַלְוִיִּם וְאָמְרוּ אֶל־כָּל־אִישׁ
טו יִשְׂרָאֵל קוֹל רָם: ס אָרוּר הָאִישׁ אֲשֶׁר יַעֲשֶׂה
פֶסֶל וּמַסֵּכָה תּוֹעֲבַת יְהוָה מַעֲשֵׂה יְדֵי חָרָשׁ וְשָׂם

the Jordan, the following shall stand on Mount Gerizim when the blessing for the people is spoken: Simeon, Levi, Judah, Issachar, Joseph, and Benjamin.   13] And for the curse, the following shall stand on Mount Ebal: Reuben, Gad, Asher, Zebulun, Dan, and Naphthali.   14] The Levites shall then proclaim in a loud voice to all the men of Israel:

15] Cursed be the man who makes a sculptured or molten image, abhorred by

12] *The following shall stand*. Not only is the construction of verses 12 and 13 uncertain, but also the role of the participants in the proceedings. It appears that the representatives of the tribes (not the tribes themselves) stood in their assigned places and that the Levites were represented along with all the others while the blessings were spoken (verse 12). Other Levites, possibly the priestly members, spoke the blessings and the curses, but only the latter function is specifically relegated to them (verse 14) [6].

On Mount Geriẓim. For the blessing, only tribes who derived their ancestry from the children of Leah and Rachel are assigned. The mountain became the Samaritans' chief place of worship, surpassing Mount Zion in sanctity.

13] *On Mount Ebal*. For the curses, the four putative descendants of Jacob's handmaidens, Bilhah

and Zilpah, are selected, plus Reuben (who lost his birthright, Gen. 49:4), and Zebulun, possibly because as Leah's youngest he was chosen to equalize the two sides of six tribes each.

15–26] The twelve curses enumerated here have no equivalent blessings, but because blessings *were* spoken (verse 12) it may be that they were the reverse of the curses. Thus, the first blessing might have been: "Blessed be the man who does not make objects to be used for idolatry" [7].

It is likely that these reprehensible actions were chosen because they would generally be committed in secret and remain unpunished by human courts [8]. The people assumed collective responsibility for such acts, of which the first and last concern a person's relationship with God (that is, with His incorporeality and His Torah) and the others with the purity of the family and with

טז בַּסָּתֶר וְעָנוּ כָל־הָעָם וְאָמְרוּ אָמֵן: ס אָרוּר

יז מַקְלֶה אָבִיו וְאִמּוֹ וְאָמַר כָּל־הָעָם אָמֵן: ס אָרוּר

יח מַסִּיג גְּבוּל רֵעֵהוּ וְאָמַר כָּל־הָעָם אָמֵן: ס אָרוּר

יט מַשְׁגֶּה עִוֵּר בַּדָּרֶךְ וְאָמַר כָּל־הָעָם אָמֵן: ס אָרוּר

כ מַטֶּה מִשְׁפַּט גֵּר־יָתוֹם וְאַלְמָנָה וְאָמַר כָּל־הָעָם
אָמֵן: אָרוּר שֹׁכֵב עִם־אֵשֶׁת אָבִיו כִּי גִלָּה כְּנַף

Deuteronomy 27
16–20

the LORD, a craftman's handiwork, and sets it up in secret.—And all the people shall respond, Amen.

16] Cursed be he who insults his father or mother.—And all the people shall say, Amen.

17] Cursed be he who moves his neighbor's landmark.—And all the people shall say, Amen.

18] Cursed be he who misdirects a blind person on his way.—And all the people shall say, Amen.

19] Cursed be he who subverts the rights of the stranger, the fatherless, and the widow.—And all the people shall say, Amen.

20] Cursed be he who lies with his father's wife, for he has removed his father's garment.—And all the people shall say, Amen.

moral behavior in various respects. It is noteworthy that four of the twelve address sexual matters. Possibly these curses were at one time part of a liturgical function and were later inserted into Deuteronomy [9].

15] *Amen.* Repeated after every curse, it is a declamation of spiritual assent.

The Hebrew is of the same root as *emunah* ("faith"); compare the (archaic) English expression "In faith!" (See also at Num. 5:22.)

16] *Insults.* מַקְלֶה (*makleh*), literally, "makes light of," the direct opposite of *kibed* ("honors"), literally, "gives weight to." In Exod. 21:17 and Lev.

20:9 the term is *mekalel*, "curses" or "reviles" one's parents; thus, the Deuteronomic prohibition goes much farther.

17] *Landmark.* See at Deut. 19:14.

18] *Who misdirects a blind person.* Cf. Lev. 19:14, "who places a stumbling block before the blind."

19] *Rights of the stranger.* So Deut. 24:17 and elsewhere in the Torah.

20] *Lies with his father's wife.* That is, his stepmother.

Removed his father's garment. See at Deut. 23:1.

כא אָבִיו וְאָמַר כָּל־הָעָם אָמֵן: ס אָרוּר שֹׁכֵב עִם־
כב כָּל־בְּהֵמָה וְאָמַר כָּל־הָעָם אָמֵן: ס אָרוּר שֹׁכֵב
עִם־אֲחֹתוֹ בַּת־אָבִיו אוֹ בַת־אִמּוֹ וְאָמַר כָּל־הָעָם
כג אָמֵן: ס אָרוּר שֹׁכֵב עִם־חֹתַנְתּוֹ וְאָמַר כָּל־הָעָם
כד אָמֵן: ס אָרוּר מַכֵּה רֵעֵהוּ בַּסָּתֶר וְאָמַר כָּל־
כה הָעָם אָמֵן: ס אָרוּר לֹקֵחַ שֹׁחַד לְהַכּוֹת נֶפֶשׁ
כו דָּם נָקִי וְאָמַר כָּל־הָעָם אָמֵן: ס אָרוּר אֲשֶׁר
לֹא־יָקִים אֶת־דִּבְרֵי הַתּוֹרָה־הַזֹּאת לַעֲשׂוֹת אוֹתָם
וְאָמַר כָּל־הָעָם אָמֵן: פ

21] Cursed be he who lies with any beast.—And all the people shall say, Amen.

22] Cursed be he who lies with his sister, whether daughter of his father or of his mother.—And all the people shall say, Amen.

23] Cursed be he who lies with his mother-in-law.—And all the people shall say, Amen.

24] Cursed be he who strikes down his neighbor in secret.—And all the people shall say, Amen.

25] Cursed be he who accepts a bribe in the case of the murder of an innocent person.—And all the people shall say, Amen.

26] Cursed be he who will not uphold the terms of this Teaching and observe them.—And all the people shall say, Amen.

21] *Lies with any beast.* Commits sodomy; see Exod. 22:18.

22] *Lies with his sister.* That is, his half sister; see Lev. 18:9; 20:17. In earlier days, down to David's time, such a relationship was permitted; see II Sam. 13:13; Gen. 20:12 (Abraham and Sarah were children of the same father but not of the same mother).

24] *Strikes down.* Kills; equivalent to the sixth commandment (Deut. 5:17).

Tradition applied this to killing someone's repu-tation [10].

In secret. He may escape human law, but he will not escape God's.

25] *Accepts a bribe.* In order to let the murderer go free; or to let an innocent person be slain in-stead. The text is ambiguous; it is also unclear whether the injunction is directed to a judge or a witness.

26] *This Teaching.* The Book of Deuteronomy. Prevailing tradition took it to mean the whole Torah [11].

Blessings and Curses[1]

Blessings and curses were closely bound to a belief in the power of speech, and both were frequently amplified by precisely circumscribed acts. Where such formulae and actions were deemed to have an independent and inevitable efficacy, which would force extra-human agencies to conform to the will of the invoker, the participants were operating in the realm of magic. Where, on the other hand, such acts were essentially submissions to the Divine, who was called upon to ratify them, blessings and curses acquired religious legitimacy. They were and are, then, forms of prayer, and thus the biblical prescriptions regarding them are to be understood. Nonetheless, the dividing line between magic and religion cannot always be clearly drawn; for instance, when Isaac said to Esau that he had already given his primary blessing away (Gen. 27:37), he spoke from a context which ascribed to his words a non-cancellable quality. The blessings and curses on Mount Gerizim and Mount Ebal had a clearly didactic purpose: they aimed at guiding the hearers to live in accordance with God's law. When God himself blessed or cursed, He could invoke himself ("By Myself I swear"; Gen. 22:16), but usually His words were tantamount to actions, for a realization of the divine will was inherent in the divine word.

Blessings and curses were usually delineated in detail; they must be executed precisely to evoke in speaker and hearer the kind of awe which would put them in touch with the supernatural Presence. They featured key words as well as special motions—such as laying on and lifting of hands, or destroying a document on which the curse was written.

While the Bible knows only one expression for blessing (*barech*, *berachah*), a number of words are used for cursing. The chief terms are *arur* (as in the chapter before us; it appears to have an operational, liturgical aspect: "cursed be he who . . ."); *alah* (which may be said to be the formulation of the curse); and *kilel* (a broad term, describing attitudes and actions; the noun *kelalah* is the usual opposite of *berachah*) [12].

Curses were included in Hittite vassal treaties; and all oaths that people swore (and swear) may be seen to contain an element of self-cursing. Thus Ruth swore that she would stay with Naomi and added that God should punish her if she broke her oath (Ruth 1:17). The legal sphere maintains to this day the connection between oath and self-curse, for the person who swears falsely thereby assumes voluntarily the consequences of the law. God too swears, although in His case the aspect of self-cursing assumes a different quality. When He invokes himself He implies: I would not be God if what I say will not come to pass.

A noteworthy aspect of the litany prescribed for the two mountains is its overt and implied emphasis on acts committed in secret. "There is a superb element in Israel's commitment, in a solemn moment, to the righteous will of God above all spheres of life, especially to a will which is operative precisely when man believes himself to be alone with himself. Israel makes itself the executor of this divine will by carrying it into the secret pathways of life" [13].

[1] This subject is also dealt with in our commentaries on Genesis, chapter 48, Numbers 6:22–27, and Leviticus, chapter 26.

GLEANINGS

A New Covenant

Three covenants did God conclude with Israel: one after the Exodus, one at Sinai, and one at this time, for the Sinaitic covenant had been abrogated by the sin of the golden calf. Therefore Moses says (verse 9): "Today you have become the people of the Lord your God."

HIZKUNI [14]

Monuments

The nations erect monuments to memorialize their conquests, victories, and heroes. Israel is to inscribe on stone the words of Torah.

ABARBANEL [15]

Stones

Expose a human "stone"[2] to God's teaching and it will be shattered.   TALMUD [16]

The power of Torah is so great that even stones are moved by it.   CHASIDIC [17]

Why the Nations Lost the Promised Land

The Torah was inscribed on the stones in seventy languages, but the nations chose to disregard it. Had they accepted it they would have been accepted into the covenant and would not have lost the Land.   TALMUD [18]

Even if they had accepted only the seven Noahide laws they would not have been driven out.

S. R. HIRSCH [19]

Secret and Public

All curses refer to secret transgressions. For public offenders there is hope of repentance; for hypocrites there is none.   CHASIDIC [20]

Misdirecting the Blind

Those too are cursed who give poor advice to the ignorant or who cause others to sin.

D. HOFFMANN [21]

The Meaning of the Curses

All blessing is denied to him who outwardly plays the pious man devoted to God but in secret denies the exclusive existence of One God and His Rule; who outwardly is respectful to his parents but inwardly considers himself vastly superior to them; who in the eyes of men preserves the reputation of an honest man but, where it is unobserved, does not hesitate to injure the rights of his neighbor to his own advantage; who is full of enthusiasm for the welfare of his neighbors, in the presence of clever and intelligent people, but pushes short-sighted and blind people into misfortune; who grovels before the powerful but denies the weak and helpless their rights; pretends to be a highly respectable member of society, to wallow in sexual licentiousness in intimate privacy (verses 20–23); who does not dig a dagger into his neighbor but, under the cloak of conversation, murders his happiness, his peace, and his honor; who enjoys the highest confidence in his community but misuses it in secret corruption; finally, also one who, even if he lives correctly and dutifully for himself, still looks with indifference on the abandonment of the duties of the Torah in his immediate and wider circles.

S. R. HIRSCH [22]

---

[2] That is, a person who has a heart of stone.

Blessings and Curses, II

The chapter before us contains an awesome array of curses that dwarf the catalogue of blessings preceding them. However, this imbalance should not be surprising, for in the Torah specific negative commandments far outnumber specific positive ones,[1] for in general it is more usual to create codes of forbidden than of desirable behavior. What sets chapter 28 aside are its detail and the expanse of its imaginative projection: whatever blessing or curse would be real to the biblical age here finds its place. The Torah promises and it threatens, and here as elsewhere it is unabashedly realistic: it assumes that, while pure love of God and His commandments is the highest rung, such height of total devotion for its own sake can be scaled only by the fewest; the majority will need earthly rewards and punishments held up before their eyes.[2]

Attempts have been made by some scholars to distinguish three catalogues of curses, starting in verses 15, 45, and 58. Others would find a "core" of blessings and curses which were greatly expanded later on. Thus, von Rad has reconstructed what he believes to be an original body of curses, with a clearly agricultural basis [2]. In any case, the whole chapter bears a striking resemblance to the vassal treaties of the Assyrian King Esar-

---

[1] Ibn Ezra (on Lev. 26:13) makes the point that "blessings are uttered in broad general terms, while curses are stated in greater detail, to awe and frighten the hearers."

[2] Maimonides sought to meliorate this idea of automatic rewards and punishments—especially as far as rainfall and drought were concerned—by terming it a necessary device in the education of a people emerging from idolatry; see also above, at chapter 11 [1].

haddon (see Commentary on Leviticus, chapter 26, and Gleanings below). The Assyrian and Hebrew texts are broadly contemporary, and there is general scholarly agreement that the former influenced the latter. In the Assyrian model, of course, there is a triangle of suzerain, vassal, and deity, while in the covenant between God and Israel only the Sovereign and His vassal are partners. The former lays down conditions and states what He will do if the latter complies or fails to comply. The catalogue of chapter 28 therefore must be seen as part of the Torah's everpresent view of Israel as a covenanted community [3].

וְהָיָה אִם־שָׁמוֹעַ תִּשְׁמַע בְּקוֹל יְהוָה אֱלֹהֶיךָ לִשְׁמֹר א

לַעֲשׂוֹת אֶת־כָּל־מִצְוֹתָיו אֲשֶׁר אָנֹכִי מְצַוְּךָ הַיּוֹם וּנְתָנְךָ

יְהוָה אֱלֹהֶיךָ עֶלְיוֹן עַל כָּל־גּוֹיֵי הָאָרֶץ: וּבָאוּ עָלֶיךָ ב

כָּל־הַבְּרָכוֹת הָאֵלֶּה וְהִשִּׂיגֻךָ כִּי תִשְׁמַע בְּקוֹל יְהוָה

אֱלֹהֶיךָ: בָּרוּךְ אַתָּה בָּעִיר וּבָרוּךְ אַתָּה בַּשָּׂדֶה: ג

בָּרוּךְ פְּרִי־בִטְנְךָ וּפְרִי אַדְמָתְךָ וּפְרִי בְהֶמְתֶּךָ שְׁגַר ד

אֲלָפֶיךָ וְעַשְׁתְּרוֹת צֹאנֶךָ: בָּרוּךְ טַנְאֲךָ וּמִשְׁאַרְתֶּךָ: ה

בָּרוּךְ אַתָּה בְּבֹאֶךָ וּבָרוּךְ אַתָּה בְּצֵאתֶךָ: יִתֵּן יְהוָה ו
ז

אֶת־אֹיְבֶיךָ הַקָּמִים עָלֶיךָ נִגָּפִים לְפָנֶיךָ בְּדֶרֶךְ אֶחָד

יֵצְאוּ אֵלֶיךָ וּבְשִׁבְעָה דְרָכִים יָנוּסוּ לְפָנֶיךָ: יְצַו ח

Deuteronomy 28

1–8

1] Now, if you obey the LORD your God, to observe faithfully all His commandments which I enjoin upon you this day, the LORD your God will set you high above all the nations of the earth.   2] All these blessings shall come upon you and take effect, if you will but heed the word of the LORD your God:

3] Blessed shall you be in the city and blessed shall you be in the country.

4] Blessed shall be the issue of your womb, the produce of your soil, and the offspring of your cattle, the calving of your herd and the lambing of your flock.

5] Blessed shall be your basket and your kneading bowl.

6] Blessed shall you be in your comings and blessed shall you be in your goings.

7] The LORD will put to rout before you the enemies who attack you; they will march out against you by a single road, but flee from you by many roads.   8] The

28:2] *Blessings shall . . . take effect.* Literally, "shall overtake you." They are pictured as having an independent existence. Compare Ps. 23:6, "goodness and mercy shall pursue me."

3] *Blessed.* Six general blessings—counting verse 4 to contain three different blessings—are enumerated, corresponding to the six tribes that bless. (Similarly, six general curses, verses 16–19, may

be seen to precede the rest.)

5] *Your basket.* For gathering the produce.
Your kneading bowl. Which utilizes the blessings that were gathered in the basket.

7] *Many roads.* Literally, "seven," often used in a broad sense; compare the English use of "dozen" or "hundred."

יְהֹוָה אִתְּךָ אֶת־הַבְּרָכָה בַּאֲסָמֶיךָ וּבְכֹל מִשְׁלַח יָדֶךָ

ט וּבֵרַכְךָ בָּאָרֶץ אֲשֶׁר־יְהֹוָה אֱלֹהֶיךָ נֹתֵן לָךְ: יְקִימְךָ יְהֹוָה לוֹ לְעַם קָדוֹשׁ כַּאֲשֶׁר נִשְׁבַּע־לָךְ כִּי תִשְׁמֹר

י אֶת־מִצְוֺת יְהֹוָה אֱלֹהֶיךָ וְהָלַכְתָּ בִּדְרָכָיו: וְרָאוּ כָּל־עַמֵּי הָאָרֶץ כִּי שֵׁם יְהֹוָה נִקְרָא עָלֶיךָ וְיָרְאוּ מִמֶּךָּ:

יא וְהוֹתִרְךָ יְהֹוָה לְטוֹבָה בִּפְרִי בִטְנְךָ וּבִפְרִי בְהֶמְתְּךָ וּבִפְרִי אַדְמָתֶךָ עַל הָאֲדָמָה אֲשֶׁר נִשְׁבַּע יְהֹוָה

יב לַאֲבֹתֶיךָ לָתֶת לָךְ: יִפְתַּח יְהֹוָה לְךָ אֶת־אוֹצָרוֹ הַטּוֹב אֶת־הַשָּׁמַיִם לָתֵת מְטַר־אַרְצְךָ בְּעִתּוֹ וּלְבָרֵךְ אֵת כָּל־מַעֲשֵׂה יָדֶךָ וְהִלְוִיתָ גּוֹיִם רַבִּים וְאַתָּה לֹא

יג תִלְוֶה: וּנְתָנְךָ יְהֹוָה לְרֹאשׁ וְלֹא לְזָנָב וְהָיִיתָ רַק

LORD will ordain blessings for you upon your barns and upon all your undertakings: He will bless you in the land which the LORD your God is giving you.   9] The LORD will establish you as His holy people, as He swore to you, if you keep the commandments of the LORD your God and walk in His ways.   10] And all the peoples of the earth shall see that the LORD's name is proclaimed over you, and they shall stand in fear of you.   11] The LORD will give you abounding prosperity in the issue of your womb, the offspring of your cattle, and the produce of your soil in the land that the LORD swore to your fathers to give you.   12] The LORD will open for you His bounteous store, the heavens, to provide rain for your land in season and to bless all your undertakings. You will be creditor to many nations, but debtor to none.

    13] The LORD will make you the head, not the tail; you will always be at the

9] *Holy people.* עַם קָדוֹשׁ (*am kadosh*). In Exod. 19:6 Israel is called גּוֹי קָדוֹשׁ (*goy kadosh*) but, while homilies have been woven around this difference, the expressions appear to have conveyed the same meaning.

10] *Is proclaimed over you.* That is, Israel belongs to God, and God lends His name to Israel; compare Isa. 4:1, "Only let us be called by Your name."

12] *Creditor.* See at 15:6.

לְמַעְלָה וְלֹא תִהְיֶה לְמָטָּה כִּי־תִשְׁמַע אֶל־מִצְוֺת

יְהֹוָה אֱלֹהֶיךָ אֲשֶׁר אָנֹכִי מְצַוְּךָ הַיּוֹם לִשְׁמֹר וְלַעֲשֽׂוֹת:

יד וְלֹא תָסוּר מִכָּל־הַדְּבָרִים אֲשֶׁר אָנֹכִי מְצַוֶּה אֶתְכֶם

הַיּוֹם יָמִין וּשְׂמֹאול לָלֶכֶת אַחֲרֵי אֱלֹהִים אֲחֵרִים

לְעָבְדָֽם: פ

טו וְהָיָה אִם־לֹא תִשְׁמַע בְּקוֹל יְהֹוָה אֱלֹהֶיךָ לִשְׁמֹר

לַעֲשׂוֹת אֶת־כָּל־מִצְוֺתָיו וְחֻקֹּתָיו אֲשֶׁר אָנֹכִי מְצַוְּךָ

הַיּוֹם וּבָאוּ עָלֶיךָ כָּל־הַקְּלָלוֹת הָאֵלֶּה וְהִשִּׂיגֽוּךָ:

טז אָרוּר אַתָּה בָּעִיר וְאָרוּר אַתָּה בַּשָּׂדֶה: אָרוּר טַנְאֲךָ

יז וּמִשְׁאַרְתֶּֽךָ: אָרוּר פְּרִי־בִטְנְךָ וּפְרִי אַדְמָתֶךָ שְׁגַר

יח אֲלָפֶיךָ וְעַשְׁתְּרֹת צֹאנֶֽךָ: אָרוּר אַתָּה בְּבֹאֶךָ וְאָרוּר

Deuteronomy 28
14–19

top and never at the bottom—if only you obey and faithfully observe the command-ments of the Lord your God which I enjoin upon you this day,   14] and do not deviate to the right or to the left from any of the commandments that I enjoin upon you this day and turn to the worship of other gods.

15] But if you do not obey the Lord your God to observe faithfully all His com-mandments and laws which I enjoin upon you this day, all these curses shall come upon you and take effect:

16] Cursed shall you be in the city and cursed shall you be in the country.

17] Cursed shall be your basket and your kneading bowl.

18] Cursed shall be the issue of your womb and the produce of your soil, the calving of your herd and the lambing of your flock.

19] Cursed shall you be in your comings and cursed shall you be in your goings.

17] *Your basket.* Verses 17 and 18 correspond to verses 5 and 4, respectively.

301

דברים כח
כ–כה

כ אַתָּה בְּצֵאתֶךָ: יְשַׁלַּח יְהֹוָה ׀ בְּךָ אֶת־הַמְּאֵרָה אֶת־
הַמְּהוּמָה וְאֶת־הַמִּגְעֶרֶת בְּכָל־מִשְׁלַח יָדְךָ אֲשֶׁר
תַּעֲשֶׂה עַד הִשָּׁמֶדְךָ וְעַד־אֲבָדְךָ מַהֵר מִפְּנֵי רֹעַ

כא מַעֲלָלֶיךָ אֲשֶׁר עֲזַבְתָּנִי: יַדְבֵּק יְהֹוָה בְּךָ אֶת־הַדָּבֶר
עַד כַּלֹּתוֹ אֹתְךָ מֵעַל הָאֲדָמָה אֲשֶׁר־אַתָּה בָא־

כב שָׁמָּה לְרִשְׁתָּהּ: יַכְּכָה יְהֹוָה בַּשַּׁחֶפֶת וּבַקַּדַּחַת
וּבַדַּלֶּקֶת וּבַחַרְחֻר וּבַחֶרֶב וּבַשִּׁדָּפוֹן וּבַיֵּרָקוֹן

כג וּרְדָפוּךָ עַד אָבְדֶךָ: וְהָיוּ שָׁמֶיךָ אֲשֶׁר עַל־רֹאשְׁךָ

כד נְחֹשֶׁת וְהָאָרֶץ אֲשֶׁר־תַּחְתֶּיךָ בַּרְזֶל: יִתֵּן יְהֹוָה אֶת־
מְטַר אַרְצְךָ אָבָק וְעָפָר מִן־הַשָּׁמַיִם יֵרֵד עָלֶיךָ

כה עַד הִשָּׁמְדָךְ: יִתֶּנְךָ יְהֹוָה ׀ נִגָּף לִפְנֵי אֹיְבֶיךָ בְּדֶרֶךְ
אֶחָד תֵּצֵא אֵלָיו וּבְשִׁבְעָה דְרָכִים תָּנוּס לְפָנָיו

Deuteronomy 28
20–25

20] The LORD will let loose against you calamity, panic, and frustration in all the enterprises you undertake, so that you shall soon be utterly wiped out because of your evildoing in forsaking Me.   **21]** The LORD will make pestilence cling to you, until He has put an end to you in the land which you are invading to occupy. **22]** The LORD will strike you with consumption, fever, and inflammation, with scorching heat and drought, with blight and mildew; they shall hound you until you perish.   **23]** The skies above your head shall be copper and the earth under you iron.   **24]** The LORD will make the rain of your land dust, and sand shall drop on you from the sky, until you are wiped out.

25] The LORD will put you to rout before your enemies; you shall march out against them by a single road, but flee from them by many roads; and you shall

---

20] *The Lord will let loose.* The Rabbis counted 98 specific curses, twice the number enumerated in Leviticus 26 [4].

22] *Consumption.* The meaning of this and the

following afflictions is not always certain.

Drought. חֶרֶב (*cherev*) usually means sword; originally the text was probably read חֹרֶב (*chorev*), which means drought, as, e.g., in Judg. 6:37.

302

כו וְהָיִיתָ לְזַעֲוָה לְכֹל מַמְלְכוֹת הָאָרֶץ: וְהָיְתָה נִבְלָתְךָ
לְמַאֲכָל לְכָל־עוֹף הַשָּׁמַיִם וּלְבֶהֱמַת הָאָרֶץ וְאֵין

כז מַחֲרִיד: יַכְּכָה יְהוָה בִּשְׁחִין מִצְרַיִם וּבַעְפֹלִים וּבַגָּרָב

כח וּבֶחָרֶס אֲשֶׁר לֹא־תוּכַל לְהֵרָפֵא: יַכְּכָה יְהוָה בְּשִׁגָּעוֹן

כט וּבְעִוָּרוֹן וּבְתִמְהוֹן לֵבָב: וְהָיִיתָ מְמַשֵּׁשׁ בַּצָּהֳרַיִם
כַּאֲשֶׁר יְמַשֵּׁשׁ הָעִוֵּר בָּאֲפֵלָה וְלֹא תַצְלִיחַ אֶת־
דְּרָכֶיךָ וְהָיִיתָ אַךְ עָשׁוּק וְגָזוּל כָּל־הַיָּמִים וְאֵין

ל מוֹשִׁיעַ: אִשָּׁה תְאָרֵשׂ וְאִישׁ אַחֵר יִשְׁגָּלֶנָּה בַּיִת תִּבְנֶה

לא וְלֹא־תֵשֵׁב בּוֹ כֶּרֶם תִּטַּע וְלֹא תְחַלְּלֶנּוּ: שׁוֹרְךָ טָבוּחַ

* כז ובטחורים קרי.
* ל ישכבנה קרי.

become a horror to all the kingdoms of the earth.   26] Your carcasses shall become food for all the birds of the sky and all the beasts of the earth, with none to frighten them off.

27] The LORD will strike you with the Egyptian inflammation, with hemorrhoids, boil-scars, and itch, from which you shall never recover.

28] The LORD will strike you with madness, blindness, and dismay.   **29]** You shall grope at noon as a blind man gropes in the dark; you shall not prosper in your ventures, but shall be constantly abused and robbed, with none to give help.

30] If you pay the bride-price for a wife, another man shall enjoy her. If you build a house, you shall not live in it. If you plant a vineyard, you shall not harvest it.

31] Your ox shall be slaughtered before your eyes, but you shall not eat of it; your

27] *Egyptian inflammation.* Likely a reference to a group of diseases considered prominent in Egypt: elephantiasis, dysentery, ophthalmia; see Deut. 7:15. Others believe the expression to refer to the plagues, see Exod. 15:26; especially the disease of boils, Exod. 9:9–10.

Hemmorrhoids. The Hebrew text says עֳפָלִים, but tradition, considering this too indelicate a word for communal reading, substituted טְחֹרִים

Today both words serve to describe the affliction with which the Philistines were reported to have been struck by divine fiat (I Sam. 5:6 ff.).

28] *Dismay.* Better, "confusion," the third of the afflictions of the mind: one cannot think, see straight, or understand.

30] *Enjoy her.* Another euphemism substituted for the written text which says "violate her"; compare verse 27. The three deprivations listed here

לְעֵינֶיךָ וְלֹא תֹאכַל מִמֶּנּוּ חֲמֹרְךָ גָּזוּל מִלְּפָנֶיךָ
וְלֹא יָשׁוּב לָךְ צֹאנְךָ נְתֻנוֹת לְאֹיְבֶיךָ וְאֵין לְךָ מוֹשִׁיעַ:

לב בָּנֶיךָ וּבְנֹתֶיךָ נְתֻנִים לְעַם אַחֵר וְעֵינֶיךָ רֹאוֹת וְכָלוֹת

לג אֲלֵיהֶם כָּל־הַיּוֹם וְאֵין לְאֵל יָדֶךָ: פְּרִי אַדְמָתְךָ
וְכָל־יְגִיעֲךָ יֹאכַל עַם אֲשֶׁר לֹא־יָדָעְתָּ וְהָיִיתָ רַק

לד עָשׁוּק וְרָצוּץ כָּל־הַיָּמִים: וְהָיִיתָ מְשֻׁגָּע מִמַּרְאֵה עֵינֶיךָ

לה אֲשֶׁר תִּרְאֶה: יַכְּכָה יְהוָה בִּשְׁחִין רָע עַל־הַבִּרְכַּיִם
וְעַל־הַשֹּׁקַיִם אֲשֶׁר לֹא־תוּכַל לְהֵרָפֵא מִכַּף רַגְלְךָ

לו וְעַד קָדְקֳדֶךָ: יוֹלֵךְ יְהוָה אֹתְךָ וְאֶת־מַלְכְּךָ אֲשֶׁר

Deuteronomy 28

32–36

ass shall be seized in front of you, and it shall not be returned to you; your flock shall be delivered to your enemies, with none to help you. **32]** Your sons and daughters shall be delivered to another people, while you look on; and your eyes shall strain for them constantly, but you shall be helpless. **33]** A people you do not know shall eat up the produce of your soil and all your gains; you shall be abused and downtrodden continually, **34]** until you are driven mad by what your eyes behold. **35]** The LORD will afflict you at the knees and thighs with a severe inflammation, from which you shall never recover—from the sole of your foot to the crown of your head.

36] The LORD will drive you, and the king you have set over you, to a nation

refer to pleasures so basic that a man was excused from army service in order to enjoy them; Deut. 20:5 ff.

32] *Helpless.* Or, "powerless." The word אֵל (*el*) means usually a (or the) divinity, but sometimes it also means "power," as in Gen. 31:29.

33] *A people you do not know.* More idiomatically:

". . . you have not even heard of."

35] *From the sole of your foot.* Compare Job 2:7. The English idiom reverses the order: "from head to toe."

36] *Will drive you.* After the defeat of the northern kingdom in 721 B.C.E. and the ensuing exile, everyone knew the terror of this threat.

תָּקִים עָלֶיךָ אֶל־גּוֹי אֲשֶׁר לֹא־יָדַעְתָּ אַתָּה וַאֲבֹתֶיךָ

לו וְעָבַדְתָּ שָּׁם אֱלֹהִים אֲחֵרִים עֵץ וָאָבֶן: וְהָיִיתָ לְשַׁמָּה לְמָשָׁל וְלִשְׁנִינָה בְּכֹל הָעַמִּים אֲשֶׁר־יְנַהֶגְךָ יְהֹוָה שָׁמָּה:

לז זֶרַע רַב תּוֹצִיא הַשָּׂדֶה וּמְעַט תֶּאֱסֹף כִּי יַחְסְלֶנּוּ

לח הָאַרְבֶּה: כְּרָמִים תִּטַּע וְעָבָדְתָּ וְיַיִן לֹא־תִשְׁתֶּה וְלֹא

לט תֶאֱגֹר כִּי תֹאכְלֶנּוּ הַתֹּלָעַת: זֵיתִים יִהְיוּ לְךָ בְּכָל־

מ גְּבוּלֶךָ וְשֶׁמֶן לֹא תָסוּךְ כִּי יִשַּׁל זֵיתֶךָ: בָּנִים וּבָנוֹת

מא תּוֹלִיד וְלֹא־יִהְיוּ לָךְ כִּי יֵלְכוּ בַּשֶּׁבִי: כָּל־עֵצְךָ

מב וּפְרִי אַדְמָתֶךָ יְיָרֵשׁ הַצְּלָצַל: הַגֵּר אֲשֶׁר בְּקִרְבְּךָ

מג יַעֲלֶה עָלֶיךָ מַעְלָה מָּעְלָה וְאַתָּה תֵרֵד מַטָּה מָּטָּה:

Deuteronomy 28
37–43

---

unknown to you or your fathers, where you shall serve other gods, of wood and stone. **37]** You shall be a consternation, a proverb, and a byword among all the peoples to which the LORD will drive you.

38] Though you take much seed out to the field, you shall gather in little, for the locust shall consume it. **39]** Though you plant vineyards and till them, you shall have no wine to drink or store, for the worm shall devour them. **40]** Though you have olive trees throughout your territory, you shall have no oil for anointment, for your olives shall drop off. **41]** Though you beget sons and daughters, they shall not remain with you, for they shall go into captivity. **42]** The cricket shall take over all the trees and produce of your land.

43] The stranger in your midst shall rise above you higher and higher, while

---

42] *Cricket.* צְלָצַל (*tzelatzal*), an onomatopoetic word that evokes a whirring sound.

43] *The stranger in your midst.* A temporary resi-

dent who would usually be there to conduct commercial affairs. He was not subject to Jewish law (though he enjoyed its protection) and hence would be exempt from the punishment allotted to the community.

מד הוּא יַלְוְךָ וְאַתָּה לֹא תַלְוֶנּוּ הוּא יִהְיֶה לְרֹאשׁ

מה וְאַתָּה תִּהְיֶה לְזָנָב: וּבָאוּ עָלֶיךָ כָּל־הַקְּלָלוֹת הָאֵלֶּה וּרְדָפוּךָ וְהִשִּׂיגוּךָ עַד הִשָּׁמְדָךְ כִּי־לֹא שָׁמַעְתָּ בְּקוֹל יְהֹוָה אֱלֹהֶיךָ לִשְׁמֹר מִצְוֹתָיו וְחֻקֹּתָיו אֲשֶׁר צִוָּךְ:

מו וְהָיוּ בְךָ לְאוֹת וּלְמוֹפֵת וּבְזַרְעֲךָ עַד־עוֹלָם: תַּחַת אֲשֶׁר לֹא־עָבַדְתָּ אֶת־יְהֹוָה אֱלֹהֶיךָ בְּשִׂמְחָה וּבְטוּב

מח לֵבָב מֵרֹב כֹּל: וְעָבַדְתָּ אֶת־אֹיְבֶיךָ אֲשֶׁר יְשַׁלְּחֶנּוּ יְהֹוָה בָּךְ בְּרָעָב וּבְצָמָא וּבְעֵירֹם וּבְחֹסֶר כֹּל וְנָתַן

מט עֹל בַּרְזֶל עַל־צַוָּארֶךָ עַד הִשְׁמִידוֹ אֹתָךְ: יִשָּׂא יְהֹוָה עָלֶיךָ גּוֹי מֵרָחֹק מִקְצֵה הָאָרֶץ כַּאֲשֶׁר יִדְאֶה הַנָּשֶׁר

you sink lower and lower: 44] he shall be your creditor, but you shall not be his; he shall be the head and you the tail.

45] All these curses shall befall you; they shall pursue you and overtake you, until you are wiped out, because you did not heed the LORD your God and keep the commandments and laws that He enjoined upon you.   46] They shall serve as signs and proofs against you and your offspring for all time.   47] Because you would not serve the LORD your God in joy and gladness over the abundance of everything, 48] you shall have to serve—in hunger and thirst, naked and lacking everything— the enemies whom the LORD will let loose against you. He will put an iron yoke upon your neck until He has wiped you out.

49] The LORD will bring a nation against you from afar, from the end of the earth, which will swoop down like the eagle—a nation whose language you do not

---

45] *All these curses.* This appears to be the beginning of an originally separate catalogue of maledictions.

46] *For all time.* Not in the literal sense, for repentance was always possible; Deut. 30:1 ff.

49–50] This catalogue has the earmarks of exilic experience, especially the vivid description of the conqueror in verse 50. The lack of compassion for the aged is ascribed to the Babylonians by Isa. 47:6 and Lam. 4:16; 5:12.

נ גּוֹי אֲשֶׁר לֹא־תִשְׁמַע לְשֹׁנוֹ: גּוֹי עַז פָּנִים אֲשֶׁר לֹא־

נא יִשָּׂא פָנִים לְזָקֵן וְנַעַר לֹא יָחֹן: וְאָכַל פְּרִי בְהֶמְתְּךָ

וּפְרִי־אַדְמָתְךָ עַד הִשָּׁמְדָךְ אֲשֶׁר לֹא־יַשְׁאִיר לְךָ

דָּגָן תִּירוֹשׁ וְיִצְהָר שְׁגַר אֲלָפֶיךָ וְעַשְׁתְּרֹת צֹאנֶךָ

נב עַד הַאֲבִידוֹ אֹתָךְ: וְהֵצַר לְךָ בְּכָל־שְׁעָרֶיךָ עַד

רֶדֶת חֹמֹתֶיךָ הַגְּבֹהֹת וְהַבְּצֻרוֹת אֲשֶׁר אַתָּה בֹּטֵחַ

בָּהֵן בְּכָל־אַרְצֶךָ וְהֵצַר לְךָ בְּכָל־שְׁעָרֶיךָ בְּכָל־

נג אַרְצְךָ אֲשֶׁר נָתַן יְהוָה אֱלֹהֶיךָ לָךְ: וְאָכַלְתָּ פְרִי־

בִטְנְךָ בְּשַׂר בָּנֶיךָ וּבְנֹתֶיךָ אֲשֶׁר נָתַן־לְךָ יְהוָה אֱלֹהֶיךָ

נד בְּמָצוֹר וּבְמָצוֹק אֲשֶׁר־יָצִיק לְךָ אֹיְבֶךָ: הָאִישׁ הָרַךְ

בְּךָ וְהֶעָנֹג מְאֹד תֵּרַע עֵינוֹ בְאָחִיו וּבְאֵשֶׁת חֵיקוֹ

נה וּבְיֶתֶר בָּנָיו אֲשֶׁר יוֹתִיר: מִתֵּת לְאַחַד מֵהֶם מִבְּשַׂר

Deuteronomy 28

50–55

understand,   50] a ruthless nation, that will show the old no regard and the young no mercy.   51] It shall devour the offspring of your cattle and the produce of your soil, until you have been wiped out, leaving you nothing of new grain, wine, or oil, of the calving of your herds and the lambing of your flocks, until it has brought you to ruin.   52] It shall shut you up in all your towns throughout your land until every mighty, towering wall in which you trust has come down. And when you are shut up in all your towns throughout your land that the LORD your God has given you,   53] you shall eat your own issue, the flesh of your sons and daughters that the LORD your God has given you, because of the desperate straits to which your enemy shall reduce you.   54] He who is most tender and fastidious among you shall be too mean to his brother and the wife of his bosom and the children he has spared   55] to share with any of them the flesh of the children that he eats,

53] *You shall eat.* That this actually happened is attested by Lam. 2:20 and 4:10 (see also commentary on Lev. 26:29 and Jer. 19:9). An Assyrian inscription from Uruk says: "We consumed the flesh of our sons and daughters" [5]. See further at verse 57.

בָּנָיו אֲשֶׁר יֹאכֵל מִבְּלִי הִשְׁאִיר־לוֹ כֹּל בְּמָצוֹר

נו וּבְמָצוֹק אֲשֶׁר יָצִיק לְךָ אֹיִבְךָ בְּכָל־שְׁעָרֶיךָ: הָרַכָּה

בְךָ וְהָעֲנֻגָּה אֲשֶׁר לֹא־נִסְּתָה כַף־רַגְלָהּ הַצֵּג עַל־

הָאָרֶץ מֵהִתְעַנֵּג וּמֵרֹךְ תֵּרַע עֵינָהּ בְּאִישׁ חֵיקָהּ

נז וּבִבְנָהּ וּבְבִתָּהּ: וּבְשִׁלְיָתָהּ הַיּוֹצֵת מִבֵּין רַגְלֶיהָ

וּבְבָנֶיהָ אֲשֶׁר תֵּלֵד כִּי־תֹאכְלֵם בְּחֹסֶר־כֹּל בַּסָּתֶר

בְּמָצוֹר וּבְמָצוֹק אֲשֶׁר יָצִיק לְךָ אֹיִבְךָ בִּשְׁעָרֶיךָ:

נח אִם־לֹא תִשְׁמֹר לַעֲשׂוֹת אֶת־כָּל־דִּבְרֵי הַתּוֹרָה הַזֹּאת

הַכְּתֻבִים בַּסֵּפֶר הַזֶּה לְיִרְאָה אֶת־הַשֵּׁם הַנִּכְבָּד

נט וְהַנּוֹרָא הַזֶּה אֵת יְהוָה אֱלֹהֶיךָ: וְהִפְלָא יְהוָה אֶת־

מַכֹּתְךָ וְאֵת מַכּוֹת זַרְעֶךָ מַכּוֹת גְּדֹלֹת וְנֶאֱמָנוֹת

because he has nothing else left as a result of the desperate straits to which your enemy shall reduce you in all your towns. **56]** And she who is most tender and dainty among you, so tender and dainty that she would never venture to set a foot on the ground, shall begrudge the husband of her bosom, and her son and her daughter, **57]** the afterbirth that issues from between her legs and the babies she bears; she shall eat them secretly, because of utter want, in the desperate straits to which your enemy shall reduce you in your towns.

58] If you fail to observe faithfully all the terms of this Teaching that are written in this book, to reverence this honored and awesome Name, the LORD your God, **59]** the LORD will inflict extraordinary plagues upon you and your offspring, strange

---

56] *Tender and dainty.* She did not walk but was carried. The image is applied by Isa. 47:1 to Babylon: "O Fair Chaldea; / Nevermore shall they call you / The tender and dainty one."

57] *Afterbirth.* This occurred during the siege of Samaria in the ninth century B.C.E. (II Kings 6:28).

58] *If you fail.* A third catalogue of curses.

59] *Lasting.* Literally, "true," that is, not apparent or temporary diseases.

ס וַחֲלָיִם רָעִים וְנֶאֱמָנִים: וְהֵשִׁיב בְּךָ אֵת כָּל־מַדְוֵה

סא מִצְרַיִם אֲשֶׁר יָגֹרְתָּ מִפְּנֵיהֶם וְדָבְקוּ בָּךְ: גַּם כָּל־
חֳלִי וְכָל־מַכָּה אֲשֶׁר לֹא כָתוּב בְּסֵפֶר הַתּוֹרָה

סב הַזֹּאת יַעְלֵם יְהֹוָה עָלֶיךָ עַד הִשָּׁמְדָךְ: וְנִשְׁאַרְתֶּם
בִּמְתֵי מְעָט* תַּחַת אֲשֶׁר הֱיִיתֶם כְּכוֹכְבֵי הַשָּׁמַיִם

סג לָרֹב כִּי־לֹא שָׁמַעְתָּ בְּקוֹל יְהֹוָה אֱלֹהֶיךָ: וְהָיָה
כַּאֲשֶׁר־שָׂשׂ יְהֹוָה עֲלֵיכֶם לְהֵיטִיב אֶתְכֶם וּלְהַרְבּוֹת
אֶתְכֶם כֵּן יָשִׂישׂ יְהֹוָה עֲלֵיכֶם לְהַאֲבִיד אֶתְכֶם
וּלְהַשְׁמִיד אֶתְכֶם וְנִסַּחְתֶּם מֵעַל הָאֲדָמָה אֲשֶׁר־אַתָּה

סד בָא־שָׁמָּה לְרִשְׁתָּהּ: וֶהֱפִיצְךָ יְהֹוָה בְּכָל־הָעַמִּים
מִקְצֵה הָאָרֶץ וְעַד־קְצֵה הָאָרֶץ וְעָבַדְתָּ שָּׁם אֱלֹהִים
אֲחֵרִים אֲשֶׁר לֹא־יָדַעְתָּ אַתָּה וַאֲבֹתֶיךָ עֵץ וָאָבֶן:

סה וּבַגּוֹיִם הָהֵם לֹא תַרְגִּיעַ וְלֹא־יִהְיֶה מָנוֹחַ לְכַף־

Deuteronomy 28
60–65

* סב קמץ בז"ק.

and lasting plagues, malignant and chronic diseases.   60] He will bring back upon you all the sicknesses of Egypt which you dreaded so, and they shall cling to you. 61] Moreover, the Lord will bring upon you all the other diseases and plagues that are not mentioned in this book of Teaching, until you are wiped out.   62] You shall be left a scant few, after having been as numerous as the stars in the skies, because you did not heed the command of the Lord your God.   63] And as the Lord once delighted in making you prosperous and many, so will the Lord now delight in causing you to perish and in wiping you out; you shall be torn from the land which you are about to invade and occupy.

64] The Lord will scatter you among all the peoples from one end of the earth to the other, and there you shall serve other gods, wood and stone, whom neither you nor your ancestors have experienced.   65] Yet even among those nations you shall find no peace, nor shall your foot find a place to rest. The Lord will give you

רַגְלֶךָ וְנָתַן יְהוָה לְךָ שָׁם לֵב רַגָּז וְכִלְיוֹן עֵינַיִם

סו וְדַאֲבוֹן נָפֶשׁ: וְהָיוּ חַיֶּיךָ תְּלֻאִים לְךָ מִנֶּגֶד וּפָחַדְתָּ

סז לַיְלָה וְיוֹמָם וְלֹא תַאֲמִין בְּחַיֶּיךָ: בַּבֹּקֶר תֹּאמַר

מִי־יִתֵּן עֶרֶב וּבָעֶרֶב תֹּאמַר מִי־יִתֵּן בֹּקֶר מִפַּחַד

לְבָבְךָ אֲשֶׁר תִּפְחָד וּמִמַּרְאֵה עֵינֶיךָ אֲשֶׁר תִּרְאֶה:

סח וְהֱשִׁיבְךָ יְהוָה מִצְרַיִם בׇּאֳנִיּוֹת בַּדֶּרֶךְ אֲשֶׁר אָמַרְתִּי

לְךָ לֹא־תֹסִיף עוֹד לִרְאֹתָהּ וְהִתְמַכַּרְתֶּם שָׁם לְאֹיְבֶיךָ

סט לַעֲבָדִים וְלִשְׁפָחוֹת וְאֵין קֹנֶה: ס אֵלֶּה דִּבְרֵי

הַבְּרִית אֲשֶׁר־צִוָּה יְהוָה אֶת־מֹשֶׁה לִכְרֹת אֶת־בְּנֵי

יִשְׂרָאֵל בְּאֶרֶץ מוֹאָב מִלְּבַד הַבְּרִית אֲשֶׁר־כָּרַת

אִתָּם בְּחֹרֵב:

* סו קמץ בז"ק.

there an anguished heart and eyes that pine and a despondent spirit. **66]** The life you face shall be precarious; you shall be in terror, night and day, with no assurance of survival. **67]** In the morning you shall say, "If only it were evening!" and in the evening you shall say, "If only it were morning!"—because of what your heart shall dread and your eyes shall see. **68]** The LORD will send you back to Egypt in galleys, by a route which I told you you should not see again. There you shall offer yourselves for sale to your enemies as male and female slaves, but none will buy.

69] These are the terms of the covenant which the LORD commanded Moses to conclude with the Israelites in the land of Moab, in addition to the covenant which He had made with them at Horeb.

66] *No assurance.* The same use of the root אמן as in verse 59, but with a negative modifier.

68] *Back to Egypt.* The ultimate threat.

None will buy. The ultimate humiliation: people will avoid you as cursed (a comparable English idiom would be "You will be a drug on the market").

69] *These are the terms.* A postscript to the preceding and also an introduction to what follows. Such bridges occur repeatedly in the Torah; see at Gen. 2:4.

Conclude . . . in the land of Moab. Meaning, in Moab the covenant was affirmed. The Deuteronomic code ends here.

In some versions verse 69 is noted as the first verse of chapter 29.

Comparisons and Uses

The catalogue invites comparisons with Exod. 23:20 ff. and Lev. 26:3 ff.

The Exodus passages are significantly different in that they are a notable exception to the expected preponderance of curses over blessings: the former are contained in a simple verse (verse 21) while the latter hold out fertility, health, and success in greater detail. The treatment in Leviticus bears a general resemblance to Deut. 28, and in some instances both have similar formulations. Nonetheless, the differences in style and wording are greater than the affinities; the Leviticus passages seem closer to Ezekiel, and Deut. 28 closer to Jeremiah.

It is most probable, therefore, that the three catalogues stem from three different traditions all of which elaborate on the consequences of God's covenant with His people [6]. It should also be noted that the Hebrew text directs itself to the individual Israelite rather than to the people as a whole, an approach often found in the Torah. The individual is considered responsible for the community; it is through his or her actions that the covenant is confirmed or endangered.

Jewish tradition has held that at one time or another all the curses of chapter 28 were fulfilled; still, Israel survived because it never totally forgot its God [7]. It became the custom, when the annual cycle of Torah readings would reach this chapter, to call up a volunteer for the curses (sometimes the synagogue's contract with the sexton included his obligation to "volunteer"). Such a person would often be called up, not in customary fashion, by his name, but rather as "He who wishes" [8]. The chapter itself would be read without interruption and in a low voice, a rule that applies also to the reading of Lev. 26:14–43. This practice reflects an old fear that, if one spoke too loudly of possible adversity, it might, in mysterious fashion, be invited to happen. In Reform services, the chapter is rarely, if ever, read in its entirety.

GLEANINGS

Despite

The promise of blessings (verse 2) is followed by the caution "if you heed" (verse 3). We are bidden to heed God *despite* the blessings.

CHASIDIC [9]

Blessed

"Blessed be you in the city" (verse 6) was interpreted by the Rabbis to mean that one should be part of a community and live close to a synagogue.

TALMUD [10]

In Your Comings . . . Your Goings (verse 6)

May you leave this world as you entered it: without sin.

TALMUD [11]

Another explanation: May your descendants not dishonor you.

MIDRASH [12]

Only if you leave this world in righteousness can you be said to have been blessed—and this can be said only of the fewest. For the majority, the rabbinic assessment applies that humanity would have been better off had it not been created at all.

CHATAM SOFER [13]

A Holy People (verse 9)

In the Book of Exodus (19:6), when calling Israel a holy people, the Torah uses the term *goy kadosh*. Here, at the end of the desert wandering, they are called *am kadosh*. In forty years they had progressed from *goy*, a nation like other nations, to *am*, a people with a spiritual purpose.

W. G. P.

The Nations

The Torah foresees that "all the peoples of the earth" will come to see God's glory (verse 10). The Hebrew (*amei ha-aretz*) can also be understood as "ignorant peoples of the earth,"[1] implying that it is Israel's task to bring God's knowledge to them.

THE GAON OF VILNA [14]

Gematria

The curses in chapter 28 contain 676 letters (in the Hebrew text), even as the word רָעוֹת ra-ot, evil occurrences) has the value of 676.[2]

Now note that God's holy name יְהוָֹה has the value of 26,[3] and 26 x 26 is 676. The hidden meaning is: The Torah threatens with רָעוֹת, but from all of them יְהוָֹה will rescue us.

CHASIDIC [15]

The Difference

In the curses of verses 17 and 18 "your basket and your kneading bowl" come before "the issue of your womb," that is, the material comes before the personal evil. In the corresponding blessings of verses 4 and 5 the order is reversed. When blessing, God begins with us; when cursing, He begins with our possessions. So He did also with Job.

D. HOFFMANN [16]

Never

The maledictions pronounced on Israel (especially the threat that the people will be "utterly wiped out," verse 20) are conditional; they take effect only if all of Israel, as a whole nation, de-

---

[1] In postbiblical Hebrew, *am ha-aretz* was understood as "peasant" and became a pejorative, the common term for a person ignorant of Torah and/or negligent in observing certain laws.

[2] ר=200; ע=70; ו=6; ת=400; added together they make 676.

[3] י=10; ה=5; ו=6; ה=5; together they make 26.

fects from the covenant. This is a degree of deterioration which has never taken place.

S. R. HIRSCH [17]

Joy of Service

We are castigated for failing to rejoice in God's service (verse 47), as it is said: "Let the heart of them rejoice that seek the Lord" (I Chron. 16:10). Someone searching for a lost article rejoices only when he finds it, but seekers after God rejoice even in the search. CHASIDIC [18]

You Shall Eat Your Own Issue (verse 53)

The text should be understood, not only in the dreadful literal sense, but also as applying to parents who are forced to eat their children's food and are cursed because of their dependence on them. CHASIDIC [19]

Horrors of War

(Describing scenes during the Roman siege of Jerusalem, 70 C.E.) It was now a miserable case, and a sight that would justly bring tears into our eyes, how men stood as to their food, while the more powerful had more than enough, and the weaker were lamenting (for want of it). But fam-ine overcomes all other passions, and it is destructive to nothing so much as to modesty; for what was otherwise worthy of reverence was in this case despised; insomuch that wives pulled the very morsels that their husbands were eating out of their very mouths, as did children to fathers, and what was still more to be pitied, so did the mothers do to their infants; and, when those that were most dear were perishing under their hands, they were not ashamed to take from them the very last drops that might preserve their lives; and, while they ate after this manner, yet were they not concealed in so doing. JOSEPHUS [20]

Past and Future

"In the morning you shall say, 'If only it were evening'" (verse 67), expressing a desperate wish for a better future. This is the way the Targum Yerushalmi understands the Hebrew. But the text can also be rendered as referring to the past: "If only it were (still yesterday) evening." This is the Talmud's way of reading [21], expressing the wish for a return of the past. For, reasons the Talmud, we know at least how things *were*, while we do not know how they *will be*—they might turn out to be worse.

Deuteronomy and Esarhaddon

Deuteronomy [22]

28:32: And the heavens over your head shall be brass, and the earth under you shall be iron.

28:27: The Lord will smite you with Egyptian inflammation . . . and with scars from which you shall never recover.

28:28-9: The Lord will smite you with madness and blindness, and confusion of mind, and you shall grope at noonday as the blind gropes in the darkness; and you shall not prosper in your ways, and you shall only be oppressed and robbed continually, and there shall be none to help you.

Esarhaddon [23]

528-31: May they (the gods) make your ground like iron so that no one can plough (cut) it. Just as rain does not fall from a brazen heaven, so may rain and dew not come upon your fields and pastures.

419-20: May Sin . . . the light of heaven and earth clothe you with leprosy; may he not order your entering into the presence of the gods or king.

422-4: May Shamash . . . not render you a just judgment (not give you a reliable decision); may he deprive you of the sight of your eyes (so that) they will wander about in darkness.

Deuteronomy	Esarhaddon
28:26: Your corpses shall be food for all birds of the heaven and for beasts of the earth.	425–7: May Ninurta . . . fell you with his swift arrow; may he fill the steppe with your corpses; may he feed your flesh to the vulture (and) the jackal.
28:30: You shall betroth a wife, and another man shall lie with her.	428–9: May Venus, the brightest of stars, make your wives lie in your enemy's lap while your eyes look (at them).
28:32: Your sons and your daughters shall be given to another people.	429–30a: May your sons not be masters of your house.
28:33: A nation which you have not known shall eat up the fruits of your ground and of your labors. . . .	430b: May a foreign enemy divide all your goods.

PART IV

Final Appeal and Farewell

With chapter 28 the Deuteronomic code came to its conclusion. Its last verse, 69,* serves as a bridge to what follows: a summation of Israel's history highlighted by the establishment of the covenant and, in covenantal style, a recapitulation of blessings and curses, with heaven and earth invoked as witnesses to this formal restatement.

Joshua is now formally appointed as the successor of Moses, and the book ends, much like the Book of Genesis, on a poetic note. A song comprises chapter 32, and a blessing, chapter 33. Then, in chapter 34, follows a brief epilogue telling of Moses' death.

The section contains two important theological statements: that future generations too will be bound by the covenant and that the book which testifies to it is openly accessible to all Israel and is not a hidden document in the possession of a special caste.

It has been noted that the section contains a number of words not found elsewhere in Deuteronomy. Examples are: לְמַעַן תַּשְׂכִּילוּ, in the sense of "that you may succeed" (29:8); אָלָה, "oath" or "sanction" (frequently in ch. 29); וַיִּתְּשֵׁם, "uprooted them" (29:27). Such linguistic variances suggest to some that these chapters came from a separate source which was later joined to the bulk of Deuteronomy. However, the integration of these chapters into the main text is such that they now form an essential part of the whole. They give the latter its literary climax and leave hearer and reader with a prophetic vision.

* In some versions (like King James, Revised Standard Version, New English Bible), Deut. 28:69 forms the first verse of chapter 29, and thus our 29:1 becomes their 29:2, etc. When referring to any verses for chapter 29, the latter method of counting will be listed in brackets, following our method of counting, i.e., 29:1 [2], 29:2 [3], etc.

The Last Oration

The final address of Moses follows the pattern made familiar by previous orations: the deeds of God are recounted as are the obligations arising therefrom for His subjects; the Sovereign's exclusive right to their loyalty is established, followed by a catalogue of consequential rewards and punishments. The address thus follows the outline of treaties between ruler and ruled which were encountered in Hittite and neo-Assyrian documents and which the Torah covenant reflects repeatedly.* The last oration does, however, present a novel feature (for Deuteronomy) in the reason given for the repetition of the covenantal framework: Israel had heretofore not fully understood the extent of God's works, because it had not had "a mind to understand or eyes to see or ears to hear" (29:3 [4])—a thought expressed in a similar way by Isaiah in his vision of God (6:9–10).

The address is characterized by broad and sweeping vigor, its words couched in striking prose, its images rich in compelling allusions. It lays down an enduring foundation for Israel's religion in that the Torah is declared to be valid for all generations, freely accessible to every member of the people, and not, as among other nations, the possession of a privileged few. The importance of these statements caused the liturgists of the Reform movement to include readings from chapter 29 in the afternoon service of Yom Kippur [1].

---

* See W. W. Hallo's essay. Von Rad calls verses 15–20 a mini-covenant and suggests that this may at one time have been the last part of Deuteronomy.

Style and choice of words distinguish the address from earlier orations. Some believe it to be a product of the Babylonian exile, when the punishments here predicted had already become bitter reality [2].

(A new weekly portion, *Nitzavim*, begins with 29:9 [10].)

א וַיִּקְרָ֤א מֹשֶׁה֙ אֶל־כָּל־יִשְׂרָאֵ֔ל וַיֹּ֖אמֶר אֲלֵהֶ֑ם אַתֶּ֣ם רְאִיתֶ֗ם אֵ֤ת כָּל־אֲשֶׁר֙ עָשָׂ֨ה יְהֹוָ֤ה לְעֵֽינֵיכֶם֙ בְּאֶ֣רֶץ

ב מִצְרַ֔יִם לְפַרְעֹ֥ה וּלְכָל־עֲבָדָ֖יו וּלְכָל־אַרְצֽוֹ: הַמַּסּוֹת֙ הַגְּדֹלֹ֔ת אֲשֶׁ֥ר רָא֖וּ עֵינֶ֑יךָ הָאֹתֹ֧ת וְהַמֹּפְתִ֛ים הַגְּדֹלִ֖ים

ג הָהֵֽם: וְלֹֽא־נָתַן֩ יְהֹוָ֨ה לָכֶ֥ם לֵב֙ לָדַ֔עַת וְעֵינַ֥יִם לִרְא֖וֹת

ד וְאָזְנַ֣יִם לִשְׁמֹ֑עַ עַ֖ד הַיּ֥וֹם הַזֶּֽה: וָאוֹלֵ֥ךְ אֶתְכֶ֛ם אַרְבָּעִ֥ים שָׁנָ֖ה בַּמִּדְבָּ֑ר לֹֽא־בָל֤וּ שַׂלְמֹֽתֵיכֶם֙ מֵֽעֲלֵיכֶ֔ם וְנַֽעַלְךָ֥

ה לֹֽא־בָֽלְתָ֖ה מֵעַ֥ל רַגְלֶֽךָ: לֶ֚חֶם לֹ֣א אֲכַלְתֶּ֔ם וְיַ֥יִן וְשֵׁכָ֖ר לֹ֣א שְׁתִיתֶ֑ם לְמַ֨עַן֙ תֵּֽדְע֔וּ כִּ֛י אֲנִ֥י יְהֹוָ֖ה

Deuteronomy 29
1–5

1] Moses summoned all Israel and said to them:

You have seen all that the Lord did before your very eyes in the land of Egypt, to Pharaoh and to all his courtiers and to his whole country: 2] the wondrous feats that you saw with your own eyes, those prodigious signs and marvels. 3] Yet to this day the Lord has not given you a mind to understand or eyes to see or ears to hear.

4] I led you through the wilderness forty years; the clothes on your back did not wear out, nor did the sandals on your feet; 5] you had no bread to eat and no wine or other liquor to drink—that you might know that I the Lord am your God.

29:3] [4] *The Lord has not given you a mind.* Despite all His labors in your behalf He could not make you appreciate Him. The idea appears to stem from a time of religious regression.

Traditional commentators wrestled with the problem posed by the text. Ibn Ezra said that the Torah here reasserts that God is the first giver of insight, and Maimonides stated that God is thus shown as the ultimate cause even of free choice [3].

Eyes . . . ears. Israel failed as a witness to God's deeds.

4] [5] *I led you.* A repetition of Deut. 8:2 ff., where the objective of God's action was said to be the education of Israel, to teach it that "man does not live on bread alone."

Note also the Hebrew terminology for "led": here it is a form of הָלַךְ not, as in Exodus and Numbers, of יָצָא and עָלָה.

5] [6] *Bread . . . wine . . . liquor.* These ordinary accoutrements of life were not available and only God sustained you.

I the Lord am your God. A formulaic ending to the statement.

<table>
<tr><td>דברים כט
ו–י</td><td>אֱלֹהֵיכֶם: וַתָּבֹאוּ אֶל־הַמָּקוֹם הַזֶּה וַיֵּצֵא סִיחֹן מֶלֶךְ־
חֶשְׁבּוֹן וְעוֹג מֶלֶךְ־הַבָּשָׁן לִקְרָאתֵנוּ לַמִּלְחָמָה וַנַּכֵּם:</td><td>ו</td></tr>
</table>

וַנִּקַּח אֶת־אַרְצָם וַנִּתְּנָהּ לְנַחֲלָה לָראוּבֵנִי וְלַגָּדִי וְלַחֲצִי

שֵׁבֶט הַמְנַשִּׁי: וּשְׁמַרְתֶּם אֶת־דִּבְרֵי הַבְּרִית הַזֹּאת

וַעֲשִׂיתֶם אֹתָם לְמַעַן תַּשְׂכִּילוּ אֵת כָּל־אֲשֶׁר תַּעֲשׂוּן:

Haftarah Ki Tavo, p. 466

פ   פ   פ

<table>
<tr><td>נצבים
Nitzavim
Deuteronomy 29
6–10</td><td>אַתֶּם נִצָּבִים הַיּוֹם כֻּלְּכֶם לִפְנֵי יְהֹוָה אֱלֹהֵיכֶם
רָאשֵׁיכֶם שִׁבְטֵיכֶם זִקְנֵיכֶם וְשֹׁטְרֵיכֶם כֹּל אִישׁ
יִשְׂרָאֵל: טַפְּכֶם נְשֵׁיכֶם וְגֵרְךָ אֲשֶׁר בְּקֶרֶב מַחֲנֶיךָ</td><td>ט

י</td></tr>
</table>

6] When you reached this place, Sihon king of Heshbon and Og king of Bashan came out to engage us in battle, but we defeated them.   **7]** We took their land and gave it to the Reubenites, the Gadites, and the half-tribe of Manasseh as their heritage.   **8]** Therefore observe faithfully all the terms of this covenant, that you may succeed in all that you undertake.

9] You stand this day, all of you, before the LORD your God—your tribal heads, your elders and your officials, all the men of Israel,   **10]** your children, your wives, even the stranger within your camp, from woodchopper to waterdrawer—

6] [7] *Sihon . . . Og.* See at 2:32 ff., 3:1 ff.

8] [9] *That you may succeed.* That you may after all understand God's marvelous deeds for you.

9] [10] *You stand this day.* The introduction which provides the setting for a ceremony of reaffirmation. The words "this day" are repeated six times in the oration and lend it rising emphasis.

10] [11] *Woodchopper . . . waterdrawer.* Lowly oc-

cupations; the Gibeonites were condemned to fill these tasks forever (Josh. 9:21 ff.). The expressions likely described declassed persons in Israel's midst.

In literary English, "hewers of wood and drawers of water" has come to stand for menial service.

Because one might have expected a contrast instead, which would have expressed the thought that everyone "from the lowest to the highest" was present, it has been suggested that both

יא מֵחֹטֵב עֵצֶיךָ עַד שֹׁאֵב מֵימֶיךָ: לְעׇבְרְךָ בִּבְרִית

יְהֹוָה אֱלֹהֶיךָ וּבְאָלָתוֹ אֲשֶׁר יְהֹוָה אֱלֹהֶיךָ כֹּרֵת

יב עִמְּךָ הַיּוֹם: לְמַעַן הָקִים־אֹתְךָ הַיּוֹם לוֹ לְעָם וְהוּא

יִהְיֶה־לְּךָ לֵאלֹהִים כַּאֲשֶׁר דִּבֶּר־לָךְ וְכַאֲשֶׁר נִשְׁבַּע

יג לַאֲבֹתֶיךָ לְאַבְרָהָם לְיִצְחָק וּלְיַעֲקֹב: וְלֹא אִתְּכֶם

לְבַדְּכֶם אָנֹכִי כֹּרֵת אֶת־הַבְּרִית הַזֹּאת וְאֶת־הָאָלָה

יד הַזֹּאת: כִּי אֶת־אֲשֶׁר יֶשְׁנוֹ פֹּה עִמָּנוּ עֹמֵד הַיּוֹם לִפְנֵי

טו יְהֹוָה אֱלֹהֵינוּ וְאֵת אֲשֶׁר אֵינֶנּוּ פֹּה עִמָּנוּ הַיּוֹם: כִּי־

אַתֶּם יְדַעְתֶּם אֵת אֲשֶׁר־יָשַׁבְנוּ בְּאֶרֶץ מִצְרָיִם וְאֵת

טז אֲשֶׁר־עָבַרְנוּ בְּקֶרֶב הַגּוֹיִם אֲשֶׁר עֲבַרְתֶּם: וַתִּרְאוּ

אֶת־שִׁקּוּצֵיהֶם וְאֵת גִּלֻּלֵיהֶם עֵץ וָאֶבֶן כֶּסֶף וְזָהָב

Deuteronomy 29
11–16

11] to enter into the covenant of the LORD your God, which the LORD your God is concluding with you this day, with its sanctions; 12] to the end that He may establish you this day as His people and be your God, as He promised you and as He swore to your fathers, Abraham, Isaac, and Jacob. 13] I make this covenant, with its sanctions, not with you alone, 14] but both with those who are standing here with us this day before the LORD our God and with those who are not with us here this day.

15] Well you know that we dwelt in the land of Egypt and that we passed through the midst of various other nations; 16] and you have seen the detestable things and the fetishes of wood and stone, silver and gold, that they keep.

"woodchopper" and "waterdrawer" had figurative meanings, the former a reference to Abraham (who took wood for the sacrifice of Isaac), the latter referring to Elijah (who used water in his contest with the Baal priests) [4].

11] [12] *To enter into the covenant.* The verb is עָבַר, which usually means "to pass over," an image

reminiscent of the "covenant between the pieces," Gen. 15.

The usual verb for concluding a pact is כָּרַת; other expressions are עָמַד (II Kings 23:3) and בָּא (II Chron. 15:12).

13] [14] *Not with you alone.* Compare Deut. 5:3 and commentary below.

דברים כט
יז–כ

אֲשֶׁר עִמָּהֶם: פֶּן־יֵשׁ בָּכֶם אִישׁ אוֹ־אִשָּׁה אוֹ מִשְׁפָּחָה
אוֹ־שֵׁבֶט אֲשֶׁר לְבָבוֹ פֹנֶה הַיּוֹם מֵעִם יְהוָה אֱלֹהֵינוּ
לָלֶכֶת לַעֲבֹד אֶת־אֱלֹהֵי הַגּוֹיִם הָהֵם פֶּן־יֵשׁ בָּכֶם
שֹׁרֶשׁ פֹּרֶה רֹאשׁ וְלַעֲנָה: וְהָיָה בְּשָׁמְעוֹ אֶת־דִּבְרֵי
הָאָלָה הַזֹּאת וְהִתְבָּרֵךְ בִּלְבָבוֹ לֵאמֹר שָׁלוֹם יִהְיֶה־
לִּי כִּי בִּשְׁרִרוּת לִבִּי אֵלֵךְ לְמַעַן סְפוֹת הָרָוָה אֶת־
הַצְּמֵאָה: לֹא־יֹאבֶה יְהוָה סְלֹחַ לוֹ כִּי אָז יֶעְשַׁן
אַף־יְהוָה וְקִנְאָתוֹ בָּאִישׁ הַהוּא וְרָבְצָה בּוֹ כָּל־הָאָלָה
הַכְּתוּבָה בַּסֵּפֶר הַזֶּה וּמָחָה יְהוָה אֶת־שְׁמוֹ מִתַּחַת
הַשָּׁמָיִם: וְהִבְדִּילוֹ יְהוָה לְרָעָה מִכֹּל שִׁבְטֵי יִשְׂרָאֵל

Deuteronomy 29
17–20

17] Perchance there is among you some man or woman, or some clan or tribe, whose heart is even now turning away from the LORD our God to go and worship the gods of those nations—perchance there is among you a stock sprouting poison weed and wormwood. **18]** When such a one hears the words of these sanctions, he may fancy himself immune, thinking, "I shall be safe, though I follow my own wilful heart"—to the utter ruin of moist and dry alike. **19]** The LORD will never forgive him; rather will the LORD's anger and passion rage against that man, till every sanction recorded in this book comes down upon him, and the LORD blots out his name from under heaven.

20] The LORD will single them out from all the tribes of Israel for misfortune,

17] [18] *Wormwood.* A bitter herb, genus *artemisia.*

18] [19] *Fancy himself immune.* Literally, "bless himself" and thereby ward off the curse.
  In medieval mystical practice, pronouncing the secret name of God was believed to have an immunizing effect.
  Moist and dry. Meaning, "everything." The combination of contrasting terms to express a totality is called "merism"; compare "good and bad" in Gen. 2:17, and the English "young and old" [5].

20] [21] *Single them out.* Hebrew, "it," that is, a tribe or clan with its members. It may be that the verse is a reference to the near destruction of one of the tribes (perhaps Simeon, which no longer appears in the blessing of Moses; see ch. 33).

כְּכֹל אָלוֹת הַבְּרִית הַכְּתוּבָה בְּסֵפֶר הַתּוֹרָה הַזֶּה:

כא וְאָמַר הַדּוֹר הָאַחֲרוֹן בְּנֵיכֶם אֲשֶׁר יָקוּמוּ מֵאַחֲרֵיכֶם וְהַנָּכְרִי אֲשֶׁר יָבֹא מֵאֶרֶץ רְחוֹקָה וְרָאוּ אֶת־מַכּוֹת הָאָרֶץ הַהִוא וְאֶת־תַּחֲלֻאֶיהָ אֲשֶׁר־חִלָּה יְהֹוָה בָּהּ:

כב גָּפְרִית וָמֶלַח שְׂרֵפָה כָל־אַרְצָהּ לֹא תִזָּרַע וְלֹא תַצְמִחַ וְלֹא־יַעֲלֶה בָהּ כָּל־עֵשֶׂב כְּמַהְפֵּכַת סְדֹם וַעֲמֹרָה אַדְמָה וּצְבֹיִים* אֲשֶׁר הָפַךְ יְהֹוָה בְּאַפּוֹ וּבַחֲמָתוֹ:

כג וְאָמְרוּ כָּל־הַגּוֹיִם עַל־מֶה עָשָׂה יְהֹוָה כָּכָה

כד לָאָרֶץ הַזֹּאת מֶה חֳרִי הָאַף הַגָּדוֹל הַזֶּה: וְאָמְרוּ עַל אֲשֶׁר עָזְבוּ אֶת־בְּרִית יְהֹוָה אֱלֹהֵי אֲבֹתָם אֲשֶׁר

כה כָּרַת עִמָּם בְּהוֹצִיאוֹ אֹתָם מֵאֶרֶץ מִצְרָיִם: וַיֵּלְכוּ וַיַּעַבְדוּ אֱלֹהִים אֲחֵרִים וַיִּשְׁתַּחֲווּ לָהֶם אֱלֹהִים אֲשֶׁר

Deuteronomy 29
21–25

* כב וצבוים קרי.

in accordance with all the sanctions of the covenant recorded in this book of Teaching. **21]** And later generations will ask—the children who succeed you, and foreigners who come from distant lands and see the plagues and diseases that the LORD has inflicted upon that land, **22]** all its soil devastated by sulfur and salt, beyond sowing and producing, no grass growing in it, just like the upheaval of Sodom and Gomorrah, Admah and Zeboiim, which the LORD overthrew in His fierce anger— **23]** all nations will ask, "Why did the LORD do thus to this land? Wherefore that awful wrath?" **24]** They will be told, "Because they forsook the covenant that the LORD, God of their fathers, made with them when He freed them from the land of Egypt; **25]** they turned to the service of other gods and worshiped them, gods whom they had not experienced and whom He had not allotted

22] [23] *Sulfur*. Older versions had "brimstone." *Upheaval of Sodom*. As told in Gen. 19:24 ff.

25] [26] *Not allotted to them*. See above, at 4:19–20.

325

כו לֹא־יְדָעוּם וְלֹא חָלַק לָהֶם: וַיִּחַר־אַף יְהוָה בָּאָרֶץ
הַהִוא לְהָבִיא עָלֶיהָ אֶת־כָּל־הַקְּלָלָה הַכְּתוּבָה

כז בַּסֵּפֶר הַזֶּה: וַיִּתְּשֵׁם יְהוָה מֵעַל אַדְמָתָם בְּאַף וּבְחֵמָה
וּבְקֶצֶף גָּדוֹל וַיַּשְׁלִכֵם אֶל־אֶרֶץ אַחֶרֶת כַּיּוֹם הַזֶּה:

כח הַנִּסְתָּרֹת לַיהוָה אֱלֹהֵינוּ וְהַנִּגְלֹת לָנוּ וּלְבָנֵינוּ עַד־
עוֹלָם לַעֲשׂוֹת אֶת־כָּל־דִּבְרֵי הַתּוֹרָה הַזֹּאת: ס

א וְהָיָה כִי־יָבֹאוּ עָלֶיךָ כָּל־הַדְּבָרִים הָאֵלֶּה הַבְּרָכָה
וְהַקְּלָלָה אֲשֶׁר נָתַתִּי לְפָנֶיךָ וַהֲשֵׁבֹתָ אֶל־לְבָבֶךָ בְּכָל־

ב הַגּוֹיִם אֲשֶׁר הִדִּיחֲךָ יְהוָה אֱלֹהֶיךָ שָׁמָּה: וְשַׁבְתָּ עַד־
יְהוָה אֱלֹהֶיךָ וְשָׁמַעְתָּ בְקֹלוֹ כְּכֹל אֲשֶׁר־אָנֹכִי מְצַוְּךָ
הַיּוֹם אַתָּה וּבָנֶיךָ בְּכָל־לְבָבְךָ וּבְכָל־נַפְשֶׁךָ:

Deuteronomy 29; 30
26–28; 1–2

to them.   26] So the LORD was incensed at that land and brought upon it all the
curses recorded in this book.   27] The LORD uprooted them from their soil in
anger, fury, and great wrath, and cast them into another land, as is still the case."

28] Concealed acts concern the LORD our God; but with overt acts, it is for us
and our children ever to apply all the provisions of this Teaching.

1] When all these things befall you—the blessing and the curse that I have set
before you—and you take them to heart amidst the various nations to which the
LORD your God has banished you,   2] and you return to the LORD your God, and
you and your children heed His command with all your heart and soul, just as I

27] [28] *Cast them.* וַיַּשְׁלִכֵם is marked by a large
ל in handwritten Torah scrolls. The reason for
this tradition is not known.
  The Mishnah applied the phrase to the Ten
Tribes exiled by the Assyrians. They were punished in accordance with the Torah's threat and
(according to R. Akiba) will also have no share in
the world-to-come [6].

28] [29] *Concealed acts.* The verse is not connected
with the preceding and appears to be a later insertion; note that it speaks of "us" instead of
"them." Perhaps it was at first a congregational
response to the Torah reading and then became
part of the text [7].
  For us and our children. Tradition prescribes
eleven dots to be placed over these words. On

ג וְשָׁב יְהֹוָה אֱלֹהֶיךָ אֶת־שְׁבוּתְךָ וְרִחֲמֶךָ וְשָׁב וְקִבֶּצְךָ

ד מִכָּל־הָעַמִּים אֲשֶׁר הֱפִיצְךָ יְהֹוָה אֱלֹהֶיךָ שָׁמָּה: אִם־

יִהְיֶה נִדַּחֲךָ בִּקְצֵה הַשָּׁמָיִם מִשָּׁם יְקַבֶּצְךָ יְהֹוָה

ה אֱלֹהֶיךָ וּמִשָּׁם יִקָּחֶךָ: וֶהֱבִיאֲךָ יְהֹוָה אֱלֹהֶיךָ אֶל־

הָאָרֶץ אֲשֶׁר־יָרְשׁוּ אֲבֹתֶיךָ וִירִשְׁתָּהּ וְהֵיטִבְךָ וְהִרְבְּךָ

ו מֵאֲבֹתֶיךָ: וּמָל יְהֹוָה אֱלֹהֶיךָ אֶת־לְבָבְךָ וְאֶת־לְבַב

זַרְעֶךָ לְאַהֲבָה אֶת־יְהֹוָה אֱלֹהֶיךָ בְּכָל־לְבָבְךָ וּבְכָל־

ז נַפְשְׁךָ לְמַעַן חַיֶּיךָ: וְנָתַן יְהֹוָה אֱלֹהֶיךָ אֵת כָּל־הָאָלוֹת

ח הָאֵלֶּה עַל־אֹיְבֶיךָ וְעַל־שֹׂנְאֶיךָ אֲשֶׁר רְדָפוּךָ: וְאַתָּה

תָשׁוּב וְשָׁמַעְתָּ בְּקוֹל יְהֹוָה וְעָשִׂיתָ אֶת־כָּל־מִצְוֹתָיו

Deuteronomy 30
3–8

enjoin upon you this day,   **3]** then the LORD your God, will restore your fortunes and take you back in love. He will bring you together again from all the peoples where the LORD your God has scattered you.   **4]** Even if your outcasts are at the ends of the world, from there the LORD your God will gather you, from there He will fetch you.   **5]** And the LORD your God will bring you to the land which your fathers occupied, and you shall occupy it; and He will make you more prosperous and more numerous than your fathers.

6] Then the LORD your God will open up your heart and the hearts of your offspring to love the LORD your God with all your heart and soul, in order that you may live.   **7]** The LORD your God will inflict all those curses upon the enemies and foes who persecuted you.   **8]** You, however, will again heed

this and the meaning of the verse, see commentary below.

30:4] *Ends of the world.* Literally, "of the heavens." See also the excerpt from Ps. 139 in Gleanings.

6] *Open up.* Literally, "circumcise"; compare 10:16, where Israel is bidden to "cut away the thickening" of its heart. Here, the verse adds the concept of God assisting in the process of repentance.

ט אֲשֶׁר אָנֹכִי מְצַוְּךָ הַיּוֹם: וְהוֹתִירְךָ יְהֹוָה אֱלֹהֶיךָ
בְּכֹל מַעֲשֵׂה יָדֶךָ בִּפְרִי בִטְנְךָ וּבִפְרִי בְהֶמְתְּךָ
וּבִפְרִי אַדְמָתְךָ לְטֹבָה כִּי יָשׁוּב יְהֹוָה לָשׂוּשׂ
עָלֶיךָ לְטוֹב כַּאֲשֶׁר־שָׂשׂ עַל־אֲבֹתֶיךָ: י כִּי תִשְׁמַע
בְּקוֹל יְהֹוָה אֱלֹהֶיךָ לִשְׁמֹר מִצְוֹתָיו וְחֻקֹּתָיו
הַכְּתוּבָה בְּסֵפֶר הַתּוֹרָה הַזֶּה כִּי תָשׁוּב אֶל־יְהֹוָה
יא אֱלֹהֶיךָ בְּכָל־לְבָבְךָ וּבְכָל־נַפְשֶׁךָ: ס כִּי הַמִּצְוָה
הַזֹּאת אֲשֶׁר אָנֹכִי מְצַוְּךָ הַיּוֹם לֹא־נִפְלֵאת הִוא
יב מִמְּךָ וְלֹא־רְחֹקָה הִוא: לֹא בַשָּׁמַיִם הִוא לֵאמֹר
מִי יַעֲלֶה־לָּנוּ הַשָּׁמַיְמָה וְיִקָּחֶהָ לָּנוּ וְיַשְׁמִעֵנוּ אֹתָהּ
יג וְנַעֲשֶׂנָּה: וְלֹא־מֵעֵבֶר לַיָּם הִוא לֵאמֹר מִי יַעֲבָר־לָנוּ
אֶל־עֵבֶר הַיָּם וְיִקָּחֶהָ לָּנוּ וְיַשְׁמִעֵנוּ אֹתָהּ וְנַעֲשֶׂנָּה:

the LORD and obey all His commandments which I enjoin upon you this day.
9] And the LORD your God will grant you abounding prosperity in all your undertakings, in the issue of your womb, the offspring of your cattle, and the
produce of your soil. For the LORD will again delight in your well-being, as He
did in that of your fathers,   10] since you will be heeding the LORD your
God and keeping His commandments and laws that are recorded in this
book of the Teaching—once you return to the LORD your God with all your heart
and soul.

11] Surely, this Instruction which I enjoin upon you this day is not too baffling
for you, nor is it beyond reach.   12] It is not in the heavens, that you should say,
"Who among us can go up to the heavens and get it for us and impart it to us, that
we may observe it?"   13] Neither is it beyond the sea, that you should say, "Who
among us can cross to the other side of the sea and get it for us and impart it to us,

---

דברים ל
יד–יט

יד כִּי־קָרוֹב אֵלֶיךָ הַדָּבָר מְאֹד בְּפִיךָ וּבִלְבָבְךָ
לַעֲשׂתוֹ: ס טו רְאֵה נָתַתִּי לְפָנֶיךָ הַיּוֹם אֶת־הַחַיִּים
טז וְאֶת־הַטּוֹב וְאֶת־הַמָּוֶת וְאֶת־הָרָע: אֲשֶׁר אָנֹכִי מְצַוְּךָ
הַיּוֹם לְאַהֲבָה אֶת־יְהוָֹה אֱלֹהֶיךָ לָלֶכֶת בִּדְרָכָיו
וְלִשְׁמֹר מִצְוֹתָיו וְחֻקֹּתָיו וּמִשְׁפָּטָיו וְחָיִיתָ וְרָבִיתָ
וּבֵרַכְךָ יְהוָֹה אֱלֹהֶיךָ בָּאָרֶץ אֲשֶׁר־אַתָּה בָא־שָׁמָּה
יז לְרִשְׁתָּהּ: וְאִם־יִפְנֶה לְבָבְךָ וְלֹא תִשְׁמָע וְנִדַּחְתָּ
יח וְהִשְׁתַּחֲוִיתָ לֵאלֹהִים אֲחֵרִים וַעֲבַדְתָּם: הִגַּדְתִּי
לָכֶם הַיּוֹם כִּי אָבֹד תֹּאבֵדוּן לֹא־תַאֲרִיכֻן יָמִים
עַל־הָאֲדָמָה אֲשֶׁר אַתָּה עֹבֵר אֶת־הַיַּרְדֵּן לָבוֹא
יט שָׁמָּה לְרִשְׁתָּהּ: הַעִדֹתִי בָכֶם הַיּוֹם אֶת־הַשָּׁמַיִם וְאֶת־
הָאָרֶץ הַחַיִּים וְהַמָּוֶת נָתַתִּי לְפָנֶיךָ הַבְּרָכָה וְהַקְּלָלָה

Deuteronomy 30
14–19

that we may observe it?"   14] No, the thing is very close to you, in your mouth and in your heart, to observe it.

15] See, I set before you this day life and prosperity, death and adversity. 16] For I command you this day, to love the LORD your God, to walk in His ways, and to keep His commandments, His laws, and His rules, that you may thrive and increase, and that the LORD your God may bless you in the land which you are about to invade and occupy.   17] But if your heart turns away and you give no heed, and are lured into the worship and service of other gods,   18] I declare to you this day that you shall certainly perish; you shall not long endure on the soil which you are crossing the Jordan to invade and occupy.   19] I call heaven and earth to witness against you this day: I have put before you life and death, blessing

---

14] *In your mouth.* As you retell the commands of Torah. Oral transmission was of supreme importance since not many people could read.

329

דברים ל

Deuteronomy 30

20

כ וּבָחַרְתָּ֙ בַּֽחַיִּ֔ים לְמַ֨עַן תִּֽחְיֶ֜ה אַתָּ֣ה וְזַרְעֶֽךָ: לְאַֽהֲבָה֙ אֶת־יְהֹוָ֣ה אֱלֹהֶ֔יךָ לִשְׁמֹ֥עַ בְּקֹל֖וֹ וּלְדָבְקָה־ב֑וֹ כִּ֣י ה֤וּא חַיֶּ֨יךָ֙ וְאֹ֣רֶךְ יָמֶ֔יךָ לָשֶׁ֣בֶת עַל־הָֽאֲדָמָ֗ה אֲשֶׁר֩ נִשְׁבַּ֨ע יְהֹוָ֧ה לַֽאֲבֹתֶ֛יךָ לְאַבְרָהָ֥ם לְיִצְחָ֖ק וּֽלְיַֽעֲקֹ֑ב לָתֵ֥ת לָהֶֽם:

Haftarah Nitzavim, p. 474

and curse. Choose life—if you and your offspring would live—   20] by loving the LORD your God, heeding His commands, and holding fast to Him. For thereby you shall have life and shall long endure upon the soil that the LORD your God swore to Abraham, Isaac, and Jacob to give to them.

330

Commitment for the Future

"I make this covenant . . . with those who are standing here . . . and with those who are not here with us this day" (29:13, 14). The reference is to future generations: they too are committed to the covenant, even though they had no voice in concluding it. This concept is essential to the continuity of Torah and of the people who are its bearers; it was expressed at the beginning of Deuteronomy and is now restated near the end (see commentary on 1:6–46, "Two Generations").[1]

That the present can and does commit the future to some extent is unquestionable. We are who we are because of our ancestors and of their achievements and failures. The fifteenth-century commentator Isaac Abarbanel compared Israel to a debtor: even as his estate is responsible for an unpaid loan, so Israel remains in debt to God for its liberation from Egypt and the gift of Eretz Yisrael. This is what the Midrash meant when it said that the souls of all the generations were present when the covenant was concluded.

But may a child not reject its inheritance? May a future Israel not choose to abandon God and Torah? It will not do so and it cannot, Abarbanel avowed—and Jewish history to this day has upheld this judgment. Already Ezekiel's strong affirmation may have referred to this question: "As I live—declares the Lord God—I *will* reign over you . . . I *will* bring you into the bond of the covenant" (Ezek. 20:33 ff.). Individuals can defect; the people as a whole cannot [8].

The Accessibility of Torah

The Torah belongs to, and therefore is the responsibility of, all the people. Clearly, the words of Deut. 30:11–14 emphasize this principle and at the same time reject the notion that Torah is secret lore, accessible only to a chosen few.

Israel had its priests, but, unlike those of Egypt's temples or of Greece's oracle places, their knowledge of God's law was not exclusive. Because of their training, knowledge, and position, their decisions had superior weight (as did those of the Rabbis in post-biblical history). However, Israel's priests dealt at all times with a law and a tradition available to all. This is the obvious meaning of verse 12: "(The Torah) is not in the heavens, that you should say, 'Who among us can go up to the heavens and get it for us and impart it to us, that we may observe it?' " The text provides its own affirmation: "No, the thing is very close to you, in your mouth and in your heart, to observe it" (verse 14).

In the religious traditions of antiquity such a commitment to universal accessibility was unique, and it had an even more profound effect on the Jewish people as the centuries passed. The study of Torah became the supreme preoccupation of the Jew; none was too humble to be excluded from the mitzvah of learning and none too prominent to be excused from it. It was a command, averred the Mishnah, that outweighed all others, for everything flowed from it [9].

The Torah, said a second-century Sage, speaks in a language that human beings can grasp [10]; it deals with the overt, not the hidden. Only the latter belongs to the realm of God, while the realm of Torah is open and accessible to all. This is the meaning implied in Deut. 29:28,[2] and stated unequivo-

---

[1] The text seems to assume that the future generations are those born into the nation as well as those who will join it voluntarily. The nation as a whole may need to reaffirm the covenant from time to time, while individuals are bound by their history and their people.

[2] The Talmud records a controversy on this verse between R. Yehudah and R. Nehemiah. Both took

cally by the Psalmist (115:16):

> The heavens belong to the Lord,
> But the earth He gave over to man.

The Torah makes clear that, though there are limits to human knowledge, these limits do not apply to the will of God as revealed in the Torah. Interpretation and elucidation may be needed, but these will be supplied by Israel and not by God.

Turning Back

In its first ten phrases Chapter 30 contains an idea fundamental to the Book of Deuteronomy and to biblical thought in general. Seven times the text uses forms of the word שׁוּב (*shuv*, turn),[3] a stylistic device that underscores the central thought: If Israel turns back to the God it has forsaken, God will graciously receive it back in turn.

In Deuteronomy the concept of turning is squarely rooted in the covenant relationship between God, the suzerain, and Israel, the servant and vassal. In Egypt, Israel had exchanged the lordship of Pharaoh for the mastery of God and, at Sinai, had confirmed the new allegiance dramatically. However, on entering the Land, exposed to the influence of Canaanite religions, Israel's loyalty to its suzerain had wavered and even lapsed. The people had strayed from single allegiance and turned to other gods, and it is such straying—and the need for turning back—that forms the subject of our chapter.

This modality of the suzerain-vassal rela-tionship governs the Deuteronomic idea of God's covenant with Israel. When Israel breaches the covenant God turns away and surrenders His people to misfortune. When Israel returns to Him, He too returns and "repents of His anger."[4] The reaffirmation of the covenant, which is the subject of chapters 29 and 30, thus contains an element of mutuality in its provision for restoration: the covenant may be broken, but it will not be abrogated, for the possibility of mutual return keeps it alive.

This view of turn and return (expressed by the term "*shuv*") antedates the formulation of the Deuteronomic text and most likely had its roots in earlier centuries, when the Sinaitic covenant still found its echo in the suzerain-vassal treaties of the ancient Near East. In Hosea (eighth century, B.C.E.), a shift is observable: now the covenant is likened to marriage, and though the wife is still subject to her master—the Hebrew for husband is *ba-al*, master—the old suzerain-vassal typology begins to pale. Turning is now identified with an attitude of the heart as much as a national show of loyalty, and the prophets, especially Hosea and Jeremiah, insistently address themselves to this theme. The need for a new national heart becomes a cornerstone of Israel's religious perceptions.

Turning back begins in Deuteronomy and Prophets as a possibility and challenge for all Israel and inevitably thereby becomes an obligation and opportunity for each indi-

---

Deut. 29:28 to refer to sin, the former stating that God holds Israel responsible for all sins committed by members of the people, even when these sins are hidden, whereas the latter said that all Israel was responsible only for overt transgressions. The verse was believed to have a concealed meaning hinted at by the Masoretes who placed diacritical dots over eleven letters of the phrase: לָנוּ וּלְבָנֵינוּ עַד עוֹלָם [11].
[3] The English translation does not convey this seven-fold occurrence. Forms of שׁוּב are found in verse 1 ("take them"); verse 2 ("return"); verse 3 ("restore," "bring again"); verse 8 ("you will again"); verse 9 ("the Lord will again"); and verse 10 ("return"). This multiple use of שׁוּב occurs also in Psalm 126, verse 1 ("restores"), and again in verse 4.
[4] The Midrash goes even further and says that God goes into exile with Israel and returns with it; see Gleanings below.

vidual (see, e.g., Jer. 36:3). The word *"teshu-vah"* does not yet occur in biblical writing in the meaning of repentance; when it appears in rabbinic sources—after the destruction of the Temple and the sacrificial cult [12]—it deals usually with an *individual's* (rather than the whole people's) transgression. God stands ready to forgive a sinner if he or she truly repents. In the order of the universe such repentance is seen to be of primal importance: of the seven things created by God even before Creation, says the Talmud, Torah stood first and repentance second.[5]

Nowhere is the difference between the spiritual life and its material counterpart more clearly seen than in the possibility of turning. In the world of nature the principle of irreversibility obtains: events move in one direction only, and once they have happened they cannot be undone. Not so with repentance: it provides for turning back the clock through a joining of human will and divine acceptance. In that sense one can understand the saying of one Sage who proclaimed the repentant sinner to be superior to one who had never sinned [14]. He meant that the reversible life of the spirit was more significant than the irreversible sweep of the rest of existence. That is why Yom Kippur became Jewry's most important holy day and the ever-present possibility of *teshuvah*, a cornerstone of Judaism.

---

[5] The other five are paradise, hell, the throne of glory, the temple, and the name of the Messiah. The inclusion of each of these is derived from a different biblical verse. That of repentance is derived from Psalm 90:2–3: "Before You brought forth the earth and the world ... You decreed, 'Return, you mortals!'" [13].

GLEANINGS

Curses and Repentance

Chapter 28 (with its imprecations) precedes chapters 29 and 30 (which extol turning back). The object of chapter 28 is to lead Israel to repent.

SEFAT EMET [15]

Concealed and Revealed (Deut. 29:28)

The final time of redemption is concealed but not its beginning, for it begins with Israel's repentance: "It is for us and our children ever to apply...." KETAV SOFER [16]

There are those who transgress secretly but perform mitzvot in public, and others who transgress openly but perform mitzvot secretly.

CHASIDIC [17]

Return

In both 30:2 and 30:10 the Torah says "return to the Lord," but the Hebrew has a subtle difference: in verse 2 the word "to" is עַד, in verse 10 it is אֶל.[6] The latter signifies a higher form of repentance, for it adds "with all your heart and soul."

MALBIM [18]

Do not read עַד (to) but עֵד (witness). When you return you will be witness to the possibility of repentance. CHASIDIC [19]

God Will Return Your Captivity (Deut. 30:3)

The word "return"[7] in this translation functions as a transitive verb, but in the Hebrew the word appears to be intransitive (שָׁב). If understood in this fashion, one would see the text to say that God himself dwells in exile with Israel

and "will return *with* (אֶת) your captivity."

RASHI [20]

Liturgy

It is customary to pronounce special blessings on the Sabbath before the arrival of the new moon (*Birkat ha-Chodesh*). The only exception is Shabbat Nitzavim (when Deut. 29:9 ff. is read), which is always the last Sabbath in the month of Elul, just before the arrival of Rosh Hashanah.

Why this omission? Because on this Sabbath God himself blesses the new month and the new year. CHASIDIC [21]

Torah Can Be Learned (Deut. 30:11)

Fools attempt to learn the whole Torah all at once, and when they fail they give up altogether. The wise study a little every day.

MIDRASH [22]

Astrology

When we are told that the Torah is not in the heavens (30:12), we are to understand that it is not found among the astrologers. MIDRASH [23]

The Reach of God

Psalm 139:7–10 speak poetically of the omnipresence of God, expanding on the theme of Deut. 30:4.

If I ascend to heaven, You are there;

If I descend to Sheol, You are there too.

If I take wing with the dawn to come to rest on the western horizon, even there Your hand will be guiding me, Your right hand be holding me fast.

---

[6] Only Buber-Rosenzweig's translation transmits this distinction, rendering עַד as *hin* (turn toward Him) and אֶל as *um* (turn back to Him).

[7] This is an alternate understanding for "restore" your fortunes.

Moses Prepares for Death

The discourses are now concluded and the Torah turns to the narrative of Moses' last days: his preparations for death, the appointment of Joshua as his successor, and the final instructions he issues to Joshua and the Levites. Then, in chapters 32 and 33, two poems follow—one a song, the other a blessing—and, in chapter 34, the account of the leader's death, which concludes the book.

Chapter 31 does not present a straightforward account. After introductory words of parting (verses 1–8), Moses charges the priests to write down the teaching and to have it read to the people once every seven years, during the Feast of Booths.

Then, with verse 14, a section begins that clearly did not originally form part of the account. It interrupts the story (which continues in verse 24) and contains Hebrew terms not otherwise found in Deuteronomy.*

(Chapter 31 constitutes a complete weekly Torah portion, *Vayelech*, the shortest in the Torah.)

---

* Examples are: Tent of Meeting, verse 14; alien gods, verse 16; break My covenant, verses 16, 20; hide My countenance, verse 17; plan (*yetzer*, as in Gen. 6:5), verse 21.

 פ   פ   פ

וילך

דברים לא

א–ד

Vayelech

Deuteronomy 31

1–4

א וַיֵּלֶךְ מֹשֶׁה וַיְדַבֵּר אֶת־הַדְּבָרִים הָאֵלֶּה אֶל־כָּל־

ב יִשְׂרָאֵל: וַיֹּאמֶר אֲלֵהֶם בֶּן־מֵאָה וְעֶשְׂרִים שָׁנָה אָנֹכִי

הַיּוֹם לֹא־אוּכַל עוֹד לָצֵאת וְלָבוֹא וַיהוָה אָמַר אֵלַי

ג לֹא תַעֲבֹר אֶת־הַיַּרְדֵּן הַזֶּה: יְהוָה אֱלֹהֶיךָ הוּא

עֹבֵר לְפָנֶיךָ הוּא־יַשְׁמִיד אֶת־הַגּוֹיִם הָאֵלֶּה מִלְּפָנֶיךָ

וִירִשְׁתָּם יְהוֹשֻׁעַ הוּא עֹבֵר לְפָנֶיךָ כַּאֲשֶׁר דִּבֶּר

ד יְהוָה: וְעָשָׂה יְהוָה לָהֶם כַּאֲשֶׁר עָשָׂה לְסִיחוֹן

וּלְעוֹג מַלְכֵי הָאֱמֹרִי וּלְאַרְצָם אֲשֶׁר הִשְׁמִיד אֹתָם:

1] Moses went and spoke these things to all Israel.   **2]** He said to them:

I am now one hundred and twenty years old, I can no longer be active. Moreover, the LORD has said to me, "You shall not go across yonder Jordan."   **3]** The LORD your God Himself will cross over at your head; and He will wipe out those nations from your path and you shall dispossess them.—Joshua is the one who shall cross at your head, as the LORD has spoken.—   **4]** The LORD will do to them as He did to Sihon and Og, kings of the Amorites, and to their countries, when He

31:1] *Moses went and spoke.* Proceeded to speak. A similar English idiom is, "went ahead and spoke."

These things. Of which he had spoken before (so the Septuagint), or of which he was about to speak. Such ambiguity is frequently found in the Torah in sentences that constitute a bridge between two accounts; see, for instance, Gen. 2:4.

2] *One hundred and twenty years old.* He spanned three generations of forty years each. One hundred and twenty is a figure which, as the multiple of the first five whole numbers ($1 \times 2 \times 3 \times 4 \times 5$), came to represent in the Torah the ideal of longevity. It also combines the decimal and duo-decimal systems (10×12). (A popular Jewish wish is, "May you live to 120 years.")

The two men who preceded and succeeded Moses in his leadership, Joseph and Joshua, fell short of his age, both dying at 110 (the ideal life span in Egypt), a figure which was also a symbolic construct: $5^2 + 6^2 + 7^2$. Similarly, Abraham, Isaac, and Jacob were said to have reached ages of structured length: Abraham, 175 (7×5^2); Isaac, 180 (5×6^2); Jacob, 147 (3×7^2) [1].

Be active. Literally, "come and go." But he was not senile, see Deut. 34:7.

Moreover. A better rendering of וְ would be "in any case." Even were I still in full strength I could not lead you across the Jordan. So, while Joshua will now stand at your head, your real leader, as always, will be God.

4] *Sihon and Og.* Compare Deut. 3:21. On Sihon's fate see 2:32 ff.; on Og's, 3:1 ff.

336

ה וּנְתָנָם יְהֹוָה לִפְנֵיכֶם וַעֲשִׂיתֶם לָהֶם כְּכָל־הַמִּצְוָה אֲשֶׁר

ו צִוִּיתִי אֶתְכֶם: חִזְקוּ וְאִמְצוּ אַל־תִּירְאוּ וְאַל־תַּעַרְצוּ

מִפְּנֵיהֶם כִּי יְהֹוָה אֱלֹהֶיךָ הוּא הַהֹלֵךְ עִמָּךְ לֹא

ז יַרְפְּךָ וְלֹא יַעַזְבֶךָּ: ס וַיִּקְרָא מֹשֶׁה לִיהוֹשֻׁעַ

וַיֹּאמֶר אֵלָיו לְעֵינֵי כָל־יִשְׂרָאֵל חֲזַק וֶאֱמָץ כִּי אַתָּה

תָּבוֹא אֶת־הָעָם הַזֶּה אֶל־הָאָרֶץ אֲשֶׁר נִשְׁבַּע יְהֹוָה

ח לַאֲבֹתָם לָתֵת לָהֶם וְאַתָּה תַּנְחִילֶנָּה אוֹתָם: וַיהֹוָה

הוּא הַהֹלֵךְ לְפָנֶיךָ הוּא יִהְיֶה עִמָּךְ לֹא יַרְפְּךָ וְלֹא

ט יַעַזְבֶךָּ לֹא תִירָא וְלֹא תֵחָת: וַיִּכְתֹּב מֹשֶׁה אֶת־

הַתּוֹרָה הַזֹּאת וַיִּתְּנָהּ אֶל־הַכֹּהֲנִים בְּנֵי לֵוִי הַנֹּשְׂאִים

Deuteronomy 31
5–9

wiped them out.   5] The LORD will deliver them up to you, and you shall deal with them in full accordance with the Instruction that I have enjoined upon you. 6] Be strong and resolute, be not in fear or in dread of them; for the LORD your God Himself marches with you: He will not fail you or forsake you.

7] Then Moses called Joshua and said to him in the sight of all Israel: Be strong and resolute, for it is you who shall go with this people into the land that the LORD swore to their fathers to give them, and it is you who shall apportion it to them. 8] And the LORD Himself will go before you. He will be with you; He will not fail you or forsake you. Fear not and be not dismayed!

9] Moses wrote down this Teaching and gave it to the priests, sons of Levi, who

5] *The Instruction that I have enjoined.* Referring to Deut. 7:1 ff., where intermarriage with these nations is prohibited and their destruction demanded.

7] *In the sight of all Israel.* That is, publicly.

Be strong and resolute. חֲזַק וֶאֱמָץ (*chazak ve-ematz*). Here, Moses says this to Joshua; God will be heard to repeat these words to Joshua after

Moses' death; and the people too will address them to their new leader (Josh. 1:6, 9, 18).

It is you. And not I, Moses.

9] *Wrote down this Teaching.* That is, the Book of Deuteronomy. But older commentators believed this to refer to the whole Torah and considered it proof that the Torah was the work of Moses.

To the priests . . . and to all the elders. He gave

י אֶת־אֲרוֹן בְּרִית יְהוָֹה וְאֶל־כָּל־זִקְנֵי יִשְׂרָאֵל: וַיְצַו
מֹשֶׁה אוֹתָם לֵאמֹר מִקֵּץ שֶׁבַע שָׁנִים בְּמֹעֵד שְׁנַת

יא הַשְּׁמִטָּה בְּחַג הַסֻּכּוֹת: בְּבוֹא כָל־יִשְׂרָאֵל לֵרָאוֹת
אֶת־פְּנֵי יְהוָֹה אֱלֹהֶיךָ בַּמָּקוֹם אֲשֶׁר יִבְחָר תִּקְרָא

יב אֶת־הַתּוֹרָה הַזֹּאת נֶגֶד כָּל־יִשְׂרָאֵל בְּאָזְנֵיהֶם: הַקְהֵל
אֶת־הָעָם הָאֲנָשִׁים וְהַנָּשִׁים וְהַטַּף וְגֵרְךָ אֲשֶׁר בִּשְׁעָרֶיךָ
לְמַעַן יִשְׁמְעוּ וּלְמַעַן יִלְמְדוּ וְיָרְאוּ אֶת־יְהוָֹה אֱלֹהֵיכֶם

יג וְשָׁמְרוּ לַעֲשׂוֹת אֶת־כָּל־דִּבְרֵי הַתּוֹרָה הַזֹּאת: וּבְנֵיהֶם
אֲשֶׁר לֹא־יָדְעוּ יִשְׁמְעוּ וְלָמְדוּ לְיִרְאָה אֶת־יְהוָֹה

Deuteronomy 31
10–13

carried the Ark of the LORD's Covenant, and to all the elders of Israel.

10] And Moses instructed them as follows: Every seventh year, the year set for remission, at the Feast of Booths,   11] when all Israel comes to appear before the LORD your God in the place which He will choose, you shall read this Teaching aloud in the presence of all Israel.   12] Gather the people—men, women, children, and the strangers in your communities—that they may hear and so learn to revere the LORD your God and to observe faithfully every word of this Teaching.   13] Their children, too, who have not had the experience, shall hear and learn to revere the

it to both the religious and civil authorities. The book was thus expressly removed from an exclusively priestly domain.

10] *Every seventh year.* Meaning, at the end of every seven years; see at Deut. 15:1 [2].

At the Feast of Booths. On Sukot, one of the three festivals when Israelites were bidden to make a pilgrimage to the sanctuary (16:16).

The Mishnah records that the reading took place at the end of the first day, and, if the first fell on the Sabbath, on the second day [3].

11] *You shall read.* This was applied to those who held supreme responsibility; at one time it was a

priest like Ezra (see Neh. 8) or the High Priest [4], at other times a king like Josiah (II Kings 23).

The Mishnah reports that King Agrippa stood up and read the following passages from Deuteronomy: 1:1–6:6; 11:13 ff.; 14:22 ff.; 17:14 ff.; 26:12 ff.; chapters 27 and 28 [5].

12] *And the strangers.* Josephus reports that the slaves, too, were in attendance at the public reading [6].

This verse and the first part of verse 13 form the opening of a Torah service in *Gates of Prayer* [7].

13] *Their children, too.* Compare 29:10.

אֱלֹהֵיכֶם כָּל־הַיָּמִים אֲשֶׁר אַתֶּם חַיִּים עַל־הָאֲדָמָה
אֲשֶׁר אַתֶּם עֹבְרִים אֶת־הַיַּרְדֵּן שָׁמָּה לְרִשְׁתָּהּ: פ

יד וַיֹּאמֶר יְהֹוָה אֶל־מֹשֶׁה הֵן קָרְבוּ יָמֶיךָ לָמוּת קְרָא
אֶת־יְהוֹשֻׁעַ וְהִתְיַצְּבוּ בְּאֹהֶל מוֹעֵד וַאֲצַוֶּנּוּ וַיֵּלֶךְ מֹשֶׁה
וִיהוֹשֻׁעַ וַיִּתְיַצְּבוּ בְּאֹהֶל מוֹעֵד: טו וַיֵּרָא יְהֹוָה בָּאֹהֶל
בְּעַמּוּד עָנָן וַיַּעֲמֹד עַמּוּד הֶעָנָן עַל־פֶּתַח הָאֹהֶל:

טז וַיֹּאמֶר יְהֹוָה אֶל־מֹשֶׁה הִנְּךָ שֹׁכֵב עִם־אֲבֹתֶיךָ וְקָם
הָעָם הַזֶּה וְזָנָה אַחֲרֵי אֱלֹהֵי נֵכַר־הָאָרֶץ אֲשֶׁר הוּא
בָא־שָׁמָּה בְּקִרְבּוֹ וַעֲזָבַנִי וְהֵפֵר אֶת־בְּרִיתִי אֲשֶׁר
יז כָּרַתִּי אִתּוֹ: וְחָרָה אַפִּי בוֹ בַיּוֹם־הַהוּא וַעֲזַבְתִּים
וְהִסְתַּרְתִּי פָנַי מֵהֶם וְהָיָה לֶאֱכֹל וּמְצָאֻהוּ רָעוֹת

Deuteronomy 31
14–17

LORD your God as long as they live in the land which you are about to cross the Jordan to occupy.

14] The LORD said to Moses: The time is drawing near for you to die. Call Joshua and present yourselves in the Tent of Meeting, that I may instruct him. Moses and Joshua went and presented themselves in the Tent of Meeting. 15] The LORD appeared in the Tent, in a pillar of cloud, the pillar of cloud having come to rest at the entrance of the tent.

16] The LORD said to Moses: You are soon to lie with your fathers. This people will thereupon go astray after the alien gods in their midst, in the land which they are about to enter; they will forsake Me and break My covenant which I made with them. 17] Then My anger will flare up against them, and I will abandon them and hide My countenance from them. They shall be ready prey; and many evils

16] *Go astray.* The Hebrew זָנָה evokes the image of adultery; compare Hos. 3:1.

According to Driver, the verse was at first meant literally and only afterwards, metaphorically [8].

17] *Hide My countenance.* See commentary below. The expression occurs nowhere else in the Torah but is found in Isaiah (8:17), Micah (3:4), and Psalms (e.g., 30:8).

רַבּוֹת וְצָרוֹת וְאָמַר בַּיּוֹם הַהוּא הֲלֹא עַל כִּי־אֵין
אֱלֹהַי בְּקִרְבִּי מְצָאוּנִי הָרָעוֹת הָאֵלֶּה: וְאָנֹכִי הַסְתֵּר
אַסְתִּיר פָּנַי בַּיּוֹם הַהוּא עַל כָּל־הָרָעָה אֲשֶׁר עָשָׂה
כִּי פָנָה אֶל־אֱלֹהִים אֲחֵרִים: וְעַתָּה כִּתְבוּ לָכֶם
אֶת־הַשִּׁירָה הַזֹּאת וְלַמְּדָהּ אֶת־בְּנֵי־יִשְׂרָאֵל שִׂימָהּ
בְּפִיהֶם לְמַעַן תִּהְיֶה־לִּי הַשִּׁירָה הַזֹּאת לְעֵד בִּבְנֵי
יִשְׂרָאֵל: כִּי־אֲבִיאֶנּוּ אֶל־הָאֲדָמָה אֲשֶׁר־נִשְׁבַּעְתִּי
לַאֲבֹתָיו זָבַת חָלָב וּדְבַשׁ וְאָכַל וְשָׂבַע וְדָשֵׁן וּפָנָה
אֶל־אֱלֹהִים אֲחֵרִים וַעֲבָדוּם וְנִאֲצוּנִי וְהֵפֵר אֶת־
בְּרִיתִי: וְהָיָה כִּי־תִמְצֶאןָ אֹתוֹ רָעוֹת רַבּוֹת וְצָרוֹת
וְעָנְתָה הַשִּׁירָה הַזֹּאת לְפָנָיו לְעֵד כִּי לֹא תִשָּׁכַח

Deuteronomy 31

18–21

and troubles shall befall them. And they shall say on that day, "Surely it is because our God is not in our midst that these evils have befallen us." **18]** Yet I will keep My countenance hidden on that day, because of all the evil they have done in turning to other gods. **19]** Therefore, write down this poem and teach it to the people of Israel; put it in their mouths, in order that this poem may be My witness against the people of Israel. **20]** When I bring them into the land flowing with milk and honey that I promised on oath to their fathers, and they eat their fill and grow fat and turn to other gods and serve them, spurning Me and breaking My covenant, **21]** and the many evils and troubles befall them—then this poem shall confront them as a witness, since it will never be lost from the mouth of their offspring.

God is not in our midst. Blaming God for not protecting His people.

19] *Write down.* Phrased in Hebrew in the plural, as if addressed to Moses and Joshua, or to all the people [9]. Moses, however, is reported as doing

the actual writing (verse 22).

This poem. Or, "song," which is contained in chapter 32.

May be My witness. That I warned them. Yet God already knows that Israel will transgress the law; see commentary below.

מִפִּי זַרְעוֹ כִּי יָדַעְתִּי אֶת־יִצְרוֹ אֲשֶׁר הוּא עֹשֶׂה הַיּוֹם בְּטֶרֶם אֲבִיאֶנּוּ אֶל־הָאָרֶץ אֲשֶׁר נִשְׁבָּעְתִּי:

כב וַיִּכְתֹּב מֹשֶׁה אֶת־הַשִּׁירָה הַזֹּאת בַּיּוֹם הַהוּא וַיְלַמְּדָהּ

כג אֶת־בְּנֵי יִשְׂרָאֵל: וַיְצַו אֶת־יְהוֹשֻׁעַ בִּן־נוּן וַיֹּאמֶר חֲזַק וֶאֱמָץ כִּי אַתָּה תָּבִיא אֶת־בְּנֵי יִשְׂרָאֵל אֶל־הָאָרֶץ

כד אֲשֶׁר־נִשְׁבַּעְתִּי לָהֶם וְאָנֹכִי אֶהְיֶה עִמָּךְ: וַיְהִי כְּכַלּוֹת מֹשֶׁה לִכְתֹּב אֶת־דִּבְרֵי הַתּוֹרָה־הַזֹּאת עַל־סֵפֶר עַד

כה תֻּמָּם: וַיְצַו מֹשֶׁה אֶת־הַלְוִיִּם נֹשְׂאֵי אֲרוֹן בְּרִית־יְהֹוָה

כו לֵאמֹר: לָקֹחַ אֵת סֵפֶר הַתּוֹרָה הַזֶּה וְשַׂמְתֶּם אֹתוֹ

For I know what plans they are devising even now, before I bring them into the land that I promised on oath.

22] That day, Moses wrote down this poem and taught it to the Israelites.

23] And He charged Joshua son of Nun: Be strong and resolute: for you shall bring the Israelites into the land which I promised them on oath, and I will be with you.

24] When Moses had put down in writing the words of this Teaching to the very end,   **25]** Moses charged the Levites who carried the Ark of the Covenant of the Lord, saying: **26]** Take this book of Teaching and place it beside the Ark of

---

21] *Plans they are devising.* God knows their יֵצֶר, their inclination to do evil, for it is indigenous to human nature (Gen. 6:5).

23] *I will be with you.* As if I were alive. The expression gives Moses' speech a suprahuman tinge.

24] *When Moses . . . .* This would follow best after verse 13 and probably stood there originally.

25] *The Levites.* That is, the priests among them; see verse 9.

26] *Take.* The Hebrew here uses an infinitive absolute (לָקֹחַ) instead of an imperative; found also, e.g., in the Decalogue (Deut. 5:12, שָׁמוֹר, and Exod. 20:8, זָכוֹר).
Contemporary languages have similar grammatical expressions; compare the German *Aufpassen!*

Place it [the book] beside the Ark. According to I Sam. 6:8, 11, 15, it was placed there in a container (*argaz*), and Targum Yerushalmi says that it was a box (*kufsa*).

Rabbi Meir (second century c.e.) had a tradition,

341

מִצַּד אֲרוֹן בְּרִית־יְהוָה אֱלֹהֵיכֶם וְהָיָה־שָׁם בְּךָ לְעֵד׃

כז כִּי אָנֹכִי יָדַעְתִּי אֶת־מֶרְיְךָ וְאֶת־עָרְפְּךָ הַקָּשֶׁה הֵן בְּעוֹדֶנִּי חַי עִמָּכֶם הַיּוֹם מַמְרִים הֱיִתֶם עִם־יְהֹוָה

כח וְאַף כִּי־אַחֲרֵי מוֹתִי׃ הַקְהִילוּ אֵלַי אֶת־כָּל־זִקְנֵי שִׁבְטֵיכֶם וְשֹׁטְרֵיכֶם וַאֲדַבְּרָה בְאָזְנֵיהֶם אֵת הַדְּבָרִים

כט הָאֵלֶּה וְאָעִידָה בָּם אֶת־הַשָּׁמַיִם וְאֶת־הָאָרֶץ׃ כִּי יָדַעְתִּי אַחֲרֵי מוֹתִי כִּי־הַשְׁחֵת תַּשְׁחִתוּן וְסַרְתֶּם מִן־ הַדֶּרֶךְ אֲשֶׁר צִוִּיתִי אֶתְכֶם וְקָרָאת אֶתְכֶם הָרָעָה בְּאַחֲרִית הַיָּמִים כִּי־תַעֲשׂוּ אֶת־הָרַע בְּעֵינֵי יְהוָה

ל לְהַכְעִיסוֹ בְּמַעֲשֵׂה יְדֵיכֶם׃ וַיְדַבֵּר מֹשֶׁה בְּאָזְנֵי כָּל־ קְהַל יִשְׂרָאֵל אֶת־דִּבְרֵי הַשִּׁירָה הַזֹּאת עַד תֻּמָּם׃

דברים לא
כז–ל

Deuteronomy 31
27–30

Haftarah Vayelech, p. 483

the Covenant of the Lord your God, and let it remain there as a witness against you.   **27]** Well I know how defiant and stiffnecked you are: even now, while I am still alive in your midst, you have been defiant toward the Lord; how much more, then, when I am dead!   **28]** Gather to me all the elders of your tribes and your officials, that I may speak all these words to them and that I may call heaven and earth to witness against them.   **29]** For I know that, when I am dead, you will act wickedly and turn away from the path which I enjoined upon you, and that in time to come misfortune will befall you for having done evil in the sight of the Lord and vexed Him by your deeds.

30] Then Moses recited the words of this poem to the very end, in the hearing of the whole congregation of Israel:

however, that the book was kept inside the ark, with the tablets [10].

As a witness against you. As a written document fortifying what was at that time an essentially oral tradition.

27] *Well I know.* From forty years of bitter experience in leading a recalcitrant people.

28] *Heaven and earth.* As ultimate witnesses, representing the infinite and the finite. Moses' song will start with invoking these two again (ch. 32).

342

Two Theological Questions

1. God's Knowledge and Human Freedom.
In verses 16 ff. God is depicted as telling Moses of Israel's future defection, as already knowing that the people will rebel against Him and that the fearful consequences of which chapter 28 had told will come to pass. If, in fact, it could be said that God anticipates the future, of what significance would human free will be? Why would God warn Israel to heed His law when He knew that they would refuse to do so? The problem is of a similar order as the confrontation between Egypt's Pharaoh and Moses: the latter pleaded with the ruler to let Israel go, but God had already informed Moses that his pleas would fall on barren ground and that God had arranged for the Pharaoh's destruction.[1]

Traditional Judaism attempted to solve the apparent contradiction between divine foreknowledge and human freedom by maintaining that while free will was given God's omniscience included a complete knowledge of human nature and the course of action people would adopt.[2]

However, when Deuteronomy was composed, these questions were not raised at all. Israel had already rebelled and suffered grievous consequences. The text does not theologize about it; rather, it phrases its judgment in the form of a prophecy which in effect has God say, "I told you so.[3] You have been proven to be stiff-necked and there-fore invited My punishment." The book never doubts that Israel could have acted differently, but the unhappy facts of history made speculation over what might have happened useless. The Torah leaves the matter there, and only later on were theological questions extrapolated from the text.

2. The Hidden God. Instead of showing compassion, the Torah says, God will hide himself when Israel sins; that is, He will be impervious to Israel's suffering and its cries for help (verses 17 and 18). From the Deuteronomic point of view—with national transgression and its consequences already having happened—the passages serve to explain God's inaction. They imply that He could have saved His people but chose not to do so, for when Israel breached the covenant God was released from His obligations as Israel's guardian and sovereign. This approach is the basic view of all prophets: Israel's misfortunes are traceable to its own misdeeds. Not God but Israel itself is to blame; God, though omnipotent, is exculpated. A repentant Israel will, however, find Him willing to reestablish the covenant on its old foundations. The wife who has gone astray will be taken back by a Husband who has never lost His love for her.

While medieval Jewish thought accepted these premises, modern post-Auschwitz thinkers have been unable to follow. They no longer believed in a God who could have saved His people from the gas chambers but chose to look away and hide His face. The Holocaust could not be understood as the monstrous result of putative sins that

---

[1] See our Commentary on Exodus, chapter 4.

[2] This conclusion is paralleled, though from a different perspective, by the view of contemporary Behaviorists who consider human action to be determined by the interaction of genetic and environmental factors. The Mishnaic phrasing was, "Everything is foreseen, nonetheless free will is given," or "Everything is in the hands of God except the fear of God" [11]. Nachmanides calls God's foreknowledge "Knowledge in potential."

[3] Prophets and Deuteronomy vigorously asserted that Israel's misfortunes were punishments from *God* and not—as antiprophetic parties suggested—from the Queen of Heaven or other deities that had been neglected (see Jer. 44:18).

Israel had committed. There remained only one alternative—short of either total disbelief or a defiant "Yet will I believe"—and that was to give up the idea of an omnipotent God. Rather, one needed to see Him as limited by human freedom. God is hidden as long as the world chooses to be alienated from Him; humanity, to whom He gave the choice to act for good or for evil, shuts Him out or lets Him in. Not God hides His face, we hide it. He took a chance on us when He created us free, and He, like us, must bear the consequences of human action. To phrase this in Deuteronomic terms: He hides himself because He must [12].

Joshua, Moses' Successor

The Torah gives us some insight into the type of person who inherited the mantle of leadership from Moses. The Book of Joshua, of course, greatly enlarges this picture.

Joshua (whom another tradition calls Hoshea), son of Nun, was an Ephraimite who had three functions assigned to him: he was Moses' personal attendant who accompanied him on his ascent of Mount Sinai; he was the guardian of the Tent; and he was a military commander who fought Amalek and whose military capacity made him the logical man to head the people in their campaign of conquering Canaan. He had previously earned his spurs by standing—at great personal risk—with Caleb against the ma-

jority of the spies; against them he proclaimed his belief that the conquest would be successful (Num. 14:6–10). He would live to be one hundred ten years, like Joseph. Thus the man who caused Israel to leave the Land was accorded the same life span as the man who would bring them back (see above, at verse 2).

Joshua became the leader of his people in a crucial time. He was now the head of the confederated tribes, he himself leading the Joseph tribe. As Moses' successor he too will be called "the servant of the Lord" and he too will be addressed by God, but he will not be God's intimate. "No personal experience to be compared with that of Moses can be glimpsed anywhere," wrote Buber [13].

In the Torah, then, Joshua is a loyal aide of his master, zealous for him and for God, courageous in defending his convictions, and successful in battle. He and Caleb were privileged to experience both the Exodus from Egypt and the conquest of the Land; that he was not like Moses does not diminish his greatness. To be chosen as the successor of the founder was in itself the mark of divine favor. For him it must have been a moment fraught with anxiety; for Moses, the investiture must have carried both regret and nostalgia. Both Joshua and Moses were human, and in their humanity they experienced the trauma of transition (see further in Gleanings).

GLEANINGS

God Knew

Before God brought Israel into the Promised Land He knew of its future sin and misery. If then, despite this, He gave the land He had promised the Fathers to their children, the latter may rest assured that the promise in the song of Moses will at some time be fulfilled.

D. HOFFMANN [14]

Liturgical

The weekly portion *Vayelech* (chapter 31) is almost always combined with the preceding one, *Nitzavim*. They are read separately only when between Rosh Hashanah and Sukot there are two Sabbaths neither of which coincides with a holy day.

הֵן

(In verse 14, when God tells Moses that death is near, He begins by saying הֵן, *hen*, "behold.")

In decreeing his death, God honored Moses by beginning with the word הֵן, the same word Moses had used in paying honor to God (Deut. 10:14).

MIDRASH [15]

The Judgment

Moses said to God: "Master of the universe, must I die after my eyes have witnessed all Your glory and power?" God replied: "What man can live and not see death (Ps. 89:49)? Were there men comparable to Abraham, Isaac, and Jacob? Yet they had to die."

And, though there was none like Moses who spoke with the Creator face to face, God said

(verse 14): "The time is drawing near for you to die."

MIDRASH [16]

Envy

Moses did not want to die.[4] But, when at the investiture of Joshua the two men went into the Tabernacle and the Cloud separated them, God spoke to Joshua alone. Afterwards Moses asked, "What did He say to you?"

Joshua replied: "When God spoke with you, did I come to know?"[5]

Thereupon Moses turned to God and told Him he was ready to die. "Better to die a hundred times than to experience even one moment of envy," he said. That is what Solomon meant: "Jealousy is cruel as the grave" (Song of Songs 8:6).

MIDRASH [17]

Joshua's Investiture

Then Joshua knelt, and Moses placed his hands upon his head and called out:

"The spirit which God put into me, I put into thee. Go in strength, and let thy might increase."

And Moses knelt by the side of Joshua and lifted his hands to heaven and prayed aloud:

"I thank Thee, O God, the God of our fathers, that Thou hast granted it to me to see the leader of Israel before Thou didst close mine eyes. And I implore Thee, God of our fathers, to strengthen his hands and to be with him as Thou hast been with me until this day."

Then he rose from his knees and called out to the people:

---

[4] More on this theme below, Gleanings on ch. 34.   [5] But another understanding is: "When God spoke with you, I knew (without asking)."

"See your leader, Joshua: Him shall ye obey!"

But among the people there was a heavyhearted silence. No tumult was raised, and no voice was heard save that of Joshua, which lamented:

"My lord, my teacher, my father!"

SHOLEM ASCH [18]

The Hidden Countenance

(After God has warned Israel against turning to alien gods, verse 16, He says that He will hide His face, verse 17.)

People will turn to man-made means to solve their problems rather than to Me—hence My countenance will be hidden.　　　SFORNO [19]

Resurrection

In traditional commentaries, verse 16 became one of the proof texts for the teaching of resurrection from death. This was based on the Hebrew sequence of the words ... הִנְּךָ שֹׁכֵב עִם אֲבֹתֶיךָ וְקָם

—literally, "You are soon to lie with your fathers and will rise . . . ."[6]

According to the Talmud, וְקָם is one of the words in the Torah where it is doubtful whether it is to be read with what precedes or with what follows, or perhaps (as here) with both [20].

Every Israelite

It says "Write down this poem"[7] (verse 19). Now the Hebrew for "write down" is phrased in the plural, implying that it is addressed to all Israel. Each Israelite has the obligation to write a scroll of the Torah (or, if he cannot do it himself, have one written in his name).　　　TALMUD [21]

This Poem May Be My Witness (verse 19)

But does God require a witness? Rather, the poem was to remind God not to judge Israel too harshly. For, though He knew their nature (verse 21), He still chose them to be His people.

MALBIM [22]

---

[6] Our translation does not reflect this reading; rather, it follows the plain sense and places a period after "your fathers" (the Masoretic punctuation places an *etnachta*—similar to a semicolon—after "your fa-

thers").

[7] "This poem" was taken to mean the whole Torah, since according to the halachah no one was permitted to copy merely parts of it.

The Song of Moses

The Bible ascribes three songs to Moses, of which two are in the Torah: one delivered after Israel's rescue from the Reed Sea, at the beginning of the desert wanderings (Exod. 15), and the other here, at the end. These two poems may therefore be seen to frame the wilderness experience, and though on the surface they appear to serve different purposes—the first a thanksgiving hymn, the second a poem of the future—they both deal with Israel's survival. At the sea, the physical existence of the nation was assured, but the forty years that followed put its spiritual future in doubt. Now, at the borders of the Promised Land, Moses celebrates the eventual realization of God's will for His people. He sings a hymn of hope to an Israel that will prevail in spirit as well as in body.*

The poem warns; it instructs; it gives hope. Israel's past history has amply demonstrated God's love and care, and these will not be found wanting in the future. Rebellion against His law may put Israel in dire straits, but in the end God will be shown not to have forgotten the people He had created. At the close of the recital, Moses is bidden to ascend Mount Nebo and prepare for death.

(Chapter 32 comprises the weekly portion *Ha'azinu*.)

---

* Psalm 90, which is also ascribed to Moses, is a prayer which shows some linguistic affinity to Deut. 32, e.g., יֻמָת in Ps. 90:15 and Deut. 32:2 [1].

האזינו	וְתִשְׁמַ֥ע הָאָ֖רֶץ אִמְרֵי־פִֽי׃	א הַאֲזִ֥ינוּ הַשָּׁמַ֖יִם וַאֲדַבֵּ֑רָה
דברים לב	תִּזַּ֤ל כַּטַּל֙ אִמְרָתִ֔י	ב יַעֲרֹ֤ף כַּמָּטָר֙ לִקְחִ֔י
א–ה	וְכִרְבִיבִ֖ים עֲלֵי־עֵֽשֶׂב׃	כִּשְׂעִירִ֣ם עֲלֵי־דֶ֔שֶׁא
	הָב֥וּ גֹ֖דֶל לֵאלֹהֵֽינוּ׃	ג כִּ֛י שֵׁ֥ם יְהֹוָ֖ה אֶקְרָ֑א
	כִּ֥י כָל־דְּרָכָ֖יו מִשְׁפָּ֑ט	ד הַצּוּר֙ תָּמִ֣ים פׇּעֳל֔וֹ
Ha'azinu	צַדִּ֥יק וְיָשָׁ֖ר הֽוּא׃	אֵ֤ל אֱמוּנָה֙ וְאֵ֣ין עָ֔וֶל
Deuteronomy 32	דּ֥וֹר עִקֵּ֖שׁ וּפְתַלְתֹּֽל׃	ה שִׁחֵ֥ת ל֛וֹ לֹ֖א בָּנָ֣יו מוּמָ֑ם
1–5		

1] Give ear, O heavens, let me speak; / Let the earth hear the words I utter! /
2] May my discourse come down as the rain, / My speech distill as the dew, / Like
showers on young growth, / Like droplets on the grass. /   3] For the name of the
LORD I proclaim; / Give glory to our God! /   4] The Rock!—His deeds are perfect, / Yea, all His ways are just; / A faithful God, never false, / True and upright
is He. /   5] Children unworthy of Him, / That crooked and twisted generation— /

32:1] *Give ear*. Heaven and earth are both fit
audience and witness to the song. Isaiah 1:2 uses
the same imagery.

2] *My discourse*. Others, "My doctrine."
In Proverbs (4:2) the Torah is called by this term:
"For I have given you good doctrine"—a phrase
that is recited at the end of the Torah service [2].

   Like droplets on the grass. So will God's teachings nourish the soul of Israel.

3] *Give glory to our God*. These words too have
become part of the Torah service in the synagogue [3].

4] *The Rock!* הַצּוּר (*Ha-Tzur*). God is repeatedly
so called in the poem, the term denoting rugged

steadfastness (compare the English idiom "like a
rock"). Jewish and Christian liturgies frequently
use this ascription; for instance: Rock of Israel,
Rock of Ages, my Rock and my Redeemer.
   In syntax, the use of a noun by which the subject
is identified with the qualities inherent in it is
called *casus pendens* [4]; compare Ps. 18:31, "God!—
His way is perfect." The Hebrew liturgy also employs this kind of address-and-description; for
instance, "the King!" [5], "the Good One," and
"the Compassionate One" [6].

5] *Children unworthy*. Literally, "non-children,"
in contrast to the faithful Father. The rendering is
but one of several of the obscure Hebrew text.
Old JPS translation had: "Is corruption His? No;
His children's is the blemish."

עַם נָבָל וְלֹא חָכָם	ו] הֲ לַיהוָה תִּגְמְלוּ־זֹאת
הוּא עָשְׂךָ וַיְכֹנְנֶךָ:	הֲלוֹא־הוּא אָבִיךָ קָּנֶךָ
בִּינוּ שְׁנוֹת דֹּר־וָדֹר	ז] זְכֹר יְמוֹת עוֹלָם
זְקֵנֶיךָ וְיֹאמְרוּ לָךְ:	שְׁאַל אָבִיךָ וְיַגֵּדְךָ
בְּהַפְרִידוֹ בְּנֵי אָדָם	ח] בְּהַנְחֵל עֶלְיוֹן גּוֹיִם
לְמִסְפַּר בְּנֵי יִשְׂרָאֵל:	יַצֵּב גְּבֻלֹת עַמִּים
יַעֲקֹב חֶבֶל נַחֲלָתוֹ:	ט] כִּי חֵלֶק יְהוָֹה עַמּוֹ
וּבְתֹהוּ יְלֵל יְשִׁמֹן	י] יִמְצָאֵהוּ בְּאֶרֶץ מִדְבָּר

Deuteronomy 32
6–10

*ו ה' רבתי והיא תיבה לעצמה.

Their baseness has played Him false. / **6]** Do you thus requite the LORD, / O dull and witless people? / Is not He the Father who created you, / Fashioned you and made you endure! / **7]** Remember the days of old, / Consider the years of ages past; / Ask your father, he will inform you, / Your elders, they will tell you: / **8]** When the Most High gave nations their homes / And set the divisions of man, / He fixed the boundaries of peoples / In relation to Israel's numbers. / **9]** For the LORD's portion is His people, / Jacob His own allotment. / **10]** He found him in

6] *Do you thus requite the Lord.* The Hebrew has an enlarged and detached ה prefixed to the divine name (though manuscripts vary on this). The reason is not clear; see Gleanings.

7] *Remember the days of old.* With Moses as the presumed speaker, the reference would be to patriarchal days [7]; in the later listener, the early days of nationhood might be evoked. In either case, the phrase testifies to history as a predominantly oral tradition.

Ages past. דֹּר־וָדֹר (*dor va-dor*), literally, "generation upon generation."

Jewish morning and afternoon prayers quote the expression in the *Amidah*: "To all generations we will make known Your greatness" [8].

8] *Gave nations their homes.* As set forth in Gen. 10. It was a fundamental belief that God had divided the earth among the nations [9]. A similar thought is expressed in Ps. 74:17.

In relation to Israel's numbers. For Israel was central in God's plan—an idea absent from Gen. 10. The Septuagint had a different Hebrew text, reading "in relation to the children of God." Revised Standard Version, New English Bible, New American Bible, and others follow this reading, which has a parallel in a Dead Sea fragment [10].

9] *The Lord's portion.* Israel belonged to God, as His treasured people (Deut. 7:6).

10] *He found him.* God is pictured as having dis-

349

יְסֹבְבֶנְהוּ יְבוֹנְנֵהוּ   יִצְּרֶנְהוּ כְּאִישׁוֹן עֵינוֹ:

^{יא} כְּנֶשֶׁר יָעִיר קִנּוֹ   עַל־גּוֹזָלָיו יְרַחֵף

יִפְרֹשׂ כְּנָפָיו יִקָּחֵהוּ   יִשָּׂאֵהוּ עַל־אֶבְרָתוֹ:

^{יב} יְהוָה בָּדָד יַנְחֶנּוּ   וְאֵין עִמּוֹ אֵל נֵכָר:

^{יג} יַרְכִּבֵהוּ עַל־בָּמֳתֵי אָרֶץ   וַיֹּאכַל תְּנוּבֹת שָׂדָי

וַיֵּנִקֵהוּ דְבַשׁ מִסֶּלַע   וְשֶׁמֶן מֵחַלְמִישׁ צוּר:

^{יד} חֶמְאַת בָּקָר וַחֲלֵב צֹאן   עִם־חֵלֶב כָּרִים

* יג ו' יתירה.   קמץ בז"ק.

Deuteronomy 32
11–14

a desert region, / In an empty howling waste. / He engirded him, watched over him, / Guarded him as the pupil of His eye. / **11]** Like an eagle who rouses his nestlings, / Gliding down to his young, / So did He spread His wings and take him, / Bear him along on His pinions; / **12]** The LORD alone did guide him, / No alien god at His side. / **13]** He set him atop the highlands, / To feast on the yield of the earth; / He fed him honey from the crag, / And oil from the flinty rock, / **14]** Curd of kine and milk of flocks; / With the best of lambs and rams, / Bulls

covered Israel in the desert (so also Hosea 9:10). Von Rad calls this a "foundling tradition," comparable to a patriarchal and Exodus tradition [11]. Jeremiah (2:2) reverses the image: Israel followed God into the wilderness.

An empty howling waste. תֹהוּ (tohu) recalls the second verse of Genesis, which says that at Creation the earth was *tohu*. As God created the earth from nothingness, so He created Israel and brought it out of the wasteland.

The adjective "howling" may refer to the voices of night animals or to a belief that the desert was inhabited by shrieking demons [12].

Pupil of His eye. Others, "apple of His eye"; the core which appears to be black (see Prov. 7:2). The word אִישׁוֹן (ishon) has also been taken as a diminutive of אִישׁ (ish, man), the miniature reflection of oneself that may be seen in another's eye [13].

This diminutive reflection is also the basic meaning of the English word "pupil."

11] *Like an eagle.* Compare Exod. 19:4.

Rouses his nestlings. To feed them as well as to teach them how to fly; so did God tend Israel in its youth. (See further in Gleanings.)

12] *The Lord alone.* The same word בָּדָד (badad) as used in Balaam's saying that Israel dwells "apart" (Num. 23:9); in both cases uniqueness and separateness go together. See further the comment on Jeshurun in verse 15.

13] *Honey . . . oil.* Both were found abundantly in ancient Canaan.

14] *Curd . . . lambs . . . rams . . . bulls . . . he-goats.* Mainstays of a people that domesticated animals.

עִם־חֵלֶב כִּלְיוֹת חִטָּה   וְאֵילִים בְּנֵי־בָשָׁן וְעַתּוּדִים

טו וְדַם־עֵנָב תִּשְׁתֶּה־חָמֶר: וַיִּשְׁמַן יְשֻׁרוּן וַיִּבְעָט

שָׁמַנְתָּ עָבִיתָ כָּשִׂיתָ   וַיִּטֹּשׁ אֱלוֹהַ עָשָׂהוּ

טז וַיְנַבֵּל צוּר יְשֻׁעָתוֹ:   יַקְנִאֻהוּ בְּזָרִים

יז בְּתוֹעֵבֹת יַכְעִיסֻהוּ:   יִזְבְּחוּ לַשֵּׁדִים לֹא אֱלֹהַ

אֱלֹהִים לֹא יְדָעוּם   חֲדָשִׁים מִקָּרֹב בָּאוּ

יח לֹא שְׂעָרוּם אֲבֹתֵיכֶם: צוּר יְלָדְךָ תֶּשִׁי

Deuteronomy 32
15–18

of Bashan and he-goats; / With the very finest wheat— / And foaming grape-blood was your drink. / **15]** So Jeshurun grew fat and kicked— / You grew fat and gross and coarse— / He forsook the God who made him / And spurned the Rock of his support. / **16]** They incensed Him with alien things, / Vexed Him with abominations. / **17]** They sacrificed to demons, no-gods, / Gods they had never known, / New ones, who came but lately, / Who stirred not your fathers' fears. / **18]** You neglected the Rock that begot you, / Forgot the God who brought you

Very finest wheat. Literally, "the kidney fat of wheat." The Hebrew idiom used the word "fat" to describe the best of a thing, whence the English expression "fat of the land" (compare also "cream of the crop").

Wheat . . . grape-blood. Products of an agricultural society. The poetic catalogue reflects a nation settled in its land.

15] *Jeshurun.* A poetic name for Israel, here occurring for the first time in the Torah. Even as *badad* in verse 12 evoked Balaam's use of it (Num. 23:9), so Balaam's *ashurenu* in that same verse is here paralleled by *jeshurun*.

Ibn Ezra traces the name Jeshurun to *yashar*, right, straight.

And kicked. Like a stubborn, spoiled mule.

Coarse. The meaning of the Hebrew is not certain. An Arabic word of similar sound means "to be gorged with food," which would fit here.

Rock of his support. Or, "of his salvation." The phrase appears in the opening of a popular Chanukah hymn, *Ma-oz Tzur Yeshuati.*

17] *Demons.* שֵׁדִים (*shedim*) is translated better as "demigods" to whom human sacrifices were offered, as Ps. 106:37 attests (the only other occurrence of *shedim* in the Bible).

The word is of Akkadian origin where it described a good and friendly spirit, a protective power [14].

No-gods. Who are adored by the no-children of verse 5 (see comment there).

New ones. Who turn out to be mere fads.

Who stirred not your fathers' fears. The meaning of the Hebrew is uncertain. Better, based on parallels to Arabic *sha-ara* and Aramaic *se-ar*: "whom your fathers did not know" (or "acknowledge"; so New English Bible).

18] *Brought you forth.* In travail, like a mother. The same feminine imagery is evoked also in Ps.

351

וַיַּרְא יְהֹוָה וַיִּנְאָץ   יט וַתִּשְׁכַּח אֵל מְחֹלְלֶךָ:

וַיֹּאמֶר אַסְתִּירָה פָנַי מֵהֶם   כ מִכַּעַס בָּנָיו וּבְנֹתָיו:

כִּי דוֹר תַּהְפֻּכֹת הֵמָּה   אֶרְאֶה מָה אַחֲרִיתָם

הֵם קִנְאוּנִי בְלֹא־אֵל   כא בָּנִים לֹא־אֵמֻן בָּם:

וַאֲנִי אַקְנִיאֵם בְּלֹא־עָם   כִּעֲסוּנִי בְּהַבְלֵיהֶם

כִּי־אֵשׁ קָדְחָה בְאַפִּי   כב בְּגוֹי נָבָל אַכְעִיסֵם:

וַתֹּאכַל אֶרֶץ וִיבֻלָהּ   וַתִּיקַד עַד־שְׁאוֹל תַּחְתִּית

אַסְפֶּה עָלֵימוֹ רָעוֹת   כג וַתְּלַהֵט מוֹסְדֵי הָרִים:

Deuteronomy 32

19–23

forth. / **19]** The LORD saw and was vexed / And spurned His sons and His daughters. / **20]** He said: / I will hide My countenance from them, / And see how they fare in the end. / For they are a treacherous breed, / Children with no loyalty in them. / **21]** They incensed Me with no-gods, / Vexed Me with their futilities; / I'll incense them with a no-folk, / Vex them with a nation of fools. / **22]** For a fire has flared in My wrath / And burned to the bottom of Sheol, / Has consumed the earth and its increase, / Eaten down to the base of the hills. / **23]** I will sweep

90:2, "Before You brought forth the earth and the world. . . ."

In the Masoretic text the י of תֶּשִׁי is written small. The reason, Ibn Ezra suggests, is that the י was a later addition and the word originally read תֶּשׁ (from the root נשה, forget, neglect), similar to תֵּט in Prov. 4:5.

19] *And His daughters.* Their mention is unusual when speaking of God.

20] *Hide My countenance.* See above, at 31:17.

Treacherous. Better, "perverse"; the Hebrew means, literally, "upside down."

No loyalty. Parallel to the no-gods and no-folk in the next verse.

21] *Futilities.* Idols that are nothing but a "puff," which is the meaning of *hevel*; see Eccles. 1:2 (where *hevel* is translated as "vanity").

No-folk. Meaning either a people who are

hardly worth mentioning or who are so uncivilized that they do not deserve the name "people." The poet may not have had any particular nation in mind, his statement meaning that when the time came God would use even barbarians for His purpose.

Fools. The word נָבָל is in assonance with הֶבֶל in the same verse.

22] *A fire.* Meaning, God's jealousy.

Sheol. A mythical place whither the dead were believed to descend. It is mentioned frequently in the Bible but is not further defined.

Eaten down. A parallel to "burned to the bottom."

23] *I will sweep.* The translation follows Ibn Ezra (who derives the word from ספה); others understand "heap" (from אסף) or "add" (from יסף).

כד חֲצִי אֲכַלֶּה־בָּם:	מְזֵי רָעָב וּלְחֻמֵי רֶשֶׁף
וְקֶטֶב מְרִירִי	וְשֶׁן־בְּהֵמֹת אֲשַׁלַּח־בָּם
כה עִם־חֲמַת זֹחֲלֵי עָפָר:	מִחוּץ תְּשַׁכֶּל־חֶרֶב
וּמֵחֲדָרִים אֵימָה	גַּם־בָּחוּר גַּם־בְּתוּלָה
כו יוֹנֵק עִם־אִישׁ שֵׂיבָה:	אָמַרְתִּי אַפְאֵיהֶם
כז אַשְׁבִּיתָה מֵאֱנוֹשׁ זִכְרָם:	לוּלֵי כַּעַס אוֹיֵב אָגוּר
פֶּן־יְנַכְּרוּ צָרֵימוֹ	פֶּן־יֹאמְרוּ יָדֵנוּ רָמָה
כח וְלֹא יְהֹוָה פָּעַל כָּל־זֹאת: כִּי־גוֹי אֹבַד עֵצוֹת הֵמָּה
כט וְאֵין בָּהֶם תְּבוּנָה: לוּ חָכְמוּ יַשְׂכִּילוּ זֹאת

Deuteronomy 32
24–29

misfortunes on them, / Use up My arrows on them: /   24] Wasting famine, ravaging plague, / Deadly pestilence, and fanged beasts / Will I let loose against them, / With venomous creepers in dust. /   25] The sword shall deal death without, / As shall the terror within, / To youth and maiden alike, / The suckling as well as the aged. /   26] I might have reduced them to naught, / Made their memory cease among men, /   27] But for fear of the taunts of the foe, / Their enemies who might misjudge / And say, "Our own hand has prevailed; / None of this was wrought by the LORD!" /   28] For they are a folk void of sense, / Lacking in all discernment. /   29] Were they wise, they would think upon this, / Gain insight

24] *Wasting famine.* The seven threats of misfortune may be an echo of the seven evil spirits noted in Mesopotamian texts [15]. They are couched in difficult poetic language. Compare also Job 3:5 (and commentaries thereon).

26] *Reduced them.* The meaning of the Hebrew is uncertain. The translation supposes that אַפְאֵיהֶם is related to פֵּאָה (corner), hence: the leftover in the corner of the field.

27] *But for fear.* God's honor needs protection,

and He "fears" that His enemies might misjudge His power.

The ascription of such a feeling to God is called anthropopathic, while the ascription of human form or action is termed anthropomorphic (see at verse 40).

28] *For they are.* There is no way of telling whether this refers to Israel's enemies or to Israel itself, but the former view fits the context better [16].

29] *Were they wise.* The enemies would come to

353

ל   יָבִינוּ לְאַחֲרִיתָם: אֵיכָה יִרְדֹּף אֶחָד אֶלֶף

   וּשְׁנַיִם יָנִיסוּ רְבָבָה   אִם־לֹא כִּי־צוּרָם מְכָרָם

לא   וַיהוָה הִסְגִּירָם: כִּי לֹא כְצוּרֵנוּ צוּרָם

לב   וְאֹיְבֵינוּ פְּלִילִים: כִּי־מִגֶּפֶן סְדֹם גַּפְנָם

   וּמִשַּׁדְמֹת עֲמֹרָה   עֲנָבֵמוֹ עִנְּבֵי־רוֹשׁ

לג   אַשְׁכְּלֹת מְרֹרֹת לָמוֹ:   חֲמַת תַּנִּינִם יֵינָם

לד   וְרֹאשׁ פְּתָנִים אַכְזָר: הֲלֹא הוּא כָּמֻס עִמָּדִי

לה   חָתֻם בְּאוֹצְרֹתָי: לִי נָקָם וְשִׁלֵּם

   לְעֵת תָּמוּט רַגְלָם   כִּי קָרוֹב יוֹם אֵידָם

Deuteronomy 32

30–35

into their future: / **30]** "How could one have routed a thousand, / Or two put ten thousand to flight, / Unless their Rock had sold them, / The Lord had given them up?" / **31]** For their rock is not like our Rock, / In our enemies' own estimation. / **32]** Ah! The vine for them is from Sodom, / From the vineyards of Gomorrah; / The grapes for them are poison, / A bitter growth their clusters. / **33]** Their wine is the venom of asps, / The pitiless poison of vipers. / **34]** Lo, I have it all put away, / Sealed up in My storehouses, / **35]** To be My vengeance and recompense, / At the time that their foot falters. / Yea, their day of disaster

---

understand that God does not permanently forsake His people. (If Israel is the subject: it would appreciate the necessity of God's chastisements.)

The phrase is frequently recited as part of the Reform Jewish funeral service.

30] *Had sold them.* Into servitude.

31] *In our enemies' own estimation.* A parenthetical aside [17].

32] *The vine.* Here used as a symbol of corruption. *Poison.* רֹשׁ, the same as רֹאשׁ in the next verse.

34] *Put away.* God uses the enemy now, but his true character is not forgotten.

כָּמֻס (*kamus*) is understood to mean כָּנֻס (*kanus*), stored up.

35] *To be My vengeance.* This accords with the Masoretic reading, but the text is likely corrupt. לִי נָקָם probably was לְיוֹם נָקָם, "against the day of vengeance"—which fits with the preceding verse (so the Septuagint, the Samaritan version, New American Bible, and New English Bible).

Old JPS and Revised Standard Version render "vengeance is Mine."

וְחָשׁ עֲתִדֹת לָמוֹ:   כִּי־יָדִין יְהוָֹה עַמּוֹ   לו

וְעַל־עֲבָדָיו יִתְנֶחָם   כִּי יִרְאֶה כִּי־אָזְלַת־יָד

וְאֶפֶס עָצוּר וְעָזוּב: וְאָמַר אֵי אֱלֹהֵימוֹ   לז

צוּר חָסָיוּ בוֹ:   אֲשֶׁר חֵלֶב זְבָחֵימוֹ יֹאכֵלוּ   לח

יִשְׁתּוּ יֵין נְסִיכָם   יָקוּמוּ וְיַעְזְרֻכֶם

יְהִי עֲלֵיכֶם סִתְרָה: רְאוּ עַתָּה כִּי אֲנִי אֲנִי הוּא   לט

וְאֵין אֱלֹהִים עִמָּדִי   אֲנִי אָמִית וַאֲחַיֶּה

מָחַצְתִּי וַאֲנִי אֶרְפָּא   וְאֵין מִיָּדִי מַצִּיל:

כִּי־אֶשָּׂא אֶל־שָׁמַיִם יָדִי   וְאָמַרְתִּי חַי אָנֹכִי לְעֹלָם: מ

אִם־שַׁנּוֹתִי בְּרַק חַרְבִּי   וְתֹאחֵז בְּמִשְׁפָּט יָדִי   מא

Deuteronomy 32
36–41

is near, / And destiny rushes upon them. / **36]** For the LORD will vindicate His people / And take revenge for His servants, / When He sees that their might is gone, / And neither bond nor free is left. / **37]** He will say: Where are their gods, / The rock in whom they sought refuge, / **38]** Who ate the fat of their offerings / And drank their libation wine? / Let them rise up to your help, / And let them be a shield unto you! / **39]** See, then, that I, I am He; / There is no god beside Me. / I deal death and give life; / I wounded and I will heal: / None can deliver from My hand. / **40]** Lo, I raise My hand to heaven / And say: As I live forever, / **41]** When I whet My flashing blade / And My hand lays hold on

36] *And take revenge.* Or, "He will repent himself" (that is, change His mind; so translated in Num. 23:19); the phrase is repeated in Ps. 135:14.

Neither bond nor free. Meaning, "no one." A merism, similar to "moist and dry," 29:18; see comment there.

37] *He will say.* Again, the subject is not clear; it is either God or the enemy. The former view appears more in consonance with the flow of the poem [18].

39] *I, I am He.* Compare Isa. 43:11, "I, I am the Lord" (where the fuller form אָנֹכִי is used, instead of אֲנִי, as here).

40] *I raise My hand to heaven.* An anthropomorphism that would be deemed an "inappropriate" expression today.

41] *Flashing blade.* Literally, "lightning of My blade" (or sword).

The image entered the "Battle Hymn of the Republic": "I have seen the fearful lightning of His terrible swift sword."

מב אַשְׁכִּיר חִצַּי מִדָּם וְחַרְבִּי תֹּאכַל בָּשָׂר אָשִׁיב נָקָם לְצָרָי וְלִמְשַׂנְאַי אֲשַׁלֵּם:

מדַּם חָלָל וְשִׁבְיָה מֵרֹאשׁ פַּרְעוֹת אוֹיֵב:

מג הַרְנִינוּ גוֹיִם עַמּוֹ כִּי דַם־עֲבָדָיו יִקּוֹם

וְנָקָם יָשִׁיב לְצָרָיו וְכִפֶּר אַדְמָתוֹ עַמּוֹ:

פ

מד וַיָּבֹא מֹשֶׁה וַיְדַבֵּר אֶת־כָּל־דִּבְרֵי הַשִּׁירָה־הַזֹּאת בְּאָזְנֵי

מה הָעָם הוּא וְהוֹשֵׁעַ בִּן־נוּן: וַיְכַל מֹשֶׁה לְדַבֵּר אֶת־

מו כָּל־הַדְּבָרִים הָאֵלֶּה אֶל־כָּל־יִשְׂרָאֵל: וַיֹּאמֶר אֲלֵהֶם
שִׂימוּ לְבַבְכֶם לְכָל־הַדְּבָרִים אֲשֶׁר אָנֹכִי מֵעִיד בָּכֶם
הַיּוֹם אֲשֶׁר תְּצַוֻּם אֶת־בְּנֵיכֶם לִשְׁמֹר לַעֲשׂוֹת אֶת־

Deuteronomy 32

42–46

judgment, / Vengeance will I wreak on My foes, / Will I deal to those who reject Me. /   42] I will make drunk My arrows with blood— / As My sword devours flesh— / Blood of the slain and the captive / From the long-haired enemy chiefs. /

43] O nations, acclaim His people! / For He'll avenge the blood of His servants, / Wreak vengeance on His foes, / And cleanse the land of His people.

44] Moses came, together with Hosea son of Nun, and recited all the words of this poem in the hearing of the people.

45] And when Moses finished reciting all these words to all Israel,   46] he said to them: Take to heart all the words with which I have warned you this day. Enjoin them upon your children, that they may observe faithfully all the terms of this

42] *With blood.* The poet describes God's victory in the accepted terms of ancient warfare.

And the captive. Who were often slain.

Long-haired enemy chiefs. Perhaps referring to the no-folk (verse 21) who had a wild appearance. The Hebrew for long-haired, *par-ot*, is in clear assonance with *par-oh*, Pharaoh, Israel's arch-enemy.

Note, however, that such wild hair had the poet's approval (Judg. 5:2), if it signified the dedication of a *nazir.*

43] *Cleanse the land.* Polluted by the enemy (or polluted by Israel's idolatry).

45] *All these words.* In the Book of Deuteronomy;

מז כָּל־דִּבְרֵי הַתּוֹרָה הַזֹּאת: כִּי לֹא־דָבָר רֵק הוּא
מִכֶּם כִּי־הוּא חַיֵּיכֶם וּבַדָּבָר הַזֶּה תַּאֲרִיכוּ יָמִים
עַל־הָאֲדָמָה אֲשֶׁר אַתֶּם עֹבְרִים אֶת־הַיַּרְדֵּן שָׁמָּה
לְרִשְׁתָּהּ:
פ

מח וַיְדַבֵּר יְהֹוָה אֶל־מֹשֶׁה בְּעֶצֶם הַיּוֹם הַזֶּה לֵאמֹר:

מט עֲלֵה אֶל־הַר הָעֲבָרִים הַזֶּה הַר־נְבוֹ אֲשֶׁר בְּאֶרֶץ
מוֹאָב אֲשֶׁר עַל־פְּנֵי יְרֵחוֹ וּרְאֵה אֶת־אֶרֶץ כְּנַעַן
אֲשֶׁר אֲנִי נֹתֵן לִבְנֵי יִשְׂרָאֵל לַאֲחֻזָּה: נ וּמֻת בָּהָר
אֲשֶׁר אַתָּה עֹלֶה שָׁמָּה וְהֵאָסֵף אֶל־עַמֶּיךָ כַּאֲשֶׁר־
מֵת אַהֲרֹן אָחִיךָ בְּהֹר הָהָר וַיֵּאָסֶף אֶל־עַמָּיו:

Deuteronomy 32
47–50

Teaching.   47] For this is not a trifling thing for you: it is your very life; through it you shall long endure on the land which you are to occupy upon crossing the Jordan.

48] That very day the Lord spoke to Moses: 49] Ascend these heights of Abarim to Mount Nebo, which is in the land of Moab facing Jericho, and view the land of Canaan which I am giving the Israelites as their holding.   50] You shall die on the mountain that you are about to ascend, and shall be gathered to your kin, as your brother Aaron died on Mount Hor and was gathered to his kin;

but traditional interpreters take it as a reference to the whole Torah.

47] *Not a trifling thing.* Literally, "not empty."

49] *Abarim.* The mountain range "beyond (the river Jordan)," seen from the perspective of Canaan. Nebo was one peak in this range. Verses 48–52 are similar to Num. 27:12–14 and probably came from the same tradition. They were not originally part of Deuteronomy but placed here

to provide the book with a sequential arrangement. One may assume that the story of the death of Moses (chapter 34) was at first told at the end of Numbers.

50] *To your kin.* The plural form of עַם (*am*, people); an English equivalent would be "your folks."

Mount Hor. Its location is uncertain; some believe it to be near Petra; others, near Kadesh-barnea. Compare Num. 20:22 ff.

However, in Deut. 10:6 Aaron is reported to have

נא עַל אֲשֶׁר מְעַלְתֶּם בִּי בְּתוֹךְ בְּנֵי יִשְׂרָאֵל בְּמֵי־מְרִיבַת
קָדֵשׁ מִדְבַּר־צִן עַל אֲשֶׁר לֹא־קִדַּשְׁתֶּם אוֹתִי בְּתוֹךְ
נב בְּנֵי יִשְׂרָאֵל: כִּי מִנֶּגֶד תִּרְאֶה אֶת־הָאָרֶץ וְשָׁמָּה לֹא
תָבוֹא אֶל־הָאָרֶץ אֲשֶׁר־אֲנִי נֹתֵן לִבְנֵי יִשְׂרָאֵל:

Deuteronomy 32
51–52

Haftarah Ha'azinu, p. 486

51] for you both broke faith with Me among the Israelite people, at the waters of Meribath-kadesh in the wilderness of Zin, by failing to uphold My sanctity among the Israelite people. **52]** You may view the land from a distance, but you shall not enter it—the land that I am giving to the Israelite people.

died at Moserah. This may be a different tradition, or Moserah may have been a place in the area of Mount Hor.

51] *For you both broke faith.* This recalls the story told in Num. 20 where the failure of Moses and Aaron, during a rebellion, led God to pronounce the judgment of death on the two leaders (see commentary there). In Deut. 3:26 and 4:21 Moses ascribes the cause of his punishment not to his own doings but to Israel's sin; on this difference see commentary on chapter 3, above.

Wilderness of Zin. In the area of Kadesh-barnea.

The Poem—Its Setting

Like the Song at the Sea (Exod. 15), the poem of Deut. 32 is also called *Shirah* (Deut. 31:30), though it is more often referred to as *Ha-azinu* ("Give ear"), the opening Hebrew word. In the affection of subsequent generations it stood close to the former,[1] but, whereas the *Shirah* at the Reed Sea is most likely of ancient origin, *Ha-azinu* has a distinctly later setting.[2]

Israel appears to be well settled in the Land, the Exodus from Egypt lies in the distant past. At the Reed Sea, idolatry had not been an issue; here it is, for centuries of intimate contact with pagan peoples have led Israel to dilute its exclusive allegiance to the One God. Apparently, the nation has suffered a series of major disasters, which the poem, in prophetic fashion, explains as just punishments for Israel's sins. The song has its parallels in Psalms 78, 105, 106 and, in prose, in Ezekiel 20. An exact time for the composition cannot be fixed; on linguistic grounds one finds the writings of Jeremiah and Ezekiel most closely related. However, since the poem does not mention exile as one of Israel's misfortunes, one may assume that its composition preceded the destruction of the Northern Kingdom by the Assyrians and the subsequent exile of the Ten Tribes.

The matter is complicated by distinctly archaic expressions and unusual ideas, such as feeding Israel on curd and honey, or the people being found by God in the desert, or the nations being numbered according to Israel's hosts.

Structure of the Poem

Ancient Hebrew poetry does not know rhyme, though it does use assonance; it is characterized primarily by rhythm, meter, parallelism, and repetition. The forty-three verses of our poem are mostly two-liners, each with two parts, the second of which is parallel to and reinforces the content of the first. Most lines have three accents (though there are a few variations). The translation of the first line reflects the Hebrew rhythm:

> Give ear, O heaven, let me speak;
> Let the earth hear the words I utter.

According to Masoretic rule, the lines are written in a special way: each line contains two phrase-parts which are separated by a central space. In Torah manuscripts the poem is thus written in two columns, a somewhat simpler arrangement than that prescribed for the *Shirah* of Exod. 15 (see there).

The structure of the poem was discussed as early as in talmudic days. The Talmud divided it into six sections, but this was done in part to provide necessary divisions for the different readers who were called to the Torah. The divisions are verses 1–6, 7–12, 13–18, 19–28, 29–39, 40–43 and are remembered by the acrostic הזי״ו ל״ך, the opening letters of each section.[3]

Our analysis [21] shows the following:

There is a prologue (1–3) and an epilogue (40–44). Between them stands the main body of the poem, its thirty-six verses falling into three parts of twelve verses each: 4–15, 16–27, 28–39. Verses 15 and 27 (which end the first two sections) are transitions to

---

[1] According to Maimonides, at least one of the two poems is to be recited at daily services [19].

[2] The "ancient origin" of Exod. 15 is, however, disputed by some scholars, and so is our rendering of

the background of Deut. 32. For instance, it has been suggested that the chapter reflects the fall of Samaria and that it belongs to exilic days.

[3] Readings 7 and 8 consist of verses 44–47 and 48–52, in the prose section which follows the poem [20].

what follows. The poem then has this structure:

1–3: prologue, calling on heaven and earth, and exalting God; 4–15: part 1, God's love for Israel; 16–27: part 2, Israel's ingratitude; 28–39: part 3, indictment of the nations and their eventual fate; 40–44: epilogue, heaven is again called as witness, and God is once more exalted.

The flow of the song is marked by a degree of repetition that gives it special intensity. Thus, the image of the discourse as life-giving rain appears four times in verse 2, as does the justice of God in verse 3. Six times in the poem the Lord is called Rock; there are no-children, no-gods, and no-folk, and the listener is strongly impressed that evil deeds will beget bitter consequences. The song has a triangular construction: its promises and warnings move between the three polarities of God, Israel, and the nations. Each depends on the actions and thoughts of the others; none—not even God himself—is seen as fully independent. In fact, this interdependence holds the poem together and almost demands that the heavens themselves become witnesses of Moses' rousing discourse.

The Ambivalence of God

At the heart of the poem stands an idea which, while not unique to the Bible, is here presented with special force. In the Torah it is expressed also in Gen. 6:5–7, and it is part of Hosea's thought (6:4; 11:8 f.). In these passages, as in the poem's verses 26–35, God is depicted as ambivalent about His course of action (note comment on verse 36). In Genesis, He is shown to have realized that the creation of humanity had been an error, and therefore He decided to destroy it—but not completely. Noah represents the door of compassion which God leaves open for himself. Hosea has God ask himself, "How can I give you up, O Ephraim? How surrender you, O Israel?" and then provides His own answer, "I have had a change of heart.... I will not act on My wrath."

In Moses' song, it is not compassion that motivates God; rather, it is His honor that must be protected. Israel is both endangered and saved because it is close to Him and is thereby involved in His needs as well. God must be seen to be God, and if Israel endangers His majesty it must suffer the consequences. At the same time, it will be rescued from perdition because God cannot allow Israel to be destroyed. The fate of the covenant people is thus forever hammered out on the anvil of history, for the ambivalence of the Divine Partner makes Israel the object both of love and of anger. The nations are the tools of God's action, but His goal is to create an evermore loyal and observant Israel. Thus does the song explain the relationship, and in the mouth of Moses it becomes a statement of fundamental belief [22].

GLEANINGS

Discourse and Speech

Of discourse, Moses says that it should come down as rain (that is, in abundance); but of speech, that it should "distill" (verse 2). Torah is discourse par excellence and it should be plentiful, but its teaching should be short and "distilled." Thus the Talmud says, "One should always teach with brevity." ABARBANEL [23]

The ה

(Verse 6 begins with a ה which is detached from the word that follows.) This ה is the end of Moses' signature. If one takes the first letters of verses 1–6 (ה, י, כ, ה, ש, ה), they add up to 345 by way of gematria which represents the value of the letters in Moses' name (משה). In this way Moses affixed his name to the book, ending his "signature" with the detached ה. MIDRASH [24]

Dull and Witless People (verse 6)

Why are two adjectives used to describe Israel's folly? Note the distinction Jeremiah makes when he says (16:11): "They deserted Me and did not keep My commandments," on which the Talmud elaborates by having God say: "Would that they forsook Me but kept My Torah, for its light would lead them to return to Me [25]. But if they are without Torah who will lead them back?"

This is what Moses meant: "Dull"—without knowledge of God; and "witless" (or wisdomless)—without the redeeming wisdom of Torah. CHAFETZ CHAYIM [26]

Another interpretation: Targum Onkelos interprets "dull and witless people" as a nation that received the Torah but did not thereby become wise. Now the Midrash uses the word נָבָל (na-val, dull) to mean "inferior variety" and says: Death, prophecy, and divine wisdom have inferior varieties. Sleep resembles but is not like death, and so are dreams an inferior reflection of prophecy, and Torah of divine wisdom [27]. Hence a people that is *naval* is one that though it has received Torah falls short of divine wisdom and is לֹא חָכָם (lo chacham, witless). THE GAON OF VILNA [28]

Ask Your Father (verse 7)

This verse was used as a proof text to support the words "who has commanded us to kindle the Chanukah lights." Whence do we know that God commanded us to do this? From this verse, for your father (and your teachers) will tell you of God's miracles and thereby will obligate you. TALMUD [29]

In Relation to Israel's Numbers (verse 8)

The plain text was taken to mean that the seventy nations who peopled the earth were a macro-image of the seventy souls whom Jacob brought to Egypt [30].

Like an Eagle (verse 11)

The simile has its foundation in the habits of the bird.

Two parent eagles were teaching their offspring, two young birds, the maneuvers of flight. Rising from the top of a mountain, they at first made small circles and the young imitated them; they paused on their wings waiting till they had made their first flight, holding them on their expanded wings when they appeared exhausted, and then took a second and larger gyration, always rising toward the sun, and enlarging their

361

circle of flight, so as to make a gradually ascending spiral. S. D. DRIVER [31]

Jeshurun Grew Fat and Kicked (verse 15)

Generally, Jeshurun is an attribute of praise, indicating a higher rung of Israel's striving. That is the problem: when Israel reaches the rung where it is worthy of being called Jeshurun, it becomes proud and kicks. CHASIDIC [32]

No-gods (verse 21)

They are called perverse because they turn God's good will into anger. RASHI

Another interpretation: Israel perverts אֵל (God) into its opposite לֹא (no) and therefore is called "a treacherous breed" (verse 20), literally a perverse breed that turns everything upside down, like אֵל into לֹא. CHASIDIC [33]

Promise and Fulfillment

In the beginning, at the burning bush, God said (Exod. 3:14): "I will be what I will be,"[4] meaning "I will redeem you from slavery and bring you into your own land." Now, in sight of the Promised Land, He speaks in the present tense, as the God who has fulfilled His promise: "I, I *am* He" (verse 39). CHATAM SOFER [34]

An Ascent

In bidding Moses to prepare for death, God says to him, "Ascend these heights" (verse 48), for it was to be a true ascent for Moses, not a descent. MIDRASH [35]

---

[4] This is one of the understandings of that verse, based on the construction of אֶהְיֶה אֲשֶׁר אֶהְיֶה in what appears to be the future tense (see commentary on Exod. 3).

וזאת הברכה

The Blessing of Moses

Jacob had blessed his sons before his death (Gen. 49), and, in the tradition of Jacob, so does Moses now bless his people. He looks at each tribe and prays for its well-being in the light of its characteristics, inclinations, and capacities. The blessing, a poem like Jacob's testament, is both prayer and prophecy. A comparison of these two blessings, as well as a consideration of the age of the poem, will be found below, in the commentary.

The blessing is quite unlike the song of Moses that precedes it (in chapter 32). There, God stood at the center; here, it is Israel that commands the hearer's attention. The song directed itself forcefully to the danger of idolatry and to God's ensuing wrath; the blessing overlooks both subjects entirely. The song soared in exciting and memorable phrases; the blessing, in comparison, is a calm assessment of Israel's past and future. In Hebrew manuscripts the blessing is set in prose form, yet its sentences clearly display a poetic rhythm. Its language has an antique flavor; some of its words are either rare or unique in the Bible; and a number of phrases are obscure and the text is not always in order. The structure of the blessing is as follows: verse 1: superscription; verses 2–5: establishing the blessing's foundation—God's kingship over Israel; verses 6–25: the catalogue of blessings; verses 26–29: conclusion, which returns to the beginning in that it extols God, the Protector of Israel.

Because verses 2–5 and 26–29 contain no blessings, some scholars have suggested that these phrases did not originally form a part of the text. However, as in a covenant (on which the blessings are ultimately founded), an exordium and a matching conclusion are necessary. They frame the main text perfectly, and there is no convincing reason to suppose them to be later additions.

(Chapter 33 begins the Torah's last weekly portion, *Vezot ha-Berachah*, so called after the opening words.)

וזאת הברכה

דברים לג
א–ד

Vezot ha-Berachah

Deuteronomy 33

1–4

א וְזֹאת הַבְּרָכָה אֲשֶׁר בֵּרַךְ מֹשֶׁה אִישׁ הָאֱלֹהִים אֶת־
ב בְּנֵי יִשְׂרָאֵל לִפְנֵי מוֹתוֹ: וַיֹּאמַר יְהֹוָה מִסִּינַי בָּא
וְזָרַח מִשֵּׂעִיר לָמוֹ הוֹפִיעַ מֵהַר פָּארָן וְאָתָה מֵרִבְבֹת
ג קֹדֶשׁ מִימִינוֹ אֵשְׁדָּת לָמוֹ: אַף חֹבֵב עַמִּים כָּל־
קְדֹשָׁיו בְּיָדֶךָ וְהֵם תֻּכּוּ לְרַגְלֶךָ יִשָּׂא מִדַּבְּרֹתֶיךָ:
ד תּוֹרָה צִוָּה־לָנוּ מֹשֶׁה מוֹרָשָׁה קְהִלַּת יַעֲקֹב:

* כ תרין מילי קרי.

1] This is the blessing with which Moses, the man of God, bade the Israelites farewell before he died.   2] He said: The LORD came from Sinai; / He shone upon them from Seir; / He appeared from Mount Paran, / And approached from Ribeboth-kodesh, / Lightning flashing at them from His right. /   3] Lover, indeed, of the people, / Their hallowed are all in Your hand. / They followed in Your steps, / Accepting Your pronouncements, /   4] When Moses charged us with the Teach-

33:1] *The man of God.* The expression occurs nowhere else in the Torah, but it does in Josh. 14:6, Psalms 90:1, Ezra 3:2, I Chron. 23:14, and II Chron. 30:16, in reference to Moses and in reference to others repeatedly in the rest of the Bible.

2] *Came from Sinai.* To reveal himself. Sinai was, so to speak, "God's mountain."

Seir . . . Mount Paran. Mountain ranges adjacent to the Negev. As the sun rises over the mountains so does God's glory rise over Israel.

Ribeboth-kodesh. A place otherwise unknown. With the Septuagint, one should probably read Meribath-kadesh, which occurs a few verses earlier, in 32:51, and provides a good parallel to Seir and Paran.

Lightning flashing. The Masorah ruled that the single word אֵשְׁדָּת be read as two words אֵשׁ דָּת, but the meaning is thereby not made any clearer. Probably, we have here another place name, in parallel with Seir, Paran, and Meribath-kadesh (Ribeboth-kodesh).

From His right. The right hand denotes strength, as in Exod. 15:6, "Your right hand, O Lord, glorious in power, Your right hand, O Lord, shatters the foe!"

3] *Lover, indeed.* Verses 3–5 are obscure, and many emendations have been offered to make sense out of what is evidently a corrupt text [1]. The above translation apostrophizes God; another possibility is to take Moses as the one who is called lover of his people [2]. Such an understanding would produce a better meaning: "O lover of the people, all His (God's) holy ones were in your care; they followed in your footsteps, accepted your pronouncements. Then the Torah with which Moses charged us became the heritage of the congregation of Jacob, and he (Moses) became king in Jeshurun, when the heads of the people assembled the tribes of Israel together."

4] *Moses charged us.* The phrase entered the Jewish prayer book. In the Ashkenazic *siddur* it is

ה וַיְהִי בִישֻׁרוּן מֶלֶךְ בְּהִתְאַסֵּף רָאשֵׁי עָם יַחַד שִׁבְטֵי

ו יִשְׂרָאֵל: יְחִי רְאוּבֵן וְאַל־יָמֹת וִיהִי מְתָיו מִסְפָּר: ס

ז וְזֹאת לִיהוּדָה וַיֹּאמַר שְׁמַע יְהֹוָה קוֹל יְהוּדָה וְאֶל־

עַמּוֹ תְּבִיאֶנּוּ יָדָיו רָב לוֹ וְעֵזֶר מִצָּרָיו תִּהְיֶה: פ

ח וּלְלֵוִי אָמַר תֻּמֶּיךָ וְאוּרֶיךָ לְאִישׁ חֲסִידֶךָ אֲשֶׁר

Deuteronomy 33

5–8

ing / As the heritage of the congregation of Jacob. / 5] Then He became King in Jeshurun, / When the heads of the people assembled, / The tribes of Israel together. / 6] May Reuben live and not die, / Though few be his numbers. / 7] And this he said of Judah: / Hear, O LORD, the voice of Judah / And restore him to his people. / Though his own hands strive for him, / Help him against his foes. / 8] And of Levi he said: / Let Your Thummim and Urim / Be with Your faithful

part of the child's morning prayer, in the Sephardic and Reform rituals, it is recited during the Torah service.

In *Gates of Prayer*, however, the text is changed to read: "The Torah commanded us by God through Moses...." [3].

5] *Jeshurun.* See at 32:15.

6] *May Reuben live.* Reuben was Jacob's first-born and came first also in the Patriarch's testament (Gen. 49:3). This blessing lacks the introduction provided for the others. A line such as "Of Reuben he said" probably preceded it. For the meaning and historical setting, see commentary below.

7] *His own hands.* If רָב is understood as an imperative, a better reading emerges: "Strengthen his hands for him"; for the verse is clearly meant as a plea to other tribes for greater support of a weakened or perhaps separated tribe (see below).

It is possible, however, that the first part of verse 7 once referred to Simeon (who has no blessing at all) [4], and the second part (perhaps plus verse 11)

to Judah. Later, after Simeon had been absorbed into Judah, its name was dropped from the blessing.

8] *Thummim and Urim.* Oracular devices, usually named in reverse order (Exod. 28:30; Lev. 8:8). Neither their origin nor the meaning of the terms is known. The devices were stones carried by the High Priest and the blind choice of one of them was believed to reveal God's will. With the rise of prophecy they gradually fell into disuse; see details in our commentary on Exod. 28.

The hope which Moses expresses is that the devices, which are in Levi's (the priestly tribe's) charge, might be truly effective.

Whom You tested. The note about the waters of Massah ("test") and Meribah ("strife") is apparently a reference to the incident reported in Exod. 17. But there it was the people of Israel who tested God. Perhaps Moses' recollection indicates that the Levites (who are not mentioned in the Exodus passage) had been part of the rebellious multitude but later became God's staunchest servants (see verse 9).

נְסִיתוֹ בְּמַסָּה תְּרִיבֵהוּ עַל־מֵי מְרִיבָה: הָאֹמֵר לְאָבִיו ט

וּלְאִמּוֹ לֹא רְאִיתִיו וְאֶת־אֶחָיו לֹא הִכִּיר וְאֶת־בָּנָו

לֹא יָדָע כִּי שָׁמְרוּ אִמְרָתֶךָ וּבְרִיתְךָ יִנְצֹרוּ: יוֹרוּ י

מִשְׁפָּטֶיךָ לְיַעֲקֹב וְתוֹרָתְךָ לְיִשְׂרָאֵל יָשִׂימוּ קְטוֹרָה

בְּאַפֶּךָ וְכָלִיל עַל־מִזְבְּחֶךָ: בָּרֵךְ יְהֹוָה חֵילוֹ וּפֹעַל יא

יָדָיו תִּרְצֶה מְחַץ מָתְנַיִם קָמָיו וּמְשַׂנְאָיו מִן־יְקוּמוּן: ס

לְבִנְיָמִן אָמַר יְדִיד יְהֹוָה יִשְׁכֹּן לָבֶטַח עָלָיו חֹפֵף יב

Deuteronomy 33
9–12

* ט בניו קרי.

one, / Whom You tested at Massah, / Challenged at the waters of Meribah; / **9]** Who said of his father and mother, / "I consider them not." / His brothers he disregarded, / Ignored his own children. / Your precepts alone they observed, / And kept Your covenant. / **10]** They shall teach Your norms to Jacob / And Your instructions to Israel. / They shall offer You incense to savor / And whole-offerings on Your altar. / **11]** Bless, O LORD, his substance, / And favor his undertakings. / Smite the loins of his foes; / Let his enemies rise no more. / **12]** Of Benjamin he said: / Beloved of the LORD, / He rests securely beside Him; / Ever does He protect

Driver suggests that the Massah-Meribah episode of the blessing has another event in mind which was not reported in the Torah [5]. The text has word plays on both Massah and Meribah.

9] *I consider them not.* Meaning that, in their utter devotion to God, they slew defectors in the golden calf episode without regard to family association (Exod. 32:27 ff.).

10] *They shall teach.* The Levites had both ritual and educational functions. The latter were in postbiblical times taken over first by scribes and then by rabbis.

Incense to savor. Literally, "they shall place incense in Your nostril" (cf. Gen. 8:21), an anthropomorphism quite acceptable in biblical times and experienced in the same fashion as references

to God's eye or ear. There was an altar for offering incense and another for bringing sacrifices.

11] *Smite the loins.* This does not seem to fit the Levites. The whole verse may have belonged to a blessing directed to Judah; see above, at verse 7.

12] *Benjamin . . . beloved of the Lord.* So called because Jerusalem was located in its territory. Thus God "dwells amid his (Benjamin's) slopes"—a translation preferable to "he (Benjamin) rests between His (God's) shoulders."

According to aggadic tradition, the courts of the Temple were located in the allotted territory of Judah, the Temple itself in Benjamin's. At the time of the division of the land, Jerusalem had belonged to the Jebusites, and after its conquest by David it straddled the border between the two tribes [6].

367

יג עָלָיו כָּל־הַיּוֹם וּבֵין כְּתֵפָיו שָׁכֵן: ס וּלְיוֹסֵף אָמַר

מְבֹרֶכֶת יְהוָֹה אַרְצוֹ מִמֶּגֶד שָׁמַיִם מִטָּל וּמִתְּהוֹם

יד רֹבֶצֶת תָּחַת: וּמִמֶּגֶד תְּבוּאֹת שָׁמֶשׁ וּמִמֶּגֶד גֶּרֶשׁ

טו יְרָחִים: וּמֵרֹאשׁ הַרְרֵי־קֶדֶם וּמִמֶּגֶד גִּבְעוֹת עוֹלָם:

טז וּמִמֶּגֶד אֶרֶץ וּמְלֹאָהּ וּרְצוֹן שֹׁכְנִי סְנֶה תָּבוֹאתָה

יז לְרֹאשׁ יוֹסֵף וּלְקָדְקֹד נְזִיר אֶחָיו: בְּכוֹר שׁוֹרוֹ הָדָר

him, / As he rests between His shoulders. / **13]** And of Joseph he said: / Blessed of the LORD be his land / With the bounty of dew from heaven, / And of the deep that couches below; / **14]** With the bounteous yield of the sun, / And the bounteous crop of the moons; / **15]** With the best from the ancient mountains, / And the bounty of hills immemorial; / **16]** With the bounty of earth and its fullness, / And the favor of the Presence in the Bush. / May these rest on the head of Joseph, / On the crown of the elect of his brothers. / **17]** Like a firstling bull in his

The text has a better meaning if חֹפֵף ("protect") is understood as "spread His wings"; creating the image that God, like an eagle guarding its young, has Benjamin rest between His shoulders; see this simile in 32:11 [7].

13] *Dew from heaven.* A better reading (following the Targum and Hebrew manuscripts) would substitute מֵעַל ("from above") for מִטָּל ("with dew"). The text would then say: "With the bounty of heaven above," which would be similar to the blessing bestowed on Joseph by Jacob (Gen. 49:25).

Deep that couches. The subterranean waters are pictured as a monster; תְּהוֹם (tehom, deep) recalls the dragon Tiamat of Mesopotamian lore (see our commentary on Gen. 1:2 and Gleanings thereon).

14] *Yield of the sun.* On whose warmth the harvest depends [8]. New English Bible translates: "ripened by the sun."

Crop of the moons. That is, of the changing

seasons; but it is possible that the expression reflects a belief in the power of the moon to influence some crops [9].

15] *Hills immemorial.* Or, "everlasting hills," an image also found in Jacob's blessing (Gen. 49:26).

16] *Presence in the Bush.* Or, "Dweller in the Bush," a reference to Moses' perceiving God as speaking out of the burning bush (Exod. 3:1 ff.). The catalogue of nature's blessings (verses 13–15) is climaxed by the privilege of God's presence.

Rest on the head of Joseph. This and the remainder of the verse are almost identical with Gen. 49:26.

For this reason, too, תָּבוֹאתָה (tavotah, "rest on" or "come upon"), which has no grammatical precedent, should be altered to תִּהְיֶיןָ (tiheyena, "shall be") as in Gen. 49:26.

17] *Firstling bull.* An image of strength. The Canaanite chief deity was called "Bull-El."

לוֹ וְקַרְנֵי רְאֵם קַרְנָיו בָּהֶם עַמִּים יְנַגַּח יַחְדָּו אַפְסֵי־ **דברים לג**

אֶרֶץ וְהֵם רִבְבוֹת אֶפְרַיִם וְהֵם אַלְפֵי מְנַשֶּׁה: ס יח—כ

יח וְלִזְבוּלֻן אָמַר שְׂמַח זְבוּלֻן בְּצֵאתֶךָ וְיִשָּׂשכָר בְּאֹהָלֶיךָ:

יט עַמִּים הַר־יִקְרָאוּ שָׁם יִזְבְּחוּ זִבְחֵי־צֶדֶק כִּי שֶׁפַע

כ יַמִּים יִינָקוּ וּשְׂפֻנֵי טְמוּנֵי חוֹל: ס וּלְגָד אָמַר

בָּרוּךְ מַרְחִיב גָּד כְּלָבִיא שָׁכֵן וְטָרַף זְרוֹעַ אַף־

Deuteronomy 33
18–20

majesty, / He has horns like the horns of the wild-ox; / With them he gores the peoples, / The ends of the earth one and all. / These are the myriads of Ephraim, / Those are the thousands of Manasseh. /   **18]** And of Zebulun he said: / Rejoice, O Zebulun, on your journeys, / And Issachar, in your tents. /   **19]** They invite their kin to the mountain, / Where they offer sacrifices of success. / For they draw from the riches of the sea / And the hidden hoards of the sand. /   **20]** And of Gad he said: / Blessed be He who enlarges Gad! / Poised is he like a lion / To tear off

---

Horns of the wild-ox. The re-em was a large-horned species (aurochs) which has since become extinct. Its strength is described in Job 39:9–12. The Psalmist sings (92:11): "You raise my horn high like that of a wild-ox."

These . . . those. Each brother is represented by one of the horns.

18] *On your journeys.* On your voyages by ship; Zebulun's territory lay along the sea (compare Gen. 49:13).

Issachar, in your tents. Issachar was profitably engaged in agriculture, but in Gen. 49:14–15 its life of ease is criticized.

Later Jewish tradition took "tents" to mean "Torah"; in the same way as Balaam's blessing was interpreted: "How fair are your tents, O Jacob" (Num. 24:5) [10].

19] *They invite their kin.* עַמִּים (amim) could also

mean "(other) peoples." Both Zebulun and Issachar were rich and apparently celebrated their success with an annual festivity to which kin or other neighboring people were invited.

To the mountain. Perhaps Mount Carmel or Mount Tabor.

Tradition took this to be a reference to the Temple mount in Jerusalem [11].

Sea . . . sand. The Jerusalem Targum speculates that part of their enterprises consisted of producing a much desired purple dye from mussels, and of making glass from the sand. Such glass making is attested to by Josephus as well as Greek and Roman sources [12].

20] *Enlarges Gad.* Which had its extensive territories east of the Jordan.

Like a lion. In I Chron. 12:9 the Gadites are described as "mighty men of valor, men trained for war, that could handle shield and spear; whose faces were like the faces of lions. . . ."

369

כא קָדְקֹד: וַיַּרְא רֵאשִׁית לוֹ כִּי־שָׁם חֶלְקַת מְחֹקֵק

סָפוּן וַיֵּתֵא רָאשֵׁי עָם צִדְקַת יְהֹוָה עָשָׂה וּמִשְׁפָּטָיו

כב עִם־יִשְׂרָאֵל: ס וּלְדָן אָמַר דָּן גּוּר אַרְיֵה יְזַנֵּק

כג מִן־הַבָּשָׁן: וּלְנַפְתָּלִי אָמַר נַפְתָּלִי שְׂבַע רָצוֹן וּמָלֵא

כד בִּרְכַּת יְהֹוָה יָם וְדָרוֹם יְרָשָׁה: ס וּלְאָשֵׁר אָמַר

בָּרוּךְ מִבָּנִים אָשֵׁר יְהִי רְצוּי אֶחָיו וְטֹבֵל בַּשֶּׁמֶן

כה רַגְלוֹ: בַּרְזֶל וּנְחֹשֶׁת מִנְעָלֶךָ וּכְיָמֶיךָ דָּבְאֶךָ:

Deuteronomy 33

21–25

arm and scalp. / **21]** He chose for himself the best, / For there is the portion of the revered chieftain, / Where the heads of the people come. / He executed the LORD's judgments / And His decisions for Israel. / **22]** And of Dan he said: / Dan is a lion's whelp / That leaps forth from Bashan. / **23]** And of Naphtali he said: / O Naphtali, sated with favor / And full of the LORD's blessing, / Take possession on the west and south. / **24]** And of Asher he said: / Most blessed of sons be Asher; / May he be the favorite of his brothers, / May he dip his foot in oil. / **25]** May your doorbolts be iron and copper, / And your security last all your days. /

21] The verse is obscure and all translations are speculative. The sense seems to be that Gad obtained an extra portion because of its devotion to God, and because it helped Israel in its conquest of Canaan after having obtained its own land at an earlier time (Num. 32; Josh. 22).

"The revered chieftain" was by tradition taken to be Moses, and "the portion" a reference to his unknown burial place [13].

22] *Dan is a lion's whelp.* In Jacob's blessing Judah is so described (Gen. 49:9), while Dan is compared to a serpent (49:17). Both lion and serpent attack suddenly. Dan's chief city was Laish, a poetic name for "lion."

Leaps forth from Bashan. An area east of Lake Kinneret. The story of Dan's settlement is told in Judg. 18. The Song of Songs (4:8) speaks of lion's

dens in the area of Mount Hermon.

23] *West and south.* Of Lake Kinneret, that is, the upper and lower Galilee. The Valley of Jezreel was then and is today the country's bread basket.

24] *Asher.* The name itself connotes happiness; see verse 29 and Ps. 1:1, "Happy is the man. . . ."

Dip his foot in oil. Olive trees abounded in Galilee.

A popular saying was: "It is easier to raise olives in Galilee than a child in the Land of Israel" [14].

25] *Your doorbolts.* The translation of this verse is speculative, although it seems clear that Moses' blessing hopes to secure Asher from the attack of enemies.

כו   אֵין כָּאֵל יְשֻׁרוּן רֹכֵב שָׁמַיִם בְּעֶזְרֶךָ וּבְגַאֲוָתוֹ שְׁחָקִים:

כז   מְעֹנָה אֱלֹהֵי קֶדֶם וּמִתַּחַת זְרֹעֹת עוֹלָם וַיְגָרֶשׁ מִפָּנֶיךָ

כח   אוֹיֵב וַיֹּאמֶר הַשְׁמֵד: וַיִּשְׁכֹּן יִשְׂרָאֵל בֶּטַח בָּדָד

עֵין יַעֲקֹב אֶל־אֶרֶץ דָּגָן וְתִירוֹשׁ אַף־שָׁמָיו יַעַרְפוּ

כט   טָל: אַשְׁרֶיךָ יִשְׂרָאֵל מִי כָמוֹךָ עַם נוֹשַׁע בַּיהֹוָה

מָגֵן עֶזְרֶךָ וַאֲשֶׁר־חֶרֶב גַּאֲוָתֶךָ וְיִכָּחֲשׁוּ אֹיְבֶיךָ לָךְ

וְאַתָּה עַל־בָּמוֹתֵימוֹ תִדְרֹךְ:   ס

Deuteronomy 33
26–29

26] O Jeshurun, there is none like God, / Riding through the heavens to help you, / Through the skies in His majesty. /   27] The ancient God is a refuge, / A support are the arms everlasting. / He drove out the enemy before you / By His command: Destroy! /   28] Thus Israel dwells in safety, / Untroubled is Jacob's abode, / In a land of grain and wine, / Under heavens dripping dew. /   29] O happy Israel! Who is like you, / A people delivered by the LORD, / Your protecting Shield, your Sword triumphant! / Your enemies shall come cringing before you, / And you shall tread on their backs. /

26] *Riding through the heavens.* Compare Ps. 68:34, "... who rides the ancient highest heavens," an expression with parallels in Ugaritic literature [15].

27] *A support are the arms everlasting.* Similar to the older translations which had "underneath are the everlasting arms." But the meaning of the whole verse is not certain, and various emendations have been proposed which yield quite different interpretations.

In the traditional ritual of the synagogue, this verse begins the last annual reading from the Torah, which takes place on Simchat Torah. The person given the honor of reciting the blessings over it is called *Chatan Torah* (Bridegroom of the Torah).

28] *Untroubled is Jacob's abode.* Or, "Jacob's fountain." Note that the word "untroubled" (Hebrew בָּדָד, *badad*) has the basic meaning "apart," isolation being regarded as an assurance of survival. (See also above, at 33:12.)

Ein Yaacov ("Fountain of Jacob") is the title of a well-known collection of tales and interpretations culled from the Talmud.

29] *Tread on their backs.* Literally, "on their high places," that is, you will triumph over them [16].

371

Comparisons

Three times in the Bible the nature and fate of the tribes are the subject of poetic creation: in the testament of Jacob (Gen. 49), in the blessing of Moses (Deut. 33), in the song of Deborah (Judg. 5). The blessing ascribed to Moses and its historic setting will be understood more clearly if one compares it with the passages in Genesis and Judges.

Name of Tribe and Location	Genesis Chapter 49	Judges Chapter 5	Deuteronomy Chapter 33
Reuben East of Jordan, near Dead Sea	First-born; powerful, but no longer the leader	Indifferent to national crisis, though not without internal conflict	Near extinction
Simeon Central Negev	Described as violent; in danger of being scattered	No mention (Josh. 5:15–16 shows that Simeonite cities have been absorbed into Judah)	No mention
Judah Northern Negev	The leading tribe; strong; seat of kings	No mention	Weak, separated from rest of people; in need of help[1]
Levi No territory	Behavior condemned; priesthood not mentioned	No mention	Praise for its courage and priestly role (which, however, is not yet assured)
Benjamin Jerusalem and north	Warlike; a "ravenous wolf"	Supported Deborah	Beloved; secure; wars are over
Joseph[2] Highlands around Samaria; half of Manasseh lies east of Jordan	Strong; blessed by God	Leading contributor to Deborah's victory	Blessed greatly; strong

[1] But see commentary above, at verse 7.
[2] In Genesis and Deuteronomy, Ephraim and Manasseh are represented by their eponymous father, Joseph.

Name of Tribe and Location	Genesis Chapter 49	Judges Chapter 5	Deuteronomy Chapter 33
Zebulun Western Jezreel, reaching to the sea	Seafaring	Holds marshal's staff; risked its life for Israel	Seafaring; successful
Issachar Eastern Jezreel	Rich lands; criticized for serving others	Supported Deborah	Agricultural; successful; not criticized
Gad East of Jordan	Strongest tribe east of Jordan, involved in warfare	Called "Gilead"; did not support Deborah	Highly praised; warlike; expansionist
Dan Originally south of Jaffa, but migrated to northernmost Galilee	Aggressive; "shall judge his people" (possibly a reference to Samson)	Did not support Deborah; went on sea expedition instead	Aggressive; strong (possible reference to Samson)
Naphtali Northern Galilee, along Lake Kinneret	Compared to a roaming hind with fawns	Praised for its contribution	Rich; "sated with favor"
Asher Southern and western Galilee	Rich	No mention	"Most blessed"; rich olive orchards; but needs secure borders

Analysis

As explained in our commentary on Gen. 49, the testament of Jacob came probably from the time of the Judges, before 1000 B.C.E., not too far removed from the particular events that gave rise to the song of Deborah. The tribes were already in Canaan but neither securely settled nor as yet united into a nation; they differed widely from one another and seem to have been bound together by faith rather than blood. The sup-

position of a common ancestry served to strengthen their still tenuous ties.

In contrast, the blessing ascribed to Moses originated in an era of greater security, which would place it several centuries later, after the monarchy had been established. Intertribal rivalries are not mentioned; no criticism is leveled against any tribe; nor is idolatry an issue. Israel is now a nation, and God—who is not mentioned in Jacob's blessing—is exalted as the people's savior, and because of Him Israel's future looks bright. This makes it probable that the poem was a hymn of national thanksgiving, perhaps recited at some ritual function, and later put into the mouth of Moses and appended to the Book of Deuteronomy.

The words spoken about Judah may give us a further key to the blessing's location in history. The tribe of Judah (which by this time had incorporated Simeon) had become separated from the rest of the nation,[3] which may be a reference to the division of the united kingdom after the death of Solomon. The song was sung in Judah and was in part a plea to the north to reunite the nation. It may have been about 900 B.C.E., a time when the Levites had already assumed an important place in the cultic system. Not unlike a prophecy, the blessing is the bearer of future hopes. Placed in the mouth of Moses it becomes "much more than an empty wish; it contains creative words which are capable of fashioning the future" [17].

For unknown reasons, the blessing suffered considerably in its early stages of transmission, resulting in a number of textual corruptions that add to the already difficult text with its antique poetic language. The poem has none of the fervor of the song of Moses; rather, it speaks to a community which on the whole enjoys material prosperity and is still secure in its relation to God. Idolatrous practices have not as yet roused the poet's ire, as they have in the song. The latter comes to us from a subsequent age when disaster had overtaken the nation—a far cry from the fairly idyllic picture drawn in the blessing.

---

[3] Reading verse 7 as we have it now.

GLEANINGS

From Criticism to Praise

(The interpretations that follow are based on the traditional assumption that Moses himself authored the blessing.)

Moses had always rebuked his people, but in the end he gives them words of hope. The Prophets learned from him.   MIDRASH [18]

Another explanation: One should connect Deut. 1:1 ("These are the words...") with 33:1 ("This is the blessing..."). Moses begins with "These are the words" (of criticism and exhortation) and ends with "This is the blessing" (containing only praise). This teaches that even in Moses' harshest words was contained the promise of blessing.

M. HACOHEN [19]

Why does Moses speak of himself as "the man of God"? To indicate that, though he spoke the blessing, the inspiration came from God.

S. R. HIRSCH [20]

Another explanation: Up 'til now Moses had been very humble, but when about to die he felt that future generations would not know who he was. He therefore reasoned: "If not now, when?"   CHASIDIC [21]

Another explanation: God had said to Moses that the hour of his death had come (31:14). Then Moses said: "All these years I have rebuked Israel, I want to leave them with a blessing." Thereupon Satan came and tried to prevent him, but Moses cast him down and blessed Israel despite him.

MIDRASH [22]

Only Israel

"The Lord came from Sinai ... Seir ... Paran" (verse 2). This is a reminder that the Torah was offered also to other nations who, however, refused it when they heard some of its laws. Only Israel accepted, and unconditionally so.

MIDRASH [23]

Another explanation: God spoke "from Sinai" in Hebrew; "from Seir" in Latin; "from Mount Paran" in Arabic; "from Ribeboth-kodesh" in Aramaic. For God offered the Torah to all nations.

MIDRASH [24]

The Threefold Cord

"This..." in verse 1 refers to the Torah, which is in itself a blessing. Why then does the text go on to speak of God and Moses? To indicate that all three participated in the blessing, and to bear out what Koheleth said (Eccles. 4:12): "A three-fold cord is not quickly broken."

MIDRASH [25]

Friendship

The Sages warn us that one should not try a friend too much, lest envy or even hatred ensue. One exception to this rule is God: His friends will always "rest securely beside Him" (verse 12).

A. I. KOOK [26]

The Portion of the Revered Chieftain (verse 21)

This refers to the grave of Moses, for, though Moses died on Mount Nebo (which is in the territory of Reuben), the angels transferred him to the portion of Gad and the Lord buried him there. The grave of Moses was one of the ten things created by God on the sixth day of Creation, at dusk, before the Sabbath [27].

MIDRASH [28]

Alone

(Taking בָּדָד, in verse 28, to mean "alone" rather than "untroubled.") Other nations rely on treaties for their safety. Israel is not secured in this way, but only by its trust in God.

M. HACOHEN [29]

PART V

Epilogue

THE DEATH OF MOSES

End and Beginning

The brief last chapter of Deuteronomy reports the death of the great leader. God shows him the Land of Promise, and the viewing of the land is both a vision of the future and an assurance that the faithful God will carry out what He swore to the Ancestors. The Torah concludes with the passing of Moses, but in the person of his successor the forward thrust of Israel's history is secured. While Joshua is not another Moses—"Never again did there arise in Israel a prophet like Moses" (verse 10)—he will be a competent leader for changing times. The only constant is God himself; because of Him the end of one era is at once the beginning of a new one. Generations may change, the God of the covenant remains the same.

In tone and style, the final verses of the book are bereft of the emotion that had erupted in the song of Moses, and neither do they contain the imagery of the blessing. The account is straightforward, and the final judgment of Moses' greatness speaks merely in terms of comparison: he was, and will remain, superior to all others who are gifted with prophecy; but the nature of his greatness will have to be culled from his life's story, not from a final assessment.

Traditional opinions varied on the authorship of chapter 34. According to one, the whole Torah was written by Moses, including all the last chapter; according to another, Joshua wrote verses 5-12; while Ibn Ezra assigned all the chapter to Joshua. He advanced two reasons: the use of the third person in chapter 34 and the silence of the text on any final return of Moses from the mountain [1]. This bold assertion later on helped to open the door for those who doubted the Mosaic authorship of other passages as well.

Modern scholars, too, though arguing from different premises, are divided on the authorship of these verses, which may at one time have stood at the end of Numbers or followed after Deut. 32:52 (the blessing being a later insertion into the text; see above, commentary on ch. 33) [2]. But such an investigation into the literary origins of the chapter is likely to remain inconclusive. For a variety of traditions have here been brought together, and this amalgam forms in itself a fitting conclusion to the Torah as we now have it in its totality. For, though the whole book was the product of different times and sources, it became in the course of centuries one book, the repository of Israel's faith and of its struggle with and for God. The final chapter now concludes this one great story or, rather, the story of its genesis and growth. The future will unfold new chapters, and the Book of Joshua will begin their recitation.

אַ וַיַּעַל מֹשֶׁה מֵעַרְבֹת מוֹאָב אֶל־הַר נְבוֹ רֹאשׁ הַפִּסְגָּה
אֲשֶׁר עַל־פְּנֵי יְרֵחוֹ וַיַּרְאֵהוּ יְהֹוָה אֶת־כָּל־הָאָרֶץ אֶת־
בַ הַגִּלְעָד עַד־דָּן: וְאֵת כָּל־נַפְתָּלִי וְאֶת־אֶרֶץ אֶפְרַיִם
וּמְנַשֶּׁה וְאֵת כָּל־אֶרֶץ יְהוּדָה עַד הַיָּם הָאַחֲרוֹן:
גַ וְאֶת־הַנֶּגֶב וְאֶת־הַכִּכָּר בִּקְעַת יְרֵחוֹ עִיר הַתְּמָרִים
דַ עַד־צֹעַר: וַיֹּאמֶר יְהֹוָה אֵלָיו זֹאת הָאָרֶץ אֲשֶׁר

Deuteronomy 34

1–4

1] Moses went up from the steppes of Moab to Mount Nebo, to the summit of
Pisgah, opposite Jericho, and the Lord showed him the whole land: Gilead as far
as Dan;   **2]** all Naphtali; the land of Ephraim and Manasseh; the whole land of
Judah as far as the Western Sea;   **3]** the Negeb; and the Plain—the valley of
Jericho, the city of palm trees—as far as Zoar.   **4]** And the Lord said to him,

34:1] *Steppes of Moab.* The river Jordan is flanked
on both sides by fertile flatlands, which on the
east were called the steppes of Moab.

Mount Nebo . . . Pisgah. Possibly one and the
same mountain, but given different names by
different traditions. Or, Pisgah may have meant a
mountain range, and Mount Nebo, the peak on
which Moses died. Today, the name Mount Nebo
is attached to an elevation that rises 2,643 feet
(805.5 meters) above sea level; it provides a good
view of much of central Israel.

The Lord showed him. There is no vantage
point from which the whole land can be seen, but
one should note that the report flavors the natural with the supernatural. Similarly, it serves no
purpose to attempt a reading of the text that
would allow for a naturalistic interpretation.

An example of the latter is to understand "as
far as Dan" (עַד דָּן) as "toward Dan."

Gilead. The area east and southeast of Lake
Kinneret.

Dan. The area of Mount Hermon which became the location of the tribe after it migrated
northward (see above, at 33:22).

2] *Naphtali.* Located west of Lake Kinneret.

Ephraim . . . Manasseh . . . Judah. The area west
of the Jordan between Kinneret and the Dead
Sea. (Part of Manasseh dwelt east of the Jordan.)

This section of the country was in 1948 occupied by the Hashemite Kingdom of Jordan and
generally referred to as West Bank. In 1967, control of the area was wrested from the Jordanians
by Israel and called *Yehudah ve-Shomron* (i.e., Judah
and Samaria).

Western Sea. The Mediterranean. Neither this
nor Mount Hermon is visible from Mount Nebo.

3] *The Plain.* The text notes its chief city, Jericho.
Its biblical name was *Kikar* ("Round") because
the area around Jericho has the appearance of a
deep dish. Its fertility was vividly described by
Josephus [3].

Zoar. The place to which Lot fled after the
destruction of Sodom and Gomorrah, Gen. 19:20 ff.
According to Josephus, Zoar was located southeast of the Dead Sea (an area that today is part of
Saudi Arabia) [4].

נִשְׁבַּעְתִּי לְאַבְרָהָם לְיִצְחָק וּלְיַעֲקֹב לֵאמֹר לְזַרְעֲךָ
ה אֶתְּנֶנָּה הֶרְאִיתִיךָ בְעֵינֶיךָ וְשָׁמָּה לֹא תַעֲבֹר: וַיָּמָת
שָׁם מֹשֶׁה עֶבֶד־יְהוָֹה בְּאֶרֶץ מוֹאָב עַל־פִּי יְהוָֹה:
ו וַיִּקְבֹּר אֹתוֹ בַגַּי בְּאֶרֶץ מוֹאָב מוּל בֵּית פְּעוֹר וְלֹא־
ז יָדַע אִישׁ אֶת־קְבֻרָתוֹ עַד הַיּוֹם הַזֶּה: וּמֹשֶׁה בֶּן־
מֵאָה וְעֶשְׂרִים שָׁנָה בְּמֹתוֹ לֹא־כָהֲתָה עֵינוֹ וְלֹא־נָס
ח לֵחֹה: וַיִּבְכּוּ בְנֵי יִשְׂרָאֵל אֶת־מֹשֶׁה בְּעַרְבֹת מוֹאָב
ט שְׁלֹשִׁים יוֹם וַיִּתְּמוּ יְמֵי בְכִי אֵבֶל מֹשֶׁה: וִיהוֹשֻׁעַ בִּן־

"This is the land of which I swore to Abraham, Isaac, and Jacob, 'I will give it to your offspring.' I have let you see it with your own eyes, but you shall not cross there."

5] So Moses the servant of the LORD died there, in the land of Moab, at the command of the LORD. **6]** He buried him in the valley in the land of Moab, near Beth-peor; and no one knows his burial place to this day. **7]** Moses was a hundred and twenty years old when he died; his eyes were undimmed and his vigor unabated. **8]** And the Israelites bewailed Moses in the steppes of Moab for thirty days. The period of wailing and mourning for Moses came to an end. **9]** Now Joshua

4] *You shall not cross there.* The Midrash embellished this brief account and told of Moses' resistance to God's judgment; see Gleanings below.

5] *At the command of the Lord.* Literally, "by the mouth of the Lord," whence the tradition arose that Moses died by a divine kiss [5].

6] *He buried him.* That is, God buried Moses. But the Hebrew construction could also be understood as "someone buried him," meaning "he was buried." This would suggest that the burial place was once known and later forgotten [6].

Ibn Ezra, basing himself on a rabbinic saying, understood "Moses buried himself," that is, he went away to die [7].

Near Beth-peor. Its location is not certain; it was somewhere east of Jericho. See at Deut. 3:29.

7] *A hundred and twenty years old.* On the symbolism of this figure, see at Deut. 31:2. Moses had been eighty years old at the time of the Exodus (Exod. 7:7).

His vigor. לֵחֹה (lechoh) occurs only here. It is probably related to *lach* (moist) and was meant as a reference to Moses' unabated (possibly sexual) capacity.

Note the opposite English idiom for an old person, "dried up."

8] *Thirty days.* As was done for Aaron; Num. 20:29. The period has remained significant in Jewish mourning practices. (See further in Gleanings.)

Wailing and mourning. The two went together; wailing was an externalized expression of grief and complemented other mourning customs.

נוּן מָלֵא רוּחַ חָכְמָה כִּי־סָמַךְ מֹשֶׁה אֶת־יָדָיו עָלָיו

וַיִּשְׁמְעוּ אֵלָיו בְּנֵי־יִשְׂרָאֵל וַיַּעֲשׂוּ כַּאֲשֶׁר צִוָּה יְהֹוָה

אֶת־מֹשֶׁה: וְלֹא־קָם נָבִיא עוֹד בְּיִשְׂרָאֵל כְּמֹשֶׁה אֲשֶׁר   י

יְדָעוֹ יְהֹוָה פָּנִים אֶל־פָּנִים: לְכָל־הָאֹתֹת וְהַמּוֹפְתִים   יא

אֲשֶׁר שְׁלָחוֹ יְהֹוָה לַעֲשׂוֹת בְּאֶרֶץ מִצְרָיִם לְפַרְעֹה

וּלְכָל־עֲבָדָיו וּלְכָל־אַרְצוֹ: וּלְכֹל הַיָּד הַחֲזָקָה וּלְכֹל   יב

הַמּוֹרָא הַגָּדוֹל אֲשֶׁר עָשָׂה מֹשֶׁה לְעֵינֵי כָּל־יִשְׂרָאֵל:

Deuteronomy 34

10–12

Haftarah Vezot ha-Berachah, p. 492

son of Nun was filled with the spirit of wisdom because Moses had laid his hands upon him; and the Israelites heeded him, doing as the LORD had commanded Moses.

10] Never again did there arise in Israel a prophet like Moses—whom the LORD singled out, face to face,   11] for the various signs and portents that the LORD sent him to display in the land of Egypt, against Pharaoh and all his courtiers and his whole country,   12] and for all the great might and awesome power that Moses displayed before all Israel.

9] *Had laid his hands.* סָמַךְ (*samach*), whence *semichah*, the general term for ordination; see at Num. 27:18 ff.

10] *Face to face.* This was the most important as-

pect of Moses' singularity (see at Num. 12:8). Deuteronomy once probably ended here.

11] *Various signs.* Most likely a later addition which recalls the Exodus as the central experience of Moses' and Israel's existence.

Moses—Man and Legend

In Jewish tradition he is called *Mosheh Rabbenu*, Moses our teacher. The cognomen combines affection and awe: he is Israel's own teacher par excellence. He was not called the lawgiver, for the law was believed to be of God. The pages of the Torah tell us what kind of man he was, and the fertile imagination of the nation he loved embellished this picture with many legends. The book was named after him[1] because he was its transmitter, not because he was its creator. With the written text, so this tradition further avers, God also gave him the Oral Law, interpretations which would be arrived at by compenent scholars in centuries to come, 'til the end of time. The revelation at Sinai encompassed the totality of the divine law and was called Torah in its wider sense. It revealed what God wanted of His people, and this will was made known to Moses, His servant and our teacher. Thus the traditional view.

A scholarly historical assessment is of needs more complex. It too proceeds from the biblical text, for it is the only source of information about Moses available to us. But, since the Torah itself is the repository of various traditions from different times, the "historical Moses" cannot be securely recovered. Scholars generally agree that Moses was indeed a historical figure who led a people of slaves out of Egypt and who gave them a religious and legal constitution. He was a man identified with the desert, with Sinai and/or Horeb, and not with Canaan itself, which for him never moved from promise to fulfillment. All else about Moses is conjectural, and so far all attempts to separate fact from later legend, or to find the Mosaic core of the Torah legislation, have failed to produce anything approaching a scholarly consensus.

What kind of person emerges when we take the Torah as a whole, without regard to its literary history? Curiously, though Moses dominates the four books from Exodus to Deuteronomy, and many incidents are reported about him, his personality remains somewhat distant. He is human but at the same time more than human; he is alive and at once statuesque, like a sculpture cast in resplendent marble. He sins, yet the nature of his sin is unclear; while in Numbers his own shortcomings cause God's judgment on him, in Deuteronomy he is said to have been punished because of Israel's transgressions. He is called a meek or humble man, yet he is wrathful like God; he is submissive to his Master, yet stands up to Him in defense of Israel for whom he is prepared to surrender his life. We cannot discern any of his feelings toward his wife and children, toward Aaron, his brother and constant co-worker, or toward Joshua, his successor.[2] He has unique access to the Divine Presence and is so secure in this relationship that when Eldad and Medad act as prophets he is not jealous of them. Above all, he loves his people; his severest castigations are rendered out of love. He assumes many roles: lawgiver, founder of the national cult, military leader, and mouthpiece of God. Not surprisingly, later generations stood in awe of him, and his very greatness prevented them from embracing him as they did David or Elijah. His towering stature bestrides the history of Israel, and thereby the history of Western civilization. He is a commanding personage in Christian and

---

[1] The term *Torat Mosheh* is already found in the Bible, e.g., Mal. 3:22; Dan. 9:11.

[2] But others' feelings toward him are occasionally recorded, see e.g., Num. 12:1 ff.

Moslem traditions and through them has helped to shape the canons of law and morality. The last verses of Deuteronomy, which report his death, are thus also prologue to the further history of Israel as well as of humanity.

(For a canvas of characterizations, see Gleanings.)

GLEANINGS

The Death of Moses

(Many of the following stories are taken from the Midrash "The Death of Moses our Teacher," which was composed to be recited on Simchat Torah, when the annual reading cycle is concluded and commenced once again. For further midrashim, see Gleanings on ch. 31.)

When Moses saw that death was imminent he said to Israel: "I have given you much trouble by teaching you Torah and mitzvot—forgive me!" They said: "Our teacher and master, you are forgiven."

Then they said: "We too have angered you often and given you much trouble, forgive us too!" He said: "You are forgiven" [8].

(The Midrash records in detail how solicitous Moses was about his successor and how he served him publicly.)

Moses did everything to ensure that Joshua was installed as Israel's leader. But, when the divine cloud descended and separated him from God and Joshua, he thought: Better a hundred deaths than feeling jealous even once!

As he was about to die his wisdom was given to Joshua. Then Moses said to God: "Until this moment I desired life, now my life is in Your hands" [9].

(Moses entered into a prolonged argument with God, giving reasons why he should not die.)

God said: "You must die because you did not sanctify Me."[3]

Moses responded: "You deal with Your creatures in mercy and forgive them once, twice, even three times—but not me!"

Said God: "You committed six sins, still I did not accuse you."

"You refused Me when I asked you to deliver your people" (Exod. 4:13).

"You accused Me of making things worse for Israel and of not having delivered the people" (Exod. 5:23).

"You tested Me twice" (in the uprising of Korah, Num. 16:29, 30).

"You slandered your people when you said: 'Listen, you rebels!'" (Num. 20:10), "and again when you called them 'a breed of sinful men'" (Num. 32:14) [10].

Moses had to die because he had slain the Egyptian taskmaster (Exod. 2:11 ff.).

God: "Did I tell you to slay the Egyptian?"

Moses: "But You killed all the first-born in Egypt!"

God: "Do you resemble Me? I cause people to die and I also revive them" [11].

Ten times is Moses' death mentioned in the Bible: eight times in Deuteronomy and twice in the Book of Joshua. For ten times it was decreed that Moses should not enter Eretz Yisrael, though the judgment was not sealed until the Court on High declared: "You shall not go across yonder Jordan" (Deut. 3:27). But Moses was unconcerned, thinking: Israel has committed many sins, yet whenever I prayed for them God answered me.

When God saw that Moses made light of the decree and did not engage in prayer, He swore to himself that Moses would not enter the Land and sealed the decree.

Moses now donned sackcloth and commenced to pray. He drew a circle and said: "I will not move until You alter the judgment." But God

---

[3] The reference is to the story told in Numbers 20.

ordered all the gates of heaven to be shut to Moses' prayer [12].

God decreed that not even Moses' bones would cross into the Promised Land. But, Moses objected, would not the bones of Joseph accompany the people? God then accused Moses of not having acknowledged his ancestry when he was called an Egyptian (Exod. 2:19), whereas Joseph had acted differently (Gen. 41:12–16) [13].

Moses prayed in fact 515 times for a reversal of the judgment. Whence do we know this? From Deut. 3:23, "I pleaded with the Lord at that time...." The Hebrew for "I pleaded" is וָאֶתְחַנַּן, the letters of which add up to 515.[4] At last God relented and allowed him at least to *view* the land [14].

Moses continued to plead his case.
"If I cannot go into the Land, let me become like one of the beasts of the field that eat its grass and drink its water and live and enjoy the world; or let me fly about like a bird gathering its food— only let my soul be like one of them."
God then said: "Enough! Never speak of this matter again!" [15].

In that hour God said: "I have heard your prayer, I Myself will bury you" [16].

When God kissed Moses and took away his soul[5] He wept, as it were. So did the heavens and the earth [17].

Why did God busy himself with Moses' burial? Because, when at the time of the Exodus everyone was looking for gold and silver, Moses looked for the coffin of Joseph. When he found it he himself carried it on his shoulders. Thus he helped to fulfill the oath of Gen. 50:25 [18].

Moses died on the seventh day of Adar and dur-

ing each hour of the day God informed him how many more hours he had to live [19].

In his view of the Land Moses had also glimpsed the future, even the time of resurrection[6] [20].

The grave of Moses is concealed from human eyes so that it would not be turned into a place of adoration [21].

Israel is called "holy" (Lev. 19:2 and elsewhere), but not Moses, not in the Torah nor in later Jewish parlance.[7]

Face to Face
Then slowly the aged
God bowed down His aged face to the aged
   mortal.
Withdrew him out of himself in kisses
into his older age. And with hands of creation
swiftly remounted to the mountain, until it
   amounted
to nothing more than the others, lightly
   surmounting
human conjecture.   R. M. RILKE [23]

The Life of Moses
The term "prophet" when used with reference both to Moses and to the others is ambiguous. The same applies, in my opinion, to his miracles and to the miracles of others.... For instance, Moses' apprehension was not like that of the Patriarchs, but greater.   MAIMONIDES [24]

I have conceived the idea of writing the life of Moses, who, according to the account of some persons, was the lawgiver of the Jews, but according to others only an interpreter of the sacred laws, the greatest and most perfect man that ever lived, having a desire to make his character fully known to those who ought not to remain in ignorance respecting him, for the glory of the laws which he left behind him has reached over the

---

[4] ו=6; א=1; ת=400; ח=8; נ=50; נ=50.
[5] See above, at verse 5.
[6] Based on reading יָם (sea, Deut. 34:2) as יוֹם (day).
[7] The expression "Holy Moses" is not traceable to

Jewish sources. It appeared first in 1855 "as an oath or expletive" and later as an expression of "surprise or amazement" [22].

whole world, and has penetrated to the very furthest limits of the universe . . . though the historians who have flourished among the Greeks have not chosen to think him worthy of mention.

PHILO [25]

Moses and Aaron

Of Moses it says that "the Israelites" wept for him (בְּנֵי יִשְׂרָאֵל, verse 8), but of Aaron that "*all the house of Israel*" did (כָּל בֵּית יִשְׂרָאֵל, Num. 20:29). This means that only the men bewailed Moses, and both men and women mourned for Aaron, because the latter had made peace between people, and thousands of children, born to parents reconciled by him, bore his name. MIDRASH [26]

Formerly I felt little affection for Moses, probably because the Hellenic spirit was dominant within me, and I could not pardon the Jewish lawgiver for his intolerance of images and every sort of plastic representation. I failed to see that, despite his hostile attitude to art, Moses was himself a great artist, gifted with the true artist's spirit. Only in him, as in his Egyptian neighbors, the artistic spirit was exercised solely upon the colossal and the indestructible. But, unlike the Egyptians, he did not shape his works out of bricks or granite. His pyramids were built of men, his obelisks hewn out of human material. A feeble race of shepherds he transformed into a people bidding defiance to the centuries—a great, eternal, holy people, God's people, an exemplar to all other peoples, the prototype of mankind; he created Israel. With greater justice than the Roman poet could this artist, the son of Amram and Yochebed the midwife, boast of having erected a monument more enduring than brass.

HEINE [27]

Moses did not establish the religious relationship between the Bene Yisrael and YHVH. He was not the first to utter that "primal sound" in enthusiastic astonishment. That may have been done by somebody long before who, driven by an irresistible force along a new road, now felt himself to be preceded along that road by "Him," the invisible one who permitted himself to be seen. But it was Moses who, on this religious relationship, established a covenant between the God and

"His people." Nothing of such a kind can be imagined except on the assumption that a relation which had come down from ancient times has been melted in the fire of some new personal experience. The foundation takes place before the assembled host; the experience is undergone in solitude. M. BUBER [28]

Hosea and Jeremiah have found sublime words to celebrate the indissoluble union between God and Israel. Feeling the full weight of this union, Moses has a deeper sense of his own indestructible attachment to Israel. He is the only one of all the men in the Bible for whom God offers to let Israel disappear and to begin history with another people. Moses refuses. In spite of the immense risks, he wishes to continue history with this people, and it is this people which will continue in history. What an absurd undertaking, contrary to the clarity of God and the realities of the situation! However, the decision of Moses is as obstinate as it is far-reaching. Today we recognize its immediate and unalterable consequences in the reassertion of the Jewish people, whose very existence seems contrary to reason and who do not fit into the ordinary scheme of things. A. NEHER [29]

Moses was a man, a human being. He was not a saint, an ascetic, one who had stripped himself of all ordinary human feelings; equally, he was not a hero in the sense in which that word was ordinarily understood in ancient times. Certainly he was in no way a demigod. He is indeed presented as a figure of incomparable greatness. But the neat and exact precision with which the dividing line between him and God is always made clear is one of the most admirable features of these narratives. There was nothing divine about Moses. Therefore neither the men of his own time nor the men of later times ever offered to him such worship as is offered to God alone. He was "the man Moses." G. VON RAD [30]

The fact that Moses himself is not shown as having lived to participate in the conquest of the Promised Land proper may well reflect, as well as the historical fact that the leader of the fugitives from Egypt who welded them into a people and gave them divinely sanctioned laws lived and died before the real conquest of Palestine was begun, the belief that the stern and bloody business of conquering a country, even if done in the implementation of a divine promise and in the interests of a divinely ordained way of life, was not the job of the lawgiver himself. . . . Moses is trapped between his ideals and the harsh practicalities involved in carrying them out. That is a not unjustifiable reading of the story as it is given to us in the biblical text.   D. DAICHES [31]

His passion for social justice, his struggle for national liberation, his triumphs and disappointments, his poetic inspiration, his gifts as a strategist and his organizational genius, his complex relationship with God and His people, his requirements and promises, his condemnations and blessings, his bursts of anger, his silences, his efforts to reconcile the law with compassion, authority with integrity—no individual, ever, anywhere, accomplished so much for so many people in so many different domains. His influence is boundless, it reverberates beyond time.   E. WIESEL [32]

Falasha Legend

(The Falashas are an ethnic group in Ethiopia who are part of the Jewish people and of its early traditions.)

God informed Moses that he would die on a Friday. Accordingly, Moses put on his shrouds every Friday and waited for the Angel of Death. . . . He saw three angels, who assumed the appearance of three young men, busying themselves with the digging of a grave. "For whom is the grave?" asked Moses. "For the beloved of God," was the reply. "If so," said Moses, "I will assist you in your work." The angels rejoined: "We know not whether the grave is big enough. Wouldst thou go down into it? The person to be buried therein is of thy size." As soon as Moses descended into the grave, he was met there by the Angel of Death, who greeted him with the words: "Peace unto thee, O Moses the son of Amram!" Moses replied: "Peace be with thee"—and he died. The angels then buried him in the grave in which he met death [33].

The Wonder

I do not pretend to understand the mystery of human transformation, the moment when the response of a man to the world about him throws upon his mind a new and wondrous light concerning the nature of our species and binds him to a vision of the future to which he gives over his life. . . . In the person of Moses was developed the paradigm of the Israelite prophet, the individual through whom God speaks to and acts upon man.

CHAIM POTOK [34]

REFERENCE NOTES

BIBLIOGRAPHY

Reference Notes

Part I *Prologue. First Discourse*

1. For an overview, see the essays by Moshe Weinfeld and Paul A. Riemann, *Interpreter's Dictionary of the Bible* [hereafter cited as *IDB*], ed. George A. Buttrick et al. (4 vols., New York and Nashville: Abingdon Press, 1962), Supplement, pp. 188 and 192 ff.; also D. N. Freedman, *ibid.*, pp. 229 ff. For a more comprehensive treatment, see M. Weinfeld, *Deuteronomy and the Deuteronomic School* (Oxford: Clarendon Press, 1972).

The Setting   DEUT. 1:1–5

1. So B. Gemser, *Vetus Testamentum* [hereafter cited as *VT*] (Leiden, Holland: E. J. Brill), 2 (1952), pp. 349–355. David Hoffmann, *Deuteronomium* (Berlin: Poppelauer, 1913–1922), *ad loc.*, compares עֵבֶר הַיַּרְדֵּן to a fixed term like Gallia Ulterior.
2. See Sifre Deut. 1; Rashi.
3. "Introducing Deuteronomy," esp. n. 7.
4. Ellis Rivkin, *The Dynamics of Jewish History* (Sarasota, Fla.: New College, 1970), p. 473; see commentary on Gen. 45:1–28 and Gleanings.
5. Quoted by B. S. Jacobson, *Meditations on the Torah* (Tel Aviv: Sinai, 1956), p. 268.
6. The latter derivation was suggested by Ben Zion Wacholder in private communication.
7. *Itture Torah*, comp. and ed. Aaron Jacob Greenberg (Tel Aviv: Yavneh, from 1965), Vol. VI, p. 2.
8. Deut. R. 1:6.
9. After Deut. R. 1:1.
10. *Itture Torah*, Vol. VI, p. 13.
11. Deut. R. 1:4.
12. Based on Ber. 8a; *Itture Torah*, Vol. VI, p. 14.
13. *Itture Torah*, Vol. VI, p. 15.

First Review   DEUT. 1:6–45

1. Sifre Deut. 1:13. So also New American Bible: men of repute.
2. San. 7b.
3. So San. 8a.
4. So Rashi; Luzzatto; for a survey of other interpretations, see *Yalkut Me'am Lo'ez* (11 vols., Jerusalem: Or Chadash, 1967–1971).
5. See Samuel R. Driver's commentary on Deuteronomy (New York: Charles Scribner's Sons, 1916).
6. Hoffmann, with sources.
7. *Min ha-Torah* (5 vols., Jerusalem: Reuben Mass, 1972), Vol. V, p. 1112.
8. Sab. 119b.
9. *Mishneh Torah* [hereafter cited as *Yad*], Hilch. San. 2; see also Deut. R. 1:10.
10. Vol. VI, p. 20.
11. *Itture Torah*, Vol. VI, p. 21, with reference to Zech. 8:16.
12. Devarim, Vol. I, p. 121.
13. *Itture Torah*, Vol. VI, p. 18.

Second Review DEUT. 1:46—3:29

1. See Weinfeld, *Deuteronomy*, pp. 70 f.

2. Joseph Reider, in his commentary on Deuteronomy (Philadelphia: Jewish Publication Society, 1937), and Hoffmann take the first view; Rashbam and Luzzatto the latter.

3. See the surveys in *Encyclopaedia Judaica* (16 vols., Jerusalem: Keter, 1972), Vol. 6, cols. 1103–1104; *Entsiklopedyah Mikra'it* (Jerusalem: Mosad Bialik, from 1955), Vol. VI, cols. 332–333, with relevant literature.

4. B.B. 121 a-b; cf. also Ta'an. 30b–31a.

5. For a traditional reconciliation of the sixty towns mentioned here and the twenty-three in I Chron. 2:22, see Hoffmann.

6. *The Jewish Antiquities*, trans. William Whiston (New York: Al Burt Co., n.d.), VIII, 2:3. On the Tar-

gum's opinion that Argob was Trachonitis of the Hellenistic period, see Reider.

7. See *IDB*, Vol. IV, p. 837; *Encyclopaedia Judaica*, Vol. 16, cols. 378 ff.

8. Vol. VI, p. 27.

9. M. Hacohen, *Al ha-Torah* (5 vols., Jerusalem: Reuben Mass, 1962), Vol. V, p. 483; based on Ber. 30 b.

10. Quoted by Hacohen, *Al ha-Torah*, Vol. V, p. 482.

11. Quoted in *Itture Torah*, Vol. VI, p. 29.

12. *Min ha-Torah*, Vol. V, p. 1128.

13. *Itture Torah*, Vol. VI, p. 31.

14. *Al ha-Torah*, Vol. V, p. 485; based on a midrash.

15. Va'etchanan 1–3.

16. Ed. Abbott, Gilbert, Hunt, and Swaim (New York: Bruce Publishing Co., 1969), p. 152.

Summary: To Observe the Law DEUT. 4:1–43

1. See Kenneth A. Kitchen, *Ancient Orient and Old Testament* (London: Tyndale Press, 1966), pp. 92 f; Dennis J. McCarthy, *Treaty and Covenant* (Rome: Pontifical Biblical Institute, 1963), p. 135.

2. See Rashi on Lev. 18:4.

3. Samson Raphael Hirsch.

4. See Sifre Deut. 58 and the parallel passage in Lev. R. 18:4, 5; also Hoffmann.

5. The Talmud, San. 38 b, opts for "God" rather than "gods."

6. So Rav in A.Z. 55a; see also Meg. 9b (where different readings are listed); Rashbam; the Church Fathers (quoted by Driver, p. 71); Hubert Junker, *Deuteronomium* (Würzburg: Echter Verlag, 1952); Carl Steuernagel, *Das Deuteronomium* (Göttingen: Vandenhoeck und Ruprecht, 1923).

7. See Rashi.

8. Deut. R. 10:4; Rashi.

9. Hag. 11b–12a.

10. See *Gates of Prayer*, ed. Chaim Stern (Reform) (New York: Central Conference of American Rabbis, 1975), p. 538; for its use in the traditional synagogue, see S. Singer–I. Abrahams, *Companion to the Daily Prayer Book* (rev. ed., London: Eyre and Spottiswoode, 1922), p. cxlix.

11. See Weinfeld, *Deuteronomy*, p. 81; *IDB*, Supplement, pp. 188 ff., where the parallels with the Davidic

covenant are explored and the changeover to a conditional covenant considered a necessary adjustment to the destruction of Jerusalem.

12. So Ibn Ezra. Some ancient versions have the plural here, as does Deut. 10:15.

13. *Das fünfte Buch Mose: Deuteronomium* (Göttingen: Vandenhoeck und Ruprecht, 1968), p. 38.

14. *Gates of Prayer*, p. 516; Standard Prayer Book, p. 93.

15. Mak. 9b–10a.

16. Epic of Erra, V, 43; on the Egyptian passage, see von Rad, *Deuteronomium*, who notes, however, that there is some doubt over its exact meaning.

17. See Maimonides, *Yad*, Hilch. Mamrim 2:9.

18. So, for instance, S. R. Hirsch, *ad* 4:2.

19. See San. 88b–89a; R. H. 28b; *Itture Torah*, Vol. VI, p. 34.

20. See W. Gunther Plaut, *The Rise of Reform Judaism* (New York: World Union for Progressive Judaism, 1963), *passim; idem, The Growth of Reform Judaism* (New York: World Union for Progressive Judaism, 1965), pp. 347 ff.

21. See *Gates of Mitzvah*, ed. Simeon J. Maslin (New York: Central Conference of American Rabbis, 1979).

22. Deut. R. 2:12. But another opinion (*ibid.*) holds that the gates of prayer are sometimes closed.

23. *Itture Torah*, Vol. VI, p. 37.

24. *Ibid.*; *Wellsprings of Torah*, ed. N. L. Alpert (2 vols., New York: Judaica Press, 1969), Vol. II, pp. 374–375.

25. Ber. 21b; Kid. 30a.

26. *Itture Torah*, Vol. VI, p. 39.

27. Based on San. 38a; see also S. R. Hirsch.

28. *Min ha-Torah*, Vol. V, pp. 1142–1143.

29. צָרַת רַבִּים חֲצִי נֶחָמָה; see also Deut. R. 2:22 and Aharon Hyman, *Otzar Divre Chachamim* (Tel Aviv: Devir, 1972), p. 490.

30. Deut. R. 2:12.

31. *Itture Torah*, Vol. VI, p. 42.

Part II *Second Discourse*

1. So von Rad, *Deuteronomium*.

The Decalogue DEUT. 4:44—5:30

1. Nachmanides on Exodus 20:2–3; Ber. 45a.

2. Von Rad, *Deuteronomium*.

3. Moshe Greenberg, *Journal of Biblical Literature* [hereafter cited as *JBL*], 75 (1957), pp. 34–39.

4. Mech. Bachodesh 7.

5. See the extensive study by G. J. Blidstein, *Judaism*, 14, 2 (1965), pp. 151–171.

6. Mech. Nezikin 5; San. 86a; Maimonides, *Yad*, Hilch. Genevah 9:1.

7. *Pesikta Rabbati* 24, ed. M. Friedmann (reprint, Tel Aviv, 1963).

8. So Elias Auerbach, *Moses* (Amsterdam: G.J.A. Ruys, 1953), p. 202.

9. So, for instance, Reider.

10. So Nachmanides; Biur; Hoffmann.

11. Mak. 23b–24a.

12. On the rabbinic position of which laws apply in Israel only, see Mishnah Kid. 1:9 and Talmud.

13. This has been emphasized by Matitiahu Tsevat, *Zeitschrift für die Alttestamentliche Wissenschaft* [hereafter cited as *ZAW*], Vol. 84 (1972), pp. 447–459. On creation and redemption, see Franz Rosenzweig, *The Star of Redemption*, trans. William W. Hallo (New York: Holt, Rinehart and Winston, 1970–1971), pp. 314, 317, 319, 359. The land has its "Sabbath of complete rest" and so does time (Lev. 23:3 and 25:4 use the expression שַׁבַּת שַׁבָּתוֹן to signify God's mastery over both).

14. Ber. 33b.

15. *Ethics of the Fathers* 3:15.

16. For a survey of Jewish thought on the subject, see *Encyclopaedia Judaica*, Vol. 7, col. 129. See also E. Urbach, *The Sages* (2 vols., Jerusalem: Magnes Press, 1975), Vol. I, pp. 256 ff.

17. Men. 29b. Another version of the Akiba story is found in Ber. 61b; see commentary on Deut. 34:1–12 and Gleanings.

18. Mak. 10a; *Yalkut Me'am Lo'ez*, Devarim, Vol. I, p. 243.

19. Commentary, *ad loc.*

20. *Moses*, p. 194.

21. *Itture Torah*, Vol. VI, pp. 423, 427.

22. *Ad loc.*; see the comment by Isaac Caro, *Toledot Yitzchak*, Parashah Yitro.

23. *Itture Torah*, Vol. VI, p. 44.

24. *Deuteronomium, ad loc.*

25. *Star of Redemption*, p. 315.

26. *Itture Torah*, Vol. VI, p. 45.

27. *Ad loc.*, based on Mech. Bachodesh 7.

28. End of Parashah Bechukotai 115b (Soncino ed.), Vol. V, p. 160.

29. *Wellsprings*, Vol. II, p. 379.

30. Meg. 21a.

The Shema DEUT. 6:1–25

1. In Matthew 22:37 it is called the greatest of the commandments.

2. *Pentateuch and Haftorahs*, ed. Joseph H. Hertz (Oxford: Oxford University Press, 1929), p. 920.

3. Kaufmann Kohler, *Jewish Theology* (New York: Macmillan, 1918), p. 90.

4. Louis Jacobs, *A Jewish Theology* (London: Darton, Longman, and Todd, 1973), p. 21.

5. So King James Version, New English Bible, and New American Bible.

6. For a survey of understandings, see Driver, p. 9;[10] Reider, *ad loc.*

7. Ber. 54a.

8. San. 74a.

9. *Shulchan Aruch*, Orach Chayim 656; Yore De'ah 249:1.

10. So M. Tsevat, *Hebrew Union College Annual* [hereafter cited as *HUCA*], 29 (1958), p. 125, n. 112. See also von Rad: *vorsprechen.*

11. See Exod. 13, reference n. 5.

12. See Deut. 11:20 and also Driver, p. 93, for similar practices among other Mediterranean peoples.

13. Hul. 17a; also Hoffmann.

14. So Nachmanides. Maimonides includes this verse in his catalogue of positive commandments (7): When taking an oath, one *must* swear by God's name.

15. Details in Hirsch and Hoffmann.

16. Von Rad.

17. Quoted in *Encyclopaedia Judaica*, Vol. 14, col. 1374.

18. For the best comprehensive, yet brief, survey of this subject, see Jacobs, *A Jewish Theology*, pp. 152 ff., and also Rosenzweig, *Star of Redemption*, pp. 173–185.

19. A point stressed by Luzzatto, Rosenzweig, and others; see also Gleanings.

20. See W. L. Moran, *Catholic Biblical Quarterly* [hereafter cited as *CBQ*], 25 (1963), pp. 77–87.

21. *HUCA*, 6 (1929), pp. 39–53.

22. Maimonides, *Yad*, Hilch. Teshuvah 10:1; Sifre Deut. 32; Hoffmann, p. 85: "Love and fear can be joined only in God." See also Tanch. 25.

23. Sifre Deut. 32.

24. *Duties of the Heart* (חוֹבוֹת הַלְּבָבוֹת), trans. Moses Hyamson (2 vols., New York: Feldheim, 1978); on the majority view, Maimonides, *Sefer ha-Mitzvot*, positive commandments (3); Nehama Leibowitz, *Studies in the Weekly Sidrah* (Jerusalem: World Zionist Organization), 7th series, 1962, pp. 301 ff.

25. Ber. 15b.

26. *Gates of Prayer*, p. 33 *passim.*

27. Mishnah Ber. 1:1–2; Talmud Ber. 2a–3a, 9b.

28. Mishnah Ber. 1:3.

29. Ber. 61b.

30. *Ad loc.*

31. Deut. R. 2:31.

32. *Theologico-Political Treatise*, 14.

33. *The Kingly Crown*, II, trans. Bernard Lewis.

34. *A Jewish Theology*, p. 37.

35. *Das Wesen des Judentums* (5th ed., Frankfurt: J. Kauffmann, 1922), p. 101.

36. The formulation of the Thirteen Principles of Faith of Maimonides (first enunciated in his commentary on the Mishnah San. 10) is printed in traditional prayer books, together with the Ten Commandments, at the end of the morning service.

37. Quoted by Hertz, p. 770.

38. *Interpreter's Bible* (12 vols., New York and Nashville: Abingdon, 1957), Vol. II, p. 373.

39. Sifre Deut. 32; see also Rashi.

40. *Yad*, Yesode ha-Torah 2:1–2.

41. *Shevet Yehudah*, quoted by Jacobson, *Meditations on the Torah*, p. 274.

42. Commentary, *ad loc.*

43. Commentary, *ad loc.*; repeated also in chasidic sayings, see *The Hasidic Anthology*, ed. Louis I. Newman (New York: Bloch, 1944), p. 115, n. 7.

44. *Itture Torah*, Vol. VI, p. 48.

45. *Star of Redemption*, p. 176.

46. *Ibid.*

47. Quoted in Hacohen, *Al ha-Torah*, Vol. V, p. 490.

48. I:833.

49. Commentary, *ad loc.*; based on the Midrash (Sifre Deut. 31).

50. Va'etchanan 269a (Soncino ed.), p. 364.

51. *Yad*, Yesode ha-Torah 10.

52. *Ad loc.*

53. לֹא עָשׂוּ לִפְנִים מִשּׁוּרַת הַדִּין (B.M. 30b).

54. Note that *A Passover Haggadah*, prepared by the Central Conference of American Rabbis, ed. Herbert Bronstein, illust. Leonard Baskin (New York: Grossman Publishers, 1974), p. 30, quotes the Hebrew of 6:20 according to the Masorah but translates אֶתְכֶם (you) as if it read אוֹתָנוּ (us).

55. *Ad loc.*

Dealing with Idolatry   DEUT. 7:1–26

1. See J. van Seters, *VT*, 22 (1972), pp. 63–81.

2. Lev. R. 17:6.

3. See *Views of the Biblical World* (5 vols., Chicago and New York: Jordan Publishing Co., 1959–1961), Vol. I, p. 258.

4. Pictured in Gaalyah Cornfeld-David N. Freed-

man, *Archaeology of the Bible: Book by Book* (New York: Harper and Row, 1976), p. 25.

5. So Yigael Yadin, *Hazor* (London and Jerusalem: Weidenfeld and Nicolson, 1975), p. 46.

6. *Moses* (Oxford and London: East and West Library, 1947), p. 105.

7. Von Rad.

8. See Stanley Gevirtz, *Patterns in the Early Poetry of Israel* (Studies in Ancient Oriental Civilization, No. 32, 1963; Chicago: University of Chicago), pp. 35 ff.

9. *Natural History*, 26:15.

10. So A. Z. 20a: לֹא תִתֵּן לָהֶם חֲנִיָּה בַּקַּרְקַע.

11. Commentary on verse 16.

12. Lines 16–18, *Ancient Near Eastern Texts* [hereafter cited as Pritchard, *ANET*], ed. James B. Pritchard (3rd ed., Princeton: Princeton University Press, 1969), p. 320.

13. Junker, commentary on 20:10–15.

14. Yeb. 76a; Kid. 68b; see S. R. Hirsch; Hoffmann, p. 91. See further *Shulchan Aruch*, Even ha-Ezer 4:9; Be-er Hetev 8.

15. See commentary on Gen. 18:8.

16. See Yehezkel Kaufmann, *The Religion of Israel* (Chicago: University of Chicago, 1960), p. 300.

17. *Year Book of the Central Conference of American Rabbis* [hereafter cited as *CCAR Year Book*], Vol. 83 (1973), pp. 57 ff.

18. See Rashi on verse 4; Yeb. 33a; Kid. 68b.

19. *Gates of Mitzvah*, pp. 36 f.

20. Erub. 22a.

21. *Ethics of the Fathers* 2:1; Tanch. Ekev 1; Rashi.

22. Hacohen, *Min ha-Torah*, Vol. V, p. 1052.

23. *Itture Torah*, Vol. VI, p. 59.

24. A. Z. 52 a-b.

25. *Ibid.*, 46a.

The Good Life   DEUT. 8:1—9:5

1. So Driver.

2. See Rashi; based on Midrash Shir ha-Shirim 4:4 ff. A more naturalistic explanation is offered by Ibn Ezra but opposed by Nachmanides.

3. See H. Brunner, *VT*, 8 (1958), pp. 428 f.

4. See Mishnah San. 6:5 and Talmud 46 a-b; Ber. 5a; B.M. 85a; Gen. R. 9:8.

5. *Guide of the Perplexed*, III,8–25.

6. Ber. 48b; Maimonides, *Yad*, Hilch. Berachot 4.

7. Ber. 35a.

8. *Shulchan Aruch*, Orach Chayim 175, 176; based on Ps. 104:14.

9. For a detailed survey, see *Encyclopaedia Judaica*, Vol. 7, cols. 835 ff.; *Yalkut Me'am Lo'ez*, Devarim, Vol. II, pp. 445 ff.

10. *The Kuzari*, trans. Hartwig Hirschfeld (New York: Pardes, 1946), 3:17.

11. Quoted in Hacohen, *Al ha-Torah*, Vol. V, p. 499.

12. *Itture Torah*, Vol. VI, p. 65.

13. *Ibid.*, p. 67.

14. *Ibid.*

15. Deut. R. 3:11.

The Stiff-Necked People   DEUT. 9:6—10:11

1. See Deut. R. 3:15.

2. Among those who count two ascents and three periods of abstinence are Luzzatto and S. R. Hirsch; Ibn Ezra takes verse 18 as an anticipatory reference to the second ascent.

3. *Ad loc.*; based on Jerusalem Shek. 6:1.

4. So Ibn Ezra; Nachmanides; based on Sifre Deut. 82. This explanation applies also to verse 3.

5. So Hoffmann, *ad loc.*: The passage about the Levites is placed here *because* they were faithful; about Aaron, *despite* his aberration.

6. An extended discussion of this theme may be found in "The 'desert motif'...," Shemaryahu Talmon, *Biblical Motifs*, ed. Alexander Altmann (Cambridge, Mass.: Harvard University Press, 1966).

7. Translation from *Gates of Repentance*, ed. Chaim Stern (New York: Central Conference of American Rabbis, 1978), pp. 269, 327.

8. Hacohen, *Al ha-Torah*, Vol. V, p. 503.

9. *Itture Torah*, Vol. VI, p. 71.

10. Quoted, *ibid.*, p. 69.

11. *Ibid.*, p. 71.

12. Ber. 8 b.
13. Men. 99 a.
14. Deut. R. 3:12.

15. *Ibid.*, 3:13.
16. *Itture Torah*, Vol. VI, p. 71.
17. *Devarim*, p. 58; based on Ber. 32 b.

The Good Land DEUT. 10:12—11:25

1. *Yad*, Hilch. Yesode ha-Torah 2:2; Hilch. Teshuvah 9:1.
2. For a detailed discussion, see M. Guttmann, *Das Judentum und seine Umwelt* (Berlin: Philo Verlag, 1927), pp. 43–114.
3. This follows Ibn Ezra. However, the Masoretic notation (introducing a pause between "witnessed" and "the lesson") would suggest a different understanding; see Hoffmann.
4. So also Hoffmann in his German rendition: *endgültig*.
5. San. 110a; Num. R. 18:19.
6. Ber. 2:2.
7. See Lenn E. Goodman, *Conservative Judaism*, XXXII, 3 (1979), pp. 36–49.
8. B. M. 59b. According to another tradition (*ibid.*), the number of such passages is forty-six; see Tosafot, *ad loc.*
9. On the often tortuous arguments of traditional exponents and the critique of Maimonides and Abarbanel, see Plaut, the *Journal of the Central Conference of American Rabbis* [hereafter cited as *CCAR Journal*] (January 1966), pp. 32–34, where the whole subject is discussed in detail.
10. Commentary on Exod. 22:20.
11. This is stressed by S. R. Hirsch, *ad* 19:33–34.
12. Data taken from *Encyclopaedia Judaica*, Vol. 9, cols. 123 ff., especially cols. 185–186.
13. *Israel's Land* (Stuttgart: Kohlhammer, 1972).
14. Gen. R. 21:6.
15. Based on the Talmud, Hul. 89a; quoted in *Itture Torah*, Vol. VI, p. 72.
16. Ber. 33b.
17. *Al ha-Torah*, Vol. V, p. 506.
18. Quoted in *Yalkut Me'am Lo'ez*, Devarim, Vol. II, p. 514.
19. Quoted in *The Hasidic Anthology*, ed. Newman, p. 48 (Circumcision on Shabbat: Talmud, Sab. 131b–132a).
20. *The Hasidic Anthology*, ed. Newman, p. 148, n. 13.
21. *Star of Redemption*, p. 240.
22. Ber. 40a; see also commentary on 21:1 ff.
23. B.B. 21a.
24. *This People Israel*, trans. Albert Friedlander (Philadelphia: Jewish Publication Society, 1965), pp. 115 f.

The Divine Command DEUT. 11:26–32

1. See R. H. Pfeiffer, *Introduction to the Old Testament* (New York: Harper and Bros., 1948), p. 227; in Christian Scriptures, John 4:20. The two mountains are pictured in *Views of the Biblical World*, Vol. I, p. 289.
2. See Driver, p. 133, who discusses in detail the difficulties of locating Gilgal.
3. Commentary on verse 26; see also *Yalkut Me'am Lo'ez*, Devarim, Vol. II, p. 599.
4. Commentary, *ad loc.*
5. Deut. R. 4:2.
6. *Ibid.*, 4:3.
7. On verse 26.
8. *Itture Torah*, Vol. VI, p. 83.
9. Sifre Deut. 54.
10. On verse 29.

The Central Sanctuary DEUT. 12:1—13:1

1. So Hoffmann, p. 135, with further references.
2. Commentary, p. 140.
3. Sifre Deut. 61.

4. There was a controversy over whether this refers to the first or second tithe; see Hoffmann, pp. 142–146.

5. See Rashi.

6. For the traditional view, see Hoffmann; Hertz, p. 939; for a summary of the critical position, von Rad, pp. 63 ff.; Steuernagel, pp. 94 f.

7. For a survey of opinions, see *IDB*, Supplement, pp. 23–25; J. Weingren, *Journal of the Ancient Near Eastern Society*, 5 (Gaster Festschrift, 1973), pp. 427–433.

8. *HUCA*, 46 (1976), pp. 19–56.

9. *Ibid.*, p. 41.

10. Jacob Milgrom offers a complex analysis of a variety of biblical terms, *HUCA*, 47 (1976), pp. 1–18.

11. For a summary of these procedures, see *Encyclopaedia Judaica*, Vol. 6, cols. 26 ff.

12. Kaufmann, *Religion of Israel*, pp. 13 ff. *passim*.

13. Sifre Deut. 59.

14. A.Z. 45b.

15. Yore De'ah 276:9; *Yalkut Me'am Lo'ez*, Devarim, Vol. II, p. 605.

16. *Deuteronomium*, p. 171.

17. Commentary on verse 19.

False Prophets DEUT. 13:2–19

1. See *Entsiklopedyah Mikra'it*, Vol. V, pp. 690 f.; *Encyclopaedia Judaica*, Vol. 13, cols. 1150 ff.; Abraham J. Heschel, *The Prophets* (New York: Burning Bush Press, 1955), *passim*.

2. See the controversy in San. 89b and Targum Jonathan.

3. So Mishnah San. 7:10; the Septuagint translates "You shall denounce him" (so that he may be tried). But Philo, *On Monarchy*, 1:7, end, thought that a "battlefield execution" was called for, as in the case of Phinehas (Num. 25:7–8).

4. See Weinfeld, *Deuteronomy*, p. 94. See there also (p. 98, n. 5), for ancient Near Eastern parallels to uterine siblings.

5. *Ad loc.* and II Corinthians 6:15.

6. San. 40a–b in explanation of Mishnah San. 5:1.

7. So M. Buber, *On the Bible: Eighteen Studies*, ed. Nahum N. Glatzer (New York: Schocken, 1968), p. 177.

8. See William W. Hallo-William K. Simpson, *The Ancient Near East: A History* (New York: Harcourt Brace Jovanovich, 1971), p. 158.

9. San. 90a; Sifre Deut. 84.

10. Ibn Ezra on Deut. 13:2.

11. Nachmanides on Deut. 13:2.

12. Rashbam on Deut. 13:2.

13. See n. 2 in Gleanings to Deut. 1:1–5.

14. *Nacherinnerung zur "Antwort" Lavaters* (Gesammelte Schriften, III, 65, 1843; Leipzig: Brockhaus). Similarly, Leibowitz, *Studies*, 1st series, 5715 Annual, Re'eh, p. 2.

15. *Deuteronomium*, p. 181.

16. Sifre Deut. 86. The Midrash calls attention to the use of סָרָה in both Deut. 13:6 (which deals with prophets) and 19:16 (which deals with witnesses).

17. Tosefta San. 14:14.

18. San. 11:5 f.

19. *Itture Torah*, Vol. VI, pp. 89–90.

20. *Ibid.*, p. 90.

21. Sotah 14a.

22. On verse 13; based on Sifre Deut. 92.

23. San. 112b. See Alexander Guttmann, *HUCA*, 40–41 (1969–1970), pp. 251–275.

24. Tosefta San. 14:1.

25. *Studies*, 2nd series, 5716 Annual, Re'eh, p. 6.

Of Food, Tithes, and Social Equity DEUT. 14:1—15:23

1. The subject is treated in detail in Mak. 21a.

2. See Luzzatto; Hoffmann, pp. 191 f.

3. Zvi Weinberg, *Beth Mikra*, 69 (1977), pp. 230–237.

4. For a survey, see *Encyclopaedia Judaica*, Vol. 6, cols. 31–34; I. Grunfeld, *The Jewish Dietary Laws* (2 vols., London: Soncino Press, 1972); Mishnah Hul. 3:6; Hul. 61b–63b; Nachmanides on Lev. 11:13.

5. See also Rashi on Lev. 11:19.

6. Further, see Hoffmann, p. 200; Sifre Deut. 103.

7. Sifre Deut. 105 takes the first, Rashi, on verse 23, the latter position.

8. Nachmanides argues this in detail, basing himself on Sifre Deut. 111, opposing Ibn Ezra.

9. Mishnah Sheb. 10:3-7; see commentary on Lev. 25.

10. Driver, p. 182, further suggests that the provision for freeing the bondwoman reflected important social changes.

11. Pritchard, *ANET*, Code of Hammurabi 40, p. 183; see Theodor H. Gaster, *Myth, Legend and Custom in the Old Testament* (New York: Harper and Row, 1969), pp. 312 ff.

12. See Hoffmann, pp. 243 ff., for the way in which traditional commentators attempted to harmonize these differences.

13. See Maria deJ. Ellis, *Journal of Cuneiform Studies*, 26 (1974), pp. 248-250.

14. See M. Weinfeld's article, *Encyclopaedia Judaica*, Vol. 15, cols. 1156-1162, where the institution of tithing is discussed in some detail; see also Kaufmann, *Religion of Israel*, pp. 189 f.

15. Yeb. 86b.

16. See the essay by Roland de Vaux, *The Bible and the Ancient Orient* (London: Darton, Longman, and Todd, 1972), pp. 252-269. For an interpretation of Isa. 66:3-4a, see J. M. Sasson, *VT*, 26 (1976), pp. 199-207.

17. Matthew 8:28-32, in the tale of the Gadarene swine.

18. Kid. 49b; on dogs, see the juxtaposition in Sab. 155b; also in Matthew 7:6. Further data are given by E. Wiesenberg, *HUCA*, 27 (1956), pp. 213-233.

19. Mishnah B.K. 7:7. On the entire subject, see *Entsiklopedyah Mikra'it*, Vol. III, pp. 90-94.

20. Kid. 36 a.

21. Vol. VI, p. 93.

22. *Ibid.*, p. 95.

23. Quoted, *ibid.*, pp. 95 f.

24. *Ibid.*, p. 96.

25. Shlomo ben Adret, quoted, *ibid.*, p. 97.

26. Quoted in *Al ha-Torah*, p. 524.

27. Abraham Samuel Benjamin Wolf; quoted, *ibid.*, p. 525.

28. *Al ha-Torah.*

29. Based on B.M. 31b.

30. *Deuteronomium*, pp. 31 f.

31. Trans. Jacobson, *Meditations on the Torah*, p. 283. The polemic is against Maimonides, *Guide*, III,48 and Nachmanides, commentary on Lev. 11:13.

32. Quoted by Leibowitz, *Studies*, 5719 Annual, Re'eh, pp. 5 f.

The Holy Days DEUT. 16:1-17

1. On new moons and sabbaths, see W. W. Hallo, *HUCA*, 48 (1977), p. 10, n. 47.

2. Sifre Deut. 129.

3. See Hoffmann, pp. 257 f.

4. So Ibn Ezra; Nachmanides; S. R. Hirsch.

5. For possible Mesopotamian analogues, see Levine-Hallo, *HUCA*, 38 (1967), pp. 45, 57.

6. See the dispute of the schools of Hillel and Shammai; Betzah 2a, 7b.

7. Sifre Deut. 131; Pes. 5b.

8. *Ad loc.*; see the discussion in Sab. 9b, 34b.

9. *The Jewish War*, trans. William Whiston (New York: Al Burt Co., n.d.), VI, 9:3.

10. One opinion, recorded in Hag. 17b, did venture this conclusion, which Ibn Ezra (on Deut. 16:7) characterizes as put forth by "the falsifiers."

11. See Hoffmann, p. 260.

12. Sifre Deut. 133; Rashi; Ibn Ezra.

13. R. H. 5a.

14. *Revolutionary Constructivism* (New York: Young Poale Zion Assoc., 1937), p. 19.

15. *Jewish Theology*, p. 462.

16. *Moses and the Vocation of the Jewish People* (New York and London: Harper/Longmans, 1959), p. 136.

17. *The Menorah Treasury*, ed. Leo W. Schwarz (Philadelphia: Jewish Publication Society, 1964), p. 712.

18. *Hegyonot Mikra* (Jerusalem: Karta, 1972), p. 259.

19. San. 39b.

20. I:554 (Emor).

21. This is based on Jerusalem Ber. 9:7 (14b): ‏אַכִּין וְרַקִּין מְעוּטִין.

22. Quoted in Hacohen, *Min ha-Torah*, Vol. V, p. 1208.

1. San. 7b.
2. Mak. 6b.
3. Sifre Deut. 153.
4. According to Hoffmann, pp. 286 f., 309, he is a judge who disobeys the high court.
5. Sifre Deut. 145.
6. Mishnah San. 2:4; also Targum Jonathan.
7. Von Rad, *Deuteronomium*.
8. Jerusalem San., end.
9. The Mishnah makes eighteen wives the maximum (San. 2:4), but already in talmudic times multiple marriages were discouraged.
10. So Rashi; based on Sifre Deut. 163.
11. Hul. 10:1.
12. Josephus, *Antiquities*, IV, 8:14.
13. Sifre Deut. 156; details in Hoffmann, pp. 310 ff.
14. See Sifre Deut. 156; Maimonides, *Sefer ha-Mitzvot*, positive commandments (173); Ibn Ezra on Deut. 17:15; Nachmanides on 17:14.
15. Ber. 58a goes so far as to suggest that even a lowly official serves only with God's consent. See also Nachmanides on verse 15.

16. Sifre Deut. 144.
17. In the commentary attributed to him, on II Chron. 19:6.
18. San. 32b.
19. Commentary on Deut. 16:20. The latter saying is also stressed in chasidic sources; see *Wellsprings*, Vol. II, p. 397; *Itture Torah*, Vol. VI, p. 110.
20. *Itture Torah*, Vol. VI, p. 110; *Yalkut Me'am Lo'ez*, Devarim, Vol. II, p. 704.
21. Commentary on verse 20; similarly *Yalkut Me'am Lo'ez*, Devarim, Vol. II, p. 705.
22. *Sefer ha-Mitzvot*, negative commandments (13); see Sifre Deut. 145.
23. Commentary on 16:22.
24. Ber. 18b.
25. *Yad*, Hilch. Berachot 11:3.
26. Mishnah R. H. 2:9.
27. Commentary on Deut. 17:15 ff.
28. Hul. 134b. See also commentary on Num. 25:13 and Gleanings.
29. *Guide*, III, 39; the order of the sentences has been reversed for the sake of this extract.

Administration of Law and State, II   DEUT. 18:9—19:21

1. Saadia's commentary (Jerusalem: Mosad Harav Kook, 1963) on Deut. 12:31; Luzzatto; Reider on the basis of Jer. 7:31; 19:5.
2. Rashi.
3. See San. 64b; Sifre Deut. 171; Nachmanides calls it "a type of witchcraft."
4. Rabbi Akiba (San. 65b) understood it to mean an astrologer, apparently relating the word to עוֹנָה, period, season. Others derived the term from עַיִן, eye, and thought מְעוֹנֵן to be an illusionist (*ibid.*); Ibn Ezra (on Lev. 19:26) took it to refer to someone predicting from the movement of clouds.
5. Sifre Deut. 171.
6. *Ibid.*, based on Ps. 58:5–6.
7. Commentary, p. 224.
8. *Deuteronomium*, p. 88.
9. Sifre Deut. 177. On the broader terminology of divine and human punishment, and, especially on יָמֻת and יוּמַת, see J. Milgrom, *Levitical Terminology* (Berkeley: University of California, 1970), pp. 5–8.

10. Sifre Deut. 179.
11. So Driver, p. 233; von Rad, p. 91; see the discussion in Sifre Deut. 185; M. Greenberg, *Entsiklopedyah Mikra'it*, Vol. VI, col. 387; idem, *IDB*, Vol. I, pp. 638 f.
12. Shev. 30a.
13. See Mak. 5b; also Hoffmann.
14. See Greenberg, *JBL*, 78 (1959), pp. 125–132; idem, *The Jewish Expression*, ed. Judah Goldin (New Haven: Yale University Press, 1970), pp. 18–37.
15. The literature on Jewish magic is considerable; see especially J. Trachtenberg, *Jewish Magic and Superstition* (New York: Behrman, 1939); *Encyclopaedia Judaica*, Vol. 11, "Magic"; Urbach, *The Sages*.
16. *Religion of Israel*, pp. 47 f.
17. *Ibid.*, p. 41.
18. *The Sages*, p. 98.
19. Quoted, *ibid.*
20. Commentary on Deut. 18:13.
21. *The Hasidic Anthology*, ed. Newman, p. 390, n. 5.
22. Sifre Deut. 175. Nachmanides supports this

view, but Hoffmann, p. 343, calls it "only a homily."

23. *Sefer ha-Mitzvot*, positive commandments (176, 182).

24. *Deuteronomium*, p. 360.

25. Sifre Deut. 188.

Administration of Law and State, III DEUT. 20:1—21:9

1. *Deuteronomium*, p. 382.
2. Dillmann, after Ewald, quoted by Driver, p. 236.
3. *Deuteronomium*, p. 94.
4. Sotah 42a–43a; Sifre Deut. 192; Hor. 12b.
5. See the controversy in Jerusalem Sotah 8:3 (22b, c).
6. Jerusalem Sotah 8:9 (23a).
7. See Sifre Deut. 194; Luzzatto; Hoffmann.
8. *Deuteronomium*, p. 94.
9. Mishnah Sotah 8:3, 4 and commentaries thereon.
10. Lev. R. 17:6.
11. See Driver, p. 240.
12. So Sifre Deut. 203.
13. Sab. 19a.
14. Mishnah Sotah 9:1,2.
15. The Talmud (Sotah 46a–b) records a controversy on this matter; see also Ziony Zevit, *JBL*, 95 (1976), pp. 377–390, who deals extensively with the *eglah arufah*.
16. Several articles on biblical warfare are easily accessible: A. Malamat, *Encyclopaedia Judaica*, Supplement, 1975–1976, pp. 166 ff.; N. Gottwald, *IDB*, Supplement, pp. 942 ff.; Y. Yadin, *World History of the Jewish People*, ed. Benjamin Mazar (New Brunswick, N.J.: Rutgers University Press, 1970), Vol. III, pp. 127 ff. The classical works on the subject are G. von Rad, *Der Heilige Krieg* (1st ed., Zurich: Zwingli Verlag, 1951), and Y. Yadin, *The Art of Warfare in Biblical Lands* (New York: McGraw-Hill, 1963).
17. Hor. 12b; he was called "the priest anointed for war" (Sotah 42b and Sifre Deut. 103). It was doubtless he who arranged a sacrifice before the campaign, as Samuel and Saul did in their day (I Sam. 7:9 and 13:9). The expression "sanctify the war" occurs in various biblical passages (e.g., Jer. 6:4 and Micah 3:5).

18. On this term and on *milchemet chovah*, see Sotah 44b.
19. Sifre Deut. 190; Mishnah Sotah 8:7.
20. See the instructive articles by Robert Gordis, *Congress bi-Weekly*, 38 (1971), pp. 19–22; E. J. Freudenstein, *Judaism*, 19, 4 (Fall 1970), pp. 406–414; J. I. Helfand, *Judaism*, 20, 3 (Summer 1971), pp. 330–335.
21. *Sefer ha-Mitzvot*, negative commandments (57).
22. Sab. 140b. For exceptions, when health was involved, see Sab. 129a; also *Yalkut Me'am Lo'ez*, Devarim, Vol. II, p. 576.
23. See Zevit, *JBL*, 95 (1976), pp. 377–390; von Rad, *Deuteronomium*, who calls the procedure "magical"; Steuernagle believes it to be a supplication to the victim for forgiveness.
24. Hoffmann, p. 394; similarly Steuernagel; Abarbanel.
25. Mishnah Sotah 9:9; also the talmudic amplification in Sotah 47a–b.
26. Commentary on 20:1.
27. *Sefer ha-Mitzvot*, negative commandments (58); *Yad*, Hilch. Melachim 7:15.
28. *Yalkut Me'am Lo'ez*, Devarim, Vol. II, p. 766.
29. *The Hasidic Anthology*, ed. Newman, p. 133, n. 3.
30. Deut. R. 5:12, 15.
31. *CCAR Year Book*, 1924, p. 91; 1955, p. 64.
32. Sotah 44a; Tosefta Sotah 7:20.
33. Devarim, Vol. II, pp. 569–570.
34. Mishnah Sotah 8:5.
35. *Itture Torah*, Vol. VI, p. 126.
36. Sotah 9:6; see the discussion of Malbim on Deut. 21:7.
37. *Studies*, 2nd series, 5716 Annual, Tetze, p. 7.
38. *Judaism*, 19, 4 (Fall 1970), p. 414.

The Social Weal, I DEUT. 21:10—22:12

1. See Sifre Deut. 212; Rashi; and especially Nachmanides.
2. M.K. 18a.

3. San. 71a; see also Mishnah San. 8:1–5, which multiplies the conditions necessary for conviction.
4. Sifre Deut. 221; San. 46b.

5. So King James Version and Revised Standard Version; similarly New American Bible. Perhaps קְלָלַת אֱלֹהִים is to be understood as "a great curse," like הַרְרֵי אֵל "great mountains."

6. See Mishnah Kilayim 8:2 ff.

7. Also Josephus, *Antiquities*, IV, 8:11.

8. See Rashi; Yeb. 3b–4a.

9. *HUCA*, 54 (1973), pp. 1 ff.

10. San. 46a–b.

11. See Mishnah San. 7:2.

12. *Guide*, II, 48; also III, 26 and 31. Maimonides attempts to reconcile his position with Mishnah Ber. 5:3; see the discussion by Jacobson, *Meditations on the Torah*, pp. 292–297.

13. Ber. 40a. On this subject, see also Isak Unna, *Tierschutz im Judentum* (Frankfurt: J. Kaufmann, 1928).

14. Hul. 142a.

15. *Ethics of the Fathers* 4:2.

16. Kid. 39b.

17. Quoted in *Itture Torah*, Vol. VI, p. 129.

18. *Ibid.*

19. San. 71a.

20. *Itture Torah*, Vol. VI, p. 133.

21. *Commentary*, p. 48.

22. *Deuteronomium*, Vol. II, p. 9.

23. San. 46b.

24. *Itture Torah*, Vol. VI, p. 136.

25. Louis Ginzberg, *The Legends of the Jews* (7 vols., Philadelphia: Jewish Publication Society, 1909–1946), Vol. VI, p. 198, n. 86.

26. Sifre Deut. 226.

27. Men. 43a.

28. *Myth*, pp. 316–318.

29. See Solomon B. Freehof, *Modern Reform Responsa* (Cincinnati: Hebrew Union College Press, 1971), p. 128, where a survey of traditional literature may also be found.

30. Deut. R. 6:7.

31. Based on Sifre Deut. 228.

32. *As a Driven Leaf* (New York: Behrman, 1939), pp. 249–250.

33. See, e.g., Ibn Ezra for one opinion, Isaac Caro, *Toledot Yitzchak*, for another; also *Itture Torah*, Vol. VI, p. 138.

The Social Weal, II   DEUT. 22:13—24:22

1. Mak. 22a–b.

2. On the subject of the slandered bride, see W. W. Hallo, *Studies Presented to A. Leo Oppenheim* (Chicago: University of Chicago Press, 1964), pp. 95–105.

3. San. 52b, 53a.

4. See the discussion in I. J. Rosenbaum, *The Holocaust and Halakhah* (New York: Ktav, 1976), p. 146; Maimonides, *Yad*, Hilch. Na'arah Betulah 1:2, puts the onus of proof on the woman who, in the city, claims she was forced.

5. So Driver, p. 260.

6. Mishnah Yeb. 4:13. On rabbinic attitudes, see S. M. Passamaneck, *HUCA*, 37 (1966), pp. 121–145.

7. Ber. 28a mentions that the intermingling of nations at the time of Sennacherib obscured the lines of descent. For the legality of Ruth's admission, see Yeb. 69a (based on the Torah's use of the masculine מוֹאָבִי).

8. This thesis is suggested in Plaut, "The Trace of Joseph," *CCAR Journal* (October 1961), pp. 29 ff.

9. So Targum Onkelos; this meaning is clearly suggested by verse 17.

10. Git. 45a.

11. For details of such practices in the ancient Near East, see Driver, p. 265.

12. See Reider, p. 217.

13. B.M. 92a; also Josephus, *Antiquities*, IV, 8:21.

14. On this, see Driver, p. 275.

15. This is, however, debated in the Talmud, B.M. 113b.

16. For an actual case in the seventh century B.C.E., see J. Naveh, *Israel Exploration Journal*, 10 (1960), pp. 129–139; D. Pardee, *Maarav*, 1 (1978), pp. 33–66.

17. For further details, see commentary on Exod. 22:24.

18. Aristotle, *Politics*, I, 10:5.

19. See the article in *Encyclopaedia Judaica*, Vol. 16, cols. 27 ff.

20. See Pritchard, ANET, Code of Hammurabi, sec. 137–140, p. 172; see the excerpt in Gleanings.

21. See Git. 90a.

22. *Antiquities*, IV, 8:23.

23. Git. 9:10.

24. Driver, p. 277; similarly Rashbam; Hoffmann.

25. See Rashi; San. 27b–28b.

26. Quoted in *Al ha-Torah*, Vol. V, p. 548.

27. Ket. 5a–b.

28. Pritchard, *ANET*, Code of Hammurabi, sec. 138, 142, p. 172.

29. Even ha-Ezer 154.

30. Deut. R. 6:8, 9.

31. Mishnah B. M. 9:13; B.M. 115a.

32. Tosefta Pe'ah 3:8, ed. S. Zuckermandl.

The Social Weal, III DEUT. 25:1—26:19

1. Cf. W. W. Hallo, *Bibliotheca Orientalis*, Vol. 33 (1976), p. 40, citing, among others, M. Stol, *Journal of Cuneiform Studies*, 25 (1973), pp. 228 f.; Samuel N. Kramer, *The Sumerians: Their History, Culture, and Character* (Chicago: University of Chicago Press, 1963), pp. 296 f. and 342, *ad* Farmer's Almanac, line 99.

2. Yeb. 24a.

3. B. K. 28a; see also Sifre Deut. 293; Rashi; S. R. Hirsch.

4. According to Reicke-Rost, *Biblisch-historisches Handwörterbuch* (Göttingen: Vandenhoeck und Ruprecht, 1964), Vol. 2, col. 1163.

5. On this, see Weinfeld, *Deuteronomy*, pp. 274 f.

6. Sifre Deut. 302.

7. See Tobit 4:17; Sirach 30:18.

8. E. R. Lachman, *JBL*, 56 (1937), pp. 53–56.

9. The sexual origins were first stressed by L. Levy, *Monatsschrift*, 62 (1918), pp. 168–170, and have been reemphasized by C. M. Carmichael, *JBL*, 96 (1977), pp. 321–336; see further Gaster, *Myth*, pp. 449–450; J. Morgenstern, *HUCA*, 7 (1930), pp. 168–170; *Jewish Encyclopedia*, ed. I. Singer (12 vols., New York: Funk and Wagnalls, 1901–1904), Vol. VI, p. 174.

10. See Mishnah Yeb. 8:4 concerning the levirate marriage of a eunuch who lived in Jerusalem in Rabbi Akiba's time; on the preference of *chalitzah* over levirate marriage, see Yeb. 39b.

11. *Encyclopaedia Judaica*, Vol. 11, cols. 128 f., where the ceremony of *chalitzah*, as practiced today, is described.

12. See author's detailed study in *CCAR Journal*, January 1962, pp. 18 ff. The Haggadah, which incorporates the prayer, takes Laban to be the Aramean who tried to destroy Jacob. M. Buber, *On the Bible*, pp. 126 ff., translates "An Aramean gone astray . . ." —a pastoral expression. He also notes that the credo uses the Divine Name 2 X 7 times.

13. *Itture Torah*, Vol. VI, p. 147.

14. Mishnah Mak. 3:10, 14, 15.

15. Sifre Deut. 286.

16. Mak. 23a.

17. In his extended commentary on these passages.

18. This is the name by which R. Abraham Wolf is commonly known; the quotation is from *Itture Torah*, Vol. VI, p. 148.

19. *Ibid.*, p. 151.

20. *Ibid.*, p. 155.

21. *Israel and Palestine* (New York: Farrar, Straus and Young, 1952), pp. 5 f.

Blessings and Curses, I DEUT. 27:1–26

1. *Deuteronomium*, p. 119.

2. See Driver. But see Sotah 35b for a different opinion; also, it appears that the reverse procedure was favored in Babylon and Greece.

3. *Antiquities*, IV, 8:44.

4. Sotah 7:5.

5. Commentary, *ad loc.*

6. Many attempts have been made to untangle these problems. Thus, Tosefta Sotah 8:9: The eldest of the Levites stood above, the others below; Driver: Some were levitical priests, others were lay or ordinary tribal members. For a detailed discussion, see Hoffmann, pp. 93–99.

7. So Mishnah Sotah 7:5.

8. So Ibn Ezra on verse 14.

9. So von Rad, *Deuteronomium*, p. 118.

10. Targum Yerushalmi; Rashi.

11. So, for instance, Rashi.

12. See A. Murtonen, *VT*, 9 (1959), pp. 158–177; H. C. Brichto, *Encyclopaedia Judaica*, Vol. 4, col. 1085.

The term *tochechot*, which later came to describe these imprecations, does not occur in the Torah.

13. Von Rad, *Deuteronomium*, p. 121.
14. Quoted in *Itture Torah*, Vol. VI, p. 160.
15. Commentary, *ad loc.*
16. Suk. 52b.
17. Attributed to the Gerer Rav: *Itture Torah*, Vol.

VI, p. 160.

18. Sotah 35b; based on Mishnah Sotah 7:5.
19. Commentary on 27:8. On the Noahide laws, see commentary on Gen. 8:15–9:29.
20. *Itture Torah*, Vol. VI, p. 161.
21. *Deuteronomium*, p. 103.
22. Commentary, p. 554.

Blessings and Curses, II   DEUT. 28:1–69

1. *Guide*, III, 30.
2. *Deuteronomium*, pp. 124–125.
3. See Exodus, Part VI, "Laws."
4. Tanch. Nitzavim 2.
5. Quoted by Junker, *Deuteronomium*.
6. A. L. Oppenheim, *Iraq*, Vol. 17 (1955), p. 79, n. 34.
7. So Nachmanides on 28:42.
8. See *Shulchan Aruch*, Orach Chayim 428:6.
9. *Itture Torah*, Vol. VI, p. 162.
10. B.M. 107a.
11. *Ibid.*
12. *Yalkut Yehudah*, Vol. 5, p. 226.
13. *Itture Torah*, Vol. VI, p. 163, in reference to the

talmudic debate, Erub. 13b.

14. *Itture Torah*, Vol. VI, p. 163.
15. *Ibid.*, p. 165.
16. *Deuteronomium*, p. 113.
17. Commentary on verse 20.
18. Ascribed to R. Simchah Bunam, *Itture Torah*, Vol. VI, p. 167.
19. *Ibid.*, p. 168.
20. *War*, VII, 10:3.
21. Sotah 49a.
22. Taken from Weinfeld, *Deuteronomy*, pp. 117 f.
23. The treaties of Esarhaddon may be found in D. J. Wiseman, *Iraq*, Vol. 20 (1958), pp. 1–99; the line citations refer to Wiseman's text.

The Last Oration   DEUT. 29:1—30:20

1. The Orthodox liturgy provides for the reading of Lev. 18:1–30.
2. So von Rad, *Deuteronomium*, p. 131.
3. *Guide*, II, 48.
4. S. Maslin, *CCAR Journal* (Fall 1975), pp. 1–6.
5. J. Krašovec, *Biblica et Orientalia*, 33 (1977); A. M. Honeyman, *JBL*, 71 (1952), pp. 11–18.
6. San. 110b.
7. So Reider.
8. See the discussion in Leibowitz, *Studies*, 3rd series, 5716 Annual, Nitzavim, on the theme of individual and collective defection; W. G. Plaut, *The Case for the Chosen People* (Garden City: Doubleday, 1964), pp. 94 f.
9. Mishnah Pe'ah 1:1.
10. Rabbi Ishmael, Jerusalem Yeb. VIII, 8d; Jerusalem Ned. I, 36c.

11. See San. 43b, and Rashi and Tosafot thereon. Num. R. 3:13 avers that the dots were introduced by Ezra.
12. See Jakob J. Petuchowski, *Judaism*, 17, 2 (1968), pp. 175–185.
13. Pes. 54a.
14. Ber. 34b.
15. *Itture Torah*, Vol. VI, p. 173.
16. *Wellsprings*, Vol. II, pp. 421 f.
17. *Itture Torah*, Vol. VI, p. 181.
18. See Leibowitz, *Studies*, 4th series, 5717 Annual, Nitzavim, pp. 3 f.; Jacobson, *Meditations on the Torah*, p. 307, n.
19. *Itture Torah*, Vol. VI, p. 184.
20. Commentary on verse 3; based on Meg. 29a.
21. *Itture Torah*, Vol. VI, p. 174.
22. Deut. R. 8:3.
23. *Ibid.*, 8:6.

Moses Prepares for Death DEUT. 31:1–30

1. See commentary on Gen. 24:1–25:18, Gleanings, "The Way of the Bible"; S. Gevirtz, *JBL*, 96 (1977), pp. 570 f.; J. G. Williams, *JBL*, 98 (1979), pp. 86 f.
2. This was the understanding in ancient days as well; see Mishnah Sotah 7:8.
3. Mishnah Sotah 7:8; also Sotah 41a.
4. Josephus, *Antiquities*, IV, 8:12.
5. Mishnah Sotah 7:8.
6. *Antiquities*, IV, *loc. cit.*
7. *Gates of Prayer*, p. 425.
8. Commentary, p. 340.
9. Nachmanides took the former view, Ibn Ezra the latter.
10. B.B. 14a.
11. *Ethics of the Fathers* 3:15. However, another interpretation of the phrase is: "Everything is *seen* (by God), and free will is given." See Urbach, *The Sages*, Vol. I, p. 257.
12. Among contemporary writers dealing with this problem are Emil. L. Fackenheim, Eliezer Berkovits, and Richard Rubenstein. Martin Buber, too, deals with the "eclipse of god," though in a somewhat different manner, in that the choice to hide or reveal Himself is God's.
13. *Moses*, p. 198.
14. *Deuteronomium*, Vol. II, p. 163.
15. Deut. R. 9:7.
16. *Ibid.*, 9:4.
17. *Ibid.*, 9:9.
18. *Moses*, trans. Maurice Samuel (New York: G. P. Putnam's Sons, 1951), p. 489.
19. On verse 20.
20. See San. 90b; Yoma 52a–b; Minchat Shai on verse 21; and the extensive discussion by Hirsch on verse 19 (pp. 620 f.).
21. San. 21b.
22. On verse 21.

The Song of Moses DEUT. 32:1–52

1. See *The Psalms Two*, ed. Mitchell Dahood (Garden City: Doubleday, 1968), p. 322: The psalm might come from the ninth century.
2. *Gates of Prayer*, p. 430; Standard Prayer Book, p. 87.
3. *Gates of Prayer*, p. 417; Standard Prayer Book, p. 83.
4. See Driver, p. 350.
5. *Gates of Repentance*, p. 97; Machzor, ed. M. Silverman (Hartford: Prayer Book Press, 1939), p. 60.
6. *Gates of Prayer*, p. 44 ("We gratefully acknowledge...."); Standard Prayer Book, pp. 62–63, "Modim."
7. So Sifre Deut. 310.
8. *Gates of Prayer*, p. 62; Standard Prayer Book, p. 55.
9. Sifre Deut. 311 comments: God gave the nations their homes so that they might not trespass upon each other.
10. See Gaster, *Myth*, p. 405, n. 1, who believes that בְּנֵי אֵל was in fact the original meaning, but since it meant "pagan gods" this reference was removed. However, in Ps. 29:1 the expression בְּנֵי אֵלִים was left standing.
11. *Deuteronomium*, p. 141.
12. So Gaster, *Myth*, p. 320, who found this belief among contemporary Bedouin.
13. So Jonah ibn Janach, *Sefer ha-Shorashim* (Berlin: H. I. Itzkowski, 1896), p. 26.
14. Driver, p. 362, relates *shedim* to the Arabic *sada*, whence *sayid* (lord, master) and the Spanish *cid*.
15. So Gaster, *Myth*, pp. 321 f.
16. Rashi and Ibn Ezra take the first position; the Midrash (Sifre Deut. 322) reports a controversy on this matter. See the discussion by Leibowitz, *Studies*, 5720 Annual, pp. 361 ff.
17. So Reider.
18. So Rashi; Ibn Ezra takes the opposite view.
19. *Yad*, Hilch. Tefilah 7:13.
20. See R. H. 31a.
21. The analysis is based on Biur. See further Jacobson, *Meditations on the Torah*, pp. 313 ff.; Leibowitz, *Studies*, 5720 Annual, p. 362; D. L. Rosenthal, *Jeschurun*, II (1915), pp. 568 f. Another division is proposed by P. W. Skehan, *CBQ*, 13 (1951), pp. 153 ff.
22. But note the "law suit" construction of the song by G. E. Wright and others (see G. E. Wright, *Israel's Prophetic Heritage*, ed. B. W. Anderson and W. Harrel-

son [New York: Harper and Bros., 1962], pp. 26 ff.) which would alter the meaning of the poem. Wright dates the song to the ninth century.

23. Commentary, *ad loc.*; the talmudic reference is to Pes. 3 b.

24. Tanch. Ha'azinu 5.

25. *Ibid.*

26. Quoted in *Itture Torah*, Vol. VI, p. 208. The talmudic reference is to Jerusalem Hag. I:7 (76c).

27. Gen. R. 17:5. The technical term for "inferior variety" is נוֹבֶלֶת.

28. Quoted in *Itture Torah*.

29. Sab. 23a.

30. So Rashi; based on Targum Yerushalmi.

31. *Deuteronomy*, p. 358, quoting from older observations. See also Buber, *On the Bible*, p. 90.

32. *Itture Torah*, Vol. VI, p. 209.

33. *Ibid.*

34. *Ibid.*, p. 213.

35. Quoted by Y. L. Ginzburg, *Yalkut Yehudah*, Vol. 5, p. 251.

The Blessing of Moses   DEUT. 33:1–29

1. This is the conclusion of Arnold B. Ehrlich, *Mikra Kifeshuto* (rev. ed., New York: Ktav, 1969), and most modern commentators. An extensive, technical discussion may be found in Tur-Sinai.

2. Still others (like Wellhausen) believe that "King in Jeshurun" (verse 5) refers to King Saul.

3. *Gates of Prayer*, p. 429.

4. The first to suggest this was R. Eliezer (2nd cent. C.E.); see Sifre Deut. 348; *Yalkut Shimoni*, I:954; H. Graetz, *Geschichte der Israeliten* (Leipzig: Oskar Leiner, 1902), Vol. 2, p. 450.

5. Commentary, pp. 398 ff.

6. See Sifre Deut. 352; based on traditions going back to Josh. 15:8 and 18:28.

7. See E. Kimron, *Beth Mikra*, 77, 2 (1979), pp. 140–141.

8. So Ibn Ezra.

9. So Rashi, while Targum Onkelos identifies "moons" with "seasons."

10. See Sifre Deut. 354.

11. So Targum Onkelos; Rashi.

12. Josephus, *War*, II, 10:2; other references in Driver, p. 410.

13. Sifre Deut. 355. See Gleanings.

14. Gen. R. 20:6.

15. See F. M. Cross, Jr.-D. N. Freedman, *JBL*, 67 (1948), pp. 191–210.

16. The translation follows Sifre Deut. 356 and Rashi.

17. Von Rad, *Deuteronomium*, p. 146.

18. Sifre Deut. 342.

19. *Al ha-Torah*, Vol. V, p. 578.

20. Commentary on verse 1.

21. *Wellsprings*, Vol. II, p. 437.

22. Quoted in Ginzberg, *Legends*, Vol. III, p. 452.

23. Sifre Deut. 343; see also Gleanings on Exod. 19.

24. Sifre Deut. 343.

25. Deut. R. 11:4.

26. *Itture Torah*, Vol. VI, p. 219.

27. *Ethics of the Fathers* 5:6; Pes. 54a.

28. Sifre Deut. 355.

29. *Al ha-Torah*, Vol. V, p. 580.

End and Beginning   DEUT. 34:1–12

1. B.B. 14b–15a; Ibn Ezra on 34:1 (based on the Paris manuscript of his commentary). How then did Joshua know about Moses' death and burial? Ibn Ezra answers: through the gift of prophecy.

2. So von Rad, *Deuteronomium*, p. 150.

3. *War*, IV, 8:3.

4. *Antiquities*, IV, 8:4.

5. So Targum Jonathan; B.B. 17a; Rashi.

6. So the old JPS translation; von Rad, *Deuteronomium*.

7. Commentary on verse 6, based on Rabbi Yishmael's interpretation in Sifre Num. 32.

8. "Petirat Mosheh Rabbenu," *Bet ha-Midrash*, ed. A. Jellinek (Jerusalem: Bamberger and Wahrmann, 1938), Vol. I, p. 126.

9. *Ibid.*, pp. 116, 127.

10. *Ibid.*, pp. 117 f.

11. *Ibid.*, p. 119.

12. *Ibid.*, pp. 120 f.; see also Deut. R. 11:10.

13. Deut. R. 2:8, in reference to Sifre Num. 135; see at 3:26 (Gleanings).

14. "Petirat Mosheh," *loc. cit.*

15. *Ibid.*

16. *Ibid.*, p. 128.

17. *Ibid.*, p. 121.

18. Deut. R. 11:7.

19. "Petirat Mosheh," pp. 122 ff. Targum Yerushalmi, 34:5 says that the seventh of Adar was the day of both Moses' birth and his death.

20. Sifre Deut. 357.

21. Midrash quoted in Ginzberg, *Legends*, Vol. VI, p. 164.

22. *Oxford English Dictionary* and *Webster's International Dictionary*, respectively.

23. "The Death of Moses," quoted in David Daiches, *Moses: The Man and His Vision* (New York: Praeger Publishers, 1975), p. 250.

24. *Guide*, II, 35.

25. *On the Life of Moses*, 1:1.

26. *Pirke de-R. Eliezer* 17, Eng. ed. Gerald Friedlander (reprint, New York: Hermon Press, 1965); *Avot de-R. Nathan* 12:3, ed. Judah Goldin (New Haven: Yale University Press, 1955).

27. Quoted in *A Passover Anthology*, ed. Philip Goodman (Philadelphia: Jewish Publication Society, 1961), pp. 190 f.

28. *Moses*, p. 55.

29. *Moses*, pp. 22 f.

30. *Moses*, p. 10.

31. *Moses*, pp. 196, 254 f.

32. *Messengers of God: Biblical Portraits and Legends* (New York: Random House, 1976), p. 182.

33. The legend is quoted by Ginzberg, *Legends*, Vol. VI, pp. 162 f., n. 952. The tradition that Moses died on Friday is also found in *Seder Olam*, 10. On Islamic tradition, see Koran, Sura VII: 141 (Al Araf); August Wünsche, *Aus Israels Lehrhallen* (6 vols., Leipzig: Eduard Pfeiffer, 1907), Vol. I, pp. 163 ff.

34. *Wanderings* (New York: Alfred A. Knopf, 1978), pp. 64, 82.

Biblical and Talmudic Abbreviations

Biblical Books

Chron.	Chronicles	Lam.	Lamentations
Deut.	Deuteronomy	Lev.	Leviticus
Eccles.	Ecclesiastes (Koheleth)	Mal.	Malachi
Exod.	Exodus	Mic.	Micah
Ezek.	Ezekiel	Neh.	Nehemiah
Gen.	Genesis	Num.	Numbers
Hab.	Habakkuk	Ob.	Obadiah
Hos.	Hosea	Prov.	Proverbs
Isa.	Isaiah	Ps.	Psalms
Jer.	Jeremiah	Sam.	Samuel
Josh.	Joshua	Zech.	Zechariah
Judg.	Judges	Zeph.	Zephaniah

Treatises of Talmud (Mishnah and Gemara)

(An English edition of the Babylonian Talmud has been published by Soncino Press, London, 1948; a translation of the Mishnah, prepared by Herbert Danby, was published by Oxford University Press in 1933.)

A.Z.	Avodah Zarah	Ket.	Ketubot
B.B.	Bava Batra	Kid.	Kiddushin
B.K.	Bava Kamma	Kil.	Kilayim
B.M.	Bava Metzia	Mak.	Makkot
Ber.	Berachot	Meg.	Megillah
Bik.	Bikkurim	M.K.	Mo'ed Katan
Erub.	Eruvin	Men.	Menachot
Git.	Gittin	Ned.	Nedarim
Hag.	Chagigah	Neg.	Nega'im
Hal.	Challah	Nid.	Niddah
Hor.	Horayot	Par.	Parah
Hul.	Chullin	Pes.	Pesachim

R.H.	Rosh Hashanah	Suk.	Sukkah
Sab.	Shabbat	Ta'an.	Ta'anit
San.	Sanhedrin	Yad.	Yadayim
Shek.	Shekalim	Yeb.	Yevamot
Shev.	Shevuot	Zeb.	Zevachim

Other Hebrew sources (not as yet translated into English) have been listed in the manner familiar to students of such texts.

Bible Translations

Consulted in the preparation of this commentary

SEPTUAGINT (attributed to seventy-two translators), third–second centuries B.C.E., Greek.

TARGUM (attributed to Onkelos), second century C.E., Aramaic.

VULGATE (by Jerome), fourth–fifth centuries C.E., Latin.

TARGUM YERUSHALMI, about fifth–sixth centuries C.E., Aramaic.

JONATHAN (attributed to Jonathan ben Uzziel), about eighth century C.E., Aramaic.

DOUAI, 1609–1610, English.

KING JAMES (also called "Authorized") VERSION, 1611, English.

MENDELSSOHN, 1780–1783, German.

THE TORAH, Jewish Publication Society, first version, 1917, American.

BUBER-ROSENZWEIG, from 1926, German.

DE VAUX, 1953, French.

REVISED STANDARD VERSION, 1953, American.

SEGOND, 1965, French.

THE TORAH, New Jewish Version, Jewish Publication Society, revised ed., 1967, American.

NEW ENGLISH BIBLE, 1970, English.

NEW AMERICAN BIBLE, 1971, American.

THE BOOK OF PSALMS, New Jewish Version, Jewish Publication Society, 1972, American.

THE PROPHETS, New Jewish Version, Jewish Publication Society, 1978, American.

Midrashic and Post-Midrashic Collections

Quoted; available wholly or in part in English

AVOT DE-R. NATHAN. Edited by Judah Goldin. New Haven: Yale University Press, 1955.

DEUT. R. Deuteronomy Rabbah. *The Midrash*, Vol. 7. London: Soncino Press, 1939.

EXOD. R. Exodus Rabbah. *The Midrash*, Vol. 3. London: Soncino Press, 1939.

GEN. R. Genesis Rabbah. *The Midrash*, Vols. 1 and 2. London: Soncino Press, 1939.

GINZBERG, LOUIS. *The Legends of the Jews*, 7 vols. Philadelphia: Jewish Publication Society, 1909–1946.

LEV. R. Leviticus Rabbah. *The Midrash*, Vol. 4. London: Soncino Press, 1939.

MA'YANAH SHEL TORAH. Edited by Alexander Zusia Friedman, 5 vols. Tel Aviv: Pe'er, 1955–1956. English edition, *Wellsprings of Torah*. Edited by N. L. Alpert, 2 vols. New York: Judaica Press, 1969.

MECH. Mechilta de-R. Yishmael. Edited by Jacob Z. Lauterbach. Philadelphia: Jewish Publication Society, 1933.

NEWMAN, LOUIS I. *The Hasidic Anthology*. New York: Bloch Publ. Co., 1944.

NUM. R. Numbers Rabbah. *The Midrash*, Vols. 5 and 6. London: Soncino Press, 1939.

PESIKTA DE-R. KAHANA. English edition by William G. Braude and Israel J. Kapstein. Philadelphia: Jewish Publication Society, 1975.

PESIKTA RABBATI. English edition by William G. Braude. New Haven: Yale University Press, 1968.

PIRKE DE-R. ELIEZER. English edition by Gerald Friedlander. Reprinted, New York: Hermon Press, 1965.

TS (TORAH SHELEMAH). M. M. Kasher, 3rd edition, from 1949: partial English edition, *Encyclopedia of Biblical Interpretation*. New York: American Biblical Encyclopedia Society, from 1953.

ZOHAR. English edition. London: Soncino Press, 1931.

Commentaries on Deuteronomy

When commentators are listed without further reference, their comment is on the verse under discussion.

The following list of commentaries contains only those works most frequently referred to in the preparation of this book. English commentaries or those available fully or partially in English translation are marked by an asterisk. English excerpts from traditional Hebrew commentaries may be found in *The Soncino Chumash*, ed. A. Cohen (Hindhead, England: Soncino Press, 1947).

Commentaries of Earlier Centuries

Saadia (ben Joseph), Babylonia, 882–942.

*Rashi (Rabbi *Shelomoh Itzchaki*), France, 1040–1105.

Rashbam (Rabbi *Shemuel ben Meir*), his grandson, c. 1085–1158.

Ibn Ezra (Abraham), Spain, 1092–1167.

*Nachmanides (Rabbi Moses ben Nachman), Spain, 1194–1270.

Ralbag (Rabbi *Levi ben Gershon*), France, 1288–1344.

Bachya (ben Asher), Spain, died 1340.

Abarbanel (Isaac), Spain–Italy, 1437–1508.

Sforno, Obadiah ben Jacob, Italy, c. 1475–1550.

*Calvin, John, Switzerland, 1509–1564.

Biur (commentary by Solomon of Dubno on the German translation of Moses Mendelssohn), Russia–Germany, 1738–1813.

Ha-ketav veha-kabbalah (commentary by J. Z. Meklenburg), Poland, 1785–1865.

Luzzatto, Samuel David, Italy, 1800–1865.

*Hirsch (Samson Raphael), Germany, 1808–1888.

Malbim (Meir *Lev ben Yechiel Michael*), Russia, 1809–1879.

Commentaries of the Twentieth Century

Kahana, Abraham. Russia–Palestine. Zhitomir: published by author, 1903.

Hoffmann, David. Germany. Berlin: Poppelauer, 1913–1922.

Schmidt, Hans. Germany. Göttingen: Vandenhoeck und Ruprecht, 1915.

*Driver, Samuel R. England. New York: Charles Scribner's Sons, 1916.

Steuernagel, Carl. Germany. Göttingen: Vandenhoeck und Ruprecht, 1923.

*Hertz, Joseph H., ed. England. Oxford: Oxford University Press, 1929–1936.

*Reider, Joseph. U.S.A. Philadelphia: Jewish Publication Society, 1937.

Cazelles, Henri. France. Paris: Les Editions du Cerf, 1950.

Junker, Hubert. Germany. Würzburg: Echter Verlag, 1952.

*Interpreter's Bible. U.S.A. New York and Nashville: Abingdon Press, 1957.

*Peake. England. London: Thomas Nelson and Sons, 1962.

*Jerome Bible Commentary. U.S.A. Englewood Cliffs: Prentice-Hall, 1968.

*Von Rad, Gerhard. Germany. Göttingen: Vandenhoeck und Ruprecht, 1968.

Commentary Aids

*[ANET] Ancient Near Eastern Texts. Edited by James B. Pritchard. Revised edition, Princeton: Princeton University Press, 1955. (Additional supplementary texts and pictures were published in 1969.)

Tur-Sinai, N. H. Peshuto shel Mikra. Jerusalem: Kiryat Sefer, 1962.

Ginsburg, Christian D. Introduction to the Massoretico-Critical Edition of the Hebrew Bible. Introduction by Harry M. Orlinsky. Reprint, New York: Ktav, 1966.

*Macmillan Bible Atlas. Edited by Y. Aharoni and M. Avi-Yonah. New York: Macmillan Co., 1968.

*Vilnay, Zev. The New Israel Atlas. Jerusalem: Israel Universities Press, 1968.

Ehrlich, Arnold B. Mikra Kifeshuto. Revised edition, New York: Ktav, 1969.

*[JPS Notes] Notes on the New Translation of the Torah. Edited by Harry M. Orlinsky. Philadelphia: Jewish Publication Society, 1969.

Selected General English Bibliography

Adam to Daniel (illustr.). Edited by G. Cornfeld. New York: Macmillan Co., 1961.

ADAR, ZVI. *The Biblical Narrative.* Jerusalem: World Zionist Organization, 1959.

ALBRIGHT, WILLIAM FOXWELL. *Yahweh and the Gods of Canaan.* Garden City: Doubleday, 1968.

ALTMANN, ALEXANDER, ed. *Biblical Motifs.* Cambridge: Harvard University Press, 1966.

BUBER, MARTIN. *Moses.* Oxford and London: East and West Library, 1947.

CHILDS, BREVARD S., *Introduction to the Old Testament.* Philadelphia: Fortress Press, 1979.

DAICHES, DAVID. *Moses: The Man and His Vision.* New York: Praeger Publishers, 1975.

Encyclopaedia Judaica. 16 vols. Jerusalem: Keter, 1972. (Annual yearbooks thereafter.)

FRAZER, JAMES G. *Folklore in the Old Testament.* 3 vols. London: Macmillan Co., 1919. Parts of this work have been updated and republished in Gaster's book (see below).

FREEHOF, SOLOMON B. *Preface to Scripture.* Cincinnati: Union of American Hebrew Congregations, 1950.

GASTER, THEODOR H. *Myth, Legend and Custom in the Old Testament.* New York: Harper and Row, 1969.

GLUECK, NELSON. *The Other Side of the Jordan.* New Haven: American School of Oriental Research, 1940.

———. *The River Jordan.* Philadelphia: Jewish Publication Society, 1946.

GORDON, CYRUS H. *Before the Bible.* New York: Harper and Row, 1962.

GUTMANN, JOSEPH, ed. *No Graven Images.* New York: Ktav, 1971.

Interpreter's Dictionary of the Bible. 4 vols. New York and Nashville: Abingdon Press, 1962. (A supplementary volume was published in 1976.)

JACOBSON, B. S. *Meditations on the Torah*. Tel Aviv: Sinai Publishing Co., 1956.

Jewish Encyclopedia. Edited by I. Singer. 12 vols. New York: Funk and Wagnalls Co., 1901–1904.

KAUFMANN, YEHEZKEL. *The Religion of Israel*. Translated and abridged by Moshe Greenberg. Chicago: University of Chicago Press, 1960.

MEEK, THEOPHILE JAMES. *Hebrew Origins*. New York: Harper and Bros., rev. ed., 1950.

ORLINSKY, HARRY M. *Ancient Israel*. Ithaca: Cornell University Press, 1954.

———. *Essays in Biblical Culture and Bible Translation*. New York: Ktav, 1974.

RIVKIN, ELLIS. *The Shaping of Jewish History*. New York: Charles Scribner's Sons, 1971.

SANDMEL, SAMUEL. *The Hebrew Scriptures*. New York: Knopf, 1963.

SIMONS, J. *The Geographical and Topographical Texts of the Old Testament*. Leiden, Holland: E. J. Brill, 1959.

SMITH, MORTON. *Palestinian Parties and Politics That Shaped the Old Testament*. New York and London: Columbia University Press, 1971.

Views of the Biblical World (illustr.). 5 vols. Chicago and New York: Jordan Publishing Co., 1959–1961.

WEINFELD, MOSHE. *Deuteronomy and the Deuteronomic School*. Oxford: Clarendon Press, 1972.

WINNETT, FREDERICK V. *The Mosaic Tradition*. Toronto: University of Toronto Press, 1949.

YADIN, YIGAEL. *The Art of Warfare in Biblical Lands*. London: Weidenfeld and Nicholson, 1963.

הפטרות

HAFTAROT

Haftarah (meaning "conclusion"; plural, *Haftarot*) was originally a special reading from the Prophets which followed the weekly Torah reading and concluded the service. In the following, *Haftarot* are provided for each Sabbath when Deuteronomy is read. The first selections are the traditional ones, the second and third alternatives have been chosen by the author from a wider range of biblical sources. Included also are *Haftarot* for the Sabbath before the New Moon (*Machar Chodesh*), the Sabbath which coincides with the New Moon (*Rosh Chodesh*), and other special Sabbaths (*Tishah b'Av, Shuvah, Sukot,* and *Atzeret-Simchat Torah*).

The translations are taken from *The Prophets* and *The Book of Psalms*, Philadelphia: Jewish Publication Society, 1978, 1972, and from *The Holy Scriptures*, 1917.

FIRST SELECTION

Isaiah

1 : 1 — 27

Chapter 1

1] The prophecies of Isaiah son of Amoz, who prophesied concerning Judah and Jerusalem in the reigns of Uzziah, Jotham, Ahaz, and Hezekiah, kings of Judah.

2] Hear, O heavens, and give ear, O earth,
For the LORD has spoken:
"I reared children and brought them up—
And they have rebelled against Me!

3] An ox knows its owner,
An ass its master's crib:
Israel does not know,
My people takes no thought."

4] Ah, sinful nation!
People laden with iniquity!
Brood of evildoers!
Depraved children!
They have forsaken the LORD,
Spurned the Holy One of Israel,
Turned their backs [on Him].

5] Why do you seek further beatings,
That you continue to offend?

א

1] חֲזוֹן יְשַׁעְיָהוּ בֶן־אָמוֹץ אֲשֶׁר חָזָה עַל־
יְהוּדָה וִירוּשָׁלָם בִּימֵי עֻזִּיָּהוּ יוֹתָם אָחָז
יְחִזְקִיָּהוּ מַלְכֵי יְהוּדָה:

2] שִׁמְעוּ שָׁמַיִם וְהַאֲזִינִי אֶרֶץ
כִּי יְהוָֹה דִּבֵּר
בָּנִים גִּדַּלְתִּי וְרוֹמַמְתִּי
וְהֵם פָּשְׁעוּ בִי:

3] יָדַע שׁוֹר קֹנֵהוּ
וַחֲמוֹר אֵבוּס בְּעָלָיו:
יִשְׂרָאֵל לֹא יָדַע
עַמִּי לֹא הִתְבּוֹנָן:

4] הוֹי גּוֹי חֹטֵא
עַם כֶּבֶד עָוֹן
זֶרַע מְרֵעִים
בָּנִים מַשְׁחִיתִים
עָזְבוּ אֶת־יְהוָֹה
נִאֲצוּ אֶת קְדוֹשׁ יִשְׂרָאֵל
נָזֹרוּ אָחוֹר:

5] עַל־מֶה תֻכּוּ עוֹד
תּוֹסִיפוּ סָרָה

Every head is ailing,
And every heart is sick.

6] From head to foot
No spot is sound:
All bruises, and welts,
And festering sores—
Not pressed out, not bound up,
Not softened with oil.

7] Your land is a waste,
Your cities burnt down;
Before your eyes, the yield of your soil
Is consumed by strangers—
A wasteland *⁻*as overthrown by strangers!*⁻*

8] Fair*ᵇ* Zion is left
Like a booth in a vineyard,
Like a hut in a cucumber field,
Like a city beleaguered.

9] Had not the LORD of Hosts
Left us some survivors,
We should be like Sodom,
Another Gomorrah.

10] Hear the word of the LORD,
You chieftains of Sodom;
Give ear to our God's instruction,
You folk of Gomorrah!

11] "What need have I of all your sacrifices?"
Says the LORD.

כָּל־רֹאשׁ לָחֳלִי

וְכָל־לֵבָב דַּוָּי:

6] מִכַּף־רֶגֶל וְעַד־רֹאשׁ

אֵין־בּוֹ מְתֹם

פֶּצַע וְחַבּוּרָה

וּמַכָּה טְרִיָּה

לֹא־זֹרוּ וְלֹא חֻבָּשׁוּ

וְלֹא רֻכְּכָה בַּשָּׁמֶן:

7] אַרְצְכֶם שְׁמָמָה

עָרֵיכֶם שְׂרֻפוֹת אֵשׁ

אַדְמַתְכֶם לְנֶגְדְּכֶם

זָרִים אֹכְלִים אֹתָהּ

וּשְׁמָמָה כְּמַהְפֵּכַת זָרִים:

8] וְנוֹתְרָה בַת־צִיּוֹן

כְּסֻכָּה בְכָרֶם

כִּמְלוּנָה בְמִקְשָׁה

כְּעִיר נְצוּרָה:

9] לוּלֵי יְהוָה צְבָאוֹת

הוֹתִיר לָנוּ שָׂרִיד כִּמְעָט

כִּסְדֹם הָיִינוּ

לַעֲמֹרָה דָּמִינוּ:

10] שִׁמְעוּ דְבַר־יְהוָה

קְצִינֵי סְדֹם

הַאֲזִינוּ תּוֹרַת אֱלֹהֵינוּ

עַם עֲמֹרָה:

11] לָמָּה לִי רֹב־זִבְחֵיכֶם

יֹאמַר יְהוָה

ᵃ⁻ᵃ Emendation yields "like Sodom overthrown"
ᵇ Lit. "Daughter"

420

"I am sated with burnt offerings of rams,
And suet of fatlings,
And blood of bulls;
And I have no delight
In lambs and he-goats.

12] That you come to appear before Me—
Who asked that *ᶜ*of you?
Trample My courts

13]   no more;
Bringing oblations is futile,⁻ᶜ
Incense is offensive to Me.
New moon and sabbath,
Proclaiming of solemnities,
ᵈ⁻Assemblies with iniquity,⁻ᵈ
I cannot abide.

14] Your new moons and fixed seasons
Fill Me with loathing;
They are become a burden to Me,
I cannot endure them.

15] And when you lift up your hands,
I will turn My eyes away from you;
Though you pray at length,
I will not listen.
Your hands are stained with crime—

16] Wash yourselves clean;
Put your evil doings
Away from My sight.
Cease to do evil;

17] Learn to do good.
Devote yourselves to justice;
*ᵉ*Aid the wronged.⁻ᵉ
Uphold the rights of the orphan;
Defend the cause of the widow.

שָׂבַעְתִּי עֹלוֹת אֵילִים

וְחֵלֶב מְרִיאִים

וְדַם פָּרִים וּכְבָשִׂים

וְעַתּוּדִים לֹא חָפָצְתִּי:

12] כִּי תָבֹאוּ לֵרָאוֹת פָּנָי

מִי בִקֵּשׁ זֹאת מִיֶּדְכֶם

רְמֹס חֲצֵרָי:

13] לֹא תוֹסִיפוּ הָבִיא מִנְחַת־שָׁוְא

קְטֹרֶת תּוֹעֵבָה הִיא לִי

חֹדֶשׁ וְשַׁבָּת קְרֹא מִקְרָא

לֹא־אוּכַל אָוֶן וַעֲצָרָה:

14] חָדְשֵׁיכֶם וּמוֹעֲדֵיכֶם שָׂנְאָה נַפְשִׁי

הָיוּ עָלַי לָטֹרַח

נִלְאֵיתִי נְשֹׂא:

15] וּבְפָרִשְׂכֶם כַּפֵּיכֶם

אַעְלִים עֵינַי מִכֶּם

גַּם כִּי־תַרְבּוּ תְפִלָּה

אֵינֶנִּי שֹׁמֵעַ

יְדֵיכֶם דָּמִים מָלֵאוּ:

16] רַחֲצוּ הִזַּכּוּ

הָסִירוּ רֹעַ מַעַלְלֵיכֶם

מִנֶּגֶד עֵינָי

חִדְלוּ הָרֵעַ:

17] לִמְדוּ הֵיטֵב

דִּרְשׁוּ מִשְׁפָּט

אַשְּׁרוּ חָמוֹץ

שִׁפְטוּ יָתוֹם

רִיבוּ אַלְמָנָה:

18] Come, ᵉ⸢let us reach an understanding⸣ᵉ"
                                          —says the LORD.

Be your sins like crimson,
They can turn snow-white;
Be they red as dyed wool,
They can become like fleece.

19] If, then, you agree and give heed,
You will eat the good things of the earth;

20] But if you refuse and disobey,
ᶠ⸢You will be devoured [by] the sword.⸣ᶠ—
For it was the LORD who spoke.

21] Alas, she has become a harlot,
The faithful city
That was filled with justice,
Where righteousness dwelt—
But now murderers.

22] Yourᵍ silver has turned to dross;
ᵉ⸢Your wine is cut with water.⸣ᵉ

23] Your rulers are rogues
And cronies of thieves,
Every one avid for presents
And greedy for gifts;
They do not judge the case of the orphan,
And the widow's cause never reaches them.

24] Assuredly, this is the declaration
Of the Sovereign, the LORD of Hosts,
The Mighty One of Israel:

ᵉ⁻ᵉ *Meaning of Heb. uncertain*
ᶠ⁻ᶠ *Or "You will be fed the sword"*
ᵍ *I.e., Jerusalem's*

18 [לְכוּ־נָא וְנִוָּכְחָה

יֹאמַר יְהֹוָה

אִם־יִהְיוּ חֲטָאֵיכֶם כַּשָּׁנִים

כַּשֶּׁלֶג יַלְבִּינוּ

אִם־יַאְדִּימוּ כַתּוֹלָע

כַּצֶּמֶר יִהְיוּ׃

19 [אִם־תֹּאבוּ וּשְׁמַעְתֶּם

טוּב הָאָרֶץ תֹּאכֵלוּ׃

20 [וְאִם־תְּמָאֲנוּ וּמְרִיתֶם

חֶרֶב תְּאֻכְּלוּ

כִּי פִּי יְהֹוָה דִּבֵּר׃

21 [אֵיכָה הָיְתָה לְזוֹנָה

קִרְיָה נֶאֱמָנָה

מְלֵאֲתִי מִשְׁפָּט

צֶדֶק יָלִין בָּהּ

וְעַתָּה מְרַצְּחִים׃

22 [כַּסְפֵּךְ הָיָה לְסִיגִים

סָבְאֵךְ מָהוּל בַּמָּיִם׃

23 [שָׂרַיִךְ סוֹרְרִים

וְחַבְרֵי גַּנָּבִים

כֻּלּוֹ אֹהֵב שֹׁחַד

וְרֹדֵף שַׁלְמֹנִים׃

יָתוֹם לֹא יִשְׁפֹּטוּ

וְרִיב אַלְמָנָה לֹא־יָבוֹא אֲלֵיהֶם׃

24 [לָכֵן נְאֻם הָאָדוֹן יְהֹוָה צְבָאוֹת

אֲבִיר יִשְׂרָאֵל

422

"Ah, I will get satisfaction from My foes;
I will wreak vengeance on My enemies!

25] I will turn My hand against you,
And smelt out your dross ʰ‑as with lye,‑ʰ
And remove your slag:

26] I will restore your magistrates as of old,
And your counselors as of yore.
After that you shall be called
City of Righteousness, Faithful City."

27] ʿZion shall be saved in the judgment;
Her repentant ones, in the retribution.ⁱ

הוֹי אֶנָּחֵם מִצָּרַי

וְאִנָּקְמָה מֵאוֹיְבִי:

25] וְאָשִׁיבָה יָדִי עָלַיִךְ

וְאֶצְרֹף כַּבֹּר סִגָּיִךְ

וְאָסִירָה כָּל־בְּדִילָיִךְ:

26] וְאָשִׁיבָה שֹׁפְטַיִךְ כְּבָרִאשֹׁנָה

וְיֹעֲצַיִךְ כְּבַתְּחִלָּה

אַחֲרֵי־כֵן יִקָּרֵא לָךְ

עִיר הַצֶּדֶק

קִרְיָה נֶאֱמָנָה:

27] צִיּוֹן בְּמִשְׁפָּט תִּפָּדֶה

וְשָׁבֶיהָ בִּצְדָקָה:

SECOND SELECTION

Amos

2 : 1-11

Chapter 2

1] Thus said the LORD:
For three transgressions of Moab,
For four, I will not revoke it:
Because he burned the bones
Of the king of Edom to lime.

ב

1] כֹּה אָמַר יְהֹוָה

עַל־שְׁלֹשָׁה פִּשְׁעֵי מוֹאָב

וְעַל־אַרְבָּעָה לֹא אֲשִׁיבֶנּוּ

עַל־שָׂרְפוֹ עַצְמוֹת

מֶלֶךְ־מוֹאָב לַשִּׂיד:

2] I will send down fire upon Moab,
And it shall devour the fortresses of Kerioth.

2] וְשִׁלַּחְתִּי־אֵשׁ בְּמוֹאָב

וְאָכְלָה אַרְמְנוֹת הַקְּרִיּוֹת

ʰ‑ʰ *Emendation yields "in a crucible"; cf. 48.10*
ⁱ *Others "Zion shall be saved by justice, | Her repentant ones by righteousness"*
ʲ *For this meaning cf. 5.16; 10.22*

And Moab shall die in tumult,
Amid shouting and the blare of horns;

3] I will wipe out the ruler from within her
And slay all her officials along with him
—said the LORD.

4] Thus said the LORD:
For three transgressions of Judah,
For four, I will not revoke it:
Because they have spurned the Teaching of the
    LORD
And have not observed His laws;
They are beguiled by the delusions
After which their fathers walked.

5] I will send down fire upon Judah,
And it shall devour the fortresses of Jerusalem.

6] Thus said the LORD:
For three transgressions of Israel,
For four, I will not revoke it:
Because they have sold for silver
Those whose cause was just,
And the needy for a pair of sandals.

7] [Ah,] you ᵃ⁻who trample the heads of the poor
Into the dust of the ground,
And make the humble walk a twisted course!⁻ᵃ
Father and son go to the same girl,
And thereby profane My holy name.

8] They recline by every altar
On garments taken in pledge,

וָמֵת בְּשָׁאוֹן מוֹאָב
בִּתְרוּעָה בְּקוֹל שׁוֹפָר:

3] וְהִכְרַתִּי שׁוֹפֵט מִקִּרְבָּהּ
וְכָל־שָׂרֶיהָ אֶהֱרוֹג עִמּוֹ
אָמַר יְהֹוָה:

4] כֹּה אָמַר יְהֹוָה
עַל־שְׁלֹשָׁה פִּשְׁעֵי יְהוּדָה
וְעַל־אַרְבָּעָה לֹא אֲשִׁיבֶנּוּ
עַל־מׇאֳסָם אֶת־תּוֹרַת יְהֹוָה
וְחֻקָּיו לֹא שָׁמָרוּ
וַיַּתְעוּם כִּזְבֵיהֶם
אֲשֶׁר־הָלְכוּ אֲבוֹתָם אַחֲרֵיהֶם:

5] וְשִׁלַּחְתִּי אֵשׁ בִּיהוּדָה
וְאָכְלָה אַרְמְנוֹת יְרוּשָׁלָ͏ִם:

6] כֹּה אָמַר יְהֹוָה
עַל־שְׁלֹשָׁה פִּשְׁעֵי יִשְׂרָאֵל
וְעַל אַרְבָּעָה לֹא אֲשִׁיבֶנּוּ
עַל־מִכְרָם בַּכֶּסֶף צַדִּיק
וְאֶבְיוֹן בַּעֲבוּר נַעֲלָיִם:

7] הַשֹּׁאֲפִים עַל־עֲפַר־אֶרֶץ
בְּרֹאשׁ דַּלִּים
וְדֶרֶךְ עֲנָוִים יַטּוּ
וְאִישׁ וְאָבִיו יֵלְכוּ
אֶל־הַנַּעֲרָה
לְמַעַן חַלֵּל אֶת־שֵׁם קׇדְשִׁי:

8] וְעַל־בְּגָדִים חֲבֻלִים
יַטּוּ אֵצֶל כָּל־מִזְבֵּחַ

ᵃ⁻ᵃ Understanding sho'afim as equivalent to shafim. Emendation yields: "Who crush
    on the ground / The heads of the poor, / And push off the road / The humble of
    the land"; cf. Job 24.4

And drink in the House of their God
Wine bought with fines they imposed.

9] Yet I
Destroyed the Amorite before them,
Whose stature was like the cedar's
And who was stout as the oak,
Destroying his boughs above
And his trunk below!

10] And I
Brought you up from the land of Egypt
And led you through the wilderness forty years,
To possess the land of the Amorite!

11] And I raised up prophets from among your
        sons
And nazirites from among your young men.
Is that not so, O people of Israel?
                        —says the Lord.

וְיֵין עֲנוּשִׁים יִשְׁתּוּ
בֵּית אֱלֹהֵיהֶם:

9] וְאָנֹכִי
הִשְׁמַדְתִּי אֶת־הָאֱמֹרִי מִפְּנֵיהֶם
אֲשֶׁר כְּגֹבַהּ אֲרָזִים גׇּבְהוֹ
וְחָסֹן הוּא כָּאַלּוֹנִים
וָאַשְׁמִיד פִּרְיוֹ מִמַּעַל
וְשׇׁרָשָׁיו מִתָּחַת:

10] וְאָנֹכִי
הֶעֱלֵיתִי אֶתְכֶם מֵאֶרֶץ מִצְרָיִם
וָאוֹלֵךְ אֶתְכֶם בַּמִּדְבָּר אַרְבָּעִים שָׁנָה
לָרֶשֶׁת אֶת־אֶרֶץ הָאֱמֹרִי:

11] וָאָקִים מִבְּנֵיכֶם לִנְבִיאִים
וּמִבַּחוּרֵיכֶם לִנְזִרִים
הַאַף אֵין־זֹאת בְּנֵי יִשְׂרָאֵל
נְאֻם־יְהֹוָה:

THIRD SELECTION

Lamentations

3 : 19 - 41

Chapter 3

19] Remember my affliction and my anguish,
The wormwood and the gall.

20] My soul has them still in remembrance,
And is bowed down within me.

21] This I recall to my mind,
Therefore have I hope.

ג

19] זְכׇר־עׇנְיִי וּמְרוּדִי
לַעֲנָה וָרֹאשׁ:

20] זָכוֹר תִּזְכּוֹר
וְתָשׁוֹחַ עָלַי נַפְשִׁי:

21] זֹאת אָשִׁיב אֶל־לִבִּי
עַל־כֵּן אוֹחִיל:

425

22] Surely the LORD's mercies are not consumed,
Surely His compassions fail not.

23] They are new every morning;
Great is Your faithfulness.

24] "The LORD is my portion," says my soul;
"Therefore will I hope in Him."

25] The LORD is good to them that wait for Him,
To the soul that seeks Him.

26] It is good that a man should quietly wait
For the salvation of the LORD.

27] It is good for a man that he bear
The yoke in his youth.

28] Let him sit alone and keep silence,
Because He has laid it upon him.

29] Let him put his mouth in the dust,
If so be there may be hope.

30] Let him give his cheek to him that smites him,
Let him be filled full with reproach.

31] For the LORD will not cast off
    For ever.
32] For though He cause grief, yet will He have
    compassion
According to the multitude of His mercies.

33] For He does not afflict willingly,
Nor grieve the children of men.

34] To crush under foot
All the prisoners of the earth,

35] To turn aside the right of a man
Before the face of the Most High,

36] To subvert a man in his cause,
The LORD approves not.

[22] חַסְדֵי יְהֹוָה כִּי לֹא־תָמְנוּ
כִּי לֹא־כָלוּ רַחֲמָיו:

[23] חֲדָשִׁים לַבְּקָרִים
רַבָּה אֱמוּנָתֶךָ:

[24] חֶלְקִי יְהֹוָה אָמְרָה נַפְשִׁי
עַל־כֵּן אוֹחִיל לוֹ:

[25] טוֹב יְהֹוָה לְקוָֹו
לְנֶפֶשׁ תִּדְרְשֶׁנּוּ:

[26] טוֹב וְיָחִיל וְדוּמָם
לִתְשׁוּעַת יְהֹוָה:

[27] טוֹב לַגֶּבֶר כִּי־יִשָּׂא
עֹל בִּנְעוּרָיו:

[28] יֵשֵׁב בָּדָד וְיִדֹּם
כִּי נָטַל עָלָיו:

[29] יִתֵּן בֶּעָפָר פִּיהוּ
אוּלַי יֵשׁ תִּקְוָה:

[30] יִתֵּן לְמַכֵּהוּ לֶחִי
יִשְׂבַּע בְּחֶרְפָּה:

[31] כִּי לֹא יִזְנַח לְעוֹלָם אֲדֹנָי:

[32] כִּי אִם־הוֹגָה וְרִחַם
כְּרֹב חֲסָדָיו:

[33] כִּי לֹא עִנָּה מִלִּבּוֹ
וַיַּגֶּה בְּנֵי־אִישׁ:

[34] לְדַכֵּא תַּחַת רַגְלָיו
כֹּל אֲסִירֵי אָרֶץ:

[35] לְהַטּוֹת מִשְׁפַּט־גָּבֶר
נֶגֶד פְּנֵי עֶלְיוֹן:

[36] לְעַוֵּת אָדָם בְּרִיבוֹ
אֲדֹנָי לֹא רָאָה:

426

37] Who is he that says, and it comes to pass,
When the LORD commands it not?

38] Out of the mouth of the Most High proceeds
   not
Evil and good?

39] Wherefore does a living man complain,
A strong man because of his sins?

40] Let us search and try our ways,
And return to the LORD.

41] Let us lift up our heart with our hands
To God in the heavens.

[37 מִי זֶה אָמַר וַתֶּהִי

אֲדֹנָי לֹא צִוָּה:

[38 מִפִּי עֶלְיוֹן לֹא תֵצֵא

הָרָעוֹת וְהַטּוֹב:

[39 מַה־יִּתְאוֹנֵן אָדָם חָי

גֶּבֶר עַל־חֲטָאָיו:

[40 נַחְפְּשָׂה דְרָכֵינוּ וְנַחְקֹרָה

וְנָשׁוּבָה עַד־יְהוָֹה:

[41 נִשָּׂא לְבָבֵנוּ אֶל־כַּפָּיִם

אֶל־אֵל בַּשָּׁמָיִם:

וָאֶתְחַנַּן

FIRST SELECTION

Isaiah
40 : 1-26

Chapter 40

1] Comfort, oh, comfort My people,
Says your God.

2] Speak tenderly to Jerusalem,
And declare to her
That her term of service is over,
That her iniquity is expiated;
For she has received at the hand of the LORD
Double for all her sins.

3] A voice rings out:
"Clear in the desert
A road for the LORD!
Level in the wilderness
A highway for our God!

4] Let every valley be raised,
Every hill and mount made low.
Let the rugged ground become level
And the ridges become a plain.

5] The Presence of the LORD shall appear,
And all flesh, as one, shall behold—
For the LORD Himself has spoken."

מ

1] נַחֲמוּ נַחֲמוּ עַמִּי
יֹאמַר אֱלֹהֵיכֶם:

2] דַּבְּרוּ עַל־לֵב יְרוּשָׁלַ͏ִם
וְקִרְאוּ אֵלֶיהָ
כִּי מָלְאָה צְבָאָהּ
כִּי נִרְצָה עֲוֹנָהּ
כִּי לָקְחָה מִיַּד יְהֹוָה
כִּפְלַיִם בְּכָל־חַטֹּאתֶיהָ:

3] קוֹל קוֹרֵא
בַּמִּדְבָּר פַּנּוּ דֶּרֶךְ יְהֹוָה
יַשְּׁרוּ בָּעֲרָבָה
מְסִלָּה לֵאלֹהֵינוּ:

4] כָּל־גֶּיא יִנָּשֵׂא
וְכָל־הַר וְגִבְעָה יִשְׁפָּלוּ
וְהָיָה הֶעָקֹב לְמִישׁוֹר
וְהָרְכָסִים לְבִקְעָה:

5] וְנִגְלָה כְּבוֹד יְהֹוָה
וְרָאוּ כָל־בָּשָׂר יַחְדָּו
כִּי פִּי יְהֹוָה דִּבֵּר:

428

6] A voice rings out: "Proclaim!"
^{a-}Another asks,^{-a} "What shall I proclaim?"
"All flesh is grass,
All its goodness like flowers of the field:

קוֹל אֹמֵר קְרָא [6
וְאָמַר מָה אֶקְרָא
כָּל־הַבָּשָׂר חָצִיר
וְכָל־חַסְדּוֹ כְּצִיץ הַשָּׂדֶה:

7] Grass withers, flowers fade
When the breath of the LORD blows on them.
Indeed, man is but grass:

יָבֵשׁ חָצִיר נָבֵל צִיץ [7
כִּי רוּחַ יְהוָה נָשְׁבָה בּוֹ
אָכֵן חָצִיר הָעָם:

8] Grass withers, flowers fade—
But the word of our God is always fulfilled!"

יָבֵשׁ חָצִיר נָבֵל צִיץ [8
וּדְבַר אֱלֹהֵינוּ יָקוּם לְעוֹלָם:

9] Ascend a lofty mountain,
O herald of joy to Zion;
Raise your voice with power,
O herald of joy to Jerusalem—
Raise it, have no fear;
Announce to the cities of Judah:
Behold your God!

עַל הַר־גָּבֹהַ עֲלִי־לָךְ [9
מְבַשֶּׂרֶת צִיּוֹן
הָרִימִי בַכֹּחַ קוֹלֵךְ
מְבַשֶּׂרֶת יְרוּשָׁלָ͏ִם
הָרִימִי אַל־תִּירָאִי
אִמְרִי לְעָרֵי יְהוּדָה
הִנֵּה אֱלֹהֵיכֶם:

10] Behold, the Lord GOD comes in might,
And His arm wins triumph for Him;
See, His reward^b is with Him,
His recompense before Him.

הִנֵּה אֲדֹנָי יְהוִה בְּחָזָק יָבוֹא [10
וּזְרֹעוֹ מֹשְׁלָה לוֹ
הִנֵּה שְׂכָרוֹ אִתּוֹ
וּפְעֻלָּתוֹ לְפָנָיו:

11] Like a shepherd He pastures His flock:
He gathers the lambs in His arms
And carries them in His bosom;
Gently He drives the mother sheep.

כְּרֹעֶה עֶדְרוֹ יִרְעֶה [11
בִּזְרֹעוֹ יְקַבֵּץ טְלָאִים
וּבְחֵיקוֹ יִשָּׂא עָלוֹת יְנַהֵל:

12] Who measured the waters with the hollow of
his hand,
And gauged the skies with a span,
And meted earth's dust with a measure,^c

מִי־מָדַד בְּשָׁעֳלוֹ מַיִם [12
וְשָׁמַיִם בַּזֶּרֶת תִּכֵּן
וְכָל בַּשָּׁלִשׁ עֲפַר הָאָרֶץ

^{a-a} *1QIs^a and Septuagint read "And I asked." (1QIs^a=manuscript^a of Isaiah found
in the first cave of Qumran, the site of the caves where the Bible manuscripts were
found in 1949–50.)*

^b *The reward and recompense to the cities of Judah; cf. Jer. 31.14, 16*

^c *Heb. shalish "third," probably a third of an ephah*

And weighed the mountains with a scale
And the hills with a balance?

13] Who has plumbed the mind of the LORD,
What man could tell Him His plan?

14] Whom did He consult, and who taught Him,
Guided Him in the way of right?
Who guided Him in knowledge
And showed Him the path of wisdom?

15] The nations are but a drop in a bucket,
Reckoned as dust on a balance;
The very coastlands He lifts like motes.

16] Lebanon is not fuel enough,
Nor its beasts enough for sacrifice.

17] All nations are as naught in His sight;
He accounts them as less than nothing.

18] To whom, then, can you liken God,
What form compare to Him?

19] The idol? A woodworker shaped it,
And a smith overlaid it with gold,
ᵈ⁻Forging links of silver.⁻ᵈ

20] As a gift, he chooses the mulberryᵉ—
A wood that does not rot—
Then seeks a skillful woodworker
To make a firm idol,
That will not topple.

21] Do you not know?
Have you not heard?

וְשָׁקַל בַּפֶּלֶס הָרִים
וּגְבָעוֹת בְּמֹאזְנָיִם:
13] מִי־תִכֵּן אֶת־רוּחַ יְהֹוָה
וְאִישׁ עֲצָתוֹ יוֹדִיעֶנּוּ:
14] אֶת־מִי נוֹעַץ וַיְבִינֵהוּ
וַיְלַמְּדֵהוּ בְּאֹרַח מִשְׁפָּט
וַיְלַמְּדֵהוּ דַעַת
וְדֶרֶךְ תְּבוּנוֹת יוֹדִיעֶנּוּ:
15] הֵן גּוֹיִם כְּמַר מִדְּלִי
וּכְשַׁחַק מֹאזְנַיִם נֶחְשָׁבוּ
הֵן אִיִּים כַּדַּק יִטּוֹל:
16] וּלְבָנוֹן אֵין דֵּי בָּעֵר
וְחַיָּתוֹ אֵין דֵּי עוֹלָה:
17] כָּל־הַגּוֹיִם כְּאַיִן נֶגְדּוֹ
מֵאֶפֶס וָתֹהוּ נֶחְשְׁבוּ־לוֹ:
18] וְאֶל־מִי תְּדַמְּיוּן אֵל
וּמַה־דְּמוּת תַּעַרְכוּ־לוֹ:
19] הַפֶּסֶל נָסַךְ חָרָשׁ
וְצֹרֵף בַּזָּהָב יְרַקְּעֶנּוּ
וּרְתֻקוֹת כֶּסֶף צוֹרֵף:
20] הַמְסֻכָּן תְּרוּמָה עֵץ
לֹא־יִרְקַב יִבְחָר
חָרָשׁ חָכָם יְבַקֶּשׁ־לוֹ
לְהָכִין פֶּסֶל לֹא יִמּוֹט:
21] הֲלוֹא תֵדְעוּ
הֲלוֹא תִשְׁמָעוּ

ᵈ⁻ᵈ Meaning of Heb. uncertain
ᵉ Heb. mesukan; *according to a Jewish tradition, preserved by Jerome, a kind of wood; a similar word denotes a kind of wood in Akkadian*

Have you not been told
From the very first?
Have you not discerned
d-How the earth was founded?-*d*

הֲלוֹא הֻגַּד מֵרֹאשׁ לָכֶם

הֲלוֹא הֲבִינֹתֶם מוֹסְדוֹת הָאָרֶץ:

22] It is He who is enthroned above the vault of
the earth,
So that its inhabitants seem as grasshoppers;
Who spread out the skies like gauze,
Stretched them out like a tent to dwell in.

22] הַיֹּשֵׁב עַל־חוּג הָאָרֶץ

וְיֹשְׁבֶיהָ כַּחֲגָבִים

הַנּוֹטֶה כַדֹּק שָׁמַיִם

וַיִּמְתָּחֵם כָּאֹהֶל לָשָׁבֶת:

23] He brings potentates to naught,
Makes rulers of the earth as nothing.

23] הַנּוֹתֵן רוֹזְנִים לְאָיִן

שֹׁפְטֵי אֶרֶץ כַּתֹּהוּ עָשָׂה:

24] Hardly are they planted,
Hardly are they sown,
Hardly has their stem
Taken root in earth,
When He blows upon them and they dry up,
And the storm bears them off like straw.

24] אַף בַּל־נִטָּעוּ

אַף בַּל־זֹרָעוּ

אַף בַּל־שֹׁרֵשׁ

בָּאָרֶץ גִּזְעָם

וְגַם נָשַׁף בָּהֶם וַיִּבָשׁוּ

וּסְעָרָה כַּקַּשׁ תִּשָּׂאֵם:

25] To whom, then, can you liken Me,
To whom can I be compared?
                    —says the Holy One.

25] וְאֶל־מִי תְדַמְּיוּנִי וְאֶשְׁוֶה

יֹאמַר קָדוֹשׁ:

26] Lift high your eyes and see:
Who created these?
He who sends out their host by count,
Who calls them each by name:
Because of His great might and vast power,
Not one fails to appear.

26] שְׂאוּ־מָרוֹם עֵינֵיכֶם וּרְאוּ

מִי־בָרָא אֵלֶּה

הַמּוֹצִיא בְמִסְפָּר צְבָאָם

לְכֻלָּם בְּשֵׁם יִקְרָא

מֵרֹב אוֹנִים וְאַמִּיץ כֹּחַ

אִישׁ לֹא נֶעְדָּר:

---

d-d Meaning of Heb. uncertain

Jeremiah

7 : 1-23

Chapter 7

1] The word which came to Jeremiah from the LORD:

2] Stand at the gate of the House of the LORD, and there proclaim this word: Hear the word of the LORD, all you of Judah who enter these gates to worship the LORD!

3] Thus said the LORD of Hosts, the God of Israel: Mend your ways and your actions, and I will *ᵃ-let you dwell*⁻ᵃ in this place.

4] Don't put your trust in illusions and say, "The Temple of the LORD, the Temple of the LORD, the Temple of the LORD are these [buildings]."
5] No, if you really mend your ways and your actions; if you execute justice between one man and another;

6] if you do not oppress the stranger, the orphan, and the widow; if you do not shed the blood of the innocent in this place; if you do not follow other gods, to your own hurt—

7] then only will I *ᵃ-let you dwell*⁻ᵃ in this place, in the land which I gave to your fathers for all time.

8] See, you are relying on illusions that are of no avail.
9] Will you steal and murder and commit adultery and swear falsely, and sacrifice to Baal, and follow other gods whom you have not experienced,ᵇ

10] and then come and stand before Me in this House which bears My name and say, "We are

ז

1] הַדָּבָר אֲשֶׁר־הָיָה אֶל־יִרְמְיָהוּ מֵאֵת יְהוָה לֵאמֹר: 2] עֲמֹד בְּשַׁעַר בֵּית יְהוָה וְקָרָאתָ שָׁם אֶת־הַדָּבָר הַזֶּה וְאָמַרְתָּ שִׁמְעוּ דְבַר־יְהוָה כָּל־יְהוּדָה הַבָּאִים בַּשְּׁעָרִים הָאֵלֶּה לְהִשְׁתַּחֲוֹת לַיהוָה:

3] כֹּה־אָמַר יְהוָה צְבָאוֹת אֱלֹהֵי יִשְׂרָאֵל הֵיטִיבוּ דַרְכֵיכֶם וּמַעַלְלֵיכֶם וַאֲשַׁכְּנָה אֶתְכֶם בַּמָּקוֹם הַזֶּה: 4] אַל־תִּבְטְחוּ לָכֶם אֶל־דִּבְרֵי־הַשֶּׁקֶר לֵאמֹר הֵיכַל יְהוָה הֵיכַל יְהוָה הֵיכַל יְהוָה הֵמָּה: 5] כִּי אִם־הֵיטֵיב תֵּיטִיבוּ אֶת־דַּרְכֵיכֶם וְאֶת־מַעַלְלֵיכֶם אִם־עָשׂוֹ תַעֲשׂוּ מִשְׁפָּט בֵּין אִישׁ וּבֵין רֵעֵהוּ: 6] גֵּר יָתוֹם וְאַלְמָנָה לֹא תַעֲשֹׁקוּ וְדָם נָקִי אַל־תִּשְׁפְּכוּ בַּמָּקוֹם הַזֶּה וְאַחֲרֵי אֱלֹהִים אֲחֵרִים לֹא תֵלְכוּ לְרַע לָכֶם: 7] וְשִׁכַּנְתִּי אֶתְכֶם בַּמָּקוֹם הַזֶּה בָּאָרֶץ אֲשֶׁר נָתַתִּי לַאֲבוֹתֵיכֶם לְמִן־עוֹלָם וְעַד־עוֹלָם: 8] הִנֵּה אַתֶּם בֹּטְחִים לָכֶם עַל־דִּבְרֵי הַשֶּׁקֶר לְבִלְתִּי הוֹעִיל: 9] הֲגָנֹב רָצֹחַ וְנָאֹף וְהִשָּׁבֵעַ לַשֶּׁקֶר וְקַטֵּר לַבָּעַל וְהָלֹךְ אַחֲרֵי אֱלֹהִים אֲחֵרִים אֲשֶׁר לֹא־יְדַעְתֶּם: 10] וּבָאתֶם וַעֲמַדְתֶּם לְפָנַי בַּבַּיִת הַזֶּה אֲשֶׁר נִקְרָא־שְׁמִי

ᵃ⁻ᵃ *Meaning of Heb. uncertain. Change of vocalization yields "dwell with you"; so Aquila and Vulgate*

ᵇ *I.e., who have not proved themselves to you; cf. Hosea 13.4*

safe"?—[Safe] to do all these abhorrent things!

11] Do you consider this House, which bears My name, to be a den of thieves? As for Me, I have been watching—declares the LORD.

12] Just go to My place at Shiloh, where I had established My name formerly, and see what I did to it because of the wickedness of My people Israel.

13] And now, because you do all these things—declares the LORD—and though I spoke to you persistently, you would not listen; and though I called to you, you would not respond—

14] therefore I will do to the House which bears My name, on which you rely, and to the place which I gave you and your fathers just what I did to Shiloh.

15] And I will cast you out of My presence as I cast out your brothers, the whole brood of Ephraim.

16] As for you, do not pray for this people, do not raise a cry of prayer on their behalf, do not plead with Me; for I will not listen to you.

17] Don't you see what they are doing in the towns of Judah and in the streets of Jerusalem?

18] The children gather sticks, the fathers build the fire, and the mothers knead dough, to make cakes for the Queen of Heaven,ᵉ and they pour libations to other gods, to vex Me.

19] Is it Me they are vexing?—says the LORD. It is rather themselves, to their own disgrace.

20] Assuredly, thus said the Lord GOD: My wrath and My fury will be poured out upon this place, on man and on beast, on the trees of the field and the fruit of the soil. It shall burn, with none to quench it.

עָלָיו וַאֲמַרְתֶּם נִצַּלְנוּ לְמַעַן עֲשׂוֹת אֵת כָּל־הַתּוֹעֵבֹת הָאֵלֶּה: 11] הַמְעָרַת פָּרִצִים הָיָה הַבַּיִת הַזֶּה אֲשֶׁר־נִקְרָא שְׁמִי עָלָיו בְּעֵינֵיכֶם גַּם אָנֹכִי הִנֵּה רָאִיתִי נְאֻם־יְהוָֹה:

12] כִּי לְכוּ־נָא אֶל־מְקוֹמִי אֲשֶׁר בְּשִׁילוֹ אֲשֶׁר שִׁכַּנְתִּי שְׁמִי שָׁם בָּרִאשׁוֹנָה וּרְאוּ אֵת אֲשֶׁר־עָשִׂיתִי לוֹ מִפְּנֵי רָעַת עַמִּי יִשְׂרָאֵל:

13] וְעַתָּה יַעַן עֲשׂוֹתְכֶם אֶת־כָּל־הַמַּעֲשִׂים הָאֵלֶּה נְאֻם־יְהוָֹה וָאֲדַבֵּר אֲלֵיכֶם הַשְׁכֵּם וְדַבֵּר וְלֹא שְׁמַעְתֶּם וָאֶקְרָא אֶתְכֶם וְלֹא עֲנִיתֶם:

14] וְעָשִׂיתִי לַבַּיִת אֲשֶׁר נִקְרָא־שְׁמִי עָלָיו אֲשֶׁר אַתֶּם בֹּטְחִים בּוֹ וְלַמָּקוֹם אֲשֶׁר־נָתַתִּי לָכֶם וְלַאֲבוֹתֵיכֶם כַּאֲשֶׁר עָשִׂיתִי לְשִׁלוֹ:

15] וְהִשְׁלַכְתִּי אֶתְכֶם מֵעַל פָּנָי כַּאֲשֶׁר הִשְׁלַכְתִּי אֶת־כָּל־אֲחֵיכֶם אֵת כָּל־זֶרַע אֶפְרָיִם:

16] וְאַתָּה אַל־תִּתְפַּלֵּל בְּעַד הָעָם הַזֶּה וְאַל־תִּשָּׂא בַעֲדָם רִנָּה וּתְפִלָּה וְאַל־תִּפְגַּע־בִּי כִּי־אֵינֶנִּי שֹׁמֵעַ אֹתָךְ: 17] הַאֵינְךָ רֹאֶה מָה הֵמָּה עֹשִׂים בְּעָרֵי יְהוּדָה וּבְחוּצוֹת יְרוּשָׁלָ͏ִם: 18] הַבָּנִים מְלַקְּטִים עֵצִים וְהָאָבוֹת מְבַעֲרִים אֶת־הָאֵשׁ וְהַנָּשִׁים לָשׁוֹת בָּצֵק לַעֲשׂוֹת כַּוָּנִים לִמְלֶכֶת הַשָּׁמַיִם וְהַסֵּךְ נְסָכִים לֵאלֹהִים אֲחֵרִים לְמַעַן הַכְעִסֵנִי: 19] הַאֹתִי הֵם מַכְעִסִים נְאֻם־יְהוָֹה הֲלוֹא אֹתָם לְמַעַן בֹּשֶׁת פְּנֵיהֶם: 20] לָכֵן כֹּה־אָמַר אֲדֹנָי יֱהוִֹה הִנֵּה אַפִּי וַחֲמָתִי נִתֶּכֶת אֶל־הַמָּקוֹם הַזֶּה עַל־הָאָדָם וְעַל־הַבְּהֵמָה וְעַל־עֵץ הַשָּׂדֶה וְעַל־פְּרִי הָאֲדָמָה וּבָעֲרָה וְלֹא תִכְבֶּה:

ᵉ I.e., the mother goddess (Ishtar, Astarte) in whose honor these cakes were baked

21] Thus said the LORD of Hosts, the God of Israel: Add your burnt offerings to your other sacrifices and eat the meat!

22] For when I freed your fathers from the land of Egypt, I did not speak with them or command them concerning burnt offerings or sacrifice.

23] But this is what I commanded them: Do My bidding, that I may be your God and you may be My people; walk only in the way that I enjoin upon you, that it may go well with you.

[21] כֹּה אָמַר יְהֹוָה צְבָאוֹת אֱלֹהֵי יִשְׂרָאֵל עֹלוֹתֵיכֶם סְפוּ עַל־זִבְחֵיכֶם וְאִכְלוּ בָשָׂר:

[22] כִּי לֹא־דִבַּרְתִּי אֶת־אֲבוֹתֵיכֶם וְלֹא צִוִּיתִים בְּיוֹם הוֹצִיאִי אוֹתָם מֵאֶרֶץ מִצְרָיִם עַל־דִּבְרֵי עוֹלָה וָזָבַח: [23] כִּי אִם־אֶת־הַדָּבָר הַזֶּה צִוִּיתִי אוֹתָם לֵאמֹר שִׁמְעוּ בְקוֹלִי וְהָיִיתִי לָכֶם לֵאלֹהִים וְאַתֶּם תִּהְיוּ־לִי לְעָם וַהֲלַכְתֶּם בְּכָל־הַדֶּרֶךְ אֲשֶׁר אֲצַוֶּה אֶתְכֶם לְמַעַן יִיטַב לָכֶם:

THIRD SELECTION

Psalms

94 : 12 - 23

Psalm 94

12] Happy is the man whom You discipline,
   O LORD,
   the man You instruct in Your teaching,

13] to give him tranquility in times of misfortune,
   until a pit be dug for the wicked.

14] For the LORD will not forsake His people;
   He will not abandon His very own.

15] Judgment shall again accord with justice
   and all the upright shall rally to it.

16] Who will take my part against evil men?
   Who will stand up for me against wrongdoers?

17] Were not the LORD my help,
   I should soon dwell in silence.

צד

[12] אַשְׁרֵי הַגֶּבֶר אֲשֶׁר־תְּיַסְּרֶנּוּ יָּהּ
וּמִתּוֹרָתְךָ תְלַמְּדֶנּוּ:

[13] לְהַשְׁקִיט לוֹ מִימֵי רָע
עַד יִכָּרֶה לָרָשָׁע שָׁחַת:

[14] כִּי לֹא־יִטֹּשׁ יְהֹוָה עַמּוֹ
וְנַחֲלָתוֹ לֹא יַעֲזֹב:

[15] כִּי־עַד־צֶדֶק יָשׁוּב מִשְׁפָּט
וְאַחֲרָיו כָּל־יִשְׁרֵי־לֵב:

[16] מִי־יָקוּם לִי עִם־מְרֵעִים
מִי־יִתְיַצֵּב לִי עִם־פֹּעֲלֵי אָוֶן:

[17] לוּלֵי יְהֹוָה עֶזְרָתָה לִּי
כִּמְעַט שָׁכְנָה דוּמָה נַפְשִׁי:

434

18] When I think my foot has given way,
Your faithfulness, O Lord, supports me.

19] When I am filled with cares,
Your assurance soothes my soul.

20] Shall the seat of injustice be Your partner,
that frames mischief by statute?

21] They band together to do away with the
righteous;
they condemn the innocent to death.

22] But the Lord is my haven;
my God is my sheltering rock.

23] He will make their evil recoil upon them,
annihilate them through their own wickedness;
the Lord our God will annihilate them.

18] אִם־אָמַרְתִּי מָטָה רַגְלִי
חַסְדְּךָ יְהֹוָה יִסְעָדֵנִי:

19] בְּרֹב שַׂרְעַפַּי בְּקִרְבִּי
תַּנְחוּמֶיךָ יְשַׁעַשְׁעוּ נַפְשִׁי:

20] הַיְחָבְרְךָ כִּסֵּא הַוּוֹת
יֹצֵר עָמָל עֲלֵי־חֹק:

21] יָגוֹדּוּ עַל־נֶפֶשׁ צַדִּיק
וְדָם נָקִי יַרְשִׁיעוּ:

22] וַיְהִי יְהֹוָה לִי לְמִשְׂגָּב
וֵאלֹהַי לְצוּר מַחְסִי:

23] וַיָּשֶׁב עֲלֵיהֶם אֶת־אוֹנָם
וּבְרָעָתָם יַצְמִיתֵם
יַצְמִיתֵם יְהֹוָה אֱלֹהֵינוּ:

FIRST SELECTION

Isaiah

49 : 14 — 51 : 3

Chapter 49

מט

14] Zion says,
"The Lord has forsaken me,
My Lord has forgotten me."

14] וַתֹּאמֶר צִיּוֹן
עֲזָבַנִי יְהוָֹה
וַאדֹנָי שְׁכֵחָנִי:

15] Can a woman forget her baby,
Or disown the child of her womb?
Though she might forget,
I never could forget you.

15] הֲתִשְׁכַּח אִשָּׁה עוּלָהּ
מֵרַחֵם בֶּן־בִּטְנָהּ
גַּם־אֵלֶּה תִשְׁכַּחְנָה
וְאָנֹכִי לֹא אֶשְׁכָּחֵךְ:

16] See, I have engraved you
On the palms of My hands,
Your walls are ever before Me.

16] הֵן עַל־כַּפַּיִם חַקֹּתִיךְ
חוֹמֹתַיִךְ נֶגְדִּי תָּמִיד:

17] Swiftly your children are coming;
Those who ravaged and ruined you shall leave
      you.

17] מִהֲרוּ בָּנָיִךְ
מְהָרְסַיִךְ וּמַחֲרִיבַיִךְ מִמֵּךְ יֵצֵאוּ:

18] Look up all around you and see:
They are all assembled, are come to you!
As I live
                    —declares the Lord—
You shall don them all like jewels,
Deck yourself with them like a bride.

18] שְׂאִי־סָבִיב עֵינַיִךְ וּרְאִי
כֻּלָּם נִקְבְּצוּ בָאוּ־לָךְ
חַי־אָנִי
נְאֻם־יְהוָֹה
כִּי כֻלָּם כָּעֲדִי תִלְבָּשִׁי
וּתְקַשְּׁרִים כַּכַּלָּה:

19] As for your ruins and desolate places
And your land laid waste—

19] כִּי חָרְבֹתַיִךְ וְשֹׁמְמֹתַיִךְ
וְאֶרֶץ הֲרִסֻתֵךְ

436

You shall soon be crowded with settlers,
While destroyers stay far from you.

20] The children ʿᵉyou thought you had lostᵉ
Shall yet say in your hearing,
"The place is too crowded for me;
Make room for me to settle."

21] And you will say to yourself,
"Who bore these for me
When I was bereaved and barren,
Exiled and disdainedᶠ—
By whom, then, were these reared?
I was left all alone—
And where have these been?"

22] Thus said the Lord GOD:
I will raise My hand to nations
And lift up My ensign to peoples;
And they shall bring your sons in their bosoms,
And carry your daughters on their backs.

23] Kings shall tend your children,
Their queens shall serve you as nurses.
They shall bow to you, face to the ground,
And lick the dust of your feet.
And you shall know that I am the LORD—
Those who trust in Me shall not be shamed.

24] Can spoil be taken from a warrior,
Or captives retrieved from a victor?

25] Yet thus said the LORD:
Captives shall be taken from a warrior

כִּי עַתָּה תֵּצְרִי מִיּוֹשֵׁב
וְרָחֲקוּ מְבַלְּעָיִךְ:

20] עוֹד יֹאמְרוּ בְאָזְנַיִךְ
בְּנֵי שִׁכֻּלָיִךְ
צַר־לִי הַמָּקוֹם
גְּשָׁה־לִּי וְאֵשֵׁבָה:

21] וְאָמַרְתְּ בִּלְבָבֵךְ
מִי יָלַד־לִי אֶת־אֵלֶּה
וַאֲנִי שְׁכוּלָה וְגַלְמוּדָה
גֹּלָה וְסוּרָה
וְאֵלֶּה מִי גִדֵּל
הֵן אֲנִי נִשְׁאַרְתִּי לְבַדִּי
אֵלֶּה אֵיפֹה הֵם:

22] כֹּה אָמַר אֲדֹנָי יְהוִה
הִנֵּה אֶשָּׂא אֶל־גּוֹיִם יָדִי
וְאֶל־עַמִּים אָרִים נִסִּי
וְהֵבִיאוּ בָנַיִךְ בְּחֹצֶן
וּבְנֹתַיִךְ עַל־כָּתֵף תִּנָּשֶׂאנָה:

23] וְהָיוּ מְלָכִים אֹמְנַיִךְ
וְשָׂרוֹתֵיהֶם מֵינִיקֹתַיִךְ
אַפַּיִם אֶרֶץ יִשְׁתַּחֲווּ־לָךְ
וַעֲפַר רַגְלַיִךְ יְלַחֵכוּ
וְיָדַעַתְּ כִּי־אֲנִי יְהוָה
אֲשֶׁר לֹא־יֵבֹשׁוּ קוָֹי:

24] הֲיֻקַּח מִגִּבּוֹר מַלְקוֹחַ
וְאִם־שְׁבִי צַדִּיק יִמָּלֵט:

25] כִּי־כֹה אָמַר יְהוָה
גַּם־שְׁבִי גִבּוֹר יֻקָּח

ᵉ⁻ᵉ Lit. "of your bereavement"   ᶠ Meaning of Heb. uncertain

And spoil shall be retrieved from a tyrant;
For I will contend with your adversaries,
And I will deliver your children.

וּמַלְקוֹחַ עָרִיץ יִמָּלֵט

וְאֶת־יְרִיבֵךְ אָנֹכִי אָרִיב

וְאֶת־בָּנַיִךְ אָנֹכִי אוֹשִׁיעַ:

26] I will make your oppressors eat their own flesh,
They shall be drunk with their own blood as with wine.
And all mankind shall know
That I the LORD am your Savior,
The Mighty One of Jacob, your Redeemer.

26] וְהַאֲכַלְתִּי אֶת־מוֹנַיִךְ אֶת־בְּשָׂרָם

וְכֶעָסִיס דָּמָם יִשְׁכָּרוּן

וְיָדְעוּ כָל־בָּשָׂר

כִּי אֲנִי יְהֹוָה מוֹשִׁיעֵךְ

וְגֹאֲלֵךְ אֲבִיר יַעֲקֹב:

Chapter 50

נ

1] Thus said the LORD:
*a*Where is the bill of divorce
Of your mother whom I dismissed?
And which of My creditors was it
To whom I sold you off?
You were only sold off for your sins,
And your mother dismissed for your crimes.

1] כֹּה אָמַר יְהֹוָה

אֵי זֶה סֵפֶר כְּרִיתוּת אִמְּכֶם

אֲשֶׁר שִׁלַּחְתִּיהָ

אוֹ מִי מִנּוֹשַׁי

אֲשֶׁר־מָכַרְתִּי אֶתְכֶם לוֹ

הֵן בַּעֲוֹנֹתֵיכֶם נִמְכַּרְתֶּם

וּבְפִשְׁעֵיכֶם שֻׁלְּחָה אִמְּכֶם:

2] Why, when I came, was no one there,
Why, when I called, would none respond?
Is my arm, then, too short to rescue,
Have I not the power to save?
With a mere rebuke I dry up the sea,
And turn rivers into desert.
Their fish stink from lack of water;
They lie dead *b*-of thirst.-*b*

2] מַדּוּעַ בָּאתִי וְאֵין אִישׁ

קָרָאתִי וְאֵין עוֹנֶה

הֲקָצוֹר קָצְרָה יָדִי מִפְּדוּת

וְאִם־אֵין־בִּי כֹחַ לְהַצִּיל

הֵן בְּגַעֲרָתִי אַחֲרִיב יָם

אָשִׂים נְהָרוֹת מִדְבָּר

תִּבְאַשׁ דְּגָתָם מֵאֵין מַיִם

וְתָמֹת בַּצָּמָא:

3] I clothe the skies in blackness
And make their raiment sackcloth.

3] אַלְבִּישׁ שָׁמַיִם קַדְרוּת

וְשַׂק אָשִׂים כְּסוּתָם:

a The mother (the country) has not been formally divorced, nor the children (the peo-
ple) sold because of poverty. Therefore there is no obstacle to their restoration
b-b Change of vocalization yields "on the parched ground"; cf. 44.3

4] ^{c-}The Lord GOD gave me a skilled tongue,
To know how to speak timely words to the
      weary.^{-c}
Morning by morning, He rouses,
He rouses my ear
To give heed like disciples.

5] The Lord GOD opened my ears,
And I did not disobey,
I did not run away.

6] I offered my back to the floggers,
And my cheeks to those who tore out my hair.
I did not hide my face
From insult and spittle.

7] But the Lord GOD will help me—
Therefore I feel no disgrace;
Therefore I have set my face like flint,
And I know I shall not be shamed.

8] My Vindicator is at hand—
Who dare contend with me?
Let us stand up together!^d
Who would be my opponent?
Let him approach me!

9] Lo, the Lord GOD will help me—
Who can get a verdict against me?
They shall all wear out like a garment,
The moth shall consume them.

10] Who among you reveres the LORD
And heeds the voice of His servant?—

4] אֲדֹנָי יֱהוִֹה נָתַן לִי לְשׁוֹן לִמּוּדִים

לָדַעַת לָעוּת אֶת־יָעֵף דָּבָר

יָעִיר בַּבֹּקֶר בַּבֹּקֶר

יָעִיר לִי אֹזֶן

לִשְׁמֹעַ כַּלִּמּוּדִים:

5] אֲדֹנָי יֱהוִֹה פָּתַח־לִי אֹזֶן

וְאָנֹכִי לֹא מָרִיתִי

אָחוֹר לֹא נְסוּגֹתִי:

6] גֵּוִי נָתַתִּי לְמַכִּים

וּלְחָיַי לְמֹרְטִים

פָּנַי לֹא הִסְתַּרְתִּי

מִכְּלִמּוֹת וָרֹק:

7] וַאדֹנָי יֱהוִֹה יַעֲזָר־לִי

עַל־כֵּן לֹא נִכְלָמְתִּי

עַל־כֵּן שַׂמְתִּי פָנַי כַּחַלָּמִישׁ

וָאֵדַע כִּי־לֹא אֵבוֹשׁ:

8] קָרוֹב מַצְדִּיקִי

מִי־יָרִיב אִתִּי

נַעַמְדָה יָּחַד

מִי־בַעַל מִשְׁפָּטִי

יִגַּשׁ אֵלָי:

9] הֵן אֲדֹנָי יֱהוִֹה יַעֲזָר־לִי

מִי־הוּא יַרְשִׁיעֵנִי

הֵן כֻּלָּם כַּבֶּגֶד יִבְלוּ

עָשׁ יֹאכְלֵם:

10] מִי בָכֶם יְרֵא יְהֹוָה

שֹׁמֵעַ בְּקוֹל עַבְדּוֹ

^{c-c} *Meaning of Heb. uncertain*
^d *I.e., as opponents in court; cf. Num. 35.12*

Though he walk in darkness
And have no light,
Let him trust in the name of the LORD
And rely upon his God.

אֲשֶׁר הָלַךְ חֲשֵׁכִים
וְאֵין נֹגַהּ לוֹ
יִבְטַח בְּשֵׁם יְהוָה
וְיִשָּׁעֵן בֵּאלֹהָיו:

11] But you are all kindlers of fire,
ᶜGirding onᶜ firebrands.
Walk by the blaze of your fire,
By the brands that you have lit!
This has come to you from My **hand**:
ᶜYou shall lie down in pain.ᶜ

11] הֵן כֻּלְּכֶם קֹדְחֵי אֵשׁ
מְאַזְּרֵי זִיקוֹת
לְכוּ בְּאוּר אֶשְׁכֶם
וּבְזִיקוֹת בִּעַרְתֶּם
מִיָּדִי הָיְתָה־זֹּאת לָכֶם
לְמַעֲצֵבָה תִּשְׁכָּבוּן:

Chapter 51

נא

1] Listen to Me, you who pursue justice,
You who seek the LORD:
Look to the rock you were hewn from.
To the quarry you were dug from.

1] שִׁמְעוּ אֵלַי
רֹדְפֵי צֶדֶק
מְבַקְשֵׁי יְהוָה
הַבִּיטוּ אֶל־צוּר חֻצַּבְתֶּם
וְאֶל־מַקֶּבֶת בּוֹר נֻקַּרְתֶּם:

2] Look back to Abraham your father
And to Sarah who brought you forth.
For he was only one when I called him,
But I blessed him and made him many.

2] הַבִּיטוּ אֶל־אַבְרָהָם אֲבִיכֶם
וְאֶל־שָׂרָה תְּחוֹלֶלְכֶם
כִּי־אֶחָד קְרָאתִיו
וַאֲבָרְכֵהוּ וְאַרְבֵּהוּ:

3] Truly the LORD has comforted Zion,
Comforted all her ruins;
He has made her wilderness like Eden,
Her desert like the Garden of the LORD.
Gladness and joy shall abide there,
Thanksgiving and the sound of music.

3] כִּי־נִחַם יְהוָה צִיּוֹן
נִחַם כָּל־חָרְבֹתֶיהָ
וַיָּשֶׂם מִדְבָּרָהּ כְּעֵדֶן
וְעַרְבָתָהּ כְּגַן־יְהוָה
שָׂשׂוֹן וְשִׂמְחָה יִמָּצֵא בָהּ
תּוֹדָה וְקוֹל זִמְרָה:

ᶜ⁻ᶜ *Emendation yields "Lighters of"*
ᶜ⁻ᶜ *Meaning of Heb. uncertain*

Isaiah

50 : 1-10

Chapter 50

נ

1] Thus said the LORD:
*Where is the bill of divorce
Of your mother whom I dismissed?
And which of My creditors was it
To whom I sold you off?
You were only sold off for your sins,
And your mother dismissed for your crimes.

1] כֹּה אָמַר יְהֹוָה
אֵי זֶה סֵפֶר כְּרִיתוּת אִמְּכֶם
אֲשֶׁר שִׁלַּחְתִּיהָ
אוֹ מִי מִנּוֹשַׁי
אֲשֶׁר מָכַרְתִּי אֶתְכֶם לוֹ
הֵן בַּעֲוֹנֹתֵיכֶם נִמְכַּרְתֶּם
וּבְפִשְׁעֵיכֶם שֻׁלְּחָה אִמְּכֶם:

2] Why, when I came, was no one there,
Why, when I called, would none respond?
Is my arm, then, too short to rescue,
Have I not the power to save?
With a mere rebuke I dry up the sea,
And turn rivers into desert.
Their fish stink from lack of water;
They lie dead *b*of thirst.*b*

2] מַדּוּעַ בָּאתִי וְאֵין אִישׁ
קָרָאתִי וְאֵין עוֹנֶה
הֲקָצוֹר קָצְרָה יָדִי מִפְּדוּת
וְאִם־אֵין־בִּי כֹחַ לְהַצִּיל
הֵן בְּגַעֲרָתִי אַחֲרִיב יָם
אָשִׂים נְהָרוֹת מִדְבָּר
תִּבְאַשׁ דְּגָתָם מֵאֵין מַיִם
וְתָמֹת בַּצָּמָא:

3] I clothe the skies in blackness
And make their raiment sackcloth.

3] אַלְבִּישׁ שָׁמַיִם קַדְרוּת
וְשַׂק אָשִׂים כְּסוּתָם:

4] *c*The Lord GOD gave me a skilled tongue,
To know how to speak timely words to the
     weary.*c*
Morning by morning, He rouses,

4] אֲדֹנָי יֱהֹוִה נָתַן לִי לְשׁוֹן לִמּוּדִים
לָדַעַת לָעוּת אֶת־יָעֵף דָּבָר
יָעִיר בַּבֹּקֶר בַּבֹּקֶר

---

a *The mother (the country) has not been formally divorced, nor the children (the peo-
     ple) sold because of poverty. Therefore there is no obstacle to their restoration*
b·b *Change of vocalization yields "on the parched ground"; cf. 44.3*
c·c *Meaning of Heb. uncertain*

He rouses my ear
To give heed like disciples.

5] The Lord GOD opened my ears,
And I did not disobey,
I did not run away.

6] I offered my back to the floggers,
And my cheeks to those who tore out my hair.
I did not hide my face
From insult and spittle.

7] But the Lord GOD will help me—
Therefore I feel no disgrace;
Therefore I have set my face like flint,
And I know I shall not be shamed.

8] My Vindicator is at hand—
Who dare contend with me?
Let us stand up together!*d*
Who would be my opponent?
Let him approach me!

9] Lo, the Lord GOD will help me—
Who can get a verdict against me?
They shall all wear out like a garment,
The moth shall consume them.

10] Who among you reveres the LORD
And heeds the voice of His servant?—
Though he walk in darkness
And have no light,
Let him trust in the name of the LORD
And rely upon his God.

יָעִיר לִי אֹ֫זֶן

לִשְׁמֹעַ כַּלִּמּוּדִים:

5] אֲדֹנָי יֱהֹוִה פָּתַֽח־לִי אֹזֶן

וְאָנֹכִי לֹא מָרִיתִי

אָחוֹר לֹא נְסוּגֹֽתִי:

6] גֵּוִי נָתַֽתִּי לְמַכִּים

וּלְחָיַי לְמֹֽרְטִים

פָּנַי לֹא הִסְתַּֽרְתִּי

מִכְּלִמּוֹת וָרֹק:

7] וַאדֹנָי יֱהֹוִה יַֽעֲזָר־לִי

עַל־כֵּן לֹא נִכְלָֽמְתִּי

עַל־כֵּן שַֽׂמְתִּי פָנַי כַּֽחַלָּמִישׁ

וָאֵדַע כִּֽי־לֹא אֵבוֹשׁ:

8] קָרוֹב מַצְדִּיקִי

מִֽי־יָרִיב אִתִּי

נַֽעַמְדָה יָּֽחַד

מִֽי־בַעַל מִשְׁפָּטִי

יִגַּשׁ אֵלָֽי:

9] הֵן אֲדֹנָי יֱהֹוִה יַֽעֲזָר־לִי

מִֽי־הוּא יַרְשִׁיעֵנִי

הֵן כֻּלָּם כַּבֶּגֶד יִבְלוּ

עָשׁ יֹאכְלֵֽם:

10] מִי בָכֶם יְרֵא יְהֹוָה

שֹׁמֵעַ בְּקוֹל עַבְדּוֹ

אֲשֶׁר הָלַךְ חֲשֵׁכִים

וְאֵין נֹגַהּ לוֹ

יִבְטַח בְּשֵׁם יְהֹוָה

וְיִשָּׁעֵן בֵּאלֹהָיו:

---

d I.e., as opponents in court; cf. Num. 35.12

442

Jeremiah

2 : 1-9

ב

[1 וַיְהִי דְבַר־יְהֹוָה אֵלַי לֵאמֹר: 2] הָלֹךְ

וְקָרָאתָ בְאָזְנֵי יְרוּשָׁלַ͏ִם לֵאמֹר כֹּה אָמַר יְהֹוָה

זָכַרְתִּי לָךְ חֶסֶד נְעוּרַיִךְ

אַהֲבַת כְּלוּלֹתָיִךְ

לֶכְתֵּךְ אַחֲרַי בַּמִּדְבָּר

בְּאֶרֶץ לֹא זְרוּעָה:

[3 קֹדֶשׁ יִשְׂרָאֵל לַיהֹוָה

רֵאשִׁית תְּבוּאָתֹה

כָּל־אֹכְלָיו יֶאְשָׁמוּ

רָעָה תָּבֹא אֲלֵיהֶם

נְאֻם־יְהֹוָה:

[4 שִׁמְעוּ דְבַר־יְהֹוָה בֵּית יַעֲקֹב

וְכָל־מִשְׁפְּחוֹת בֵּית יִשְׂרָאֵל:

[5 כֹּה אָמַר יְהֹוָה

מַה־מָּצְאוּ אֲבוֹתֵיכֶם בִּי עָוֶל

כִּי רָחֲקוּ מֵעָלָי

וַיֵּלְכוּ אַחֲרֵי הַהֶבֶל וַיֶּהְבָּלוּ:

[6 וְלֹא אָמְרוּ אַיֵּה יְהֹוָה

הַמַּעֲלֶה אֹתָנוּ מֵאֶרֶץ מִצְרָיִם

הַמּוֹלִיךְ אֹתָנוּ בַּמִּדְבָּר

בְּאֶרֶץ עֲרָבָה וְשׁוּחָה

בְּאֶרֶץ צִיָּה וְצַלְמָוֶת

Chapter 2

1] The word of the LORD came to me, saying,
2] Go proclaim to Jerusalem: Thus said the LORD:
I accounted to your favor
The devotion of your youth,
Your love as a bride—
How you followed Me in the wilderness,
In a land not sown.

3] Israel was holy to the LORD,
The first fruits of His harvest.
All who ate of it were held guilty;
Disaster befell them
              —declares the LORD.

4] Hear the word of the LORD, O House of Jacob,
Every clan of the House of Israel!

5] Thus said the LORD:
What wrong did your fathers find in Me
That they abandoned Me
And went after delusion and were deluded?

6] They never asked themselves, "Where is the
      LORD,
Who brought us up from the land of Egypt,
Who led us through the wilderness,
A land of deserts and pits,
A land of drought and darkness,

A land no man had traversed,
Where no human being had dwelt?"

7] I brought you to this country of farm land
To enjoy its fruit and its bounty;
But you came and defiled My land,
You made My possession abhorrent.

8] The priests never asked themselves, "Where is
    the LORD?"
The guardians of the Teaching ignored Me;
The rulers*a* rebelled against Me,
And the prophets prophesied by Baal
And followed what can do no good.

9] Oh, I will go on accusing you
                    —declares the LORD—
And I will accuse your children's children!

בְּאֶרֶץ לֹא־עָבַר בָּהּ אִישׁ
וְלֹא־יָשַׁב אָדָם שָׁם:

7] וָאָבִיא אֶתְכֶם אֶל־אֶרֶץ הַכַּרְמֶל
לֶאֱכֹל פִּרְיָהּ וְטוּבָהּ
וַתָּבֹאוּ וַתְּטַמְּאוּ אֶת־אַרְצִי
וְנַחֲלָתִי שַׂמְתֶּם לְתוֹעֵבָה:

8] הַכֹּהֲנִים לֹא אָמְרוּ אַיֵּה יְהוָֹה
וְתֹפְשֵׂי הַתּוֹרָה לֹא יְדָעוּנִי
וְהָרֹעִים פָּשְׁעוּ בִי
וְהַנְּבִיאִים נִבְּאוּ בַבַּעַל
וְאַחֲרֵי לֹא־יוֹעִלוּ הָלָכוּ:

9] לָכֵן עֹד אָרִיב אִתְּכֶם
נְאֻם־יְהוָֹה
וְאֶת בְּנֵי בְנֵיכֶם אָרִיב:

---

a Lit. "shepherds"; cf. 3.15; 23.1 ff.

444

ראה

FIRST SELECTION

Isaiah

54 : 11 — 55 : 5

נד

Chapter 54

11] Unhappy, storm-tossed one, uncomforted!
I will lay carbunclesᵈ as your building stones
And make your foundations of sapphires.

12] I will make your battlements of rubies,
Your gates of precious stones,
The whole encircling wall of gems.

13] And all your children shall be disciples of the
    LORD,
And great shall be the happiness of your children;

14] You shall be established through righteousness.
You shall be safe from oppression,
And shall have no fear;
From ruin, and it shall not come near you.

15] ᵉSurely no harm can be done
Without My consent:
Whoever would harm you
Shall fall because of you.

16] It is I who created the smith
To fan the charcoal fire

[11] עֲנִיָּה סֹעֲרָה לֹא נֻחָמָה
הִנֵּה אָנֹכִי מַרְבִּיץ בַּפּוּךְ אֲבָנַיִךְ
וִיסַדְתִּיךְ בַּסַּפִּירִים:

[12] וְשַׂמְתִּי כַּדְכֹד שִׁמְשֹׁתַיִךְ
וּשְׁעָרַיִךְ לְאַבְנֵי אֶקְדָּח
וְכָל־גְּבוּלֵךְ לְאַבְנֵי־חֵפֶץ:

[13] וְכָל־בָּנַיִךְ לִמּוּדֵי יְהֹוָה
וְרַב שְׁלוֹם בָּנָיִךְ:

[14] בִּצְדָקָה תִּכּוֹנָנִי
רַחֲקִי מֵעֹשֶׁק
כִּי־לֹא תִירָאִי
וּמִמְּחִתָּה כִּי לֹא־תִקְרַב אֵלָיִךְ:

[15] הֵן גּוֹר יָגוּר
אֶפֶס מֵאוֹתִי
מִי־גָר אִתָּךְ
עָלַיִךְ יִפּוֹל:

[16] הִנֵּה אָנֹכִי בָּרֵאתִי חָרָשׁ
נֹפֵחַ בְּאֵשׁ פֶּחָם

ᵈ *Taking* puch *as a by-form of* nofech; *so already Rashi*

ᵉ *Meaning of verse uncertain*

445

And produce the tools for his work;
So it is I who create
The instruments of havoc.

17] No weapon formed against you
Shall succeed.
And every tongue that contends with you at law
You shall defeat.
Such is the lot of the servants of the LORD.
Such their triumph through Me
         —declares the LORD.

Chapter 55

1] Ho, all who are thirsty,
Come for water,
Even if you have no money;
Come, buy food and eat:
Buy food without money,
Wine and milk without cost.

2] Why do you spend money for what is not
    bread,
Your earnings for what does not satisfy?
Give heed to Me,
And you shall eat choice food
And enjoy the richest viands.

3] Incline your ear and come to Me;
Hearken, and you shall be revived.
And I will make with you an everlasting covenant,
The enduring loyalty promised to David.

4] ᵃ⁻As I made him a leaderᵇ of peoples,
A prince and commander of peoples,

ומוֹצִיא כְלִי לְמַעֲשֵׂהוּ

וְאָנֹכִי בָּרָאתִי

מַשְׁחִית לְחַבֵּל:

[17] כָּל־כְּלִי יוּצַר עָלַיִךְ

לֹא יִצְלָח

וְכָל־לָשׁוֹן תָּקוּם־אִתָּךְ לַמִּשְׁפָּט

תַּרְשִׁיעִי זֹאת נַחֲלַת עַבְדֵי יְהֹוָה

וְצִדְקָתָם מֵאִתִּי

נְאֻם־יְהֹוָה:

נה

[1] הוֹי כָּל־צָמֵא

לְכוּ לַמַּיִם

וַאֲשֶׁר אֵין־לוֹ כָּסֶף

לְכוּ שִׁבְרוּ וֶאֱכֹלוּ

וּלְכוּ שִׁבְרוּ בְּלוֹא־כֶסֶף

וּבְלוֹא מְחִיר יַיִן וְחָלָב:

[2] לָמָּה תִשְׁקְלוּ־כֶסֶף בְּלוֹא־לֶחֶם

וִיגִיעֲכֶם בְּלוֹא לְשָׂבְעָה

שִׁמְעוּ שָׁמוֹעַ אֵלַי

וְאִכְלוּ־טוֹב

וְתִתְעַנַּג בַּדֶּשֶׁן נַפְשְׁכֶם:

[3] הַטּוּ אָזְנְכֶם וּלְכוּ אֵלַי

שִׁמְעוּ וּתְחִי נַפְשְׁכֶם

וְאֶכְרְתָה לָכֶם בְּרִית עוֹלָם

חַסְדֵי דָוִד הַנֶּאֱמָנִים:

[4] הֵן עֵד לְאוּמִּים נְתַתִּיו

נָגִיד וּמְצַוֵּה לְאֻמִּים:

ᵃ⁻ᵃ *Cf. II Sam. 22.44–45* ǁ *Ps. 18.44–45*
ᵇ *Cf. Targum; others* "witness"

446

5] So you shall summon a nation you did not
    know,
And a nation that did not know you
Shall come running to you⁻ᵃ—
For the sake of the LORD your God,
The Holy One of Israel who has glorified you.

[5 הֵן גּוֹי לֹא־תֵדַע תִּקְרָא

וְגוֹי לֹא־יְדָעוּךָ אֵלֶיךָ יָרוּצוּ

לְמַעַן יְהֹוָה אֱלֹהֶיךָ

וְלִקְדוֹשׁ יִשְׂרָאֵל כִּי פֵאֲרָךְ:

SECOND SELECTION

Joshua

8 : 30 - 35

ח

Chapter 8

30] At that time Joshua built an altar to the
LORD, the God of Israel, on Mount Ebal,

31] as
Moses, the servant of the LORD, had commanded
the Israelites—as is written in the Book of the
Teaching of Mosesᵈ—an altar of unhewn stone
upon which no iron had been wielded. They offered on it burnt offerings to the LORD, and
brought sacrifices of well-being.

32] And there,
on the stones, he inscribed a copy of the Teaching
which Moses had written for the Israelites.

33] All Israel—stranger and citizen alike—with
their elders, officials, and magistrates, stood on
either side of the Ark, facing the levitical priests
who carried the Ark of the LORD's Covenant. Half
of them faced Mount Gerizim and half of them
faced Mount Ebal, as Moses the servant of the
LORD had commanded them of old, in order to
bless the people of Israel.

34] After that, he read
all the words of the Teaching, the blessing and
the curse, just as is written in the Book of the
Teaching.ᵉ

35] There was not a word of all that
Moses had commanded which Joshua failed to
read in the presence of the entire assembly of
Israel, including the women and children and the
strangers who accompanied them.

[30 אָז יִבְנֶה יְהוֹשֻׁעַ מִזְבֵּחַ לַיהֹוָה אֱלֹהֵי
יִשְׂרָאֵל בְּהַר עֵיבָל: 31] כַּאֲשֶׁר צִוָּה מֹשֶׁה
עֶבֶד־יְהֹוָה אֶת־בְּנֵי יִשְׂרָאֵל כַּכָּתוּב בְּסֵפֶר
תּוֹרַת מֹשֶׁה מִזְבַּח אֲבָנִים שְׁלֵמוֹת אֲשֶׁר לֹא־
הֵנִיף עֲלֵיהֶן בַּרְזֶל וַיַּעֲלוּ עָלָיו עֹלוֹת לַיהֹוָה
וַיִּזְבְּחוּ שְׁלָמִים: 32] וַיִּכְתָּב־שָׁם עַל־הָאֲבָנִים
אֵת מִשְׁנֵה תּוֹרַת מֹשֶׁה אֲשֶׁר כָּתַב לִפְנֵי בְּנֵי
יִשְׂרָאֵל: 33] וְכָל־יִשְׂרָאֵל וּזְקֵנָיו וְשֹׁטְרִים
וְשֹׁפְטָיו עֹמְדִים מִזֶּה וּמִזֶּה לָאָרוֹן נֶגֶד הַכֹּהֲנִים
הַלְוִיִּם נֹשְׂאֵי אֲרוֹן בְּרִית־יְהֹוָה כַּגֵּר כָּאֶזְרָח
חֶצְיוֹ אֶל־מוּל הַר־גְּרִזִים וְהַחֶצְיוֹ אֶל־מוּל הַר־
עֵיבָל כַּאֲשֶׁר צִוָּה מֹשֶׁה עֶבֶד־יְהֹוָה לְבָרֵךְ
אֶת־הָעָם יִשְׂרָאֵל בָּרִאשֹׁנָה: 34] וְאַחֲרֵי־כֵן
קָרָא אֶת־כָּל־דִּבְרֵי הַתּוֹרָה הַבְּרָכָה וְהַקְּלָלָה
כְּכָל־הַכָּתוּב בְּסֵפֶר הַתּוֹרָה: 35] לֹא־הָיָה
דָבָר מִכֹּל אֲשֶׁר־צִוָּה מֹשֶׁה אֲשֶׁר לֹא־קָרָא
יְהוֹשֻׁעַ נֶגֶד כָּל־קְהַל יִשְׂרָאֵל וְהַנָּשִׁים וְהַטַּף
וְהַגֵּר הַהֹלֵךְ בְּקִרְבָּם:

ᵈ See Deut. 27.3–8   ᵉ See Deut. 27.11–28.68

Psalms

24 : 1 - 10

Psalm 24

כד

1] A psalm of David.
The earth is the LORD's and all that it holds,
the world and its inhabitants.

2] For He founded it upon the ocean,
set it on the nether-streams.

3] Who may ascend the mountain of the LORD?
Who may stand in His holy place?—

4] He who has clean hands and a pure heart,
who has not taken a false oath by My[a] life
or sworn deceitfully.

5] He shall carry away a blessing from the LORD,
a just reward from God, his deliverer.

6] Such are the people[b] who turn to Him,
Jacob, who seek Your presence.   Selah

7] O gates, lift up your heads!
Up high, you everlasting doors,
so the King of Glory may come in!

8] Who is the King of Glory?—
the LORD, mighty and valiant,
the LORD, valiant in battle.

[1] לְדָוִד מִזְמוֹר
לַיהֹוָה הָאָרֶץ וּמְלוֹאָהּ
תֵּבֵל וְיֹשְׁבֵי בָהּ:

[2] כִּי־הוּא עַל־יַמִּים יְסָדָהּ
וְעַל־נְהָרוֹת יְכוֹנְנֶהָ:

[3] מִי־יַעֲלֶה בְהַר־יְהֹוָה
וּמִי־יָקוּם בִּמְקוֹם קׇדְשׁוֹ:

[4] נְקִי כַפַּיִם וּבַר־לֵבָב
אֲשֶׁר לֹא־נָשָׂא לַשָּׁוְא נַפְשִׁי
וְלֹא נִשְׁבַּע לְמִרְמָה:

[5] יִשָּׂא בְרָכָה מֵאֵת יְהֹוָה
וּצְדָקָה מֵאֱלֹהֵי יִשְׁעוֹ:

[6] זֶה דּוֹר דֹּרְשָׁיו
מְבַקְשֵׁי פָנֶיךָ יַעֲקֹב סֶלָה:

[7] שְׂאוּ שְׁעָרִים רָאשֵׁיכֶם
וְהִנָּשְׂאוּ פִּתְחֵי עוֹלָם
וְיָבוֹא מֶלֶךְ הַכָּבוֹד:

[8] מִי זֶה מֶלֶךְ הַכָּבוֹד
יְהֹוָה עִזּוּז וְגִבּוֹר
יְהֹוָה גִּבּוֹר מִלְחָמָה:

---

[a] *Ancient versions and some mss. read "His"*
[b] *Lit. "generation"*

9] O gates, lift up your heads!
Lift them up, you everlasting doors,
so the King of Glory may come in!

10] Who is the King of Glory?—
the LORD of Hosts,
He is the King of Glory!   *Selah*

9] שְׂאוּ שְׁעָרִים רָאשֵׁיכֶם
וְשְׂאוּ פִּתְחֵי עוֹלָם
וְיָבֹא מֶלֶךְ הַכָּבוֹד:

10] מִי הוּא זֶה מֶלֶךְ הַכָּבוֹד
יְהוָֹה צְבָאוֹת הוּא מֶלֶךְ הַכָּבוֹד סֶלָה:

FIRST SELECTION

Isaiah

51 : 12 — 52 : 12

נא

Chapter 51

12] I, I am He who comforts you!
What ails you that you fear
Man who must die,
Mortals who fare like grass?

12] אָנֹכִי אָנֹכִי הוּא מְנַחֶמְכֶם
מִי־אַתְּ וַתִּירְאִי
מֵאֱנוֹשׁ יָמוּת
וּמִבֶּן־אָדָם חָצִיר יִנָּתֵן:

13] You have forgotten the LORD your Maker,
Who stretched out the skies and made firm the
        earth!
And you live all day in constant dread
Because of the rage of an oppressor
Who is aiming to cut [you] down.
Yet of what account is the rage of an oppressor?

13] וַתִּשְׁכַּח יְהוָה עֹשֶׂךָ
נוֹטֶה שָׁמַיִם וְיֹסֵד אָרֶץ
וַתְּפַחֵד תָּמִיד כָּל־הַיּוֹם
מִפְּנֵי חֲמַת הַמֵּצִיק
כַּאֲשֶׁר כּוֹנֵן לְהַשְׁחִית
וְאַיֵּה חֲמַת הַמֵּצִיק:

14] *a*Quickly the crouching one is freed;
He is not cut down and slain,
And he shall not want for food.

14] מִהַר צֹעֶה לְהִפָּתֵחַ
וְלֹא־יָמוּת לַשַּׁחַת
וְלֹא יֶחְסַר לַחְמוֹ:

15] For I the LORD your God—
Who stir up the sea into roaring waves,
Whose name is LORD of Hosts—

15] וְאָנֹכִי יְהוָה אֱלֹהֶיךָ
רֹגַע הַיָּם וַיֶּהֱמוּ גַּלָּיו
יְהוָה צְבָאוֹת שְׁמוֹ:

16] *h*-Have put My words in your mouth
And sheltered you with My hand;-*h*

16] וָאָשִׂם דְּבָרַי בְּפִיךָ
וּבְצֵל יָדִי כִּסִּיתִיךָ

---

*a Meaning of verse uncertain. Emendation yields (cf. Jer. 11.19; Job 14.7–9) "Quickly
  the tree buds anew; | It does not die though cut down, | And its sap does not fail"*
h-h I.e., I have chosen you to be a prophet-nation; cf. 49.2; 59.21

I, who planted*i* the skies and made firm the earth,
Have said to Zion: You are My people!

לִנְטֹעַ שָׁמַיִם וְלִיסֹד אָרֶץ
וְלֵאמֹר לְצִיּוֹן עַמִּי אָתָּה:

17] Rouse, rouse yourself!
Arise, O Jerusalem,
You who from the LORD's hand
Have drunk the cup of His wrath,
You who have drained to the dregs
The bowl, the cup of reeling!

17] הִתְעוֹרְרִי הִתְעוֹרְרִי
קוּמִי יְרוּשָׁלַםִ
אֲשֶׁר שָׁתִית מִיַּד יְהֹוָה
אֶת־כּוֹס חֲמָתוֹ
אֶת־קֻבַּעַת כּוֹס הַתַּרְעֵלָה
שָׁתִית מָצִית:

18] She has none to guide her
Of all the sons she bore;
None takes her by the hand,
Of all the sons she reared.*j*

18] אֵין מְנַהֵל לָהּ
מִכָּל־בָּנִים יָלָדָה
וְאֵין מַחֲזִיק בְּיָדָהּ
מִכָּל־בָּנִים גִּדֵּלָה:

19] These two things have befallen you:
Wrack and ruin—who can console you?
Famine and sword—*k*how shall I*-k* comfort you?

19] שְׁתַּיִם הֵנָּה קֹרְאֹתַיִךְ
מִי יָנוּד לָךְ
הַשֹּׁד וְהַשֶּׁבֶר
וְהָרָעָב וְהַחֶרֶב
מִי אֲנַחֲמֵךְ:

20] Your sons lie in a swoon
At the corner of every street—
Like an antelope caught in a net—
Drunk with the wrath of the LORD,
With the rebuke of your God.

20] בָּנַיִךְ עֻלְּפוּ
שָׁכְבוּ בְּרֹאשׁ כָּל־חוּצוֹת
כְּתוֹא מִכְמָר
הַמְלֵאִים חֲמַת־יְהֹוָה
גַּעֲרַת אֱלֹהָיִךְ:

21] Therefore,
Listen to this, unhappy one,
Who are drunk, but not with wine!

21] לָכֵן
שִׁמְעִי־נָא זֹאת עֲנִיָּה
וּשְׁכֻרַת וְלֹא מִיָּיִן:

22] Thus said the LORD, your Lord,
Your God who champions His people:

22] כֹּה־אָמַר אֲדֹנַיִךְ יְהֹוָה
וֵאלֹהַיִךְ יָרִיב עַמּוֹ

---

i Emendation yields "stretched out"; cf. Syriac version and v. 13

j To guide a drunken parent home was a recognized filial duty in ancient Canaan and Egypt

k-k Several ancient versions render "who can"

Herewith I take from your hand
The cup of reeling,[1]
The bowl, the cup of My wrath;
You shall never drink it again.

23] I will put it in the hands of your tormentors,
Who have commanded you,
"Get down, that we may walk over you"—
So that you made your back like the ground,
Like a street for passers-by.

Chapter 52

1] Awake, awake, O Zion!
Clothe yourself in splendor;
Put on your robes of majesty,
Jerusalem, holy city!
For the uncircumcised and the unclean
Shall never enter you again.

2] Arise, shake off the dust,
Sit [on your throne], Jerusalem!
Loose the bonds from your neck,
O captive one, Fair Zion!

3] For thus said the LORD:
You were sold for no price,
And shall be redeemed without money.

4] For thus said the Lord GOD:
Of old, My people went down
To Egypt to sojourn there;

הִנֵּה לָקַחְתִּי מִיָּדֵךְ
אֶת־כּוֹס הַתַּרְעֵלָה
אֶת־קֻבַּעַת כּוֹס חֲמָתִי
לֹא־תוֹסִיפִי לִשְׁתּוֹתָהּ עוֹד:

23] וְשַׂמְתִּיהָ בְּיַד־מוֹגַיִךְ
אֲשֶׁר־אָמְרוּ לְנַפְשֵׁךְ
שְׁחִי וְנַעֲבֹרָה
וַתָּשִׂימִי כָאָרֶץ גֵּוֵךְ
וְכַחוּץ לַעֹבְרִים:

נב

1] עוּרִי עוּרִי
לִבְשִׁי עֻזֵּךְ צִיּוֹן
לִבְשִׁי בִּגְדֵי תִפְאַרְתֵּךְ
יְרוּשָׁלַ͏ִם עִיר הַקֹּדֶשׁ
כִּי לֹא יוֹסִיף יָבֹא־בָךְ עוֹד
עָרֵל וְטָמֵא:

2] הִתְנַעֲרִי מֵעָפָר
קוּמִי שְּׁבִי יְרוּשָׁלָ͏ִם
הִתְפַּתְּחִי מוֹסְרֵי צַוָּארֵךְ
שְׁבִיָּה בַּת־צִיּוֹן:

3] כִּי־כֹה אָמַר יְהֹוָה
חִנָּם נִמְכַּרְתֶּם
וְלֹא בְכֶסֶף תִּגָּאֵלוּ:

4] כִּי כֹה אָמַר אֲדֹנָי יֱהֹוִה
מִצְרַיִם יָרַד־עַמִּי בָרִאשֹׁנָה
לָגוּר שָׁם

---

[1] A figure of speech for a dire fate; cf. Jer. 25.15 ff.

But Assyria has robbed them,
Giving nothing in return.[a]

5] What therefore do I gain here?
         —declares the LORD—
For My people has been carried off for nothing,
Their mockers howl
         —declares the LORD—
And constantly, unceasingly,
My name is reviled.

6] Assuredly, My people shall learn My name,
Assuredly [they shall learn] on that day
That I, the one who promised,
Am now at hand.

7] How welcome on the mountain
Are the footsteps of the herald
Announcing happiness,
Heralding good fortune,
Announcing victory,
Telling Zion, "Your God is King!"

8] Hark!
Your watchmen raise their voices,
As one they shout for joy;
For every eye shall behold
The LORD's return to Zion.

9] Raise a shout together,
O ruins of Jerusalem!
For the LORD will comfort His people,
Will redeem Jerusalem.

10] The LORD will bare His holy arm
In the sight of all the nations,

וְאַשּׁוּר בְּאֶפֶס עֲשָׁקֽוֹ׃

5] וְעַתָּה מַה־לִּי־פֹה

נְאֻם־יְהֹוָה

כִּי־לֻקַּח עַמִּי חִנָּם

מֹשְׁלָו יְהֵילִילוּ

נְאֻם־יְהֹוָה

וְתָמִיד כָּל־הַיּוֹם

שְׁמִי מִנֹּאָץ׃

6] לָכֵן יֵדַע עַמִּי שְׁמִי

לָכֵן בַּיּוֹם הַהוּא

כִּי־אֲנִי־הוּא הַמְדַבֵּר הִנֵּנִי׃

7] מַה־נָּאווּ עַל־הֶהָרִים

רַגְלֵי מְבַשֵּׂר

מַשְׁמִיעַ שָׁלוֹם

מְבַשֵּׂר טוֹב

מַשְׁמִיעַ יְשׁוּעָה

אֹמֵר לְצִיּוֹן מָלַךְ אֱלֹהָיִךְ׃

8] קוֹל צֹפַיִךְ נָשְׂאוּ קוֹל

יַחְדָּו יְרַנֵּנוּ

כִּי עַיִן בְּעַיִן יִרְאוּ

בְּשׁוּב יְהֹוָה צִיּוֹן׃

9] פִּצְחוּ רַנְּנוּ יַחְדָּו

חָרְבוֹת יְרוּשָׁלָ͏ִם

כִּי־נִחַם יְהֹוָה עַמּוֹ

גָּאַל יְרוּשָׁלָ͏ִם׃

10] חָשַׂף יְהֹוָה אֶת־זְרוֹעַ קָדְשׁוֹ

לְעֵינֵי כָּל־הַגּוֹיִם

---

[a] *Whereas the Israelites themselves sought hospitality in Egypt, Assyria (i.e., the Chaldean Empire) has exiled them by force*

And the very ends of earth shall see
The victory of our God.

11] Turn, turn away, touch naught unclean
As you depart from there;
Keep pure, as you go forth from there,
You who bear the vessels of the LORD![b]

12] For you will not depart in haste,
Nor will you leave in flight;
For the LORD is marching before you,
The God of Israel is your rear guard.

וְרָאוּ כָּל־אַפְסֵי־אָרֶץ
אֵת יְשׁוּעַת אֱלֹהֵינוּ:
11] סוּרוּ סוּרוּ צְאוּ מִשָּׁם
טָמֵא אַל־תִּגָּעוּ
צְאוּ מִתּוֹכָהּ
הִבָּרוּ נֹשְׂאֵי כְּלֵי יְהוָה:
12] כִּי לֹא בְחִפָּזוֹן תֵּצֵאוּ
וּבִמְנוּסָה לֹא תֵלֵכוּן
כִּי־הֹלֵךְ לִפְנֵיכֶם יְהוָה
וּמְאַסִּפְכֶם אֱלֹהֵי יִשְׂרָאֵל:

SECOND SELECTION

First Samuel

8 : 1-22

Chapter 8

1] When Samuel grew old, he appointed his sons judges over Israel. 2] The name of his first-born son was Joel, and his second son's name was Abijah; they sat as judges in Beer-Sheba. 3] But his sons did not follow in his ways; they were bent on gain, they accepted bribes, and they subverted justice. 4] All the elders of Israel assembled and came to Samuel at Ramah, 5] and they said to him, "You have grown old, and your sons have not followed your ways. Therefore appoint a king for us, to govern us like all other nations." 6] Samuel

ח

1] וַיְהִי כַּאֲשֶׁר זָקֵן שְׁמוּאֵל וַיָּשֶׂם אֶת־בָּנָיו שֹׁפְטִים לְיִשְׂרָאֵל: 2] וַיְהִי שֶׁם־בְּנוֹ הַבְּכוֹר יוֹאֵל וְשֵׁם מִשְׁנֵהוּ אֲבִיָּה שֹׁפְטִים בִּבְאֵר שָׁבַע: 3] וְלֹא־הָלְכוּ בָנָיו בִּדְרָכָיו וַיִּטּוּ אַחֲרֵי הַבָּצַע וַיִּקְחוּ־שֹׁחַד וַיַּטּוּ מִשְׁפָּט: 4] וַיִּתְקַבְּצוּ כֹּל זִקְנֵי יִשְׂרָאֵל וַיָּבֹאוּ אֶל־שְׁמוּאֵל הָרָמָתָה: 5] וַיֹּאמְרוּ אֵלָיו הִנֵּה אַתָּה זָקַנְתָּ וּבָנֶיךָ לֹא הָלְכוּ בִּדְרָכֶיךָ עַתָּה שִׂימָה־לָּנוּ מֶלֶךְ לְשָׁפְטֵנוּ כְּכָל־הַגּוֹיִם: 6] וַיֵּרַע

[b] Cf. Ezra 1.7–8; 5.14–15

was displeased that they said "Give us a king to govern us." Samuel prayed to the LORD,

7] and the LORD replied to Samuel, "Heed the demand of the people in everything they say to you. For it is not you that they have rejected; it is Me they have rejected as their king. 8] Like everything else they have done ever since I brought them out of Egypt to this day—forsaking Me and worshiping other gods—so they are doing to you. 9] Heed their demand; but warn them solemnly, and tell them about the practices of any king who will rule over them."

10] Samuel reported all the words of the LORD to the people, who were asking him for a king.

11] He said, "This will be the practice of the king who will rule over you: He will take your sons and appoint them as his charioteers and horsemen, and they will serve as outrunners for his chariots. 12] He will appoint them as his chiefs of thousands and of fifties; or they will have to plow his fields, reap his harvest, and make his weapons and the equipment for his chariots. 13] He will take your daughters as perfumers, cooks, and bakers. 14] He will seize your choice fields, vineyards, and olive groves, and give them to his courtiers. 15] He will take a tenth part of your grain and vintage and give it to his eunuchs and courtiers. 16] He will take your male and female slaves, your choice ᵃ⁻young men,⁻ᵃ and your asses, and put them to work for him. 17] He will take a tenth part of your flocks, and you shall become his slaves. 18] The day will come when you cry out because of the king whom you yourselves have chosen; and the LORD will not answer you on that day."

ᵃ⁻ᵃ *Septuagint reads "cattle"*

הַדָּבָר בְּעֵינֵי שְׁמוּאֵל כַּאֲשֶׁר אָמְרוּ תְּנָה־לָּנוּ מֶלֶךְ לְשָׁפְטֵנוּ וַיִּתְפַּלֵּל שְׁמוּאֵל אֶל־יְהֹוָה: 7 וַיֹּאמֶר יְהֹוָה אֶל־שְׁמוּאֵל שְׁמַע בְּקוֹל הָעָם לְכֹל אֲשֶׁר־יֹאמְרוּ אֵלֶיךָ כִּי לֹא אֹתְךָ מָאָסוּ כִּי־אֹתִי מָאֲסוּ מִמְּלֹךְ עֲלֵיהֶם: 8 כְּכָל־הַמַּעֲשִׂים אֲשֶׁר־עָשׂוּ מִיּוֹם הַעֲלֹתִי אֹתָם מִמִּצְרַיִם וְעַד־הַיּוֹם הַזֶּה וַיַּעַזְבֻנִי וַיַּעַבְדוּ אֱלֹהִים אֲחֵרִים כֵּן הֵמָּה עֹשִׂים גַּם־לָךְ: 9 וְעַתָּה שְׁמַע בְּקוֹלָם אַךְ כִּי־הָעֵד תָּעִיד בָּהֶם וְהִגַּדְתָּ לָהֶם מִשְׁפַּט הַמֶּלֶךְ אֲשֶׁר יִמְלֹךְ עֲלֵיהֶם:

10 וַיֹּאמֶר שְׁמוּאֵל אֵת כָּל־דִּבְרֵי יְהֹוָה אֶל־הָעָם הַשֹּׁאֲלִים מֵאִתּוֹ מֶלֶךְ: 11 וַיֹּאמֶר זֶה יִהְיֶה מִשְׁפַּט הַמֶּלֶךְ אֲשֶׁר יִמְלֹךְ עֲלֵיכֶם אֶת־בְּנֵיכֶם יִקָּח וְשָׂם לוֹ בְּמֶרְכַּבְתּוֹ וּבְפָרָשָׁיו וְרָצוּ לִפְנֵי מֶרְכַּבְתּוֹ: 12 וְלָשׂוּם לוֹ שָׂרֵי אֲלָפִים וְשָׂרֵי חֲמִשִּׁים וְלַחֲרֹשׁ חֲרִישׁוֹ וְלִקְצֹר קְצִירוֹ וְלַעֲשׂוֹת כְּלֵי־מִלְחַמְתּוֹ וּכְלֵי רִכְבּוֹ: 13 וְאֶת־בְּנוֹתֵיכֶם יִקָּח לְרַקָּחוֹת וּלְטַבָּחוֹת וּלְאֹפוֹת: 14 וְאֶת־שְׂדוֹתֵיכֶם וְאֶת־כַּרְמֵיכֶם וְזֵיתֵיכֶם הַטּוֹבִים יִקָּח וְנָתַן לַעֲבָדָיו: 15 וְזַרְעֵיכֶם וְכַרְמֵיכֶם יַעְשֹׂר וְנָתַן לְסָרִיסָיו וְלַעֲבָדָיו: 16 וְאֶת־עַבְדֵיכֶם וְאֶת־שִׁפְחוֹתֵיכֶם וְאֶת־בַּחוּרֵיכֶם הַטּוֹבִים וְאֶת־חֲמוֹרֵיכֶם יִקָּח וְעָשָׂה לִמְלַאכְתּוֹ: 17 צֹאנְכֶם יַעְשֹׂר וְאַתֶּם תִּהְיוּ־לוֹ לַעֲבָדִים: 18 וּזְעַקְתֶּם בַּיּוֹם הַהוּא מִלִּפְנֵי מַלְכְּכֶם אֲשֶׁר בְּחַרְתֶּם לָכֶם וְלֹא־יַעֲנֶה יְהֹוָה אֶתְכֶם בַּיּוֹם הַהוּא:

19] But the people would not listen to Samuel's warning. "No," they said. "We must have a king over us,

20] that we may be like all the other nations: Let our king rule over us and go out at our head and fight our battles."

21] When Samuel heard all that the people said, he reported it to the LORD.

22] And the LORD said to Samuel, "Heed their demands and appoint a king for them." Samuel then said to the men of Israel, "All of you go home."

19] וַיְמָאֲנוּ הָעָם לִשְׁמֹעַ בְּקוֹל שְׁמוּאֵל וַיֹּאמְרוּ לֹא כִּי אִם־מֶלֶךְ יִהְיֶה עָלֵינוּ:

20] וְהָיִינוּ גַם־אֲנַחְנוּ כְּכָל־הַגּוֹיִם וּשְׁפָטָנוּ מַלְכֵּנוּ וְיָצָא לְפָנֵינוּ וְנִלְחַם אֶת־מִלְחֲמֹתֵינוּ: 21] וַיִּשְׁמַע שְׁמוּאֵל אֵת כָּל־דִּבְרֵי הָעָם וַיְדַבְּרֵם בְּאָזְנֵי יְהוָה: 22] וַיֹּאמֶר יְהוָה אֶל־שְׁמוּאֵל שְׁמַע בְּקוֹלָם וְהִמְלַכְתָּ לָהֶם מֶלֶךְ וַיֹּאמֶר שְׁמוּאֵל אֶל־אַנְשֵׁי יִשְׂרָאֵל לְכוּ אִישׁ לְעִירוֹ:

THIRD SELECTION

Jeremiah

23 : 13-22

Chapter 23

13] In the prophets of Samaria
I saw a repulsive thing:
They prophesied by Baal
And led My people Israel astray.

14] But what I see in the prophets of Jerusalem
Is something horrifying:
Adultery and false dealing.
They encourage evildoers,
So that no one turns back from his wickedness.
To Me they are all like Sodom,
And [all] its inhabitants like Gomorrah.

15] Assuredly, thus said the LORD of Hosts concerning the prophets:
I am going to make them eat wormwood

כג

13] וּבִנְבִיאֵי שֹׁמְרוֹן רָאִיתִי תִפְלָה

הִנַּבְּאוּ בַבַּעַל

וַיַּתְעוּ אֶת־עַמִּי אֶת־יִשְׂרָאֵל:

14] וּבִנְבִאֵי יְרוּשָׁלַ͏ִם רָאִיתִי שַׁעֲרוּרָה

נָאוֹף וְהָלֹךְ בַּשֶּׁקֶר

וְחִזְּקוּ יְדֵי מְרֵעִים

לְבִלְתִּי־שָׁבוּ אִישׁ מֵרָעָתוֹ

הָיוּ־לִי כֻלָּם כִּסְדֹם

וְיֹשְׁבֶיהָ כַּעֲמֹרָה:

15] לָכֵן כֹּה־אָמַר יְהוָה צְבָאוֹת עַל־הַנְּבִאִים

הִנְנִי מַאֲכִיל אוֹתָם לַעֲנָה

And drink a bitter draft;
For from the prophets of Jerusalem
Godlessness has gone forth to the whole land.

וְהִשְׁקִתִים מֵי־רֹאשׁ

כִּי מֵאֵת נְבִיאֵי יְרוּשָׁלַם

יָצְאָה חֲנֻפָּה לְכָל־הָאָרֶץ:

16] Thus said the LORD of Hosts:
Do not listen to the words of the prophets
Who prophesy to you.
They are deluding you,
The prophecies they speak are from their own
    minds,
Not from the mouth of the LORD.

16] כֹּה־אָמַר יְהוָה צְבָאוֹת

אַל־תִּשְׁמְעוּ עַל־דִּבְרֵי הַנְּבִאִים

הַנִּבְּאִים לָכֶם

מַהְבִּלִים הֵמָּה אֶתְכֶם

חֲזוֹן לִבָּם יְדַבֵּרוּ

לֹא מִפִּי יְהוָה:

17] They declare to men who despise Me:
"The LORD has said:
All shall be well with you";
And to all who follow their willful hearts they
    say:
"No evil shall befall you."

17] אֹמְרִים אָמוֹר לִמְנַאֲצַי

דִּבֶּר יְהוָה

שָׁלוֹם יִהְיֶה לָכֶם

וְכֹל הֹלֵךְ בִּשְׁרִרוּת לִבּוֹ אָמְרוּ

לֹא־תָבוֹא עֲלֵיכֶם רָעָה:

18] But he who has stood in the council of the
    LORD,
And seen, and heard His word—
He who has listened to His word must obey.[d]

18] כִּי מִי עָמַד בְּסוֹד יְהוָה

וְיֵרֶא וְיִשְׁמַע אֶת־דְּבָרוֹ

מִי־הִקְשִׁיב דְּבָרוֹ וַיִּשְׁמָע:

19] [e]Lo, the storm of the LORD goes forth in fury,
A whirling storm,
It shall whirl down upon the heads of the wicked.

19] הִנֵּה סַעֲרַת יְהוָה

חֵמָה יָצְאָה וְסַעַר מִתְחוֹלֵל

עַל רֹאשׁ רְשָׁעִים יָחוּל:

20] The anger of the LORD shall not turn back
Till it has fulfilled and completed His purposes.[-e]
In the days to come
You shall clearly perceive it.

20] לֹא יָשׁוּב אַף־יְהוָה

עַד־עֲשֹׂתוֹ

וְעַד־הֲקִימוֹ מְזִמּוֹת לִבּוֹ

בְּאַחֲרִית הַיָּמִים

תִּתְבּוֹנְנוּ בָהּ בִּינָה:

21] I did not send those prophets,
But they rushed in;

21] לֹא־שָׁלַחְתִּי אֶת־הַנְּבִאִים

וְהֵם רָצוּ

[d] *Change of vocalization yields "announce it"; cf. vv. 22, 28*
[e-e] *This section constitutes the word of God to which Jeremiah refers*

I did not speak to them,
Yet they prophesied.

22] If they have stood in My council,
Let them announce My words to My people
And make them turn back
From their evil ways and wicked acts.

לֹא־דִבַּרְתִּי אֲלֵיהֶם

וְהֵם נִבָּאוּ:

22] וְאִם־עָמְדוּ בְּסוֹדִי

וְיַשְׁמִעוּ דְבָרַי אֶת־עַמִּי

וִישִׁבוּם מִדַּרְכָּם הָרָע

וּמֵרֹעַ מַעַלְלֵיהֶם:

FIRST SELECTION

Isaiah

54 : 1 - 10

Chapter 54

1] Shout, O barren one,
You who bore no child!
Shout aloud for joy,
You who did not travail!
For the children of the wife forlorn
Shall outnumber those of the espoused
        —said the LORD.

2] Enlarge the site of your tent,
a-Extend the size of your dwelling,-*a*
Do not stint!
Lengthen the ropes, and drive the pegs firm.

3] For you shall spread out to the right and the
    left;
Your offspring shall dispossess nations!*b*
And shall people the desolate towns.

4] Fear not, you shall not be shamed;
Do not cringe, you shall not be disgraced.
For you shall forget
The reproach of your youth,
And remember no more
The shame of your widowhood.

5] For He who made you will espouse you—
His name is "LORD of Hosts";
The Holy One of Israel will redeem you,
Who is called "God of all the Earth."

נד

1] רָנִּי עֲקָרָה לֹא יָלָדָה
פִּצְחִי רִנָּה וְצַהֲלִי לֹא־חָלָה
כִּי־רַבִּים בְּנֵי־שׁוֹמֵמָה
מִבְּנֵי בְעוּלָה אָמַר יְהֹוָה:

2] הַרְחִיבִי מְקוֹם אׇהֳלֵךְ
וִירִיעוֹת מִשְׁכְּנוֹתַיִךְ יַטּוּ אַל־תַּחְשֹׂכִי
הַאֲרִיכִי מֵיתָרַיִךְ וִיתֵדֹתַיִךְ חַזֵּקִי:

3] כִּי־יָמִין וּשְׂמֹאול תִּפְרֹצִי
וְזַרְעֵךְ גּוֹיִם יִירָשׁ
וְעָרִים נְשַׁמּוֹת יוֹשִׁיבוּ:

4] אַל־תִּירְאִי כִּי־לֹא תֵבוֹשִׁי
וְאַל־תִּכָּלְמִי כִּי־לֹא תַחְפִּירִי
כִּי בֹשֶׁת עֲלוּמַיִךְ תִּשְׁכָּחִי
וְחֶרְפַּת אַלְמְנוּתַיִךְ לֹא תִזְכְּרִי־עוֹד:

5] כִּי בֹעֲלַיִךְ עֹשַׂיִךְ
יְהֹוָה צְבָאוֹת שְׁמוֹ
וְגֹאֲלֵךְ קְדוֹשׁ יִשְׂרָאֵל
אֱלֹהֵי כׇל־הָאָרֶץ יִקָּרֵא:

a-a Lit. "Let the cloths of your dwelling extend"
b I.e., the foreigners who had occupied regions from which Israelites had been exiled;
  cf. II Kings 17.24

6] The LORD has called you back
As a wife forlorn and forsaken.
Can one cast off the wife of his youth?
                    —said your God.

7] For a little while I forsook you.
But with vast love I will bring you back.

8] In slight anger, for a moment,
I hid My face from you;
But with kindness everlasting
I will take you back in love
                    —said the LORD your Redeemer.

9] For this to Me is like the waters[c] of Noah:
As I swore that the waters of Noah
Nevermore would flood the earth,
So I swear that I will not
Be angry with you or rebuke you.

10] For the mountains may move
And the hills be shaken,
But my loyalty shall never move from you,
Nor My covenant of friendship be shaken
                    —said the LORD, who takes you back in love.

‏6] כִּי־כְאִשָּׁה עֲזוּבָה‎

‏וַעֲצוּבַת רוּחַ קְרָאָךְ יְהֹוָה‎

‏וְאֵשֶׁת נְעוּרִים‎

‏כִּי תִמָּאֵס אָמַר אֱלֹהָיִךְ׃‎

‏7] בְּרֶגַע קָטֹן עֲזַבְתִּיךְ‎

‏וּבְרַחֲמִים גְּדוֹלִים אֲקַבְּצֵךְ׃‎

‏8] בְּשֶׁצֶף קֶצֶף הִסְתַּרְתִּי פָנַי רֶגַע מִמֵּךְ‎

‏וּבְחֶסֶד עוֹלָם רִחַמְתִּיךְ‎

‏אָמַר גֹּאֲלֵךְ יְהֹוָה׃‎

‏9] כִּי־מֵי נֹחַ זֹאת לִי‎

‏אֲשֶׁר נִשְׁבַּעְתִּי מֵעֲבֹר מֵי־נֹחַ‎

‏עוֹד עַל־הָאָרֶץ‎

‏כֵּן נִשְׁבַּעְתִּי‎

‏מִקְּצֹף עָלַיִךְ וּמִגְּעָר־בָּךְ׃‎

‏10] כִּי הֶהָרִים יָמוּשׁוּ‎

‏וְהַגְּבָעוֹת תְּמוּטֶינָה‎

‏וְחַסְדִּי מֵאִתֵּךְ לֹא־יָמוּשׁ‎

‏וּבְרִית שְׁלוֹמִי לֹא תָמוּט‎

‏אָמַר מְרַחֲמֵךְ יְהֹוָה׃‎

---

[c] Other Heb. mss. and the ancient versions read "days"

460

SECOND SELECTION

Isaiah

5 : 1 - 16

Chapter 5

ה

1] Let me sing for my beloved
A song of my lover about his vineyard.
My beloved had a vineyard
⁻On a fruitful hill.⁻

1] אָשִׁירָה נָּא לִידִידִי

שִׁירַת דּוֹדִי לְכַרְמוֹ

כֶּרֶם הָיָה לִידִידִי

בְּקֶרֶן בֶּן־שָׁמֶן:

2] He broke the ground, cleared it of stones,
And planted it with choice vines.
He built a watchtower inside it,
He even hewed a wine press in it;
For he hoped it would yield grapes.
Instead, it yielded wild grapes.

2] וַיְעַזְּקֵהוּ וַיְסַקְּלֵהוּ

וַיִּטָּעֵהוּ שֹׂרֵק

וַיִּבֶן מִגְדָּל בְּתוֹכוֹ

וְגַם־יֶקֶב חָצֵב בּוֹ

וַיְקַו לַעֲשׂוֹת עֲנָבִים

וַיַּעַשׂ בְּאֻשִׁים:

3] "Now, then,
Dwellers of Jerusalem
And men of Judah,
You be the judges
Between Me and My vineyard:

3] וְעַתָּה

יוֹשֵׁב יְרוּשָׁלַם

וְאִישׁ יְהוּדָה

שִׁפְטוּ־נָא בֵּינִי וּבֵין כַּרְמִי:

4] What more could have been done for My vine-
yard
That I failed to do in it?
Why, when I hoped it would yield grapes,
Did it yield wild grapes?

4] מַה־לַּעֲשׂוֹת עוֹד לְכַרְמִי

וְלֹא עָשִׂיתִי בּוֹ

מַדּוּעַ קִוֵּיתִי לַעֲשׂוֹת עֲנָבִים

וַיַּעַשׂ בְּאֻשִׁים:

5] Now I am going to tell you
What I will do to My vineyard:
I will remove its hedge,
That it may be ravaged;

5] וְעַתָּה אוֹדִיעָה־נָּא אֶתְכֶם

אֵת אֲשֶׁר־אֲנִי עֹשֶׂה לְכַרְמִי

הָסֵר מְשׂוּכָּתוֹ

וְהָיָה לְבָעֵר

⁻ *Meaning of Heb. uncertain*

461

I will break down its wall,
That it may be trampled.

6] And I will *make it a desolation;*
It shall not be pruned or hoed,
And it shall be overgrown with briers and thistles.
And I will command the clouds
To drop no rain on it."

7] For the vineyard of the LORD of Hosts
Is the House of Israel,
And the seedlings he lovingly tended
Are the men of Judah.
*b*And He hoped for justice,
But behold, injustice;
For equity,
But behold, iniquity!

8] Ah,
Those who add house to house
And join field to field,
Till there is room for none but you
To dwell in the land!

9] In my hearing [said] the LORD of Hosts:
Surely, great houses
Shall lie forlorn,
Spacious and splendid ones
Without occupants.

10] For ten acres of vineyard

פָּרֹץ גְּדֵרוֹ

וְהָיָה לְמִרְמָס:

6] וַאֲשִׁיתֵהוּ בָתָה

לֹא יִזָּמֵר וְלֹא יֵעָדֵר

וְעָלָה שָׁמִיר וָשָׁיִת

וְעַל הֶעָבִים אֲצַוֶּה

מֵהַמְטִיר עָלָיו מָטָר:

7] כִּי כֶרֶם יְהוָה צְבָאוֹת

בֵּית יִשְׂרָאֵל

וְאִישׁ יְהוּדָה

נְטַע שַׁעֲשׁוּעָיו

וַיְקַו לְמִשְׁפָּט

וְהִנֵּה מִשְׂפָּח

לִצְדָקָה

וְהִנֵּה צְעָקָה:

8] הוֹי מַגִּיעֵי בַיִת בְּבַיִת

שָׂדֶה בְשָׂדֶה יַקְרִיבוּ

עַד אֶפֶס מָקוֹם

וְהוּשַׁבְתֶּם לְבַדְּכֶם

בְּקֶרֶב הָאָרֶץ:

9] בְּאָזְנָי יְהוָה צְבָאוֹת

אִם־לֹא בָּתִּים רַבִּים

לְשַׁמָּה יִהְיוּ

גְּדֹלִים וְטוֹבִים

מֵאֵין יוֹשֵׁב:

10] כִּי עֲשֶׂרֶת צִמְדֵּי־כֶרֶם

---

a-a Meaning of Heb. uncertain

b This sentence contains two word plays: "And He hoped for mishpat, / And there
is mispach" (exact meaning uncertain); "For tzedakah, / But there is tze'akah"
(lit. "outcry")

Shall yield just one *bath*,[c]
And a field sown with a *homer* of seed
Shall yield a mere *ephah*.

11] Ah,
Those who chase liquor
From early in the morning,
And till late in the evening
Are inflamed by wine!

12] [d]Who, at their banquets,
Have[-d] lyre and lute,
Timbrel, flute, and wine;
But who never give a thought
To the plan of the LORD,
And take no note
Of what He is designing.

13] Assuredly,
My people will suffer exile
For not giving heed,
Its multitude victims of hunger
And its masses parched with thirst.

14] Assuredly,
Sheol has opened wide its gullet
And parted its jaws in a measureless gape;
And down into it shall go
That splendor and tumult,
That din and revelry.

15] Yea, man is bowed,
And mortal brought low;
Brought low is the pride of the haughty.

16] And the LORD of Hosts is exalted by judgment,
The Holy God proved holy by retribution.

יַעֲשׂוּ בַּת אֶחָת

וְזֶרַע חֹמֶר

יַעֲשֶׂה אֵיפָה:

11] הוֹי מַשְׁכִּימֵי בַבֹּקֶר

שֵׁכָר יִרְדֹּפוּ

מְאַחֲרֵי בַנֶּשֶׁף

יַיִן יַדְלִיקֵם:

12] וְהָיָה כִנּוֹר וָנֶבֶל

תֹּף וְחָלִיל וָיַיִן מִשְׁתֵּיהֶם

וְאֵת פֹּעַל יְהֹוָה

לֹא יַבִּיטוּ

וּמַעֲשֵׂה יָדָיו לֹא רָאוּ:

13] לָכֵן גָּלָה עַמִּי

מִבְּלִי־דָעַת

וּכְבוֹדוֹ מְתֵי רָעָב

וַהֲמוֹנוֹ צִחֵה צָמָא:

14] לָכֵן הִרְחִיבָה שְּׁאוֹל נַפְשָׁהּ

וּפָעֲרָה פִיהָ לִבְלִי־חֹק

וְיָרַד הֲדָרָהּ וַהֲמוֹנָהּ

וּשְׁאוֹנָהּ וְעָלֵז בָּהּ:

15] וַיִּשַּׁח אָדָם

וַיִּשְׁפַּל־אִישׁ

וְעֵינֵי גְבֹהִים תִּשְׁפַּלְנָה:

16] וַיִּגְבַּהּ יְהֹוָה צְבָאוֹת בַּמִּשְׁפָּט

וְהָאֵל הַקָּדוֹשׁ נִקְדַּשׁ בִּצְדָקָה:

[c] *I.e., of wine. The bath was the liquid equivalent of the ephah; and the homer was
ten baths or ephahs (Ezek. 45.11)*

[d-d] *Emendation yields "Whose interests are" (mish'ehem, from sha'ah "to turn
to" 17.7, 8; 31.1)*

463

Proverbs

28 : 1-14

Chapter 28

כח

1] The wicked flee when no man pursues;
But the righteous are secure as a young lion.

2] For the transgression of a land many are the
princes thereof;
But by a man of understanding and knowledge established order shall long continue.

3] A poor man that oppresses the weak
Is like a sweeping rain which leaves no food.

4] They that forsake the law praise the wicked;
But such as keep the law contend with them.

5] Evil men understand not justice;
But they that seek the LORD understand all things.

6] Better is the poor that walks in his integrity,
Than he that is perverse in his ways, though
he be rich.

7] A wise son observes the teaching;
But he that is a companion of gluttonous men
shames his father.

8] He that augments his substance by interest
and increase,
Gathers it for him that is gracious to the poor.

9] He that turns away his ear from hearing
the law,
Even his prayer is an abomination.

10] Whoso causes the upright to go astray in an
evil way,
He shall fall himself into his own pit;
But the whole-hearted shall inherit good.

11] The rich man is wise in his own eyes;
But the poor that has understanding searches
him through.

1] נָסוּ וְאֵין־רֹדֵף רָשָׁע
וְצַדִּיקִים כִּכְפִיר יִבְטָח׃

2] בְּפֶשַׁע אֶרֶץ רַבִּים שָׂרֶיהָ
וּבְאָדָם מֵבִין יֹדֵעַ כֵּן יַאֲרִיךְ׃

3] גֶּבֶר רָשׁ וְעֹשֵׁק דַּלִּים
מָטָר סֹחֵף וְאֵין לָחֶם׃

4] עֹזְבֵי תוֹרָה יְהַלְלוּ רָשָׁע
וְשֹׁמְרֵי תוֹרָה יִתְגָּרוּ בָם׃

5] אַנְשֵׁי־רָע לֹא־יָבִינוּ מִשְׁפָּט
וּמְבַקְשֵׁי יְהוָה יָבִינוּ כֹל׃

6] טוֹב־רָשׁ הוֹלֵךְ בְּתֻמּוֹ
מֵעִקֵּשׁ דְּרָכַיִם וְהוּא עָשִׁיר׃

7] נוֹצֵר תוֹרָה בֵּן מֵבִין
וְרֹעֶה זוֹלְלִים יַכְלִים אָבִיו׃

8] מַרְבֶּה הוֹנוֹ בְּנֶשֶׁךְ וְתַרְבִּית
לְחוֹנֵן דַּלִּים יִקְבְּצֶנּוּ׃

9] מֵסִיר אָזְנוֹ מִשְּׁמֹעַ תּוֹרָה
גַּם־תְּפִלָּתוֹ תּוֹעֵבָה׃

10] מַשְׁגֶּה יְשָׁרִים בְּדֶרֶךְ רָע
בִּשְׁחוּתוֹ הוּא־יִפּוֹל
וּתְמִימִים יִנְחֲלוּ־טוֹב׃

11] חָכָם בְּעֵינָיו אִישׁ עָשִׁיר
וְדַל מֵבִין יַחְקְרֶנּוּ׃

12] When the righteous exult, there is great glory;
But when the wicked rise, men must be sought
for.

13] He that covers his transgressions shall not
prosper;
But whoso confesses and forsakes them shall obtain mercy.

14] Happy is the man that fears always;
But he that hardens his heart shall fall into evil.

12] בַּעֲלֹץ צַדִּיקִים רַבָּה תִפְאָרֶת
וּבְקוּם רְשָׁעִים יְחֻפַּשׂ אָדָם:

13] מְכַסֶּה פְשָׁעָיו לֹא יַצְלִיחַ
וּמוֹדֶה וְעֹזֵב יְרֻחָם:

14] אַשְׁרֵי אָדָם מְפַחֵד תָּמִיד
וּמַקְשֶׁה לִבּוֹ יִפּוֹל בְּרָעָה:

כי תבוא

FIRST SELECTION

Isaiah

60 : 1- 22

Chapter 60

1] Arise, shine, for your light has dawned;
The Presence of the LORD has shone upon you!

2] Behold! Darkness shall cover the earth,
And thick clouds the peoples;
But upon you the LORD will shine,
And His Presence be seen over you.

3] And nations shall walk by your light;
Kings, by your shining radiance.

4] Raise your eyes and look about:
They have all gathered and come to you.
Your sons shall be brought from afar,
Your daughters like babes on shoulders.

5] As you behold, you will glow;
Your heart will throb and thrill—
For the wealth of the sea[a] shall pass on to you,
The riches of nations shall flow to you.

6] Dust clouds of camels shall cover you,
Dromedaries of Midian and Ephah.

ס

1] קוּמִי אוֹרִי כִּי־בָא אוֹרֵךְ
וּכְבוֹד יְהוָה עָלַיִךְ זָרָח:

2] כִּי־הִנֵּה הַחֹשֶׁךְ יְכַסֶּה־אֶרֶץ
וַעֲרָפֶל לְאֻמִּים
וְעָלַיִךְ יִזְרַח יְהוָה
וּכְבוֹדוֹ עָלַיִךְ יֵרָאֶה:

3] וְהָלְכוּ גוֹיִם לְאוֹרֵךְ
וּמְלָכִים לְנֹגַהּ זַרְחֵךְ:

4] שְׂאִי סָבִיב עֵינַיִךְ וּרְאִי
כֻּלָּם נִקְבְּצוּ בָאוּ־לָךְ
בָּנַיִךְ מֵרָחוֹק יָבֹאוּ
וּבְנֹתַיִךְ עַל־צַד תֵּאָמַנָה:

5] אָז תִּרְאִי וְנָהַרְתְּ
וּפָחַד וְרָחַב לְבָבֵךְ
כִּי־יֵהָפֵךְ עָלַיִךְ הֲמוֹן יָם
חֵיל גּוֹיִם יָבֹאוּ לָךְ:

6] שִׁפְעַת גְּמַלִּים תְּכַסֵּךְ
בִּכְרֵי מִדְיָן וְעֵיפָה

[a] *Emendation yields "coastlands"*

466

They all shall come from Sheba;
They shall bear gold and frankincense,
And shall herald the glories of the LORD.

כֻּלָּם מִשְּׁבָא יָבֹאוּ

זָהָב וּלְבוֹנָה יִשָּׂאוּ

וּתְהִלֹּת יְהֹוָה יְבַשֵּׂרוּ:

7] All the flocks of Kedar shall be assembled for
    you,
The rams of Nebaioth shall serve your needs;
They shall be welcome offerings on My altar,
And I will add glory to My glorious House.

7 כָּל־צֹאן קֵדָר יִקָּבְצוּ לָךְ

אֵילֵי נְבָיוֹת יְשָׁרְתוּנֶךְ

יַעֲלוּ עַל־רָצוֹן מִזְבְּחִי

וּבֵית תִּפְאַרְתִּי אֲפָאֵר:

8] Who are these that float like a cloud,
Like doves to their cotes?

8 מִי־אֵלֶּה כָּעָב תְּעוּפֶינָה

וְכַיּוֹנִים אֶל־אֲרֻבֹּתֵיהֶם:

9] ᵇ⁻Behold, the coastlands await me,⁻ᵇ
With ᶜ⁻ships of Tarshish⁻ᶜ in the lead,
To bring your sons from afar,
And theirᵈ silver and gold as well—
For the name of the LORD your God,
For the Holy One of Israel, who has glorified you.

9 כִּי־לִי אִיִּים יְקַוּוּ

וָאֳנִיּוֹת תַּרְשִׁישׁ בָּרִאשֹׁנָה

לְהָבִיא בָנַיִךְ מֵרָחוֹק

כַּסְפָּם וּזְהָבָם אִתָּם

לְשֵׁם יְהֹוָה אֱלֹהַיִךְ

וְלִקְדוֹשׁ יִשְׂרָאֵל כִּי פֵאֲרָךְ:

10] Aliens shall rebuild your walls,
Their kings shall wait upon you—
For in anger I struck you down,
But in favor I take you back.

10 וּבָנוּ בְנֵי־נֵכָר חֹמֹתַיִךְ

וּמַלְכֵיהֶם יְשָׁרְתוּנֶךְ

כִּי בְקִצְפִּי הִכִּיתִיךְ

וּבִרְצוֹנִי רִחַמְתִּיךְ:

11] Your gates shall always stay open—
Day and night they shall never be shut—
To let in the wealth of the nations,
With their kings in procession.

11 וּפִתְּחוּ שְׁעָרַיִךְ תָּמִיד

יוֹמָם וָלַיְלָה לֹא יִסָּגֵרוּ

לְהָבִיא אֵלַיִךְ חֵיל גּוֹיִם

וּמַלְכֵיהֶם נְהוּגִים:

12] For the nation or the kingdom
That does not serve you shall perish;
Such nations shall be destroyed.

12 כִּי־הַגּוֹי וְהַמַּמְלָכָה

אֲשֶׁר לֹא־יַעַבְדוּךְ יֹאבֵדוּ

וְהַגּוֹיִם חָרֹב יֶחֱרָבוּ:

ᵇ⁻ᵇ *Emendation yields "The vessels of the coastlands are gathering"*
ᶜ⁻ᶜ *Probably a type of large ship*
ᵈ *I.e., of the people of the coastlands*

467

13] The majesty of Lebanon shall come to you—
Cypress and pine and box—
To adorn the site of My Sanctuary,
To glorify the place where My feet rest.

14] Bowing before you, shall come
The children of those who tormented you;
Prostrate at the soles of your feet
Shall be all those who reviled you;
And you shall be called
"City of the LORD,
Zion of the Holy One of Israel."

15] Whereas you have been forsaken,
Rejected, with none passing through,
I will make you a pride everlasting,
A joy for age after age.

16] You shall suck the milk of the nations,
Suckle at royal breasts.ᵉ
And you shall know
That I the LORD am your Savior,
I, The Mighty One of Jacob, am your Redeemer.

17] Instead of copper I will bring gold,
Instead of iron I will bring silver;
Instead of wood, copper;
And instead of stone, iron.
And I will appoint Well-being as your
    government,
Prosperity as your officials.

18] The cry "Violence!"
Shall no more be heard in your land,
Nor "Wrack and ruin!"
Within your borders.
And you shall name your walls "Victory"
And your gates "Renown."

13] כְּבוֹד הַלְּבָנוֹן אֵלַיִךְ יָבוֹא
בְּרוֹשׁ תִּדְהָר וּתְאַשּׁוּר יַחְדָּו
לְפָאֵר מְקוֹם מִקְדָּשִׁי
וּמְקוֹם רַגְלַי אֲכַבֵּד:

14] וְהָלְכוּ אֵלַיִךְ שְׁחוֹחַ
בְּנֵי מְעַנַּיִךְ
וְהִשְׁתַּחֲווּ עַל־כַּפּוֹת רַגְלַיִךְ
כָּל־מְנַאֲצָיִךְ
וְקָרְאוּ לָךְ עִיר יְהוָה
צִיּוֹן קְדוֹשׁ יִשְׂרָאֵל:

15] תַּחַת הֱיוֹתֵךְ עֲזוּבָה
וּשְׂנוּאָה וְאֵין עוֹבֵר
וְשַׂמְתִּיךְ לִגְאוֹן עוֹלָם
מְשׂוֹשׂ דּוֹר וָדוֹר:

16] וְיָנַקְתְּ חֲלֵב גּוֹיִם
וְשֹׁד מְלָכִים תִּינָקִי
וְיָדַעַתְּ כִּי־אֲנִי יְהוָה
מוֹשִׁיעֵךְ וְגֹאֲלֵךְ אֲבִיר יַעֲקֹב:

17] תַּחַת הַנְּחֹשֶׁת אָבִיא זָהָב
וְתַחַת הַבַּרְזֶל אָבִיא כֶסֶף
וְתַחַת הָעֵצִים נְחֹשֶׁת
וְתַחַת הָאֲבָנִים בַּרְזֶל
וְשַׂמְתִּי פְקֻדָּתֵךְ שָׁלוֹם
וְנֹגְשַׂיִךְ צְדָקָה:

18] לֹא־יִשָּׁמַע עוֹד חָמָס בְּאַרְצֵךְ
שֹׁד וָשֶׁבֶר בִּגְבוּלָיִךְ
וְקָרָאת יְשׁוּעָה חוֹמֹתַיִךְ
וּשְׁעָרַיִךְ תְּהִלָּה:

ᵉ Lit. "breasts of kings" or "breasts of kingdoms"

468

19] No longer shall you need the sun
For light by day,
Nor the shining of the moon
For radiance [by night*];
For the Lord shall be your light everlasting,
Your God shall be your glory.

20] Your sun shall set no more,
Your moon no more withdraw;
For the Lord shall be a light to you forever,
And your days of mourning shall be ended.

21] And your people, all of them righteous,
Shall possess the land for all time;
They are the shoot that I planted,
My handiwork in which I glory.

22] The smallest shall become a clan;
The least, a mighty nation.
I the Lord will speed it in due time.

[19] לֹא־יִהְיֶה־לָּךְ עוֹד הַשֶּׁמֶשׁ

לְאוֹר יוֹמָם

וּלְנֹגַהּ הַיָּרֵחַ לֹא־יָאִיר לָךְ

וְהָיָה־לָךְ יְהוָה לְאוֹר עוֹלָם

וֵאלֹהַיִךְ לְתִפְאַרְתֵּךְ׃

[20] לֹא־יָבוֹא עוֹד שִׁמְשֵׁךְ

וִירֵחֵךְ לֹא יֵאָסֵף

כִּי יְהוָה יִהְיֶה־לָּךְ לְאוֹר עוֹלָם

וְשָׁלְמוּ יְמֵי אֶבְלֵךְ׃

[21] וְעַמֵּךְ כֻּלָּם צַדִּיקִים

לְעוֹלָם יִירְשׁוּ אָרֶץ

נֵצֶר מַטָּעַי מַעֲשֵׂה יָדַי לְהִתְפָּאֵר׃

[22] הַקָּטֹן יִהְיֶה לָאֶלֶף

וְהַצָּעִיר לְגוֹי עָצוּם

אֲנִי יְהוָה בְּעִתָּהּ אֲחִישֶׁנָּה׃

SECOND SELECTION

Joshua

4 : 1-24

Chapter 4

1] When the entire nation had finished crossing the Jordan, the Lord said to Joshua,

2] "Select twelve men from among the people, one from each tribe,

3] and instruct them as follows: Pick up twelve stones from the spot exactly in the middle of the Jordan, where the priests' feet are standing; take them along with

ד

[1] וַיְהִי כַּאֲשֶׁר־תַּמּוּ כָל־הַגּוֹי לַעֲבוֹר אֶת־

הַיַּרְדֵּן וַיֹּאמֶר יְהוָה אֶל־יְהוֹשֻׁעַ לֵאמֹר׃

[2] קְחוּ לָכֶם מִן־הָעָם שְׁנֵים עָשָׂר אֲנָשִׁים אִישׁ־

אֶחָד אִישׁ־אֶחָד מִשָּׁבֶט׃ [3] וְצַוּוּ אוֹתָם לֵאמֹר

שְׂאוּ־לָכֶם מִזֶּה מִתּוֹךְ הַיַּרְדֵּן מִמַּצַּב רַגְלֵי

הַכֹּהֲנִים הָכִין שְׁתֵּים־עֶשְׂרֵה אֲבָנִים וְהַעֲבַרְתֶּם

So 1QIsᵃ, Septuagint, and Targum

you and deposit them in the place where you will spend the night."

4] Joshua summoned the twelve men whom he had designated among the Israelites, one from each tribe;

5] and Joshua said to them, "Walk up to the Ark of the LORD your God, in the middle of the Jordan, and each of you lift a stone onto his shoulder—corresponding to the number of the tribes of Israel.

6] This shall serve as a symbol among you: in time to come, when your children ask, 'What is the meaning of these stones for you?'

7] you shall tell them, 'The waters of the Jordan were cut off because of the Ark of the LORD's Covenant; when it passed through the Jordan, the waters of the Jordan were cut off.' And so these stones shall serve the people of Israel as a memorial for all time."

8] The Israelites did as Joshua ordered. They picked up twelve stones, corresponding to the number of the tribes of Israel, from the middle of the Jordan—as the LORD had charged Joshua—and they took them along with them to their night encampment and deposited them there.

9] Joshua also set up twelve stones in the middle of the Jordan, at the spot where the feet of the priests bearing the Ark of the Covenant had stood; and they have remained there to this day.

10] The priests who bore the Ark remained standing in the middle of the Jordan until all the instructions that the LORD had ordered Joshua to convey to the people had been carried out. And so the people speedily crossed over, ᵃ⁻just as Moses had assured Joshua in his charge to him.⁻ᵃ

11] And when all the people finished crossing, the Ark of the LORD and the priests advanced to the head of the people.

12] The Reubenites, the Gadites, and the half-tribe of Manasseh went across armedᵇ in the

אוֹתָם עִמָּכֶם וְהִנַּחְתֶּם אוֹתָם בַּמָּלוֹן אֲשֶׁר־תָּלִינוּ בוֹ הַלָּיְלָה:

4 וַיִּקְרָא יְהוֹשֻׁעַ אֶל־שְׁנֵים הֶעָשָׂר אִישׁ אֲשֶׁר הֵכִין מִבְּנֵי יִשְׂרָאֵל אִישׁ־אֶחָד אִישׁ־אֶחָד מִשָּׁבֶט: 5 וַיֹּאמֶר לָהֶם יְהוֹשֻׁעַ עִבְרוּ לִפְנֵי אֲרוֹן יְהֹוָה אֱלֹהֵיכֶם אֶל־תּוֹךְ הַיַּרְדֵּן וְהָרִימוּ לָכֶם אִישׁ אֶבֶן אַחַת עַל־שִׁכְמוֹ לְמִסְפַּר שִׁבְטֵי בְנֵי־יִשְׂרָאֵל: 6 לְמַעַן תִּהְיֶה זֹאת אוֹת בְּקִרְבְּכֶם כִּי־יִשְׁאָלוּן בְּנֵיכֶם מָחָר לֵאמֹר מָה הָאֲבָנִים הָאֵלֶּה לָכֶם: 7 וַאֲמַרְתֶּם לָהֶם אֲשֶׁר נִכְרְתוּ מֵימֵי הַיַּרְדֵּן מִפְּנֵי אֲרוֹן בְּרִית־יְהֹוָה בְּעָבְרוֹ בַּיַּרְדֵּן נִכְרְתוּ מֵי הַיַּרְדֵּן וְהָיוּ הָאֲבָנִים הָאֵלֶּה לְזִכָּרוֹן לִבְנֵי יִשְׂרָאֵל עַד־עוֹלָם:

8 וַיַּעֲשׂוּ־כֵן בְּנֵי־יִשְׂרָאֵל כַּאֲשֶׁר צִוָּה יְהוֹשֻׁעַ וַיִּשְׂאוּ שְׁתֵּי־עֶשְׂרֵה אֲבָנִים מִתּוֹךְ הַיַּרְדֵּן כַּאֲשֶׁר דִּבֶּר יְהֹוָה אֶל־יְהוֹשֻׁעַ לְמִסְפַּר שִׁבְטֵי בְנֵי־יִשְׂרָאֵל וַיַּעֲבִרוּם עִמָּם אֶל־הַמָּלוֹן וַיַּנִּחוּם שָׁם:

9 וּשְׁתֵּים עֶשְׂרֵה אֲבָנִים הֵקִים יְהוֹשֻׁעַ בְּתוֹךְ הַיַּרְדֵּן תַּחַת מַצַּב רַגְלֵי הַכֹּהֲנִים נֹשְׂאֵי אֲרוֹן הַבְּרִית וַיִּהְיוּ שָׁם עַד הַיּוֹם הַזֶּה:

10 וְהַכֹּהֲנִים נֹשְׂאֵי הָאָרוֹן עֹמְדִים בְּתוֹךְ הַיַּרְדֵּן עַד תֹּם כָּל־הַדָּבָר אֲשֶׁר־צִוָּה יְהֹוָה אֶת־יְהוֹשֻׁעַ לְדַבֵּר אֶל־הָעָם כְּכֹל אֲשֶׁר־צִוָּה מֹשֶׁה אֶת־יְהוֹשֻׁעַ וַיְמַהֲרוּ הָעָם וַיַּעֲבֹרוּ:

11 וַיְהִי כַּאֲשֶׁר־תַּם כָּל־הָעָם לַעֲבוֹר וַיַּעֲבֹר אֲרוֹן־יְהֹוָה וְהַכֹּהֲנִים לִפְנֵי הָעָם:

12 וַיַּעַבְרוּ בְּנֵי־רְאוּבֵן וּבְנֵי־גָד וַחֲצִי שֵׁבֶט הַמְנַשֶּׁה חֲמֻשִׁים לִפְנֵי בְּנֵי יִשְׂרָאֵל כַּאֲשֶׁר דִּבֶּר

ᵃ⁻ᵃ Connection of clause uncertain; cf. Deut. 31.7–8   ᵇ Meaning of Heb. uncertain

470

van of the Israelites, as Moses had charged them.ᶜ
13] About forty thousand shock troops went across, at the instance of the LORD, to the steppes of Jericho for battle.

14] On that day the LORD exalted Joshua in the sight of all Israel, so that they revered him all his days as they had revered Moses.

[5] The LORD said to Joshua,
16] "Command the priests who bear the Ark of the Pact to come up out of the Jordan."
17] So Joshua commanded the priests, "Come up out of the Jordan."
18] As soon as the priests who bore the Ark of the LORD's Covenant came up out of the Jordan, and the feet of the priests stepped onto the dry ground, the waters of the Jordan resumed their course, flowing over its entire bed as before.

19] The people came up from the Jordan on the tenth day of the first month, and encamped at Gilgal on the eastern border of Jericho.

20] And Joshua set up in Gilgal the twelve stones they had taken from the Jordan.

21] He charged the Israelites as follows: "In time to come, when your children ask their fathers, 'What is the meaning of those stones?'
22] tell your children: 'Here the Israelites crossed the Jordan on dry land.'

23] For the LORD your God dried up the waters of the Jordan before you until you crossed, just as the LORD your God did to the Sea of Reeds, which

He dried up before us until we crossed.   24] Thus all the peoples of the earth shall know how mighty is the hand of the LORD, and you shall fear the LORD your God always."

ᶜ See Num. 32.20–22

אֲלֵיהֶם מֹשֶׁה: 13] כְּאַרְבָּעִים אֶלֶף חֲלוּצֵי הַצָּבָא עָבְרוּ לִפְנֵי יְהוָה לַמִּלְחָמָה אֶל עַרְבוֹת יְרִיחוֹ:

14] בַּיּוֹם הַהוּא גִּדַּל יְהוָה אֶת־יְהוֹשֻׁעַ בְּעֵינֵי כָּל־יִשְׂרָאֵל וַיִּרְאוּ אֹתוֹ כַּאֲשֶׁר יָרְאוּ אֶת־מֹשֶׁה כָּל־יְמֵי חַיָּיו:

15] וַיֹּאמֶר יְהוָה אֶל־יְהוֹשֻׁעַ לֵאמֹר: 16] צַוֵּה אֶת־הַכֹּהֲנִים נֹשְׂאֵי אֲרוֹן הָעֵדוּת וְיַעֲלוּ מִן הַיַּרְדֵּן: 17] וַיְצַו יְהוֹשֻׁעַ אֶת־הַכֹּהֲנִים לֵאמֹר עֲלוּ מִן־הַיַּרְדֵּן: 18] וַיְהִי כַּעֲלוֹת הַכֹּהֲנִים נֹשְׂאֵי אֲרוֹן בְּרִית־יְהוָה מִתּוֹךְ הַיַּרְדֵּן נִתְּקוּ כַּפּוֹת רַגְלֵי הַכֹּהֲנִים אֶל הֶחָרָבָה וַיָּשֻׁבוּ מֵי־הַיַּרְדֵּן לִמְקוֹמָם וַיֵּלְכוּ כִתְמוֹל־שִׁלְשׁוֹם עַל־כָּל־גְּדוֹתָיו:

19] וְהָעָם עָלוּ מִן־הַיַּרְדֵּן בֶּעָשׂוֹר לַחֹדֶשׁ הָרִאשׁוֹן וַיַּחֲנוּ בַּגִּלְגָּל בִּקְצֵה מִזְרַח יְרִיחוֹ: 20] וְאֵת שְׁתֵּים עֶשְׂרֵה הָאֲבָנִים הָאֵלֶּה אֲשֶׁר לָקְחוּ מִן־הַיַּרְדֵּן הֵקִים יְהוֹשֻׁעַ בַּגִּלְגָּל: 21] וַיֹּאמֶר אֶל־בְּנֵי יִשְׂרָאֵל לֵאמֹר אֲשֶׁר יִשְׁאָלוּן בְּנֵיכֶם מָחָר אֶת־אֲבוֹתָם לֵאמֹר מָה הָאֲבָנִים הָאֵלֶּה: 22] וְהוֹדַעְתֶּם אֶת־בְּנֵיכֶם לֵאמֹר בַּיַּבָּשָׁה עָבַר יִשְׂרָאֵל אֶת־הַיַּרְדֵּן הַזֶּה: 23] אֲשֶׁר־הוֹבִישׁ יְהוָה אֱלֹהֵיכֶם אֶת־מֵי הַיַּרְדֵּן מִפְּנֵיכֶם עַד־עָבְרְכֶם כַּאֲשֶׁר עָשָׂה יְהוָה אֱלֹהֵיכֶם לְיַם־סוּף אֲשֶׁר־הוֹבִישׁ מִפָּנֵינוּ עַד־עָבְרֵנוּ: 24] לְמַעַן דַּעַת כָּל־עַמֵּי הָאָרֶץ אֶת־יַד יְהוָה כִּי חֲזָקָה הִיא לְמַעַן יְרָאתֶם אֶת־יְהוָה אֱלֹהֵיכֶם כָּל־הַיָּמִים:

Isaiah

35 : 1 - 10

Chapter 35

1] The arid desert shall be glad,
The wilderness shall rejoice
And shall blossom like a rose.ª

2] It shall blossom abundantly,
It shall also exult and shout.
It shall receive the glory of Lebanon,
The splendor of Carmel and Sharon.
They shall behold the glory of the LORD,
The splendor of our God.

3] Strengthen the hands that are slack;
Make firm the tottering knees!

4] Say to the anxious of heart,
"Be strong, fear not;
Behold your God!
Requital is coming,
The recompense of God—
He Himself is coming to give you triumph."

5] Then the eyes of the blind shall be opened.
And the ears of the deaf shall be unstopped,

6] Then the lame shall leap like a deer,
And the tongue of the dumb shall shout aloud;
For waters shall burst forth in the desert,
Streams in the wilderness.

לה

‎1] יְשֻׂשׂוּם מִדְבָּר וְצִיָּה
וְתָגֵל עֲרָבָה
וְתִפְרַח כַּחֲבַצָּלֶת:

‎2] פָּרֹחַ תִּפְרַח וְתָגֵל
אַף גִּילַת וְרַנֵּן
כְּבוֹד הַלְּבָנוֹן נִתַּן־לָהּ
הֲדַר הַכַּרְמֶל וְהַשָּׁרוֹן
הֵמָּה יִרְאוּ כְבוֹד־יְהֹוָה
הֲדַר אֱלֹהֵינוּ:

‎3] חַזְּקוּ יָדַיִם רָפוֹת
וּבִרְכַּיִם כֹּשְׁלוֹת אַמֵּצוּ:

‎4] אִמְרוּ לְנִמְהֲרֵי־לֵב
חִזְקוּ אַל־תִּירָאוּ
הִנֵּה אֱלֹהֵיכֶם נָקָם יָבוֹא
גְּמוּל אֱלֹהִים
הוּא יָבוֹא וְיֹשַׁעֲכֶם:

‎5] אָז תִּפָּקַחְנָה עֵינֵי עִוְרִים
וְאָזְנֵי חֵרְשִׁים תִּפָּתַחְנָה:

‎6] אָז יְדַלֵּג כָּאַיָּל פִּסֵּחַ
וְתָרֹן לְשׁוֹן אִלֵּם
כִּי־נִבְקְעוּ בַמִּדְבָּר מַיִם
וּנְחָלִים בָּעֲרָבָה:

ª *Lit. "crocus"*

472

7] Torrid earth shall become a pool;
Parched land, fountains of water;
The home of jackals, a pasture[b];
The abode [of ostriches],[c] reeds and rushes.

[7] וְהָיָה הַשָּׁרָב לַאֲגַם
וְצִמָּאוֹן לְמַבּוּעֵי מָיִם
בִּנְוֵה תַנִּים רִבְצָהּ
חָצִיר לְקָנֶה וָגֹמֶא:

8] And a highway shall appear there,
Which shall be called the Sacred Way.
No one unclean shall pass along it,
But it shall be for them.[d]
[e]No traveler, not even fools, shall go astray.[e]

[8] וְהָיָה־שָׁם מַסְלוּל וָדֶרֶךְ
וְדֶרֶךְ הַקֹּדֶשׁ יִקָּרֵא לָהּ
לֹא־יַעַבְרֶנּוּ טָמֵא וְהוּא־לָמוֹ
הֹלֵךְ דֶּרֶךְ וֶאֱוִילִים לֹא יִתְעוּ:

9] No lion shall be there,
No ferocious beast shall set foot on it—
These shall not be found there.
But the redeemed shall walk it;

[9] לֹא־יִהְיֶה שָׁם אַרְיֵה
וּפְרִיץ חַיּוֹת בַּל־יַעֲלֶנָּה
לֹא תִמָּצֵא שָׁם
וְהָלְכוּ גְּאוּלִים:

10] And the ransomed of the Lord shall return,
And come with shouting to Zion,
Crowned with joy everlasting.
They shall attain joy and gladness,
While sorrow and sighing flee.

[10] וּפְדוּיֵי יְהֹוָה יְשֻׁבוּן
וּבָאוּ צִיּוֹן בְּרִנָּה
וְשִׂמְחַת עוֹלָם עַל־רֹאשָׁם
שָׂשׂוֹן וְשִׂמְחָה יַשִּׂיגוּ
וְנָסוּ יָגוֹן וַאֲנָחָה:

[b] Meaning of Heb. uncertain. Emendation yields "a marsh"
[c] Cf. 34.13
[d] Emendation yields "for His people"
[e-e] Meaning of Heb. uncertain

FIRST SELECTION

Isaiah

61 : 10 — 63 : 9

Chapter 61

סא

10] I greatly rejoice in the LORD,
My whole being exults in my God.
For He has clothed me with garments of triumph,
Wrapped me in a robe of victory,
Like a bridegroom adorned with a turban,
Like a bride bedecked with her finery.

10] שׂוֹשׂ אָשִׂישׂ בַּיהֹוָה

תָּגֵל נַפְשִׁי בֵּאלֹהַי

כִּי הִלְבִּישַׁנִי בִּגְדֵי־יֶשַׁע

מְעִיל צְדָקָה יְעָטָנִי

כֶּחָתָן יְכַהֵן פְּאֵר

וְכַכַּלָּה תַּעְדֶּה כֵלֶיהָ:

11] For as the earth brings forth her growth
And a garden makes the seed shoot up,
So the Lord GOD will make
Victory and renown shoot up
In the presence of all the nations.

11] כִּי כָאָרֶץ תּוֹצִיא צִמְחָהּ

וּכְגַנָּה זֵרוּעֶיהָ תַצְמִיחַ

כֵּן אֲדֹנָי יֱהֹוִה יַצְמִיחַ

צְדָקָה וּתְהִלָּה נֶגֶד כָּל־הַגּוֹיִם:

Chapter 62

סב

1] For the sake of Zion I will not be silent,
For the sake of Jerusalem I will not be still,
Till her victory emerge resplendent
And her triumph like a flaming torch.

1] לְמַעַן צִיּוֹן לֹא אֶחֱשֶׁה

וּלְמַעַן יְרוּשָׁלַ͏ִם לֹא אֶשְׁקוֹט

עַד־יֵצֵא כַנֹּגַהּ צִדְקָהּ

וִישׁוּעָתָהּ כְּלַפִּיד יִבְעָר:

2] Nations shall see your victory,
And every king your majesty;
And you shall be called by a new name
Which the LORD Himself shall bestow.

2] וְרָאוּ גוֹיִם צִדְקֵךְ

וְכָל־מְלָכִים כְּבוֹדֵךְ

וְקֹרָא לָךְ שֵׁם חָדָשׁ

אֲשֶׁר פִּי יְהֹוָה יִקֳּבֶנּוּ:

3] You shall be a glorious crown
In the hand of the Lord,
And a royal diadem
In the palm of your God.
4] Nevermore shall you be called "Forsaken,"
Nor shall your land be called "Desolate";
But you shall be called "I delight in her,"
And your land "Espoused."
For the Lord takes delight in you,
And your land shall be espoused.

5] As a youth espouses a maiden,
ᵃ⁻Your sonsᵃ shall espouse you;
And as a bridegroom rejoices over his bride,
So will your God rejoice over you.

6] Upon your walls, O Jerusalem,
I have set watchmen,
Who shall never be silent
By day or by night.
O you, the Lord's remembrancers,ᵇ
Take no rest

7] And give no rest to Him,
Until He establish Jerusalem
And make her renowned on earth.

8] The Lord has sworn by His right hand,
By His mighty arm:
Nevermore will I give your new grain
To your enemies for food,
Nor shall foreigners drink the new wine
For which you have labored.

וְהָיִ֛ית עֲטֶ֥רֶת תִּפְאֶ֖רֶת בְּיַד־יְהֹוָ֑ה 3]
וּצְנִ֥יף מְלוּכָ֖ה בְּכַף־אֱלֹהָֽיִךְ׃
לֹא־יֵאָמֵר֩ לָ֨ךְ ע֜וֹד עֲזוּבָ֗ה 4]
וּלְאַרְצֵךְ֙ לֹא־יֵאָמֵ֥ר עוֹד֙ שְׁמָמָ֔ה
כִּ֣י לָ֗ךְ יִקָּרֵא֙ חֶפְצִי־בָ֔הּ
וּלְאַרְצֵ֖ךְ בְּעוּלָ֑ה
כִּי־חָפֵ֤ץ יְהֹוָה֙ בָּ֔ךְ
וְאַרְצֵ֖ךְ תִּבָּעֵֽל׃
כִּֽי־יִבְעַ֤ל בָּחוּר֙ בְּתוּלָ֔ה 5]
יִבְעָל֖וּךְ בָּנָ֑יִךְ
וּמְשׂ֤וֹשׂ חָתָן֙ עַל־כַּלָּ֔ה
יָשִׂ֥ישׂ עָלַ֖יִךְ אֱלֹהָֽיִךְ׃
עַל־חוֹמֹתַ֣יִךְ יְרוּשָׁלַ֗͏ִם 6]
הִפְקַ֙דְתִּי֙ שֹֽׁמְרִ֔ים
כׇּל־הַיּ֧וֹם וְכׇל־הַלַּ֛יְלָה תָּמִ֖יד
לֹ֣א יֶחֱשׁ֑וּ
הַמַּזְכִּרִים֙ אֶת־יְהֹוָ֔ה
אַל־דֳּמִ֖י לָכֶֽם׃
וְאַל־תִּתְּנ֥וּ דֳמִ֖י ל֑וֹ 7]
עַד־יְכוֹנֵ֞ן וְעַד־יָשִׂ֧ים אֶת־יְרֽוּשָׁלַ֛͏ִם
תְּהִלָּ֖ה בָּאָֽרֶץ׃
נִשְׁבַּ֧ע יְהֹוָ֛ה בִּימִינ֖וֹ 8]
וּבִזְר֣וֹעַ עֻזּ֑וֹ
אִם־אֶתֵּן֩ אֶת־דְּגָנֵ֨ךְ ע֤וֹד
מַֽאֲכָל֙ לְאֹ֣יְבַ֔יִךְ
וְאִם־יִשְׁתּ֤וּ בְנֵֽי־נֵכָר֙ תִּירוֹשֵׁ֔ךְ
אֲשֶׁ֖ר יָגַ֥עַתְּ בּֽוֹ׃

ᵃ⁻ᵃ *Change of vocalization yields "He who rebuilds you"*
ᵇ *I.e., the watchmen just mentioned*

9] But those who harvest it shall eat it
And give praise to the LORD;
And those who gather it shall drink it
In My sacred courts.

10] Pass through, pass through the gates!
Clear the road for the people;
Build up, build up the highway,
Remove the rocks!
Raise an ensign over the peoples!

11] See, the LORD has proclaimed
To the end of the earth:
Announce to Fair Zion,
Your Deliverer is coming!
See, his reward is with Him,
His recompense before Him.[c]

12] And they shall be called, "The Holy People,
The Redeemed of the LORD,"
And you shall be called, "Sought Out,
A City Not Forsaken."

Chapter 63

1] Who is this coming from Edom,
In crimsoned garments from Bozrah—
[Who is] this, majestic in attire,
[a]Pressing forward[a] in His great might?
"It is I, who contend victoriously,
[b]Powerful to give triumph."[b]

9] כִּי מְאַסְפָיו יֹאכְלֻהוּ
וְהִלְלוּ אֶת־יְהוָֹה
וּמְקַבְּצָיו יִשְׁתֻּהוּ
בְּחַצְרוֹת קָדְשִׁי:

10] עִבְרוּ עִבְרוּ בַּשְּׁעָרִים
פַּנּוּ דֶּרֶךְ הָעָם
סֹלּוּ סֹלּוּ הַמְסִלָּה
סַקְּלוּ מֵאֶבֶן
הָרִימוּ נֵס עַל־הָעַמִּים:

11] הִנֵּה יְהוָֹה הִשְׁמִיעַ
אֶל־קְצֵה הָאָרֶץ
אִמְרוּ לְבַת־צִיּוֹן
הִנֵּה יִשְׁעֵךְ בָּא
הִנֵּה שְׂכָרוֹ אִתּוֹ
וּפְעֻלָּתוֹ לְפָנָיו:

12] וְקָרְאוּ לָהֶם עַם־הַקֹּדֶשׁ
גְּאוּלֵי יְהוָֹה
וְלָךְ יִקָּרֵא דְרוּשָׁה
עִיר לֹא נֶעֱזָבָה:

סג

1] מִי־זֶה בָּא מֵאֱדוֹם
חֲמוּץ בְּגָדִים מִבָּצְרָה
זֶה הָדוּר בִּלְבוּשׁוֹ
צֹעֶה בְּרֹב כֹּחוֹ
אֲנִי מְדַבֵּר בִּצְדָקָה
רַב לְהוֹשִׁיעַ:

[c] The recompense to the cities of Judah; cf. Jer. 31.14, 16

[a-a] Meaning of Heb. uncertain; emendation yields "striding"
[b-b] Change of vocalization yields "Who contest triumphantly"; cf. 19.20

2] Why is your clothing so red,
Your garments like his who treads grapes?[c]

3] "I trod out a vintage alone;
[d-]Of the peoples[-d] no man was with Me.
I trod them down in My anger,
Trampled them in My rage;
Their life-blood[e] bespattered My garments,
And all My clothing was stained.

4] For I had planned a day of vengeance,
And My year of redemption arrived.

5] Then I looked, but there was none to help;
I stared, but there was none to aid—
So My own arm wrought the triumph,
And [f-]My own rage[-f] was My aid.

6] I trampled peoples in My anger,
[g-]I made them drunk with[-g] My rage,
And I hurled their glory to the ground."

7] I will recount the kind acts of the LORD,
The praises of the LORD—
For all that the LORD has wrought for us,
The vast bounty to the House of Israel
That He bestowed upon them
According to His mercy and His great kindness.

8] He thought: Surely they are My people,
Children who will not play false.
[h-]So He was their Deliverer.

מַדּוּעַ אָדֹם לִלְבוּשֶׁךָ [2
וּבְגָדֶיךָ כְּדֹרֵךְ בְּגַת:

פּוּרָה דָּרַכְתִּי לְבַדִּי [3
וּמֵעַמִּים אֵין־אִישׁ אִתִּי
וְאֶדְרְכֵם בְּאַפִּי
וְאֶרְמְסֵם בַּחֲמָתִי
וְיֵז נִצְחָם עַל־בְּגָדַי
וְכָל־מַלְבּוּשַׁי אֶגְאָלְתִּי:

כִּי יוֹם נָקָם בְּלִבִּי [4
וּשְׁנַת גְּאוּלַי בָּאָה:

וְאַבִּיט וְאֵין עֹזֵר [5
וְאֶשְׁתּוֹמֵם וְאֵין סוֹמֵךְ
וַתּוֹשַׁע לִי זְרֹעִי
וַחֲמָתִי הִיא סְמָכָתְנִי:

וְאָבוּס עַמִּים בְּאַפִּי [6
וַאֲשַׁכְּרֵם בַּחֲמָתִי
וְאוֹרִיד לָאָרֶץ נִצְחָם:

חַסְדֵי יְהֹוָה אַזְכִּיר [7
תְּהִלֹּת יְהֹוָה
כְּעַל כֹּל אֲשֶׁר־גְּמָלָנוּ יְהֹוָה
וְרַב־טוּב לְבֵית יִשְׂרָאֵל
אֲשֶׁר־גְּמָלָם כְּרַחֲמָיו
וּכְרֹב חֲסָדָיו:

וַיֹּאמֶר אַךְ־עַמִּי הֵמָּה [8
בָּנִים לֹא יְשַׁקֵּרוּ
וַיְהִי לָהֶם לְמוֹשִׁיעַ:

---

[c] Lit. "in a press"   [d-d] Emendation yields "Peoples, and. . . ."   [e] Meaning of Heb. uncertain

[f-f] Many mss. read vetzidkati "My victorious [right hand]"; cf. 59.16

[g-g] Many mss. and Targum read "I shattered them in"; cf. 14.25

[h-h] Ancient versions read "So He was their Deliverer | 9] In all their troubles. | No

9] In all their troubles He was troubled,
And the angel of His Presence delivered them.⁻ᴬ
In His love and pity
He Himself redeemed them,
Raised them, and exalted them
All the days of old.

בְּכָל־צָרָתָם לוֹ צָר [9

וּמַלְאַךְ פָּנָיו הוֹשִׁיעָם

בְּאַהֲבָתוֹ וּבְחֶמְלָתוֹ

הוּא גְאָלָם

וַיְנַטְּלֵם וַיְנַשְּׂאֵם

כָּל־יְמֵי עוֹלָם:

SECOND SELECTION

Isaiah

51 : 1-16

Chapter 51

1] Listen to Me, you who pursue justice,
You who seek the LORD:
Look to the rock you were hewn from,
To the quarry you were dug from.

נא

שִׁמְעוּ אֵלַי [1

רֹדְפֵי צֶדֶק

מְבַקְשֵׁי יְהֹוָה

הַבִּיטוּ אֶל־צוּר חֻצַּבְתֶּם

וְאֶל־מַקֶּבֶת בּוֹר נֻקַּרְתֶּם:

2] Look back to Abraham your father
And to Sarah who brought you forth.
For he was only one when I called him,
But I blessed him and made him many.

הַבִּיטוּ אֶל־אַבְרָהָם אֲבִיכֶם [2

וְאֶל־שָׂרָה תְּחוֹלֶלְכֶם

כִּי־אֶחָד קְרָאתִיו

וַאֲבָרְכֵהוּ וְאַרְבֵּהוּ:

3] Truly the LORD has comforted Zion,
Comforted all her ruins;
He has made her wilderness like Eden,
Her desert like the Garden of the LORD.

כִּי־נִחַם יְהֹוָה צִיּוֹן [3

נִחַם כָּל־חָרְבֹתֶיהָ

וַיָּשֶׂם מִדְבָּרָהּ כְּעֵדֶן

וְעַרְבָתָהּ כְּגַן־יְהֹוָה

[so ketiv] angel or messenger, / His own Presence delivered them." Cf. Deut. 4.37
which yields "He Himself"

478

Gladness and joy shall abide there,
Thanksgiving and the sound of music.

4] Hearken to Me, *ᵃ⁻My people,⁻ᵃ*
And give ear to Me, O *ᵃ⁻My nation,⁻ᵃ*
For teaching shall go forth[b] from Me,
My way for the light of peoples.
In a moment I will bring it:

5] The triumph I grant is near,
The success I give has gone forth.
My arms shall *ᶜ⁻provide for⁻ᶜ* the peoples;
The coastlands shall trust in Me,
They shall look to My arm.

6] Raise your eyes to the heavens,
And look upon the earth beneath:
Though the heavens should melt away like smoke,
And the earth wear out like a garment,
And its inhabitants die out *ᵈ⁻as well,⁻ᵈ*
My victory shall stand forever,
My triumph shall remain unbroken.

7] Listen to Me, you who care for the right,
O people who lay My instruction to heart!
Fear not the insults of men,
And be not dismayed at their jeers;

8] For the moth shall eat them up like a garment,
The worm[e] shall eat them up like wool.
But My triumph shall endure forever,
My salvation through all the ages.

שָׂשׂוֹן וְשִׂמְחָה יִמָּצֵא בָהּ
תּוֹדָה וְקוֹל זִמְרָה:

4 הַקְשִׁיבוּ אֵלַי עַמִּי
וּלְאוּמִּי אֵלַי הַאֲזִינוּ
כִּי תוֹרָה מֵאִתִּי תֵצֵא
וּמִשְׁפָּטִי לְאוֹר עַמִּים אַרְגִּיעַ:

5 קָרוֹב צִדְקִי
יָצָא יִשְׁעִי
וּזְרֹעַי עַמִּים יִשְׁפֹּטוּ
אֵלַי אִיִּים יְקַוּוּ
וְאֶל־זְרֹעִי יְיַחֵלוּן:

6 שְׂאוּ לַשָּׁמַיִם עֵינֵיכֶם
וְהַבִּיטוּ אֶל־הָאָרֶץ מִתַּחַת
כִּי־שָׁמַיִם כֶּעָשָׁן נִמְלָחוּ
וְהָאָרֶץ כַּבֶּגֶד תִּבְלֶה
וְיֹשְׁבֶיהָ כְּמוֹ־כֵן יְמוּתוּן
וִישׁוּעָתִי לְעוֹלָם תִּהְיֶה
וְצִדְקָתִי לֹא תֵחָת:

7 שִׁמְעוּ אֵלַי יֹדְעֵי צֶדֶק
עַם תּוֹרָתִי בְלִבָּם
אַל־תִּירְאוּ חֶרְפַּת אֱנוֹשׁ
וּמִגִּדֻּפֹתָם אַל־תֵּחָתּוּ:

8 כִּי כַבֶּגֶד יֹאכְלֵם עָשׁ
וְכַצֶּמֶר יֹאכְלֵם סָס
וְצִדְקָתִי לְעוֹלָם תִּהְיֶה
וִישׁוּעָתִי לְדוֹר דּוֹרִים:

ᵃ⁻ᵃ *Several mss. read "O peoples . . . O nations"; cf. end of this verse and verse 5*
ᵇ *I.e., through My servant Israel; cf. 42.1–5; 49.6*
ᶜ⁻ᶜ *Lit. "judge"*   ᵈ⁻ᵈ *Emendation yields "like gnats"*
ᵉ *Heb. sas, another word for "moth"*

9] Awake, awake, clothe yourself with splendor,
O arm of the LORD!
Awake as in days of old,
As in former ages!
It was you that hacked Rahab*f* in pieces,
That pierced the Dragon.*f*

9] עוּרִי עוּרִי לִבְשִׁי־עֹז

זְרוֹעַ יְהֹוָה

עוּרִי כִּימֵי קֶדֶם

דֹּרוֹת עוֹלָמִים

הֲלוֹא אַתְּ־הִיא הַמַּחְצֶבֶת רַהַב

מְחוֹלֶלֶת תַּנִּין:

10] It was you that dried up the Sea,
The waters of the great deep;
That made the abysses of the Sea
A road the redeemed might walk.

10] הֲלוֹא אַתְּ־הִיא הַמַּחֲרֶבֶת יָם

מֵי תְּהוֹם רַבָּה

הַשָּׂמָה מַעֲמַקֵּי־יָם

דֶּרֶךְ לַעֲבֹר גְּאוּלִים:

11] So let the ransomed of the LORD return,
And come with shouting to Zion,
Crowned with joy everlasting.
Let them attain joy and gladness,
While sorrow and sighing flee.

11] וּפְדוּיֵי יְהֹוָה יְשׁוּבוּן

וּבָאוּ צִיּוֹן בְּרִנָּה

וְשִׂמְחַת עוֹלָם עַל־רֹאשָׁם

שָׂשׂוֹן וְשִׂמְחָה יַשִּׂיגוּן

נָסוּ יָגוֹן וַאֲנָחָה:

12] I, I am He who comforts you!
What ails you that you fear
Man who must die,
Mortals who fare like grass?

12] אָנֹכִי אָנֹכִי הוּא מְנַחֶמְכֶם

מִי־אַתְּ וַתִּירְאִי מֵאֱנוֹשׁ יָמוּת

וּמִבֶּן־אָדָם חָצִיר יִנָּתֵן:

13] You have forgotten the LORD your Maker,
Who stretched out the skies and made firm the
      earth!
And you live all day in constant dread
Because of the rage of an oppressor
Who is aiming to cut [you] down.
Yet of what account is the rage of an oppressor?

13] וַתִּשְׁכַּח יְהֹוָה עֹשֶׂךָ

נֹטֶה שָׁמַיִם וְיֹסֵד אָרֶץ

וַתְּפַחֵד תָּמִיד כָּל־הַיּוֹם

מִפְּנֵי חֲמַת הַמֵּצִיק

כַּאֲשֶׁר כּוֹנֵן לְהַשְׁחִית

וְאַיֵּה חֲמַת הַמֵּצִיק:

14] *g*Quickly the crouching one is freed;
He is not cut down and slain,
And he shall not want for food.

14] מִהַר צֹעֶה לְהִפָּתֵחַ

וְלֹא־יָמוּת לַשַּׁחַת

וְלֹא יֶחְסַר לַחְמוֹ:

---

f Names of primeval monsters

*g Meaning of verse uncertain. Emendation yields (cf. Jer. 11.19; Job 14.7–9) "Quickly
the tree buds anew; | It does not die though cut down, | And its sap does not fail"*

15] For I the LORD your God—
Who stir up the sea into roaring waves,
Whose name is LORD of Hosts—

16] h-Have put My words in your mouth
And sheltered you with My hand;-h
I, who planted[i] the skies and made firm the earth,
Have said to Zion: You are My people!

15] וְאָנֹכִי יְהוָה אֱלֹהֶיךָ
רֹגַע הַיָּם וַיֶּהֱמוּ גַּלָּיו
יְהוָה צְבָאוֹת שְׁמוֹ:
16] וָאָשִׂים דְּבָרַי בְּפִיךָ
וּבְצֵל יָדִי כִּסִּיתִיךָ
לִנְטֹעַ שָׁמַיִם וְלִיסֹד אָרֶץ
וְלֵאמֹר לְצִיּוֹן
עַמִּי אָתָּה:

THIRD SELECTION

Jeremiah

31 : 27-36

Chapter 31

27] See, a time is coming—declares the LORD—when I will sow the House of Israel and the House of Judah with seed of men and seed of cattle;

28] and just as I was watchful over them to uproot and to pull down, to overthrow and to destroy and to bring disaster, so I will be watchful over them to build and to plant—declares the LORD.

29] In those days, they shall no longer say, "Fathers have eaten sour grapes and children's teeth are blunted."[k]

30] But everyone shall die for his own sins: whosoever eats sour grapes, his teeth shall be blunted.

31] See, a time is coming—declares the LORD—when I will make a new covenant with the House of Israel and the House of Judah.

לא

27] הִנֵּה יָמִים בָּאִים נְאֻם־יְהוָה וְזָרַעְתִּי אֶת־
בֵּית יִשְׂרָאֵל וְאֶת־בֵּית יְהוּדָה זֶרַע אָדָם וְזֶרַע
בְּהֵמָה: 28] וְהָיָה כַּאֲשֶׁר שָׁקַדְתִּי עֲלֵיהֶם
לִנְתוֹשׁ וְלִנְתוֹץ וְלַהֲרֹס וּלְהַאֲבִיד וּלְהָרֵעַ כֵּן
אֶשְׁקֹד עֲלֵיהֶם לִבְנוֹת וְלִנְטוֹעַ נְאֻם־יְהוָה:
29] בַּיָּמִים הָהֵם לֹא־יֹאמְרוּ עוֹד אָבוֹת אָכְלוּ
בֹסֶר וְשִׁנֵּי בָנִים תִּקְהֶינָה: 30] כִּי אִם־אִישׁ
בַּעֲוֹנוֹ יָמוּת כָּל־הָאָדָם הָאֹכֵל הַבֹּסֶר תִּקְהֶינָה
שִׁנָּיו:
31] הִנֵּה יָמִים בָּאִים נְאֻם־יְהוָה וְכָרַתִּי אֶת־
בֵּית יִשְׂרָאֵל וְאֶת־בֵּית יְהוּדָה בְּרִית חֲדָשָׁה:

---

h-h *I.e., I have chosen you to be a prophet-nation; cf. 49.2; 59.21*
i *Emendation yields "stretched out"; cf. Syriac version and v. 13*
k *Others "set on edge"*

32] It
will not be like the covenant I made with their
fathers, when I took them by the hand to lead
them out of the land of Egypt, a covenant which
they broke, so that I rejected[1] them—declares the
LORD.

33] But such is the covenant I will make
with the House of Israel after these days—declares
the LORD: I will put My Teaching into their in-
most being and inscribe it upon their hearts.
Then I will be their God, and they shall be My
people.

34] No longer will they need to teach
one another and say to one another, "Heed the
LORD"; for all of them, from the least of them to
the greatest, shall heed Me—declares the LORD.
For I will forgive their iniquities,
And remember their sins no more.

35] Thus said the LORD,
Who established the sun for light by day,
The laws of moon and stars for light by night,
Who stirs up the sea into roaring waves,
Whose name is LORD of Hosts:

36] If these laws should ever be annulled by Me
—declares the LORD—
Only then would the offspring of Israel cease
To be a nation before Me for all time.

לֹא כַבְּרִית אֲשֶׁר כָּרַתִּי אֶת־אֲבוֹתָם בְּיוֹם [32
הֶחֱזִיקִי בְיָדָם לְהוֹצִיאָם מֵאֶרֶץ מִצְרָיִם אֲשֶׁר־
הֵמָּה הֵפֵרוּ אֶת־בְּרִיתִי וְאָנֹכִי בָּעַלְתִּי בָם נְאֻם־
יְהֹוָה: 33] כִּי זֹאת הַבְּרִית אֲשֶׁר אֶכְרֹת אֶת־
בֵּית יִשְׂרָאֵל אַחֲרֵי הַיָּמִים הָהֵם נְאֻם־יְהֹוָה
נָתַתִּי אֶת־תּוֹרָתִי בְּקִרְבָּם וְעַל־לִבָּם אֶכְתֲּבֶנָּה
וְהָיִיתִי לָהֶם לֵאלֹהִים וְהֵמָּה יִהְיוּ־לִי לְעָם:
34] וְלֹא יְלַמְּדוּ עוֹד אִישׁ אֶת־רֵעֵהוּ וְאִישׁ
אֶת־אָחִיו לֵאמֹר דְּעוּ אֶת־יְהֹוָה כִּי כוּלָם
יֵדְעוּ אוֹתִי לְמִקְטַנָּם וְעַד־גְּדוֹלָם נְאֻם־יְהֹוָה
כִּי אֶסְלַח לַעֲוֺנָם
וּלְחַטָּאתָם לֹא אֶזְכָּר־עוֹד:

35] כֹּה אָמַר יְהֹוָה
נֹתֵן שֶׁמֶשׁ לְאוֹר יוֹמָם
חֻקֹּת יָרֵחַ וְכוֹכָבִים
לְאוֹר לָיְלָה רֹגַע הַיָּם וַיֶּהֱמוּ גַלָּיו
יְהֹוָה צְבָאוֹת שְׁמוֹ:

36] אִם־יָמֻשׁוּ הַחֻקִּים הָאֵלֶּה מִלְּפָנַי
נְאֻם־יְהֹוָה
גַּם זֶרַע יִשְׂרָאֵל יִשְׁבְּתוּ
מִהְיוֹת גּוֹי לְפָנַי כָּל־הַיָּמִים:

[1] *Taking ba'alti as equivalent to bahalti; cf. 3.14*

וילך

Isaiah

55 : 6 — 56 : 8

Chapter 55

נה

6] Seek the Lord while He can be found,
Call to Him while He is near.

6] דִּרְשׁוּ יְהוָה בְּהִמָּצְאוֹ

קְרָאֻהוּ בִּהְיוֹתוֹ קָרוֹב:

7] Let the wicked give up his ways,
The sinful man his plans;
Let him turn back to the Lord,
And He will pardon him;
To our God,
For He freely forgives.

7] יַעֲזֹב רָשָׁע דַּרְכּוֹ

וְאִישׁ אָוֶן מַחְשְׁבֹתָיו

וְיָשֹׁב אֶל־יְהוָה וִירַחֲמֵהוּ

וְאֶל־אֱלֹהֵינוּ כִּי־יַרְבֶּה לִסְלוֹחַ:

8] For My plans are not your plans,
Nor are My ways*e* your ways*e*
                    —declares the Lord.

8] כִּי לֹא מַחְשְׁבוֹתַי מַחְשְׁבוֹתֵיכֶם

וְלֹא דַרְכֵיכֶם דְּרָכָי

נְאֻם יְהוָה:

9] But as the heavens are high above the earth,
So are My ways*e* high above your ways*e*
And My plans above your plans.

9] כִּי־גָבְהוּ שָׁמַיִם מֵאָרֶץ

כֵּן גָּבְהוּ דְרָכַי מִדַּרְכֵיכֶם

וּמַחְשְׁבֹתַי מִמַּחְשְׁבֹתֵיכֶם:

10] For as the rain or snow drops from heaven
And returns not there,
But soaks the earth
And makes it bring forth vegetation,
Yielding *d*seed for sowing and bread for eating,*d*

10] כִּי כַּאֲשֶׁר יֵרֵד הַגֶּשֶׁם וְהַשֶּׁלֶג מִן־הַשָּׁמַיִם

וְשָׁמָּה לֹא יָשׁוּב

כִּי אִם־הִרְוָה אֶת־הָאָרֶץ

וְהוֹלִידָהּ וְהִצְמִיחָהּ

וְנָתַן זֶרַע לַזֹּרֵעַ וְלֶחֶם לָאֹכֵל:

e Emendation yields "words"; cf. v. 11 and 40.8
d-d Lit. "seed for the sower and bread for the eater"

11] So is the word that issues from My mouth:
It does not come back to Me unfulfilled,
But performs what I purpose,
Achieves what I sent it to do.

12] Yea, you shall leave* in joy and be led home
    secure.
Before you, mount and hill shall shout aloud,
And all the trees of the field shall clap their hands.

13] Instead of the brier, a cypress shall rise;
Instead of the nettle, a myrtle shall rise.
These shall stand as a testimony to the LORD,
As an everlasting sign that shall not perish.

Chapter 56

1] Thus said the LORD:
Observe what is right and do what is just;
For soon My salvation shall come,
And My deliverance be revealed.

2] Happy is the man who does this,
The man who holds fast to it:
Who keeps the sabbath and does not profane it,
And stays his hand from doing any evil.

3] Let not the foreigner say,
Who has attached himself to the LORD,
"The LORD will keep me apart from His people";
And let not the eunuch say,
"I am a withered tree."

4] For thus said the LORD:
"As regards the eunuchs who keep My sabbaths,

---

* I.e., leave the Babylonian exile

כֵּן יִהְיֶה דְבָרִי אֲשֶׁר יֵצֵא מִפִּי [11
לֹא־יָשׁוּב אֵלַי רֵיקָם
כִּי אִם־עָשָׂה אֶת־אֲשֶׁר חָפַצְתִּי
וְהִצְלִיחַ אֲשֶׁר שְׁלַחְתִּיו:
כִּי־בְשִׂמְחָה תֵצֵאוּ וּבְשָׁלוֹם תּוּבָלוּן [12
הֶהָרִים וְהַגְּבָעוֹת יִפְצְחוּ לִפְנֵיכֶם רִנָּה
וְכָל־עֲצֵי הַשָּׂדֶה יִמְחֲאוּ־כָף:
תַּחַת הַנַּעֲצוּץ יַעֲלֶה בְרוֹשׁ [13
וְתַחַת הַסִּרְפָּד יַעֲלֶה הֲדַס
וְהָיָה לַיהוָה לְשֵׁם
לְאוֹת עוֹלָם לֹא יִכָּרֵת:

נו

כֹּה אָמַר יְהוָה [1
שִׁמְרוּ מִשְׁפָּט וַעֲשׂוּ צְדָקָה
כִּי־קְרוֹבָה יְשׁוּעָתִי לָבוֹא
וְצִדְקָתִי לְהִגָּלוֹת:
אַשְׁרֵי אֱנוֹשׁ יַעֲשֶׂה־זֹּאת [2
וּבֶן־אָדָם יַחֲזִיק בָּהּ
שֹׁמֵר שַׁבָּת מֵחַלְּלוֹ
וְשֹׁמֵר יָדוֹ מֵעֲשׂוֹת כָּל־רָע:
וְאַל־יֹאמַר בֶּן־הַנֵּכָר [3
הַנִּלְוָה אֶל־יְהוָה לֵאמֹר
הַבְדֵּל יַבְדִּילַנִי יְהוָה מֵעַל עַמּוֹ
וְאַל־יֹאמַר הַסָּרִיס
הֵן אֲנִי עֵץ יָבֵשׁ:
כִּי־כֹה אָמַר יְהוָה [4
לַסָּרִיסִים אֲשֶׁר יִשְׁמְרוּ אֶת־שַׁבְּתוֹתַי

Who have chosen what I desire
And hold fast to My covenant—

5] I will give them, in My House
And within My walls,
A monument and a name
Better than sons or daughters.
I will give them an everlasting name
Which shall not perish.

6] As for the foreigners
Who attach themselves to the LORD,
To minister to Him.
And to love the name of the LORD,
To be His servants—
All who keep the sabbath and do not profane it,
And who hold fast to My covenant—

7] I will bring them to My sacred mount
And let them rejoice in My house of prayer.
Their burnt offerings and sacrifices
Shall be welcome on My altar;
For My House shall be called
A house of prayer for all peoples."

8] Thus declares the Lord GOD,
Who gathers the dispersed of Israel:
"I will gather still more to those already
    gathered."

וּבָחֲרוּ בַּאֲשֶׁר חָפָצְתִּי

וּמַחֲזִיקִים בִּבְרִיתִי:

5] וְנָתַתִּי לָהֶם בְּבֵיתִי

וּבְחוֹמֹתַי

יָד וָשֵׁם

טוֹב מִבָּנִים וּמִבָּנוֹת

שֵׁם עוֹלָם אֶתֶּן־לוֹ

אֲשֶׁר לֹא יִכָּרֵת:

6] וּבְנֵי הַנֵּכָר

הַנִּלְוִים עַל־יְהוָֹה לְשָׁרְתוֹ

וּלְאַהֲבָה אֶת־שֵׁם יְהוָה

לִהְיוֹת לוֹ לַעֲבָדִים

כָּל־שֹׁמֵר שַׁבָּת מֵחַלְּלוֹ

וּמַחֲזִיקִים בִּבְרִיתִי:

7] וַהֲבִיאוֹתִים אֶל־הַר קָדְשִׁי

וְשִׂמַּחְתִּים בְּבֵית תְּפִלָּתִי

עוֹלֹתֵיהֶם וְזִבְחֵיהֶם

לְרָצוֹן עַל־מִזְבְּחִי

כִּי בֵיתִי בֵּית־תְּפִלָּה יִקָּרֵא

לְכָל־הָעַמִּים:

8] נְאֻם אֲדֹנָי יֱהֹוִה

מְקַבֵּץ נִדְחֵי יִשְׂרָאֵל

עוֹד אֲקַבֵּץ עָלָיו לְנִקְבָּצָיו:

FIRST SELECTION

Second Samuel

22 : 1-51

Chapter 22

1] ᵃDavid addressed the words of this song to the LORD, after the LORD had saved him from the hands of all his enemies and from the hands of Saul.

2] He said:
O LORD, my crag, my fastness, my deliverer!

3] O ᵇ⁻God, the rock⁻ᵇ wherein I take shelter:
My shield, my ᶜ⁻mighty champion,⁻ᶜ my fortress and refuge!
My savior, You who rescue me from violence!

4] ᵈ⁻All praise! I called on the LORD,⁻ᵈ
And I was delivered from my enemies.

5] For the breakers of Death encompassed me,
The torrents of Belialᵉ terrified me;

6] The snares of Sheol encircled me,
The toils of Death engulfed me.

כב

1] וַיְדַבֵּר דָּוִד לַיהוָה אֶת־דִּבְרֵי הַשִּׁירָה
הַזֹּאת בְּיוֹם הִצִּיל יְהוָה אֹתוֹ מִכַּף כָּל־אֹיְבָיו
וּמִכַּף שָׁאוּל:

2] וַיֹּאמַר:
יְהוָה סַלְעִי וּמְצֻדָתִי וּמְפַלְטִי־לִי:

3] אֱלֹהֵי צוּרִי אֶחֱסֶה־בּוֹ
מָגִנִּי וְקֶרֶן יִשְׁעִי
מִשְׂגַּבִּי וּמְנוּסִי
מֹשִׁעִי מֵחָמָס תֹּשִׁעֵנִי:

4] מְהֻלָּל אֶקְרָא יְהוָה
וּמֵאֹיְבַי אִוָּשֵׁעַ:

5] כִּי אֲפָפֻנִי מִשְׁבְּרֵי־מָוֶת
נַחֲלֵי בְלִיַּעַל יְבַעֲתֻנִי:

6] חֶבְלֵי שְׁאוֹל סַבֻּנִי
קִדְּמֻנִי מֹקְשֵׁי־מָוֶת:

ᵃ This poem occurs again as Ps. 18, with a number of variations, some of which are cited in the following notes

ᵇ⁻ᵇ Lit. "the God of my rock"; Ps. 18.3 "my God, my rock"

ᶜ⁻ᶜ Lit. "horn of rescue"

ᵈ⁻ᵈ Construction of Heb. uncertain

ᵉ I.e., the nether world, like "Death" and "Sheol"

7] In my anguish I called on the LORD,
Cried out to my God;
In His abode*ᶠ* He heard my voice,
My cry entered His ears.

8] Then the earth rocked and quaked,
The foundations of heaven*ᵍ* shook—
Rocked by His indignation.

9] Smoke went up from His nostrils,
From His mouth came devouring fire;
Live coals blazed forth from Him.

10] He bent the sky and came down,
Thick cloud beneath His feet.

11] He mounted a cherub and flew;
ʰ-He was seen-*ʰ* on the wings of the wind.

12] He made pavilions of darkness about Him,
Dripping clouds, huge thunderheads;

13] In the brilliance before Him
Blazed fiery coals.

14] The LORD thundered forth from heaven,
The Most High sent forth His voice;

15] He let loose bolts, and scattered them;*ⁱ*
Lightning and, put them to rout.

16] The bed of the sea was exposed,
The foundations of the world were laid bare
By the mighty roaring of the LORD,
At the blast of the breath of His nostrils.

בַּצַּר־לִי אֶקְרָא יְהוָֹה [7

וְאֶל־אֱלֹהַי אֶקְרָא

וַיִּשְׁמַע מֵהֵיכָלוֹ קוֹלִי

וְשַׁוְעָתִי בְּאָזְנָיו:

וַיִּתְגָּעַשׁ וַתִּרְעַשׁ הָאָרֶץ [8

מוֹסְדוֹת הַשָּׁמַיִם יִרְגָּזוּ

וַיִּתְגָּעֲשׁוּ כִּי־חָרָה לוֹ:

עָלָה עָשָׁן בְּאַפּוֹ [9

וְאֵשׁ מִפִּיו תֹּאכֵל

גֶּחָלִים בָּעֲרוּ מִמֶּנּוּ:

וַיֵּט שָׁמַיִם וַיֵּרַד [10

וַעֲרָפֶל תַּחַת רַגְלָיו:

וַיִּרְכַּב עַל־כְּרוּב וַיָּעֹף [11

וַיֵּרָא עַל־כַּנְפֵי־רוּחַ:

וַיָּשֶׁת חֹשֶׁךְ סְבִיבֹתָיו סֻכּוֹת [12

חַשְׁרַת־מַיִם עָבֵי שְׁחָקִים:

מִנֹּגַהּ נֶגְדּוֹ [13

בָּעֲרוּ גַּחֲלֵי־אֵשׁ:

יַרְעֵם מִן־שָׁמַיִם יְהוָֹה [14

וְעֶלְיוֹן יִתֵּן קוֹלוֹ:

וַיִּשְׁלַח חִצִּים וַיְפִיצֵם [15

בָּרָק וַיָּהֹם:

וַיֵּרָאוּ אֲפִקֵי יָם [16

יִגָּלוּ מֹסְדוֹת תֵּבֵל

בְּגַעֲרַת יְהוָֹה

מִנִּשְׁמַת רוּחַ אַפּוֹ:

ᶠ Lit. "Temple"
ᵍ Ps. 18.8 "mountains"
ʰ⁻ʰ Ps. 18.11 "Gliding"
ⁱ I.e., the enemies in v. 4

17] He reached down from on high, He took me,
Drew me out of the mighty waters;[i]

18] He rescued me from my enemy so strong,
From foes too mighty for me.

19] They attacked me on my day of calamity,
But the LORD was my stay.

20] He brought me out to freedom,
He rescued me because He was pleased with me.

21] The LORD rewarded me according to my
merit,
He requited the cleanness of my hands.

22] For I have kept the ways of the LORD
And have not been guilty before my God;

23] I am mindful of all His rules
And have not departed from His laws.

24] I have been blameless before Him,
And have guarded myself against sinning—

25] And the LORD has requited my merit,
According to my purity in His sight.

26] With the loyal You deal loyally;
With the blameless hero,[k] blamelessly.

27] With the pure You act in purity,
And with the perverse You are wily.

28] To humble folk You give victory,
[l-]And You look with scorn on the haughty.[-l]

29] You, O LORD, are my lamp;
The LORD lights up my darkness.

[17] יִשְׁלַח מִמָּרוֹם יִקָּחֵנִי
יַמְשֵׁנִי מִמַּיִם רַבִּים:

[18] יַצִּילֵנִי מֵאֹיְבִי עָז
מִשֹּׂנְאַי כִּי אָמְצוּ מִמֶּנִּי:

[19] יְקַדְּמֻנִי בְּיוֹם אֵידִי
וַיְהִי יְהֹוָה מִשְׁעָן לִי:

[20] וַיֹּצֵא לַמֶּרְחָב אֹתִי
יְחַלְּצֵנִי כִּי־חָפֵץ־בִּי:

[21] יִגְמְלֵנִי יְהֹוָה כְּצִדְקָתִי
כְּבֹר יָדַי יָשִׁיב לִי:

[22] כִּי שָׁמַרְתִּי דַּרְכֵי יְהֹוָה
וְלֹא רָשַׁעְתִּי מֵאֱלֹהָי:

[23] כִּי כָל־מִשְׁפָּטָיו לְנֶגְדִּי
וְחֻקֹּתָיו לֹא־אָסוּר מִמֶּנָּה:

[24] וָאֶהְיֶה תָמִים לוֹ
וָאֶשְׁתַּמְּרָה מֵעֲוֹנִי:

[25] וַיָּשֶׁב יְהֹוָה לִי כְּצִדְקָתִי
כְּבֹרִי לְנֶגֶד עֵינָיו:

[26] עִם־חָסִיד תִּתְחַסָּד
עִם־גִּבּוֹר תָּמִים תִּתַּמָּם:

[27] עִם־נָבָר תִּתָּבָר
וְעִם־עִקֵּשׁ תִּתַּפָּל:

[28] וְאֶת־עַם עָנִי תּוֹשִׁיעַ
וְעֵינֶיךָ עַל־רָמִים תַּשְׁפִּיל:

[29] כִּי־אַתָּה נֵרִי יְהֹוָה
וַיהֹוָה יַגִּיהַּ חָשְׁכִּי:

---

[i] Cf. v. 5

[k] Ps. 18.26 "man"

[l-l] Lit. "And lower Your eyes on the haughty"; Ps. 18.28 "But haughty eyes You
humble"

30] With You, I can rush a barrier,[m]
With my God, I can scale a wall.

31] The way of God is perfect,
The word of the Lord is pure.
He is a shield to all who take refuge in Him.

32] Yea, who is a god except the Lord,
Who is a rock except God—

33] The God, [n]my mighty stronghold,[n]
Who kept[o] my path secure;

34] Who made my legs like a deer's,
And set me firm on the[p] heights;

35] Who trained my hands for battle,
So that my arms can bend a bow of bronze!

36] You have granted me the shield of Your
protection
[q]And Your providence has made me great.[q]

37] You have let me stride on freely,
And my feet have not slipped.

38] I pursued my enemies and wiped them out,
I did not turn back till I destroyed them.

39] I destroyed them, I struck them down;
They rose no more, they lay at my feet.

40] You have girt me with strength for battle,
Brought low my foes before me,

41] Made my enemies turn tail before me,
My foes—and I wiped them out.

כִּי בְכָה אָרוּץ גְּדוּד [30
בֵּאלֹהַי אֲדַלֶּג־שׁוּר:

הָאֵל תָּמִים דַּרְכּוֹ [31
אִמְרַת יְהֹוָה צְרוּפָה
מָגֵן הוּא לְכֹל הַחֹסִים בּוֹ:

כִּי מִי־אֵל מִבַּלְעֲדֵי יְהֹוָה [32
וּמִי־צוּר מִבַּלְעֲדֵי אֱלֹהֵינוּ

הָאֵל מָעוּזִּי חָיִל [33
וַיַּתֵּר תָּמִים דַּרְכִּי:

מְשַׁוֶּה רַגְלַי כָּאַיָּלוֹת [34
וְעַל בָּמֹתַי יַעֲמִדֵנִי:

מְלַמֵּד יָדַי לַמִּלְחָמָה [35
וְנִחַת קֶשֶׁת־נְחוּשָׁה זְרֹעֹתָי:

וַתִּתֶּן־לִי מָגֵן יִשְׁעֶךָ [36
וַעֲנֹתְךָ תַרְבֵּנִי:

תַּרְחִיב צַעֲדִי תַּחְתֵּנִי [37
וְלֹא מָעֲדוּ קַרְסֻלָּי:

אֶרְדְּפָה אֹיְבַי וָאַשְׁמִידֵם [38
וְלֹא אָשׁוּב עַד־כַּלּוֹתָם:

וָאֲכַלֵּם וָאֶמְחָצֵם וְלֹא יְקוּמוּן [39
וַיִּפְּלוּ תַּחַת רַגְלָי:

וַתַּזְרֵנִי חַיִל לַמִּלְחָמָה [40
תַּכְרִיעַ קָמַי תַּחְתֵּנִי:

וְאֹיְבַי תַּתָּה לִּי עֹרֶף [41
מְשַׂנְאַי וָאַצְמִיתֵם:

---

[m] Cf. post-biblical gedudiyot, "walls," Aramaic gudda, "wall"

[n-n] Ps. 18.33 "who girded me with might"

[o] Meaning of Heb. uncertain; Ps. 18.33 "made"

[p] Taking bamotai as a poetic form of bamot; cf. Hab. 3.19; others "my"

[q-q] Meaning of Heb. uncertain

42] They looked,[r] but there was none to deliver;
To the Lord, but He answered them not.

42] יִשְׁעוּ וְאֵין מֹשִׁיעַ
אֶל־יְהוָה וְלֹא עָנָם׃

43] I pounded them like dust of the earth,
Stamped, crushed them like dirt of the streets.

43] וְאֶשְׁחָקֵם כַּעֲפַר־אָרֶץ
כְּטִיט חוּצוֹת אֲדִקֵּם אֶרְקָעֵם׃

44] You have rescued me from the strife of peoples,[s]
[t]Kept me to be[t] a ruler of nations;
Peoples I knew not must serve me.

44] וַתְּפַלְּטֵנִי מֵרִיבֵי עַמִּי
תִּשְׁמְרֵנִי לְרֹאשׁ גּוֹיִם
עַם לֹא־יָדַעְתִּי יַעַבְדֻנִי׃

45] Aliens have cringed before me,
Paid me homage at the mere report of me.

45] בְּנֵי נֵכָר יִתְכַּחֲשׁוּ־לִי
לִשְׁמוֹעַ אֹזֶן יִשָּׁמְעוּ לִי׃

46] Aliens have lost courage
[q]And come trembling out of their fastnesses.[q]

46] בְּנֵי נֵכָר יִבֹּלוּ
וְיַחְגְּרוּ מִמִּסְגְּרוֹתָם׃

47] The Lord lives! Blessed is my rock!
Exalted be God, the rock
Who gives me victory;

47] חַי־יְהוָה וּבָרוּךְ צוּרִי
וְיָרֻם אֱלֹהֵי צוּר יִשְׁעִי׃

48] The God who has vindicated me
And made peoples subject to me,

48] הָאֵל הַנֹּתֵן נְקָמֹת לִי
וּמוֹרִיד עַמִּים תַּחְתֵּנִי׃

49] Rescued me from my enemies,
Raised me clear of my foes,
Saved me from lawless men!

49] וּמוֹצִיאִי מֵאֹיְבָי
וּמִקָּמַי תְּרוֹמְמֵנִי
מֵאִישׁ חֲמָסִים תַּצִּילֵנִי׃

50] For this I sing Your praise among the nations
And hymn Your name:

50] עַל־כֵּן אוֹדְךָ יְהוָה בַּגּוֹיִם
וּלְשִׁמְךָ אֲזַמֵּר׃

51] [u]Tower of victory[u] to His king,
Who deals graciously with His anointed,
With David and his offspring evermore.

51] מִגְדּוֹל יְשׁוּעוֹת מַלְכּוֹ
וְעֹשֶׂה־חֶסֶד לִמְשִׁיחוֹ
לְדָוִד וּלְזַרְעוֹ עַד־עוֹלָם׃

[r] *Ps. 18.42 "cried"*

[s] *So some mss. and the Septuagint; most mss. and the printed editions "my people"*

[t-t] *Ps. 18.44 "made me"*

[q-q] *Meaning of Heb. uncertain*

[u-u] Ketiv *Ps. 18.51 reads "Who accords wondrous victories"*

SECOND SELECTION

Psalms

78 : 1-8

Psalm 78

1] A *maskil* of Asaph.
Give ear, my people, to my teaching,
turn your ear to what I say.

2] I will expound a theme,
hold forth on the lessons of the past,

3] things we have heard and known,
that our fathers have told us.

4] We will not withhold them from their children,
telling the coming generation
the praises of the LORD and His might,
and the wonders He performed.

5] He established a decree in Jacob,
ordained a teaching in Israel,
charging our fathers
to make them known to their children,

6] that a future generation might know
—children yet to be born—
and in turn tell their children

7] that they put their confidence in God,
and not forget God's great deeds,
but observe His commandments,

8] and not be like their fathers,
a wayward and defiant generation,
a generation whose heart was inconstant,
whose spirit was not true to God.

עח

‏1] מַשְׂכִּיל לְאָסָף‎
‏הַאֲזִינָה עַמִּי תּוֹרָתִי‎
‏הַטּוּ אָזְנְכֶם לְאִמְרֵי־פִי:‎

‏2] אֶפְתְּחָה בְמָשָׁל פִּי‎
‏אַבִּיעָה חִידוֹת מִנִּי־קֶדֶם:‎

‏3] אֲשֶׁר שָׁמַעְנוּ וַנֵּדָעֵם‎
‏וַאֲבוֹתֵינוּ סִפְּרוּ־לָנוּ:‎

‏4] לֹא נְכַחֵד מִבְּנֵיהֶם לְדוֹר אַחֲרוֹן‎
‏מְסַפְּרִים תְּהִלּוֹת יְהֹוָה‎
‏וֶעֱזוּזוֹ וְנִפְלְאוֹתָיו אֲשֶׁר עָשָׂה:‎

‏5] וַיָּקֶם עֵדוּת בְּיַעֲקֹב‎
‏וְתוֹרָה שָׂם בְּיִשְׂרָאֵל‎
‏אֲשֶׁר צִוָּה אֶת־אֲבוֹתֵינוּ‎
‏לְהוֹדִיעָם לִבְנֵיהֶם:‎

‏6] לְמַעַן יֵדְעוּ דּוֹר אַחֲרוֹן‎
‏בָּנִים יִוָּלֵדוּ‎
‏יָקֻמוּ וִיסַפְּרוּ לִבְנֵיהֶם:‎

‏7] וְיָשִׂימוּ בֵאלֹהִים כִּסְלָם‎
‏וְלֹא יִשְׁכְּחוּ מַעַלְלֵי־אֵל‎
‏וּמִצְוֹתָיו יִנְצֹרוּ:‎

‏8] וְלֹא יִהְיוּ כַּאֲבוֹתָם‎
‏דּוֹר סוֹרֵר וּמֹרֶה‎
‏דּוֹר לֹא־הֵכִין לִבּוֹ‎
‏וְלֹא־נֶאֶמְנָה אֶת־אֵל רוּחוֹ:‎

491

וזאת הברכה

Joshua

1 : 1-18

Chapter 1

1] After the death of Moses the servant of the LORD, the LORD said to Joshua son of Nun, Moses' attendant:

2] "My servant Moses is dead. Prepare to cross the Jordan, together with all this people, into the land which I am giving to the Israelites. 3] Every spot on which your foot treads I give to you, as I promised Moses.

4] Your territory shall extend from the wilderness and the Lebanon to the Great River, the River Euphrates [on the east] —the whole Hittite country—and up to the Mediterranean[a] Sea on the west.

5] No man shall be able to resist you as long as you live. As I was with Moses, so I will be with you; I will not fail you or forsake you.

6] "Be strong and resolute, for you shall apportion to this people the land that I swore to their fathers to give them.

7] But you must be very strong and resolute to observe faithfully all the Teaching that My servant Moses enjoined upon you. Do not deviate from it to the right or to the left, that you may be successful wherever you go. 8] Let not this Book of the Teaching cease from

א

1] וַיְהִ֗י אַחֲרֵ֛י מ֥וֹת מֹשֶׁ֖ה עֶ֣בֶד יְהֹוָ֑ה וַיֹּ֤אמֶר יְהֹוָה֙ אֶל־יְהוֹשֻׁ֣עַ בִּן־נ֔וּן מְשָׁרֵ֥ת מֹשֶׁ֖ה לֵאמֹֽר:

2] מֹשֶׁ֥ה עַבְדִּ֖י מֵ֑ת וְעַתָּה֩ ק֨וּם עֲבֹ֜ר אֶת־הַיַּרְדֵּ֣ן הַזֶּ֗ה אַתָּה֙ וְכׇל־הָעָ֣ם הַזֶּ֔ה אֶל־הָאָ֕רֶץ אֲשֶׁ֧ר אָנֹכִ֛י נֹתֵ֥ן לָהֶ֖ם לִבְנֵ֥י יִשְׂרָאֵֽל: 3] כׇּל־מָק֗וֹם אֲשֶׁ֨ר תִּדְרֹ֧ךְ כַּף־רַגְלְכֶ֛ם בּ֖וֹ לָכֶ֣ם נְתַתִּ֑יו כַּֽאֲשֶׁ֥ר דִּבַּ֖רְתִּי אֶל־מֹשֶֽׁה: 4] מֵהַמִּדְבָּר֩ וְהַלְּבָנ֨וֹן הַזֶּ֜ה וְעַד־הַנָּהָ֤ר הַגָּדוֹל֙ נְהַר־פְּרָ֔ת כֹּ֖ל אֶ֣רֶץ הַֽחִתִּ֑ים וְעַד־הַיָּ֤ם הַגָּדוֹל֙ מְב֣וֹא הַשָּׁ֔מֶשׁ יִֽהְיֶ֖ה גְּבֽוּלְכֶֽם: 5] לֹֽא־יִתְיַצֵּ֥ב אִישׁ֙ לְפָנֶ֔יךָ כֹּ֖ל יְמֵ֣י חַיֶּ֑יךָ כַּֽאֲשֶׁ֨ר הָיִ֤יתִי עִם־מֹשֶׁה֙ אֶֽהְיֶ֣ה עִמָּ֔ךְ לֹ֥א אַרְפְּךָ֖ וְלֹ֥א אֶעֶזְבֶֽךָּ:

6] חֲזַ֖ק וֶֽאֱמָ֑ץ כִּ֣י אַתָּ֗ה תַּנְחִיל֙ אֶת־הָעָ֣ם הַזֶּ֔ה אֶת־הָאָ֕רֶץ אֲשֶׁר־נִשְׁבַּ֥עְתִּי לַֽאֲבוֹתָ֖ם לָתֵ֥ת לָהֶֽם: 7] רַק֩ חֲזַ֨ק וֶֽאֱמַ֜ץ מְאֹ֗ד לִשְׁמֹ֤ר לַֽעֲשׂוֹת֙ כְּכׇל־הַתּוֹרָ֗ה אֲשֶׁ֤ר צִוְּךָ֙ מֹשֶׁ֣ה עַבְדִּ֔י אַל־תָּס֥וּר מִמֶּ֖נּוּ יָמִ֣ין וּשְׂמֹ֑אול לְמַ֣עַן תַּשְׂכִּ֔יל בְּכֹ֖ל אֲשֶׁ֥ר תֵּלֵֽךְ: 8] לֹֽא־יָמ֡וּשׁ סֵ֩פֶר֩ הַתּוֹרָ֨ה הַזֶּ֜ה מִפִּ֗יךָ

your lips, but recite it day and night, so that you may observe faithfully all that is written in it. Only then will you prosper in your undertakings and only then will you be successful.

9] "I charge you: Be strong and resolute; do not be terrified or dismayed, for the LORD your God is with you wherever you go."

10] Joshua thereupon gave orders to the officials of the people:

11] "Go through the camp and charge the people thus: Get provisions ready, for in three days' time you are to cross the Jordan, in order to enter and occupy the land which the LORD your God is giving you as a possession."

12] Then Joshua said to the Reubenites, the Gadites, and the half-tribe of Manasseh,

13] "Remember what Moses the servant of the LORD enjoined upon you, when he said: 'The LORD your God is granting you a haven; He is assigning this territory to you.'

14] Let your wives, children, and livestock remain in the land which Moses assigned to you *b-*on this side of*-b* the Jordan; but every one of your fighting men shall go across armed*c* in the van of your kinsmen. And you shall assist them

15] until the LORD has given your kinsmen a haven, such as you have, and they too have gained possession of the land which the LORD your God has assigned to them. Then you may return to the land on the east side of the Jordan, which Moses the servant of the LORD assigned to you as your possession, and you may occupy it."

16] They answered Joshua, "We will do everything you have commanded us and we will go wherever you send us.

וְהָגִיתָ בּוֹ יוֹמָם וָלַיְלָה לְמַעַן תִּשְׁמֹר לַעֲשׂוֹת כְּכָל־הַכָּתוּב בּוֹ כִּי־אָז תַּצְלִיחַ אֶת־דְּרָכֶךָ וְאָז תַּשְׂכִּיל:

9 הֲלוֹא צִוִּיתִיךָ חֲזַק וֶאֱמָץ אַל־תַּעֲרֹץ וְאַל־תֵּחָת כִּי עִמְּךָ יְהֹוָה אֱלֹהֶיךָ בְּכֹל אֲשֶׁר תֵּלֵךְ:

10 וַיְצַו יְהוֹשֻׁעַ אֶת־שֹׁטְרֵי הָעָם לֵאמֹר:

11 עִבְרוּ בְּקֶרֶב הַמַּחֲנֶה וְצַוּוּ אֶת־הָעָם לֵאמֹר הָכִינוּ לָכֶם צֵידָה כִּי בְּעוֹד שְׁלֹשֶׁת יָמִים אַתֶּם עֹבְרִים אֶת־הַיַּרְדֵּן הַזֶּה לָבוֹא לָרֶשֶׁת אֶת־הָאָרֶץ אֲשֶׁר יְהֹוָה אֱלֹהֵיכֶם נֹתֵן לָכֶם לְרִשְׁתָּהּ:

12 וְלָראוּבֵנִי וְלַגָּדִי וְלַחֲצִי שֵׁבֶט הַמְנַשֶּׁה אָמַר יְהוֹשֻׁעַ לֵאמֹר: 13 זָכוֹר אֶת־הַדָּבָר אֲשֶׁר צִוָּה אֶתְכֶם מֹשֶׁה עֶבֶד־יְהֹוָה לֵאמֹר יְהֹוָה אֱלֹהֵיכֶם מֵנִיחַ לָכֶם וְנָתַן לָכֶם אֶת־הָאָרֶץ הַזֹּאת: 14 נְשֵׁיכֶם טַפְּכֶם וּמִקְנֵיכֶם יֵשְׁבוּ בָּאָרֶץ אֲשֶׁר נָתַן לָכֶם מֹשֶׁה בְּעֵבֶר הַיַּרְדֵּן וְאַתֶּם תַּעַבְרוּ חֲמֻשִׁים לִפְנֵי אֲחֵיכֶם כֹּל גִּבּוֹרֵי הַחַיִל וַעֲזַרְתֶּם אוֹתָם: 15 עַד אֲשֶׁר־יָנִיחַ יְהֹוָה לַאֲחֵיכֶם כָּכֶם וְיָרְשׁוּ גַם־הֵמָּה אֶת־הָאָרֶץ אֲשֶׁר־יְהֹוָה אֱלֹהֵיכֶם נֹתֵן לָהֶם וְשַׁבְתֶּם לְאֶרֶץ יְרֻשַּׁתְכֶם וִירִשְׁתֶּם אוֹתָהּ אֲשֶׁר נָתַן לָכֶם מֹשֶׁה עֶבֶד יְהֹוָה בְּעֵבֶר הַיַּרְדֵּן מִזְרַח הַשָּׁמֶשׁ:

16 וַיַּעֲנוּ אֶת־יְהוֹשֻׁעַ לֵאמֹר כֹּל אֲשֶׁר־צִוִּיתָנוּ נַעֲשֶׂה וְאֶל־כָּל־אֲשֶׁר תִּשְׁלָחֵנוּ נֵלֵךְ:

b-b Lit. "across"

c Meaning of Heb. uncertain

17] We will obey you just as we obeyed Moses; let but the LORD your God be with you as He was with Moses!

18] Any man who flouts your commands and does not obey every order you give him shall be put to death. Only be strong and resolute!"

[17 כְּכֹל אֲשֶׁר־שָׁמַעְנוּ אֶל־מֹשֶׁה כֵּן נִשְׁמַע אֵלֶיךָ רַק יִהְיֶה יְהֹוָה אֱלֹהֶיךָ עִמָּךְ כַּאֲשֶׁר הָיָה עִם־מֹשֶׁה: 18] כָּל־אִישׁ אֲשֶׁר־יַמְרֶה אֶת־פִּיךָ וְלֹא־יִשְׁמַע אֶת־דְּבָרֶיךָ לְכֹל אֲשֶׁר־תְּצַוֶּנּוּ יוּמָת רַק חֲזַק וֶאֱמָץ:

494

Isaiah

66 : 1–24

Chapter 66

סו

1] Thus said the LORD:
The heaven is My throne
And the earth is My footstool:
Where could you build a house for Me.
What place could serve as My abode?

[1] כֹּה אָמַר יְהֹוָה
הַשָּׁמַיִם כִּסְאִי
וְהָאָרֶץ הֲדֹם רַגְלָי
אֵי־זֶה בַיִת אֲשֶׁר תִּבְנוּ־לִי
וְאֵי־זֶה מָקוֹם מְנוּחָתִי:

2] All this was made by My hand,
And thus it all came into being
—declares the LORD.
Yet to such a one I look:
To the poor and broken-hearted,
Who is concerned about My word.

[2] וְאֶת־כָּל־אֵלֶּה יָדִי עָשָׂתָה
וַיִּהְיוּ כָל־אֵלֶּה
נְאֻם־יְהֹוָה
וְאֶל־זֶה אַבִּיט
אֶל־עָנִי וּנְכֵה־רוּחַ
וְחָרֵד עַל־דְּבָרִי:

3] ^aAs for those who slaughter oxen and slay humans,
Who sacrifice sheep and immolate^b dogs,
Who present as oblation the blood of swine,
Who offer^c incense and worship false gods—
Just as they have chosen their ways
And take pleasure in their abominations,

[3] שׁוֹחֵט הַשּׁוֹר מַכֵּה־אִישׁ
זוֹבֵחַ הַשֶּׂה עֹרֵף כֶּלֶב
מַעֲלֵה מִנְחָה דַּם־חֲזִיר
מַזְכִּיר לְבֹנָה מְבָרֵךְ אָוֶן
גַּם־הֵמָּה בָּחֲרוּ בְּדַרְכֵיהֶם
וּבְשִׁקּוּצֵיהֶם נַפְשָׁם חָפֵצָה:

---

^a *Vv. 3–4 refer to practitioners of idolatrous rites; cf. v. 17 and 57.5–8; 65.1–12*
^b *Lit. "break the necks of"*
^c *Heb.* mazkir *refers to giving the "token portion"* (azkarah); *cf. Lev. 2.2*

4] So will I choose to mock them,
To bring on them the very thing they dread.
For I called and none responded,
I spoke and none paid heed.
They did what I hold evil
And chose what I do not want.

5] Hear the word of the LORD,
You who are concerned about His word!
Your kinsmen who hate you,
Who spurn you because of Me,[d] are saying,
"Let the LORD manifest His Presence,
So that we may look upon your joy."
But theirs shall be the shame.

6] Hark, tumult from the city,
Thunder from the Temple!
It is the thunder of the LORD
As He deals retribution to His foes.

7] Before she labored, she was delivered;
Before her pangs came, she bore a son.

8] Who ever heard the like?
Who ever witnessed such events?
Can a land pass through travail
In a single day?
Or is a nation born
All at once?
Yet Zion travailed
And at once bore her children!

[4 גַּם־אֲנִי אֶבְחַר בְּתַעֲלֻלֵיהֶם

וּמְגוּרֹתָם אָבִיא לָהֶם

יַעַן קָרָאתִי וְאֵין עוֹנֶה

דִּבַּרְתִּי וְלֹא שָׁמֵעוּ

וַיַּעֲשׂוּ הָרַע בְּעֵינַי

וּבַאֲשֶׁר לֹא־חָפַצְתִּי בָּחָרוּ׃

[5 שִׁמְעוּ דְּבַר־יְהֹוָה

הַחֲרֵדִים אֶל־דְּבָרוֹ

אָמְרוּ אֲחֵיכֶם שֹׂנְאֵיכֶם

מְנַדֵּיכֶם לְמַעַן שְׁמִי

יִכְבַּד יְהֹוָה

וְנִרְאֶה בְשִׂמְחַתְכֶם

וְהֵם יֵבֹשׁוּ׃

[6 קוֹל שָׁאוֹן מֵעִיר

קוֹל מֵהֵיכָל

קוֹל יְהֹוָה

מְשַׁלֵּם גְּמוּל לְאֹיְבָיו׃

[7 בְּטֶרֶם תָּחִיל יָלָדָה

בְּטֶרֶם יָבוֹא חֵבֶל לָהּ וְהִמְלִיטָה זָכָר׃

[8 מִי־שָׁמַע כָּזֹאת

מִי רָאָה כָּאֵלֶּה

הֲיוּחַל אֶרֶץ

בְּיוֹם אֶחָד

אִם־יִוָּלֵד גּוֹי

פַּעַם אֶחָת

כִּי־חָלָה

גַּם־יָלְדָה צִיּוֹן אֶת־בָּנֶיהָ׃

---

[d] Lit. "My name"

9] Shall I who bring on labor not bring about
   birth?
                    —says the LORD.
Shall I who cause birth shut the womb?
                    —said your GOD.

10] Rejoice with Jerusalem and be glad for her,
All you who love her!
Join in her jubilation,
All you who mourned over her—

11] That you may suck from her breast
Consolation to the full,
That you may draw from her bosom^e
Glory to your delight.

12] For thus said the LORD:
I will extend to her
Prosperity like a stream,
The wealth of nations
Like a wadi in flood;
And you shall drink of it.
You shall be carried on shoulders
And dandled upon knees.

13] As a mother comforts her son
So I will comfort you;
You shall find comfort in Jerusalem.

14] You shall see and your heart shall rejoice,
Your limbs shall flourish like grass.
The power of the LORD shall be revealed
In behalf of His servants;
But He shall rage against His foes.

9] הַאֲנִי אַשְׁבִּיר וְלֹא אוֹלִיד

יֹאמַר יְהֹוָה

אִם־אֲנִי הַמּוֹלִיד

וְעָצַרְתִּי

אָמַר אֱלֹהָיִךְ׃

10] שִׂמְחוּ אֶת־יְרוּשָׁלַ͏ִם וְגִילוּ בָה

כָּל־אֹהֲבֶיהָ

שִׂישׂוּ אִתָּהּ מָשׂוֹשׂ

כָּל־הַמִּתְאַבְּלִים עָלֶיהָ׃

11] לְמַעַן תִּינְקוּ

וּשְׂבַעְתֶּם מִשֹּׁד תַּנְחֻמֶיהָ

לְמַעַן תָּמֹצּוּ

וְהִתְעַנַּגְתֶּם מִזִּיז כְּבוֹדָהּ׃

12] כִּי־כֹה אָמַר יְהֹוָה

הִנְנִי נֹטֶה־אֵלֶיהָ

כְּנָהָר שָׁלוֹם

וּכְנַחַל שׁוֹטֵף

כְּבוֹד גּוֹיִם

וִינַקְתֶּם

עַל־צַד תִּנָּשֵׂאוּ

וְעַל־בִּרְכַּיִם תְּשָׁעֳשָׁעוּ׃

13] כְּאִישׁ אֲשֶׁר אִמּוֹ תְּנַחֲמֶנּוּ

כֵּן אָנֹכִי אֲנַחֶמְכֶם

וּבִירוּשָׁלַ͏ִם תְּנֻחָמוּ׃

14] וּרְאִיתֶם וְשָׂשׂ לִבְּכֶם

וְעַצְמוֹתֵיכֶם כַּדֶּשֶׁא תִפְרַחְנָה

וְנוֹדְעָה יַד־יְהֹוָה

אֶת־עֲבָדָיו

וְזָעַם אֶת־אֹיְבָיו׃

^e *Cf. Akkadian* zizu, *Arabic* zizat *"udder"*

497

15] See, the LORD is coming with fire—
His chariots are like a whirlwind—
To vent His anger in fury,
His rebuke in flaming fire.

16] For with fire will the LORD contend,
With His sword, against all flesh;
And many shall be the slain of the LORD.

17] Those who sanctify and purify themselves to enter the groves, ⁱ-imitating one in the center,-ⁱ eating the flesh of the swine, the reptile, and the mouse, shall one and all come to an end—declares the LORD.
18] ᵍFor I [know] their deeds and purposes.

[The time] has come to gather all the nations and tongues; they shall come and behold My glory.
19] I will set a sign among them, and send from them survivors to the nations: to Tarshish, Pul, and Lud—that draw the bow—to Tubal, Javan, and the distant coasts, that have never heard My fame nor beheld My glory. They shall declare My glory among these nations.

20] And out of all the nations, said the LORD, they shall bring all your brothers on horses, in chariots and drays, on mules and dromedaries, to Jerusalem My holy mountain as an offering to the LORD—just as the Israelites bring an offering in a pure vessel to the House of the LORD.
21] And from them likewise I will take some to be ʰ-levitical priests,-ʰ said the LORD.

22] For as the new heaven and the new earth
Which I will make

כִּי־הִנֵּה יְהֹוָה בָּאֵשׁ יָבוֹא [15
וְכַסּוּפָה מַרְכְּבֹתָיו
לְהָשִׁיב בְּחֵמָה אַפּוֹ
וְגַעֲרָתוֹ בְּלַהֲבֵי־אֵשׁ:
כִּי בָאֵשׁ יְהֹוָה נִשְׁפָּט [16
וּבְחַרְבּוֹ אֶת־כָּל־בָּשָׂר
וְרַבּוּ חַלְלֵי יְהֹוָה:

הַמִּתְקַדְּשִׁים וְהַמִּטַּהֲרִים אֶל־הַגַּנּוֹת [17
אַחַר אַחַת בַּתָּוֶךְ אֹכְלֵי בְּשַׂר הַחֲזִיר וְהַשֶּׁקֶץ
וְהָעַכְבָּר יַחְדָּו יָסֻפוּ נְאֻם־יְהֹוָה: [18 וְאָנֹכִי
מַעֲשֵׂיהֶם וּמַחְשְׁבֹתֵיהֶם:

בָּאָה לְקַבֵּץ אֶת־כָּל־הַגּוֹיִם וְהַלְּשֹׁנוֹת וּבָאוּ
וְרָאוּ אֶת־כְּבוֹדִי: [19 וְשַׂמְתִּי בָהֶם אוֹת
וְשִׁלַּחְתִּי מֵהֶם פְּלֵיטִים אֶל־הַגּוֹיִם תַּרְשִׁישׁ
פּוּל וְלוּד מֹשְׁכֵי קֶשֶׁת תֻּבַל וְיָוָן הָאִיִּים
הָרְחֹקִים אֲשֶׁר לֹא־שָׁמְעוּ אֶת־שִׁמְעִי וְלֹא־
רָאוּ אֶת־כְּבוֹדִי וְהִגִּידוּ אֶת־כְּבוֹדִי בַּגּוֹיִם:
וְהֵבִיאוּ אֶת־כָּל־אֲחֵיכֶם מִכָּל־הַגּוֹיִם מִנְחָה [20
לַיהֹוָה בַּסּוּסִים וּבָרֶכֶב וּבַצַּבִּים וּבַפְּרָדִים
וּבַכִּרְכָּרוֹת עַל הַר קָדְשִׁי יְרוּשָׁלַם אָמַר
יְהֹוָה כַּאֲשֶׁר יָבִיאוּ בְנֵי יִשְׂרָאֵל אֶת־הַמִּנְחָה
בִּכְלִי טָהוֹר בֵּית יְהֹוָה: [21 וְגַם־מֵהֶם אֶקַּח
לַכֹּהֲנִים לַלְוִיִּם אָמַר יְהֹוָה:

כִּי כַאֲשֶׁר הַשָּׁמַיִם הַחֲדָשִׁים וְהָאָרֶץ הַחֲדָשָׁה [22
אֲשֶׁר אֲנִי עֹשֶׂה

ⁱ-ⁱ Meaning of Heb. uncertain
ᵍ Exact construction of this verse uncertain; for the insertions in brackets, cf. Kimchi
ʰ-ʰ Some Heb. mss. read "priests and Levites"

Shall endure by My will
                   —declares the LORD—
So shall your seed and your name endure.

23] And new moon after new moon,
And sabbath after sabbath,
All flesh shall come to worship Me
                   —said the LORD.

24] They shall go out and gaze
On the corpses of the men who rebelled against
    Me:
Their worms shall not die,
Nor their fire be quenched;
They shall be a horror
To all flesh.

And new moon after new moon,
And sabbath after sabbath,
All flesh shall come to worship Me
                   —said the LORD.

עֹמְדִים לְפָנַי

נְאֻם־יְהֹוָה

כֵּן יַעֲמֹד זַרְעֲכֶם וְשִׁמְכֶם:

‫23‬ וְהָיָה מִדֵּי־חֹדֶשׁ בְּחָדְשׁוֹ

וּמִדֵּי שַׁבָּת בְּשַׁבַּתּוֹ

יָבוֹא כָל־בָּשָׂר לְהִשְׁתַּחֲוֹת לְפָנַי

אָמַר יְהֹוָה:

‫24‬ וְיָצְאוּ וְרָאוּ

בְּפִגְרֵי הָאֲנָשִׁים הַפֹּשְׁעִים בִּי

כִּי תוֹלַעְתָּם לֹא תָמוּת

וְאִשָּׁם לֹא תִכְבֶּה

וְהָיוּ דֵרָאוֹן

לְכָל־בָּשָׂר:

וְהָיָה מִדֵּי־חֹדֶשׁ בְּחָדְשׁוֹ

וּמִדֵּי שַׁבָּת בְּשַׁבַּתּוֹ

יָבוֹא כָל־בָּשָׂר לְהִשְׁתַּחֲוֹת לְפָנַי

אָמַר יְהֹוָה:

מחר חדש

First Samuel

20 : 18-42

Chapter 20

18] Jonathan said to him, "Tomorrow will be the new moon; and you will be missed when your seat remains vacant.*ʰ*

19] So the day after tomorrow, go down *ⁱ⁻*all the way*⁻ⁱ* to the place where you hid *ⁱ⁻*the other time,*ⁱ⁻* and stay close to the Ezel stone.

20] Now I will shoot three arrows to one side of it, as though I were shooting at a mark,

21] and I will order the boy to go and find the arrows. If I call to the boy, 'Hey! the arrows are on this side of you,' be reassured*ᵏ* and come, for you are safe and there is no danger—as the LORD lives!

22] But if, instead, I call to the lad, 'Hey! the arrows are beyond you,' then leave, for the LORD has sent you away.

23] As for the promise we made to each other,*ˡ* may the LORD be [witness] between you and me forever."

24] David hid in the field. The new moon came, and the king sat down to partake of the meal.

25] When the king took his usual place on the seat by the wall, Jonathan rose*ᵐ* and Abner sat down at Saul's side; but David's place remained vacant.

ʰ At the festal meal
ⁱ⁻ⁱ Lit. "very much"
ⁱ⁻ʲ Lit. "on the day of the incident"; see 19.2 ff.
ᵏ Lit. "accept it"
ˡ See vv. 12–17
ᵐ Force of Heb. uncertain; Septuagint "faced him"

כ

18] וַיֹּאמֶר־לוֹ יְהוֹנָתָן מָחָר חֹדֶשׁ וְנִפְקַדְתָּ כִּי יִפָּקֵד מוֹשָׁבֶךָ׃ 19] וְשִׁלַּשְׁתָּ תֵּרֵד מְאֹד וּבָאתָ אֶל־הַמָּקוֹם אֲשֶׁר־נִסְתַּרְתָּ שָּׁם בְּיוֹם הַמַּעֲשֶׂה וְיָשַׁבְתָּ אֵצֶל הָאֶבֶן הָאָזֶל׃ 20] וַאֲנִי שְׁלֹשֶׁת הַחִצִּים צִדָּה אוֹרֶה לְשַׁלַּח־לִי לְמַטָּרָה׃ 21] וְהִנֵּה אֶשְׁלַח אֶת־הַנַּעַר לֵךְ מְצָא אֶת־הַחִצִּים אִם־אָמֹר אֹמַר לַנַּעַר הִנֵּה הַחִצִּים מִמְּךָ וָהֵנָּה קָחֶנּוּ וָבֹאָה כִּי־שָׁלוֹם לְךָ וְאֵין דָּבָר חַי־יְהוָֹה׃ 22] וְאִם־כֹּה אֹמַר לָעֶלֶם הִנֵּה הַחִצִּים מִמְּךָ וָהָלְאָה לֵךְ כִּי שִׁלַּחֲךָ יְהוָֹה׃ 23] וְהַדָּבָר אֲשֶׁר דִּבַּרְנוּ אֲנִי וָאָתָּה הִנֵּה יְהוָֹה בֵּינִי וּבֵינְךָ עַד־עוֹלָם׃

24] וַיִּסָּתֵר דָּוִד בַּשָּׂדֶה וַיְהִי הַחֹדֶשׁ וַיֵּשֶׁב הַמֶּלֶךְ אֶל־הַלֶּחֶם לֶאֱכוֹל׃ 25] וַיֵּשֶׁב הַמֶּלֶךְ עַל־מוֹשָׁבוֹ כְּפַעַם בְּפַעַם אֶל־מוֹשַׁב הַקִּיר וַיָּקָם יְהוֹנָתָן וַיֵּשֶׁב אַבְנֵר מִצַּד שָׁאוּל וַיִּפָּקֵד

26] That day, however, Saul said nothing. "It's accidental," he thought. *ⁿ*-"He must be unclean and not yet cleansed."-*ⁿ*

27] But on the day after the new moon, the second day, David's place was vacant again. So Saul said to his son Jonathan, "Why didn't the son of Jesse*ᵒ* come to the meal yesterday or today?"

28] Jonathan answered Saul, "David begged leave of me to go to Bethlehem.

29] He said, 'Please let me go, for we are going to have a family feast in our town and my brother has summoned me to it. Do me a favor, let me slip away to see my kinsmen.' That is why he has not come to the king's table."

30] Saul flew into a rage against Jonathan. "You son of a perverse, rebellious woman!" he shouted. "I know that you side with the son of Jesse—to your shame, and to the shame of your mother's nakedness!

31] For as long as the son of Jesse lives on earth, neither you nor your kingship will be secure. Now then, have him brought to me, for he is marked for death."

32] But Jonathan spoke up and said to his father, "Why should he be put to death? What has he done?"

33] At that, Saul threw*ᵖ* his spear at him to strike him down; and Jonathan realized that his father was determined to do away with David.

34] Jonathan rose from the table in a rage. He ate no food on the second day of the new moon, because he was grieved about David, and because his father had humiliated him.

35] In the morning, Jonathan went out into the open for the meeting with David accompanied by a young boy.

36] He said to the boy, "Run ahead and find the arrows that I shoot." And as

מְקוֹם דָּוִד: 26] וְלֹא־דִבֶּר שָׁאוּל מְאוּמָה בַּיּוֹם הַהוּא כִּי אָמַר מִקְרֶה הוּא בִּלְתִּי טָהוֹר הוּא כִּי־לֹא טָהוֹר: 27] וַיְהִי מִמָּחֳרַת הַחֹדֶשׁ הַשֵּׁנִי וַיִּפָּקֵד מְקוֹם דָּוִד וַיֹּאמֶר שָׁאוּל אֶל־יְהוֹנָתָן בְּנוֹ מַדּוּעַ לֹא־בָא בֶן־יִשַׁי גַּם־תְּמוֹל גַּם־הַיּוֹם אֶל־הַלָּחֶם: 28] וַיַּעַן יְהוֹנָתָן אֶת־שָׁאוּל נִשְׁאֹל נִשְׁאַל דָּוִד מֵעִמָּדִי עַד־בֵּית לָחֶם: 29] וַיֹּאמֶר שַׁלְּחֵנִי נָא כִּי זֶבַח מִשְׁפָּחָה לָנוּ בָּעִיר וְהוּא צִוָּה־לִי אָחִי וְעַתָּה אִם־מָצָאתִי חֵן בְּעֵינֶיךָ אִמָּלְטָה נָּא וְאֶרְאֶה אֶת־אֶחָי עַל־כֵּן לֹא־בָא אֶל־שֻׁלְחַן הַמֶּלֶךְ:

30] וַיִּחַר־אַף שָׁאוּל בִּיהוֹנָתָן וַיֹּאמֶר לוֹ בֶּן־נַעֲוַת הַמַּרְדּוּת הֲלוֹא יָדַעְתִּי כִּי־בֹחֵר אַתָּה לְבֶן־יִשַׁי לְבָשְׁתְּךָ וּלְבֹשֶׁת עֶרְוַת אִמֶּךָ: 31] כִּי כָל־הַיָּמִים אֲשֶׁר בֶּן־יִשַׁי חַי עַל־הָאֲדָמָה לֹא תִכּוֹן אַתָּה וּמַלְכוּתֶךָ וְעַתָּה שְׁלַח וְקַח אֹתוֹ אֵלַי כִּי בֶן־מָוֶת הוּא: 32] וַיַּעַן יְהוֹנָתָן אֶת־שָׁאוּל אָבִיו וַיֹּאמֶר אֵלָיו לָמָּה יוּמַת מֶה עָשָׂה: 33] וַיָּטֶל שָׁאוּל אֶת־הַחֲנִית עָלָיו לְהַכֹּתוֹ וַיֵּדַע יְהוֹנָתָן כִּי־כָלָה הִיא מֵעִם אָבִיו לְהָמִית אֶת־דָּוִד: 34] וַיָּקָם יְהוֹנָתָן מֵעִם הַשֻּׁלְחָן בָּחֳרִי־אָף וְלֹא־אָכַל בְּיוֹם־הַחֹדֶשׁ הַשֵּׁנִי לֶחֶם כִּי נֶעְצַב אֶל־דָּוִד כִּי הִכְלִמוֹ אָבִיו:

35] וַיְהִי בַבֹּקֶר וַיֵּצֵא יְהוֹנָתָן הַשָּׂדֶה לְמוֹעֵד דָּוִד וְנַעַר קָטֹן עִמּוֹ: 36] וַיֹּאמֶר לְנַעֲרוֹ רֻץ מְצָא נָא אֶת־הַחִצִּים אֲשֶׁר אָנֹכִי מוֹרֶה הַנַּעַר

ⁿ⁻ⁿ Heb. construction unclear

ᵒ To refer to a person merely as "the son (ben) of . . ." is slighting; cf. 10.11; 20:30, 31; Isa. 7:4

ᵖ As in 18.11, change of vocalization yields "raised"

the boy ran, he shot the arrows past him. 37] When the boy came to the place where the arrows shot by Jonathan had fallen, Jonathan called out to the boy, "Hey, the arrows are beyond you!"

38] And Jonathan called after the boy, "Quick, hurry up. Don't stop!" So Jonathan's boy gathered the arrows and came back to his master.—

39] The boy suspected nothing; only Jonathan and David knew the arrangement.—

40] Jonathan handed the gear to his boy and told him, "Take these back to the town."

41] When the boy got there, David [q]emerged from his concealment at[q] the Negeb.[r] He flung himself face down on the ground and bowed low three times. They kissed each other and wept together; David wept the longer.

42] Jonathan said to David, "Go in peace! For we two have sworn to each other in the name of the LORD: 'May the LORD be [witness] between you and me, and between your offspring and mine, forever!' "

רָץ וְהוּא־יָרָה הַחֵצִי לְהַעֲבִרוֹ׃ 37] וַיָּבֹא
הַנַּעַר עַד־מְקוֹם הַחֵצִי אֲשֶׁר יָרָה יְהוֹנָתָן
וַיִּקְרָא יְהוֹנָתָן אַחֲרֵי הַנַּעַר וַיֹּאמֶר הֲלוֹא
הַחֵצִי מִמְּךָ וָהָלְאָה׃ 38] וַיִּקְרָא יְהוֹנָתָן אַחֲרֵי
הַנַּעַר מְהֵרָה חוּשָׁה אַל־תַּעֲמֹד וַיְלַקֵּט נַעַר
יְהוֹנָתָן אֶת־הַחִצִּים וַיָּבֹא אֶל־אֲדֹנָיו׃ 39] וְהַנַּעַר
לֹא־יָדַע מְאוּמָה אַךְ יְהוֹנָתָן וְדָוִד יָדְעוּ אֶת־
הַדָּבָר׃ 40] וַיִּתֵּן יְהוֹנָתָן אֶת־כֵּלָיו אֶל־הַנַּעַר
אֲשֶׁר־לוֹ וַיֹּאמֶר לוֹ לֵךְ הָבֵיא הָעִיר׃ 41] הַנַּעַר
בָּא וְדָוִד קָם מֵאֵצֶל הַנֶּגֶב וַיִּפֹּל לְאַפָּיו אַרְצָה
וַיִּשְׁתַּחוּ שָׁלֹשׁ פְּעָמִים וַיִּשְּׁקוּ אִישׁ אֶת־רֵעֵהוּ
וַיִּבְכּוּ אִישׁ אֶת־רֵעֵהוּ עַד־דָּוִד הִגְדִּיל׃

42] וַיֹּאמֶר יְהוֹנָתָן לְדָוִד לֵךְ לְשָׁלוֹם אֲשֶׁר
נִשְׁבַּעְנוּ שְׁנֵינוּ אֲנַחְנוּ בְּשֵׁם יְהוָה לֵאמֹר יְהוָה
יִהְיֶה בֵּינִי וּבֵינֶךָ וּבֵין זַרְעִי וּבֵין זַרְעֲךָ עַד־
עוֹלָם׃

[q-q] *Lit. "rose up from beside"*

[r] *Identical with the "Ezel Stone," v. 19*

Hosea

14 : 2 - 10

Chapter 14

2] Return, O Israel, to the Lord your God,
For you have fallen because of your sin.

3] Take words with you
And return to the Lord.
Say to Him:
ᵃ"Forgive all guilt
And accept what is good;
Instead of bulls we will pay
[The offering of] our lips."*ᵃ*

4] Assyria shall not save us,
No more will we ride on steeds;*ᵇ*
Nor ever again will we call
Our handiwork our god,
Since in You alone orphans find pity!"

5] I will heal their affliction,*ᶜ*
Generously will I take them back in love;
For My anger has turned away from them.*ᵈ*

יד

2] שׁוּבָה יִשְׂרָאֵל עַד יְהֹוָה אֱלֹהֶיךָ

כִּי כָשַׁלְתָּ בַּעֲוֺנֶךָ:

3] קְחוּ עִמָּכֶם דְּבָרִים

וְשׁוּבוּ אֶל־יְהֹוָה

אִמְרוּ אֵלָיו

כָּל־תִּשָּׂא עָוֺן

וְקַח־טוֹב

וּנְשַׁלְּמָה פָרִים שְׂפָתֵינוּ:

4] אַשּׁוּר לֹא יוֹשִׁיעֵנוּ

עַל־סוּס לֹא נִרְכָּב

וְלֹא־נֹאמַר עוֹד

אֱלֹהֵינוּ לְמַעֲשֵׂה יָדֵינוּ

אֲשֶׁר־בְּךָ יְרֻחַם יָתוֹם:

5] אֶרְפָּא מְשׁוּבָתָם

אֹהֲבֵם נְדָבָה

כִּי שָׁב אַפִּי מִמֶּנּוּ:

ᵃ⁻ᵃ Meaning of Heb. uncertain
ᵇ I.e., we will no longer depend on an alliance with Egypt; cf. II Kings 18.24 ‖ Isa.
  36.9; Isa. 30.16
ᶜ For this meaning of meshuvah *see Jer. 2.19; 3.22*
ᵈ Heb. "him"

6] I will be to Israel like dew;
He shall blossom like the lily,
He shall strike root like a ͤ⁻Lebanon tree.⁻ͤ

אֶהְיֶ֤ה כַטַּל֙ לְיִשְׂרָאֵ֔ל

יִפְרַ֖ח כַּשּֽׁוֹשַׁנָּ֑ה

וְיַ֥ךְ שָׁרָשָׁ֖יו כַּלְּבָנֽוֹן׃

7] His boughs shall spread out far,
His beauty shall be like the olive tree's,
His fragrance like that of Lebanon.

יֵלְכוּ֙ יֽוֹנְקוֹתָ֔יו

וִיהִ֥י כַזַּ֖יִת הוֹד֑וֹ

וְרֵ֥יחַֽ ל֖וֹ כַּלְּבָנֽוֹן׃

8] They who sit in his shade shall be revived:
They shall bring to life new grain,
They shall blossom like the vine;
His scent shall be like the wine of Lebanon.ᶠ

יָשֻׁ֨בוּ֙ יֹשְׁבֵ֣י בְצִלּ֔וֹ

יְחַיּ֥וּ דָגָ֖ן וְיִפְרְח֣וּ כַגָּ֑פֶן

זִכְר֖וֹ כְּיֵ֥ין לְבָנֽוֹן׃

9] Ephraim [shall say]:
"What more have I to do with idols?
When I respond and look to Him,
I become like a verdant cypress."
ᵃ⁻Your fruit is provided by Me.⁻ᵃ

אֶפְרַ֕יִם

מַה־לִּ֥י ע֖וֹד לָֽעֲצַבִּ֑ים

אֲנִ֤י עָנִ֙יתִי֙ וַאֲשׁוּרֶ֔נּוּ

אֲנִ֙י כִּבְר֣וֹשׁ רַֽעֲנָ֔ן

מִמֶּ֖נִּי פֶּרְיְךָ֥ נִמְצָֽא׃

10] He who is wise will consider these words,
He who is prudent will take note of them.
For the paths of the LORD are smooth;
The righteous can walk on them,
While sinners stumble on them.

מִ֤י חָכָם֙ וְיָ֣בֵֽן אֵ֔לֶּה

נָב֖וֹן וְיֵֽדָעֵ֑ם

כִּֽי־יְשָׁרִ֞ים דַּרְכֵ֣י יְהֹוָ֗ה

וְצַדִּקִים֙ יֵ֣לְכוּ בָ֔ם

וּפֹשְׁעִ֖ים יִכָּ֥שְׁלוּ בָֽם׃

ͤ⁻ͤ *Emendation yields "poplar"*
ᶠ *Emendation yields "Helbon"; cf. Ezek. 27.18*
ᵃ⁻ᵃ *Meaning of Heb. uncertain*

Micah

7 : 18-20

Chapter 7

18] Who is a God like You,
Forgiving iniquity
And remitting transgression;
Who has not maintained His wrath forever
Against the remnant of His own people,
Because He loves graciousness!

19] He will take us back in love;
He will cover up our iniquities,
You will hurl all our[i] sins
Into the depths of the sea.

20] You will keep faith with Jacob,
Loyalty to Abraham,
As You promised on oath to our fathers
In days gone by.

ז

[18] מִי־אֵל כָּמוֹךָ
נֹשֵׂא עָוֹן וְעֹבֵר עַל־פֶּשַׁע
לִשְׁאֵרִית נַחֲלָתוֹ
לֹא־הֶחֱזִיק לָעַד אַפּוֹ
כִּי־חָפֵץ חֶסֶד הוּא:

[19] יָשׁוּב יְרַחֲמֵנוּ
יִכְבֹּשׁ עֲוֹנֹתֵינוּ
וְתַשְׁלִיךְ בִּמְצֻלוֹת יָם
כָּל־חַטֹּאתָם:

[20] תִּתֵּן אֱמֶת לְיַעֲקֹב
חֶסֶד לְאַבְרָהָם
אֲשֶׁר־נִשְׁבַּעְתָּ לַאֲבֹתֵינוּ
מִימֵי קֶדֶם:

Joel

2 : 15-27

Chapter 2

15] Blow a horn in Zion,
Solemnize a fast,
Proclaim an assembly!

16] Gather the people,
Bid the congregation purify themselves.[d]

ב

[15] תִּקְעוּ שׁוֹפָר בְּצִיּוֹן קַדְּשׁוּ־צוֹם
קִרְאוּ עֲצָרָה:
[16] אִסְפוּ־עָם
קַדְּשׁוּ קָהָל

---

[i] Heb. "their" [d] Cf. Exod. 19.10; Zeph. 1.7

Bring together the old,
Gather the babes
And the sucklings at the breast;
Let the bridegroom come out of his chamber,
The bride from her canopied couch.

17] Between the portico and the altar,
Let the priests, the LORD's ministers, weep
And say:
"Oh, spare Your people, LORD!
Let not Your possession become a mockery,
To be taunted by nations!
Let not the peoples say,
'Where is their God?'"

18] Then the LORD was roused
On behalf of His land
And had compassion
Upon His people.
19] In response to His people
The LORD declared:
"I will grant you the new grain,
The new wine, and the new oil,
And you shall have them in abundance.
Nevermore will I let you be
A mockery among the nations.

20] I will drive the northerner[e] far from you,
I will thrust it into a parched and desolate land—
Its van to the Eastern Sea[f]
And its rear to the Western Sea;[g]
And the stench of it shall go up,
And the foul smell rise."
For [the LORD] shall work great deeds.

קִבְצוּ זְקֵנִים אִסְפוּ עוֹלָלִים וְיֹנְקֵי שָׁדָיִם

יֵצֵא חָתָן מֵחֶדְרוֹ
וְכַלָּה מֵחֻפָּתָהּ:

17] בֵּין הָאוּלָם וְלַמִּזְבֵּחַ

יִבְכּוּ הַכֹּהֲנִים מְשָׁרְתֵי יְהוָֹה

וְיֹאמְרוּ

חוּסָה יְהוָֹה עַל־עַמֶּךָ

וְאַל־תִּתֵּן נַחֲלָתְךָ לְחֶרְפָּה

לִמְשָׁל־בָּם גּוֹיִם

לָמָּה יֹאמְרוּ בָעַמִּים

אַיֵּה אֱלֹהֵיהֶם:

18] וַיְקַנֵּא יְהוָֹה לְאַרְצוֹ

וַיַּחְמֹל עַל־עַמּוֹ:

19] וַיַּעַן יְהוָֹה וַיֹּאמֶר לְעַמּוֹ

הִנְנִי שֹׁלֵחַ לָכֶם אֶת־הַדָּגָן

וְהַתִּירוֹשׁ וְהַיִּצְהָר

וּשְׂבַעְתֶּם אֹתוֹ

וְלֹא־אֶתֵּן אֶתְכֶם עוֹד

חֶרְפָּה בַּגּוֹיִם:

20] וְאֶת־הַצְּפוֹנִי אַרְחִיק מֵעֲלֵיכֶם

וְהִדַּחְתִּיו אֶל־אֶרֶץ צִיָּה וּשְׁמָמָה

אֶת־פָּנָיו אֶל־הַיָּם הַקַּדְמֹנִי

וְסֹפוֹ אֶל־הַיָּם הָאַחֲרוֹן

וְעָלָה בָאְשׁוֹ

וְתַעַל צַחֲנָתוֹ

כִּי הִגְדִּיל לַעֲשׂוֹת:

---

[e] I.e., the locusts. Emendation yields "My multitude"; cf. "nation" (1.6), "horde,"
  "army," and "host" (2.2, 5, 11, and 25)
[f] The Dead Sea
[g] The Mediterranean Sea

21] Fear not, O soil, rejoice and be glad;
For the LORD has wrought great deeds.

22] Fear not, O beasts of the field,
For the pastures in the wilderness
Are clothed with grass.
The trees have borne their fruit;
Fig tree and vine
Have yielded their strength.

23] O children of Zion, be glad,
Rejoice in the LORD your God.
For He has given you the early rain in [His]
    kindness,
Now He makes the rain fall [as] formerly—
The early rain and the late—

24] And threshing floors shall be piled with grain,
And vats shall overflow with new wine and oil.

25] "I will repay you *h*-for the years-*h*
Consumed by swarms and hoppers,
By grubs and locusts,
The great army I let loose against you.

26] And you shall eat your fill
And praise the name of the LORD your God
Who dealt so wondrously with you—
My people shall be shamed no more.

27] And you shall know
That I am in the midst of Israel:
That I the LORD am your God
And there is no other.
And My people shall be shamed no more."

[21] אַל־תִּירְאִי אֲדָמָה

גִּילִי וּשְׂמָחִי

כִּי־הִגְדִּיל יְהוָה לַעֲשׂוֹת:

[22] אַל־תִּירְאוּ בַּהֲמוֹת שָׂדַי

כִּי דָשְׁאוּ נְאוֹת מִדְבָּר

כִּי־עֵץ נָשָׂא פִרְיוֹ

תְּאֵנָה וָגֶפֶן נָתְנוּ חֵילָם:

[23] וּבְנֵי צִיּוֹן

גִּילוּ וְשִׂמְחוּ בַּיהוָה אֱלֹהֵיכֶם

כִּי־נָתַן לָכֶם אֶת־הַמּוֹרֶה לִצְדָקָה

וַיּוֹרֶד לָכֶם גֶּשֶׁם

מוֹרֶה וּמַלְקוֹשׁ בָּרִאשׁוֹן:

[24] וּמָלְאוּ הַגְּרָנוֹת בָּר

וְהֵשִׁיקוּ הַיְקָבִים תִּירוֹשׁ וְיִצְהָר:

[25] וְשִׁלַּמְתִּי לָכֶם אֶת־הַשָּׁנִים

אֲשֶׁר אָכַל הָאַרְבֶּה

הַיֶּלֶק וְהֶחָסִיל וְהַגָּזָם

חֵילִי הַגָּדוֹל אֲשֶׁר שִׁלַּחְתִּי בָּכֶם:

[26] וַאֲכַלְתֶּם אָכוֹל וְשָׂבוֹעַ

וְהִלַּלְתֶּם אֶת־שֵׁם יְהוָה אֱלֹהֵיכֶם

אֲשֶׁר־עָשָׂה עִמָּכֶם לְהַפְלִיא

וְלֹא־יֵבֹשׁוּ עַמִּי לְעוֹלָם:

[27] וִידַעְתֶּם כִּי בְקֶרֶב יִשְׂרָאֵל אָנִי

וַאֲנִי יְהוָה אֱלֹהֵיכֶם וְאֵין עוֹד

וְלֹא־יֵבֹשׁוּ עַמִּי לְעוֹלָם:

h-h Emendation yields "double what was"

507

FIRST SELECTION

Zechariah

14:7-9, 16-21

Chapter 14

7] But there shall be a continuous day—only the Lord knows when—of neither day nor night, and there shall be light at eventide.

8] In that day, fresh water shall flow from Jerusalem, part of it to the Eastern Sea*d* and part to the Western Sea,*e* throughout the summer and winter.

9] And the Lord shall be king over all the earth; in that day there shall be one Lord with one name.*f*

- - -

16] All who survive of all those nations that came up against Jerusalem shall make a pilgrimage year by year to bow low to the King Lord of Hosts and to observe the Feast of Booths.

17] Any of the earth's communities that does not make the pilgrimage to Jerusalem to bow low to the King Lord of Hosts shall receive no rain.

18] However, if the community of Egypt does not make this pilgrimage, it shall not be visited by the same affliction with which the Lord will

יד

7] וְהָיָה יוֹם־אֶחָד הוּא יִוָּדַע לַיהוָֹה לֹא־יוֹם וְלֹא־לָיְלָה וְהָיָה לְעֵת־עֶרֶב יִהְיֶה־אוֹר:

8] וְהָיָה בַּיּוֹם הַהוּא יֵצְאוּ מַיִם־חַיִּים מִירוּשָׁלַם חֶצְיָם אֶל־הַיָּם הַקַּדְמוֹנִי וְחֶצְיָם אֶל־הַיָּם הָאַחֲרוֹן בַּקַּיִץ וּבָחֹרֶף יִהְיֶה:

9] וְהָיָה יְהוָֹה לְמֶלֶךְ עַל־כָּל־הָאָרֶץ בַּיּוֹם הַהוּא יִהְיֶה יְהוָֹה אֶחָד וּשְׁמוֹ אֶחָד:

- - -

16] וְהָיָה כָּל־הַנּוֹתָר מִכָּל־הַגּוֹיִם הַבָּאִים עַל־יְרוּשָׁלָם וְעָלוּ מִדֵּי שָׁנָה בְשָׁנָה לְהִשְׁתַּחֲוֺת לְמֶלֶךְ יְהוָֹה צְבָאוֹת וְלָחֹג אֶת־חַג הַסֻּכּוֹת:

17] וְהָיָה אֲשֶׁר לֹא־יַעֲלֶה מֵאֵת מִשְׁפְּחוֹת הָאָרֶץ אֶל־יְרוּשָׁלַם לְהִשְׁתַּחֲוֺת לְמֶלֶךְ יְהוָֹה צְבָאוֹת וְלֹא עֲלֵיהֶם יִהְיֶה הַגָּשֶׁם: 18] וְאִם־מִשְׁפַּחַת מִצְרַיִם לֹא־תַעֲלֶה וְלֹא בָאָה וְלֹא עֲלֵיהֶם תִּהְיֶה הַמַּגֵּפָה אֲשֶׁר יִגֹּף יְהוָֹה אֶת־הַגּוֹיִם אֲשֶׁר

---

d I.e., the Dead Sea; cf. Joel 2.20

e I.e., the Mediterranean Sea; cf. Joel 2.20

f I.e., the Lord alone shall be worshiped and shall be invoked by His true name

strike the other nations that do not come up to observe the Feast of Booths.[i]

19] Such shall be the punishment of Egypt and of all other nations that do not come up to observe the Feast of Booths.

20] In that day, even the bells on the horses shall be inscribed "Holy to the LORD." The metal pots in the House of the LORD shall be like the basins before the altar;

21] indeed, every metal pot in Jerusalem and in Judah shall be holy to the LORD of Hosts. And all those who sacrifice shall come and take of these to boil [their sacrificial meat] in; in that day there shall be no more traders[k] in the House of the LORD of Hosts.

לֹא יַעֲלוּ לָחֹג אֶת־חַג הַסֻּכּוֹת: 19] וְאֹת תִּהְיֶה חַטַּאת מִצְרָיִם וְחַטַּאת כָּל־הַגּוֹיִם אֲשֶׁר לֹא יַעֲלוּ לָחֹג אֶת־חַג הַסֻּכּוֹת:

20] בַּיּוֹם הַהוּא יִהְיֶה עַל־מְצִלּוֹת הַסּוּס קֹדֶשׁ לַיהוָֹה וְהָיָה הַסִּירוֹת בְּבֵית יְהוָֹה כַּמִּזְרָקִים לִפְנֵי הַמִּזְבֵּחַ: 21] וְהָיָה כָּל־סִיר בִּירוּשָׁלַםִ וּבִיהוּדָה קֹדֶשׁ לַיהוָֹה צְבָאוֹת וּבָאוּ כָּל־הַזֹּבְחִים וְלָקְחוּ מֵהֶם וּבִשְּׁלוּ בָהֶם וְלֹא־יִהְיֶה כְנַעֲנִי עוֹד בְּבֵית־יְהוָֹה צְבָאוֹת בַּיּוֹם הַהוּא:

SECOND SELECTION

Ecclesiastes

1 : 1–18

Chapter 1

א

1] The words of Koheleth, the son of David, king in Jerusalem.
2] Vanity of vanities, says Koheleth; Vanity of vanities, all is vanity.

3] What profit has man of all his labor Wherein he labors under the sun?

4] One generation passes away, and another generation comes; And the earth abides for ever.

5] The sun also arises, and the sun goes down, And hastens to his place where he arises.

1] דִּבְרֵי קֹהֶלֶת בֶּן־דָּוִד מֶלֶךְ בִּירוּשָׁלָםִ:

2] הֲבֵל הֲבָלִים אָמַר קֹהֶלֶת הֲבֵל הֲבָלִים הַכֹּל הָבֶל:

3] מַה־יִּתְרוֹן לָאָדָם בְּכָל־עֲמָלוֹ שֶׁיַּעֲמֹל תַּחַת הַשָּׁמֶשׁ:

4] דּוֹר הֹלֵךְ וְדוֹר בָּא וְהָאָרֶץ לְעוֹלָם עֹמָדֶת:

5] וְזָרַח הַשֶּׁמֶשׁ וּבָא הַשָּׁמֶשׁ וְאֶל־מְקוֹמוֹ שׁוֹאֵף זוֹרֵחַ הוּא שָׁם:

---

[i] *Because Egypt is not dependent on rain, it will suffer some other punishment, presumably that described in v. 12*

[k] *To sell ritually pure vessels*

509

6] The wind goes toward the south,
And turns about to the north;
It turns about continually in its circuit,
And the wind returns again to its circuits.

7] All the rivers run into the sea,
Yet the sea is not full;
Unto the place where the rivers go,
There they go again.

8] All things toil to weariness;
Man cannot utter it,
The eye is not satisfied with seeing,
Nor the ear filled with hearing.

9] That which has been is that which shall be,
And that which has been done is that which shall
   be done;
And there is nothing new under the sun.

10] Is there a thing whereof it is said: "See, this is
new"?—it has been already, in the ages which
were before us.

11] There is no remembrance
of them of former times; neither shall there be
any remembrance of them of latter times that are
to come, among those that shall come after.

12] I Koheleth have been king over Israel in
Jerusalem.

13] And I applied my heart to seek
and to search out by wisdom concerning all things
that are done under heaven; it is a sore task that
God has given to the sons of men to be exercised
therewith.

14] I have seen all the works that
are done under the sun; and, behold, all is vanity
and a striving after wind.

15] That which is crooked cannot be made
   straight;
And that which is wanting cannot be numbered.

16] I spoke with my own heart, saying:"Lo, I have
gotten great wisdom, more also than all that were

הוֹלֵךְ אֶל־דָּרוֹם [6

וְסוֹבֵב אֶל־צָפוֹן

סוֹבֵב סֹבֵב הוֹלֵךְ הָרוּחַ

וְעַל־סְבִיבֹתָיו שָׁב הָרוּחַ:

כָּל־הַנְּחָלִים הֹלְכִים אֶל־הַיָּם [7

וְהַיָּם אֵינֶנּוּ מָלֵא

אֶל־מְקוֹם שֶׁהַנְּחָלִים הֹלְכִים

שָׁם הֵם שָׁבִים לָלָכֶת:

כָּל־הַדְּבָרִים יְגֵעִים [8

לֹא־יוּכַל אִישׁ לְדַבֵּר

לֹא־תִשְׂבַּע עַיִן לִרְאוֹת

וְלֹא־תִמָּלֵא אֹזֶן מִשְּׁמֹעַ:

מַה־שֶּׁהָיָה הוּא שֶׁיִּהְיֶה [9

וּמַה־שֶּׁנַּעֲשָׂה הוּא שֶׁיֵּעָשֶׂה

וְאֵין כָּל־חָדָשׁ תַּחַת הַשָּׁמֶשׁ:

יֵשׁ דָּבָר שֶׁיֹּאמַר רְאֵה־זֶה חָדָשׁ הוּא כְּבָר [10

הָיָה לְעֹלָמִים אֲשֶׁר הָיָה מִלְּפָנֵנוּ: אֵין [11

זִכְרוֹן לָרִאשֹׁנִים וְגַם לָאַחֲרֹנִים שֶׁיִּהְיוּ לֹא־

יִהְיֶה לָהֶם זִכָּרוֹן עִם שֶׁיִּהְיוּ לָאַחֲרֹנָה:

אֲנִי קֹהֶלֶת הָיִיתִי מֶלֶךְ עַל־יִשְׂרָאֵל [12

בִּירוּשָׁלָ͏ִם: וְנָתַתִּי אֶת־לִבִּי לִדְרוֹשׁ וְלָתוּר [13

בַּחָכְמָה עַל כָּל־אֲשֶׁר נַעֲשָׂה תַּחַת הַשָּׁמָיִם

הוּא עִנְיַן רָע נָתַן אֱלֹהִים לִבְנֵי הָאָדָם לַעֲנוֹת

בּוֹ: רָאִיתִי אֶת־כָּל־הַמַּעֲשִׂים שֶׁנַּעֲשׂוּ תַּחַת [14

הַשָּׁמֶשׁ וְהִנֵּה הַכֹּל הֶבֶל וּרְעוּת רוּחַ:

מְעֻוָּת לֹא־יוּכַל לִתְקֹן [15

וְחֶסְרוֹן לֹא־יוּכַל לְהִמָּנוֹת:

דִּבַּרְתִּי אֲנִי עִם־לִבִּי לֵאמֹר אֲנִי הִנֵּה [16

הִגְדַּלְתִּי וְהוֹסַפְתִּי חָכְמָה עַל כָּל־אֲשֶׁר־הָיָה

before me over Jerusalem"; yea, my heart has had great experience of wisdom and knowledge. 17] And I applied my heart to know wisdom, and to know madness and folly—I perceived that this also was a striving after wind.

18] For in much wisdom is much vexation;
And he that increases knowledge increases sorrow.

לְפָנַי עַל־יְרוּשָׁלָ͏ִם וְלִבִּי רָאָה הַרְבֵּה חָכְמָה וָדָעַת: 17] וָאֶתְּנָה לִבִּי לָדַעַת חָכְמָה וְדַעַת הֹלֵלוֹת וְשִׂכְלוּת יָדַעְתִּי שֶׁגַּם־זֶה הוּא רַעְיוֹן רוּחַ:

18] כִּי בְּרֹב חָכְמָה רָב־כָּעַס וְיוֹסִיף דַּעַת יוֹסִיף מַכְאוֹב:

חול המועד סכות

Ezekiel

38:18—39:7

לח

Chapter 38

18] On that day, when Gog sets foot on the soil of Israel—declares the Lord GOD—My raging anger shall flare up.

19] For I have decreed in My indignation and in My blazing wrath: On that day, a terrible earthquake shall befall the land of Israel.

20] The fish of the sea, the birds of the sky, the beasts of the field, all creeping things that move on the ground, and every human being on earth shall quake before Me. Mountains shall be overthrown, cliffs shall topple, and every wall shall crumble to the ground.

21] *d-*I will then summon the sword against him throughout My mountains*-d*—declares the Lord GOD—and every man's sword shall be turned against his brother. 22] I will punish him with pestilence and with bloodshed; and I will pour torrential rain, hailstones, and sulfurous fire upon him and his hordes and the many peoples with him.

23] Thus will I manifest My greatness and My holiness, and make Myself known in the sight of many nations. And they shall know that I am the LORD.

18] וְהָיָה בַּיּוֹם הַהוּא בְּיוֹם בּוֹא גוֹג עַל־אַדְמַת יִשְׂרָאֵל נְאֻם אֲדֹנָי יֱהוִֹה תַּעֲלֶה חֲמָתִי בְּאַפִּי: 19] וּבְקִנְאָתִי בְאֵשׁ־עֶבְרָתִי דִּבַּרְתִּי אִם־לֹא בַּיּוֹם הַהוּא יִהְיֶה רַעַשׁ גָּדוֹל עַל אַדְמַת יִשְׂרָאֵל: 20] וְרָעֲשׁוּ מִפָּנַי דְּגֵי הַיָּם וְעוֹף הַשָּׁמַיִם וְחַיַּת הַשָּׂדֶה וְכָל־הָרֶמֶשׂ הָרֹמֵשׂ עַל־הָאֲדָמָה וְכֹל הָאָדָם אֲשֶׁר עַל־פְּנֵי הָאֲדָמָה וְנֶהֶרְסוּ הֶהָרִים וְנָפְלוּ הַמַּדְרֵגוֹת וְכָל־חוֹמָה לָאָרֶץ תִּפּוֹל: 21] וְקָרָאתִי עָלָיו לְכָל־הָרַי חֶרֶב נְאֻם אֲדֹנָי יֱהוִֹה חֶרֶב אִישׁ בְּאָחִיו תִּהְיֶה: 22] וְנִשְׁפַּטְתִּי אִתּוֹ בְּדֶבֶר וּבְדָם וְגֶשֶׁם שׁוֹטֵף וְאַבְנֵי אֶלְגָּבִישׁ אֵשׁ וְגָפְרִית אַמְטִיר עָלָיו וְעַל־אֲגַפָּיו וְעַל־עַמִּים רַבִּים אֲשֶׁר אִתּוֹ: 23] וְהִתְגַּדִּלְתִּי וְהִתְקַדִּשְׁתִּי וְנוֹדַעְתִּי לְעֵינֵי גּוֹיִם רַבִּים וְיָדְעוּ כִּי־אֲנִי יְהוָה:

---

d-d Meaning of Heb. uncertain

512

1] And you, O mortal, prophesy against Gog and say: Thus said the Lord GOD: I am going to deal with you, O Gog, chief prince of Meshech and Tubal!

2] I will turn you around and *-drive you on,-*[a] and I will take you from the far north and lead you toward the mountains of Israel. 3] I will strike your bow from your left hand and I will loosen the arrows from your right hand. 4] You shall fall on the mountains of Israel, you and all your battalions and the peoples who are with you; and I will give you as food to carrion birds of every sort and to the beasts of the field, 5] as you lie in the open field. For I have spoken—declares the Lord GOD.

6] And I will send a fire against Magog and against those who dwell secure in the coastlands. And they shall know that I am the LORD.

7] I will make My holy name known among My people Israel, and never again will I let My holy name be profaned. And the nations shall know that I the LORD am holy in Israel.

וְאַתָּה בֶן־אָדָם הִנָּבֵא עַל־גּוֹג וְאָמַרְתָּ [1] כֹּה אָמַר אֲדֹנָי יְהוִֹה הִנְנִי אֵלֶיךָ גּוֹג נְשִׂיא רֹאשׁ מֶשֶׁךְ וְתֻבָל: [2] וְשֹׁבַבְתִּיךָ וְשִׁשֵּׁאתִיךָ וְהַעֲלִיתִיךָ מִיַּרְכְּתֵי צָפוֹן וַהֲבִאוֹתִיךָ עַל־הָרֵי יִשְׂרָאֵל: [3] וְהִכֵּיתִי קַשְׁתְּךָ מִיַּד שְׂמֹאולֶךָ וְחִצֶּיךָ מִיַּד יְמִינְךָ אַפִּיל: [4] עַל־הָרֵי יִשְׂרָאֵל תִּפּוֹל אַתָּה וְכָל־אֲגַפֶּיךָ וְעַמִּים אֲשֶׁר אִתָּךְ לְעֵיט צִפּוֹר כָּל־כָּנָף וְחַיַּת הַשָּׂדֶה נְתַתִּיךָ לְאָכְלָה: [5] עַל־פְּנֵי הַשָּׂדֶה תִּפּוֹל כִּי אֲנִי דִבַּרְתִּי נְאֻם אֲדֹנָי יְהוִֹה: [6] וְשִׁלַּחְתִּי־אֵשׁ בְּמָגוֹג וּבְיֹשְׁבֵי הָאִיִּים לָבֶטַח וְיָדְעוּ כִּי־אֲנִי יְהוָה: [7] וְאֶת־שֵׁם קָדְשִׁי אוֹדִיעַ בְּתוֹךְ עַמִּי יִשְׂרָאֵל וְלֹא־אַחֵל אֶת־שֵׁם־קָדְשִׁי עוֹד וְיָדְעוּ הַגּוֹיִם כִּי־אֲנִי יְהוָה קָדוֹשׁ בְּיִשְׂרָאֵל:

---

a-a Meaning of Heb. uncertain

Joshua

1 : 1-18

Chapter 1

1] After the death of Moses the servant of the LORD, the LORD said to Joshua son of Nun, Moses' attendant:

2] "My servant Moses is dead. Prepare to cross the Jordan, together with all this people, into the land which I am giving to the Israelites. 3] Every spot on which your foot treads I give to you, as I promised Moses.

4] Your territory shall extend from the wilderness and the Lebanon to the Great River, the River Euphrates [on the east] —the whole Hittite country—and up to the Mediterranean[a] Sea on the west.

5] No man shall be able to resist you as long as you live. As I was with Moses, so I will be with you; I will not fail you or forsake you.

6] "Be strong and resolute, for you shall apportion to this people the land that I swore to their fathers to give them.

7] But you must be very strong and resolute to observe faithfully all the Teaching that My servant Moses enjoined upon you. Do not deviate from it to the right or to the left, that you may be successful wherever you go.

8] Let not this Book of the Teaching cease from

א

1] וַיְהִי אַחֲרֵי מוֹת מֹשֶׁה עֶבֶד יְהוָה וַיֹּאמֶר יְהוָה אֶל־יְהוֹשֻׁעַ בִּן־נוּן מְשָׁרֵת מֹשֶׁה לֵאמֹר: 2] מֹשֶׁה עַבְדִּי מֵת וְעַתָּה קוּם עֲבֹר אֶת־הַיַּרְדֵּן הַזֶּה אַתָּה וְכָל־הָעָם הַזֶּה אֶל־הָאָרֶץ אֲשֶׁר אָנֹכִי נֹתֵן לָהֶם לִבְנֵי יִשְׂרָאֵל: 3] כָּל־מָקוֹם אֲשֶׁר תִּדְרֹךְ כַּף־רַגְלְכֶם בּוֹ לָכֶם נְתַתִּיו כַּאֲשֶׁר דִּבַּרְתִּי אֶל־מֹשֶׁה: 4] מֵהַמִּדְבָּר וְהַלְּבָנוֹן הַזֶּה וְעַד־הַנָּהָר הַגָּדוֹל נְהַר־פְּרָת כֹּל אֶרֶץ הַחִתִּים וְעַד־הַיָּם הַגָּדוֹל מְבוֹא הַשֶּׁמֶשׁ יִהְיֶה גְּבוּלְכֶם: 5] לֹא־יִתְיַצֵּב אִישׁ לְפָנֶיךָ כֹּל יְמֵי חַיֶּיךָ כַּאֲשֶׁר הָיִיתִי עִם־מֹשֶׁה אֶהְיֶה עִמָּךְ לֹא אַרְפְּךָ וְלֹא אֶעֶזְבֶךָּ: 6] חֲזַק וֶאֱמָץ כִּי אַתָּה תַּנְחִיל אֶת־הָעָם הַזֶּה אֶת־הָאָרֶץ אֲשֶׁר־נִשְׁבַּעְתִּי לַאֲבוֹתָם לָתֵת לָהֶם: 7] רַק חֲזַק וֶאֱמַץ מְאֹד לִשְׁמֹר לַעֲשׂוֹת כְּכָל־הַתּוֹרָה אֲשֶׁר צִוְּךָ מֹשֶׁה עַבְדִּי אַל־תָּסוּר מִמֶּנּוּ יָמִין וּשְׂמֹאול לְמַעַן תַּשְׂכִּיל בְּכֹל אֲשֶׁר תֵּלֵךְ: 8] לֹא־יָמוּשׁ סֵפֶר הַתּוֹרָה הַזֶּה מִפִּיךָ

[a] Heb. "Great"

514

your lips, but recite it day and night, so that you may observe faithfully all that is written in it. Only then will you prosper in your undertakings and only then will you be successful.

9] "I charge you: Be strong and resolute; do not be terrified or dismayed, for the LORD your God is with you wherever you go."

10] Joshua thereupon gave orders to the officials of the people:

11] "Go through the camp and charge the people thus: Get provisions ready, for in three days' time you are to cross the Jordan, in order to enter and occupy the land which the LORD your God is giving you as a possession."

12] Then Joshua said to the Reubenites, the Gadites, and the half-tribe of Manasseh,

13] "Remember what Moses the servant of the LORD enjoined upon you, when he said: 'The LORD your God is granting you a haven; He is assigning this territory to you.'

14] Let your wives, children, and livestock remain in the land which Moses assigned to you *b*-on this side of-*b* the Jordan; but every one of your fighting men shall go across armed*c* in the van of your kinsmen. And you shall assist them

15] until the LORD has given your kinsmen a haven, such as you have, and they too have gained possession of the land which the LORD your God has assigned to them. Then you may return to the land on the east side of the Jordan, which Moses the servant of the LORD assigned to you as your possession, and you may occupy it."

16] They answered Joshua, "We will do everything you have commanded us and we will go wherever you send us.

וְהָגִ֤יתָ בּוֹ֙ יוֹמָ֣ם וָלַ֔יְלָה לְמַ֙עַן֙ תִּשְׁמֹ֣ר לַעֲשׂ֔וֹת כְּכָל־הַכָּת֖וּב בּ֑וֹ כִּי־אָ֛ז תַּצְלִ֥יחַ אֶת־דְּרָכֶ֖ךָ וְאָ֥ז תַּשְׂכִּֽיל׃

9 הֲל֤וֹא צִוִּיתִ֙יךָ֙ חֲזַ֣ק וֶאֱמָ֔ץ אַֽל־תַּעֲרֹ֖ץ וְאַל־תֵּחָ֑ת כִּ֤י עִמְּךָ֙ יְהֹוָ֣ה אֱלֹהֶ֔יךָ בְּכֹ֖ל אֲשֶׁ֥ר תֵּלֵֽךְ׃

10 וַיְצַ֣ו יְהוֹשֻׁ֔עַ אֶת־שֹׁטְרֵ֥י הָעָ֖ם לֵאמֹֽר׃

11 עִבְר֣וּ ׀ בְּקֶ֣רֶב הַֽמַּחֲנֶ֗ה וְצַוּ֤וּ אֶת־הָעָם֙ לֵאמֹ֔ר הָכִ֥ינוּ לָכֶ֖ם צֵידָ֑ה כִּ֞י בְּע֣וֹד ׀ שְׁלֹ֣שֶׁת יָמִ֗ים אַתֶּם֙ עֹֽבְרִים֙ אֶת־הַיַּרְדֵּ֣ן הַזֶּ֔ה לָבוֹא֙ לָרֶ֣שֶׁת אֶת־הָאָ֔רֶץ אֲשֶׁר֙ יְהֹוָ֣ה אֱלֹֽהֵיכֶ֔ם נֹתֵ֥ן לָכֶ֖ם לְרִשְׁתָּֽהּ׃

12 וְלָרֽאוּבֵנִי֙ וְלַגָּדִ֔י וְלַחֲצִ֖י שֵׁ֣בֶט הַֽמְנַשֶּׁ֑ה אָמַ֥ר יְהוֹשֻׁ֖עַ לֵאמֹֽר׃ 13 זָכוֹר֙ אֶת־הַדָּבָ֔ר אֲשֶׁ֨ר צִוָּ֥ה אֶתְכֶ֛ם מֹשֶׁ֥ה עֶֽבֶד־יְהֹוָ֖ה לֵאמֹ֑ר יְהֹוָ֤ה אֱלֹהֵיכֶם֙ מֵנִ֣יחַ לָכֶ֔ם וְנָתַ֥ן לָכֶ֖ם אֶת־הָאָ֥רֶץ הַזֹּֽאת׃ 14 נְשֵׁיכֶ֣ם טַפְּכֶ֞ם וּמִקְנֵיכֶ֗ם יֵשְׁבוּ֙ בָּאָ֔רֶץ אֲשֶׁ֨ר נָתַ֥ן לָכֶ֛ם מֹשֶׁ֖ה בְּעֵ֣בֶר הַיַּרְדֵּ֑ן וְאַתֶּם֩ תַּעַבְר֨וּ חֲמֻשִׁ֜ים לִפְנֵ֣י אֲחֵיכֶ֗ם כֹּ֚ל גִּבּוֹרֵ֣י הַחַ֔יִל וַעֲזַרְתֶּ֖ם אוֹתָֽם׃ 15 עַ֠ד אֲשֶׁר־יָנִ֨יחַ יְהֹוָ֥ה ׀ לַֽאֲחֵיכֶם֮ כָּכֶם֒ וְיָרְשׁ֣וּ גַם־הֵ֔מָּה אֶת־הָאָ֕רֶץ אֲשֶׁר־יְהֹוָ֥ה אֱלֹֽהֵיכֶ֖ם נֹתֵ֣ן לָהֶ֑ם וְשַׁבְתֶּ֞ם לְאֶ֤רֶץ יְרֻשַּׁתְכֶם֙ וִֽירִשְׁתֶּ֣ם אוֹתָ֔הּ אֲשֶׁ֣ר ׀ נָתַ֣ן לָכֶ֗ם מֹשֶׁה֙ עֶ֣בֶד יְהֹוָ֔ה בְּעֵ֥בֶר הַיַּרְדֵּ֖ן מִזְרַ֥ח הַשָּֽׁמֶשׁ׃

16 וַֽיַּעֲנ֔וּ אֶת־יְהוֹשֻׁ֖עַ לֵאמֹ֑ר כֹּ֤ל אֲשֶׁר־צִוִּיתָ֙נוּ֙ נַֽעֲשֶׂ֔ה וְאֶֽל־כָּל־אֲשֶׁ֥ר תִּשְׁלָחֵ֖נוּ נֵלֵֽךְ׃

---

b-b Lit. "across"

c Meaning of Heb. uncertain

515

17] We will obey you just as we obeyed Moses; let but the Lord your God be with you as He was with Moses!

18] Any man who flouts your commands and does not obey every order you give him shall be put to death. Only be strong and resolute!"

[17] כְּכֹל אֲשֶׁר־שָׁמַעְנוּ אֶל־מֹשֶׁה כֵּן נִשְׁמַע אֵלֶיךָ רַק יִהְיֶה יְהֹוָה אֱלֹהֶיךָ עִמָּךְ כַּאֲשֶׁר הָיָה עִם־מֹשֶׁה: [18] כָּל־אִישׁ אֲשֶׁר־יַמְרֶה אֶת־פִּיךָ וְלֹא־יִשְׁמַע אֶת־דְּבָרֶיךָ לְכֹל אֲשֶׁר־תְּצַוֶּנּוּ יוּמָת רַק חֲזַק וֶאֱמָץ:

Jeremiah

8:13–9:23

Chapter 8

ח

13] *ᵃ⁻I will make an end of them⁻ᵃ*
        —declares the Lord:
No grapes left on the vine,
No figs on the fig tree,
The leaves all withered;
ᵇ⁻Whatever I have given them is gone.⁻ᵇ

13] אָסֹף אֲסִיפֵם

נְאֻם־יְהֹוָה

אֵין עֲנָבִים בַּגֶּפֶן

וְאֵין תְּאֵנִים בַּתְּאֵנָה

וְהֶעָלֶה נָבֵל

וָאֶתֵּן לָהֶם יַעַבְרוּם:

14] Why are we sitting by?
Let us gather into the fortified cities
And meet our doom there.
For the Lord our God has doomed us,
He has made us drink a bitter draft.
Because we sinned against the Lord.

14] עַל־מָה אֲנַחְנוּ יֹשְׁבִים

הֵאָסְפוּ וְנָבוֹא אֶל־עָרֵי הַמִּבְצָר

וְנִדְּמָה־שָּׁם

כִּי יְהֹוָה אֱלֹהֵינוּ הֲדִמָּנוּ

וַיַּשְׁקֵנוּ מֵי־רֹאשׁ

כִּי חָטָאנוּ לַיהֹוָה:

15] We hoped for good fortune, but no happiness
    came;
For a time of relief—instead there is terror!

15] קַוֵּה לְשָׁלוֹם וְאֵין טוֹב

לְעֵת מַרְפֵּה וְהִנֵּה בְעָתָה:

16] The snorting of their horses was heard from
    Dan;
At the loud neighing of their steeds
The whole land quaked.
They came and devoured the land and what was
    in it,
The towns and those who dwelt in them.

16] מִדָּן נִשְׁמַע נַחְרַת סוּסָיו

מִקּוֹל מִצְהֲלוֹת אַבִּירָיו

רָעֲשָׁה כָּל־הָאָרֶץ

וַיָּבוֹאוּ וַיֹּאכְלוּ אֶרֶץ וּמְלוֹאָהּ

עִיר וְיֹשְׁבֵי בָהּ:

*ᵃ⁻ᵃ Meaning of Heb. uncertain; change of vocalization yields "Their fruit harvest has
    been gathered in"*
ᵇ⁻ᵇ Meaning of Heb. uncertain

17] Lo, I will send serpents against you,
Adders that cannot be charmed,
And they shall bite you
—declares the LORD.

כִּי הִנְנִי מְשַׁלֵּחַ בָּכֶם נְחָשִׁים [17
צִפְעֹנִים אֲשֶׁר אֵין־לָהֶם לָחַשׁ
וְנִשְּׁכוּ אֶתְכֶם
נְאֻם־יְהֹוָה:

18] *b*When in grief I would seek comfort,*-b*
My heart is sick within me.

מַבְלִיגִיתִי עֲלֵי יָגוֹן [18
עָלַי לִבִּי דַוָּי:

19] *c*"Is not the LORD in Zion,
Is not her King within her?
Why then did they anger Me with their images,
With alien futilities?"
Hark! The outcry of my poor people
From the land far and wide:

הִנֵּה־קוֹל שַׁוְעַת בַּת־עַמִּי [19
מֵאֶרֶץ מַרְחַקִּים
הַיהֹוָה אֵין בְּצִיּוֹן
אִם־מַלְכָּהּ אֵין בָּהּ
מַדּוּעַ הִכְעִסוּנִי בִּפְסִלֵיהֶם
בְּהַבְלֵי נֵכָר:

20] "Harvest is past,
Summer is gone,
But we have not been saved."

עָבַר קָצִיר [20
כָּלָה קָיִץ
וַאֲנַחְנוּ לוֹא נוֹשָׁעְנוּ:

21] Because my people is shattered I am shattered;
I am dejected, seized by desolation.

עַל־שֶׁבֶר בַּת־עַמִּי הָשְׁבָּרְתִּי [21
קָדַרְתִּי שַׁמָּה הֶחֱזִיקָתְנִי:

22] Is there no balm in Gilead,
Can no physician be found?
Why has healing not yet
Come to my poor people?

הַצֳרִי אֵין בְּגִלְעָד [22
אִם־רֹפֵא אֵין שָׁם
כִּי מַדּוּעַ לֹא עָלְתָה אֲרֻכַת
בַּת־עַמִּי:

23] Oh, that my head were water,
My eyes a fount of tears!
Then would I weep day and night
For the slain of my poor people.

מִי־יִתֵּן רֹאשִׁי מַיִם [23
וְעֵינִי מְקוֹר דִּמְעָה
וְאֶבְכֶּה יוֹמָם וָלַיְלָה
אֵת חַלְלֵי בַת־עַמִּי:

b-b Meaning of Heb. uncertain
c Here God is speaking

1] Oh, to be in the desert,
At an encampment for wayfarers!
Oh, to leave my people,
To go away from them—
For they are all adulterers,
A band of rogues.

2] They bend their tongues like bows;
They are valorous in the land
For treachery, not for honesty;
They advance from evil to evil.
And they do not heed Me
            —declares the LORD.

3] Beware, every man of his friend!
Trust not even a brother!
For every brother takes advantage,
Every friend ᵃ˙is base in his dealings.˙ᵃ

4] One man cheats the other,
They will not speak truth;
They have trained their tongues to speak falsely;
ᵇ˙They wear themselves out working iniquity.

5] You dwell in the midst of deceit.
In their deceit,˙ᵇ they refuse to heed Me
            —declares the LORD.

6] Assuredly, thus said the LORD of Hosts:
Lo, I shall smelt and assay them—
ᵇ˙For what else can I do because of My poor people?˙ᵇ

1] מִי־יִתְּנֵנִי בַמִּדְבָּר
מְלוֹן אֹרְחִים
וְאֶעֶזְבָה אֶת־עַמִּי
וְאֵלְכָה מֵאִתָּם
כִּי כֻלָּם מְנָאֲפִים
עֲצֶרֶת בֹּגְדִים:

2] וַיַּדְרְכוּ אֶת־לְשׁוֹנָם קַשְׁתָּם
שֶׁקֶר וְלֹא לֶאֱמוּנָה
גָּבְרוּ בָאָרֶץ
כִּי מֵרָעָה אֶל־רָעָה יָצָאוּ
וְאֹתִי לֹא־יָדָעוּ
נְאֻם־יְהוָה:

3] אִישׁ מֵרֵעֵהוּ הִשָּׁמֵרוּ
וְעַל־כָּל־אָח אַל־תִּבְטָחוּ
כִּי כָל־אָח עָקוֹב יַעְקֹב
וְכָל־רֵעַ רָכִיל יַהֲלֹךְ:

4] וְאִישׁ בְּרֵעֵהוּ יְהָתֵלּוּ
וֶאֱמֶת לֹא יְדַבֵּרוּ
לִמְּדוּ לְשׁוֹנָם דַּבֶּר־שֶׁקֶר
הַעֲוֵה נִלְאוּ:

5] שִׁבְתְּךָ בְּתוֹךְ מִרְמָה
בְּמִרְמָה מֵאֲנוּ דַעַת־אוֹתִי
נְאֻם־יְהוָה:

6] לָכֵן כֹּה אָמַר יְהוָה צְבָאוֹת
הִנְנִי צוֹרְפָם וּבְחַנְתִּים
כִּי־אֵיךְ אֶעֱשֶׂה מִפְּנֵי בַּת־עַמִּי:

ᵃ˙ᵃ Others "go about as a talebearer among"; meaning of Heb. unknown
ᵇ˙ᵇ Meaning of Heb. uncertain

7] Their tongue is a sharpened arrow,
They use their mouths to deceive.
One speaks to his fellow in friendship,
But lays an ambush for him in his heart.

8] Shall I not punish them for such deeds?
—says the LORD—
Shall I not bring retribution
On such a nation as this?

9] For the mountains I take up weeping and
wailing,
For the pastures in the wilderness, a dirge.
They are laid waste; no man passes through,
And no sound of cattle is heard.
Birds of the sky and beasts as well
Have fled and are gone.

10] I will turn Jerusalem into rubble,
Into dens for jackals;
And I will make the towns of Judah
A desolation without inhabitants.

11] What man is so wise
That he understands this?
To whom has the LORD's mouth spoken,
So that he can explain it:
Why is the land in ruins,
Laid waste like a wilderness,
With none passing through?

12] The LORD replied: Because they forsook
the Teaching I had set before them. They did not
obey Me and they did not follow it,
13] but
followed their own willful heart and followed

7] חֵץ שָׁחוּט לְשׁוֹנָם

מִרְמָה דִבֵּר

בְּפִיו שָׁלוֹם אֶת־רֵעֵהוּ יְדַבֵּר

וּבְקִרְבּוֹ יָשִׂים אָרְבּוֹ:

8] הַעַל־אֵלֶּה לֹא־אֶפְקָד־בָּם

נְאֻם־יְהֹוָה

אִם־בְּגוֹי אֲשֶׁר כָּזֶה

לֹא תִתְנַקֵּם נַפְשִׁי:

9] עַל־הֶהָרִים אֶשָּׂא בְכִי וָנֶהִי

וְעַל־נְאוֹת מִדְבָּר קִינָה

כִּי נִצְּתוּ מִבְּלִי־אִישׁ עֹבֵר

וְלֹא שָׁמְעוּ קוֹל מִקְנֶה

מֵעוֹף הַשָּׁמַיִם וְעַד־בְּהֵמָה

נָדְדוּ הָלָכוּ:

10] וְנָתַתִּי אֶת־יְרוּשָׁלַ͏ִם לְגַלִּים

מְעוֹן תַּנִּים

וְאֶת־עָרֵי יְהוּדָה

אֶתֵּן שְׁמָמָה מִבְּלִי יוֹשֵׁב:

11] מִי־הָאִישׁ הֶחָכָם

וְיָבֵן אֶת־זֹאת

וַאֲשֶׁר דִּבֶּר פִּי־יְהֹוָה אֵלָיו

וְיַגִּדָהּ

עַל־מָה אָבְדָה הָאָרֶץ

נִצְּתָה כַמִּדְבָּר

מִבְּלִי עֹבֵר:

12] וַיֹּאמֶר יְהֹוָה עַל־עָזְבָם אֶת־תּוֹרָתִי אֲשֶׁר

נָתַתִּי לִפְנֵיהֶם וְלֹא־שָׁמְעוּ בְקוֹלִי וְלֹא־הָלְכוּ

בָהּ: 13] וַיֵּלְכוּ אַחֲרֵי שְׁרִרוּת לִבָּם וְאַחֲרֵי

the Baalim, as their fathers had taught them.
14] Assuredly, thus said the Lord of Hosts, the God of Israel: I am going to feed that people wormwood and make them drink a bitter draft.

15] I will scatter them among nations which they and their fathers never knew; and I will dispatch the sword after them until I have consumed them.

16] Thus said the Lord of Hosts:
Listen!
Summon the dirge-singers, let them come;

17] Send for the skilled women, let them come.
Let them quickly start a wailing for us,
That our eyes may run with tears,
Our pupils flow with water.

18] For the sound of wailing
Is heard from Zion:
How we are despoiled!
How greatly we are shamed!
Ah, we must leave our land,
Abandon^e our dwellings!

19] Hear, O women, the word of the Lord,
Let your ears receive the word of His mouth,
And teach your daughters wailing,
And one another lamentation.

20] For death has climbed through our windows,
Has entered our fortresses,
To cut off babes from the streets,
Young men from the squares.

הַבְּעָלִים אֲשֶׁר לִמְּדוּם אֲבוֹתָם: 14] לָכֵן כֹּה־אָמַר יְהֹוָה צְבָאוֹת אֱלֹהֵי יִשְׂרָאֵל הִנְנִי מַאֲכִילָם אֶת־הָעָם הַזֶּה לַעֲנָה וְהִשְׁקִיתִים מֵי־רֹאשׁ: 15] וַהֲפִצוֹתִים בַּגּוֹיִם אֲשֶׁר לֹא יָדְעוּ הֵמָּה וַאֲבוֹתָם וְשִׁלַּחְתִּי אַחֲרֵיהֶם אֶת־הַחֶרֶב עַד כַּלּוֹתִי אוֹתָם:

16] כֹּה אָמַר יְהֹוָה צְבָאוֹת
הִתְבּוֹנְנוּ
וְקִרְאוּ לַמְקוֹנְנוֹת וּתְבוֹאֶינָה
וְאֶל־הַחֲכָמוֹת שִׁלְחוּ וְתָבוֹאנָה:

17] וּתְמַהֵרְנָה וְתִשֶּׂנָה עָלֵינוּ נֶהִי
וְתֵרַדְנָה עֵינֵינוּ דִּמְעָה
וְעַפְעַפֵּינוּ יִזְּלוּ־מָיִם:

18] כִּי קוֹל נְהִי
נִשְׁמַע מִצִּיּוֹן
אֵיךְ שֻׁדָּדְנוּ
בֹּשְׁנוּ מְאֹד
כִּי־עָזַבְנוּ אָרֶץ
כִּי הִשְׁלִיכוּ מִשְׁכְּנוֹתֵינוּ:

19] כִּי־שְׁמַעְנָה נָשִׁים דְּבַר־יְהֹוָה
וְתִקַּח אָזְנְכֶם דְּבַר־פִּיו
וְלַמֵּדְנָה בְנוֹתֵיכֶם נֶהִי
וְאִשָּׁה רְעוּתָהּ קִינָה:

20] כִּי־עָלָה מָוֶת בְּחַלּוֹנֵינוּ
בָּא בְּאַרְמְנוֹתֵינוּ
לְהַכְרִית עוֹלָל מִחוּץ
בַּחוּרִים מֵרְחֹבוֹת:

^e Lit. "They abandoned"

21] Speak thus—says the LORD:
The carcasses of men shall lie
Like dung upon the fields,
Like sheaves behind the reaper,
With none to pick them up.

22] Thus said the LORD:
Let not the wise man glory in his wisdom;
Let not the strong man glory in his strength;
Let not the rich man glory in his riches.

23] But only in this should one glory:
In his earnest devotion to Me.
For I the LORD act with kindness,
Justice, and equity in the world;
For in these I delight
                                —declares the LORD.

[21] דַּבֵּר כֹּה נְאֻם־יְהֹוָה
וְנָפְלָה נִבְלַת הָאָדָם
כְּדֹמֶן עַל־פְּנֵי הַשָּׂדֶה
וּכְעָמִיר מֵאַחֲרֵי הַקּוֹצֵר
וְאֵין מְאַסֵּף:

[22] כֹּה אָמַר יְהֹוָה
אַל־יִתְהַלֵּל חָכָם בְּחָכְמָתוֹ
וְאַל־יִתְהַלֵּל הַגִּבּוֹר בִּגְבוּרָתוֹ
אַל־יִתְהַלֵּל עָשִׁיר בְּעָשְׁרוֹ:

[23] כִּי אִם־בְּזֹאת יִתְהַלֵּל הַמִּתְהַלֵּל
הַשְׂכֵּל וְיָדֹעַ אוֹתִי
כִּי אֲנִי יְהֹוָה עֹשֶׂה חֶסֶד
מִשְׁפָּט וּצְדָקָה בָּאָרֶץ
כִּי־בְאֵלֶּה חָפַצְתִּי
נְאֻם־יְהֹוָה:

תשעה באב – מנחה

Isaiah

55 : 6 — 56 : 8

נה

Chapter 55

6] Seek the Lord while He can be found,
Call to Him while He is near.

7] Let the wicked give up his ways,
The sinful man his plans;
Let him turn back to the Lord,
And He will pardon him;
To our God,
For He freely forgives.

8] For My plans are not your plans,
Nor are My ways^e your ways^e
               —declares the Lord.

9] But as the heavens are high above the earth,
So are My ways^e high above your ways^e
And My plans above your plans.

10] For as the rain or snow drops from heaven
And returns not there,
But soaks the earth
And makes it bring forth vegetation,
Yielding ^dseed for sowing and bread for eating,^{-d}

6] דִּרְשׁוּ יְהֹוָה בְּהִמָּצְאוֹ
קְרָאֻהוּ בִּהְיוֹתוֹ קָרוֹב:

7] יַעֲזֹב רָשָׁע דַּרְכּוֹ
וְאִישׁ אָוֶן מַחְשְׁבֹתָיו
וְיָשֹׁב אֶל־יְהֹוָה וִירַחֲמֵהוּ
וְאֶל־אֱלֹהֵינוּ כִּי־יַרְבֶּה לִסְלוֹחַ:

8] כִּי לֹא מַחְשְׁבוֹתַי מַחְשְׁבוֹתֵיכֶם
וְלֹא דַרְכֵיכֶם דְּרָכָי
נְאֻם יְהֹוָה:

9] כִּי־גָבְהוּ שָׁמַיִם מֵאָרֶץ
כֵּן גָּבְהוּ דְרָכַי מִדַּרְכֵיכֶם
וּמַחְשְׁבֹתַי מִמַּחְשְׁבֹתֵיכֶם:

10] כִּי כַּאֲשֶׁר יֵרֵד הַגֶּשֶׁם וְהַשֶּׁלֶג מִן־הַשָּׁמַיִם
וְשָׁמָּה לֹא יָשׁוּב
כִּי אִם־הִרְוָה אֶת־הָאָרֶץ
וְהוֹלִידָהּ וְהִצְמִיחָהּ
וְנָתַן זֶרַע לַזֹּרֵעַ וְלֶחֶם לָאֹכֵל:

---

^e *Emendation yields "words"; cf. v. 11 and 40.8*

^{d-d} *Lit. "seed for the sower and bread for the eater"*

11] So is the word that issues from My mouth:
It does not come back to Me unfulfilled,
But performs what I purpose,
Achieves what I sent it to do.

12] Yea, you shall leave° in joy and be led home
secure.
Before you, mount and hill shall shout aloud,
And all the trees of the field shall clap their hands.

13] Instead of the brier, a cypress shall rise;
Instead of the nettle, a myrtle shall rise.
These shall stand as a testimony to the LORD,
As an everlasting sign that shall not perish.

Chapter 56

1] Thus said the LORD:
Observe what is right and do what is just;
For soon My salvation shall come,
And My deliverance be revealed.

2] Happy is the man who does this,
The man who holds fast to it:
Who keeps the sabbath and does not profane it,
And stays his hand from doing any evil.

3] Let not the foreigner say,
Who has attached himself to the LORD,
"The LORD will keep me apart from His people";
And let not the eunuch say,
"I am a withered tree."

4] For thus said the LORD:
"As regards the eunuchs who keep My sabbaths,

° I.e., leave the Babylonian exile

נו

11] כֵּן יִהְיֶה דְבָרִי אֲשֶׁר יֵצֵא מִפִּי
לֹא־יָשׁוּב אֵלַי רֵיקָם
כִּי אִם־עָשָׂה אֶת־אֲשֶׁר חָפַצְתִּי
וְהִצְלִיחַ אֲשֶׁר שְׁלַחְתִּיו:
12] כִּי־בְשִׂמְחָה תֵצֵאוּ וּבְשָׁלוֹם תּוּבָלוּן
הֶהָרִים וְהַגְּבָעוֹת יִפְצְחוּ לִפְנֵיכֶם רִנָּה
וְכָל־עֲצֵי הַשָּׂדֶה יִמְחֲאוּ־כָף:
13] תַּחַת הַנַּעֲצוּץ יַעֲלֶה בְרוֹשׁ
וְתַחַת הַסִּרְפַּד יַעֲלֶה הֲדַס
וְהָיָה לַיהוָה לְשֵׁם
לְאוֹת עוֹלָם לֹא יִכָּרֵת:

נו

1] כֹּה אָמַר יְהוָה
שִׁמְרוּ מִשְׁפָּט וַעֲשׂוּ צְדָקָה
כִּי־קְרוֹבָה יְשׁוּעָתִי לָבוֹא
וְצִדְקָתִי לְהִגָּלוֹת:
2] אַשְׁרֵי אֱנוֹשׁ יַעֲשֶׂה־זֹּאת
וּבֶן־אָדָם יַחֲזִיק בָּהּ
שֹׁמֵר שַׁבָּת מֵחַלְּלוֹ
וְשֹׁמֵר יָדוֹ מֵעֲשׂוֹת כָּל־רָע:
3] וְאַל־יֹאמַר בֶּן־הַנֵּכָר
הַנִּלְוָה אֶל־יְהוָה לֵאמֹר
הַבְדֵּל יַבְדִּילַנִי יְהוָה מֵעַל עַמּוֹ
וְאַל־יֹאמַר הַסָּרִיס
הֵן אֲנִי עֵץ יָבֵשׁ:
4] כִּי־כֹה אָמַר יְהוָה
לַסָּרִיסִים אֲשֶׁר יִשְׁמְרוּ אֶת־שַׁבְּתוֹתַי

Who have chosen what I desire
And hold fast to My covenant—

5] I will give them, in My House
And within My walls,
A monument and a name
Better than sons or daughters.
I will give them an everlasting name
Which shall not perish.

6] As for the foreigners
Who attach themselves to the LORD,
To minister to Him.
And to love the name of the LORD,
To be His servants—
All who keep the sabbath and do not profane it,
And who hold fast to My covenant—

7] I will bring them to My sacred mount
And let them rejoice in My house of prayer.
Their burnt offerings and sacrifices
Shall be welcome on My altar;
For My House shall be called
A house of prayer for all peoples."

8] Thus declares the Lord GOD,
Who gathers the dispersed of Israel:
"I will gather still more to those already
      gathered."

וּבָחֲרוּ בַּאֲשֶׁר חָפָצְתִּי

וּמַחֲזִיקִים בִּבְרִיתִי:

5] וְנָתַתִּי לָהֶם בְּבֵיתִי

וּבְחוֹמֹתַי

יָד וָשֵׁם

טוֹב מִבָּנִים וּמִבָּנוֹת

שֵׁם עוֹלָם אֶתֶּן־לוֹ

אֲשֶׁר לֹא יִכָּרֵת:

6] וּבְנֵי הַנֵּכָר

הַנִּלְוִים עַל־יְהֹוָה לְשָׁרְתוֹ

וּלְאַהֲבָה אֶת־שֵׁם יְהֹוָה

לִהְיוֹת לוֹ לַעֲבָדִים

כָּל־שֹׁמֵר שַׁבָּת מֵחַלְּלוֹ

וּמַחֲזִיקִים בִּבְרִיתִי:

7] וַהֲבִיאוֹתִים אֶל־הַר קָדְשִׁי

וְשִׂמַּחְתִּים בְּבֵית תְּפִלָּתִי

עוֹלֹתֵיהֶם וְזִבְחֵיהֶם

לְרָצוֹן עַל־מִזְבְּחִי

כִּי בֵיתִי בֵּית־תְּפִלָּה יִקָּרֵא

לְכָל־הָעַמִּים:

8] נְאֻם אֲדֹנָי יֱהֹוִה

מְקַבֵּץ נִדְחֵי יִשְׂרָאֵל

עוֹד אֲקַבֵּץ עָלָיו לְנִקְבָּצָיו:

Torah Blessings

Before reading the Torah

בָּרְכוּ אֶת־יְיָ הַמְבֹרָךְ!

בָּרוּךְ יְיָ הַמְבֹרָךְ לְעוֹלָם וָעֶד!

בָּרוּךְ אַתָּה, יְיָ אֱלֹהֵינוּ, מֶלֶךְ הָעוֹלָם, אֲשֶׁר בָּחַר־בָּנוּ מִכָּל־הָעַמִּים וְנָתַן־לָנוּ אֶת־תּוֹרָתוֹ. בָּרוּךְ אַתָּה, יְיָ, נוֹתֵן הַתּוֹרָה.

Praise the Lord, to whom our praise is due!

Praised be the Lord, to whom our praise is due, now and for ever!

Blessed is the Lord our God, Ruler of the universe, who has chosen us from all peoples by giving us His Torah. Blessed is the Lord, Giver of the Torah.

◆ ◆

After reading the Torah

בָּרוּךְ אַתָּה, יְיָ אֱלֹהֵינוּ, מֶלֶךְ הָעוֹלָם, אֲשֶׁר נָתַן לָנוּ תּוֹרַת אֱמֶת וְחַיֵּי עוֹלָם נָטַע בְּתוֹכֵנוּ. בָּרוּךְ אַתָּה, יְיָ, נוֹתֵן הַתּוֹרָה.

Blessed is the Lord our God, Ruler of the universe, who has given us a Torah of truth, implanting within us eternal life. Blessed is the Lord, Giver of the Torah.

Haftarah Blessings

Before reading the Haftarah

בָּרוּךְ אַתָּה, יְיָ אֱלֹהֵֽינוּ, מֶֽלֶךְ הָעוֹלָם, אֲשֶׁר בָּחַר
בִּנְבִיאִים טוֹבִים וְרָצָה בְדִבְרֵיהֶם הַנֶּאֱמָרִים בֶּאֱמֶת.
בָּרוּךְ אַתָּה, יְיָ, הַבּוֹחֵר בַּתּוֹרָה וּבְמֹשֶׁה עַבְדּוֹ
וּבְיִשְׂרָאֵל עַמּוֹ וּבִנְבִיאֵי הָאֱמֶת וָצֶֽדֶק.

Blessed is the Lord our God, Ruler of the universe, who
has chosen faithful prophets to speak words of truth.
Blessed is the Lord, for the revelation of Torah, for Moses
His servant and Israel His people, and for the prophets of
truth and righteousness.

◆ ◆

After reading the Haftarah

בָּרוּךְ אַתָּה, יְיָ אֱלֹהֵֽינוּ, מֶֽלֶךְ הָעוֹלָם, צוּר כָּל־
הָעוֹלָמִים, צַדִּיק בְּכָל־הַדּוֹרוֹת, הָאֵל הַנֶּאֱמָן, הָאוֹמֵר
וְעוֹשֶׂה, הַמְדַבֵּר וּמְקַיֵּם, שֶׁכָּל־דְּבָרָיו אֱמֶת וָצֶֽדֶק.

Blessed is the Lord our God, Ruler of the universe, Rock
of all creation, Righteous One of all generations, the
faithful God whose word is deed, whose every command
is just and true.

*נֶאֱמָן אַתָּה הוּא יְיָ אֱלֹהֵֽינוּ, וְנֶאֱמָנִים דְּבָרֶֽיךָ, וְדָבָר
אֶחָד מִדְּבָרֶֽיךָ אָחוֹר לֹא־יָשׁוּב רֵיקָם, כִּי אֵל מֶֽלֶךְ
נֶאֱמָן וְרַחֲמָן אָֽתָּה. בָּרוּךְ אַתָּה, יְיָ, הָאֵל הַנֶּאֱמָן בְּכָל־
דְּבָרָיו.

*You are the Faithful One, O Lord our God, and faithful
is Your word. Not one word of Yours goes forth without
accomplishing its task, O faithful and compassionate God
and King. Blessed is the Lord, the faithful God.

*These paragraphs are omitted from many Reform services.

*רַחֵם עַל־צִיּוֹן כִּי הִיא בֵּית חַיֵּינוּ, וְלַעֲלוּבַת נֶפֶשׁ תּוֹשִׁיעַ בִּמְהֵרָה בְּיָמֵינוּ. בָּרוּךְ אַתָּה, יְיָ, מְשַׂמֵּחַ צִיּוֹן בְּבָנֶיהָ.

*Show compassion for Zion, our House of Life, and banish all sadness speedily, in our own day. Blessed is the Lord, who brings joy to Zion's children.

*שַׂמְּחֵנוּ, יְיָ אֱלֹהֵינוּ, בְּאֵלִיָּהוּ הַנָּבִיא עַבְדֶּךָ, וּבְמַלְכוּת בֵּית דָּוִד מְשִׁיחֶךָ, בִּמְהֵרָה יָבֹא וְיָגֵל לִבֵּנוּ. עַל־כִּסְאוֹ לֹא־יֵשֵׁב זָר וְלֹא־יִנְחֲלוּ עוֹד אֲחֵרִים אֶת־כְּבוֹדוֹ. כִּי בְשֵׁם קָדְשְׁךָ נִשְׁבַּעְתָּ לּוֹ שֶׁלֹּא־יִכְבֶּה נֵרוֹ לְעוֹלָם וָעֶד. בָּרוּךְ אַתָּה, יְיָ, מָגֵן דָּוִד.

*Lord our God, bring us the joy of Your kingdom: let our dream of Elijah and David bear fruit. Speedily let redemption come to gladden our hearts. Let Your solemn promise be fulfilled: David's light shall not for ever be extinguished!

Blessed is the Lord, the Shield of David.

עַל־הַתּוֹרָה וְעַל־הָעֲבוֹדָה וְעַל־הַנְּבִיאִים וְעַל־יוֹם הַשַּׁבָּת הַזֶּה, שֶׁנָּתַתָּ־לָנוּ, יְיָ אֱלֹהֵינוּ, לִקְדֻשָּׁה וְלִמְנוּחָה, לְכָבוֹד וּלְתִפְאָרֶת, עַל־הַכֹּל, יְיָ אֱלֹהֵינוּ, אֲנַחְנוּ מוֹדִים לָךְ, וּמְבָרְכִים אוֹתָךְ. יִתְבָּרַךְ שִׁמְךָ בְּפִי כָּל־חַי תָּמִיד לְעוֹלָם וָעֶד. בָּרוּךְ אַתָּה, יְיָ, מְקַדֵּשׁ הַשַּׁבָּת.

For the Torah, for the privilege of worship, for the prophets, and for this Shabbat that You, O Lord our God, have given us for holiness and rest, for honor and glory, we thank and bless You. May Your name be blessed for ever by every living being.

Blessed is the Lord, for the Sabbath and its holiness.

*These paragraphs are omitted from many Reform services.